THE SWORD OF LUCHANA

The Sword of Luchana

Baldomero Espartero and the Making of Modern Spain, 1793–1879

ADRIAN SHUBERT

UNIVERSITY OF TORONTO PRESS
Toronto Buffalo London

© Adrian Shubert 2021
This edition has been published by arrangement
with Galaxia Gutenberg, S.L., Barcelona (Spain)
University of Toronto Press
Toronto Buffalo London
utorontopress.com
Printed in the U.S.A.

ISBN 978-1-4875-0860-9 (cloth)
ISBN 978-1-4875-3859-0 (EPUB)
ISBN 978-1-4875-3858-3 (PDF)

Toronto Iberic

Publication cataloguing information is available from Library
and Archives Canada.

This book has been published with the help of a grant from the Federation
for the Humanities and Social Sciences, through the Awards to Scholarly
Publications Program, using funds provided by the Social Sciences and
Humanities Research Council of Canada.

University of Toronto Press acknowledges the financial assistance to its
publishing program of the Canada Council for the Arts and the Ontario
Arts Council, an agency of the Government of Ontario.

To my Jacinta

In civil wars, there is neither glory for the victors nor deprecation for the vanquished. Remember that when peace is reborn, everything is mixed together and the story of suffering and defeat, of triumphs and conquests will be seen as the shared patrimony of those who earlier fought on opposite sides.
– Baldomero Espartero, 1837

Neither surrender nor embraces of Vergara ... nor anything other than total and definitive victory.
– Emilio Mola, 1936

The nineteenth century, which we would have desired to erase from our history, is the negation of the Spanish spirit.
– Francisco Franco, 1950

Contents

List of Illustrations   ix

Acknowledgments   xi

Introduction   3
  1 From Gránatula to America, February 1793–February 1815   16
  2 Defender of the Empire, February 1815–November 1825   35
  3 Defender of the Throne, November 1825–September 1836   59
  4 Commander in Chief, September 1836–August 1839   94
  5 The Reluctant Revolutionary, August 1839–May 1841   129
  6 Regent of the Realm, May 1841–July 1843   163
  7 Exile and Return, July 1843–July 1854   196
  8 "The Personification of Liberty," July 1854–July 1856   224
  9 The Retiree of Logroño, July 1856–September 1868   255
 10 "King or President?" September 1868–December 1870   288
 11 The Necessary Man, January 1871–March 1876   315
Epilogue: Death and Afterlife, March 1876–   331

Notes   355

Bibliography   423

Index   443

Illustrations

1	The Night of Luchana	6
2	Espartero in material culture: ceramic plate	8
3	Portrait of Jacinta Martínez de Sicilia y Santa Cruz, 1840	62
4	Portrait of Jacinta Martínez de Sicilia y Santa Cruz, 1847	63
5	Espartero's charge at the Battle of Guadarmino, May 1839	118
6	The Embrace of Vergara, August 1839	127
7	"Songs sung in honour of the Duke of Victory at the serenade on 14 July 1840"	147
8	Portrait of Espartero as regent, 1841	165
9	A fan writes to Espartero on his return from exile, 1850	218
10	A fan's drawing of Espartero, 1850	219
11	Espartero enters Madrid, July 1854	230
12	"Let the national will be done," 1854	232
13	*Carte de visite*, Espartero in civilian clothes, c. 1860	276
14	"Espartero: King or President?," 1868	297
15	King Alfonso XII visits Espartero, 1875	327
16	Portrait of Jacinta, 1878	333
17	Transfer of the remains of Espartero and his wife, 1889	340
18	Spanish Civil War cartoon satirizing a Luchana-style negotiated peace, 1937	347

Acknowledgments

Researching and writing a book such as this requires time and money, and I have enjoyed the good fortune of having both. An Insight Grant from the Social Sciences and Humanities Research Council of Canada allowed me to undertake research in Spain and the United Kingdom as well as hire research assistants there and in Portugal and Argentina. A Killam Research Fellowship from the Canada Council for the Arts gave me the luxury of two years during which I could devote myself to writing full time.

Historians also need sources, and I have been extremely fortunate here as well. The late Pablo Montesino-Espartero y Juliá, fifth Duque de la Victoria, and the current Duke, his son Pablo Montesino-Espartero y Velasco, have been models of generosity. They gave me full access to the private papers of Baldomero Espartero and full freedom in using them. This book could not have been written without them.

I am grateful to the many institutions that gave me the opportunity to present earlier versions of my ideas and receive invaluable comments and suggestions: the Department of Contemporary History and the History of America at the University of Santiago de Compostela, the Department of Contemporary History at the University of Valencia, the Department of Contemporary History at the University of the Basque Country, the Department of Modern and Contemporary History at the Autonomous University of Barcelona, the Department of Contemporary Humanities at the University of Alicante, the Contemporary History Seminar at the Ortega y Gasset University Institute, the Department of History at Trent University, the Department of History at Tel Aviv University, the Re-imaging Democracy in the Nineteenth Century Mediterranean project at Oxford University, the Centre for the History of Ibero-America at Leeds University, the Leeds Library, and the Empires, Nations and Sovereignty Research Group at the Pompeu Fabra University.

Finally, I want to thank the many friends and colleagues whose help and encouragement over many years has enriched this book: Myles Ali, Mikel Alberi Sagardia, Gregorio Alonso, Teresa Álvarez González, José Álvarez Junco, Daniel Aquillué Domínguez, Xavier Andreu Miralles, Raúl Martín Arranz, Lurdes Azpiazu Aizpiolea, Edward Baker, Isabel Burdiel, Mónica Burguera, Antonio Cazorla-Sánchez, María Cifuentes, Boyd Cochran, Chris Cunningham, Josep Fradera, Gregorio de la Fuente Monge, Albert García Balañá, Irene González González, Tony Graham, Arthur Haberman, Abril Liberatore, Marcel Martel, Jani Mauricio, Bàrbara Molas Gregorio, Asís Montesino-Espartero, Javier Moreno Luzón, Xosé Manoel Núñez Seixas, Juan Pro Ruiz, Oriol Regué Sendrós, Jordi Roca Vernet, Oscar Rodríguez Barreira, Mari Cruz Romeo Mateo, Manuel Santirso Rodríguez, Vicent Sanz, and Miguel Torrens.

THE SWORD OF LUCHANA

Introduction

The Spanish civil war was already into its fourth year. It was being fought with such viciousness and brutality that Great Britain had intervened to negotiate a code of conduct for the treatment of prisoners. The Carlist rebels, ultra-reactionary defenders of the claim to the throne of Prince Carlos, the uncle of the infant queen Isabel II, had besieged Bilbao for three weeks in 1835 and were once again laying siege to this major port. Capturing it, they anticipated, would bring the international recognition that had eluded them until now as well as providing a badly needed source of revenue. And the city looked like an easy target, cut off from the rest of liberal Spain and defended by only a small, ill-provisioned garrison.

The bombardments began on 25 October 1836 and soon blasted a massive breach in the walls. After an attempt to take the city in a frontal assault failed, the rebels changed their strategy, seizing the various forts that defended Bilbao and blocking the Nervión River. By 17 November, the city was surrounded, and its surrender seemed close at hand. The one remaining fort fell on 27 November. The Carlists called on the city to surrender, but its commander, General Evaristo San Miguel, refused. His bravado covered over the increasingly desperate conditions being endured by the residents, especially members of the National Militia, who had been pulled from their employment, and their families. Food was running low and bread was rationed. The bread that was available was "black" and so bad that it was making people ill. Some residents were even eating cats – when they could find them. On 14 December, the city authorities sent a desperate telegram to the government army: "There are biscuits for only two days, we have no flour or provisions. The garrison is discouraged and the population is suffering greatly." Then typhus hit.[1]

Morale was worsened by the failure of the main loyalist army, under General Baldomero Espartero, to relieve the city. Since arriving in

Portugalete, thirteen kilometres downriver, at the end of November, the army had made various sorties along both sides of the Nervión but had been unable to raise the siege. By mid-December, the high command was divided on how to proceed. Should the army cross to the right bank of the river and attempt an attack from there? Even though only a minority of his generals, as well as the British military observer Colonel William Wylde, were in favour, Espartero decided to take the chance.

The attack took place on 24 December. The weather was atrocious: torrential rain in the morning turned to sleet and then, by late afternoon, when the attack was to start, became a "Canadian snow storm."[2] What would be known as the Battle of Luchana began with a sophisticated amphibious operation. At 4:00 in the afternoon, eight companies of troops boarded launches and rafts which were towed upriver by two British naval vessels, covered by four Spanish gun boats. Aided by the snow, they were able to land behind the foremost Carlist battery and launch a surprise attack. After the Carlists fled and as engineers repaired the Luchana bridge the rafts were brought up and turned into a temporary bridge enabling the troops to cross. After they captured the strategic summit of Monte de Cabras, the Carlists began to fight back. "Combat quickly became lethal; both sides were firing point blank; the ground was littered with corpses, and the howling of the hurricane drowned out the cries of the wounded." The weather was so bad that the fighting stopped for a while. At midnight, the temperature was ten below zero.[3]

Espartero had been horribly plagued by kidney stones throughout the campaign and was agonizing in bed when the attack began. When Lieutenant Edward Vicars, a British officer attached to Espartero's headquarters, first met him,

> he was lodged in a miserable habitation which seemed to be somewhere between a barn and a dwelling house, the floor covered with straw and Indian corn, wool and feathers, the debris of old beds, without other furniture than the bed the General was stretched on, and a few old chairs. He was surrounded by a medical attendant and some of his staff, a cigar in his mouth, and holding out for our inspection a stone about the size of a pea, which he had just passed. He had been relieved from the extreme of agony but looked the picture of distress and misery, his mind ill at ease from the great and awful responsibility he felt was on his shoulders while his frame was wracked an torn by a grievous and painful disease.

One can almost see Vicars grimacing as he concluded, "I assure you the Lieutenant of Engineers did not, on leaving the chamber, envy the general in chief of the army of the north."[4]

When General Marcelino Oráa, who had been in command, came to Espartero's tent around midnight and told him that the Carlists were putting up such fierce resistance, Espartero called for his orderly: "Tomás ... bring my uniform and my boots." Oráa's attempts to dissuade him from getting up produced only "two or three obscenities." A feverish Espartero dressed and marched to the launches and, after crossing the river, mounted his horse, standing in his stirrups because he was in too much pain to sit down.[5] He had, he later told his wife, decided "enter Bilbao or die trying."[6]

After forming up the troops, Oráa had the bugle sound the charge. Espartero put himself at the head of one of the columns and addressed the men before him: "Comrades," the time to show the world what they were made of had arrived. After the winter hardships they had endured, queen and fatherland demanded one last great effort:

> Such valiant soldiers as you need no more than a single cartridge, and you will use that only when absolutely necessary. With the points of bayonets which are accustomed only to victory we will bring this great enterprise to an end, we will whip the enemies of our adored queen, we will crush them. Along with you, I, the first soldier, the first among you, will see them die or abandon the field laden with ignominy, hurrying to their lairs to hide it. Let us march, then, into combat; let us march to finish the job we have begun, then grasp the victor's crown that awaits us, and finally, let us march to save and embrace our brothers, who have so valorously imitated our example by defending the national cause inside the walls of the immortal city of Bilbao.[7]

More than thirty years later, a sergeant from the Gerona Volunteers recalled how the sound of Espartero's "sonorous voice" urging them on to Bilbao revived "our frozen and mutilated bodies, weakened by hunger and fatigue."[8]

Espartero then had his men move forward in silence, and when they came upon a body of Carlist troops he led the charge, cheering for the queen and freedom. "The bullets, the shrapnel, the grenades, a powerful snowstorm and a terrible hurricane," he told his wife, "offered a most impressive spectacle." The enemy fled. The road to Bilbao lay open. It was now five in the morning. Being on the battlefield had itself been a cure for his suffering. "When the bayonet charge began all my ailments disappeared."[9]

Figure 1 The Night of Luchana. Nineteenth Century Album, Museo Zumalakarregi.

At 8:00 that morning Espartero led his army into Bilbao. It was Christmas Day and there was more than one saviour to celebrate.[10] "How I am alive," he told Vicars, "I cannot tell."[11]

The news did not reach Madrid until New Year's Day, but when it did, the capital was ecstatic. This obscure general became a national hero almost overnight.[12] The government published a special issue of the official *Gazette* with Espartero's dispatch to the minister of war.[13] As it was a holiday, the blind men and women who usually waited outside the National Print Works to collect and distribute the *Gazette* were not there. Instead, the task was taken up by natives of Bilbao resident in the capital and "anxious to spread the great news to the public," who gave the paper away for free. Accounts of the battle spread rapidly and took precedence over everything else. As the news reached the city's theatres, audiences demanded that performances be interrupted so that Espartero's dispatch could be read out. In one theatre the audience, "considering the place too constricted for the great emotions they were feeling," poured out into the street to celebrate.[14]

When parliament met the next day, the great victory at Bilbao was the sole topic. Joaquín María López, the interior minister and one of the greatest orators of an age known for its oratory, delivered a speech so powerful that people learned it by heart and remembered it for decades. Salustiano Olózaga, another famed speaker, was for once at a loss for words and found himself needing to "release the ecstasy" that news of Espartero's victory had created.[15] Over the next few days the queen regent decreed and Cortes voted to award the title of *beneméritos* [distinguished] to all the defenders of Bilbao and a medal to all members of the garrison, grant the city the titles "very noble and very loyal" and "unvanquished," rebuild the buildings which had been destroyed, and provide a pension for the widows and orphans of the men who fell during the siege. A new square being built in Madrid was to be called the Plaza de Bilbao. Espartero was ennobled as Count of Luchana by royal decree.[16]

The government also engaged "the greatest propaganda tool at its disposal" to publicize the glorious news. On 5 February 1837, in all the country's cathedrals, and in "the oldest parishes in the towns without one," there were "solemn funeral rites" in memory of those who died during the siege and in the final battle.[17] The voice of the Catholic Church, much of which rejected Carlism and remained loyal to Queen Isabel, reached much further into the corners of Spain than that of the government, and from pulpits across the country Spaniards heard the clergy mourning the dead, celebrating the victory, and praising the general whose name most had never before heard. In the great cathedral of El Pilar in Zaragoza, Canon Policarpo Romea spoke repeatedly of "immortal Espartero" and "Espartero the hero." Miguel Moragues began his sermon in the cathedral of Palma de Mallorca with a quote from the book of Maccabees about the need to die trying to save one's brothers or face dishonour before asking, "In whose lips better than in those of the brave Espartero do these heroic words belong?"[18] In Cervera, Antonio Vila described Espartero as nothing less than the hand of God:

> The captain sent by the Lord, clothed in his power and preceded by a column of fire, marches with his intrepid legions, leaps over the deepest valleys and tallest parapets, gives the signal and in a single blast the trumpets and drums uproot the cedars of Lebanon, destroy the forts of Moab, destroy the walls of Jericho, and, in the name of the Lord makes his triumphal entry into the city over the bodies of the enemy.[19]

Preaching in Madrid's San Isidro church, Pedro Rico y Amat made the greatest comparison of all: Espartero led his army into the liberated city "the same day in which the liberator of nations, Jesus Christ, came to the world to save us and make us free."[20]

Figure 2 Espartero in material culture: ceramic plate. Museo Nacional de Cerámica y de las Artes Suntuarias González Martí.

Glorifying Luchana, and Espartero with it, was not the monopoly of official institutions Souvenirs were produced to meet popular demand: maps, lithographs showing Espartero leading the charge, and an engraving with eighteen vignettes of the most memorable parts of the battle, with Espartero's "daring and valour" in a starring role.[21] There were poems and songs. One of the most popular, *El sitio de Bilbao: rasgo épico* by Gerónimo Morán, a nineteen-year-old from Valladolid, urged "fervent Spaniards" to imitate "the determination of Espartero in the fight."[22] And there were plays. Manuel Bretón de los Herreros's *Las improvisaciones*, which was performed in Madrid at the end of January, highlighted Espartero as the saviour of the city, as did *El Sitio de Bilbao* by Antonio García Gutiérrez, which debuted on 11 March, a love story set in Bilbao during the siege. Espartero was not a character, but he was the hero. The play ends with "Espartero's rangers" entering the city as a voice cries out, perhaps for the first time in public, a pairing that would become famous: "Long live liberty. Long live Espartero!"[23]

Luchana was not a battle that would "go down in the annals of military history," as Espartero characteristically boasted to his wife, but he was right in calling it "a fatal blow to the faction" even if it would take another thirty-two months before the Carlists gave up the struggle in the Basque Country and Navarra and another eleven after that before the war was entirely won.[24] But Luchana, which came at the midpoint in his long life, was a crucial turning point for Espartero himself. Spain's new hero was forty-three years old, and in many ways his life had already been an extraordinary one, the product of his abilities and the tumultuous, often disastrous circumstances facing Spain in the age of war and revolution that began with the French Revolution of 1789.

Born in 1793, Joaquín Baldomero Fernández Espartero was the ninth child of a cartwright from the small town of Granátula de Calatrava in La Mancha. After completing a degree at the Universidad de Almagro, itself a rarity in the Spain of the time, in 1809 at the age of sixteen he volunteered for the army to fight against the French as a common soldier. He took advantage of the new openness of the officer corps under the anti-Napoleonic regime and became a lieutenant. When that war ended he volunteered again, this time to go to America to defend the empire against movements fighting to liberate the colonies. In almost ten years of fighting he rose to the rank of brigadier general. The outbreak of the Carlist War in October 1833, in which Prince Carlos challenged the right to the throne of his three-year-old niece, Isabel II, gave him the opportunity to rise still further, and a few months before Luchana he had been named commander in chief of the Army of the North. Espartero was far from unique. In this age of unrelenting warfare, many military men enjoyed similarly meteoric careers.

What came after 24 December 1836, however, was truly exceptional, a story worthy of Stendhal or Gabriel García Márquez, a life to which only a handful of others could be compared. In August 1839, he brought the war in the north to an end with a negotiated peace that earned him the unofficial but enduring title of "Pacificador de España" [Peacemaker of Spain]. He followed this with an impressive campaign in the Maestrazgo, which defeated the Carlists completely. Then, in short order, he became the hero of Progressive liberalism, prime minister, and, in May 1841, regent of the realm. A little more than two years later he was overthrown by a military uprising supported by some members of his own party and went into exile in Great Britain, where he spent four and a half years before being allowed to return to Spain. Then, facing revolution in July 1854, Queen Isabel called him to power, but he lasted only two years before being forced out again. This time he was allowed to remain in the country, and he returned to Logroño, his wife's birthplace and his adopted home, where he remained for the rest of his life. Stunningly, the failure of both his moments in power did not destroy his popularity. When Isabel was chased from the throne in September 1868, there was an impressive campaign to make the seventy-five-year-old Espartero king, and he famously refused an invitation from the revolutionary government to be considered for the role. Until the consolidation of the restored Bourbon dynasty after 1875, his return to office was repeatedly seen as a solution to political crises.

Surprisingly, there is no full-scale biography of this remarkable life. This one benefits from the major renewal the genre has experienced in recent years.[25] Biographers now select their subjects from a much wider pool of possibilities than before.[26] Even the life of the "great man," the traditional hunting ground of many biographers, was reinvigorated by taking as a focus the ways in which the life was presented at the time and remembered, appropriated, and used afterwards.[27] Biographers are increasingly writing what Sabine Loriga has called "biographical history," in which the biographer is driven by broader historical questions as much as, or even more than, by the actual individual being studied.[28]

This biography of Espartero shares this approach. It tells the story of Espartero's life in a traditional way, but it also seeks to cast light on broad aspects of Spain's modern history and contribute to the emerging, more sophisticated understanding of the nineteenth century.[29] As I was writing, three such questions emerged; two of them brought an additional protagonist to the book.

The first question was political culture and national identity. The extent to which there was a shared national identity and where it came from has been the major question in historiography of nineteenth-century Spain. The long-standing concern with the supposed deficiencies of the Spanish state and the belief that it had produced an inadequate nationalization, especially when compared to an idealized French model, has more recently given way to a focus on culture and society and on non-state, non-elite, and regional or local agents of nationalization.[30] This new historiography has produced a very different picture, one in which "the chronology of Spanish nation building has changed substantially." The nation now appears as a catalyst of popular affective and mobilizing loyalty earlier than was thought. This was certainly true in the case of national symbols such as flags and songs, where there was "an undeniable expansion of Spanish nationalism" which touched even "certain areas of the rural world and the popular classes.' Espartero was at the very centre of such mobilization, of what the nation "mean[t] to ordinary people" who, through their autonomous activity, could "construe a national identity out of elements that are not always handed out to them by the elite ... [and] fashion their own national heroes and narratives."[31]

The protagonist here is collective, what Isabel Burdiel has called the "chorus of voices" that created competing stories about their contemporaries.[32] In this case, it consists of the many thousands of ordinary people all over the country who admired, even revered, the man they saw as the unyielding champion of liberty and, especially, the bringer of peace after a long and brutal civil war. It was these people, and the entrepreneurs who catered to them by producing lithographs, *aleluyas*, and affordable images and books, who through decades and across generations kept alive what I call the cult of Espartero, a cult to which only those of Napoleon and Garibaldi compare.[33] It was these people who made Espartero Spain's first political celebrity and real public figure, as well as the incarnation of public morality and of the liberal, and even the democratic, nation.[34] This collective voice was composed of large numbers of individual ones, the vast majority of which were, at the time, anonymous or not even heard publicly. Here I will name them whenever possible.

The second question was gender. Across the Atlantic world, the construction of liberal and republican political systems and societies was accompanied by the need to define the gender dimensions of the new order. Just what the age of revolution meant for women has been a long-standing question. Did it kill off a recognized public role for – at least – elite women, or did women continue to have a public role despite their banishment from the formal institutions of politics? Were the new societies structured around a strict public/private dichotomy in which women were consigned to the purdah of domesticity, or were their public spheres sufficiently capacious for women to stake out a domain, either as individuals or collectively?[35]

These questions apply to Spain as well, and there is now a substantial and sophisticated literature that paints a much more textured and complex picture of the creation of a liberal state and society there during the first half of the nineteenth century. The old vision of a failed and backward country has been replaced by one that sees a real liberal revolution that brought about a profound and meaningful rupture from the *ancien régime*. This revisionist interpretation has extended to concepts of gender and the place of women. As historians have looked beyond prescriptive literature and developed an understanding of political activity that is not limited to elections and legislatures – where the exclusion of women was unambiguous – they have seriously modified early ideas about the separation of the spheres and the banishment of women from public life.[36]

Rather than being predetermined, the roles of women were the focus of debates in which women participated, and which were themselves a constitutive part of the liberal revolution. These debates did not simply pit liberals against their opponents. The place of women in the new order was one of a number of key issues over which the two main branches of Spanish liberalism, Progressives and Moderates, had fundamental differences. Both groups were less modern political parties than amalgams of notables and their followers. Progressives favoured a broader suffrage, a more decentralized state that made municipal governments autonomous, a system that gave parliament more power than the monarch, a more hard-nosed attitude to the Catholic Church, and the restoration of the National Militia, a citizens' militia first established by the Constitution of 1812. They also advocated what Mónica Burguera calls "a project of gradual social transformation which counted on the active public presence of women." The years between the creation of the Constitution of 1337 and the fall of the Espartero regency in 1843, when the Progressives were in power for much of the time, were crucial in allowing the creation of a "respectable public femininity" centred on education and philanthropy.[37] Only later was the domestic archetype known as the "angel of the hearth," after a phrase popularized by María del Pilar Sinués de Marco in her massive 1859 best-seller *El Ángel del Hogar*, consolidated.[38]

The protagonist here is María Jacinta Guadalupe Martínez de Sicilia y Santa Cruz. She married Espartero in 1827, when she was only sixteen years old, and they were a couple for fifty-one years, until her death in 1878. Jacinta, as I will call her throughout the book,[39] came to play an important role in Espartero's career and, more significantly, was widely known to have done so. She was also an impressive woman in her own right: well-read, well-connected, sharp-tongued, with ideas of her own, she went from a provincial upbringing in Logroño to functioning in the most elevated social and political circles. No less a person than Lord Palmerston, who knew Jacinta when she was in her thirties, described her as "a very superior woman."[40] If the sources had permitted, I would have written a double biography. In the end, I settled for giving her as prominent a role as possible.

The final question was historical memory. This has been a topic of considerable academic and public interest and controversy in Spain over the past fifteen to twenty years, although this interest has been directed almost exclusively to the Spanish Civil War and the Franco regime.[41] The leading figure of Spain's nineteenth-century history, the most famous Spaniard of his time, remains both contentious and essentially orphaned. He has critics but no advocates. While questions of historical memory regarding the nineteenth century and its civil wars cannot begin to match the level of emotion surrounding those of the twentieth, Espartero's example makes it clear that the question and, to some extent, the emotions persist and that conflicts over memory are not limited to the recent past. In a country with such a tumultuous political history, which endured two bloody and debilitating civil wars within a hundred years, in which a vicious forty-year dictatorship contaminated the symbols and expressions of national feeling, and in which the fundamental nature of the nation was in play, the cultures of memory are particularly complex. Historical memory in Spain remains long but fragmented and conflictual, especially where potential "national" heroes are concerned. This question does not have a protagonist, which, perhaps, is all that needs to be said.

This biography also benefits from what we might call an "Espartero moment." After many years, even decades, in which they had almost totally ignored him, historians have begun to show an interest in Espartero, although this still remains limited to a handful of articles and three books devoted to specific moments or aspects of Espartero's life.[42] I have also been extremely fortunate with sources. I had the good fortune to enjoy access to a new and immensely valuable source: Espartero's private papers, which are in the possession of the current Duque de la Victoria. And while the press is far from a new source, the digital collections in the National Library of Spain's Hemeroteca Digital and the Ministry of Culture's Biblioteca Virtual de Prensa Histórica have made it possible to use the press in ways which would have been unthinkable in the analogue age.[43]

And Espartero himself? After reading his entire archive with its thousands of documents, I still find him elusive. Little inclined to introspection or to explaining himself in public, he kept no diary and did not write memoirs or an autobiography. (The one time he did publish an explanation of his conduct, it was written by someone else under commission from Jacinta.) Only in his letters to her did he express himself fully and openly, and these exist only for the one occasion in their long marriage when they were apart for an extended period of time, the years of the Carlist War and its immediate aftermath. Little in the rest of his voluminous correspondence reveals much about his thoughts, beliefs, or motivations. The next best sources are reports of their conversations with him by people such as Ángel Fernández de los Ríos and Arthur Aston, the British ambassador in Madrid during Espartero's regency.[44] As a result, we do not know what he sought to achieve, beyond sustaining the monarchy, or what he thought about such monumental issues as the Catholic Church or slavery.

There was no single coherent or consistent Espartero. As a soldier, his unlimited physical courage, even recklessness, brought him success after success on the battlefield. As a commander, he was both a fierce disciplinarian who did not shy away from the firing squad as a punishment and someone who genuinely cared for his men, was economical with their lives, and even used his personal resources to keep them fed and clothed. As a commander in chief he was far from being a Wellington, a Napoleon, or a Grant, but his caution saved him from defeat and made it possible for him to win the war in the end. He was a man of war who understood that a military solution is not always the best one. He was supremely self-confident, even arrogant. During the final years of the Carlist War, he came to feel that he had a privileged and unique understanding of the needs and desires of the Spanish people. He was a Spanish nationalist for whom national unity was the holy grail and he its champion. Today we might say that he believed his own press clippings. He was an ardent monarchist who spent all his public life sustaining the threatened throne of Isabel II but who, as an old man, endorsed a new dynasty and then the First Republic as emanations of the "national will." He valued loyalty to friends above almost all else and he practised it in his political life, to his great cost. He was a devoted and doting husband who was emotionally dependent on the wife who did so much to advance his career.

The most important things about Espartero were these. While he revelled in adulation, he was not ambitious, at least not in the same way as many of his contemporaries, civilian or military. He craved neither office nor power, and he certainly did not enjoy the real work of political life. He did not understand politicians, but neither did they understand him. The general who could electrify his men with his harangues and was so decisive on the battlefield was almost tongue-tied in parliament and dithered at moments of political crisis, but he came closer to being a truly constitutional head of state than anyone before 1870. This striking juxtaposition of "passivity and dynamism" was something he shared with Ulysses S. Grant, who was in a number of ways a comparable figure. Both were nobodies "who became almost everything." Both fought a brutal civil war which they ended with gestures they hoped would lead to reconciliation. And after their military triumphs, they both had political careers that have been the subject of controversy.[45] Despite his wealth, Espartero was a man of simple tastes who shunned the pomp and glamour of Madrid and whose favourite hobby was planting trees. He was honest at a time when Spaniards felt this was sorely lacking in public life. He saw himself as Cincinnatus, but a closer model was George Washington, with whom he was frequently compared. Garry Wills's description of the first United States president as "a virtuoso of resignations … who gained his power by his willingness to give it up" fits Espartero well.[46] Both Cincinnatus and Washington were exemplars of republican virtue, but there was little room for that in Espartero's Spain. In an age which thrived on melodramatic novels[47] the way our own thrives on *Game of Thrones* and reality television, he – and Jacinta – were the virtuous protagonists of a melodrama playing out in real time.

1

From Gránatula to America, February 1793–February 1815

On 28 February 1793, Antonio Alfonso Treviño y Carrillo performed a baptism in the church of Santa Ana in the small town of Gránatula de Calatrava, in the region of La Mancha in central Spain. The parents, Antonio Fernández Espartero and Josefa Álvarez, looked on as their day-old son, held by his godmother, Antonia Molina, was baptized with the names Joaquín Baldomero.

Gránatula de Calatrava was an out of the way and undistinguished place, although it stands only a few kilometres away from the ruins of Oretum, the ancient town of the Iberians. The baptismal font must have had special meaning for earlier inhabitants: it originally stood in the church of San Miguel in Añavete and was carried to Gránatula by the residents of that hamlet when it was abandoned in the sixteenth century.[1] Until 1712, when King Philip V granted it the status of autonomous *villazgo* [chartered town], Gránatula was under the control of Almagro, twelve kilometres away.[2] In response to a questionnaire sent out by the Cardinal Archbishop of Toledo, Francisco Antonio de Lorenzana, in 1773, the parish priest described the local economy as producing "wheat, barley, rye, millet, oil, wine, turnips, the most exquisite peppers in La Mancha, and other edible legumes … There are no factories as the largest part of the male population works in agriculture, but the women do fine lace work for the merchants of Almagro who provide them with the thread."[3]

The first modern census in Spain, commissioned by the Count of Floridablanca in 1787, confirmed the priest's description of Gránatula as a place dominated by agriculture. The town had a population of 2,036, with men slightly outnumbering women. It was also a very young population, with 40 per cent of the inhabitants under sixteen years old. (The broader eighteenth-century trend of demographic growth was certainly in evidence there.) Of the 472 people who reported an occupation, 67 were *labradores*, which meant that they owned or leased the land they farmed, while 274 were *jornaleros*, day labourers, almost all of whom would have worked on those farms. The remaining townspeople with a recorded occupation included 37 artisans, 51 servants, 12 students, 12 people attached to the Church, including one employee of the Inquisition, 6 merchants or shopkeepers, 4 employees receiving a salary from the king, 1 scribe, and 1 lawyer. There were also 4 *hidalgos*, men who claimed noble status although they did not have a title of any sort, and three claiming the *fuero militar* [to be under military jurisdiction], which meant they were or had been in the armed forces.

Antonio Fernández Espartero (1747–1818) was one of the artisans, a wagon maker and carpenter. This was a family trade; his father, Manuel Fernández Espartero, is mentioned in the *Catastro de Ensenada*, compiled in the 1750s, as one of three "master cartwrights" in Gránatula,[4] and Antonio's eldest son, Vicente, carried on after him. Antonio seems to have had some education, as well as a certain local social standing, serving as a mediator in disputes that found their way to the municipal government. His wife, Josefa Vicenta Álvarez de Toro y Molina (1749–1815), was born in the smaller town of Villamayor de Calatrava, some 40 kilometres away. Her family's roots there were not deep. Her mother, Angela de Molina, was from Granátula, but her father, Pedro Alvarez, had moved to Villamayor from Mérida, in Extremadura, 250 kilometres to the west. What prompted him to make such an unusual move and how he earned his living are not clear; unlike most men who had occupations other than agriculture, Pedro Alvarez is not mentioned by name in the *Catastro de Ensenada*. Even so, Josefa's family was connected to the local notables. Her godfather, Mateo Muñoz Bastante, was a notary; he was also one of the local informants for the Catastro.[5]

Antonio and Josefa had a large family. Joaquín Baldomero, born when both his parents were in their mid-forties, was the youngest of nine children, three girls and six boys. Three of the older boys became priests, and one of them, Manuel José Hilario, was a Dominican friar in the convent of Almagro, which ran the university there. One of the girls became a nun. Very little is known about Espartero's childhood. One of his first biographers claimed that he showed his military proclivities early on, that people who knew him as a child said that he was very fond of playing soldier, "even building a wooden contraption in his father's workshop which could throw stones further and with greater force than those of his playmates."[6]

We have only two pieces of evidence suggesting how Espartero got on with his parents. The 1818 letter to his father, written from America when he was twenty-five, begins with almost hyperbolic endearments and shows that he wrote home often.

> My dear father: is it possible that since I left Cádiz I have not had the glory of knowing the situation of those who brought me into the world? That I haven't received a single reply to the letters I wrote from Margarita Island, Cumana, Puerto Cabello, Caracas, Puerto Velo y Panama, all the ports of the mainland, and that the same has happened to those I wrote from Payta, Lima, Cuzco, and other places in Peru, where I am now? I can only attribute this unexpected development to your having died, for only in this way could the love of the best of fathers cease.
>
> Nevertheless, my heart tells me that you and my dear mother are still alive, and I predict that the day will come when we have the joy of giving each other a thousand embraces and enjoying in the company of my siblings and other relatives the satisfactions which come from such a long absence.

Sadly, his father was buried the very day Espartero was writing this letter. His mother had died three years earlier.[7] On the other hand, Espartero did not seem much impressed with his father's status in Granátula. In 1837, years after he himself married a woman who had inherited large amounts of land, he advised his brother Francisco on marriage choices for his daughters: "if they marry it should be with landowners or honest farmers with a comfortable income ... Do not let them marry artisans of any kind."[8]

Espartero received an unusual amount of education for the time. He studied Latin and rhetoric with a friend of his father, Antonio Meoro, who was also a carpenter. (As regent, Espartero would unsuccessfully try to appoint one of Meoro's sons, Anacleto Meoro Sánchez, bishop of Gerona.) This was enough to get Espartero into the University of Almagro, where he started his studies in 1806 at the age of thirteen.

Founded in 1574 by the medieval military order of Calatrava, which controlled so much of La Mancha, and connected to the Dominican convent of Nuestra Señora del Rosario, the University of Almagro initially offered degrees in arts, medicine, law, and theology. Following the reform of Spanish universities under Charles III, it taught physics, metaphysics, logic, and grammar as well as theology. With the exception of grammar, all the subjects were taught by monks. By the 1790s, the university was in decline, and in July 1807, while Espartero was in the midst of his studies, Almagro was included in a list of eleven "lesser universities" to be closed, although that did not happen until 1824.[9]

Espartero graduated from Almagro in 1808 with a degree in *filosofía* [humanities]. Given the trajectory of his three brothers, he was likely destined for the clergy. (Espartero valued education, at least for boys: in a letter to his family sent from Potosí, Peru, in 1818 he told his brothers, "If Paco and Vicente have sons they should make sure to give them a good education.")[10] Whatever plans Espartero's father may have had for him, or he had for himself, they were disrupted by events emanating from faraway Paris.

The outbreak of the French Revolution posed major military and political challenges for Spain. A war with the French Republic in 1793–5 had demonstrated the country's military weakness and led to the Second Treaty of San Idefonso in 1796, which made the two countries allies. But even before this war, there were serious tensions between elements in the government that favoured reform and those that resisted any significant change. From 1792 to 1798 and from 1801 to 1808, Spain's government was in the hands of Manuel Godoy, a louche former Guards officer from an impoverished noble family who was widely reputed to be the lover of Queen María Luisa. Godoy attempted a number of reforms to increase government revenues and strengthen the country's military, but these only further antagonized the aristocracy, the Church, and some sectors of the army while doing nothing to lessen Napoleon's distrust of his ally, or his belief that Spain was mismanaging the vast resources flowing in from America.[11]

Following his defeat of Prussia and Russia in the War of the Fourth Coalition (1806–7), Napoleon turned his attention to the Iberian peninsula. In order to launch an attack on Portugal, which remained outside his Continental System blockade of Great Britain, Napoleon forced Godoy to sign the Treaty of Fontainebleau (17 October 1807). French troops were authorized to pass through Spain so that a joint French-Spanish army could march on Lisbon. Portugal would be dismembered, with Godoy himself being given the southern third. What Napoleon's plans for Spain itself were at this point is unclear, but internal political developments soon provided him with an opportunity to take control.

The heir to the throne, Prince Fernando, deeply resented his father for favouring Godoy, whom he hated intensely.[12] This made the prince the natural ally of the elements at court which opposed Godoy's reforms, and at their urging he wrote secretly to Napoleon requesting his protection. When the king learned of this, he arrested Fernando and ordered his collaborators into internal exile. Napoleon responded to these events by sending fifty thousand troops into northern Spain. In February 1808, he sent additional troops and ordered their commander, Marshal Joachim

Murat, to march on Madrid. The court withdrew to Aranjuez, south of the capital. There, on 18 March, the aristocratic dissidents, in league with Fernando, provoked a popular uprising; the following day Godoy was arrested and King Carlos forced to abdicate in favour of his son. The new king received a rapturous reception when he entered Madrid on 24 March, but the real power there was Murat, who refused to recognize Fernando's authority. Moreover, Carlos had had second thoughts about his abdication and appealed to Napoleon to restore him to the throne. With the disposition of the Spanish crown in his hands, Napoleon acted decisively. He summoned Carlos and Fernando to the French town of Bayonne, where he forced them both to abdicate and appointed his brother Joseph Bonaparte the new king of Spain. Some Spaniards rallied to the new monarch, seeing him as the agent of the reforms they were seeking. In this they were right: on 7 July, Joseph issued Spain's first constitution, the Constitution of Bayonne. The people who collaborated with the Napoleonic regime considered themselves patriots but became known pejoratively as *afrancesados* [Frenchified ones].[13]

By this time, an anti-French revolution had broken out. On 2 May 1808, a popular uprising shook Madrid, although the French re-established control the next day. (These events were captured by Francisco Goya in his two magnificent paintings *The Second of May, 1808, or the Charge of the Mamelukes* and *The Third of May, 1808 in Madrid, or The Executions on Príncipe Pío Hill*.) News from Madrid and Bayonne then set off a series of uprisings across the country, starting in Asturias on 9 May, affecting the rest of the north and spreading like a chain reaction southwards. The established institutions of power were discredited by their collaboration with the French or collapsed entirely and were replaced by a patchwork of municipal and provincial juntas with political outlooks ranging from reactionary to liberal. The junta in Asturias even made the revolutionary proclamation that "sovereignty always resides in the people."[14]

The struggle against the French, which would last until 1814, later became known as the War of Independence, but this name hides its complex nature and the diverse motives which led Spaniards to take up arms. It was, as José Álvarez Junco describes it, "a very complicated combination of causes ... a series of lesser conflicts which came together in time and fed into each other." It was an anti-French war driven less by "an exaltation of one's own" than by a xenophobic "hatred of the foreigner." It was a religious war, a "crusade against modern enlightened Jacobin atheism," and a social protest against the seigneurial system in which lords' homes or properties were attacked. It was a war driven more by "local patriotism" than by a sense of Spanish nationalism. And it was all this in the context of an international war between France and Great Britain and a civil war between Spanish elites.[15]

The provincial juntas proclaimed themselves sovereign, declared war on Napoleon, and began raising armies based on citizen militias. Some even sent delegations to London to try and negotiate with the British government. In September, representatives of the eighteen provincial juntas met in Aranjuez and created a thirty-five-man Junta Central Suprema y Gubernativa del Reino to serve as the national government in the king's absence. This Junta Central, which was forced by the French advance to relocate to Seville, was never able to properly establish its authority, especially in the absence of any military success after an initial victory at Bailén in July 1808, although it did sign a military alliance with Great Britain in January 1809. It also took a decision that would have staggering consequences, not just for the war against the French but for the rest of Spain's nineteenth century: On 22 May it issued a decree calling for a General and Extraordinary Cortes.

The General Cortes was the Castilian version of the assemblies, such as Parliament in England and the Estates General in France, that were created in much of western Europe in the thirteenth century. Convoked by the monarch to accede to his requests for money, the Cortes was composed of representatives of the three estates into which medieval society was divided: the clergy, the nobility, and the commoners. From the sixteenth century, however, the Cortes became increasingly less influential, and in the eighteenth century they were called for the sole purpose of acknowledging the heir to the throne.

The new General Cortes was designated "Extraordinary" and it had to deal with a truly extraordinary situation. Spain had two kings, or possibly three: Napoleon's brother José I, and two Bourbon claimants, the last legitimate king, Carlos IV, whom Napoleon had bought off, and his son, Fernando VII, whom he had put under arrest. Spanish elites were divided. French forces occupied much of the country but had to deal with an intense guerrilla war in the north and more traditional military resistance from the forces of the Junta Central and its British allies.[16] In principle, the Cortes's mandate was to oversee the war effort and pass whatever laws it deemed necessary to ensure victory. In practice, it would go much further than that.[17] The Cortes came into being only after a long, complex, and controversial process that dragged on for two years. At its heart was the way the assembly would be structured. Would it be a gathering of the old corporate bodies or would it be a parliament of the Spanish people? The latter won out, but, given the French occupation, elections could not be held in much of the country.

By the time the Cortes began its deliberations in September 1810, French power in Spain was at its height.

The war against the French, which would last until April 1814, opened up opportunities for military careers that were unthinkable earlier. Espartero's was one of these. In 1809, he accompanied his brother Manuel on a trip to Baza, in the province of Granada. It was here that he made the decision to volunteer for the army. His service record notes that on 1 November 1809 Espartero joined the Ciudad Real Infantry Regiment as a "soldado distinguido," someone who "joined a military unit and later became cadet and continued in the military as an officer."[18] Espartero never commented directly on what motivated him to volunteer, but the authors of a biography published when he was seventy-five quote him as saying that he "obeyed only the instinct of national salvation, propelled by his fighting temperament and by the development of his strength and agility, which made him think of the foreigner as someone who could frighten only children."[19]

Espartero would see action very quickly, but his first experience as a soldier cannot have been a happy one. His unit was part of the Army of La Mancha, the spearhead of the last Spanish offensive of the war, which would conclude on 19 November 1809 with the shattering defeat at Ocaña. The plan was for three Spanish armies to converge on Madrid from the south, west, and north. Arthur Wellesley (the future Duke of Wellington) was opposed to it at the time. The British military historian William Napier later called it "an extreme example of military rashness."[20] He could have added incompetence.

The Army of La Marcha massed at a place called Santa Cruz de Mudela, only forty-one kilometres southeast of Espartero's home town. It was an impressive force compared to other Spanish armies: fifty thousand men including almost six thousand cavalry, with new uniforms and equipment, and sixty cannon. Napier describes the soldiers as "young, robust and full of self-confidence," and in these words one can see the sixteen-year-old Espartero on his first military adventure.[21] On the other hand, Colonel Roche, a British officer attached to the staff of General Juan Carlos de Areizaga, who had only recently taken command, saw something very different: "[N]othing can exceed the general discontent, dissatisfaction and demoralization of the mass of the people and of the army."[22]

Espartero had been a soldier for only two days when the army began its northward march. For five days it advanced quickly, covering twenty-five kilometres per day. Then Areizaga stopped and allowed the French, under the command of Marshal Soult, to gain the advantage. Areizaga's forces outnumbered Soult's, fifty thousand to thirty-four thousand, but his position was much weaker; military historians have described it as "miserably defective" and "appalling."[23] The Spanish infantry initially fought well, but the superiority of the French cavalry soon turned the battle into a rout. "The whole army then dissolved in chaos. Entire divisions laid down their arms whilst the rest of the troops scattered in all directions. A few troops on the left maintained their order and conducted a gallant rearguard action."[24] Was Espartero's regiment one of these? The battle had lasted less than four hours, but "an army of fifty thousand men had been ruined."[25] Spanish losses were horrendous: eighteen thousand casualties as well as fifty of the sixty cannon and large quantities of other weapons and supplies. Many of the soldiers who fled the battlefield deserted.

What lessons did the neophyte soldier draw from this experience? Decades later he reportedly told two of his biographers that the battle stripped him of his preconceptions about the French – and the Spaniards. Before Ocaña, "I didn't realize that there could be other men as privileged by nature as Spaniards"; afterwards he knew that "the French knew how to fight ... I began to see things as they were ... That was when I began to be a man."[26] Would he also have agreed with Charles Oman's devastating judgment on his commanding general? "For a combination of rashness and vacillation it excels that of any other Spanish general during the whole war ... In the actual moment of conflict he seems to have remained in a hypnotized condition in his church tower, hardly issuing an order and allowing the fight to go as it pleased."[27]

Ocaña changed the strategic situation radically. Before the battle, the French had not moved much south of Madrid. Their victory left the road to southern Spain open, with only the Army of Extremadura and the disorganized remnants of Areizaga's force to stop them. Napoleon had taken advantage of his victory over the Habsburgs at the Battle of Wagram in July 1809 to send significant reinforcements to Spain. On 19 January 1810, an army of sixty thousand men invaded Andalucía. Facing little resistance, they reached Seville, the capital of the Junta Central, by the 31st, but the Junta had already abandoned the city and retreated to Cádiz, where it arrived on 28 January 1810.[28]

Soon after Ocaña, Espartero was in Seville. There he left the Ciudad Real regiment on 24 December to join the Volunteer Battalion of the University of Toledo, retaining his rank of "soldado distinguido." This unusual unit was part of the patriotic response to the French invasion, and especially the victory at Bailén. In a decision that had no precedent, but which was followed by a number of other Spanish universities, in August 1808 the University of Toledo created a volunteer force of students. By December it was in Seville, assigned to maintaining order in the city. On 1 December 1809, the ruling Junta Central authorized the creation of a new military academy to train officers that was open to members of the University Battalion.[29] Was it this opportunity that led Espartero to transfer there only three weeks later? In any case, the French advance forced both the Batallón Universitario and the academy out of Seville. On 2 February 1810, and only days ahead of the French forces, the battalion arrived in Cádiz as part of the Army of Extremadura. For the next three years, Cádiz and its environs would be Espartero's home.

Even in normal times, Cádiz was exceptional among Spanish cities. Long a major port, in 1717 it was given the monopoly on all trade with Spain's American empire, replacing Seville, which had enjoyed this privilege since 1503. This role brought the city a new prosperity, one which even the abolition of the monopoly and the proclamation of "imperial free trade" in 1778 did not diminish. If anything, Cádiz became even more prosperous. The 1790s were a kind of golden age as Cádiz became a global emporium, connecting America, Africa, Asia, and Europe. It was also well connected to the major financial centres of Europe.[30] Given these extensive international connections, it is not surprising that Cádiz was home to a large foreign population. The 1801 census showed that in a city of 57,837 people, there were 2,823 foreigners, about 5 per cent of the total.[31] Many *forasteros* (outsiders) from other parts of Spain, especially the northern regions of Cantabria and the Rioja, were also part of the city's commercial life. Among them was Domingo de Santa Cruz, a twenty-three-year-old from Logroño, who would play an important role in Espartero's later life.

The economy of Cádiz had survived a major commercial crisis in 1786, but it could not overcome the damage caused by the wars of the French Revolution. The alliance with France made Spain an enemy of Great Britain: hundreds of ships – and their cargoes – were lost to British attacks, and dozens of merchant houses and insurance companies declared bankruptcy. Even more significantly, the wars provided the British the opportunity they had long sought to break Spain's monopoly of trade with its American empire. In this respect, the Battle of Trafalgar in 1805, in which the British admiral Horatio Nelson defeated a combined Spanish-French fleet, was a devastating economic blow.[32]

The time Espartero spent in and around Cádiz was far from normal. The French offensive in Andalucía drove tens of thousands of refugees into the city, and by 1810 its population was almost double the fifty-seven thousand people of 1801.[33] And for over two years, Cádiz was a city under siege. On 6 February, the French commander, Marshal Victor, demanded that the city surrender. The ruling junta refused. According to legend, it sent back its response written on a cigarette paper: "The city of Cádiz, loyal to the principles it has sworn, recognizes no king other than His Majesty Fernando VII."[34] After an initial attack, which was easily resisted, the French settled in for a siege of the city.

The siege of Cádiz was unusual in many ways. The city sits on one of the islands in the Bay of Cádiz. A nine-kilometre-long causeway separates it from another island, the Isla de León, which itself is separated from the mainland by the Caño de Sancti Petri, an area of salt marshes formed by a narrow strip of the Atlantic Ocean. Only one bridge, which dated from Roman times, connected the Isla de León to the mainland, and Spanish forces successfully held it throughout the siege. On the other hand, the city was surrounded on three sides by the sea and was vulnerable to naval attack. A combined British-Dutch force had captured and sacked the city in 1596. Nelson's fleet bombarded the city without much effect in the summer of 1797 and maintained a blockade until 1802.

The French were in no position to attempt a similar blockade, and Napoleon ignored Joseph's requests for naval assistance. The events of 1808 had made Great Britain and Spain allies rather than enemies, and the Spaniards quickly forced the French naval squadron in Cádiz Bay to surrender. With the Royal Navy now defending Cádiz rather than attacking it, the city had no problem getting the supplies it needed to withstand the siege. According to the Count of Toreno, a leading liberal of the day, "not even snow was lacking; it was brought from the far mountains by ship and used to make sorbets."[35] The besieging army, at the end of long supply lines, was much worse off. In March 1812, the Regency even had to issue a decree forbidding the sale of food to the enemy.[36]

The best the French could do was to bombard the city, but initially these attacks were irregular and ineffective. Few projectiles actually landed in Cádiz and those caused little damage and claimed few victims. According to Alcalá Galiano, the bombardment was as much "the butt of jokes" as a subject of concern.[37] Then, in March 1812, the bombardment became more sustained: over the course of fifteen days the French fired 515 grenades, but 475 landed in the bay. Their aim improved in May, and certain districts of the city were abandoned, but then, on 25 August, the French abandoned the siege and withdrew.

Most significantly, Cádiz was the capital of free Spain, and this Cádiz was a centre of political energy, excitement, and innovation superseded only by Paris during the first years of the French Revolution. Benito Pérez Galdós conveyed some of this energy in his novel *Cádiz*, published in 1874. Calle Ancha [Broad Street] was the place that the latest news and gossip about war and politics were spread and discussed. It was also the centre of the publishing world. "There the first issues of those innocent little newspapers, butterflies born in the tepid warmth of the freedom of the press, were passed from hand to hand ... Some were absolutist and enemies of reform; others more liberal and defenders of the new laws. Ancha Street brought together all the patriotism and all the fanaticism of the time."[38] The source of this ferment was the Cortes, which started its sessions in a converted theatre on the Isla de León on 24 September 1810 before moving to the Oratory of San Felipe Neri in Cádiz itself in February 1811.

The retreat from Seville had left the Junta Central totally discredited, and at the end of January 1810 it handed power to a five-man Regency Council and dissolved itself. The new Regency was a much more conservative body than its predecessor and delayed calling the Cortes until 18 June, when it announced that the assembly would meet on the Isla de León starting in August. The Cortes finally opened on 24 September 1810 with 102 deputies present. After a religious service, the deputies took an oath to uphold "the Roman, Catholic, Apostolic religion, not allowing any other to enter these realms," to defend national integrity, preserve King Fernando and try to liberate him, and defend the country's laws. After responding "we so swear," two by two they touched the Bible and proceeded into the nearby theatre where they would meet.[39] Despite this traditional beginning, the revolutionary nature of the Cortes became evident almost immediately. In the brief opening session, the deputies passed Decree 1, which proclaimed that "national sovereignty" resided in the Cortes, and that Fernando's abdication was null and void, not just because it had been coerced but "principally because it lacked the consent of the Nation."[40] And this was only the beginning.

At the end of August 1810, the Batallón Universitario was dissolved, and on 1 September its members, Espartero included, entered the re-established Military Academy located on the Isla de Leon, about fourteen kilometres from the city.[41] By the end of 1810, there were 647 students. The period of study was to be brief, in theory only six months, and the curriculum skewed towards technical and tactical subjects: shooting, regulations, fortifications, concepts of artillery, tactics, and cavalry and infantry manoeuvres took up half the students' time while various branches of mathematics and military drawing occupied 35 per cent. The rest was split between history and geography (10 per cent) and riding and fencing (5 per cent). This was not just a matter of wartime exigency. The Academy's founder, Mariano Gil de Bernabé, a lieutenant colonel of artillery, believed that young men with a university education, whatever the discipline, were good officer material. In the proposal he sent to the Junta Central in August 1809 he wrote: "We cannot doubt that in the same way as lands suited to delicate seeds quickly produce their tasty fruits, students prepared by the most sublime studies must, in little time, know everything an excellent officer needs."[42]

The regulations of the new Academy specified that cadets must have at least three years of university study. Traditionally, the most prestigious branches of the officer corps, the Guards, artillery, and cavalry, were the monopoly of the nobility, and when the Academy was set up in Seville, students had to be able to demonstrate "circumstances of good birth (Proof of Nobility)."[43] If this had actually been respected in Seville, it was ignored on the Isla de León. And to drive home the message that it was creating a radically new Spain, on 17 August 1811 the Cortes of Cádiz issued a decree formally opening officer training to "all the sons of honourable Spaniards ... without need for evidence of nobility." This was, as the decree proclaimed, a demonstration of "the appreciation which Spaniards of all classes deserve for their heroic efforts in the current circumstances of the fatherland as its faces its evil oppressors."[44]

The Academy was established in a building that had belonged to the Spanish navy. The cadets lived there, although it quickly became too small and had to be supplemented with an encampment of seventy tents set out in front of the building. The students, known as "Gilitos" after Gil de Bernabé, were divided into eight units, each of which had a sergeant and two corporals. Daily activities, including prayer, were set out in the regulations. The day began at 5:00 a.m. when the cadets were woken and the sergeants inspected their dress and cleanliness. Then they went to the classroom building for a general inspection, after which, "marching in the same rigorous formation," they returned to barracks for "manoeuvres and formations." From 8:00 until 10:00 a.m. they were in class, and for the next two hours there was private study. After eating lunch at noon, they went to their rooms until 3:00 p.m. when they returned to class. Three days a week they would read "the public papers" and the other three they would be instructed "in the obligations of officers, sergeants, corporals, and enlisted men," in how to prepare dispatches, lists, abstracts from reviews, and all classes of reports. Mathematics and its applications came from 3:30 to 5:30. Then they returned to the barracks for weapons training and manoeuvres. There was an hour and a half of free time from 6:00 until 7:30 during which the cadets "can walk and amuse themselves in the vicinity of the barracks, being able to play those games which, because of their simplicity, had been banished by effete cultured society." Dinner was at 7:30, after which "they will pray the rosary." From 8:00 until 10:00

they were in study hall. Then it was bedtime. In addition, there was a weekly session of shooting practice, and once a month the cadets went into the field to practise designing fortifications. On holidays, they studied from 7:00 until 8:00, after which they could spend time "either doing religious exercises or in amusing themselves honestly" and, if they wanted, going to the city "whether for religious exercises or to entertain themselves in an honest way." They were to demonstrate at all times "a noble bearing corresponding to their education and principles; therefore entering unseemly houses is forbidden."[45]

Did Espartero and his classmates take advantage of the opportunity to go to "the island" to walk by the theatre two kilometres away where the Cortes met from 24 September 1810 until 20 February 1811, dates which coincided almost exactly with Espartero's time on the Isla de León? Did he perhaps attend one or more of the sessions? He certainly would have heard about the debates in which the deputies of this novel institution were determining the future of the country. Did he and his fellow cadets discuss the debates and decisions of Spain's first parliament among themselves? It was almost certainly here that Espartero was first exposed to the advanced political ideas of liberals like Agustín Arguelles, the priest Diego Muñoz Torrero, and the young Count of Toreno. And was it here, where liberalism combined with defence of Spain against the foreign invader, where Espartero began to make these ideas his own?

Until early 1811, Espartero split his time between studying and "performing services on the front line." One of his early biographers reports that a "respectable and completely reliable person" told him that while Espartero "went on a scouting party or on roadblocks he always tried to distinguish himself through some valiant action, often bringing fruit, vegetables and other things from the enemy camp to share with his comrades."[46] Then, in February 1811, he was sent to the Portazgo battery, a crucial defensive position not far from the bridge that connected the Isla de León to the mainland. On 5 March, he saw his first action since Ocaña, at the Battle of Pinar de Chiclana.

When the Regency learned that Marshal Soult was withdrawing some of his troops from the siege to pursue the Duke of Wellington, it decided to attack the French from the rear. Spanish and British troops left Cádiz on 26 February and sailed eastward to land at Tarifa and Algeciras the next day. However, the Spanish commander, General Manuel La Peña, chose not to proceed inland and left the British troops under Sir Thomas Graham facing a larger French force. Even after Graham managed to overcome this disadvantage and cause the French significant losses, La Peña refused to engage, preferring to return to Cádiz over a pontoon bridge across the salt marshes. As a result, the French were able to renew their blockade. Whatever Espartero actually saw and experienced during the battle – some Spanish troops were with Graham so he might have been involved in the fighting – he was undoubtedly aware of the very public and vicious controversy between Graham and La Peña that erupted afterwards.[47]

Espartero remained at the Military Academy until the end of 1811. His grades were solid: "Good" in arithmetic, algebra, geometry, and fortifications, and "outstanding" in tactics.[48] In December 1811 Espartero was one of forty-nine cadets at the Academy who were allowed to sit the exams for the newly established training school for military engineers in Cádiz itself. (The Engineering Corps had a well-established reputation as being the most demanding branch of the Spanish army.) He was accepted and on 1 January 1812 he was promoted to second lieutenant in the Royal Engineering Corps. He was just two months short of his nineteenth birthday.

From its opening in September 1810 until its dissolution three years later, the Cortes would hold 1,788 sessions.[49] Its work would be revolutionary. On 6 August 1811, the Cortes passed a law abolishing seigneurial jurisdiction, the rights of the nobility to administer justice and impose fiscal obligations over a large part of Spanish territory, as well as eliminating the status of "vassal." It also did away with fiscal and labour impositions on Indigenous people in America that had existed for centuries. In February 1813, it abolished the Inquisition. The Cortes also made a major contribution to the global political vocabulary: it was there that the word "liberal," applied to the advocates of freedom of the press and other reforms, was first used to designate a political party or position. Their opponents were known pejoratively as *serviles* [servile ones].[50]

The crowning achievement of the Cortes, however, was the drafting and proclamation of the Political Constitution of the Spanish Monarchy, better known as the Constitution of Cádiz or the Constitution of 1812. Its 371 articles set out the framework for a radically new Spain, a nation of citizens "of both hemispheres" who were the source of sovereignty. This aspiration to create a transatlantic nation made Spanish liberalism unique.[51] Spain would be a nation that was "free and independent, and [not] the property of any family or person." Its government was to be a "moderate, hereditary monarchy," but the power to make the laws lay "in the Cortes, with the king." In fact, the Cortes, which had only a single chamber and was elected by a relatively democratic franchise, men over the age of twenty-one with no property qualification, was a powerful body. The king's ability to override its decisions or to act independently was limited. He could not make treaties or impose taxes on his own, and "under no pretext whatsoever [could he] prevent the meeting of the Cortes, at the times or under the circumstances directed by the Constitution; nor suspend nor dissolve them; nor, in any way whatsoever, check or embarrass their deliberations." When he appeared before the Cortes he had to do so "without a guard and accompanied only by the persons appointed for receiving and accompanying him on his return."[52] One Portuguese diplomat later denounced the Constitution of Cádiz as "a republican constitution, whose head, even if called a king, has less power and less dignity than the president of the United States."[53]

The Constitution was proclaimed on 19 March 1812, which was both the day that Fernando VII had become king after the events of Aranjuez in March 1808 and the feast of San José, the name day of Joseph Bonaparte. (The day also gave the constitution its popular nickname, "La Pepa.") It was a day for celebration. The festivities were, in Alcalá Galiano's words, "happy and singular," even if the circumstances did not allow "great luxury." The centrepiece was a Te Deum, but as the cathedral was within range of the French guns, it was moved to the more secure Carmelite convent. Then the "new law" was posted "on a number of platforms in the most public places of the city, with the wording used in royal proclamations." As the "solemn act" was about to begin, a storm, which had been threatening since the previous day, broke. The "hurricane and the rain ... barely registered amidst the outbursts of enthusiasm and joy ... The celebration began, the bells tolled, the artillery of the fortifications and the naval vessels thundered ... All the while, the wind and the rain grew into a fury, and the result was the strangest spectacle imaginable."[54] Was Espartero among the crowds? Did he stop to read the "new law"? And what was he thinking as the city celebrated the new constitution?

Espartero's time at the artillery academy started well enough: in the exams in September 1812, on a grading scheme which ran from "outstanding" to "very good," "good," "average," and "poor," he got "good" in all his courses except for drawing, where he received an "average." His grades deteriorated the next year as he started paying much less attention to his classes. Perhaps it was the move from the Isla de León to Cádiz itself, where the engineering school was located and where the distractions were much greater, as an early biographer suggests.[55] Did these distractions include strolling along the Calle Ancha, taking in the gossip about politics and literature and frequenting the cafés where politics were being discussed? Or perhaps the "unseemly houses" the regulations had put off limits? Whatever he was doing, when exam time came in March 1813, his results were worse than the previous September, which meant that he had to repeat the classes. There was also a note that "if he had applied himself he would have got better grades, since his aptitude is average." Espartero's earliest biographers claim that these bad grades were due at least in part to "a certain personal conflict which ... for reasons that had nothing to do with his classes but rather with the rashness typical of his age, Espartero had with one of the professors."[56] The authors of a biography that was published in 1868 quote him as saying, "I was always stung by impatience. The slowness of the training bored and tormented me. I was an officer of a specialist corps at eighteen years old, more or less, but I wasn't getting the opportunities I wanted to fight. I more desired the activity of light units to the monotony of class and the frivolous diversions of Cádiz. I knew neither fear nor danger, until experience taught me to be cautious."[57] Although showing caution on the battlefield would be something Espartero never really learned.

He did not accept these results passively. On 6 April 1813, he and two other cadets, José Moreno Núñez and Manuel Benito, sent a petition to the director of the Academy.

> The impression made on us and the surprise caused to others by the sensitive news we received yesterday has put us in the mood to seek out all the means by which we can recover our lost honour. We always count on the protection of Your Excellency, whose heart and generous character we know well. We see two ways of obtaining our goal: a comparative exam with various individuals who passed, the other a hearing and a ruling by those comrades whom you most trust together with the professors you deem appropriate.[58]

The director refused to take any action and Espartero refused to repeat his courses. Three weeks later, Espartero was out of the academy and serving as a second lieutenant in the Second Soria Infantry Regiment.

By this time, the war was effectively over. The French had been pushed back to the Pyrenees, and although Soult did launch a new counteroffensive, it failed to turn the tide. Anglo-Spanish forces entered France in October, and on 11 December, Napoleon signed the Treaty of Valencay, restoring Fernando VII to the Spanish throne. Even so, the fighting continued until Napoleon's final defeat and abdication in April 1814.

Espatero's posting took him to a new part of Spain, the Mediterranean coast, the Vall d'Uxo, forty-five kilometres north of Valencia, and then further north, into Catalonia. The British military historian Charles

Oman commented that "[n]othing from the point of view of military narrative can be less interesting than the last six months of the war on the Catalan side." The Soria Regiment was part of General Elío's Second Army, which the British commander, William Clinton, left "to settle down to the interminable sieges, or rather blockades, of Saguntum, Tortosa, Lérida and the smaller French garrisons of the East."[59] Espartero was part of this side-show, and did not take part in any of the major battles of the waning months of the war. From October to December 1813, his unit participated in the siege of Tortosa, about 180 kilometres south of Barcelona, and he was present at two minor encounters: at Cherta on 9 November and Amposta on 22 November.

In February 1814, the commander of the Soria Regiment, General Pedro Villacampa, was named captain general of New Castile. This prestigious posting took him to Madrid, and his regiment went with him. What Espartero did while he was in the capital is not known, although he was able to witness the arrival of Fernando VII and the restoration of absolutism that it brought.[60] Fernando had returned to Spain on 24 March 1814. On 4 May, in Valencia, he issued a decree nullifying everything that had happened in his absence: "[T]he constitution and those decrees [are] null and void, now and forever, as if those events never happened and … my subjects have absolutely no obligation to respect them or follow them."[61] Fernando had also secretly named a new captain general of Castile, the reactionary General Francisco de Eguía, who ordered liberal leaders arrested and then sat by as rioters sacked the Cortes, which had started meeting in Madrid on 15 January 1814, and destroyed the monument to the Constitution. Many of the liberals who were not arrested fled into exile. In July, Fernando restored the Inquisition.

At the beginning of September 1814, Espartero made a decision that would have incalculable consequences for the rest of his life, opening up possibilities that would have been unthinkable otherwise.

The French invasion of Spain in 1808, Napoleon's deposition of the king, and the crisis of legitimacy these events had created also provoked uprisings across Spain's American empire. When the astonishing news of events in Spain reached America, they caused much confusion. Many *americanos* understood their loyalty as being to the king, personally, and not to an abstract entity called Spain. Nor did they automatically accept the authority of a new junta based in Seville which claimed to speak for the monarch. The result was what John Chasteen has called "a slow-motion crisis of legitimacy" based on a single, powerful question, "Who should rule in the name of the King?"[62] When they learned of the retreat of the Spanish junta to Cádiz, *americanos* across the empire, from New Spain (Mexico) to Venezuela, New Granada (Colombia), Buenos Aires, and even remote Chile, answered the question by creating their own juntas.

These juntas claimed to govern in the king's name – in Caracas it called itself the Junta to Preserve the Rights of Fernando VII – and in this they had much popular support. At the same time, many included radicals inspired by French and American ideas who aspired to make their homelands independent, while beneath the cries of "Long live the king!" lay varying degrees of resentment against the European-born Spaniards who wielded so much political and economic power and the pent-up anger of Indigenous people, slaves, and mixed-race people in a world where race defined status. The multiple fault lines in these complex colonial societies all but guaranteed that any challenge to Spanish rule would go well beyond a simple confrontation between royalists and advocates of independence.

Fernando VII needed the colonies and the revenue they provided to run an effective government, and he quickly ordered a major military expedition to set sail for America as soon as possible. For many Spanish officers who had fought against the French on Spanish soil, fighting a colonial war on the other side of the Atlantic was not an appealing task; as a result, there was an "avalanche" of requests for transfers from officers whose units had been selected for service in America.[63] Espartero's Soria Regiment had not been chosen, but in September he requested a transfer to the Extremadura Regiment, which had been. Espartero never explained why he made this decision, but the most likely reason was a mixture of adventure and ambition. (The possibility of being left without a position, a career, or a salary as the government reduced the officer corps by as much as 75 per cent could also have been a factor.) One of his biographers claims that he "saw the road to the thirst for glory that has so dominated him open"; another wrote that his "character naturally took him towards great enterprises [and] he could not ignore the voice of the fatherland."[64] Espartero had also found a real vocation: "it never occurred to me that there could be a better occupation for a man than to live with soldiers, participate in their fatigues, listen to their stories and adventures during the nightly bivouac, and at the sound of reveille start to march, charging the enemy when the sun illuminated the battlefield."[65] But might politics have also played a role? Did Espartero already consider himself a liberal and see service in America as an opportunity to get away from the restored absolutism and the repression that Fernando had brought to Spain?

Espartero's admirers tell a story about an early run-in with his new commander, Pablo Morillo. Morillo (1775–1837) was himself an outstanding example of the unprecedented careers that the war had made possible: having started as a simple soldier at the age of thirteen, he became a militia officer in 1808 and then rose all the way to lieutenant general. When Espartero requested some leave to visit his family, and by this time he had been away for five years, Morillo turned him down, supposedly saying that the request was "not at all military" and displayed "the soul of a mammy's boy." To which Espartero, putting his hand on his sword, replied, "My general, if anyone other than Your Excellency had said such things to me my answer would have been a short one … with the sword." This bold reply impressed Morillo, who then granted the leave, but Espartero, "fearing he would be taken for a coward," refused to take it and did so only after Morillo insisted repeatedly.[66]

In February 1815, the frigate *Carlota* set sail from Cádiz accompanied by five warships and forty-one other vessels carrying some twelve thousand soldiers. Days short of his twenty-second birthday, Espartero was one of them. He was about to encounter a new war and a new world.

2

Defender of the Empire, February 1815–November 1825

When the great expeditionary force set sail from Cádiz, the men expected that they would be heading to the Río de la Plata to fight the insurgency that had started there in 1810. However, once Morillo opened his orders, they learned that their destination was not Buenos Aires but Terra Firme, or Venezuela. According to one Spanish soldier, this news provoked "general consternation ... We all knew that in Buenos Aires and Montevideo the rebels were divided, that one side awaited the king's troops in order to join them, while in Venezuela they were fighting a war without quarter and with a savage ferocity."[1]

This characterization of the war in Venezuela was no exaggeration. A national congress had declared independence on 5 July 1811, but a number of important cities refused to accept the authority of Caracas. Rule by rich creoles, and Simón Bolívar was one of the richest, quickly provoked a revolt of black slaves and mixed-race *pardos*, which, in turn, allowed royalist forces to regain control of the country by July 1812. The slaves soon revived their revolt when they realized that, for them, rule by royalists or patriots was indistinguishable. Bolívar had escaped to New Granada and from there he led a tiny army back to Venezuela. The cruelty of the restored Spanish regime prompted him to declare a "war to the death."[2] Bolívar entered Caracas in August 1813 and in January 1814 he had been named president of the second republic, but the fighting was far from over. The slaves continued their revolt, but this was overshadowed by the mixed-race cowboy cavalry of the vast grasslands of the *llanos*. Led by a Spaniard named Tomás Boves, the *llaneros* repeatedly defeated republican forces and drove Bolívar into exile once again. Bolívar had had many Spaniards executed without trial; Boves oversaw numerous atrocities, including the murder of women and children.

By the time Espartero arrived in Venezuela in April 1815, royalist forces were back in control, Bolívar was in Jamaica, and resistance to Spanish rule had been reduced to a few small guerrilla operations. Morillo's first objective was Margarita Island, with its strategically important location off the eastern coast of Venezuela and close to the mouth of the Orinoco River, but the rebels who held it surrendered without a fight. Morillo then decided that the situation in Venezuela was sufficiently secure that he could, as his instructions directed, take part of his forces to New Granada and even send some to Peru. In May, Espartero's unit, the Extremadura Battalion, left for Panama, from where it sailed to Callao, the port of Lima.[3]

Of all Spain's American dominions, Peru was the least troubled by political unrest in the years after 1808.[4] The viceroyalty had been badly shaken by the violence of the Indigenous uprising led by Tupac Amaru in 1780, and memories of this traumatic event remained strong, cementing the loyalty of the creole elite to the crown. This did not mean that royal authorities in Peru could ignore what was going on elsewhere. Chile was part of the viceroyalty, and the creation of a Junta Provisional there in 1811 was a challenge to Spanish authority, but by October 1814 Viceroy José Fernando de Abascal had defeated the Chileans.

Buenos Aires presented a more persistent threat. In 1776 Charles III redrew imperial jurisdictions to create a new viceroyalty, Río de la Plata, with its capital in Buenos Aires, which was given the territory known as Upper Peru, now the country of Bolivia, including the wealthy mining city of Potosí. In the spring of 1811, forces of the Buenos Aires junta tried to invade Peru itself from Upper Peru but were defeated at the Battle of Huaqi. The defeat made it possible for Abascal to restore the provinces lost in 1776 to his viceroyalty, and they would remain under Peruvian control until the final Spanish defeat in December 1824. This did not mean the provinces were at peace. On the one hand, the government in Buenos Aires tried to reconquer them in 1813 and 1815. On the other, the region saw an ongoing guerrilla struggle against royalist forces. It was here, in the province of Charcas, on the border with what is now Argentina, that Espartero would spend his first four years in Peru, fighting a counter-insurgency.

Although he had been in the army for more than five years before shipping out for America, Espartero actually saw limited action in the war against Napoleon, and the fighting he did was in traditional set-piece battles, such as Ocaña in October 1809 or in the blockade of Tortosa in October through December 1813. What awaited him in Upper Peru was very different. During the war against the French, Spanish forces had had guerrillas on their side; in Peru, they had to fight against them. In his memoirs, Spanish officer Andrés García Camba wrote that "the lack of knowledge of this completely new type of war ... and the unfavourable impression that [we] had cavalierly formed about the enemy was the cause of a number of rash and costly actions."[5] This was not the type of warfare Espartero had studied in the military academy or seen on the battlefields in Spain. It was a vicious conflict, as counter-insurgencies often are: the reprisals the Spaniards took against insurgents included burning towns and public displays of the heads of executed enemies. After defeating a guerrilla leader, one royalist commander sent his head to the viceroy, "having distributed the other parts of his body to the diverse places that he had stirred up." In at least one instance, Spanish troops committed mass rapes.[6]

Espartero's unit arrived in Peru in September 1815. Very shortly afterwards, some of the troops mutinied. Most accounts of the incident say that it was provoked by soldiers not being paid on time.[7] Two soldiers were shot and six imprisoned. Espartero's later obsession with ensuring that his soldiers were paid and well equipped, even using his own money if he had to, probably started with this episode.

The following July, the Extremadura Battalion was sent to Upper Peru. Espartero would spend the next four years there and on the border with the Argentine provinces of Salta and Jujuy, where he had to confront the gauchos. García Camba described them as "men of the country, with excellent horses and all armed with machetes, sabres, or rifles which they used on horseback with surprising ability, approaching our troops with such confidence, ease, and sangfroid that European soldiers were astonished the first time they set eyes on those extraordinary horsemen." They were, in his view, equal or superior to "the celebrated Mamelukes or famous Cossacks."[8]

Espartero shared this admiration for the enemy. In the one surviving letter home during his time in America, written in Potosí in January 1818, he told his father that they were "natural warriors, valiant soldiers and better suited for this type of war than [we] are." He had also decided that only with massive reinforcements from Spain, "twenty or thirty thousand men," and harsh measures could the "seed of revolution" be eliminated. "I am completely convinced," he wrote, "that softness was not the prudent approach, but rigour is; only this way" would the royalists prevail. He even admitted to having committed what today we would consider war crimes. "I can assure you, my father, that I am far from being a bloodthirsty person, and no one knows better than you the sensitivity of my heart, but I also say that *I have had to devastate villages and make all their residents victims because this was the only way to ensure the peace of America for a few years.*"[9]

Espartero's service record lists the actions in which he participated in those years. In 1816 and 1817, he commanded a column of five hundred men in "the pacification of the province of Charcas ... On 7, 9, 10, and 11 February in Icla, Mollecitos, Montegrande, and Oroncota he completely defeated the chiefs Prudencio Zárate and Pereira, seizing all the arms and horses and taking forty-nine prisoners ... On 13 and 19 March and 5 April he assisted in other actions and in one, after completely defeating the enemy he found himself alone among an enemy vanguard and managed to capture it by pretending to be the [rebel] commander Fernández."[10] The "pacification" of Charcas also included the vengeance exacted on the city of La Paz by the regiment's commander, General Mariano Ricafort, after an uprising in which the Spanish governor and other "Europeans and royalists" were killed. Seven men went before the firing squad and were "shot in the back" – not allowing them to face their executioners was an additional humiliation – and the bodies of six were hung on the gibbet for twenty-one hours. Five more were executed in the same way the next day, but only after two of them had been "dragged by a pack animal." All five bodies were displayed for a day, and one, belonging to "el Choconapi, commander of the insurgent Indians," was drawn and quartered; the "quarters, along with his head, were displayed in the town of Italaque, where he had committed his crimes." There was more to come, equally gruesome and even more theatrical. Five days later, a group were executed, backs to the firing squad, their bodies hung for forty-eight hours before three of them, all brothers, were drawn and quartered and their heads distributed, one hung, along with an arm, at the entrances to Lima and Potosí, the third sent to the town of Placa, where it and three hands were nailed to the wall of the government building. In addition to this brutal display, Ricafort imposed massive fines.[11]

The Extremadura Battalion was part of the army commanded by General José de la Serna that invaded Argentina in the spring of 1817. After they had quickly taken the city of Salta, problems with supplies and unending attacks by gauchos forced the expedition to retreat and then leave Argentina altogether.[12] That fall Espartero was tasked with constructing trenches around the cities of Potosí and La Plata and the fortifications of Tarabuco and La Laguna as well as mapping the provinces of Arequipa and the provinces of Upper Peru.[13] In 1819, he was still commanding five hundred men, still chasing guerrilla chieftans, and still engaging in small-scale actions. His was one of two columns sent to chase down rebels in the Mojo valley, a campaign that involved "fifty days of uninterrupted marches." Espartero was relieved after "leaving the villages tranquil," but had to return a few months later to deal with more partisan bands there. In May and June 1820, he was part of a brief royalist incursion into Jujuy and Salta.[14]

While Espartero was fighting guerrillas in Upper Peru, the events that would prove decisive for the fate of the Viceroyalty were taking place elsewhere. This was the work of the Argentinian general José de San Martín. He was born in the Viceroyalty of Río de La Plata, in the border outpost of Yaypeyú, in 1778. His father was a soldier and a Spaniard, and when José was seven, the family moved back to Spain. After some schooling there, at the age of eleven, he joined the army as a cadet. His service in wars in North Africa and then against the French led to his reaching the rank of lieutenant colonel by 1811. Discontented at how American interests were being treated in the Cortes of Cádiz, he resigned from the Spanish army and returned to America. Arriving in Buenos Aires in March 1812, he was immediately given command of a regiment in the rebel army.[15]

After seeing the defeat of three attempted invasions through Upper Peru, San Martín came up with an audacious alternative: conquer Chile and use it as the base for a seaborne invasion of Peru. In January 1817, he led the army he had spent more than two years building from scratch out of Mendoza, across the Andes, and into Chile. After defeating royalist forces at the battle of Chacabuco (12 February 1817), he entered the capital, Santiago, two days later. In April 1818, he soundly defeated an expedition to reconquer Chile at the Battle of Maipú.

His Chilean base secure, San Martín proceeded with the next stage in the strategy: building a navy. Ships were purchased from Great Britain and the United States, as well as captured from the Spaniards, and the new Chilean fleet was put under the command of Thomas Alexander, Lord Cochrane, a brilliant officer who had been dismissed from the Royal Navy in 1814 following his conviction for stock fraud. (Cochrane was well known to Spanish authorities, for privateering and attacking the royalist navy since 1811.) Only in 1820 were preparations for the invasion of Peru complete, and on 20 August the armada carrying San Martín's army set sail from Valparaíso. They disembarked at Pisco, some two hundred kilometres from Lima, on 8 September.

San Martín arrived at a particularly difficult moment for the Spanish authorities. Only four days earlier, Viceroy Joaquín de la Pezuela had received dramatic and unsettling news from Spain: the Constitution of Cádiz had been restored.

Fernando VII's abrogation of the Constitution of 1812 and his annulment of all the changes that had taken place since 1808 had generated much discontent. Between 1815 and 1819 there were four failed attempts to make a revolution and restore constitutional government, led by discontented army officers. (This military intervention in politics would continue throughout most of the nineteenth century and become one of the distinctive features of Spanish politics.) The fifth succeeded. Ironically, it came from the troops who were about to embark from Cádiz to reinforce the royalist armies in America. On 1 January 1820, Rafael de Riego rebelled in the town of Cabezas de San Juan in the name of the Constitution of 1812. Initially, Riego received no support and found himself marching his forces through Andalucía hoping to find some. Eventually, liberal officers in a number of cities joined in, and on 9 March, Fernando reluctantly agreed to rule under the Constitution.[16]

The change in political regime in Spain also produced a new attitude towards the American conflicts among the authorities in Madrid. Almost immediately, the government decided to open negotiations with what it called the "dissidents." The idea of negotiating would be a constant throughout the short, three-year life of the constitutional regime, although the approach would change significantly in 1822.[17] The first phase began with a Royal Order issued on 11 April 1820 – "in which His Majesty wants to end the war in America by any possible means" – and the Instructions for the Commissioners, which were issued four days later. The overriding message was that the commissioners were to get the "dissidents" to accept the Constitution, which meant renouncing independence as a goal. Word of these developments did not reach Peru for six months; only four days after it did, San Martín landed his army at Pisco, and three days after that Pezuela invited him to negotiate. San Martín accepted on 15 September, the same day that the Constitution was officially proclaimed in Lima. Discussions began at Miraflores, just outside the capital on 25 September, and continued on and off into the new year despite the obvious obstacle of the independence issue.

When word of the revolution reached Upper Peru, it prompted Espartero to make the first public statement of his political ideas. He expressed his support for the constitution not in a letter or a manifesto but in a poem, the first of a number he would write. It began: "A while ago Mother Spain caught / between the most outrageous despotism / and ambitious sons dominated by their private interests / Could not even console herself in the hope / of recovering her lost liberty" and concluded "Now, comrades, we are free / to celebrate such fortunate news / Let the oppressed spirit fill with pride / Exchange lamentations for loud cheers!"[18]

San Martín remained at Pisco for six weeks before taking his troops to Huacho, about 120 kilometres north of Lima, where he proclaimed that his goal was "to destroy forever Spanish domination" in Peru, but only through a "peaceful victory" based on the Peruvians' decision that they wanted independence.[19] As a large number of municipalities across northern Peru declared for independence, San Martín's strategy appeared to be working. These developments and the presence of invaders so close to the vice-regal capital exacerbated a crisis that had been developing for four years.

When Espartero arrived in Peru, the army of Alto Perú was under the command of Joaquín de la Pezuela. The next year, Pezuela was appointed viceroy and replaced by José de la Serna. Unlike Pezuela, who had been in America since 1803, La Serna was a veteran of the war against Napoleon who arrived in Peru only in 1816. There was tension between the two men from the outset. La Serna disagreed with the viceroy's analysis of the military situation, and on more than one occasion he refused to obey the viceroy's orders. Tensions only worsened as the military situation deteriorated in 1820. In February, Cochrane captured the major Spanish naval base of Valdivia, giving the Chileans total command of the sea. Pezuela's military strategy was to defend Lima at all costs, an approach that La Serna rejected because he believed that the city was indefensible and not essential to the defence of Peru as a whole. La Serna was supported by a group of officers who were also veterans of the war against the French and relatively recent arrivals in Peru, men such as José de Canterac, Gerónimo Valdés, and Andrés García Camba.

These discontented soldiers found support in an influential faction of Lima's merchants. Naval superiority allowed the Chileans to blockade Peruvian ports, which created shortages of wheat and other key goods. Pezuela's attempts to deal with this situation by ending the merchants' monopoly on trade made enemies of this powerful part of the Lima elite.[20] On 5 November 1820, Cochrane's squadron seized the Spanish warship *Esmeralda* in the port of Callao. A month later, the Numancia Regiment deserted and joined San Martín. By the end of 1820, Pezuela's authority had become "a matter of public debate." His personal honesty was being questioned and even his wife was being criticized for her conduct.[21]

The situation came to a head on 29 January 1821 when nineteen high-ranking officers presented Pezuela with the ultimatum of Aznapuquio. His policies, they wrote, had put Peru "on the edge of a precipice" and his government "does not enjoy the confidence of the army or the towns and thus is respected by no one." Peru needed "a leader who can inspire such confidence and whom the enemy will respect," and La Serna was that leader. If Pezuela did not transfer command to him in two hours, the army would force him to do so.[22] When the deadline passed, the viceroy received a second letter, this one giving him an additional forty-five minutes to comply before the army marched on Lima. After calling a meeting of his War Council, Pezuela resigned in favour of La Serna. He was then taken to his country residence, where he and his family were kept under armed guard and, for the first few days, in total isolation.[23] For the first time in the centuries-long history of the Spanish empire in America, a viceroy was removed by a military coup.

While these dramatic events were taking place, Espartero was 1,700 kilometres away, in the town of Oruro in Upper Peru. Just a few weeks before, in December 1820, he had disrupted another conspiracy "against the king hatched by the governor of Oruro, officers of the Royal Treasury, the commander of the garrison, and various other individuals."[24] After uncovering evidence that a Captain Pedro Nordenflich was involved in a conspiracy to rebel against the royalist authorities, Espartero had him and the other suspected conspirators arrested. Nordenflich was tried by a summary court martial and quickly executed, although there has been some debate over whether Espartero denied him an appropriate trial.[25]

Espartero was far too junior to have been part of the conspiracy against Pezuela, and his was not one of the names on the ultimatum presented to the viceroy, but he had served under a number of those who did sign: Mariano Ricafort, with whom he had sailed to Venezuela in 1815, Gerónimo Valdés, and Antonio Seoane.[26] His career certainly took off after La Serna became viceroy. In his first five years in America, he had received only two promotions, moving from lieutenant to captain in September 1816 and segundo comandante in August 1817. In the next two years and nine months, he was promoted five times, all the way to brigadier general and chief of the General Staff of the army of southern Peru. The first of these promotions came less than a month after the coup against Pezuela.[27]

Viceroy La Serna followed the instructions from Madrid to negotiate with San Martín, even though it meant delaying his plan to abandon Lima. The two men met in early June 1821, but once again the talks foundered on the question of independence: La Serna refused to contemplate it, even in the form of a constitutional monarchy ruled by a member of the Spanish royal house as San Martín proposed. La Serna then took the radical step of abandoning Lima. Cuzco, in the Andes, would be the new vice-regal capital. San Martín entered Lima six days later, and three days after that a public meeting of the city's elite voted for independence. On 28 July, San Martín made the formal declaration of Peruvian independence and was named protector, effectively dictator.

In 1822, now Lieutenant Colonel Espartero was transferred to Arequipa with his regiment. Founded in 1540, the city of some thirty thousand, built from the volcanic sand of the surrounding desert, was a little more than a hundred kilometres from the Pacific coast through a desert of blazing white sand.[28] Arequipa was a very different world from the highlands where he had spent most of his time in America. It seems he had earned a reputation among his comrades as a poet: "my friends begged me," he wrote on the first page of a small folder entitled "My pastime," "to compose something" about the strange things they saw there. Espartero himself was struck by "the latest fashion of the Petimetres" – dandies. The women made a particular impression, and not a positive one: "they sing and play making a thousand strange and improper gestures and movements, using the Italian language but so badly that not even the mother who bore it would recognize it." The result was a "Dialogue between Lisipo and Tolomeo" in which Espartero skewers the pretensions of the men and women of the city.[29]

From the second half of the eighteenth century on, direct trade with Spain was one of the bulwarks of Arequipa's economy. The city was one of only five places in the Americas where the powerful merchants of Cinco Gremio Mayores of Madrid established outlets, and it gained in commercial importance following the declaration of Peruvian independence in 1821.[30] As a result, Arequipa attracted many ambitious traders from Spain, and Espartero got to know some of them. One was Francisco Murrieta. Originally from Sopuerta in Vizcaya, he had moved to Lima, where he developed a flourishing business and married a wealthy Peruvian woman, Mariana García Lemoine. He moved to Arequipa in 1821, and their son Luciano was born there the following year. Espartero knew the family, and Luciano would later prove to be one of his most loyal followers and closest friends.[31]

While Espartero was settling into Arequipa, the first Peruvian congress met in September 1822. San Martín, whose regime had become increasingly unpopular, stepped down as head of the government and left the country. He was replaced by a triumvirate, which decided to go on the offensive and attack the royalists' Andean stronghold. The idea was to exploit what they saw as the enemy's weak point: the ports between Callao and Valparaíso, known as the *Intermedios*. Troops would land at one of the ports and then march inland to connect with the rebels in Upper Peru. General Rudecindo Alvarado's four-thousand-man División Libertadora del Sur arrived at Arica on 3 December 1822, where it remained, inactive for three weeks, a delay that gave La Serna the opportunity to concentrate the widely dispersed royalist forces on the endangered area.

For the royalists, the key figure in the campaign would be Gerónimo Valdés (1784–1855). In a number of ways, Valdes's career resembled that of Espartero. He had been studying civil and canon law at the University of Oviedo when Napoleon invaded Spain. He immediately joined the army and attained the rank of lieutenant colonel by the time the war was over. In 1816, he volunteered for service in America and was one of the officers who arrived in Peru with La Serna. Valdés was involved in the coup against Viceroy Pezuela, and was probably its mastermind. He was both respected by his superiors and admired by his troops. William Miller, the Englishman who fought with San Martín and became a general in the Peruvian army, described Valdés as "the soul of the Spanish army."[32] With a small but high-quality force, which included Espartero's Battalion of the Centre, Valdés made short work of Alvarado's army, sending them fleeing for the coast after two battles in three days.

These battles – Torata (19 January 1823) and Moquegua (21 January) – were Espartero's breakthrough moment and a display of the valour, flair, and even recklessness on the battlefield that would later help make him a national hero. At Torata, he led a bold charge, which José Canterac, the Spanish commander, described this way in his official report: "During this operation I ordered Colonel Baldomero Espartero to attack the right [flank] of the Peruvian legion … his men made only one charge and they charged with bayonets drawn … Espartero killed one of the enemy officers in the middle of his unit but his horse was killed and he received three glorious wounds at almost the same moment. The total defeat of the enemy's right made a significant contribution to our victory."[33] Years later, Espartero himself would describe these events this way: "the young Espartero … commanded the vanguard of the army. The enemy had greater numbers and at a crucial moment Espartero, at the head of a small column, leads an impetuous bayonet charge against the enemy's right flank, kills the commander in hand-to-hand combat, crushes the enemy, and decides the victory." Despite "an arm hanging from his neck," he disobeyed an order to remain in hospital and played a significant role in the battle of Moquegua only two days later.[34] For these two feats, he was promoted to full colonel and recommended for the prestigious Cross of San Fernando.

When news of these defeats reached Lima, they provoked another of the political crises that would plague independent Peru. A military mutiny overthrew the ruling Triumvirate and installed José de la Riva Agüero as president. Riva Agüero built up Peru's military capacity at the same time as he sought to negotiate with La Serna. When this initiative failed, he ordered Andrés de Santa Cruz to lead a second expedition to invade the south through the *Intermedios*, having already arranged support from a force from Colombia and Chile. The five-thousand-man expedition landed at Arica in June, quickly taking the towns of Tacna and Moquegua and marching on to La Paz as the small remaining royalist forces withdrew in the face of a much more numerous enemy.[35]

On the royalist side, Valdes's victories in the south prompted La Serna to attack Lima. Espartero's regiment, still under Valdés's command, was ordered to march from Arequipa. It was a long march, some 1,100 kilometres, which Espartero undertook "in spite of having open wounds." They did not arrive until June 1823, but by then, President Riva Agüero and the Congress had abandoned the capital and fled to the castle of Callao. Espartero took part in a siege of the castle from 19 June until 2 July.[36] During the siege, Congress deposed Riva Agüero and put Bolivar's subordinate Antonio José de Sucre in charge.

When La Serna learned about Santa Cruz's expedition, he ordered Valdés to take an army that included Espartero's regiment to go south to confront it. This meant yet another journey of more than a thousand kilometres. They arrived in time to fight Santa Cruz at Zepita, on the shores of Lake Titicaca, on 25 August, a battle that Santa Cruz won. Soon, however, Santa Cruz's army would be fleeing for the coast with Valdés in pursuit. According to Daniel O'Leary, one of Bolívar's generals, "the withdrawal turned into a flight; discipline evaporated; the officers disobeyed the general and the men disobeyed the officers; the desertion was disgraceful; everything was confusion; the army ceased to exist."[37]

When the campaign against the Peruvians ended in October, Espartero was promoted yet again, to brigadier. He was also named chief of the General Staff of the Army of the South based in Arequipa. Before he could settle into this new position, however, developments that had begun in Madrid two years before would send him back to the border with Argentina entrusted with a new kind of mission.

In mid-1821 the government in Madrid learned that its negotiating strategy had failed completely. As the Spanish authorities were discussing how to handle the colonial situation, the Marqués of Valle-Umbroso and General Antonio Seoane, whom Viceroy La Serna had sent to Spain to report on the situation in Peru following the deposition of Pezuela in January, finally arrived. With this additional information, the Cortes decided to take another stab at negotiations, but by now the earlier confidence that the American dominions could be saved had given way to the recognition that many were already lost.[38] Once again, commissioners were selected to be sent to each territory. The two who went to Buenos Aires, Antonio Luis Pereira and Luis de la Robla, succeeded in negotiating a Preliminary Peace Agreement with the government of Buenos Aires that was signed on 4 July 1823. This document, which looked forward to a "treaty of peace and friendship" between Spain and the United Provinces of the Río de la

Plata, called for an eighteen-month armistice during which full commercial relations would be restored and a definitive peace treaty negotiated. This treaty, however, would not be limited to Spain and the United Provinces alone. The Buenos Aires legislature had authorized the negotiations on the condition that no treaty could be signed "until fighting had ended in all the new States of the American continent and their independence was recognized." Three days after the Agreement was signed, letters were sent to the governments of Chile, Peru, and Colombia.[39] For their part, the Spanish commissioners wrote to La Serna informing him of the agreement as well as of the French invasion of Spain that had taken place in April.

The Buenos Aires foreign minister, Bernardino Rivadavia, then requested that La Serna allow a representative, General Juan Gregorio de las Heras, to travel to Cuzco to negotiate the treaty with him. Las Heras was familiar with Peru. Born in Buenos Aires in 1780, he was in business there until the British invaded in 1806. He joined the army to defend the city, but when it rejected the authority of the Junta Central in Spain in May 1810, he chose to fight against Spain. He remained in the army and worked with San Martín in building the army that would invade Chile in 1817. During the invasion of Peru in 1820, he was San Martín's chief of the General Staff; he participated in the occupation of Lima in July 1821 and served as an adviser to San Martín during his time as protector. When San Martín renounced this office in 1823, Las Heras returned to Buenos Aires.[40]

Las Heras left Buenos Aires expecting to meet with La Serna. As he travelled towards the border, he successfully negotiated the adherence of the provinces of Córdoba, Santiago del Estero, and Salta and learned from Rivadavia that Tucumán, Chile, and Colombia had also signed. On 22 October, he wrote to La Serna requesting permission to discuss the proposed treaty with him. In a strong military position and not well disposed to the treaty, especially one that would recognize the independence of all of Spanish America, La Serna refused to meet Las Heras or even let him enter Peruvian territory. Instead, he decided to send Espartero as his delegate with instructions to discuss the agreement the Spanish commissioners had signed with the "Government of Buenos Aires."[41] His formal instructions ordered Espartero to meet Las Heras at the town of Tupiza, in southernmost Upper Peru near the border with Argentina, where he would discuss "the points contained in the agreement" that the Spanish commissioners had signed with the government of Buenos Aires Less than a week later, La Serna changed the venue; until he himself had heard the proposals, Las Heras should not go beyond the village of Humaguaca.[42]

Espartero and Las Heras exchanged a series of letters that crossed each other, which would be a problem until they actually met face to face in Salta on 9 December. An initial friendly exchange, in which Las Heras complimented Espartero on "your well-known virtues" and looked forward to discussions that would restore, "in an intimate and unbreakable way, the reciprocal friendship and great understanding between a glorious nation, formerly the Metropolis, and the states of this hemisphere which have shown themselves worthy of their emancipation, first by their efforts and now by their moderation,"[43] was followed by one in which Las Heras expressed surprise and concern at being informed of the change of venue ordered by the viceroy. His mission, he said, was limited to getting the viceroy's acceptance of the Agreement; he had expected that the negotiations would be straightforward, but this was clearly not the case. Las Heras then set out six points for Espartero to communicate to Cuzco. Point five was the crucial one – and would prove to be a deal breaker: the "essentially continental interests of America" meant that Las Heras could make no decisions without the approval of the representative his government had sent to the independent government in Lima. He also had express orders to communicate directly with that representative.[44]

Las Heras wrote again two days later, this time to forward documents that he had received from Buenos Aires. These included two official letters from the Spanish commissioners as well as copies of Buenos Aires newspapers reporting on events in Spain. The latter gave him "indescribable pleasure," as they recounted "the progress of arms of the Spanish nation under a representative government against the invaders of Louis XVIII." (That France, invoking the Holy Alliance, had invaded Spain would, literally, have been news to Espartero.) But these newspapers also served Las Heras's purpose. As he pointed out, they carried reports on the sessions of the Spanish Cortes, including one of the Overseas Committee about finding a peaceful way to end the conflict in America. It was time, Las Heras wrote, that "European and American Spaniards ... take their quarrels before the court of reason and humanity." Spain was simply on the wrong side of history, and Espartero and his companions had no reason for shame: "you have sustained your national dignity ... and made yourselves worthy of Spain's gratitude for your actions in face of the irresistible force of destiny."[45] In his reply acknowledging receipt of the documents, Espartero accepted an invitation to meet in Salta. He also wrote, in words that Las Heras would throw back at him, that everything he had set out in his letter of 25 November was "reasonable ... completely in line with my commission and not at all far from my desires."[46]

When the two men finally met in Espartero's lodgings in Salta, what Las Heras described as "the divergence of opinions and the incompatability of principles" quickly became clear.[47] The day after the initial meeting, Espartero sent Las Heras a six-point document that was "completely in line with the instructions of my government." 1) The Andes Division would be withdrawn from Peruvian territory within four months of the treaty being signed; 2) the United Provinces of the Río de la Plata would provide absolutely no military or naval assistance to Colombia, Chile, or Peru during the eighteen-month armistice; 3) commercial relations would be limited to items produced in Spain, Peru, and the United Provinces; 4) the border between the United Provinces and "the possessions of the Spanish nation that it occupies by force of arms" would be clearly defined; 5) the two governments should take the necessary measures to permit commerce to continue; and 6) once ratified, the treaty would be widely publicized.[48] Las Heras's frustration came through in his reply. He had, he thought, made it clear that the "continental system" was the "foundation of American policy" and thus an essential component of any agreement. He then quoted Espartero's own words, about these proposals being completely reasonable and within his mandate. Working together was a "cardinal dogma" for the "newborn states" and accepting the proposals would mean "deserting the defensive alliance." These proposals were "inadmissible" as well as "entirely inconsistent" with Espartero's earlier letter. Las Heras concluded with three proposals of his own: that the 4 July agreement was "beneficial for Spain and its forces in Upper Peru"; that Spain's own independence was "connected to the independence of America"; and that the duration of the ceasefire in the agreement favoured Spanish forces, and these benefits "will be even greater under the definitive peace treaty."[49]

Espartero's reply was lengthy. There had been no previous indication that the negotiations were to go beyond the Spanish authorities in Peru and the "Free People of the Union [of Río de la Plata]." The viceroy considered that Chile and the government in Lima were "a secondary matter" and for that reason he had authorized Espartero to deal only with the government of Buenos Aires, and with those of Salta and Tucumán should they wish to subscribe to the Convention. If he had known that Las Heras had a "continental" mandate, the viceroy would happily have received him in Cuzco. There was nothing in the Preliminary Agreement that even hinted at "continental interests" and, moreover, there was no contradiction between what Espartero wrote on 30 November and 10 December. They were clearly at a stalemate, and as they could do nothing that their respective governments would approve, "our meetings should end for now." Espartero had written to Viceroy La Serna asking him to meet with Las Heras. He had no authority to allow Las Heras "to travel into the interior of Peru," but would travel with him to Selocha or Mojo, on the border, if he wanted.[50]

Both men now decided that further conversations were pointless. For Las Heras, Espartero was constrained by "the narrow limits of his instructions," which allowed him to negotiate only with the United Provinces, while the "soul" of his own mandate was "a continental goal." The Preliminary Agreement did contain "a continental idea," and, through the initiative of the government of Buenos Aires, the final treaty was aiming at a "continental peace." Even the instructions that the Spanish Cortes had given the commissioners "include all the provinces of Spanish America." Under the circumstances, a meeting with Viceroy La Serna was essential. However, both Espartero's conduct in their meetings and La Serna's official communications made clear the viceroy's "resentment against the Spanish commissioners" for having negotiated something "so important and so transcendent" without his knowledge.[51] Espartero had already decided that, absent a meeting between Las Heras and La Serna, "we can do nothing at all, nothing,"[52] and recommended that Las Heras be allowed to go to Cuzco to speak with the viceroy face to face. In the meantime, he had made an independent decision: he would take Las Heras to the Peruvian town of Tojo, where they would await the viceroy's orders.[53] They left Salta on 22 January, and while Las Heras went to Tupiza, where he arrived on 2 February, Espartero headed to Potosí to get "the necessary guarantees" for Las Heras and to collect the correspondence that La Serna had sent there.[54]

On 19 January 1824, the viceroy had issued new instructions based on the reports Espartero had filed up to 16 December. Las Heras had introduced "inconvenient matters which we had not known about and could not have foreseen" and was asking the royalist authorities to consider "something very grave" for which they had no mandate from Madrid. La Serna rejected out of hand the claim that the government of Chile and the "dissident" government in Lima were covered by the Preliminary Agreement and he told Espartero that "Sr. Heras' *new ideas*" should not prevent him from relaying proposals that might come from Salta "or other places" interested in agreements that will "prevent evil and bring reciprocal benefits." He also authorized Espartero to "proceed using all legitimate means" available to him to let other "dissident" governments know they could negotiate with him. Most significantly, none of this "can be presumed to constitute a recognition of their so-called independence."[55]

The meeting between Las Heras and La Serna never took place. On 10 February, the viceroy ordered Espartero to return to Cuzco because "special circumstances prevent any new discussions." To Las Heras he wrote that he required instructions from Madrid before he could discuss a document that included any government other than that of Buenos Aires, and, given the time that this communication would take, Las Heras should return "to his territory as the reason for his mission had ended." Given this "completely unexpected result," Las Heras left for Salta on 13 February. He would remain there until he received instructions from his government and he hoped that, so long as he was there, Espartero would consider "negotiations still open."[56]

Despite stumbling in his initial reply to Las Heras, Espartero stuck to his mandate and, by not reaching any agreement, he achieved the outcome the viceroy wanted. His exchanges with Las Heras involved possible political intrigues as well as diplomatic negotiations. After arriving in Salta on 16 October, Las Heras received two confidential letters regarding the situation in Peru. One said that General Pedro Olañeta, the Spanish military commander in Upper Peru, was violently opposed to a peace treaty; "such dirty dealings should not be done even with Guinea."[57] A Spanish-born merchant who had made himself wealthy during a long stay in Peru, Olañeta joined the army when the independence wars broke out in the Río de la Plata and rose to the rank of general. A fierce absolutist, he was unhappy with the constitutional regime that had been in place since 1820 and with La Serna and his coterie of apparently liberal officers. Olañeta also felt that the viceroy was cutting him out of important issues, such as the peace negotiations with Las Heras.[58]

Espartero had been in Salta only a few days when he too began hearing disquieting things about Olañeta. His adjutant, Captain Celestino Pérez, relayed rumours that Olañeta would rebel and that "many residents said this was a good thing." Espartero's initial reaction was that this was a ruse to spread suspicion among the royalists. He raised it with Las Heras, who, after many requests, showed Espartero a letter which "came down to [Olañeta] having resolved to retain absolute command of the southern provinces, abandoning his obedience to the viceroy and declaring war on him, for which he had four thousand men and the co-operation of the province of Salta."[59]

News of the defeat of the constitutional government and King Fernando's revocation of the Constitution, which came via Buenos Aires and which Olañeta received before La Serna, was the cue for his revolt at the end of January. These were the "special circumstances" that the viceroy mentioned in recalling Espartero on 10 February. Olañeta's troops attacked those of General José Santos de La Hera in Potosí and forced them to take refuge in the mint. When he learned of this episode, La Serna ordered Olañeta to Cuzco to explain himself. His response was to issue a manifesto addressed "the peoples of Peru" in the name of "the principles of Religion" and "loyalty to the Sovereign," denouncing "the most scandalous corruption" and "poison of false Philosophy" which had led "some innovators" to shamelessly profane crown and religion with "the most sacriligious profanities … unbridled libertinism … the total overturning of order and the grossest arbitriness." A week later he proclaimed the abolition of the constitution and the restoration of the absolutist system.[60]

Before Las Heras could leave Tupiza, he was able to do a major favour for Espartero. As a supporter of La Serna and a known liberal, Espartero had reason to fear falling into Olañeta's hands. Las Heras hid Espartero in his house and then helped him get out of Tupiza.[61] From there Espartero made his way to Potosí, where he took independent political action for the first time, attacking the rebel general in a manifesto every bit as fiery and vitriolic as Olañeta's own. Swallowing his liberalism, Espartero began with "Vivas" to "religion, king and nation." He then denounced Olañeta as a traitor who wanted to join the rebels of the Río de la Plata and as a "hypocrite" who wrapped himself in the "sacred name of our religion." The viceroy, Espartero claimed, was on his way and, after dealing with this "shameless thief [and] well-known smuggler," would make public this "perfidious person's horrendous plot." Espartero concluded by describing his own motives: "the love he professes for the inhabitants of Peru and the determination with which he has always defended the rights of the Spanish nation, of the king, and of religion."[62]

The revolt had serious consequences for the royalist military position. Olañeta commanded some four thousand of the eighteen thousand royalist troops; and Valdés, whom La Serna had sent to deal with him, commanded another three thousand.[63] Unable to defeat Olañeta militarily, Valdés came to an agreement with him, leaving Olañeta in command of the army of Upper Peru in return for his promise to recognize La Serna as viceroy, follow his orders, and provide him with financial support.[64] Olañeta reneged on his commitment and then, in June, ignored La Serna's order that he submit or leave Peru. Once again, Valdés was ordered to suppress the revolt.

It was in this context that La Serna learned of further dramatic events in Spain. At the Congress of Verona in October 1822, the reactionary great powers of Europe authorized the king of France to put down the revolutionary regime in Spain. A French army, known as the Hundred Thousand Sons of Saint Louis, crossed the border on 7 April 1823. They met little resistance, and on 30 September, the government, which had retreated to Cádiz, agreed to release Fernando.[65] The next day, the king issued a decree abolishing the constitution and annulling all laws passed by the Cortes.[66] The period of absolutist reaction that became known as the "Ominous Decade" had begun. It took five months for the news to reach La Serna in Cuzco, and it came not directly from Spain but through Buenos Aires and then through Olañeta. On 8 March 1824, La Serna abolished the Constitution in Peru, but his decree makes clear just how extreme his lack of information was. "The Royal Decree of last October 1 has just reached my hands on a sheet of plain, undated paper; for these reasons, its authenticity remains uncertain."[67]

This "civil war among royalists" provided the independence forces with an unexpected, and badly needed, break. When he returned to Peru in the fall of 1823, Simón Bolívar was pessimistic about what he found, with "Peruvian affairs [in] a peak of anarchy" and the "enemy army ... well organized, united, strong, energetic and capable."[68] Things only got worse at the start of 1824. The leaders of the Peruvian government defected and went over to the royalist side. The royalists now controlled all but one province of the viceroyalty and had even managed to retake Lima, which was in a state of complete chaos. Bolívar himself fell ill and was out of action until March.

While the royalists were fighting each other, the final act in the Peruvian war began. After months of rebuilding his army and training it to fight at high altitude, Bolívar, "possessed by the demon of war and ... about to end this fight one way or the other," marched out of his stronghold of Trujillo.[69] He was true to his word. The first battle took place on 6 August at Junín, but Valdés and his army were still in Upper Peru fighting Olañeta. The royalists retreated after only forty-five minutes, and insurgent morale rose. La Serna then decided to unite his forces and go after Bolívar. Following months of playing cat and mouse in the mountains, the two tired armies finally met at Ayacucho on 9 December. The independence army, with Sucre in command, won. La Serna received multiple wounds and was captured, so it fell to Canterac to surrender. The royalist defence of Peru was effectively over.

Olañeta's revolt may have undermined the royalists at a key moment, but he was driven by his loyalty to King Fernando and was not about to abandon Spanish territory to rebels. He remained in control of the province of Charcas, in present-day Bolivia, and rejected invitations to join Bolívar and Sucre. In March 1825, he found himself caught between Sucre's forces advancing from the north and those of Juan Antonio

Álvarez de Arenales, the governor of the Argentine province of Salta, advancing from the south. Facing a hopeless situation, Olañeta's troops began to desert, and in April he died, probably at the hands of his own soldiers.

Although he had been in America since 1815, Espartero was not present for the two climactic battles of the war. Instead, he was on his way to Spain as the viceroy's emissary to inform the king and government of the situation in Peru. La Serna's explanation for choosing Espartero suggests that he was confused or misinformed about Espartero's background: "I believe Espartero is suitable, especially as he is the nephew of the current minister of war and justice, García de la Torre."[70] In his letter to the minister of state, La Serna gave very different, and more credible, reasons for sending Espartero: "as much for his character and skills as for having been fighting in this part of the monarchy since 1816 [sic], Espartero has exact and uncommon knowledge of these provinces ... and for his great love for the Royal Service despite his damaged health" from the wounds he had received at Torata. Espartero's lengthy service included "two sieges, a retreat, and thirty-eight actions" and was marked by "undeniable evidence of his military knowledge and extraordinary valour ... tied to his honesty, zeal and decisiveness in the service of the king." La Serna also requested that the king confirm the "interim titles" that he had awarded Espartero. The viceroy's letter revealed the vacuum in which he had been operating. Since assuming office more than three years before, he had not "received a single reply to the continual official communiques that I have sent to His Majesty's government."[71]

Espartero sailed from Quilca for Spain on the British ship *Tiber* on 5 June 1824. To fund the voyage, he turned to another of his merchant contacts in Arequipa. Lucas de la Cotera was Murrieta's business partner, the most important merchant in Arequipa, and the chief financier of the royalist government between 1821 and 1824. Cotera gave Espartero six thousand pesos "so that he can travel to the peninsula carrying the documents of His Excellency the viceroy."[72]

Cotera and Murrieta had probably helped Espartero before. During his time in Peru, Espartero had managed to acquire a considerable amount of money. How he came by it is a mystery. Unlike some other Spaniards serving in Peru, he did not marry into a wealthy local family. Later Peruvian documents, including some in Quechua, accused Spanish officers, referred to as Jews and heretics, of profaning churches and stealing their treasures.[73] The one explanation that has been given is that he won his money at cards. An early biography claims that on one occasion he won six thousand ounces of gold in a single night and that just before his final departure from Peru he won a thousand ounces from a German who had been one of Bolívar's adjutants.[74] These explanations fit the image of Espartero as a louche card sharp later favoured by his enemies.[75]

His acquaintance with leading merchants like Murrieta and Cotera is a more likely explanation. Certainly, by late 1822 Espartero was in a position to send money back to Europe. In November, he arranged with Juan de Arrache, a ship's captain who had worked with Murrieta and was moving to Europe, to send 15,000 pesos to be invested. Arrache's letter to Espartero suggests that this was their first business dealing: he explains who his contacts and agents are in Bordeaux, Madrid, Cádiz, Santander, and La Coruña. He also explains that the actual transfer would be done by Cristóbal Murrieta, who was based in Río de Janeiro, and that Arrache himself would embark from there on a French ship, the *Telegraph*.[76] Arrache had expected to go to Spain, but when he arrived in Bordeaux on 10 April 1823 he found that the French intervention against the liberal government prevented him from crossing the border. He had not heard anything about the French warship *Clorinda*, which had been carrying Espartero's money – and his own – so given the state of war between France and Spain, "I gave orders to London and have received assurances about all the funds."[77] As it turned out, after Arrache left Rio, Murrieta sent the money on a British ship destined for Portsmouth. The transaction costs were astronomical: of the 15,000 pesos in cash that Espartero gave Arrache in Arequipa on 8 November 1822 he was left with only a little over 10,000. This was sold in London for a total of £2,227, worth 56,283 francs, of which 55,905 were invested in French bonds at 5 per cent interest, providing Espartero with an annual income of 2,700 francs paid in two instalments. In December 1824, his return was 1,350 francs, which was transferred to Madrid, with a 50-franc charge.[78]

Espartero added to his nest egg during his diplomatic mission to Spain. While in Bordeaux waiting to return to Peru, he informed Arrache, who was now in Paris, that he wanted to buy more French bonds to bring his income up to 5,000 francs and sent him three letters of exchange worth a total of 48,000 francs, issued in Madrid the previous month, with which to purchase the requisite amount of the 5 per cent consolidated bonds.[79] These were significant amounts of money. The £2,227 would have been worth almost £140,000 in purchasing power in 2001, and the additional 48,000 francs he added in 1824 another £118,000. His annual interest of 5,000 francs, equivalent to £200, represented a respectable middle-class annual salary in Britain at the time and, for a woman, would have produced a "living" that would have made her an attractive marriage partner.[80]

Espartero arrived at Cádiz on 28 September and then left for Madrid, where he arrived on 12 October. (Santiago Donoso García says that he stopped en route in Granátula, although there is no evidence for this.)[81] According to an eyewitness, the king received the documents Espartero was carrying "with the greatest pleasure and joy, and warmly applauded [La Serna's] conduct and that of [his] officers, whom he described as 'virtuous commanders and soldiers' ... In sum, the king wanted the ceremony of receiving the flags [which had been seized from the enemy], which took place on his birthday, to be as splendid as possible and he ordered Espartero to put on the medal of San Fernando and enter with the flags at the moment of the kissing of hands." Later in life, Espartero had a reputation for the "harangues" with which he motivated his troops: how did he feel addressing this "immense gathering" of Spain's ruling elites while offering these "trophies" to the king? Fernando was certainly happy with what he heard: "You cannot imagine the pleasure and satisfaction that this good king feels for your loyal army," a gratitude he demonstrated with a shower of honours that included the title of Count of the Andes for La Serna and promotion to field marshal and the Gran Cruz de San Fernando for Valdés. He also approved all the promotions and awards that La Serna had made as viceroy, including the five promotions he had given to Espartero.[82]

By mid-December, Espartero was in the French port of Bayonne preparing to return to Peru. The passport issued by the Spanish consul in Bordeaux describes him as five feet two inches tall, with an uncovered forehead, black hair and eyebrows, brown eyes, a sharp nose, a close-cut beard, a regular mouth, and olive-coloured skin. On 30 December, three weeks after the decisive defeat at Ayacucho, accompanied by two servants, one white and one "of colour," Espartero embarked on the *L'Ange Gardien* carrying instructions for the viceroy of a realm that had ceased to exist, save for the lone fortress of Callao where General José Ramón Rodil held out with manic determination until 23 January 1826.[83]

L'Ange Gardien docked in Quilca in early May 1825. Espartero disembarked wearing his military uniform; the Peruvian authorities immediately arrested him as a spy. He was eventually released and allowed to return to Spain, but this episode is possibly the most confusing, and certainly the most romanticized, of his American career. As usual, Espartero himself said little about it publicly. In the letter to a friend published in 1846, he wrote that Bolívar treated him with "an unequalled inhumanity." He spent three months in the "gloomiest cell of the public jail" of

Arequipa, expecting to be executed at any moment. When his health deteriorated, and after Bolívar had left the city, he was transferred to a hospital from which "I managed to escape and board the French commercial vessel *Telegraph*, in which I returned to Bordeaux."[84]

In fact, Espartero owed his escape from possible execution to a number of other people. In some accounts, it hinged on a love triangle involving a woman, Espartero, and Bolívar. According to the Count of Romanones, a former lover of Espartero's had become Bolívar's mistress, and while Espartero refused to ask her to intercede on his behalf because "he did not consider it decent to do so," some of his friends did. "Using all her powers of seduction she had little problem in getting the desired pardon." Espartero's joy at being released was "much diminished" when he learned how his freedom had been attained.[85] The Peruvian writer Ciro Alegría offered a different variant of this romantic tale in his 1969 short story "Entre Bolívar, Espartero y un Extra."[86] Written long after the events and long after Espartero had become famous, both these tales belong more to the realm of legend than of fact.

Contemporary documents in Espartero's archive tell a less romantic story. When Espartero returned from Peru in December 1825, he petitioned the Spanish government for funds to help him travel from France to Spain. This petition included statements from people who were witnesses to the events. Espartero was arrested as soon as he disembarked and taken to Arequipa, where he was put in an "ignominious jail." He was tried as a spy; the main charge against him was having thrown overboard the official documents he was carrying. (Apparently the one thing he held on to were the documents confirming the promotions that Viceroy La Serna had made.) When the magistrate ruled that there was no evidence to try Espartero on this charge and that he should be treated as a prisoner of war, Bolívar handed the case to more compliant judges. Because of his bad health, Espartero was sent to a military hospital, where the doctor, "specifically assigned by Bolívar," treated him "brutally." Finally, the intervention of unnamed friends convinced Bolívar to let Espartero leave Peru on the same ship that was to carry the officers and soldiers who had surrendered at Ayacucho. (José Segundo Flórez mentions Juan Seco Amarelo, Antonio González, Antonio Seoane, and Facundo Infante. The last three were liberals who had fled Spain following the suppression of the constitutional regime in 1823. The connection with Espartero would later benefit all three, but, in the meantime, Infante would have a particularly unusual career, serving as interior minister in the government of independent Bolivia under Antonio José de Sucre between 1826 and 1828 and then living in Buenos Aires and Peru before returning to Spain in 1834.)[87] One thing that comes through in all these accounts is Bolívar's determination to have Espartero declared a spy. José Vidart, who had been Espartero's secretary during the negotiations with Las Heras, claimed that Bolívar was driven by the desire to seize the *L'Ange Garde*, the French ship on which Espartero had travelled. This claim would appear to be substantiated by the fact that the ship's captain was himself put on trial for knowingly transporting a Spanish officer, a violation of French neutrality.[88]

Espartero left Peru for the final time on 1 August on board the *Telegraph*. He would never return to the continent where he had spent almost ten years. Even though he published almost nothing about his life, many years later Espartero did publicly recognize the importance of his American experience. The American conflict, "fought constantly and on an almost daily basis, made me as a soldier by dint of repetition." (One hundred years later, Francisco Franco would say much the same thing about his time in Morocco. Neither man would have to wait very long to apply in Spain what he had learned fighting in the colonies.) His diplomatic mission was a bonus: "I had not thought of being a *politician* until the viceroy of Peru assigned me to those meetings in Salta ... these made me understand that I was capable of being a *diplomat*."[89] These few lines are reasonably revealing, but they remain a serious understatement. His American years were absolutely crucial to Espartero's future: he had proven himself on the battlefield, received promotions that propelled him far beyond any rank he would have achieved in Spain, amassed a small fortune, and developed an imposing network of comrades and allies.

The *Telegraph* also carried twenty-seven of the Spanish officers who had surrendered at Ayacucho and accepted Sucre's offer to return them to Spain, as well as two women who were accompanying them. The government of Peru paid for their passage and set out in detail how they were to be treated. Each officer was to have a "cot" near the cabin where his wife and family slept. The Spaniards were to eat at two or three tables: the seating plan was to be determined by the ship's captain in consultation with the highest-ranking officer, but everyone would receive the same food. There would be two meals each day: one at 9:00 in the morning, the other at 4:00 in the afternoon. The menu was limited, consisting of "more or less the following: unlimited biscuits, one plate each of rice, dried legumes, salted meat, fresh meat, and salted fish, two ounces of cheese, a half bottle of wine, an eighth of a bottle of rum, oil, vinegar, pepper and salt," but the cook was to prepare the meals differently each day. Espartero had to pay his own way and may have bought himself better conditions, including, perhaps, the "first cabin," which the captain could assign as he wished. He was accompanied by

Arrache's teenaged nephew Manuel Váldez. Espartero was good with children and seems to have been engaging company for the young boy; Arrache was "firmly convinced that [the boy] had not missed his father."[90]

After a voyage of almost four months, the *Telegraph* docked in Bordeaux in November 1825. It had been eighteen months since Espartero first set out on his mission to the court and he had spent fully eleven of them on board ship. He was exhausted and his health was "ruined due to my wounds and having endured three consecutive voyages between Spain and Peru."[91] Now he had to try and make his way in the "ominous decade" of Fernando VII's second restoration.

3

Defender of the Throne, November 1825–September 1836

Espartero faced a dangerous environment as he sought to relaunch his military career in the peninsula. King Fernando VII had learned lessons from his first, tumultuous restoration and worked hard to make the second more secure. The army was a crucial focus of this effort. After 1814, Liberal officers had been his most persistent and dangerous enemies. Now the officer corps was subjected to a political purge, and starting in 1825, the minister of war, the Marqués de Zambrano, sought to reduce the size of the army and make it more professional.[1] In confronting these challenges, Espartero enjoyed two powerful assets. The first was his lengthy and impressive military record. The second, and much more crucial, was the extensive support network of the comrades with whom he had fought in Peru, the men who had signed the ultimatum to Viceroy Pezuela and who had helped further Espartero's career afterwards. These were the men who would come to be known as the "ayacuchos."[2]

Even though many of them were initially left "in barracks," without significant commands because they were responsible for "losing the empire," they remained in the army and were able to provide support for Espartero's petition for funds to travel to Madrid and explain his conduct to the Court. Gerónimo Valdés's comments were typical: during his years in Peru, Espartero's "political and military conduct were irreproachable and his adhesion to the person of the king, our lord, was constant."[3] And in a report on officers who had come back from Peru that he prepared for General Manuel Llauder, the inspector general of infantry, Valdés wrote that Espartero "has great valour, talent and his loyalty to the king, our lord, is well known … His military instinct and ability to take advantage of the enemy's mistakes mean that he will one day be a brigadier general."[4]

In addition to his military connections from Peru, Espartero had a civilian agent, Francisco Pérez Alonso, looking out for his financial and other interests in Madrid. Pérez Alonso was a man of some stature, a merchant who moved in the highest levels of Madrid's financial life: in 1825 and 1826 he was a member of the board of directors of the Banco de San Carlos, created in 1782 as Spain's first national bank, and between 1830 and 1833 he served as an advisor to its successor, the Banco Español de San Fernando.[5] How Espartero came to know him is a mystery. Perhaps Cotera and Murrieta, his merchant friends from Peru, provided the contact? It was Pérez Alonso who put Espartero's petition in "the hands of the war minister." He also had to fight Espartero's impatience to get to the capital, warning him that if he tried to go without official permission he would not "be allowed to get beyond Vitoria." A friend of his had a friend in the ministry who would make sure Espartero's request got into the right hands, and another was going to the ministry daily to see if the authorization had been granted. As it turned out, Espartero would not reach Madrid: on 13 February 1826, he was ordered to report to Pamplona, where he was left "in barracks." When he arrived, he was in a bad way: his eyes were bothering him and his "wounds were bursting open."[6]

The letters from his comrades in arms all emphasized Espartero's "well-known loyalty" to the king, and while this was the only logical thing to do under the circumstances, it was also an accurate description of Espartero's political ideas. The man who would come to be revered as the champion of liberalism and identified with the slogan "Let the national will be done!" was still much more a royalist and a defender of the "fatherland" than a liberal. Or perhaps there was no such contradiction: one of Espartero's defining traits would always be deference towards what, at the moment, he considered the legitimate political authority.

Any liberal beliefs Espartero might have held did not prevent him from asking to serve the absolutist king after he returned from America, as they had not prevented Valdés and others who had served La Serna in Peru. One more episode suggests that Espartero's royalism and respect for established authority, and perhaps his career prospects, trumped his liberalism. In November 1826, after returning to Pamplona from the spa town of Bañeras where he had gone to help restore his health, Espartero wrote to the government denouncing a liberal conspiracy. He had met one of "those liberal emigrés who have done so much damage to the king and the fatherland" at the spa, and one of them told him that "in London they had formed a committee headed by [Francisco Espoz y Mina]" that had "sent agents to provincial capitals in order to reach into the villages and even the army. The goal of these traitors is to overthrow the government, extinguish the royal family and proclaim the Emperor of Brazil King of Spain and Portugal."[7] This was vague stuff, and the government almost certainly knew about the junta in London, but the value of the information matters less than the fact that, at this point in his life, Espartero was prepared to denounce liberals to the absolutist authorities.

Espartero passed the purification process, but like many other officers, he found that his career was stagnating. In the reduced peacetime army, military duties consisted of uneventful garrison life, and advancement was hard to come by. His last promotion in Peru had been in October 1823; his next one would not come until February 1834. While he was at the spa in France, Pérez Alonso advised him to return directly to Pamplona and stay there. Word was that there were no commands going in New Castile for officers like him.[8] Then, after two years without a real posting, on 2 May 1828 he was granted a transfer to Logroño with the roles of comandante de Armas and president of the Junta de Agravios.[9] Was he paying bribes to get approval for such requests? In September, Pérez Alonso acknowledged receipt of a letter in which Espartero authorized him to "give the sweets to those who have had a hand in the quick issuing of the Royal Order."[10]

There was a powerful reason for requesting Logroño: on 13 September 1827 Espartero had married a *riojana*, María Jacinta Guadalupe Martínez de Sicilia y Santa Cruz. This would turn out to be one of the most important decisions of his life. Not only was he marrying a formidable woman who would contribute to advancing his career, but he was also marrying into a family with economic power and social influence which, when circumstances changed, would provide the base for a political career.

Jacinta came from a radically different background and had had radically different life experiences from Baldomero. Barely past her sixteenth birthday, she was an orphan. Her father had died when she was only eight months old, her mother when she was five. On her father's side, Jacinta descended from the historic local urban elite. Her mother was the daughter of Domingo de Santa Cruz. He was a self-made man: the son of a landless labourer who had gone into colonial commerce and become a merchant, a banker, and, after buying property in the disentailment of Church lands in the 1790s and 1820s, the largest landowner in the city. His two sons were ardent liberals who had been jailed at the end of the Trienio; Domingo fled the city after getting them out of jail in 1824. Jacinta brought a lot to the marriage: an entailed property inherited from her father comprising a forty-one-hectare estate and a number of houses in the city as well as other belongings her guardian

Figure 3 Portrait of Jacinta Martínez de Sicilia y Santa Cruz, 1840. Colección Madrazo, Comunidad de Madrid.

administered for her. All told, this was worth some eight hundred thousand *reales*, a considerable fortune.[11]

Jacinta was a devout Catholic, but we know nothing about her education. Perhaps it was similar to that of Juana de la Vega, the future Countess of Mina. The two women's lives shared some striking parallels and they would later become good friends. Born five years earlier than Jacinta, she too was the daughter of a wealthy liberal family in a provincial city and she too got married at the age of sixteen to a much older military man from a very different social background, the forty-year-old former guerrilla leader Francisco Espoz y Mina.[12] Jacinta was also a beautiful and elegant woman. Three years after the marriage, when Baldomero was stationed in Barcelona, one of his colleagues described her as "much sought after by Barcelona society, and with good reason, since … she was one of the most stylish and attractive of the women."[13]

Figure 4 Portrait of Jacinta Martínez de Sicilia y Santa Cruz, 1847.
Museo de La Rioja, Logroño.

It is not clear how or when the two met. It might have been in Bañeras – Jacinta would go there frequently later in life – or in Pamplona, where she had relatives.[14] By April 1827, Espartero was writing Jacinta a poem. It was about a man who wished to be the confidant of two young women, "a much sought-after position," but was it really a declaration of love? If they chose him, he said, "I promise, obediently, to do all you tell me … And fervently / I fall at your feet / And beg, implore and beseech / Your merciful decree."[15] The first record of Espartero's presence in Logroño was his signature on the marriage contract, which was concluded on 10 August 1827. There seems to have been a rush to have the wedding performed. The marriage contract dictated that it happen as quickly as possible, and dispensing with "the reading of the three banns" in both Pamplona and Logroño sped things along.[16] The economic aspects of the marriage were also set out in detail. Jacinta brought the entailed estate established by her father, along with "other plentiful belongings, rights and shares" which were being administered by her grandfather. These would be handed over to Baldomero, while he would bring "all his moneys, shares and rights" into the marriage. Many years later he described Jacinta's contribution as "lands and houses, modest belongings but no money."[17]

The formal contract, which was notarized on 11 July 1829, set out Baldomero's financial status. At the time of the marriage he had 700,000 *reales* "in cash" invested in a Paris bank. He had liquidated those investments on his honeymoon and invested all but 80,000 *reales* in Spain. There were loans to individuals and the purchase of some properties. There were also investments with bankers and agents, including 18,487 *reales* with "grandfather D. Domingo de Santa Cruz." Finally, there were 20,000 *reales* in the house.[18]

The marriage has all the appearances of being arranged, with a young girl being married off to a much older man she may have barely known. The marriage agreements make it seem like a clear-headed business agreement. There was certainly a lot of property and money in play. This resembles the "economic and political transaction" involving family members and outsiders that Stephanie Koontz identifies as the traditional, patriarchal form of marriage. Or what Pilar Muñoz López described for elite families during the Restoration of the late nineteenth century, for whom the choice of a spouse was "powerfully mediated by the family" and the woman was "simply a piece in the matrimonial strategies designed by her family."[19] Domingo de Santa Cruz had certainly been strategic when it came to marrying his own children: his daughter, Jacinta's mother, married twice, both times into families of the old Logroño elite, while his two sons married into families like their own.[20] Why would he have chosen Espartero as a husband for his granddaughter? His background and social position were very different from those who married his own children. And in 1827 it was not evident that the military was the key to a brilliant future. The one obvious thing Espartero had in his favour was his money.

The newlyweds spent their honeymoon in Paris, where they stayed through January 1828. They shopped, buying Jacinta's "trousseau, jewels, and everything necessary for the house in Logroño where we would live." They also devoted themselves to renovating the house that Jacinta had inherited from her father, which had been uninhabited since 1812. As well as changing the layout of the rooms, they completely refurnished it, buying "necessary furniture, decorations, silverware and utensils." Espartero was not an ostentatious man, but he liked quality, so he surely did as the popular British *Stranger's Guide* advised, making their "purchases for home at the best shops – they are cheapest in the end." Perhaps they also visited the long list of sights the *Guide* recommended: the Tuileries, the Louvre, Invalides, the Chamber of Deputies and of Peers, Notre Dame, the Gobelins manufactory, the flower market, "all the bridges ... all the theatres, some of the balls," the catacombs "(if not of a nervous habit)," and, of course, asking a "French friend to show you the morgue in the morning, and to give you the history." Among the people they would visit was Joaquín María Ferrer, whom Baldomero had known in Peru and who would play a role in his later career.[21] They also attended to financial matters, liquidating Baldomero's investments "in order to take them to Spain to be invested." Arranging his finances included giving his old Peru acquaintance Lucas de la Cotera, who had returned to South America, a "power of attorney" to collect debts of 15,000 *pesos* owed to him in Arequipa. These first eight months of married life cost Baldomero a great deal, 195,702 *reales* or almost a quarter of his fortune.[22]

Shortly after their marriage, Baldomero wrote another poem for Jacinta: "Dialogue between Catisa and Celia on occasion of learning that the French garrison would leave Pamplona in October 1827." Espartero was still technically posted in Pamplona, so the departure of the French troops stationed there since the invasion of 1823 would have been of considerable interest to him. In the poem, however, the only consequence of the news is its impact on the love lives of the two women. "Who will entertain us?" asks Catisa, to which her friend replies that, should the troops leave, "no one will love us," and in "such a difficult situation" the only thing to do is "renounce being a woman." Catisa does not agree; she will go wherever she can continue to enjoy "the greatest of all pleasures." What other choice does a woman have, Catisa asks. Not many, according to Celia, "And therefore I am inclined / That we renounce / the world and the moment they leave / bury ourselves in a convent / and devote ourselves to God." This "strange thought" shocks Catisa. Doesn't Celia understand that, locked away from the world's diversions, "Our passions will become even more inflamed"? The dialogue ends here with a note "to be continued."[23] It is a curious poem to write for a new wife. Was it a statement of Baldomero's views on women, with the brothel and the convent the only options for certain kinds of women? Or was he playing to Jacinta's religiosity?

Living in Logroño in his own home and surrounded by Jacinta's family was undoubtedly comfortable, and having an actual posting was certainly better than not having one, but his work was bureaucratic and far from exciting. His main tasks were arranging lodgings for officers temporarily in the city and dealing with the question of a tax rebate to which military men were entitled. This second task brought him into an extended conflict with the city council.[24] He also served on various committees and was involved in ceremonial events: accompanying two aldermen to call on the new bishop of Calahorra and attending the service held when Fernando VII's third wife died.[25]

Baldomero accepted Pérez Alonso's invitation that he and Jacinta visit Madrid to take in the celebrations for the marriage of King Fernando and his fourth wife, María Cristina de Borbón-Dos Sicilias, in December 1829. Baldomero had aleady been to the capital twice, at the end of the war against Napoleon and on his diplomatic mission for Viceroy La Serna; this was probably Jacinta's first visit. Through a friend, Pérez Alonso managed to find them "a room on the best square in the Capital … so that Doña Jacinta can watch the most important part of the festivities without leaving; it's not large but it is decent."[26]

Above all, for an ambitious thirty-five-year-old, serving as a military bueaucrat in an irsignificant city did not promise advancement, and Pérez Alonso was working his contacts to get Espartero a better posting. In May 1829 he heard from one that the Third Light, based in Gerona, needed a colonel. He had also inquired about a place in the Royal Guard, "but he was told that would be very difficult."[27] Shortly afterwards, Espartero petitioned the captain general of Old Castile for command of a regiment. His request was sent to Madrid with a favourable professional and political recommendation: his name did not appear on any of the lists of "prohibited Societies." Finally, in October 1830, he was given command of the Soria regiment, the same one he had joined after leaving the military academy.[28]

The regiment was part of the Barcelona garrison, which put Espartero under the command of the Conde de España. He was responsible for what Manuel Santirso Rodríguez calls a "campaign of terror" against local liberals that included thirty-two public executions and four hundred deportations as well as numerous fines for suspected liberals and the closing down of the cafés and other places where they met. He even had the cannon in the Ciudadela fired "to announce the executions to the entire city."[29] As an obedient officer, Espartero followed orders and "when necessary authorized the excesses committed against liberals," as one of his biographers put it. On 30 July 1831, he signed the decision of a military tribunal to sentence Estevan Dolla and Juan Novell to death for having conspired with General Espoz y Mina.[30]

The Soria regiment was transferred to Palma de Mallorca on 1 November 1831 and would remain there until December 1833. During his time on the island, Espartero reportedly fought a duel with one of his junior officers.[31] Towards the end of the posting, the regiment was inspected by the captain general of the Balearic Islands, General Juan Antonio Monet, another of Espartero's acquaintances from Peru. He gave a glowing report on the state of the regiment, and Espartero himself passed with flying colours, personally, professionally, and politically: "Loyalty to the king, our lord. Strong and well proven. Religiosity. Well known."[32]

While Espartero was off in Mallorca, conspiracies swirled around the throne. Until October 1830, Fernando VII was childless, and his younger brother, the ultra-reactionary Carlos María Isidro, fully expected to become king. An unbending supporter of the traditional absolute monarchy, Carlos was unhappy with the policies followed by Fernando after his second restoration in 1823, which produced a new centralization of power that favoured the crown at the expense of the jurisdictional rights of the aristocracy and the autonomous authority of the Church. Carlos had powerful supporters in the State Council, the Church, and the Royalist Volunteers, the anti-liberal militia created in June 1823, while the "War of the Aggrieved," the uprising of ultra-royalists in 1827, demonstrated that he had popular support in rural areas in Catalonia, Valencia, and the Basque Provinces.[33]

Fernando married for a fourth time in December 1829, and his new wife, María Cristina, soon became pregnant. Immediately after this, on 3 April 1830, Fernando published the Pragmatic Sanction, a decision of the Cortes of 1789 that had never been promulgated, nullifying the Bourbon dynasty's Salic Law, which prohibited women from ruling. Their first child, Isabel, was born in October. (A second daughter, Luisa Fernanda, was born in January 1832.) Then, in the fall of 1832, Fernando fell so seriously ill that it was believed he would soon die. Under pressure, much of it from foreign diplomats, María Cristina persuaded the king to retract the Pragmatic Sanction, thereby reinstating Carlos as his heir. However, Fernando recovered and appointed a new, more moderate government headed by Francisco Cea Bermúdez, which quickly removed Carlos's sympathizers from positions of political and military influence and issued a limited amnesty for liberals. Fernando publicly restored the Pragmatic Sanction on 31 December 1832; six months later, on 20 June, the civic, religious, and military officials of the realm swore allegiance to the infant queen. Carlos had been allowed to go into exile in Portugal in March 1833, but this did not prevent a rash of "arrests, minor revolts and rumors of conspiracy," many of them involving the Royalist Volunteers.[34] Carlos refused to take the oath of allegiance and avoided obeying Fernando's order to move from Portugal to the Papal States. At the same time, he also refused to act openly against the king.

Fernando VII died on 29 September 1833. Under the terms of his will, María Cristina became guardian of their two daughters and queen regent until Isabel was old enough to reign in her own right. As soon as news of his brother's death reached him, Carlos issued the Abrantes Manifesto proclaiming himself king of Spain.[35] It concluded by urging "Spanish Catholics who love me [not to] kill, harm, rob or commit the slightest excess," but by the time any of them could have heard these words many were already rebelling in his name. The first uprising, in Talavera de la Reina on the night of 2 October, was quickly put down by the army. In Old Castile, the Basque Provinces and Navarra, however, things were very different. Carlists, as his supporters came to be known, were able to take control of a number of cities, including Bilbao, Vitoria, and Logroño, as well as large parts of the Basque Provinces. By the end of November, Cristino forces, as those who supported María Cristina and her daughter were called, had taken back the major cities and done great damage to the Carlists everywhere except Navarra. There, Tomás Zumalacárregi, a previously undistinguished colonel who had been dismissed from his post as military governor of El Ferrol for absolutist sympathies, was busy turning guerrilla bands into the makings of a Carlist army.[36]

The First Carlist War had begun.[37] It would last almost seven years, more than double the length of the Spanish Civil War of the 1930s, and would be much more lethal than its more famous successor.[38] Although the Carlist War would end without the mass exile, incarceration, and executions that followed the Civil War, the psychological scars were profound and contributed in no small part to Espartero's lasting popularity. The war would also make Espartero's career. It was one of those "times of crisis" that weaken the hold of the "customs, laws and institutions" which prevail in "ordinary times" and make possible the *"irruption"* into leading parts in history of people who until then had been destined to only supporting roles.[39]

When news of the Carlist revolt reached Palma, Espartero requested permission to take his regiment to the Basque Provinces to combat it. This was a matter of loyalty to the crown, of vanquishing "the enemies of the throne ... that the late king entrusted to our swords."[40] Disembarking with the First Battalion at Grao (Valencia) on 20 December 1833, he was immediately ordered to put down a Carlist uprising in Xátiva led by Mariano Magraner, a young lawyer and notary who had managed to put together a force of between one hundred and four hundred men. They were no match for Espartero's troops; Magraner was arrested, and, under orders from the captain general, Espartero had him tried by a court martial. He was executed on Christmas Day despite numerous pleas for clemency, including from the Marquis of Montortal, in whose house Espartero was lodging. The execution of Magraner earned Espartero recognition from María Cristina for the "great zeal he has shown for the rights of my august daughter,"[41] the first of many such expressions of gratitude. A few days later he received an order to go to Madrid to report to Géronimo Valdes, his old Peru comrade now commander in chief of the Army of the North. Valdés named him commander of the province of Vizcaya.[42] Espartero was going to the main theatre of the war.

Immediately after taking up his position in Bilbao, Espartero began a seemingly endless pursuit of Carlist guerrilla bands through the Vizcayan mountains. It must have reminded him of Peru. His service record reports that he set out from Bilbao on 14 January "in pursuit of the rebels with whom he had engagements on the 14th, 15th, 16th, 17th and 18th." On the 19th he arrived in Durango, where he established a garrison. He left three days later to continue his pursuit and had an engagement every day between 22 and 26 January. He then came to the defence of the Guernica garrison, which was under assault, and after chasing off the attackers fought an engagement near Bermeo before returning to Bilbao. He remained there for a little over two weeks, seeing to the city's fortifications and those of Portugalete and Olaviaga. Then, on 17 February, Espartero received word that the Carlists were again attacking Guernica. He arrived that same day and entered the city after a "fierce encounter." The Carlists returned the next day, and Espartero held out for a week before, "without supplies and down to twenty cartridges per man," he abandoned Guernica in the middle of the night of 23 February.

For the relief and defence of Guernica, Espartero was promoted to field marshal. In September, he successfully requested that the promotion be made retroactive from 3 March to 17 February, the day he entered the city.[43] This was a small thing, two weeks' seniority, but symptomatic of an important aspect of Espartero's personality: his intense concern that he receive the greatest possible recognition for his military accomplishments.

After leaving his wounded at Mundaca, he proceeded to Bermeo, which had been occupied by the Carlists, and retook it before returning to Bilbao on the 24th. Three days later, he "set out after the faction once again." And on it went through the spring.[44] In early April, he found himself outnumbered and facing a frontal attack: "My answer was to cry 'No quarter today; Long live Isabel II; Draw bayonets.' My valiant ones repeated my words and this terrified the enemy and was their ruin."

Among the prisoners was the leader of "this horde of bandits, a self-styled brigadier ... who was executed, according to the law."[45]

This is the official record, but thanks to Baldomero's remarkable correspondence with Jacinta while he was on campaign, and perhaps unique in the context of nineteenth-century Spain, we can see what he actually thought about the war. Baldomero undoubtedly gave an over-optimistic account of his achievements: the enemy "fear me like the devil and when I approach they don't know where to hide," but the frustration and weariness caused by the endless pursuit of an enemy whom he could not really defeat still came through. On 6 March, he wrote from Durango that "I don't rest for a moment; I am always marching through these rugged mountains." Five days later: "I am fine but there are no words for how hard I am working. I don't get a moment's rest."[46] On the other hand, he was also in his element: "You know my greatest passion is the glories that Mars can offer."[47] The enemy feared him, and "my rapid movements drive them crazy," but he didn't have enough troops to do the job: "With two thousand more men I'd deal with them in two weeks and then go to Navarra and Álava and do the same, but they don't send me reinforcements and that limits what I can do."[48] This would be the first of many complaints about troop shortages.[49] Espartero was particularly proud of his men taking few casualties. He mentioned this repeatedly. In a skirmish near Portugalete, "the field was covered with the bodies of the enemy and we suffered only three wounded and a few banged up." He was one of them: "a bullet scraped my left leg [but] that did not stop me from continuing my pursuit."[50]

The local political authorities were impressed with Espartero's efforts. When he requested a transfer at the end of March, the city government of Bilbao immediately spoke out against it. Espartero had compensated for the inadequate number of men under his command with "his rapid movements" and his "untiring energy, military skill and local knowledge." When his commander confirmed that Espartero would stay on, the city council was "filled with pleasure" and urged him to provide more troops. The enemy now had some eight thousand men and Espartero had only two thousand to deal with them. Even "this valiant general" who had won a number of "heroic victories" could do only so much. Neither he nor his men were "made of iron."[51]

Espartero was still at it in May. He wrote from Munguía at 8 at night on the 16th: "After not resting for three days and nights," he finally caught up with the enemy. If they felt safe in the "imposing positions" they were wrong. "[N]othing can resist the bayonets of my bravos," and two flanking movements forced them "to abandon their stronghold and flee across open country.[52] "General Helter Skelter [Bullebulle]," as he called himself, set off again on 2 June with four thousand men. This expedition included an engagement in which Espartero launched a successful surprise attack after a twenty-five-kilometre march over difficult terrain during the dead of night. For Vidal Delgado, the idea that a general commanding a division would leave his headquarters to lead an operation that would normally be run by a colonel was one of Espartero's "madnesses" but also one of the things that endeared him to his men.[53]

By the summer Espartero was facing a new challenge: Zumalacárregi had come to Vizcaya and was enjoying "free run of the mountains."[54] On 15 July, he wrote from Bermeo: "The enemy run like the deer but I fly like the Eagle ... I am exhausted and at times I think I have discovered perpetual motion."[55] He spent the first part of August in Navarra, Álava y Guipúzcoa, chasing the Pretender, but then it was back to his raids in Vizcaya. In September, cholera hit Bilbao, and Espartero decided to head to Guernica "so that it doesn't feed off this group of valiant men who accompany me."[56]

Numerous skirmishes, lots of prisoners taken, and an abundance of weapons seized, but what did it amount to? The Carlist bands kept reappearing and by September 1834 they had become more daring, attacking such major towns as Bermeo and Vergara. An English-language biography that Espartero commissioned while he was in exile in London after 1843, but which was never published, explained that the Carlists enjoyed "the good will and enthusiasm of [Vizcaya's] inhabitants ... always watched by men placed on every hill as so many telegraphs destined to give immediate notice of all they observed," he was at a permanent disadvantage. On top of that, Carlist tactics meant that "the victory of one day was no security for the next."[57]

Cristino strategy, Baldomero complained, was "useless since all we do is run after a swift shadow we never catch, and if we do, the outcome is indecisive." He had his own plan, which he sent to the government that month. The first step was to pacify Vizcaya, "the fire that sustains the sparks in Castile and the bands in Guipúzcoa and Álava." Bands from other provinces must not enter Vizcaya without pursuit, and it was essential that his troops not be ordered out of the province. The next step, asserting control over the coast, was almost in hand. The heart of Espartero's plan was to establish "a system of garrisons and flying columns" that would undertake a "constant and sustained persecution, control the countryside and make political decisions effective." He would need 4,500 men for three flying columns and 300 more for garrisons, considerably more than the 3,500 he had available.

His years in Peru had taught him that the problem was not simply a military one. It was also essential to declare a state of war in the province. Civil authority had shown itself to be entirely inadequate, and "people with money and connections just laugh at all the crimes they commit." Only "rigorous measures from a hand that does not waver" would do the job This was always a problem in civil wars, but the situation in Vizcaya was more difficult than most because of the *fueros* [local privileges], which, in his opinion, "only get in the way of whatever good one might achieve ... *Where everything is war, everything should be under military control*." These privileges also obstructed proper provisioning of the troops. Vizcaya was a "supremely rich place," but the queen's troops went hungry and ill clothed while the rebels "get abundant resources everywhere."[58]

Given this attitude, it is not surprising that by the autumn the Bilbao city council was demanding that Espartero be replaced for not displaying the proper deference to the local authorities, even treating "legitimate authorities, known as patriots and supporters of the just cause, as if they were rebels." The same men who only a few months earlier had praised his knowledge of the country now demanded a commander "who is familiar with its customs and who is experienced in the specifics of this class of conflict."[59] The discontent was only fuelled when Espartero stated his need for a "voluntary or forced loan of forty thousand *duros*." When the authorities baulked and invoked "our wise laws," Espartero was outraged. "Who can refuse such a patriotic action without receiving a permanent stain of ignominy ... I cannot believe such an aberration."[60]

As the winter of 1834 came on, little changed. Not everyone agreed with his approach: "Many say my system is foolhardy," but it was the "only way to teach this scum a lesson ... it produces good results as our troops are encouraged while the rebels are seized by a Homeric fear."[61] Later he defeated and captured the priest and guerrilla leader José María Ibarreche. In one of his few comments on religion, Espartero reported that "this apostate to our most holy religion expiated his crimes before the firing squad."[62] He was still complaining about not having enough troops to do the job, on top of which the weather was awful – "it has been snowing and we suffer greatly in these horrible trails."[63]

These "unceasing marches" and occasional skirmishes continued into 1835. At least now he had a decent-sized force, more than four thousand men, but even so, at times it seemed he was chasing phantoms. And worst of all, he was getting no support. "I have no idea what the Army of Navarra is doing."[64] Then, in February, he returned to Bilbao "after twelve continuous days marching through the snow."[65] In March, he was again escorting convoys and fruitlessly chasing the local rebels with General Manuel Latre. There were significant skirmishes on 28 March and 2 April which left him "very happy" because "I had very few losses," even though he had another horse shot out from under him and two of his aides de camp were wounded.[66]

John Francis Bacon, a British merchant living in Bilbao, considered these incessant manoeuvres evidence of Espartero's inability to find an effective way to deal with Zumalacárregi. The Carlists were able to "dance him and his division around round and round the province," although they never could get him to divide his troops. "It was [his] custom to march out with his column for a few days and then to return and stay a week or fortnight in Bilbao." These excursions were limited to the main roads, "so that the Carlists, in derision, nicknamed him el 'ordinario de Durango' – the Durango Courier." There were no gains, but "he had escaped being beaten, which was at least something."[67]

At the end of March there was confusion about his future. He had heard that he was going to be transferred to Navarra but he hoped it wouldn't happen, as "I know this country well and I am needed here." Then his successor presented himself in Bilbao even though Espartero hadn't received his own orders, and he refused to hand over command, "so no one can say I am eager to get away from danger." He had written to Madrid "in a foul humour and I just might send them all to hell and go home." In the end, he was promoted to commander of all the Basque Provinces on 1 May.[68]

The war had been fought with unusual viciousness from the outset. By May 1834, George Villiers, the British ambassador in Madrid, was telling London that it "is characterized by a policy of ferocious reprisals almost without parallel in modern times."[69] (He exaggerated: the war in the Vendée in 1793–4, which resembled the Carlist War in many respects, was incomparably more savage.)[70] Successive Cristino commanders had promised rivers of blood, but in December 1834 Espoz y Mina upped the rhetorical ante, declaring a "war of extermination" and burning entire villages. Espartero contributed to the brutality. In December 1834, he defeated the guerrilla band led by the priest Pedro Barreneche, who was captured and immediately shot. After a clumsy attempt by a farmer from the village of Luyando to assassinate Espartero on 23 January 1835, his soldiers "burned Luyando to the ground." For their part, Carlist commanders matched terror with terror, frequently executing prisoners in batches of more than one hundred.[71] There was at least one incident of Carlists publicly humiliating women after capturing a town.[72]

Espartero had other responses to Carlist atrocities. After the execution of eight soldiers, "two women, and a child" in Ochandiano in May 1834, he issued a general order forbidding reprisals. "There will be no executions," he told his superior; "both my character and my convictions oppose such atrocities, which I consider useless." Economic penalties against people who harboured Carlist fighters, "whose property and families are secure in our midst," would be more effective. He was also going to "round up men with their hair cut short … all who wear it that way are rebels since the peaceful farmer lets it grow long to his shoulders."[73]

The war was closely followed outside of Spain, especially in Great Britain, where *The Times* ran regular twice-weekly reports. All this violence shocked foreigners, none more so than King George IV, who urged his foreign minister, the Duke of Wellington, to do something. Wellington sent Lord Eliot, who had served in the British embassy in Madrid in the 1820s, to negotiate a prisoner exchange agreement.[74] Eliot arrived in Spain on 16 April 1835 and within ten days had persuaded the two commanders, Zumalacárregi and Valdés, to agree to what would become known as the Eliot Convention. The final amendments were negotiated, and Valdés signed the document over dinner at Espartero's house in Logroño on 27 April. Zumalacárregi signed at his headquarters the next day. Espartero's contribution to the negotiations was minimal at best. Colonel John Gurwood, who accompanied Eliot, recorded that "[i]n the amendments proposed Córdova seemed to be the ostensible negotiator – Valdés said very little, Espartero less." His house was also the site of a meeting between the Cristino commanders and Zumalacárregi's representative, General Joaquín Montenegro, at which lists of prisoners were exchanged.[75]

The Convention, which covered the Basque Provinces and Navarra, set out a system of regular prisoner exchanges, "two or three times a month" and more often if circumstances permitted. Exchanges would be made "in proportion to the number of prisoners held by each side," with rank being taken into account in the case of officers. People who were not prisoners of war would not be executed "for their opinions" unless they had been tried and convicted by a proper military court, and each side would "religiously respect and leave free" the sick and wounded so long as they had "a certificate from a military surgeon."[76] The Convention succeeded in reducing the killing of prisoners, but only in the northern theatre of the war, and even there Carlos's Durango Decree denied its protections to foreigners captured carrying weapons.

Elsewhere, and especially in the eastern Meastrazgo region, the atrocities continued unabated.

The signing of the Eliot Convention took place only days after Zumalacárregi had inflicted a humiliating defeat on Valdés at the battle of Améscoas.[77] This was the prelude to a Carlist offensive that culminated in the siege of Bilbao in June. Amidst the gloom, there was a bright spot for Espartero. After Iriarte, his successor as commander of Vizcaya, suffered a major defeat, some two hundred men holed up in a convent in Guernica, "which they defended heroically." As soon as he heard about the events, Espartero set out through a "torrential rain," put the enemy to flight, and rescued the defenders. As he told his friend, Colonel Ramón Solano, "When they saw me they all embraced me and, with tears of joy in their eyes, exclaimed: only our general, our father, could be our Saviour."[78] His General Order of 4 May demonstrated once again how Espartero recognized the bravery of his men and the values that he cherished. Addressing them in a very personal way, he emphasized that they all had a share in this heroic event. "Here, comrades, is the fruit of the brutal marches you have undertaken ... without your fortitude and your suffering ... these comrades would have been lost. You have saved them; you return them to their families and to the fatherland, and I thank you for it."[79]

As he defeated one Cristino general after another in the spring of 1835, Zumalacárregi seemed invincible. Espartero was not spared: on 2 June, he suffered his greatest defeat of the war at Monte Descarga. In his letter to Jacinta written four days after the battle, Baldomero described suffering "some insignificant losses" after the Carlists attacked his rearguard.[80] The reality was very different. After conferring with his senior officers at 7:00 p.m., Espartero decided to abandon the heights. When the withdrawal started an hour later, it was already dark. His force was overtaken by a small detachment of Carlist cavalry, but the result was that "they scattered ... and the rearguard was overtaken by confusion and discourgament." Espartero kept his own head and, putting himself "at the point of greatest danger," vainly tried to rally his men, who "either didn't hear him or who were so filled with panic that they couldn't obey." He tried to hold his ground, "in valiant man to man combat," but was "swept along by the fugitives." Twelve hundred men were lost and the retreat continued all the way to Bilbao.[81]

Within a week after Monte Descarga, the Carlist offensive had left the Cristinos with the cities of Bilbao, Pamplona, San Sebastián, Vitoria, and little else. Zumalacárregi wanted to attack Madrid but was overruled by Carlos, who, desperately needing foreign recognition and financial support, insisted that Bilbao was the priority.[82] The siege of Bilbao started on 10 June, but the Carlists lacked the artillery to bombard the city effectively. On 15 June, Zumalacárregi was shot in the knee; initially the wound did not seem serious, but he died nine days later. The Carlists continued the siege for another week until, "after a short exchange of gunfire," Espartero and Latre were able to enter the city on 1 July.[83]

What was Espartero doing during the siege? His service record reports only two items. One was his support for Latre at the Puente de Castrejana on 23 June, where, he told Jacinta, "our brave soldiers ignored bullets, shells, and grenades." The second was a "risky operation" in which he took a "small escort" across enemy-held territory to convince the new commander in chief, General José Santos de la Hera, who had ordered Espartero and Latre to withdraw, to bring the reinforcements they needed to relieve Bilbao. La Hera was one of the "ayacuchos" who had supported Espartero's reincorporation into the army in 1826, but Espartero did not bite his tongue, sending his old comrade a fiercely worded letter in which he theatened to "rip up my sash [and] reject the name of Spaniard" if La Hera ignored his and Latre's advice to attack Bilbao. La Hera himself would "be covered in ignominy. Don't think this is harsh language; the interests of the fatherland and our friends demand it. I repeat: Early tomorrow in Balmaseda even if the world is in flames."[84] Espartero later claimed responsibility for breaking the siege. In Bilbao "everyone knows that it is because of me the enemy raised the siege," but again he was concerned about the "envy" which would "distort things, especially as I write to nobody because the welfare of my fatherland concerns me too much and I have time for nothing else."[85]

What should have been a great moment was quickly ruined when *El Eco del Comercio*, the principal Progressive newspaper, published his letter to La Hera without his permission. The blame lay with what Espartero considered two of his, and Spain's, greatest enemies: envy and political partisanship. "My motive is to earn a good reputation … but I believe I work in vain because the truth is covered up or distorted, either by party spirit or because envy exercises its dark influence among us … I repeat that I want nothing more than to live as a man removed from all contact with the affairs of the great world."[86]

Much like the Spanish Civil War of the 1930s, the First Carlist War was a highly internationalized conflict. This should not be surprising: ever since the defeat of Napoleon, any serious political change in a European state was immediately the concern of the Great Powers and their Concert of Europe. The internationalization of the war was even more likely following the signing, in April 1834, of the Quadruple Alliance by Great Britain, France, Spain, and Portugal, which was engaged in its own, quite similar, civil war between constitutionalists and absolutists. For the British Whig government, its prime movers, the alliance was a means of defending constitutional government in western Europe, although Tories, including the Duke of Wellington, denounced it as a dangerous innovation. Under the treaty, the Portuguese government promised to do everything possible to get Don Carlos to leave its territory. In return, the Spanish government would send troops into Portugal to fight on the government side, Great Britain would use its navy to support the Portuguese and Spanish armies, and France would remain uninvolved until the other three signatories requested its assistance. The Alliance was bolstered by some "Additional Articles" signed four months later. France agreed to control the border with Spain to prevent "men, arms, or warlike stores" from reaching the Carlists, Great Britain committed itself to providing Spain with the arms and materiel it needed and to assist "with a Naval Force." Portugal agreed to assist "with such means as may be in [its] power."[87]

By the spring of 1835, Zumalacárregi's success in the Basque Country forced a reluctant but desperate government to request French troops and British naval support. This request was rejected, but one to allow the recruiting of volunteers was granted. The French sent 4,100 men from the Algerian Legion.[88] There was also a 2,500-man Portuguese Legion, which was actually part of the Portuguese army, and a Belgian Auxiliary Legion, which included Portuguese and Italians as well as veterans of the Belgian revolution. Espartero welcomed foreign intervention. The arrival of the French would lead, he thought, to a negotiated solution. In January 1836, after he had observed them for a while, he described the French Legion as "superb."[89] Both he and Jacinta welcomed rumours in the spring of 1836 that France would be sending more men because it meant that the war would soon be over. Baldomero was certain that "this alone would be enough for the enemy to dissolve."[90]

The largest and most significant foreign unit was the 9,500-man British Auxiliary Legion, which arrived in Spain in the fall of 1835.[91] This was Espartero's first serious encounter with British military men and it was love at first sight. He was particularly impressed with the Legion's commander, George de Lacy Evans. The forty-eight-year-old Evans was a member of parliament with decidedly radical views. He was also an experienced soldier who had volunteered for the army at nineteen, served in India and Mauritius, and fought in the Peninsular War, the War of 1812, and at the Battle of Waterloo. He was a short and wiry man with a dark complexion that, in the eyes of one of his officers, made him look more like a Spaniard than an Englishman. He bore such a striking resemblance to Espartero that "both Spanish and English soldiers mistook the one for the other."[92] Curiously, Baldomero made the same observation in a letter to Jacinta: "I am becoming a total Englishman; not even my colour is a problem since it's the same as Evans'. The women of Bilbao ... say I resemble [him] a lot." The English were, he wrote a week later, "very fine people and superb officers. I have become English." Evans had aleady invited him to visit England when the war was over. "Of course, we are counting on you because Mistress Evans is a haughty girl who, her husband tells me, speaks good Spanish. She would love to see the Rioja beauty in London." Baldomero spoke to the British officers in French.[93]

In January 1836, he told Jacinta that he was greatly pleased with the British: "my countryman is my countryman" was how he put it, but his national pride was ruffled when Evans was named commander of the Army of the Left. As an individual he was "pleased ... since Evans is a good sort, but as a Spaniard I dislike it, especially when I see that even the ordinary soldier feels the same." A few weeks later his opinion of the British Legion and Evans had changed sharply. As a commander, "he only gets in the way."[94] By May, he was calling him "that brute" who fought "like a Tartar."[95] Evans's opinion of Espartero was more favourable, even though he had been interfering with his command. He called him "an honest and most zealous man ... I like General Espartero much and ... I am ready to serve with him in any manner that may be agreeable to him and that the government may direct."[96]

The death of Zumalacárregi and the failure to take Bilbao marked the end of the first phase of the war. Largely due to his military genius, Carlism had established itself as "a political and military alternative" in the north. In the next phase, which would last until October 1837, the Carlists would try to extend their success to other parts of Spain.[97] On the government side, shortly after the end of the siege, Luis Fernández de Córdova replaced La Hera as commander in chief. His first major initiative was the battle of Mendigorría on 16 July.

Mendigorría would prove to be the largest battle of the entire war, with thirty-six thousand Cristino troops facing twenty-four thousand Carlists under Zumalacárregi's successor, Vicente González Moreno. The Carlists, who had taken up a position with a river at their backs, were forced to retreat across the bridge that was their only escape route. Don Carlos himself barely got away. After capturing the formidable Cerro de la Corona, Espartero led a bayonet charge against the fleeing defenders of the bridge during which his horse was shot twice; even so, he gave up the chase only when ordered to do so by Fernández de Córdova, and then with great reluctance. The Carlists lost some two thousand men, the Cristinos over one thousand.[98] More importantly, in their first engagement without Zumalacárregi at their head, the Carlists had been badly defeated.

Baldomero was "full of joy" for his part in the "brilliant" battle, and for the public recognition he received. They had "completely vanquished twenty-six enemy batallions." He had "worked as I never had before, and had lots of luck." Fernández de Córdova had "showered me with praise" and the "vivas to General Espartero echoed throughout the army ... The soldiers were all heroes; it is hard to explain [their] enthusiasm ... I deserved this public applause and as I aspire to nothing more, I am happy."[99] His pleasure didn't last long. Two weeks later, the battle had become very much a lost opportunity: "we should have captured the entire enemy army and the Pretender as well ... I will always believe that we had it all in our hands and another such opportunity is not likely to present itself."[100] In this he was right.

The war then returned to its habitual pattern as Espartero again pursued the Carlists across the Basque Provinces. At 10 in the morning on 10 August, he wrote Jacinta that he had just returned to Logroño "in a brutal heat after many forced marches." But he wouldn't get much rest: that night he would be off again for Haro to start operations along the Ebro. It was the same in September, "not a moment's rest." On the other hand, "so long as I'm moving I am all right. I was not born to sit around."[101]

Now he had another, more personal grievance as well. A rumour that the war minister, the Marqués de las Amarillas, was going to remove him from his post "upset me so much that I asked Córdova to let me go home." He had even ignored his commander's pleas and made the same request to the queen regent. After all, he was "the centre of gravity of the army."[102] Soon there were press reports, as well as rumours among the troops, that Espartero's resignation had been accepted.[103] In the end, the war minister assured Córdova that it was all the work of "the enemies who seek to undermine our spirit ... Tell this worthy commander that I value him especially and that the queen regent is very satisfied with his services."[104] The question was finally resolved at the end of August when Espartero received a Royal Order, "full of flattery," refusing his request. He took it philosophically. "At the end of the day, we serve the fatherland and the innocent queen, and if we fail we will lament our misfortune but we will not feel remorse for not having done our best."[105]

Then Espartero was seriously wounded. Operating as part of the Army of the Reserve under General Joaquín Ezpeleta, on 11 September he encountered a large Carlist force about ten kilometres from Bilbao.

Ezpeleta ordered a retreat. Espartero was among the last to withdraw and when he arrived at the Bolueta bridge, he found it controlled by the enemy. Here was the kind of situation he relished. His position was critical: "I had eleven battalions behind me, a horde of marksmen on my flanks, [and] only my General Staff and four hussar orderlies by my side ... Followed by a small column we fell quickly on the bridge. I shot out a lancer's brains with my pistol and then we fought with our sabres. Then my comrades from the infantry arrived and the enemy briefly yielded the opening I desired." Not everyone had crossed when the enemy attacked the bridge. "My hussars and I fell on them again and this charge pushed them back again; we were all mixed together; I didn't have time to load my pistols; but imitating my hussars and inspired by their valour, I also landed some good thrusts." The infantry were able to cross the bridge, but Espartero left the scene with a wound from a lance and a bullet in one arm. "I didn't mention it for a half an hour because there were few of us and it was necessary not to cause any discouragement."[106]

The battle took place so close to Bilbao that people there could witness Espartero's heroics, and, as he told Jacinta, they "are delirious about me."[107] John Richardson, an officer with the British Legion who observed the battle from the city through his telescope, confirmed Espartero's valour. "More than once the bridge was taken and retaken while Espartera [sic], who had come to the scene full of shame and indignation at the conduct of his men, was seen to tear his hair and court the loss of life no longer valuable to him. In fact, on being remonstrated with on the danger to which he unnecessarily exposed himself, he replied 'that he courted danger and did not wish to survive the day'. But though the bullets of the enemy spared him not ... His wish was not realized."[108] For this action, he was awarded the Gran Cruz de Isabel la Católica. To Jacinta, Baldomero downplayed the seriousness of his wound: "I am as lucky in war as I am in love ... The wound was so clean that in a few days I will be well ... The pus has started to form; I have no fever and only the food torments me." He also complained about another lost opportunity. Ezpeleta had been under orders to be cautious, "and that is how we miss the best opportunities."[109]

While he was recovering, Espartero learned of the rewards doled out for the action at Mendigorría. He was furious. "I alone" was responsible for the victory, but while there were "one new lieutenant general, four field marshals, and a clutch of brigadiers," he had received only the Gran Cruz de Isabel la Católica when he deserved a more important decoration. Jacinta needed to discuss the matter with "those who have influence with the government."[110]

By mid-October, Espartero had returned to duty even though he didn't have full movement in his shoulder. Now another issue, one driven by the government's financial straits, had arisen: foregoing salaries. Baldomero did not approve. It would be better if everyone gave what he could from his private resources, "since those who are in the field need all their salary, which isn't enough anyway, and only those who have private means can afford to forego it." If it were imposed, he would give up his salary even if he were not on campaign, as it wouldn't be right to "be any less than the others. I will do what the other generals do." In the end, he renounced 10 per cent of his salary for the duration of the conflict.[111]

In early November, he was at Castrobarto, "a miserable village" in the Losa Valley where he was waiting for the British Legion. His health was good, "but continually moving around is getting to me." As the winter came on, the cold hit, it snowed "horribly," and he was getting fed up with the "unending marches."[112] John Richardson described the frustration of this type of warfare and the challenges of the terrain.

> There is something very dispiriting and discouraging in going out day after day in the expectation of an affair, and yet as often returning to our respective barracks without even getting sight of the enemy ... [The terrain] abounds in passes which an army, worn down by incessant toil, would have found difficulty in carrying. Once, and for nearly half a league, our route lay through one of these passes, bounded on the right by a precipice of many hundred feet of perpendicular descent, and on the left by a tall crag, nearly a musket shot in height, the bold yet regular sides of which assimilated it rather to some tower of strength, the work of human hands than the sport of capricious nature.[113]

In December, Espartero got a break from this incessant movement, spending almost three weeks fortifying the town of Ariñez amidst a "hideous cold."[114]

Espartero had a reputation for doing everything possible to ensure the well-being of his troops. He was also a ferocious disciplinarian, and in December 1835 he imposed a punishment so striking that it brought his name before parliament.

During an action in Labastida (Álava) the previous month, some *chapelgorris*, members of a volunteer unit from the province of Guipúzcoa, had killed a priest and plundered the church. The bishop of Calahorra complained to Espartero, and the matter also came to the attention of the government. He ordered an inquiry and three men were arrested, but more "horrible crimes and sacrileges" followed, so Espartero decided to take drastic measures.[115] "If the wrongdoers do not appear," he announced in his General Order for 13 December, "if their accomplices and those who should know who they were do not identify them, then luck will determine who will die." Exemplary punishment was "indispensable ... The public is saying you committed the crimes and you have to show your parents, your families, and the entire world that you are not the authors of such acts against religion."[116]

Captain John Richardson of the British Legion witnessed the events. The *chapelgorris* were marched to a raised ground along the Miranada road, where

> they found a body of 6000 infantry, the horse artillery which had preceded them from Vitoria, and a considerable number of cavalry all drawn up. Having completed the ascent they were halted, and ordered to pile their arms, from which they were commanded to move some distance. The cavalry now rode up between the Chapelgorris and their muskets, forming a guard to these latter. Then for the first time, the poor fellows began to form a suspicion of what was intended against them, and several moved as if to repossess themselves of their arms, but the cavalry drove them back and they were left helpless. Espartero, who commanded in person at this scene, now ordered that lots should be cast for decimation. The command was obeyed, and the unfortunates stood apart from their astonished and indignant comrades. The first ten of this devoted number were again selected, and these were inevitably to die.[117]

Four days later, Baldomero set out his theory of discipline to Jacinta. "You may say I am too harsh," but maintaining discipline required "punishing with an iron fist." If his soldiers adored him it was not because he let them do what they wanted, "but because I treat them justly, because I am with them in their hardships, their suffering and their moments of glory. They know I love them like a father and punish them like a fair judge." He would continue to punish every "offence" as he always had, and if "this division is as brave as it is obedient and if it loves its general it is because the men see him as the first in facing danger, the first in sharing their privations, an inseparable companion in the good and the bad."[118]

Not everyone agreed. Joaquín María Ferrer, a parliamentarian for Guipúzcoa, whom Espartero had visited while honeymooning in Paris, demanded Espartero's "head."[119] The matter was referred to Fernández de Córdova, who demanded an explanation, which Espartero provided in a lengthy document dated 4 January 1836. Those "idiots" in Madrid had no business judging his decisions; nor did they have any idea about the army – although Ferrer had served in Peru. Espartero explained what had happened in great detail, including claiming that the villagers were so terrified of reprisals that they wouldn't talk to the investigating officer. Fearing that if nothing were done, the robberies would continue, he decided that exemplary punishment was the only recourse. Nor was he in the least repentant; if anything, he should have punished the officers too, since they were "as guilty as the rest."[120]

Jacinta had read about the incident in parliament and immediately written to Baldomero. His reply revealed his contempt and disdain for his critics. "In the end, Chiquita, I stand by my acts but I will also remember that canaille to greet them as they deserve when they are within range of my boot."[121] When some *chapelgorri* officers, "as thieving, murderous and sacrilegious as their men," published a letter in the press, he "and every other officer was scandalized that it is permitted to publish such libel, which undermines discipline horribly." But he was not above fighting the matter out in public. He was sending an article he had writtten to Seoane and his other friends in Madrid for them to place in the papers. Nor would this be the last one; "I am lazy about writing but I write like the devil when I need to."[122] The publication and distribution of Espartero's *Dictamen* provoked Ferrer to publish a rebuttal in February, including letters from *chapelgorri* officers claiming that their men were innocent, as well as a letter he and another parliamentarian, Juan Esteban de Izaga, sent to the minister of war demanding a full inquiry into the events.[123] In the end, there was no inquiry and the matter faded away.

For all its severity, Espartero's punishment of the *chapelgorris* did not achieve its intended effect. Word that some soldiers had left camp and attacked food convoys produced a new order dated 2 February 1836 theatening such actions with immediate court martial, with those convicted to be "sentenced to death by firing squad." Anyone, officers included, who tolerated or concealed any crime would pay "with their persons and their jobs." He concluded by addressing his men as "your friend and comrade" and reminding them that he had always "made every effort [to ensure] that they lacked nothing, as circumstances permitted." However, men who did not blindly obey their superiors were not worthy of such attention; nor were they "worthy to live among you."[124]

The *chapelgorri* controversy did not disturb Espartero's fighting spirit. With an operation planned at Arlabán, "I am excited … at the head of my comrades in arms I am invincible." The unending days and the bad weather quickly took their toll, however. The 17th of January was "a brutal day. From the moment I got up until 10 at night I was riding through the mountains in a dense fog and heavy rain with nothing to eat."[125] Then came Fernández de Córdova's first, failed attempt to dislodge the Carlists from Arlabán and with it a major falling out between him and Espartero, whom he apparently blamed for the failure. Once again Jacinta was to be Baldomero's intermediary with the "our trusted friends" in Madrid, who were to deliver his protest to the minister personally. He was fed up with "the lies and intrigues of our fraud of a commander ... He says that at Arlabán General Espartero did not arrive until 1:00 when I had reached the peak just after 10." Yet again he was talking about resigning. "If they remove me from this army we will go home. I don't want another posting. Is it my fault that the soldiers and officers cheer me whenever they see me? And what's unusual about this when for the last two years I have shared their dangers and privations as well as their glories?"[126] He was fed up with working on behalf of "ignorance and ingratitude," especially when his men were being made to pay for it by being sent to build fortifications "on this damn mountain ... with a metre of snow, as removed from the world as if we were in the middle of the ocean." Only his "love of country" prevented him from going home and "telling all those charlatans and cowards to screw themselves.'[127] He also sent a letter to the editors of *La Revista Mensajera* giving his version of the events at Arlabán.[128]

At the start of March, Espartero was at the Peña de Orduña keeping an eye on the enemy to make sure they didn't march on Bilbao or Portugalete. He was far from pleased and his patience was running out.[129] The pleasure of a successful attack at Orduña on 5 March soon gave way to frustration over yet another failure to follow up effectively.[130] There was another victory at the Peña de Unzá on 19 March, where Espartero, fearing that he would be left with "a weak and extended line in enemy territory," ignored Fernández de Córdova's orders to divide his forces. Given his success, there was little Fernández de Córdova could say.[131] The battle, "the most military action of the entire campaign," against a much larger force "on frightening ground," moved Baldomero to unusual flights of poetry. "I write with only a poor candlelight, surrounded by my wounded men and overwhelmed with fatigue as I was on horseback from 5 in the morning until 10 at night, wearing out three of my mounts. I didn't have even a drop of water the whole day, and my spirit was working more than my body ... In the midst of the bloody conflict I remembered ... my beloved mistress [dueña]."[132] He also waved off criticism of such a senior general leading a cavalry charge. It was a matter of taking advantage of the moment, and the only way of achieving "the happy results I proposed ... I know this war and I also know that generals who do not follow my example, or that of the Gran Capitán, will achieve nothing."[133]

Fernández de Córdova wanted to reward Espartero by proposing him to be a *gentilhombre* but when he saw that "I wasn't happy with it he said that as a reward for my last two actions ... he would request the sash of María Luisa" for Jacinta. Baldomero was thrilled that "the idol of my love" be so honoured. And she deserved it, since "everybody knows that if I am fearless in the face of danger it is because of Jacinta, whom I adore." She should stay in Madrid so that María Cristina could give her the sash personally, and she should tell Mendizábal y Almodóvar that this would "please me more than being made a lieutenant general." Baldomero got his wish: Jacinta was awarded the Sash of the Noble Ladies of María Luisa.[134]

April ended and May began with eight days in the Zuya valley. Even though it was spring, there was "half a metre of snow" and no expectation of better weather.[135] Then came the second battle of Arlabán, "five days of continuous combat" between 22 and 26 May. On the first day, Espartero "completely defeated ... nine enemy battalions," but when the battle was over, the Carlists remained in control of the heights. For the Cristinos, Arlabán was, at best, a stand-off; it was also effectively the end of Fernández de Córdova's command.[136]

Immediately after the battle, Fernández de Córdova went to Madrid to discuss the situation with the government and issued "a very pompous general order" leaving Espartero in temporary command. He was pessimistic about the situation of the army, and until sufficient resources were available, the only viable strategy was "a purely defensive one along the entire line." In other words, Espartero should do nothing. The political situation was little better, offering only "wretched problems," and it was essential to keep a close watch that the army remained "impervious to ... party spirit." If there were any disturbances of public order, he should always remember that they were fighting for "liberty, order, the throne of Isabel II and obedience to the laws."[137]

Taking over from Fernández de Córdova, Espartero lamented, was "the greatest sacrifice I can make for my fatherland."[138] He had aleady complained about being "totally occupied with so much paper," and after only a few days in the top job he was "bored with so much writing and so many complicated matters ... Today I am drowning in paper and won't even have time to eat."[139] Such complaints about paperwork would be a recurring theme as he moved up the chain of command. Much to Baldomero's relief, the commander returned on 19 June.[140]

He did not have to wait long to get away from the paperwork he so detested.

While Fernández de Córdova was in Madrid, a new promotion list was announced and Espartero was not included. This oversight provoked a twenty-page letter of complaint to María Cristina, one of the longest documents he would ever write. The letter reveals a number of important aspects of his thinking: pride in his military effectiveness and popularity with the army; concern for recognition; dislike of "parties" and the divisiveness they cause; and belief that he had a unique understanding of the true needs of the "fatherland."

The letter is an account of his exploits in the north from the start of his service there, and the story has one ongoing theme: how his efforts had been continually undercut by successive commanders in chief, and especially Fernández de Córdova, who, driven by jealousy of the "general enthuasism for me," had sought to have him removed from active command almost as soon as he had arrived. Fernández de Córdova was a disastrous commander, unable to take advantage of the "most favourable circumstances" he inherited. In addition, Espartero was denied the promotion he deserved, while other officers, including some under his command, were promoted. The first battle of Arlabán, where Fernández de Córdova ordered him to withdraw from the heights he had taken, produced the "decline and disgrace of our cause." The second was a failure even though he had captured the key position. "When soldiers like ours are led by the example of a general like Baldomero Espartero they are invincible," but Fernández de Córdova was not Espartero. After the battle, Espartero had made the sacrifice of taking temporary command even though he was ordered to take no initiatives. This was not the way war should be waged. Fernández de Córdova's absence turned out to be much longer than he had indicated and Espartero had figured out why. "I detect the parties." He, in contrast, was "all about the fatherland." Finally, he had been left out of the latest round of promotions. Fernández de Córdova was responsible for this gross injustice, but the blatant favouritism affected all ranks, causing "discouragement and disgust in the army." He concluded by begging María Cristina to act. Whether or not Espartero actually sent this letter, shortly after he wrote it and the day Fernández de Córdova returned from Madrid, he was promoted to lieutenant general.[141]

There was much more to the First Carlist War than a dispute over who would succeed to the Spanish throne. It involved a number of what Isabel Burdiel describes as "fundamental political questions."[142] The war represented the full explosion of the conflicts that had racked Spain since the Napoleonic invasion: between absolutism and liberalism, on the one hand, and between competing versions of liberalism, on the other. On the Cristino side, once the conflict began, the course of the war and the course of politics would play off each other, leading from moderate absolutism to liberalism and then to a struggle between timid and more radical visions of liberalism. How would Espartero, who so far had both celebrated the Constitution of 1812 and acted as a loyal agent of the absolutist throne, navigate these turbulent political waters?

Shortly after Espartero arrived in the Basque Country, the queen regent made a daring political move. In an effort to create as much support as possible for her daughter's cause, she dismissed Cea Bermúdez and on 15 January 1834 appointed the former liberal exile Francisco Martínez de la Rosa as prime minister. Three months later she issued the Royal Statute, which has frequently been described as analogous to the Charter granted by Louis XVIII in 1814. It allowed for elections, but only on the narrowest of terms.[143] This new political horizon tempted Baldomero: on 8 June, he wrote from Bilbao asking Jacinta to tell "our friends that I would be happy to be a deputy for Logroño, for the sole purpose of working for the well-being and prosperity of the Rioja."[144] He was not elected. Espartero said little about politics after this, although he clearly saw it as problematic and, at best, a sacrifice to be endured for the good of the country. New elections were held in February 1836, and Jacinta's uncle, Francisco Javier de Santa Cruz, was elected for Logroño. This meant that the uncle had to leave home, which Baldomero saw as one of the sacrifices which "we are all obliged to make for the fatherland." But this did not put him off: "Tell uncle Javier ... that I will be a deputy when the time comes."[145]

A few weeks later, after Jacinta must have written about the *bullangas*, the anticlerical riots which took place in Barcelona on 25 July, he told her curtly that he didn't want to talk about them, since "it puts me in a bad mood to see that they are leading us to the precipice."[146] In September, Baldomero told her that the prime minister had written to Fernández de Córdova about María Cristina's concerns over "divisions and parties" in the army. Baldomero had aleady sent a letter saying she could "count on the entire army," mostly because of his own popularity, and "I always speak of the queen with the greatest enthusiasm." Even so, he urged Jacinta, who was in Madrid, to see the war minister as soon as possible; his letter would dispel "the government's unfounded fears about the army."[147] Did it not occur to him that having the army under the influence of a single general might not be reassuring?

In January 1836, in the midst of the controversy over his decimation of the *chapelgorris*, he heard that Fernández de Córdova was going to be removed from command. The blame lay with "the natterings of the deputies from these provinces and Navarra, which do more harm to the cause than the enemy ... especially when they encourage indiscipline."[148] His impatience with the politicians only grew as 1836 wore on. "Party spirit paralyses everything," he told Jacinta in May, "*I do not belong to any.*"[149] Jacinta kept her husband well informed about political developments. In late May, she wrote to him about the newly appointed Istúriz government. It would not last long, he thought; the war minister, Antonio Seoane, "is a joke." The word was that Fernández de Córdova "will end up as foreign minister, war minister, prime minister and *generalísimo*. Others say dictator." As far as Baldomero was concerned, "I want it to end so I can go home and tell all of them to go to hell. They are all canaille and xxx." Perhaps Jacinta was keeping him too well informed: on 16 June he said simply, "Don't talk to me about politics. I don't want to talk about it either."[150]

Finally, in August there was something positive. On 15 May, María Cristina had replaced Mendizábal as prime minister with the much more conservative Francisco Javier de Istúriz, and when the Cortes received him with a non-confidence vote, she dissolved it. This was the catalyst for a series of local uprisings that started in Málaga in late July and then spead through Andalucía and up the Mediterranean coast. The events culminated on the evening of 12 August in La Granja, the summer palace north of Madrid, when the garrison, backed by some of the Royal Guard, rebelled and demanded the restoration of the Constitution of 1812. After midnight María Cristina met with a delegation of the rebels led by a Sergeant Alejandro Gómez. Until dawn she did her best to put them off before relenting and signing a decree restoring the Constitution on an interim basis until a Cortes could decide whether to keep it or create a new one. María Cristina named José María Calatrava, a Progressive, as president of the Council of Ministers, and he brought back Mendizábal as minister of finance. This was "the point of no return of the Spanish revolution."[151]

Baldomero welcomed word of what he called "the events of Madrid and all the provinces ... The revolution is finally here and I detect a fortunate future on the horizon."[152] But what exactly about this revolution was he celebrating? The restoration of the Constitution of 1812? The promise of a new constitution? The prospect of better funding for the war effort from a Progressive government? Or of further advancement for himself?

The death of Zumalacárregi and subsequent setbacks in June and July 1835 led to a major change in Carlist strategy: rather than limit their efforts to the north, they decided to send a force to Catalonia, where a small-scale guerrilla war was being fought. This expedition, which lasted from mid-August until November 1835, was sufficiently successful that a second one, under Miguel Gómez, was sent to the northwest in June 1836. Starting with three thousand men, Gómez had Cristino armies chasing him across a good part of the national territory for the next six months. The Gómez expedition was in many ways a remarkable feat, but it failed totally in its mission of provoking Carlist uprisings in Asturias and Galicia, and when Gómez returned to Carlist territory in the Basque Provinces he was arrested and put on trial for disobeying orders.[153]

Espartero was charged with hunting Gómez down. The British military observer Colonel William Wylde considered the expeditions a major mistake, which "ought to lead to their ruin. [Espartero] ought to crush Gómez, not a man ought to escape." If the Cristino generals "did their duty with common vigilance and energy," the Carlists would be defeated.[154] It did not turn out this way.

Gómez set off at 2 am on 26 June; Espartero, "with six battalions and two squadrons of hussars," began his pursuit two days later. Before leaving, he addressed his troops. As their general and "companion," he was aware of the "difficult marches *we* face." (His use of the first-person plural emphasized that he would face the hardships with them.) They were fighting "to liberate your homes and your families," and he had no doubt that they would be victorious so long as they maintained "unity, discipline and blind obedience to your superiors."[155]

Things started badly. On 27 June, General Juan Tello's Reserve division suffered a major defeat at Baranda. If Espartero hadn't arrived when he did, "it would have been a total disaster." Then he encountered a problem that he would find repeatedly: the weakness and docility of the Cristino garrisons.[156] On 3 July, after "horrible heat and incessant marches," he was at the border between Palencia and Asturias and would catch Gómez soon, "if ... the troops in Asturias hold the enemy in one of the passes ... for only half a day." He was astonished that the troops from Castile and Asturias hadn't seized "the passes that lead into Asturias; they can be held with very few men." He was even more surprised when he learned that they had abandoned Oviedo to the enemy.[157]

While in Siero he was informed about incidents of soldiers stealing in the villages they passed through, and he devoted his general order of 4 July to this question. Such a breach of discipline and violation of "the virtues of the men I am proud to command should incite your imagination against the perpetrators," especially when he had directed "all my efforts to ensuring you lack nothing." Any future theft, "however small," would bring immediate execution, and "the officers will answer to me for it." Part of their mission was "to protect, not destroy, the property of the locals"; if they completed it, "the people will bless you and you will always merit the love of your General."[158]

By the time Espartero reached Oviedo on 9 July, Gómez had aleady abandoned the city and headed for Galicia. Espartero was going to follow, but he had to feed his troops. According to Luis de Evans, after a long time "without any food whatsoever," the men got "a quarter pound of poor quality bread."[159] Espartero had received no word from the government and felt "abandoned by everyone except the steadfastness of my brave soldiers," who were "without rations or even the time to eat them."[160] As they prepared to head to Galicia, Espartero addressed the shortage of food. He had warned them about the many days of "uninterrupted marches, burned by the sun and hindered by the harshness of the terrain." Despite his best efforts, they did not have enough food. The "violence" and "looting" by the enemy had left the land "devastated" and unable to supply them. The only thing that cheered him was seeing that his "companions" retained their "enthusiasm and determination."[161]

Gómez had entered Galicia without resistance and Espartero followed. From Lugo he sent a letter to the government describing the situation. Gómez had been able to march through Santander, Palencia, and Leon and into Asturias "without firing a shot." He had even been able to attack a government convoy and capture a large sum of money. Espartero's faith in victory was wavering. "I foresee that when I reach the miserable villages where the enemy has aleady been and sucked the little juice they have, the grave shortages my men have aleady suffered will be repeated and they may become discouraged, especially when they see that the money I have requested in order to feed them has not been forthcoming."[162] Espartero's talk about hardships and lack of food was more than just rhetoric. He had been forced to start his pursuit of Gómez without time to properly supply his division. Money and food were problems almost from the start. Only three days after setting out, he sent the quartermaster in Santander an urgent request for funds. Some money was available, but getting his hands on it was a problem; in Gijón he rented a launch and urged the quartermaster to send the money there. He convinced the city government and cathedral chapter of Oviedo to advance him thirty thousand *duros*. The hardships followed into Galicia. While he was asking the quartermaster for twenty thousand *duros* "or whatever was possible," he was receiving a petition from the director of the Gran Hospital Real to rescind an order claiming all the bread intended for the patients.[163] The problems continued in Leon. Espartero's request to the city council for twelve thousand rations of bread only got him the runaround. The best he could manage were "biscuits ... in pieces from all the journeys they have made."[164] It was little better in Palencia, where the chapter eventually agreed to provide six thousand *duros* but delayed in actually delivering them.[165] Espartero even had to mobilize his own family's resources to supply his army: Jacinta's uncle, Francisco Javier de Santa Cruz, ended up delivering one hundred thousand *reales* to the military auditor in Logroño.[166] It would not be the only time he did so.

Espartero's army arrived in Santiago on 20 July, the day after Gómez's departure, and remained there until 23 July. Gómez had received considerable support in the city, and in response Espartero issued an edict theatening dire punishment for anyone who did not immediately turn over any weapons, horses, or anything else belonging to the Carlists, or for any village which provided the enemy with supplies. Anyone who joined the "rebels" and did not present himself within six days would be considered a traitor, "and punished according to the laws."[167] From Santiago, he returned to Lugo. He could not praise his men enough, but the local troops were a different matter. "If they were really soldiers," they would hold the enemy long enough for him to catch up. Their failure to do so before was "disgraceful."[168]

At the end of July, he was back in Asturias, "worn out by this awful campaign." By now the pursuit had covered 750 kilometres. He tried to outflank the Carlists, but Gómez learned about the manoeuvre and went through the mountains to Castile. Baldomero's latest plan was to catch up with him by way of the Pajares pass, but it would not work "if the other troops operate as they have done until now."[169] He entered Leon on 5 August, but Gómez had abandoned the city the day before. Three days later, Espartero finally got the battle he had been hoping for. His relentless pursuit forced Gómez to stand and fight. He chose the Puerto de Tarna as the place. (One Carlist commander claimed that in Tarna "they told us Espartero had ordered [the town] sacked for three hours when he passed through before.")[170] This plan was disrupted when Espartero advanced much more quickly than anticipated and the encounter took place at Escaro (Leon). The Carlists suffered abundant casualties and those who escaped "are totally dispersed among these rugged mountains." Even so, Gómez survived to continue his expedition, so it was not the "complete destruction" Espartero claimed.[171]

Gómez had planned to return to Asturias and Galicia, but, according to one of his senior officers, Espartero's "active persecution" forced him to head for Old Castile instead.[172] Stopping in Potes (Santander),

Espartero found time to write a letter to the editors of *El Español* in which he repeated some of his favourite themes: the bravery of his troops, his own personal disinterest in reward, and the eagerness of others to claim credit they did not deserve.[173]

Baldomero complained about being worn out by the campaign, but he always assured Jacinta that he was well. On 20 August, however, he was so ill that he had to travel in a cart rather than on horseback. The next day he announced to his troops the proclamation of the Constitution of 1812 by the "heroine of the century, the immortal Cristina." On 23 August, in what must have been a painful decision, he handed command to General Isidro Alaix. By this time, he had covered 1,480 kilometres in just under two months. His general order said that the change in command would be "for a few days ... The day I am at your head again will be one of the happiest of my life."[174] On the 24th he felt well enough to accompany the army to Lerma, but the 50-kilometre journey left him in a "fatal prostration" owing to what the doctors diagnosed as "intestinal fevers," which they treated with "quinine sulfanta." He was, they said, "very weak due as much to his meagre diet and loss of blood from the numerous leeches that were applied. Also, the inflamation caused by his chronic illness which ... has complicated the secondary fever, which currently prevails in this region." Only on 31 August did his condition begin to improve.[175]

Jacinta did not learn about Baldomero's illness until 2 September. From Lerma he wrote that "I have recovered from my fevers but these damn doctors have left me very weak from applying so many leeches ... In two or three weeks I will be able to leave for Burgos and then Logroño." The following day he was feeling much better but he had not yet left Lerma as the doctors "fear my great weakness will cause a relapse." He would set out the next day and be home by 7 September. On the 4th he was in Burgos, "pretty weak but I travelled well on horseback and I feel stronger"; on the 5th he eached Bribiesca, feeling "as if I had never been sick." He also told Jacinta that "there is no doubt I owe my life" to Francisco Linaje.[176] It was a debt he would honour at great cost to himself.

Fernández de Córdova had pondered resigning his command since at least April. Rumours to this effect were circulating within the Army of the North, while in Madrid there were questions about his loyalty to the cause.[177] In July, he begged Ambassador Villiers to convince María Cristina to accept his resignation, which she did, albeit with reluctance.[178] Espartero was nobody's first choice as his successor. Pedro Sarsfield refused to return the post he had held at the start of the war. José Ramón

Rodil did accept but was ordered to take up the chase after Gómez first, and he named Espartero as his temporary replacement. His failure brought Espartero the permanent job. On 16 September, a month after coming into office, Calatrava's Progressive government appointed Espartero commander in chief of the Army of the North and viceroy of Navarra, although because of his illness he took up command only nine days later.[179] The British were not impressed. Villiers told Palmerston that he had made every effort to prevent the appointment.[180] Wylde considered it "a very unfortunate selection," while de Lacy Evans felt it "impossible to place confidence in his judgement."[181]

The post had been a revolving door ever since the start of the conflict. Sarsfield had been followed by Quesada, Valdés, Rodil, Espoz y Mina, Valdés again, and Fernández de Córdova, the only one to last more than a few months. Now, after almost three years of war, it was Espartero's turn.

4

Commander in Chief, September 1836–August 1839

Espartero inherited an army that Ambassador Villiers described as "dismembered, discontented, without pay, without rations, and as it appears, without hope."[1] A few days after taking command, Espartero described a similar situation to War Minister Rodil. Lacking "all resources and provisions … and with all the symptoms of a schism," the army was in a "sad and pitiful" state. The potential consequences were dire: "the dissatisfaction and anxiety of the troops grows more frightening," producing "disorder" that "perverts discipline … No one can predict where it might lead."[2]

His first Order of the Day, issued at Logroño, where he was still recuperating from his illness, did not hide the magnitude of the challenge from the troops. "Companions," it began, "the situation is critical … the lack of resources for your basic needs is what most distresses me." He was counting on their "love, constancy, endurance and heroism" because, without them, "I will be able to do nothing." Then his tone changed. His soldiers had shown themselves to be valiant and long suffering, but these qualities would not be enough to bring victory unless they were accompanied by "the most iron discipline." Without this "valour and strength count for little" but with it "we will always be victorious." Anything less than their "blind obedience to your superiors" would bring "the censure of the fatherland" as well as the loss of "my esteem" and the punishment set out in the regulations.[3]

Baldomero was soon complaining to Jacinta about his new job: He was "commander in chief of documents, not operations."[4] This would soon change when the Carlists subjected Bilbao to a second siege, testimony to just how little had been accomplished under Fernández de Córdova.[5] Espartero received news of the siege while he was in Villarcayo (Burgos). His initial reaction was to reinforce the city's garrison, but, fearing another possible Carlist expedition, he decided to remain where he was. Then, having learned that the Carlists were attacking "boldly," he set out for Bilbao, although "continuous snow and wind like a hurricane" stranded him in the "miserable town" of Bercedo. After leaving three battalions at Portugalete, near Bilbao, he returned south, only to head north again after learning that the city's situation was serious. After "horrible marches on unpassable roads in frightening weather," he arrived in Castro Urdiales, about forty kilometres from Bilbao, on 21 November.[6]

En route he sent a lengthy letter in English to Evans. The Carlists had obstructed "all the roads by which troops can move to the relief of that place" and were perfectly aware that "my forces are insufficient to force their lines."[7] Evans felt that Espartero was really asking him to raise the siege while "you might move back with your army to the Ebro without being obliged to compromise it in a serious action with the enemy." Lord John Hay, who was present when the letter arrived, felt that "if it had not been for the perserverance of Col. Wylde, I am afraid [Espartero] would never have approached Portugalete and would even now have fled from Bilbao."[8] For Villiers, Espartero was simply "a frightened man shrinking from responsibility and knowing he was about to undertake that which it is probable he should fail in performing ... You may depend upon it he is doing the best he can and very bad that best is."[9]

With the land routes under Carlist control, Espartero decided to send his army by water. Things went well at first, but then violent storms forced a halt for three days. By then Espartero had already reached Portugalete by land: the Carlist commander Bruno de Villareal, worried about troops at his rear, had withdrawn and left Somorrostro clear. As this was taking place, Baldomero confided his worries to Jacinta. He knew he was taking a big risk. "My movement on Bilbao is reckless and not military but in these circumstances I must risk everything ... The present operation worries me less, however, than what I should do if I save Bilbao ... How terrible is the situation of a general in a civil war. My garden, my garden!!!"[10]

It took Espartero a month to get from Portugalete to Bilbao, a distance of twelve kilometres. He made his first attempt on 27 November. The Carlists had destroyed the bridges across the Galindo and Cadagua rivers, but he was able to cross the first using a pontoon bridge built by British and Spanish sailors. Heavy enemy fire stopped the advance at the second, and Espartero decided to return to Portugalete, even though Wylde offered the guns of the *Saracen* to cover his crossing. During the retreat, Wylde reported, Espartero "allowed his troops, without reproof, wantonly to plunder and burn the fine village of Baracaldo."[11]

A council of his generals at 8 am on 30 November unanimously agreed that the next attempt should come along the other bank of the Nervión. Espartero's troops crossed the river using a floating bridge; with his usual hyperbole, he told Jacinta that it was "perhaps the greatest in military history."[12] After spending the night at Algorta, they started marching towards Bilbao but were forced to stop after advancing only eight kilometres because the Luchana bridge over the Asua was cut. Espartero then sought Wylde's advice on the best attack route; Wylde proposed crossing the Asua at Luchana and with the guns on the *Saracen* providing artillery support. Espartero agreed.[13] Before the plan could be put into effect, however, one of his officers defected and it had to be cancelled. On 6 December, the army returned to Portugalete. Two days later he made another attempt along the left bank, only to be stopped again at the Cadagua River.

The British were beside themselves. Wylde felt that Espartero was "completely overwhelmed by the weight of responsibility thrown upon him" and had "not the slightest confidence ... in any of his plans from one hour to the other."[14] Richard de la Saussaye, serving with the Legion, sent Villiers an astonishing tirade in which he described Espartero as "pottering about the riverside like a rheumatic otter telling people que no está para esas cosas" [he is not up to such things].[15]

A Carlist attack forced the army back to Portugalete, which produced grumbling through the ranks of the unpaid, badly fed, inadequately clothed, and, in some cases, unshod men. Espartero was now having serious doubts about his ability to save Bilbao. Then, on 16 December, he issued "a spirited address" to his troops.[16] This was not a retreat but a way of conserving their energies for "the glorious events ahead." He closed by promising he would be "generous in giving prizes on the battlefield; I will not lose sight of any of your heroic acts."[17] Whatever the effect of Espartero's words, morale could only have been helped by the arrival two days later of a British ship bringing two thousand pairs of shoes.[18]

The army again crossed to the right bank on 19 and 20 December. Espartero also ordered diversionary operations to distract the Carlists from the real target. On 22 December, the day before the attack was originally scheduled, Spanish and British ships unleashed an artillery barrage on Carlist positions.[19] That same day Espartero told Jacinta not to worry because "the commander in chief does not expose himself."[20] She undoubtedly knew her husband well enough not to be comforted. The complex amphibious operation finally got underway on 24 December, despite horrific cold and a raging snowstorm. After rising from his sickbed to lead a reckless cavalry charge, Espartero led his army into a battered but jubilant Bilbao on Christmas morning.[21]

Once in the city, Espartero gave a speech in which he praised its garrison, militia, and citizens. He also lauded the contribution of their British allies, and Colonel Wylde in particular.[22] His first General Order after the triumph praised his men for the bravery that "has made you immortal." They had promised to shed their blood, and they had done so; he had promised them victory, and he had delivered.[23]

Espartero's troops spent the following days collecting the materiel that the Carlists had abandoned. There was so much snow that, two weeks after the battle, "the bodies, hundreds of friends and enemies, remain covered on the battlefield, a hideous sight."[24] The conditions his men had to endure embarrassed him. "The sick lack a roof, a bed and the necessary food," he told the war minister. "The wounded go without bandages, the healthy without clothes or rations." By the end of February he was using his own credit to get a supply contract with some Bilbao merchants, "since they look on the credit of Her Majesty's Government with pure contempt."[25]

Despite his complaints, Espartero was also enjoying the praise and gifts that poured in.[26] But the praise was far from universal. Luchana brought Espartero fame and noble titles, but it did not win him the respect and confidence of his political masters. Villiers was disposed to be a little more generous than before: "we must be just towards a man suffering agonies from the stone and who leaves his bed on such a dreadful night ... in order to put himself at the head of his battalion to storm a fortress which was considered impregnable," and whose first thought, at the moment of victory, "was to thank the British officers," but his overall opinion remained unchanged. Espartero was "a moral coward [who] does not dare risk operations he knows he has not the abilities to direct." On the other hand, there was "literally no one else to put in [his] place."[27] Key members of the cabinet shared this view. Prime Minister Calatrava was "constantly complaining about the lack of a general" and even considered replacing Espartero with a foreigner. Espartero was too popular with the public and, especially, the army to replace, so they decided to direct the war from Madrid through an Auxiliary War Committee.[28] Here was perhaps the first example of a theme which would repeat itself over the years: while political elites would have little respect for Espartero and even write him off as a force, he continued to enjoy a deep popularity among ordinary Spaniards, civilians as well as soldiers.

Why was Espartero so popular with the troops? For his critics, it was because he refused to impose discipline, even though his decimation of the *chapelgorris* a year before had caused a scandal. There were, however, other, more compelling reasons. Holding firm to the first lesson he had learned in America, Espartero did everything possible, including using his own and his family's financial resources, to ensure that his men were fed, clothed, and paid. He was also economical with their lives. He shared the dangers of battle, repeatedly putting his own life at risk by leading cavalry charges, part of his gift of being able to connect with them. In his general orders and his speeches, he addressed them as his "comrades," a custom which Jacinta disliked but which, he told her, was crucial to his connection to his men: "I am sorry you do not like my word comrades but I cannot stop using it. The soldiers know me by it and it electrifies them. If you saw its magical effect, you would enjoy using it as much as I do."[29]

After Luchana, the question for the Cristinos was how to follow up their victory. Villiers and the government wanted to go on the offensive immediately, and to give priority to closing the French frontier, although Villiers and Wylde both recognized that Mendizábal's idea that Espartero live off the country was foolish. "The only things needful are supplies of all sorts and MONEY – without this last, Espartero cannot enter into the heart of the enemy's country or strike a serious blow. Pray therefore move the government upon this point and support Espartero."[30] Still, an immediate offensive was the decision. On 7 January, the Auxiliary Committee presented its plan, designed by Sarsfield and strongly backed by Villiers, which thus became known as the "English plan." Armies commanded by Espartero, Sarsfield, and Evans were to cut the border, "abandon several fortified places," and launch co-ordinated attacks on the Carlist heartland.[31]

The plan also involved Espartero sending reinforcements to both Evans and Sarsfield, something he refused to do. Wylde found that Espartero was "so ill that there is no getting at him to talk him out of [his] state of apathy and determination to do nothing," while an exasperated Evans had given up on co-operation.[32] Once things got underway, however, Espartero did indeed send reinforcements, and Evans radically revised his opinions. He had "completely convinced me," he wrote on 30 March, "of his sincerity and good disposition towards the cause. I cannot now be mistaken in him."[33]

The plan, which had been designed in Madrid and forced on the commander in chief, was an absolute disaster, in part because the Carlists had learned of it in advance. Espartero accomplished his mission, taking Durango on 12 March, but Sarsfield and Evans completely failed in theirs. The climax came at Oriamendi on 16 March, where the British Legion suffered a humiliating rout. This allowed the Carlist commander to turn his full attention on Espartero, who was forced to return to Bilbao, where he arrived after a seven-hour fight during which he lost five hundred men and was wounded in the left arm.[34]

From Bilbao, he sent Jacinta his longest letter thus far. The plan "was Sarsfield's, not mine," and his only role had been to do what he had been told. "Madrid continues to give orders ... This is not being a commander in chief and I assure you that only being totally, totally committed to the fatherland is stopping me from abandoning this thorny job."[35] He also complained about the "armchair patriots" in Madrid who criticized him without knowing the reality of the situation: "a yard of snow and 2,500 men are down with the flu." As for criticism in the British press, "I have decided to ignore the papers."[36]

Following the failure of the "English plan," Espartero was allowed to command without supervision from Madrid. His own plan, which involved cutting Carlist supply lines by closing the French border and taking the war to the heart of enemy territory, was not radically different, although it was both more cautious and more realistic as it did not involve complex operations at the height of a brutal winter.[37] He was confident it would produce positive results by May.[38] The campaign started auspiciously enough with the capture of the town of Hernani. Before the battle, he urged his men to treat prisoners humanely: "valiant men like you see an enemy only on the battlefield; once they have surrendered you generously extend your hand and avoid useless bloodshed." Then, with his "characteristic generosity," Espartero let Evans and the Legion lead the assault.[39] After Hernani, the Legion and a Spanish division took Irún and Fuentarrabia, effectively closing the French border.

Espartero now issued two important proclamations. The first promised that any Carlist soldier, from general down to sergeant, who surrendered along with a number of men "equal to that they command" within a month and either joined Espartero's army or went home would have his rank recognized. Those who surrendered on their own would be accepted at one rank lower if they had never served in the Cristino army and at their actual rank if they had. Ordinary soldiers who surrendered would have the choice of joining his army or returning home. He concluded with some observations on civil war that, one hundred years later, another commander in chief would have done well to heed. "In civil wars, there is no glory for the victors nor shame for the vanquished. Remember that when peace is reborn everything is mixed together and that the story of suffering and disasters, of triumphs and conquests, will be the shared patrimony of those who fought on opposing sides."[40] In the second, he asked the people of the Basque

Provinces and Navarra what they had gained by following those who "who do not tire of deceiving you" and for whom they had endured so much. Now was the time to put down their arms and return to their homes and families, secure that they would "find the protection that your misfortunes have earned you." Once the month was up, the war would resume, and "you will have only yourselves to blame."[41] Taken together, these proclamations constituted the core of the later Agreement of Vergara.

While Espartero was launching his successful offensive, the Constituent Cortes which had been elected in October 1836 approved the new constitution on 22 May 1837.[42] (Espartero was elected for Logroño, receiving all nine of the votes cast.)[43] The Cortes was dominated by Progressives, but the Constitution of 1837 was different from the Constitution of 1812, which had been their traditional rallying cry, and far removed from the revolutionary implications of the events which had brought them to power. A compromise with more timid liberal ideas, it broke with both absolutism and the parliamentary monarchy of 1812, creating something new with more of a balance between the Crown and the Cortes. At the same time, the Constitution left a number of key questions, including the creation of municipal governments, to be resolved by later laws, and this, as well as different understandings of the real power of the Crown, would become the catalyst for intense conflict over fundamental ideas.[44] Baldomero had received the news of the La Granja events with great enthusiasm. In his letters to Jacinta, however, he said nothing about the new constitution, although he would soon become closely identified with it, as a rare piece of Manises ceramic demonstrates.[45]

Espartero's autonomy was soon interrupted by another Carlist expedition. Led by the Pretender himself, the goal of the so-called Royal Expedition was to end the war through a negotiated solution with María Cristina, who, terrified by the La Granja mutiny, had let the king of Naples know that she was willing to come to an arrangement with Carlos. An imposing force of 11,000 soldiers and 1,200 cavalry left Estella (Navarra) on 15 May and crossed the Ebro River five days later. After defeating Cristino armies at Huesca and Barbastro on 24 May and 2 June and fighting a number of minor skirmishes in Catalonia and Valencia, the Carlists crossed the Maestrazgo and, on 4 August, captured Segovia, only ninety kilometres from the gates of the weakly guarded capital.[46] When the Carlists arrived on the outskirts of Madrid and it looked as though the war might be lost, María Cristina started negotiating with the Pretender.

The threat posed by the Royal Expedition led the government to again take control from Espartero. Demoted to a secondary position, he resigned on 5 July, but that same day he received orders putting him in charge of the pursuit. After almost four years fighting exclusively in the north, Baldomero set off for Aragón, "a very different theatre."[47] British journalist John Moore, who was travelling with Espartero's army, left a powerful account of the hardships it had to endure.

> [F]or five days the troops had no other food whatever but the little meat remaining from the slaughtered sheep, fortunately secured near Fortanete, and a very few bullocks that had been driven with the army all the way from Logroño: there was neither bread, biscuit, salt, nor wine, and the water to be met with was very often in a most unwholesome state. The forage for the cavalry was completely exhausted; and the horses were drooping and dying daily; for they had nothing to eat but a scanty picking of straw, and here and there a little wheat in the ear culled from some patch of land which had escaped the notice of the Carlists. Add to this, unceasing marches over steep and flinty mountainous paths – great numbers of the men being literally barefoot – under a scorching sun.[48]

At Teruel, the British attaché reported, Espartero "was obliged to offer bills on his house at Logroño" to acquire rations.[49]

As Espartero was chasing the Pretender through Aragón, María Cristina named him minister of war. He turned it down, claiming he was unqualified "to direct that complicated machinery of the State." He was absolutely right.[50] He might well have added that he detested paperwork and desk jobs. He was not, he told Jacinta, going to accept a position that "I can't undertake with dignity." As always, he sought her approval: "I believe you will approve of my decision."[51]

When news of the Carlist capture of Segovia reached the capital, a frantic government ordered Espartero to march to Madrid. He received the order in Daroca (Zaragoza), 260 kilometres away; a week later he was in Madrid.[52] His stay there lasted just two weeks, but it was incredibly intense and saw his first serious involvement in politics.

General Antonio Seoane met Espartero and his army on the outskirts of Madrid to urge him not to enter the city. Espartero insisted: he had promised his men that they would parade before the queen and the queen mother. He then went to the palace, where he met with María Cristina for more than two hours. He supposedly told her that he "belonged to no party" and that his "only motto was Isabel II."[53] This certainly sounds like him. Espartero's men got their parade on 13 August. They were in "brilliant condition" and received an enthusiastic reception.[54] So did their commander. "Rarely has a citizen been given such flattering reception" was the assessment of one newspaper.[55]

A few days later, eighty officers of the Royal Guard and of the Second Brigade, both stationed in towns near Madrid, mutinied, demanding a change of government. Far from spontaneous, this was the fruit of conservative efforts to use the army to reverse the events of August 1836. Espartero went to Aravaca and convinced the men to march to Segovia with a promise that there would be a new government once the enemy had been defeated. After sending two separate envoys to Pozuelo with the same promise, he was forced to go there himself and meet with Manuel de Mazarredo y Mazzaredo and Colonel Roncali, a man who, months before, he had described in a letter to Jacinta as "one of those many busybodies who care only about their own interests."[56] He wound up asking them to tell their men to return to duty, and that "if necessary, I will become dictator." This provided a temporary solution, but when the mutineers discovered that they were to go to Segovia, they demanded to be released from duty. Espartero agreed and then promoted a number of sergeants to take their place. According to Mazzaredo, "he shouted, cried, snivelled, offered them promotions, said that with them he had no need for officers and God knows what other things that undermined discipline."[57]

Unlike in the past and, as we shall see, in the future, this time Espartero chose to respond with leniency. He petitioned María Cristina for clemency because the episode had been "unimportant."[58] To Jacinta, he described the events as merely "a passing passion." To both he emphasized that what mattered was the loyalty of the troops, "always with their General Espartero."[59]

Lacking "sufficient power to remove the General in Chief," Calatrava tendered his government's resignation.[60] María Cristina asked Espartero to become the new prime minister and war minister. He didn't want the top job, but if María Cristina insisted, he would have to "take it on and taste being supreme general (generalísimo) of the armies, president of the council and heaven knows what else." In reality, all he wanted was "my home without having to command or be commanded," but a "public man cannot evade his responsibilities."[61] A "public man" – this was a phrase he had never used before, either about himself or about the politicians he had so often denounced. Was he starting to see himself as something more than a simple soldier at the service of queen and country? On 19 August Espartero informed María Cristina that, if she insisted, he would head the ministry, "because I have undertaken to accept even the most terrible undertaking on Your Majesty's behalf."[62] Once the cabinet was in place, with Eusebio Bardají as prime minister and Evaristo San Miguel as interim minister of war, he resigned. He was now, he told Jacinta, "free of such a heavy burden."[63]

For Luis Garrido Muro, Espartero had planned the political manoeuvres, starting with his refusal to accept the War Ministry back in the summer, "as if it were a military encircling movement." He had prevented the Moderates from coming to power and avoided "the counter-revolution some hoped for." Best of all, the new government "bore [his] seal." And when, in December, Bardají was replaced by Ofalia, a non-party man whose top priority was to end the war, "Espartero's needs were fully met."[64] This is an astonishing achievement, especially for a political neophyte. Would Espartero's subsequent performance justify such a judgment? But Espartero himself was not so sure of the situation. Even after he had the government he wanted, he warned Jacinta, who was in France, that the "tempest" continued and that she should remain there until "the sky in the Peninsula clears."[65]

Espartero set out after the Carlists on 27 August, but they managed to elude him, and on 12 September, they appeared on the outskirts of the capital, which was defended by little more than the National Militia. This was Carlos's great moment, but, for reasons that remain unexplained, instead of attacking he ordered a retreat.[66] Espartero, who arrived in Madrid the next day, pursued them and on 19 September won a major victory at Aranzueque (Guadalajara). The defeat so disgusted Carlist general Ramón Cabrera that he took his forces back to the Maestrazgo. This was effectively the end of the Royal Expedition, although it was only on 24 October that Carlos and his remaining men crossed back into Navarra. Espartero did not follow.[67] Months later, Lieutenant George Turner, who was in discussions with the Carlists, reported that they would have surrendered if Espartero had continued his pursuit.[68]

With the Royal Expedition finally defeated, Espartero could turn his mind to another serious matter. Between April and August, the army had been shaken by a series of mutinies, almost all of them related to money.[69] On 24 June, the Logroño garrison rebelled because it had not been paid, and nine days later soldiers of the Princesa regiment refused to go into action for the same reason. During the mutiny, the Count of Mirasol, the commander, was punched and his adjutant killed. In mid-August, in Miranda del Ebro, General Ceballos Escalera, who was replacing Espartero while he was pursuing the Carlist expedition, was killed by troops who believed, incorrectly, that he had been hoarding their pay.[70] In Vitoria the next day, enraged – and unpaid – soldiers killed the military governor, a deputy, and a number of other civilians. Finally, on 26 August, General Sarsfield was bayoneted to death by his troops and his naked body defiled in the main square of Pamplona. Another general and four civilians were also killed.[71]

Espartero arrived in Miranda del Ebro on 28 October to deal with the mutineers. On 30 October, he had the regiment responsible for Escalera's death form up in a square on the outskirts of the town with the cavalry positioned behind them. As a "sepulchral silence" descended, Espartero rode into the middle of the square and dismissed his adjutants. Alone, sword in hand and "in that stentorian voice of his," he announced that they were there to deal with a scandal which had dishonoured the army and "hugely torments my spirit." As their "comrade" who shared their hardships on the battlefield, he would do anything to prevent their honour from being attacked, since "your honour is my honour." Were they his "shield"? he asked, to which, "excited by the words of their commander," the men yelled yes. Then, reaching a new level of intimacy, he recounted how "a bloodied ghost ... his body torn to shreds" had appeared to him in a dream. "Look at me ... avenge my grievance ... save the fatherland," it said. "I promised to do it. Do you know who it was? My beloved friend, the valiant General Escalera, the terror of the enemies of our sacred liberty, that most honest Spaniard, that convinced patriot, that untiring hero who worked to bring us victory that terrible night of Luchana ... Do you remember him? Well (his voice shaking), he lives no longer." Then, pointing his sword towards the town, he cried that "some assassins" in the pay of the Carlists had murdered "a favourite son of the fatherland," a man who was "worthy of being your friend because he was mine." The criminals, men from the Segovia provincial regiment, were among them now, "their foul breath" contaminating the air they all breathed, and if they were not identified, the regiment would be "decimated immediately." The threat worked: ten men were identified and, after receiving the last rites, were shot. Thirty-six others were sentenced to life in the fortress at Ceuta, and the regiment itself was dissolved and its men distributed among other units.[72] From Miranda, Espartero went to Pamplona to deal with those responsible for the deaths of Sarsfield and Mendivil. On 14 November, a court martial passed the death sentence on two officers and eight sergeants as well as on a number who had fled. Other officers were stripped of their rank and/or sentenced to prison.[73]

Following the executions, Baldomero told Jacinta that that the "army has never been in better shape nor the men shown me greater signs of their esteem, which is no small thing."[74] He told María Cristina that the punishments had been harsh but necessary and the army was now "as disciplined as it was loyal. Never have men of all ranks given me greater and more repeated proof of their affection and respect."[75] Wylde, who was present in Miranda del Ebro, reported that Espartero's "act of justice was extremely well received" by the troops and that only Espartero, "so popular with the soldiers that he can do what he pleases with them without risk," could have carried it off.[76]

The Royal Expedition had failed, but the Carlist cause was still alive. Cabrera was back in his stronghold in the east, where the war reached unprecedented levels of brutality. In the north, Espartero would soon be chasing new Carlist expeditions. In addition to the unending sparring with the government over what he repeatedly called the "absolute lack of resources," he found himself dealing with a ministry which would work hard to get rid of him. More than ever, Espartero was fighting on two fronts.

Claiming ill health, Espartero again submitted his resignation in November.[77] Even though the enemy were "demoralized" and his army "admirably disciplined," the government remained a problem. The snow was already falling, but his men had "only summer trousers" and there were no "buildings in which to shelter them."[78] If this situation did not change he could not continue as commander in chief.[79]

On 16 December, Ofalía succeeded Bardají as prime minister. Espartero was again named minister of war, and again he refused He even refused to name an alternative.[80] The new interior minister, the Marquis of Someruelos, was a friend, and starting on New Year's Day 1838 Espartero sent him a remarkable series of letters, many of them unusually lengthy for him, in which he voiced his complaints about government actions and set out his views on politics.

The new government's failure to provide the necessary resources had left the army in a "distressing situation," and recent War Ministry decisions on promotions, especially Narváez's, were not "in harmony with my principles of justice."[81] Espartero's refusal to recommend a new war minister stemmed from his refusal "to get mixed up in government actions." That said, for the war effort to be effective, the "influential people who consider themselves strategists," even though they lack the necessary knowledge, should be cleared out of the ministry so that "the commander in chief [has] exclusive influence in the War Ministry, since he needs the complete confidence of the government. If this is not the case, he must be removed and replaced with someone more capable."[82]

Espartero also offered some general political advice. He himself was above political party – "I've never belonged to one and never will" – and it would be best if governments were the same.[83] He was furious with the "filthy newspapers," which were, he claimed, the reason the war was dragging on.[84] And he was angry at how the Crown had been weakened. The man who had rejoiced at news of the events of La Granja was now lamenting that the royal prerogative had been undermined.[85] Finally, Espartero made an astonishing assertion about his own importance. Only the "magic prestige with all classes that luck has granted me" was holding the army together, but even this was not infinite, and if it were eaten away, "Goodbye Isabel II! Goodbye fatherland!!!"[86]

In February, the war minister, General Carratalá, asked Espartero to assume command of the Army of the Centre as well and to provide his views on how to prosecute the war.[87] Unsurprisingly, he refused the second command, but he did have ideas about how the war should be fought.[88] With the conflict spreading to other parts of the country, the first step was to declare nationwide a state of war, leaving the military "sweeping powers [and] freedom of action," something he had proposed back in 1835. Every district should have a military court to deal with "rebellion and disloyalty," and the civil authorities needed to keep a close watch on all people "suspected of disaffection." Of course, the government had to ensure that the army had sufficient men and resources to prosecute the war properly. Given the type of enemy they were facing, generals should be both "intrepid and active." His "rapid movements" had countered the Carlist strategy of launching more expeditions, but the extended lines he had to protect and the change of season were making this much more difficult. The government should create a new force with the sole mission of hunting these expeditions, "leaving [the enemy] without a moment's rest." In the meantime, Espartero would pursue any new expeditions, and this meant his army could not be dismembered. In the north, "leniency and indulgence" had to give way to "just rigour ... crops should be cut down; all foodstuffs collected, and those which cannot be taken away destroyed ... Villages abandoned by their inhabitants razed to the ground." It was essential to rekindle among Cristino loyalists "the enthusiasm and determination sapped by the rebels' terror." Finally, commanders must have the "unlimited confidence" of the government so they could "operate with complete freedom."

As to governing, it was necessary "to make oneself loved and respected," and this required a four-pronged approach. One must be "conciliatory so that the gangs that so harm our cause disappear." One must be "independent to avoid all outside or personal influence." One must be "objective so that rewards go to those with merit and punishments to those who deserve them." And one must be "circumspect so that decisions are always based on results, utility, and the common good." Choosing important government figures must be done with "the greatest tact and precision," since having "unblemished people of known probity who will act energetically" in key positions is the best way to assure public opinion.[89]

Around the same time, Espartero sent a long letter to his friend and second in command, Manuel de Latre, in which he set out his political thinking and his sense of self. Some of it comes from his standard vocabulary, especially his invocation of queen and country and his denunciation of parties and "factions," but other parts do not, especially his presentation of himself as a Spanish everyman. Given its unusual length and level of detail, it deserves to be cited in full.

> I will never belong to parties or factions; I am a Spaniard who belongs entirely to the general body of my countrymen and my sole motto will always be *Everything for my queen, everything for my fatherland*. I desire nothing nor aspire to anything since I need nothing from anyone. As you well know, the magic prestige I have among my comrades in arms is not just with the enlisted men ... it starts with you, who are my second, and ends with the last drummer. This prodigious prestige comes not only from being the dean in this campaign, nor from my always being an inseparable comrade in glories, hardships, and dangers, nor from my constant fortune on the battlefield. The main cause of this prestige comes from my inalterable system of not being a party man nor allowing myself to be swayed by personal affections ... The Spanish soldier is not stupid and knows how to think and reason in his own way. I wish that all the ministers would follow this system; then we would soon see the happy end to this disastrous struggle. Unfortunately, ministers generally belong to a gang, must accommodate to the demands of their party, commit a thousand injustices, become hateful, and in such a situation there is no throne, nor peace, nor order, nor justice. But the day will come when we have such longed-for goods. In addition to her talent and good intentions, the queen regent has a beautiful heart and it may well happen that a man of known honour and known record will say to her, "My Lady, do not fear these men of factions, whose knowledge of the throne and fatherland stops at their own interests. Your Majesty should and can count on the general mass of the nation, on the good Spaniards. You can and should count on an army as valiant as it is virtuous that knew how to sacrifice itself in the name of Your Majesty, innocent Isabel, and this unfortunate fatherland. Choose five good men for your councillors, which will not be difficult among ten million. Choose them without fear and the Throne of your sublime daughter will be strengthened with the peace of happiness of the Spanish people, who will obey you always as their mother, their liberator."[90]

In the meantime, the government had been seeking a new war minister. Espartero's old commander, Fernández de Córdova, was offered the job – along with that of commander in chief of the army, and later even the presidency of the government – but he turned them all down. Espartero was outraged. Fernández de Córdova was one of those "men who will only serve their own interests."[91] In the end, the post went to José Carratalá, someone whom Espartero knew well from Peru and whom he deemed to lack entirely the necessary qualities.[92]

After encouraging Someruelos to show his letters to María Cristina and the day after he told Latre that she needed an "a man of known honour" to advise her, Espartero wrote to the queen regent directly. Despite everything he had done for the cause, the current government neither trusted nor supported him, undoubtedly because he was not a party man. He repeated his lament about the "most absolute abandonment" of his army and closed by asking her to protect Colonel Benito Miranda, his childhood friend who was likely to be dismissed from his position in the War Ministry because Espartero had recommended him.[93] And when Miranda was indeed dismissed, Espartero approached María Cristina again. Three ministers, Castro, Mon, and Carratalá, "have declared war on me," and without the confidence of the government he could not continue as commander in chief.[94] In this context, Espartero's threat to resign was, as Luis Garrido Muro says, "close to straightforward blackmail," and it worked. Carratalá was soon replaced as war minister by Latre, and Espartero's protégé Genaro Gamiz also got a job in the ministry.[95] This would be only one of many occasions on which he would wield such a threat and on which it would be effective.

On 23 February Espartero sent a letter to Congress setting out his grievances. The government had ignored his repeated warnings about the "absolute lack of resources" facing the Army of the North, and now only "extraordinary measures" could ward off serious consequences. Deputies should demand to see all his letters to the cabinet since the previous October so that it "would become aware of the critical situation" of the army and take appropriate action.[96] Even though Congress president Manuel Barrio Ayuso did not present the letter to the legislature, the matter still became public.[97] On 2 March, Espartero gave a speech to his troops in Haro in which he repeated the complaints he had made so many times in writing and announced that he had written to the Cortes. *El Eco del Comercio* printed the speech, which in turn led to a debate in the Congress.[98]

Almost as if they had been waiting for this drama to end, in mid-March the Carlists launched yet another expedition, this one led by Count Ignacio de Negri.[99] Starting on 17 March, the chase took Espartero to Burgos, Palencia, and Leon, before he could deliver the coup de grace. After a nighttime march "through a horrific, freezing darkness along impassable roads," he caught up with Negri at Fresno de Rodilla

(Burgos) on 27 April. As dawn broke, at the head of a contingent of some eighty cavalry, Espartero "charged so decisively" that only Negri himself and a small number of men escaped capture.[100] Lieutenant Lynn described it as "an act of great gallantry but rashness," but Villiers, who had come to recognize Espartero's importance, was horrified and urged Lynn to remind Espartero that he was "*indispensable* to his country and that his life should not be exposed to the same hazards as the lowest soldier … I cannot but think that the magic influence he exercises over his troops would be the same if they knew he was witnessing their conduct at the distance usually maintained by all commanders in chief." Espartero's reward for this victory was to be named captain general, the highest rank in the army.[101]

During the pursuit of Negri, another test of wills over personnel issues took place when the government transferred Espartero's chief of staff, Antonio Van Halen, without even consulting him. Once again, Espartero appealed to the queen regent, this time with an explicit threat: she had to choose between him on the one hand and Mon and Castro on the other, since "in this matter there is no middle ground." But that was precisely how the question was resolved: both Van Halen and the ministers remained where they were.[102] It was perhaps a Solomonic solution, but an angry Espartero vented his frustrations against the "Strategists" whose "theories and gang spirit" were doing more damage than the Carlists. He was "fed up and disgusted," but he felt especially badly that María Cristina was surrounded by "so many rascals without a fatherland [or] honour … with no interests beyond their own and those of their gangs … Poor fatherland!!!"[103]

Espartero's next major initiative was the capture of Peñacerrada (Álava) in June. Before attacking the town itself, Espartero had to overcome the imposing castle of Uziharra which defended it. He began with an artillery barrage at dawn on 20 June, but the walls were so thick that he ordered two battalions of rangers to scale them. Even though the ladders were too short, his men stuck with it, and after "an hour of admirable, unbelievable combat" they achieved their objective. This time even the enemy was worthy of praise. "[T]he defenders were brave, really brave and my generous and valiant Rangers spared their lives."[104] The attack on Peñacerrada itself came the next morning. It began with another unproductive artillery barrage but climaxed, as it did so often with Espartero, in a cavalry charge. "I put myself at the head of my hussars. The clash against their lances, bayonets, guns and artillery was cruel, but everything yielded to valour." (Espartero didn't know it, but the Carlist defeat would have an important consequence: Juan Antonio Guergué was replaced as commander by Rafael Maroto.) Lieutenant

Lynn thought that Espartero had "exposed himself" too much, but he was impressed with how he treated the prisoners, letting them choose between joining his army, joining Juan Antonio Muñagorri's force, or even returning to their homes.[105]

Afterwards the Hussars named him their honorary colonel. This was precisely the recognition he most craved. "It will be beautiful," he wrote.[106] And when his Hussar uniform eventually arrived, he was thrilled. "It's magnificent and it suits me perfectly." He also enjoyed the glamorous ball given in his honour in Vitoria on 2 July. On his arrival, "three young people placed a crown of laurel on my head." After he said a few words in reponse to the mayor, "there were many cheers ... youngsters sang the Hymn of Luchana."[107]

Between battles, however, life was boring and burdensome, "full of hard work and so much paper," he complained to Jacinta as he oversaw repairs to the walls of Peñacerrada. Then came an incident which reveals much about his personality. Dressed "in a way that they couldn't help but recognize me, I rode within sixty metres" of an enemy battery, which fired on him. Jacinta might think this "madness," but he did not. "I am convinced death does not want me ... it detests me and flees from me ... I like things with spirit, alive ... very much alive, like lightning."[108]

Espartero's next offensive move was to take the town of Labraza on 15 July. Estella, which he planned to use as the base for an invasion of the Carlist strongholds, was to follow, but he had again been forced to call on his personal credit to raise one and a half million *reales*. Then repeated bad news: the failure of General Oráa's siege of Morella, the defeat of Colonel Coba's First Light Infantry, and the advance of the guerrilla-priest Merino into Castilla led him to abandon the Estella operation "so that we don't lose the Castiles."[109]

As in America, this was a war that involved the local population, and that did not usually mean trying to win hearts and minds. In January, Espartero had issued an edict banning all "games of chance ... cards, darts, lotteries, and roulette" which were not legally authorized, in bars and cafés, and other public and private places. Then in June he lightened the blockade he had put in place in December 1835. Rather than "depriving the enemy of resources," it had hurt the economy of the loyal provinces and seriously reduced their ability to supply his troops. On the other hand, he also ordered "the expulsion of people whose sons are fighting for the enemy." Finally, on 27 November, "convinced of the evils caused by the use of berets, a special badge" of the enemy, he prohibited soldiers and civilians from wearing them.[110]

The treatment of prisoners again became an issue when the Carlists executed six Cristino soldiers in the spring of 1838. Espartero threatened to retaliate in kind but was stopped when Lord John Hay and Villiers put pressure on the government.[111] Espartero was far from pleased, as he made clear to the prime minister. He had ordered the executions because he was "the chief defender of my soldiers," and reprisals were simply "self defence." His own image and authority also depended on them. Without reprisals, "I should lose the magical illusion which fortune has granted to me."[112] There was a second incident in November when Carlist general Juan Manuel Martín de Balmaseda executed twenty-five Cristino soldiers who had surrendered in Álava. This time Espartero gave the British no chance to intervene: he had an equal number of prisoners from Balmaseda's own unit executed the very next day. This was, he told his troops, "repugnant to my heart," but it was the only means he had left to protect them from "such atrocious scenes." Wylde, who opposed the idea of reprisals in principle, told Villers that in this instance Espartero was justified because "the indignation of the soldiery was so great ... that had he not done so the discipline of his army would have been gravely affected."[113]

Oráa's failure to take Morella changed much more than Espartero's campaign plans. Towards the end of June, the tensions with the government heated up again. Having his friend Latre in the War Ministry had not helped for very long; in fact, it almost became his undoing. Shortly after Peñacerrada, he again complained to María Cristina about "my enemies" Castro and Mon, who were doing everything in their power to eliminate him. He certainly did not need an Auxiliary War Committee or "those who insist on calling themselves Strategists" giving him campaign plans which "would be criminal to put into practice."[114] He also complained to Wylde about Leopoldo O'Donnell, commander of the Army of Biscay, who had been furnished with private instructions, not only without his having been consulted on the subject, but without his having been informed afterwards.[115] A few weeks later, his complaints about Castro and Mon took on an extra edge: If they remained in office, "I cannot nor should not remain in command, or in any other post."[116] He got the answer he had hoped for: Espartero was "the one whom my daughter's cause needs more."[117] However, he had also sent a copy of this second letter to Latre, who leaked it to the press as part of a plot with Fernández de Córdova to discredit him.[118] *El Correo Nacional* even threw Espartero's American past in his face, warning Spaniards that "divisions among our generals were to blame for the loss of such vast possessions."[119]

On 7 August the cabinet and the presidents of the Congress and the Senate, as well the Duke of Frías, Istúriz, and Martínez de la Rosa, met to confront the crisis. After four hours of debate the cabinet offered its resignation, but María Cristina refused to accept it. Ofalía then offered to undo some of the things that had so angered Espartero and assured him that any sense of enmity from Castro and Mon was nothing more than "a misunderstanding or exaggeration."[120] Espartero was not the least bit mollified. The end result of the affair, he told María Cristina, was to make him look like "a dictator who violated the Constitution and the royal prerogative, when I am their most zealous defender." How could he face the enemy calmly when he was always looking over his shoulder, worried that his enemies at home would take advantage of any opportunity "to take shots at the fame I have acquired at such cost"? It was now absolutely impossible "to achieve the necessary harmony between [him] and the aforementioned ministers." She had to choose.[121] It was not a difficult choice, since María Cristina knew that for the question that really mattered to her, saving the throne, Espartero was "worth more than Mon and Castro, than the entire cabinet." Above all, "while the war continues the opinion of the generals carries as much weight [as] or more than that of [parliamentary] majorities."[122]

After learning of Oráa's withdrawal from Morella, Espartero wrote the queen regent again. The entire letter was a tirade against the cabinet for the lamentable state in which it had left his army. He had kept things going, "using my property and my wife's as collateral, and with the magic of my prestige." María Cristina herself had found four million *reales* to cover his credit temporarily, but the efforts of an individual like himself could be no more than a stopgap and could not be repeated. If the government couldn't do its job, it should "admit it and leave the Crown free to name new ministers because this prerogative is the only guarantee that monarchs in representative governments have of not being slaves."[123]

News of the defeat at Morella finally brought the government down. After "greater than normal" difficulty in finding a new ministry, the Duke of Frías took office on 6 September. When Espartero made it clear that the war minister "should be identified with the commander in chief," both Frías and María Cristina asked him who should have the job. It was a question he had been asked many times before and he had always refused to propose names. This time he did: "General Isidro Alaix."[124] Alaix was still recovering from the serious wounds he had received a couple of weeks earlier, and there was a revolving door of acting ministers, including Frías himself, until he arrived in Madrid at the end of November.[125]

Like Ofalía before him, Frías soon sought ways of reducing the government's reliance on Espartero. His solution was Ramón María Narváez.

During the1820s, Narváez had been a more consistent liberal than Espartero, spending eight months as a prisoner in France after the events of 1823, refusing to take the oath of loyalty to Fernando VII, and returning to the army only after the monarch's death. Serving under Fernández de Córdova, he received three promotions in ten months; he also shifted to the right politically. In November 1836, the government put him in charge of pursuing the Gómez expedition when it had crossed into central and southern Spain, but he was replaced by Alaix. After resigning and then changing his mind, Narváez refused to obey orders to go to the north to serve under Espartero. He even took his case public in a pamphlet. A change of cabinet spared him a court martial, and then, in September 1837, he was ordered to create a new army based in Andalucía. He was also promoted to field marshal.[126] Narváez despised Espartero, whom he described as "that utter idiot who does nothing but lie and issue false dispatches." If anyone could show him that Espartero had "done anything good in this war, Luchana included, I will let myself be castrated."[127]

After a successful campaign against the Carlists in the centre and south, Narváez entered an enthusiastic Madrid on 14 October. That same day, he sent a strategy paper to the cabinet, which was adopted immediately. The war's centre of gravity, he claimed, had shifted from the north to Aragón and Catalonia, and Cabrera was now the Cristinos' most dangerous enemy. His solution was to create a new, large, and autonomous force, which he called the Army of the Reserve, to fight him. Narváez was proposing nothing less than a complete change in military strategy, and with it a change in military leadership – and political influence. The latter certainly suited the government, which "in one week" turned from Espartero to Narváez "purely for political survival."[128]

On 25 October, the *Gaceta* published a decree creating a forty-thousand-man Army of the Reserve. Narváez was given command as well as sweeping powers, including overriding the captains general.[129] Espartero responded immediately, writing an *Exposición* to María Cristina on 31 October.[130] When this published seventeen-page pamphlet appeared in Madrid on 12 November, it flew off the shelves and "circulated widely" across the country.[131] Espartero's pamphlet hit some of his favourite themes, especially his distrust of politicians and partisanship. How did this measure get approved so quickly? And without any proper consultation? Why was he, the commander in chief, not asked for his opinion? Creating this new army "when those that exist lack the basic necessities for fighting a war" was "monstrous" and would destroy those armies and bring "immediate demoralization." Worse, it would threaten the throne itself; the queen regent had to act, appointing a new government consisting of "six pure, strong and wise councillors ... free of all party spirit." Only this would create the "unity and order" needed to defeat the enemy and bring peace.[132]

Narváez's new influence evaporated even before Espartero drafted his document, a casualty of "one of the most obscure and confusing ... episodes ... of the Regency." On 28 October, the war minister ordered Narváez to bring troops into the capital to prevent some rumoured disturbances. These never materialized, and the next day General Quiroga, the captain general of New Castile, resigned, charging that this had happened without his knowledge. When María Cristina rejected the resignation, Narváez resigned and two days later left the capital for his home town of Loja.[133] But Narváez still had much further to fall. In late November, he and Fernández de Córdova were involved in a failed uprising in Seville.[134]

Espartero responded with another pamphlet.[135] Here was an opportunity to get rid of his rivals and he took it, calling for the death penalty for Narváez and Fernández de Cordóva. It was time to apply the law and to punish disobedience and indiscipline as he had done in Miranda del Ebro and Pamplona. They had been responsible for "an atrocious attack on the social order and state security" that required "exemplary punishment. Before the law, social distinctions must disappear."[136] When the Cortes voted unanimously to try the two men, they fled the country. Narváez's exile took him to Gibraltar, Tangiers, Marseilles, and Paris. In the North African city, he wrote a manifesto defending himself against Espartero's charges.[137] In private letters, he raged against the "beast," the "vile man," whose "ambition and criminal pretensions" knew no limits and who, he claimed, had tried to have him assassinated.[138] For now, at least, Narváez was powerless to do anything about it.

All of this was contributing to profound political instability. By the time that Alaix arrived in Madrid, the country had been without a government for ten days. Frías had resigned on 20 November and, despite an agreement between their respective leaders, the two main parties had been unable to put together a coalition government. On 3 December, Alaix, a man who had known no life outside the army and whom Villiers described as an "ignorant brute," found himself as caretaker prime minister.[139] A proper government finally took office on 9 December with the sixty-year-old diplomat Evaristo Pérez de Castro as prime minister and Alaix in the War Ministry. Alaix had already dissolved Narváez's reserve army; he now disbanded the Auxiliary War Council that had so angered Espartero. Espartero himself was named commander of the Royal Guard, but he turned it down because "it would give rise to slander" and suggested that Valdés be appointed instead. He also recommended that María Cristina promote both Alaix and Van Halen. Espartero was, Villiers wrote, "the most effective King" Spain had had in fifty years.[140]

Luis Garrido Muro describes the new administration as a "blank slate waiting for its new master to dictate the script,"[141] yet the government had been in office only three days when Espartero began to express his doubts, and his unhappiness took months to dissipate. Baldomero spent his forty-sixth birthday in a foul mood. "So much paper, so much misery and a government that does nothing," he complained to Jacinta. "Last night I sent a bad-humoured letter to the regent and an even worse one to the government, who are a bunch of scatterbrains."[142] Once again he put his personal property on the line, signing credits for 2,851,500 *reales*.[143]

Espartero was mistaken in his misgivings: Alaix proved to be exactly the kind of war minister he needed. "What you propose will be done, what you request will be granted," Alaix wrote in July 1839.[144] Soon 80 per cent of the budget was going to the army. Once these resources began to flow, Espartero would deliver on his promises of victory.

On 9 February, the day after María Cristina had suspended the sitting of the Cortes, Alaix informed Espartero that the regent was "anxious" that the upcoming campaign "be executed with all possible care" and had requested that Espartero detail what he needed.[145] It was a blank cheque, at least as regarded money, but for Espartero that was not enough. Victory also required a different approach to the war itself: "Seek out the enemy untiringly. Hurt them with frequent and forced marches ... And undertake unplanned operations to capitalize on unexpected demands." Above all, military authorities must not be subject to any "obstacle" that would impede their ability to conduct the war and carry out "the pacification of the country." There should be "military commissions to render summary judgment on any sign of defection or any sort of crime that might have favoured the Pretender's cause." The approach was easily summarized: "rigorous treatment for our enemies and protection for the loyalists."[146]

As 1839 got underway, Baldomero was spending a frustrating time pursuing Maroto. Then, on 19 February, he received stunning news: Maroto had executed four generals, his predecessor Guergué among them, and two officials of the Carlist administration.[147] This dramatic episode was the culmination of internal tensions and conflicts among the Carlists which went back to the defeat of the Royal Expedition in October 1837. Immediately after returning to Navarra, the Pretender had issued the Arciniega manifesto in which he took personal responsibility for what had happened. This was followed by a purge of military and political leaders, which brought Catholic ultras to power, including Guergué as chief of the general staff. After the defeat at Peñacerrada only seven months later, he was replaced by Maroto, who sought to bring more moderate people into the Carlist government. It was this "sordid struggle for power" which led to the executions at Estella on 18 February 1839. Don Carlos declared Maroto a traitor but quickly reversed himself.[148]

For Baldomero, this was welcome news. The internal struggles were far from over, he told Jacinta. Maroto could count on the rank and file but not on many of the officers. "The clergy is also against him and remains a strong enemy as it is Lent and they are hard at work."[149] He was also in the field and not complaining of boredom. His headquarters at Alcanadre (Rioja) were far from luxurious, but he wrote about them almost as if he were on a camping trip: "There are no beds but we have no shortage of fleas that XXXX all over. I am doing well."[150]

On 23 March Espartero sent the government his campaign plan. It was an echo of what he had told Alaix a couple of weeks earlier. The war had been allowed to drag on because the government had followed "badly understood humanitarian sentiments" when "justly and opportunely executed rigour" would have saved many lives. Other than having recourse to the "degrading" arbitration of foreign nations, there were only two ways to end the war. He favoured a full military occupation of rebel territory, but the country lacked the resources for it. The other was "the devastation of rebel-occupied territory," and for this he needed government approval. He wasn't optimistic that Madrid would go along because "it won't be very pretty."[151] Much to his surprise, he received a free hand to employ "all the rigour needed to secure victory."[152]

Espartero needed one more thing: freedom from "the terror of a responsibility unconnected to the art of war, which falls exclusively on him who commands an army." In other words, he did not want to be undermined by politics. If the government did not feel able to provide this, he had a solution, one which revealed his ongoing distaste for political parties and his views on the workings of representative government, at least during times of war.

> Dissolve the Cortes, immediately call new elections, and have the government use all possible means to ensure that they are won by people from

outside the parties who truly love the fatherland; get a majority that will support the Crown's councillors, approve the bills they present, which, during the war, should be only those necessary to remove obstacles to and provide resources for victory. In sum, with the social order established on firm and respected foundations, power serves as a support for the army.[153]

By the time Espartero wrote this, the sittings of the Cortes had been suspended for two months. It would be another two before it was dissolved.

By mid-April Espartero was on his way to Ramales. Getting there was difficult, as the Carlists had severely damaged the road. The repairs took five days despite "non-stop work and the large number of men employed." Taking the town was secondary to getting Maroto to fight, but Maroto refused, withdrawing whenever Baldomero got close.[154] He was ready to attack Ramales on 1 May but was prevented by "the damn weather ... The roads, or rather the paths through this scrub, are impassible and the constant fog, rain, and snow keep visibility below twenty paces. I am absolutely furious." He was also "always soaked, with mud even in my sideburns."[155] The assault finally came at dawn on 8 May. It began with an artillery barrage that lasted for eight hours and ended with a bayonet charge in which half of his escort took part, "as the terrain prevented all of it from participating."[156]

The fort at Guadarmino overlooking Ramales remained. After three days of artillery barrages, "determined to save the blood of these brave men," Espartero led a direct attack. British journalist John Moore was there.

> Espartero, on horseback[,] was in advance of all, cheering and encouraging his men, and exposing himself to the hottest fire. All his aides-de-camp had their horses either killed or wounded, and Colonel Urbina, commanding the escort, was mortally wounded. A musket ball struck Espartero's horse on the forehead but it glanced off without seriously injuring the animal; the General's coat was also torn by a musket ball, and a third lodged in another part of his uniform. It was astonishing that he was not shot, for ... he was in advance of his escort and of the troops, when the balls were pouring down upon them from the thickly lined parapet and the fort – officers and men, and horses, falling around him. His presence and example were invaluable; the troops boldly advanced under his eye, and the result was that when they had nearly gained the summit of the fortified heights, the enemy abandoned them and fled.[157]

Guadarmino was "a little hot," Baldomero told Jacinta. Three days later he sent her a long letter describing the events and explaining his

Figure 5 Espartero's charge at the Battle of Guadarmino, May 1839. Nineteenth Century Album, Museo Zumalakarregi.

conduct. The province of Santander was "assured," and he was now after Maroto "to hit him where it hurts." She shouldn't worry about him: If he put himself in harm's way, "it is because it's suitable." At Guadarmino it was the difference between taking two hundred casualties and two thousand. "I must be at the head of my men because when they see me they are each worth a thousand."[158] On 1 June María Cristina issued a Royal Decree naming Espartero Duke of Victory, a grandee first class, the highest category of nobility.[159]

Carlist resistance now all but disappeared as Maroto retreated in the face of Espartero's advance. By 27 May he was in Orduña, where he stopped to repair the defences and build a hospital which he described with his characteristic hyperbole: "Nowhere in the world are there better equipped hospitals ... for the wounded. I saw to it they lacked for nothing and they were even deluxe, as the English say." He was itching to finish Maroto off but "the damned weather" left him "fed up" and kept him in Orduña much longer than he wanted.[160] (He also hoped that Diego de León, "the Ney of the Army of the North," would do the same to Elío in Navarra.)[161]

From Orduña he planned to move into rebel terriory, "to squeeze the enemy, increase pressure on his resources and further weaken his morale, or oblige him to fight." Amurrio would be his "strategic point."[162] Espartero arrived there on 11 June after Maroto withdrew without a fight and set to work building fortifications to cover the roads which converged there. The work here also took longer than expected and he would not leave for almost two months. Then he heard that Maroto had abandoned Balmaseda. When Baldomero's troops entered the town, they found that the Carlists had blown up the castle and burned the barracks, "which doesn't bother me as it's not a place I'm interested in."[163]

On 19 June, Wylde brought Palmerston up to date on the military developments. Espartero had abandoned his original idea of building a line of communication "from Villarcayo to the coast by Ramales" in favour of one "from the Ebro to Bilbao," which was "much more conducive to [ending the war in these provinces] …The effect has already been produced by our advance to [Amurrio] and the evidence of its being the General's intention to keep permanent possession of the country he has gained afforded by the erection of redoubts at each point as we go on, has been much greater than I anticipated." Wylde also had praise for Alaix, who "had done more for the Army than any of his predecessors" by making it possible for Espartero "to form magazines and by keeping the troops more regularly supplied with pay and clothing than they have been for the last three years."[164]

As July began, Baldomero was still in Amurrio, "bored" by work on the fortifications.[165] He "daily supervised and directed [the works] for several hours," and his presence "gave life and activity to the working parties."[166] The enemy had tried to get some of his men to desert by offering bribes, and some did until "I caught three seductors and had them shot immediately." Maroto tried to lure him into attacking Areta, but "I don't shed blood to take points that are useless to us." Elsewhere, his order to "deprive the enemy of the harvest has been executed only partly, but I believe [Diego de] León will do everything possible."[167]

This stage of the campaign in the north coincided with elections which took place on 24 July. These gave Baldomero another opportunity to vent his distaste for politicians of all stripes. The only people who should serve as deputies were "those who don't want to do so and who, elected only for their virtues … accept only for the good of the fatherland, in which case *none of the so-called Moderates and Exalteds would be chosen* … That multitude of miserable ambition-ridden [men] who will stop at nothing to achieve their goals annoys me as much as it does you."[168] As far as the press was concerned, "newspapers are insulting but one must arm oneself with patience and ignore them."[169] Three days later he wrote to the prime minister and war minister demanding that Fernando Fernández de Córdova be subjected to a court martial for a letter about Espartero's conduct during the events of August 1837 that had appeared in a number of papers. The right to "write freely, without prior censorship ... the greatest and most useful political right, must be respected" because it was in the Constitution. "Good liberals" had designed it "to anathematize contrary acts, stop absolutist tendencies, and limit abuses," but it was only "opportune and convenient" when the political system was consolidated and the country at peace. He himself had always been "unconcerned ... about censorship of the ill-informed ... press" but he had never imagined that a military officer would publicly censure his superior as Fernández de Córdova had done, "the most grave crime recognized in our military laws."[170]

In March, Espartero's grievance had been more with Fernández de Córdova than with the press. Another episode in July revealed what he thought about press freedom itself. On 7 July, the government banned *El Guirigay*, ostensibly for publishing an article defaming María Cristina.[171] Espartero sent a letter supporting the government's decision which was published in two papers. As a defender of the Constitution, he deplored "that pernicious licence ... of that miserable clique ... A worthless group of immoral men ... That class of men without titles to recommend them, without property to ensure the good faith of their exaggerated maxims ... and without virtues recognized by accomplishments." Freedom to write and to publish should be defended, but not when "it endangers the health of the fatherland." The press was contributing to the divisions that were weakening the war effort, but worst of all was "the remarkable scandal of seeing the sacred and inviolable person of the queen regent publicy abused." The government was right to have banned the paper.[172]

Jacinta also became involved in the politics of the moment. After the elections, she received a letter from former finance minister Pío Pita Pizarro asking her to serve as a go-between with her husband. (Pita knew Jacinta from his time as governor in Logroño. She was also a friend of his wife.) He was enclosing a letter for Espartero; it was in a separate, sealed envelope, but she should feel free to read it before deciding whether to forward it. He was sending it through her because, when he had been finance minister in 1837, things had happened "that might make him question my consistent and loyal friendship." Since then he had written Espartero two letters without receiving a reply.[173]

Baldomero's correspondence with Jacinta makes no reference to this letter, but it might help explain some comments on political parties not long after he would have received it. "When the parties work with such ardour and perfidy one must be careful with all of them. I will never join either of the two extremes; they are equally rabble." A pox on both their houses but also, for the first time, some distinction between the two. "Believe, my dear, that I know men and things well and I work with this belief. The rabble rousers of the two gangs will find me as much an obstacle as the Carlists do, but don't doubt that those of the party that calls itself Moderate hate me more."[174]

Espartero was finally able to leave Amurrio on 8 August. Before he did, Maroto issued a proclamation that Cristino soldiers faced death in return for their "odious conduct ... you sack and burn everything, nothing escapes."[175] Maroto spoke "with all his boastfulness" on paper but he still refused to fight.[176] On 14 August, Espartero attacked Maroto's "formidably entrenched" positions between Villareal and Arlabán.[177] Wylde said that the Carlists "defended their positions very badly"; Espartero said that "never were they so cowardly."[178] Even with the campaign clearly in its last stages, Espartero refused to play it safe, leading his escort up the thickly forested heights. "How our horses kept their footing I know not," Moore wrote. "The paths were torturous; the branches and twigs, held aside by the horseman next in advance, swung back again with a force which, if not avoided, would have sent one rolling down the steep ... Still the General kept on, and we maintained our places as close to him as possible."[179]

On 22 August, Espartero marched into Durango, "the Pretender's capital."[180] There he again addressed his troops. They were reaching the end of the successful campaign he had planned, one which had started by replacing "the softness and leniency that had so emboldened our enemy ... with a prudent rigour": reprisals, the expulsion of Carlists' families, the burning of crops had worked. Now that defeat was inevitable, those who surrendered "will be admitted as members of a family with the past forgotten and a fraternal reconciliation that will make peace endure."[181] Six days later his army entered Vergara to enthusiastic cheers of "Long live peace!"[182]

The idea of hastening the end of the war by dividing the Pretender and the hardcore supporters of his cause from those for whom the dynastic issue mattered much less than others, such as the Basque *fueros*, had been around since at least 1837. This would indeed turn out to be the path to peace, but finding it would take time and involve many different actors.

The first attempt to do so was Juan Antonio de Muñagorri's "peace and *fueros*" campaign. Muñagorri was a notary and iron foundry owner from the Guipuzcoan town of Berastegui. As the war cut into his businesses, he and other Basque notables came up with a policy to "separate the interests of the Basque Provinces from those of Don Carlos."[183] He pitched his idea to the government in 1837, but only after the Ofalía cabinet succeeded in arranging a loan for the purpose could he launch his movement. In April 1838, he announced he would form a new army and invited Carlist deserters to join him. The uprising was a failure and Muñagorri had to flee to France.[184] He tried again in the spring of 1839 and managed to capture the fort of Urdax. Espartero was not thrilled about having another armed force present. Muñagorri was welcome to enter Carlist territory and fight the Carlists, "but the instant he admits a deserter from the liberal army, he will be persecuted as an enemy." He refused to meet with Muñagorri, and when Muñagorri managed to get a meeting with Alaix he found that the cabinet refused to endorse his new plan in case it "contradicted the plans of the commander in chief."[185] By this time, Muñagorri's project was being overtaken by events on the ground.

Espartero undertook his own initiative shortly after receiving carte blanche from the government in March 1839. On the one hand, he sought to exacerbate the divisions among the enemy by distributing documents that "by exciting the passions, will complicate matters among the rebels." (He made no mention of Eugenio Aviraneta, who was doing exactly this from his base in Bayona, and he may well have been taking credit for Aviraneta's work.)[186] His other initiative was much more significant. With Jacinta often serving as intermediary, he had been receiving voluminous reports on Maroto and the Carlists from Agustín Fernández de Gamboa, the Spanish consul in Bayona. Now he opened a direct line of communication with Maroto, sending him "a code we can use to communicate safely." Espartero rejected Maroto's initial demands but he promised "to issue a Royal Order in my name offering their current positions to all who join [you] to form part of my army in order to pacify the nation under the banner of Isabel II, constitutional queen." If this were insufficient he would give Maroto the "stronghold" he requested "if Don Carlos and his family" were delivered to him. They would be "respected" and allowed to choose their place of residence once peace had been restored. At this point Maroto broke off negotiations "in an irritating and indecorous manner."[187]

At the same time, Espartero was approached by the Marquis of Miraflores, who, from his post as Spain's ambassador in Paris, was overseeing attempts to build "a party for the Crown" composed of moderate liberals and former Carlists with Espartero as the necessary military strongman.[188] His goals were a negotiated peace with the Carlists, closer relations with France, and the creation of a strong "purely Spanish" government, "the product of a system of social reconstruction that is not reactionary." Espartero found Miraflores' ideas "brilliant" and his principles "solid ... I look on the intrigues of the political parties with equal disdain." Spain had to end the war itself but it would not be able to do so "until society is made moral, spirits united, the throne obeyed, the government respected ... and an honest and economical administration created." What Miraflores was proposing was essentially a version of what Espartero himself had just sent to the minister of war.

Encouraged by this reply, Miraflores urged María Cristina to keep Espartero in command at all costs and wrote again, setting out his plan in more detail, most of which was devoted to undoing the disentailment and restoring key elements of the Old Regime. Since a face-to-face meeting was impossible, Miraflores sent a Colonel Hezeta to Espartero's headquarters in Amurrio in July. Hezeta discovered that Espartero was not prepared to be the "saviour" that Miraflores wanted. "If the government and the Cortes consider it opportune to recognize the *fueros*, I can only obey," he told Hezeta. He did not "interfere in political questions"; his duty was to maintain discipline in the army, lead it to victory, and uphold and obey the government. It was not his place to undertake political initiatives. "You should tell the Marquis that I quite like [what] he has suggested but those are matters for the Cortes and the government."[189]

British military officers, especially Lord John Hay and William Wylde, also played a major role in the discussions that brought a negotiated peace to the north, although Espartero established very clear limits. He welcomed foreign military assistance but he was adamant that the peace be a Spanish one. He "stated very candidly to myself and to General Maroto at the commencement of the negotiations," Wylde recalled, "that he wished to conclude them if possible without any foreign mediation, saying that it was a quarrel among Spaniards and should be made up between Spaniards." When the final, culminating meeting between the two commanders took place, Wylde was not invited.[190]

Even before the battle of Hernani, and with Alaix's knowledge, the British had sent Lieutenant Turner to convey possible peace terms, including "a law to secure the *fueros* ... which would pass without difficulty, besides which Navarra and the Basque Provinces would be exempted from all contributions for one year." A number of Carlist officers, including General Elío, the commander in Navarra, expressed interest, but the initiative went no further.[191] A few months later, Lord John Hay was putting out similar feelers.[192] Throughout the ups and downs of Muñagorri's activities, Hay had remained in contact with Basque military leaders, urging them not to abandon the idea of a "peace and *fueros*" solution, and on 14 July, Maroto asked to meet with him personally. After the meeting on 27 July, Hay travelled to Amurrio to meet with Espartero, who rejected Maroto's proposal for an armistice as a delaying tactic and too vague to justify "a suspension of hostilities for a single day." (Wylde agreed that, if Espartero accepted, it would be "a gross dereliction of his duty.")[193] To Alaix, Espartero dismissed it as "the bad faith of a rebel general."[194] Espartero had his own terms for Maroto, which Hay then delivered. They were basically the same as those he had put forward in March: "acknowledging the Queen's right to the throne, the Constitution, and the Basque Fueros, under some modifications, and of the rank and pay of the officers under his orders being guaranteed." He had government authorization for such terms, "so far as the Government itself, at least, was empowered to offer them by the Constitution, without the consent of the Cortes, which was necessary with regard to the Fueros."[195]

Espartero did not hold out much hope and he was right. When Maroto heard Espartero's terms, he decided to wait on events and proceed no further.[196] On 17 August, Maroto sent his secretary to Espartero's headquarters under a flag of truce requesting a three-day ceasefire. Again Espartero refused. He then asked Madrid for advice on two crucial questions. The first was the need to indemnify the Carlist soldiers who "prefer to return home" instead of joining the Cristino army. This would be resolved by an assurance that there would be twenty, and possibly twenty-five, million *reales* available for this purpose. The second issue was the *fueros*, which were "in the power of the Cortes, not the government." Alaix replied two days later. The government would do everything possible to raise the twenty-five million "without delay," and while the *fueros* were a matter for the Cortes, the government "formally commits itself to proposing to it their concession or modification, as is most suitable."[197]

Without informing Maroto, the next day another Carlist general, Simón de la Torre, sent an emissary to "treat for peace with the Duke" bearing what Espartero called "the same demands" as Maroto, including the *fueros*, to which Espartero gave the same reply. At this point Espartero made it clear that he needed Madrid to provide "clear and categorical instructions."[198] Espartero sent Brigadier Zavala to hear Maroto's response, which remained "unfavourable on account of the question of the Fueros.' Repeated exchanges produced no progress "until the 24th, when an aide-de-camp of Maroto's came to request a further suspension of hostilities, and Brigadier Zavala returned with him to say that the Duke would not consent to any suspension of hostilities until Maroto had declared himself; and he also sent by Brigadier

Zavala the original of the Royal Order signed by the five Ministers containing the same conditions as those communicated through Colonel Linares." Finally satisfied, Maroto agreed to meet with Espartero the next day.[199]

The meeting started well. The two commanders embraced and went into a nearby farmhouse where they talked alone for a half-hour before summoning Wylde, Espartero's secretary Linaje, and Carlist general Juan Antonio de Urbiztondo. Serious disagreements soon emerged, and Maroto sent Urbiztondo to consult with some of his battalion commanders. He returned two hours later accompanied by a deputation which urged Maroto "not to consent to the slightest modification of the Fueros." The conversation ended there. In Wylde's view, Espartero's conduct was "consistent and extremely conciliatory, and he has fully proved his sincere desire for peace." Espartero left "convinced ... that the question will be decided by force."[200]

Two days later Espartero sent Maroto his final offer. It had three parts. First, Maroto's generals and officers would have their positions recognized. If they wished, they could serve with the Cristino army until the war was over. Second, Maroto would hand over all his artillery and other weapons. Finally, Espartero would quickly "remind the government to fulfil its offer of formally proposing that the Cortes grant or modify the *fueros* of Vizcaya and Guipúzcoa." No mention was made of Don Carlos.[201] Urbiztondo and some other representatives met with Espartero at 10 the next morning "and agreed to the best possible terms available to us."[202]

The final document consisted of ten articles, but the first two were the most crucial.

> **First article**. Captain General Baldomero Espartero will strongly recommend to the government it fulfil his offer of formally proposing to the Cortes the concession or modification of the *fueros*.
>
> **Second article**. The positions, rank, and decorations of the generals, officers, NCOs, and other individuals belonging to the army of Lieutenant General Rafael Maroto will be respected ... They will have the choice of defending the Constitution of 1837, the throne of Isabel II and the regency of her august mother, or retiring to their homes.[203]

Years later, in his *Vindicación*, Maroto complained that Espartero had never considered Maroto's proposals and ignored "my repeated requests for a suspension of hostilities."[204] What he was really saying was that Espartero had done his job well. Enjoying the military advantage and aware that Maroto's political position in the Carlist camp was increasingly precarious, he insisted on the terms he had initially offered. In doing so, Espartero stayed within his mandate and was scrupulous in not offering anything beyond what the government had authorized and in respecting the authority of the Cortes.

There would still be one hiccup before the formal signing, which was to take place in Vergara on 31 August. When Espartero arrived there on 30 August, he found Maroto accompanied by only his staff and a few other senior officers. Not one of the units specified in the agreement had "obeyed his order to march on [V]ergara," as they seriously doubted that the Cortes would approve the *fueros*. "This unlooked-for event seemed to paralyze everybody. No one knew what to answer." Finally, De la Torre and Urbiztondo went to speak with the troops and returned that evening "bringing with them a copy of the Convention … signed by the Commandant of every battalion for themselves and their men and a promise to march to [Vergara] the next day."[205]

The public ceremony took place on 31 August. When John Moore awoke that morning, "the hum of happy voices pervaded the streets." Side by side, Espartero and Maroto rode through the streets of Vergara to the Oñate road. Immediately on leaving the town, Moore saw "the divisions of the Royal and Provincial Guard of the Queen's army and the brilliant regiments of the *Princesa* Hussars drawn up a little to the left and right of the road … On a small mound on the right were grouped the general and superior officers of the Carlist army who had entered into the Convention, and Maroto's staff." The Carlist soldiers, "[t]he varied hues of their *boynas* – white, red or blue; and the picturesque shape of those caps, adorned with long gold or silver tassels fixed on the centre of the crown, and pendant on one side, made a singular effect." As Espartero arrived, "the military bands of the Queen's regiments struck up; the Carlist drums beat to arms, and the whole of the troops formed rapidly; the Carlist and Queen's facing each other – for the first time not in hostile array. The Duke with his cortege road along the double line and was saluted by each with the honours due to his rank. Maroto was by his side." Then Espartero, "with that soldier-like eloquence and that frank energy by which he is distinguished," addressed the two armies which had been fighting each other for almost six years.[206] "I addressed them," he reported to Madrid, "with all the feelings in my heart, saying that all Spaniards, the fatherland, and the queen would recognize them eternally for the great act of fraternally joining with my army to consolidate the peace all so desired."[207]

Figure 6 The Embrace of Vergara, August 1839.
Nineteenth Century Album, Museo Zumalakarregi.

The Carlist forces arrived at Vergara separately, and Espartero had to repeat his speech three times. Moore reported the one to the volunteers from Guipúzcoa, which he thought the most impressive.

"Guipuzcoans!

All Spaniards demand peace; all are anxious for union and that the shedding of Spanish blood should cease. In coming forward, as you do now to effect this grand object, you are entitled to the gratitude of your country, to that of the government and of the Queen. Henceforth let there be but one cry – union and peace!

Those of you who wish to retire to your homes may do so at once; those who feel inclined to remain with us will be received as brethren.

I well know this province. In early life I visited it – in peaceful times – and I learned to value its happy state. I have enjoyed the hospitality of *guipuzcoanos*; I have danced the *zorzico* with your young people." Here there was a spontaneous and universal burst of *vivas!* from the *Guipuzcoanos* ...

"Hear me," cried the Duke in the midst of these heartfelt cheers. "My desire is to see you all restored to this happy state; that you may return to comfort your aged parents from whom you have been so long separated; that you may mingle with your relatives and friends and be happy.

"Now," he continued, "go and embrace your brethren who are drawn up beside you – those gallant soldiers of mine who are all anxious to receive you as brothers – embrace them with the same sincerity as I now do your General Maroto".

Espartero then embraced Maroto, after which, "elevating his manly voice so as to be heard in every direction, he cried, "Long live peace! Long live the Union ... Long live the Queen!" ... Then glancing along the line, he gave the word of command in fine military style to the late Carlist battalions to ... stand at ease, which they obeyed in due form. On leaving the ground he desired that they should pile their arms and go mingle with his own soldiers. They joyfully did so." It was, Moore concluded, "a grand and gratifying spectacle."[208] Maroto called it a "sublime act."[209] Urbiztondo could not find the words to describe it.[210] Of course, Baldomero made time during that climactic day to write to Jacinta. "Today," he said simply, "has been glorious."[211]

5

The Reluctant Revolutionary, August 1839–May 1841

The war in the north was over, but fighting continued to rage in the east, where the fractured landscape and its mountaintop towns and forts were the perfect terrain for an experienced and ruthless guerrilla commander like Ramón Cabrera. Espartero would soon assume command there but first he had to attend to some housekeeping in the Basque Provinces and Navarra.

On 1 September Espartero issued a statement to "the Basque and Navarrese peoples" continuing his message of reconciliation – "*I have proclaimed PEACE*" – and it had been received "passionately." However, if the Basques and Navarrese did not join "the theatre of reconciliation" where former enemies had "sacrificed their differences for the good of our unfortunate fatherland," he would bring his "numerous, battle-hardened and disciplined army" to bear."[1] Over the following days, more Carlist units surrendered and handed over their weapons. Jacinta would be "crazy with pleasure since my glories are your glories."[2]

Espartero left Vergara on 6 September to hunt down the Pretender. In addition to seizing vast quantities of weapons, in Ozcoz he discovered "a magnificent carriage built in Oñate for Don Carlos," which he proudly sent to María Cristina. On 14 September, Espartero got word that Don Carlos was in Urdax, about nine kilometres from his position in Elisondo. After a brief battle, the Pretender and his remaining troops crossed into France. It was a culminating moment. "I have enjoyed today more than the 31st in Vergara, if such a thing were possible … Carlos's pride has driven him to prefer cutting such a poor figure among the French *to surrendering to the man he called his vassal.*"[3]

Espartero now took his victory lap. He left Urdax on the 18th and headed for Pamplona. At Villalba he was met by the provincial authorities, who gave him a public breakfast before "he was .. conducted in triumph" to Pamplona.⁴ "Amidst so much glory I thought only of my adored Jacinta whom I desired to see the[se] displays of gratitude and admiration."⁵ The *Centinela de los Pirineos* reported that, while Espartero was in the city, soldiers of the two armies "shook hands and embraced each other."⁶ Wylde was impressed by the desire for peace: "in many instances the women have taken their arms away from their brothers and husbands" and delivered them to government authorities.⁷

On 23 September, Espartero reached Viana en route to Logroño. At 1:00 in the afternoon, the bells rang and the National Militia formed up outside the house where he would be staying while the city government and a delegation from the cathedral rushed to meet him on the outskirts of the city. The crowds were immense. Seventy-year-old women danced "crazily" in the streets. Then word circulated that the Duchess of Victory was on her way and soon a new peal of bells announced her arrival.⁸ Logroño greeted Espartero in the manner of a Roman conqueror. After speeches by the local authorities, he was put onto "a triumphal carriage … that was led by militiamen to his house." Along the way, the horses pulling it were unhitched and the carriage was pulled by people who could barely make their way through the joyous throng spilling into the streets. There were four nights of illuminations, a special show at the theatre, three bullfights, and two balls, one of which was given by Jacinta.⁹

After a week at home, Espartero left for Aragón. The towns along the way to Zaragoza "received us with an enthusiasm that approached madness," but the Aragonese capital outdid anything he had experienced so far. "This morning I attended mass at the Pilar [cathedral]; I arrived there amidst an immense throng. There was no room to stand. The *vivas* did not stop even in the temple, but when I stood to kiss the hand of the Virgin all was confusion. When I left the chuch I was afraid I'd be stripped naked by the many embraces."¹⁰ Other good news awaited him in Zaragoza: Jacinta had been named a *Dama* of Queen Isabel. This meant she would be going to Madrid and could convey his messages to María Cristina personally. She would be, as he put it later, "a living letter."¹¹

From Zaragoza, he directed his "voice of reconciliation" to the residents of Aragón and Valencia. The past would be forgotten and they could return to their homes and families under the protection of someone "who prefers the glory of the peacemaker to that of the triumphant warrior." However, with those who chose to fight on, he would be "implacable."¹²

As his army moved further into Aragón, Espartero found a more forbidding situation than the one he knew from the Basque Provinces. The countryside "appears to have suffered much more from the effects of the war in every respect," Wylde observed, while "Cabrera's ferocious punishments" had "excited such terror amongst the inhabitants" that the Cristinos found themselves without any sources of information.[13] With winter setting in and rations running low, Espartero decided to wait. An enemy like Cabrera, "whose tactics are to avoid all encounters," could not be defeated militarily "in such a desolate season." Work on Espartero's line of fortifications was going well; a road from his headquarters at Mas de las Matas to facilitate the movement of supplies and artillery was under construction; and ovens were being built to deal with the difficulty of moving food. In the meantime, flying columns would patrol and others would enter rebel territory, "harassing them as much as possible" in preparation for "a complete pacification." This required, however, that the government provide him the resources he needed.[14]

The months after Vergara were a turning point in Espartero's political development. From a vehemently non-partisan, or rather anti-partisan, position, he shifted towards support for the Progressives, a movement which would be confirmed in the Mas de la Mata Manifesto that was published in the *Eco del Comercio* on 9 December. What was happening politically to account for such a significant change?

Those were certainly turbulent months. The elections held on 24 July produced a massive Progressive majority, "an unprecedented disaster" for the government. Backed by the queen regent, the cabinet did everything it could to avoid a dissolution, but then it too began to fall apart. The Cortes was dissolved on 18 November and new elections called for January 1840. This time the Moderates were better prepared and the government made effective use of the administration to ensure a strong majority.[15]

Before the dissolution, the Cortes did one thing of great significance: on 7 October, it unanimously approved a law confirming the *fueros* of the Basque Provinces and Navarra. At one point during the session, Alaix and Olózaga embraced on the floor of the chamber, with the former "repeatedly shouting effusively ... 'This is the Embrace of Vergara.'" "[E]xtraordinarily moved ... and animated by the same spirit of reconciliation," the deputies and ministers "rushed to imitate that noble example, hugging each other repeatedly."[16] This vision of national unity transcending partisanship would take on an almost mystical status in Espartero's mind as a demonstration of what politics should be.

Less than a month after Vergara, Espartero was venting his anger with the government to William Wylde. Always concerned with recognition, he felt they had attempted to "deprive him of a part of *the credit which is justly his due* in having brought about the late events." On the other hand, he was "particularly pleased" with the Progressives.[17] He was also upset that Van Halen had not been restored to his position of chief of the staff from which he had been removed without any consultation.[18]

Just after the dissolution of the Cortes, Espartero explained his political ideas to a French military observer, Colonel Genil. He had always refused María Cristina's requests to head the government or to serve in it. In part, this was practical – he could not be a minister and fight the war – but there was another, deeper reason. "I neither can nor want to appear to be a dictator" because this would cost him "[a]ll the moral force attached to my unquestioned personal honesty, loyalty as a citizen and faithful soldier." What he most wanted was for the queen regent to be free to act "constitutionally as she understands it." This was a sweeping prerogative that included her right to choose the ministers she wanted and to "impose the direction she judges best for the good of the country." The only thing that mattered was "the queen's freedom of action and will ... Under the shade of my sword" she needed only "six statesmen ... who dare govern following their conscience and the voice of their sovereign."[19]

Then, on 2 December, *El Eco del Comercio* published an article repeating what ministers were saying: that Espartero had advised that "they act illegally and [was] ready to support them with force."[20] Espartero was incensed, and a letter signed by his secretary, Francisco Linaje, soon appeared in the *Eco de Aragón* and then the Madrid press. Espartero was, he wrote, dismayed by "the loss of reason, the partisan animosities, and the rancour" that had followed the display of unity on 7 October, and disappointed in the conduct of the government. Of course, these were only "the expressions of an isolated opinion that does not imply criticism of the ministers or the deputies." The Duke of Victory "wants only that *the public be convinced that anything said about his involvement in matters of state is untrue*. His personal opinion is that THE CORTES SHOULD NOT HAVE BEEN DISSOLVED." He had not offered to use force against the government or the constitution, and "under no circumstances does he want to *distract the army from its principal object*, which is to destroy the fierce armed enemies who resist pacification."[21]

What immediately became known as the Mas de las Matas Manifesto hit the political world like a shell fired from Espartero's heaviest artillery piece. Here was his complete public repudiation of the Moderates.[22] Even before it appeared in Madrid, the ministers had seen the version published in Zaragoza, and the cabinet collectively complained to María

Cristina, demanding nothing less than a declaration that Espartero disown Linaje's letter.[23] The queen regent immediately wrote to Espartero, who confirmed that he had instructed Linaje to write it. The ministers had pestered him despite his known aversion "to getting mixed up in government business." No one had contradicted the claim made by the *Eco del Comercio* which harmed his reputation. The unity of 7 October had been broken for partisan purposes at a time when the last thing Spain wanted was "rancour between the parties." Despite all this he would have stayed silent if his name had not been associated with these manoeuvres. The idea that he was nothing more than "an automaton who allows himself to be manipulated" infuriated him, but what truly "pierces my heart" was that the ministers had told María Cristina, "The Mother of the People," that his conduct contradicted what he had always said.[24] "My secretary ... does, and did, what I tell him," he told Jacinta.[25]

The incident further turned Espartero against "that clique [of] near Carlists" who wanted to remove him from command.[26] His agent in Paris, "the Danish dog," kept him informed of their scheming, and his visit at the end of January "has left me stunned." María Cristina was surrounded by "the spirit of evil."[27] But Baldomero remained sceptical of the Progressives as well. From the frigid conditions of the Maestrazgo front he denounced both the Moderates and "the so-called Progressives" as "equally intolerant ... they both want power so they can "exploit mine."[28]

Espartero decided in January that he would launch the Maestrazgo campaign before the winter came to an end. The conditions impressed even him, who had fought for years in the Andes. "There were," he told War Minister Narváez, "deserts comparable to those in Arabia, such is the miserable condition to which the war has reduced this already unwelcoming country." Still, he assured the minister that with the money he had already received and the other resources that he had been promised, the war in Aragón and Valencia would be over by summer and that in Catalonia by the fall.[29] The well-conceived, well-prepared, and well-executed campaign plan rendered these estimates conservative.

Espartero set out from Mas de las Matas on 18 February with 91,079 men, 6,189 cavalry, and 4,463 officers, split almost equally between his slightly larger Army of the North and the Army of the Centre, to which he had appointed Leopoldo O'Donnell commander.[30] This campaign would be very different from his previous ones. It consisted of attacking Carlist-held castles and would be centred on the use of heavy artillery. The cavalry charges which Espartero so enjoyed would have a much smaller role, and he would take no part in them.

The first target was the castle of Segura de los Baños (Teruel). "We have nowhere to lodge and wood is scarce," he told Jacinta on the eve of the attack.[31] The castle surrendered after a short artillery barrage on Espartero's forty-seventh birthday. Next came Castellote (Teruel), a bigger challenge, which fell on 26 March following an artillery barrage lasting three days. After the surrender, Espartero told his men that their prisoners "were Spaniards ... who had shown their courage; my heart is sensitive to spilling Spanish blood so show your generosity with those who surrender.' From Castellote, they could see the most daunting target of all, Cabrera's capital, Morella.[32]

After a brief return to Mas de las Matas and a short stay in Aguaviva, on 25 April Espartero established his headquarters in Monroyo (Teruel), near the border with Castellón. The army left Monroyo on 19 May, but terrible rain, snow, and fog kept it from reaching Morella until the 23rd. Morella is built on a high hill and is completely surrounded by walls. The thirteenth-century castle, encircled by nearly two kilometres of walls of its own, stands on the Mola, a rocky promontory, more than one hundred metres above the town. Morella had withstood Oráa's attack in the summer of 1838, but he did not have the heavy siege guns that Espartero possessed. Lieutenant Lynn, who had replaced Wylde as British military observer at Espartero's headquarters, reported that Espartero had "begun to make extensive preparations" for Morella "early in the year, while he was occupied with Segura and Castellote."[33]

The bombardment began on 27 May and became more intense over the next two days. More than seven thousand projectiles were fired on the morning of the 29th alone. Espartero demanded unconditional surrender and on 30 May he got it, although he did grant the Carlist commander's request that his men be allowed to march out of the town carrying their weapons. To his "comrades in glory and danger" he proclaimed the end of the war in Aragón and invoked the Spanishness of their opponents, as well as his desire not to expose them to unnecessary danger, to explain his decision to forego an assault on the city.[34] Colonel Edward Mitchell, another British observer, "felt proud" to have witnessed an operation which had been carried out "with such skill and vigour on the part of the General in Chief, with celerity and science on the part of the Engineers and the artillery, and gallantry and zeal on the part of the Spanish soldiers."[35] For this action, Espartero received yet another title, Duke of Morella, and was awarded the Toisón de Oro.[36]

After resting his men for a few days, Espartero set out after Cabrera, who had crossed the Ebro into Tarragona, falling back to Berga (Barcelona). He arrived at Lérida on 9 June, being received along the way as a "conqueror and peacemaker." At one village, the local schoolmaster recited a poem he had written in Espartero's honour "expressive of gratitude for the blessings of peace," which was then sung by a group of boys whom he accompanied on guitar.[37] While in Lérida, Espartero announced the end of the "rigorous methods" he had imposed in October. This did not apply, however, to the families of those who continued to fight, who would continue to be subject to having their property seized.[38]

Espartero remained in Lérida until 26 June before heading towards Berga, Cabrera's stronghold, where he arrived on 4 July. He received an enthusiastic reception en route. Approaching Cellent, John Moore saw a road "thronged with the inhabitants, as was the long narrow street of the town, and the elevated spots beyond it. Men, women and children greeted Espartero with the utmost enthusiasm."[39] He also issued an edict in Catalan threatening severe penalties for people who assisted the rebels. On the other hand, rebels who presented themselves to the authorities would be given a safe conduct to live where they chose.[40] Espartero didn't expect Cabrera to put up a struggle and he was right. After a very brief battle, Espartero entered the nearly deserted town at 10 in the morning on 4 July. Two days later Cabrera fled to France with "some six thousand bandits not counting priests, monks, and other riffraff."[41] On 7 July, Espartero made one final proclamation to his men: thanks to their "constancy and valour," their "demonstrations of confidence, loyalty, suffering and patriotism," they had achieved "the triumph of the holiest of causes."[42]

The war was over. It had not been a total war perhaps, but it had mobilized vast numbers of people. The Madrid government had called up some 370,000 men, and by 1840 the Cristino army was 300,000 strong. There were also more than 400,000 armed members of the militia. It had also been a lethal war: 100,000 dead, another 100,000 wounded, and swathes of the country devastated. Reflecting on the state of Spain after Vergara but before the final defeat of the Carlists, Francisco Pareja de Alarcón observed that "the true value of the advantages of peace is only appreciated after having lived through the bloody scenes of a war of extermination."[43] For many Spaniards at the time, and for long afterwards, this peace would be synonymous with Espartero, "the Peacemaker of Spain."

As Espartero was conducting his campaign in the Maestrazgo, the climactic battle between Moderates and Progressives was being fought in Madrid over the question of municipal government, one of the issues the framers of the Constitution of 1837 had left unsettled. The Municipal Government Law, which was introduced on 21 March 1840, eliminated the powers of municipal governments almost entirely. For the Moderates this was crucial to their goal of having "the government or its agents take control of ... all public spaces." For the Progressives, whose strength lay at the municipal level, it amounted to a political death sentence, and they used every possible parliamentary tactic to stall it. After an attempt to appeal to the queen mother failed, they turned to Espartero. This was a measure of their desperation: before the 1840 election they had been planning to get rid of him as commander in chief.[44] Many of his political ideas – the emphasis on order, the distrust of the press, and, above all, the powerful belief in the prerogatives of the Crown – were much closer to those of their Moderate rivals. On the other hand, in his suspicion of political parties and "cliques" and the disunity they caused, in his criticism of unjustified political ambition, and in his overriding concern for the national interest, what he called the "happiness of the fatherland," he was already very much a Progressive.[45] In the late spring and early summer, "city governments and militia units began to write to him ... inundating his headquarters with dozens and dozens of letters" in which they praised him as "the foremost defender of the constitutional throne," "the captain of the century," and "the new Cid," and begged him to "turn his glance to Madrid" in order to stop the looming destruction of local government, the constitution, and political liberty itself.[46]

María Cristina also had hopes for Espartero as the military leader of a much more conservative, even reactionary, political project. She took his side against the government on a number of issues which arose in early 1840 and she also continued their private correspondence, both directly and through Jacinta.[47] Now, she decided, it was time to meet face to face, preferably away from Madrid, as there were "many things that cannot be properly explained in writing."[48] Using Isabel's longstanding skin condition as an excuse, she manufactured a reason to travel to Catalonia. The cabinet did its best to convince her to change her mind and, when that failed, to delay her departure as much as possible. They also tried, without success, to convince her to travel via Valencia rather than Zaragoza, as Espartero requested.[49]

The royal party of 121 people finally set out from Madrid on 11 June. Accompanying María Cristina, Queen Isabel, and her sister were the prime minister, the war minister, and the navy minister. Jacinta was part of the entourage, something which did not sit well with traditional court circles.[50] A week later, they arrived in Zaragoza, where, according to some accounts, Jacinta received more cheers than the royal family. The *Eco de Aragón* even printed a poem dedicated to her.[51]

As he awaited María Cristina's arrival, Espartero received two letters on the political situation. The first, dated 8 June and written partially in code, emphasized the need for a change of government, partly because the current one "does not agree with [your] doctrines" and partly because it was so discredited that a revolution was possible. The queen regent would be opposed because she "has much sympathy" for some of the ministers. The informant, probably Valentín Ferraz, one of Espartero's comrades from America and one who had vouched for him when he had to meet Fernando VII's political purity test, then included a list of possible ministers for a cabinet headed by Espartero.[52] The second letter, dated twelve days later, called for a government composed of people – and names were mentioned – whose "honesty and observed conduct inspire confidence in the Nation and who can gather a majority from the healthy part of the parties." The writer had no doubt that María Cristina would take Espartero's advice above that of her ministers, but if it came to a discussion in a cabinet meeting with María Cristina and Espartero present it was very possible that he would lose, "because you are not as malicious or as experienced as your rivals." Espartero had to be very careful to avoid getting trapped, especially "displeasing the queen."[53]

While the royal party was on the road, Madrid was on tenterhooks: "everyone in his shell, awaiting the conversation between Her Majesty and the Duke."[54] It finally arrived in Lérida on the night of 24 June. Espartero had prepared a truly royal welcome. Accompanied by his staff and the British and French military observers, "all in full uniform," he rode out to meet them. Then, "with torch-bearers on each side of the royal carriage, bands playing martial airs, the veteran soldiers presenting arms, the officers saluting with their swords, the regimental banners waving," the procession entered the city as fireworks went off and a salute was fired.[55]

Espartero's first meeting was with Navy Minister Sotelo, a friend to whom he expressed what Sotelo called "some general ideas." Then he met with María Cristina herself. It was a frustrating encounter, "a dance of gestures and silences, of answers as misguided as the questions," as Isabel Burdiel characterizes it. He wanted her to dismiss the entire cabinet, refuse to sanction the Law of Municipalities, and dissolve the Cortes. He refused to suggest new ministers but firmly rejected María Cristina's proposal of Francisco Javier de Istúriz as prime minister: "He wanted nothing to do with the Big Shots [santones] of the parties." The conversation ended with nothing settled.[56]

The royal party left the next day. Espartero accompanied them but, to avoid detracting from the reception given to María Cristina and the queen, "whenever the nature of the ground permitted," he separated from the royal procession as it was about to enter a town, "leading us over fields and across ditches, and other rough and difficult places – flanking the villages or towns as it were – and bringing us out perhaps half a mile beyond, and then rejoining the royal cortege."[57] Espartero had arranged that María Cristina would review the troops at Cervera. Before she began, he gave a speech in which he stated that the upcoming campaign would be enhanced with María Cristina "leading operations as General in Chief."[58] She refused the offer, one more example of her refusal to take any meaningful role in the war.[59]

They parted ways on 29 June as Espartero headed to Manresa to prepare the attack on Berga. During their final conversation, he insisted on the need for a new government, and this time he presented names: other than the military ministers, both of whom were his friends, they were on the list sent by his Madrid informer. These were a mixed bag of Progressives, Moderates, and one non-party person. Not one of them could remotely be considered a "Big Shot." This was the strong and non-partisan government for which Espartero had been clamouring. María Cristina was not impressed and insisted that Istúriz be included. The meeting ended with Espartero promising that Valdés would prepare a program for his government.[60]

Espartero was not entirely happy with how things were going, including the government program that Linaje had drafted for Valdés. On 8 July, he sent Jacinta a lengthy letter on the political situation. She was well informed about what was going on, had her own opinions, and, once again, was serving as her husband's go-between. From his letter of 25 June: "I see that Valdés has discussed the project with you ... I do not share your opinion, not his, not that of the Señora [María Cristina] ... What we need is to keep the 'Big Shots' [like Istúriz] from centre stage because ... they are all 'gang members' ... But, in the end, the Señora wants him and I will not oppose, although the results will end up making us cry." The proposed program was even worse. Everyone "will think it was my work, and [it] would neutralize all my previous efforts, having worked so effectively for queen and country. *It may be good for some people that the new cabinet start with the laws before the Cortes being approved, but not for me. I will not have anything to do with such a calamity.*" The only real solution was the one he had repeated "a million times" and one Jacinta should repeat to Valdés and *"to the Señora if you want."* Despite her "noble sentiments [and] beautiful heart, in the end María Cristina was a woman," unable to resist the influence of the "servile, ambitous and ignorant rascals ... who will lead us to a frightening revolution."[61]

By this time, the program which Espartero was criticizing had already been delivered to María Cristina in Barcelona. It was much more of a compromise than what he himself wanted: dissolution of the Cortes followed by new elections in which "the parties will not intrigue to bring out their new Big Shots," and the replacement of all bills currently before the legislature with new ones "in harmony with the constitution." It also included the need to ensure that the Basque *fueros* did not trigger "demands from other provinces for equal or greater rights."[62] This was much closer to what the Progressives had been advocating, evidence that their letter writing campaign had worked.[63]

Espartero arrived in Barcelona on 14 July. The city had welcomed María Cristina warmly enough on her arrival three weeks earlier, even if she had to endure seeing banners with articles of the Constitution hung from lampposts along the Ramblas and the article on municipal government illuminated on the façade of the city hall, and "everywhere" listen to the cheers directed at the Duchess of Victory.[64]

That reception paled compared to the full-blown "civic festival" that greeted Espartero.[65] The city council had to be careful not to mount a more magnificent show than it had for the queen regent, but, even so, "more than eighty thousand people went out to receive him," the crowd reaching fifteen kilometres from the city centre. He was met by a delegation from the city council and responded to their greetings that this was "happiest day of my life." The crowds were so thick that Espartero could "barely move through that fanatical multitude that kissed his hands, hugged his knees and gazed upon him in tears of enthusiasm ... all the way to his lodgings." He then came out onto the balcony to salute the crowds again. It was an unprecedented display, the first "mass demonstration" in the city's history.[66]

That night, the municipal government offered a serenade outside Espartero's residence. There was even a song dedicated to him set to nothing less than the music of the famous liberal anthem named after the martyr of the Revolution of 1820, the Hymn of Riego! When the music was over, Espartero gave a short speech from his balcony: "We have fought for seven years to secure the throne of Isabel II, the Constitution of 1837, and national independence. For such dear objectives we will continue to fight, to the death if necessary. (Loud shouts: yes, to the death.) This is the oath of all good Spaniards, and also of a soldier who does what he promises."[67]

Espartero immediately requested an interview with the queen regent, but the conversation which had started in Lérida would not continue for long. Angered by Espartero's immense popularity, María Cristina immediately gave the Law of Municipalities royal sanction. From there events speeded up incredibly during what Andrés Borrego called "days of passion and vertigo."[68] Isabel Burdiel paints a picture of a María Cristina increasingly isolated and not fully aware of the magnitude of what was happening around her.[69] Espartero was not isolated but he was on a new and unfamiliar battlefield, one where the valiant cavalry charges and the inspiring harangues that had been so central to his success were irrelevant. He was playing for the highest stakes in a game whose rules he barely knew. He had reason to be nervous.

The very night of his serenade, Espartero rejected requests from Valdés and others to compromise. When he learned the next morning that María Cristina had signed the law, the news made him physically ill, "grief stricken and angered," in Jacinta's words.[70] He then wrote a letter of resignation. The "rush" with which María Cristina had sanctioned the municipal government law despite his willingness to be part of a new government was a "total snub" and undeniable evidence that she had lost confidence in him. He would go home "to my retreat." His final word was to request compensation for "valiant, long-suffering and worthy people of all classes" who had fought under him.[71]

Jacinta delivered the letter on 16 July. María Cristina's immediate reaction was to resign the regency, but after lengthy discussions her ministers convinced her that the only viable course of action was to ask Espartero to form a government with the names he had already proposed. She invited him to meet with her at 2 in the afternoon of 18 July.[72] The meeting was an extraordinary one. It could not have been easy for Espartero. He had always proclaimed his unflinching loyalty to the "Mother of the Spaniards" and blamed what he saw as her mistakes on the self-serving clique that surrounded her. Now she had taken the final step, and he had to confront her directly. He was at an emotional fever pitch; at times he forgot the decorum due to royalty and had to apologize. He spoke plainly, "with a soldier's frankness," and reminded her, as he had so many times, that the army was "devoted to him."[73] He complained "bitterly" that she had not accepted his resignation; demanded that she choose "*Between the ministry and me*"; and warned that "the people were very upset" with the cabinet and that if she allowed it to remain in office they would find themselves "knee deep in blood!"[74]

After the meeting, María Cristina decided to name a new government headed by Espartero, but not with the ministers he had proposed. According to an anonymous diary, a crowd in front of the city hall "began to shout vivas to the constitution ... and demand the fall of the ministry. They started to build barricades; no one offered the least resistance." Another crowd went to Espartero's residence, where they repeated the same cries. He came onto the balcony and proclaimed that "while he was alive the fundamental law was safe," after which they returned to city hall. The diarist claimed that Linaje was behind it, but it was, in fact, Van Halen. Espartero himself was not involved; Van Halen later said that "if [Espartero] had known ... nothing would have happened."[75] Around 12:30, Espartero headed for the palace followed by cheering crowds. Along with Jacinta, Van Halen, Valdés, and some of his staff, he met with María Cristina as the demonstrations continued. "There were shots, and cries of *death to the queens* ... someone shouted long live Baldomero I." On leaving the meeting, Espartero assured the crowd that the queen regent had dismissed the government and would accept his demands. It was all over by 3:30 in the morning.[76] For María Cristina it had been La Granja all over again, although this time with "generals ... in charge." The next morning, she appointed a new government headed by Antonio González, who had played a role in getting Bolívar to commute the death sentence on Espartero in 1825.[77]

The city remained tense, and on 21 July there was a street fight between the queen regent's supporters and those of Espartero. As María Cristina set out on her daily excursion accompanied by Jacinta, a crowd approached her carriage shouting "*long live the absolutist regency, death to progress, death to Espartero* and similar things." When the carriage reached the waterfront, some people directed "vulgar insults" at Jacinta, who, María Cristina reported, "was furious ... when we got out she came straight to me to say that ... if she could she would fry such tedious cheers with her curses ... she didn't complain when the cheers were for her." Such was the provocation that a mass of "the true people of Barcelona" descended on them "giving blows," leaving two or three dead and a number roughed up. Espartero then arrived at the head of two battalions to restore order. The next day he declared the city in a state of siege.[78] One wonders which angered him more, the offence and fright felt by María Cristina or the insults to his wife.

On 22 July, María Cristina told her ministers that she wanted to return to Madrid by way of Valencia, but Espartero's resistance kept her in the city for another month. During this time, she reasserted herself politically. She refused to endorse the cabinet's program; González and his colleagues resigned and were replaced on 12 August by a more moderate ministry headed by Valentín Ferraz. She also refused to consult Espartero about appointing new army commanders and managed to meet with Diego de León, one of the generals who resented Espartero's presumption to speak for the entire army.[79]

The queen regent finally left Barcelona on 22 August, which spared her from having to endure the festivities on the anniversary of the Embrace of Vergara on 31 August. Her absence freed the city government to celebrate Espartero's great victory as it truly wished to do, which included presenting him with a "triumphal crown" carried on a silver platter. After the ceremony, there was a banquet at city hall where "a transparent portrait of Espartero" hung next to one of George Washington and another of the queen. That night there was a "general illumination" and a dance "for the people" in the city's four principal squares.[80] This was precisely the kind of recognition Espartero sought, but he was not entirely happy because, once again, the authorities had neglected the ordinary enlisted man. "Not a dime so the poor soldier can have a good meal on such a memorable day. I will see if I can pay for something myself ... They all call the people 'shirtless' ... but they think only of how to take their shirts!!"[81]

Espartero remained in Barcelona, where he had assumed the roles of military and civil governor, but complained about being out of touch with what was going on at court. He visited the factories, where he found the people "very happy," and he was confident of "soon unifying all spirits."[82] He was also keeping track, as best he could, of the manoeuvrings of his opponents. The "Danish dog" informed him about what was going on in Paris, "that the Señora wrote to important people in London and Paris, and he describes what they are planning. It's horrible! Declare your husband a traitor and put him beyond the law."[83] He was confident he could prevent the "abyss" that was coming, since "I know the public spirit well."[84] Above all, he was indignant that "the Señora ... would get rid of me to further the plans ... of such ignorant, cowardly and perficious men."[85] All he wanted, he told Jacinta, was "to see you where you should be: at your husband's side or in your home."[86]

Then, suddenly, the spotlight moved to Madrid. Ever since María Cristina and the court had left in June, taking much of the city's garrison with them, the power of the central government over the capital had been severely weakened. Progressives controlled local political institutions, with city hall in the hands of more advanced elements of the party. And there was a ten-thousand-man National Militia undergoing a "neverending indoctrination in constitutional nationalism or patriotism."[87] When news of the new cabinet arrived, "the agitation became more pronounced," wrote another of Espartero's informants, "Cigarrero."[88] With a large and excited crowd in and around city hall, the government distributed arms and appealed to other municipal governments. It then met jointly with the provincial Deputation and the militia commanders and created a Provisional Governing Junta headed by the mayor, Joaquín María Ferrer. An attempt by the captain general to quash the uprising failed when most of his troops joined the rebels. The Provisional Junta now commanded some twenty thousand men. One of its first acts was to request that Espartero give his blessing to the movement, but, his faith in María Cristina still intact, he was not prepared to abet a revolution.[89]

The revolt spread quickly to other cities. Zaragoza was one of the first. Its municipal government issued a proclamation on 3 September praising Espartero, the "virtuous Peacemaker of the realm" who had refused to serve as the "vile instrument of the tyranny of a few." Spain had "powerful" need "of a Washington."[90]

On 5 September, the government decided to send Espartero to suppress the revolution by force. María Cristina also wrote privately the same day, playing on his concerns about having lost her confidence. "Be great facing these disorders as you have been against usurpation and you will see how great is the gratitude of your queen."[91] Espartero was beyond such enticements. He refused to "tyrannize [the fatherland] by supporting a party that wants its misery and abandoning another that desires its happiness." Here was an unequivocal statement that he had become a Progressive. But there was more: she and the government were ordering him to spill "precious [Spanish] blood," and when he read the order, "my body and my soul suffered more than when" he heard that "the Law of Municipalities received sanction, and the blood of Berga was still warm."[92] Espartero replied in what he described as a "reverent exposition." María Cristina was still being manipulated by "an egotistical clique of ... bastard Spaniards." The events in Madrid and Zaragoza were not a revolutionary threat to social order but the work of "the liberal party ... men of wealth and good standing ... who, fearful of a return to despotism, have taken up arms" to defend the throne. Even some military units had joined them, and if he were to send his army to Madrid he doubted his men would fire on them. She could still salvage the situation with "a clear manifesto" defending the Constitution, dissolving the Cortes, and allowing the new one to reconsider the laws passed by its predecessor, the same program he had been promoting for months. If she didn't do this, then the consequences would be incalculable.[93] In other words, he was refusing to obey. Jacinta thought that Baldomero should have resigned. He disagreed. That is what someone less "committed than I to the good of my fatherland and the consolidation of the throne" would have done. All his advice to the "Señora" had been for her own good, but she had chosen to heed "others more self-interested, more perfidious, and more full of ignorance."[94]

"Everything changed" when Espartero's document arrived in Valencia. "Baltasara," the persona María Cristina used in private letters to her husband, thought it was "little gentlemanly." Even O'Donnell "said yielding was the only alternative." María Cristina appointed a Progressive cabinet under Vicente Sancho, but when only one of the ministers agreed to serve, she played her final card, placing herself "entirely in [Espartero's] hands," as she told British chargé d'affaires Arthur Aston. On 16 September, María Cristina's supporter General Francisco Javier Azpiroz wrote Espartero a frantic letter calling him "the only one who can prevent the dissolution threatening our unfortunate country."[95] "In spite of myself," Espartero agreed. Jacinta should tell the Señora "to convince herself, by God, that the heart of this soldier is always honourable and without ambition." On 24 September, he received royal authorization to go to Madrid to consult with potential ministers and ensure that they were willing to serve. "With this goal alone," he set out the next morning[96]

In the meantime, he received a visit from Manuel Cortina, who had been sent by the Madrid Junta to sound him out on the possibility of a co-regency. This had not been one of the demands made on 1 September, but since then, as the revolution had spread across the country, a second, more radical option had emerged: the creation of a Junta Central composed of representatives of all the juntas, as had happened in 1808. Espartero made it clear that this was something he would resist "by all possible means."[97]

Espartero's arrival in Madrid on 29 September was another triumph. By the time he reached the Alcalá Gate at 2:00 in the afternoon, the militia and troops from the garrison had been lining the route for hours. He was greeted by a delegation from the city council as well as functionaries, officers, and guildsmen, and, after an exchange of short speeches, he got into a "magnificent, specially prepared carriage" which carried him to the Casa de la Panadería, where he was greeted by the Provisional Junta and the Deputation. For the next two and a half hours he reviewed a military parade. That night there was "one of the most well attended serenades that [Madrid] has ever seen."[98] This was followed by three days of festivities dedicated to Espartero, which included banquets, a bullfight, a display of horsemanship, and a theatrical function. The Calle de Alcalá was even renamed Duke of Victory.[99] There was also a performance of a new play by Bretón de los Herreros that closed with the debut of the *Himno a Espartero*, written by the actor Julián Romea.[100]

The next day Espartero met with the city council, the Deputation, and the Provisional Junta to discuss the composition and program of the new government. The ministers were all Progressives, from "the most moderate part" of the party. In a private meeting with Evaristo San Miguel, Espartero gave "an immediate and decided refusal" to his request to create a Junta Central. He was also convinced by Antonio González that any changes to the status of the regency should be the decision of the "Cortes *alone*."[101] María Cristina approved the cabinet on 3 October, and on 6 October Espartero, accompanied by all but one of his ministers, set out for Valencia.

After Luchana, the government had promoted a cult of Espartero as hero. As the military victories piled up in the spring of 1839, that cult was reinvigorated, but this time the impetus for the Espartero cult came not from the national government, which placed María Cristina and the rest of the royal family at the centre of the peace celebrations in Madrid, but from below: from local governments, militia units, and individual Spaniards.[102]

From Vergara through the revolution of September 1840, celebrations organized by local governments across the country hailed Espartero as a hero. These were particularly elaborate and enthusiastic in places such as Zaragoza, Barcelona, Valencia, and Madrid where Espartero actually appeared, but he was often at the heart of the celebrations even where he was not present. When news of the fall of Morella reached Valencia on 4 June, the city exploded with joy. A stage was erected in the city hall square and a portrait of "the hero of the Spains" placed under a canopy. The municipal government scrambled to organize a parade, at the centre of which a "triumphal carriage" carried Espartero's portrait adorned with a laurel crown.[103] In Jerez de la Frontera, where the celebrations started on Isabel's birthday, a portrait of Espartero was placed in "a triumphal carriage which [was] driven through the streets."[104]

Poets of all levels of ability dedicated their efforts to praising Espartero. Valencia produced a number of such poems, some commissioned by the municipal government.[105] Many other poems were written without official stimulus and represented genuine, grass-roots admiration. One published in Zaragoza late in 1839 presented the man who "ended the fratricidal war" as the heir to El Cid and Pelayo, the king who stopped the Muslim conquest of Spain.[106] The Barcelona-based actress and prolific playwright Francisca Navarro commemorated the first anniversary of Vergara with a poem in which she gave Espartero all the credit for peace: "To whom is this glory owed? / to the Duke of Victory."[107] She also wrote a play, *El 30 de Agosto de 1839 en los campos de Vergara o el sueño feliz y el ramo de oliva*, which was never presented or published, which she sent to Espartero. He must have been thrilled: in addition to presenting him as the "great heaven-sent soldier ... who has pacified the realm," it called on Spaniards to reject the terms "victor and vanquished" and "think of parties no more."[108] Finally, an aspiring teenage poet in Badajoz by the name of Carolina Coronado, who would later become one of Spain's leading Romantic poets, was inspired to dedicate some verses to the "Happy Duke of Victory," the "nuncio of peace."[109]

The cult of Espartero was also nourished in the intimate setting of the family. Republican politician and future president of the First Republic Emilio Castelar, who was born in 1832, told the Constituent Cortes in 1869, "I will always remember those Christmas nights when we sat around the fire with my parents, and when the rain splattered on the windows, they would say. 'Son, bless General Espartero because he won the war and gave us peace.'"[110] An admirer from Villena wrote, "When I was very young, my parents taught me to speak the name Espartero with the veneration and enthusiasm due the man who ensured Liberty in our beloved Spain."[111] We can get a sense of what peace meant from a letter Espartero received from María Antonia Piños from Monroyo (Teruel). Cabrera's flight had allowed her "beloved papa" to return home, and since then "we have been at peace and we do not stop blessing him who gave it to us ... how welcome in this house your name is."[112]

Naming children after Espartero was another aspect of the cult. Few parental acts are more laden with meaning than choosing names for children, especially when those names are political. Later in his life, Espartero would receive letters from some of these namesakes or their parents. Baldomero Martínez, an aspiring opera singer from Mahón, was one. His deceased father, he wrote, in January 1869, had been a "loyal follower of [your] cause." He was going to dedicate his upcoming debut concert to Espartero, "the person I most admire and respect ... Your portrait will be in the place of honour."[113] In his memoirs, General Romualdo Nogués, who was born in Borja (Zaragoza) in 1822, recounts that in 1836 a child in the neighbouring town of Ainzón was baptized "Cristino," but "if he had been born between '40 and '56 he would have been called Baldomero, after Espartero."[114]

Another example of the transmission of the Espartero cult was the *romance*.[115] Originally part of oral tradition, *romances* were also produced in cheap printed versions which were often sold in the streets by vendors who hung them from strings. Starting with Vergara, Espartero became a feature of these important vectors of popular culture, especially those produced in Barcelona. Published *romances* were both manifestations of

The Reluctant Revolutionary, 1839–1841 147

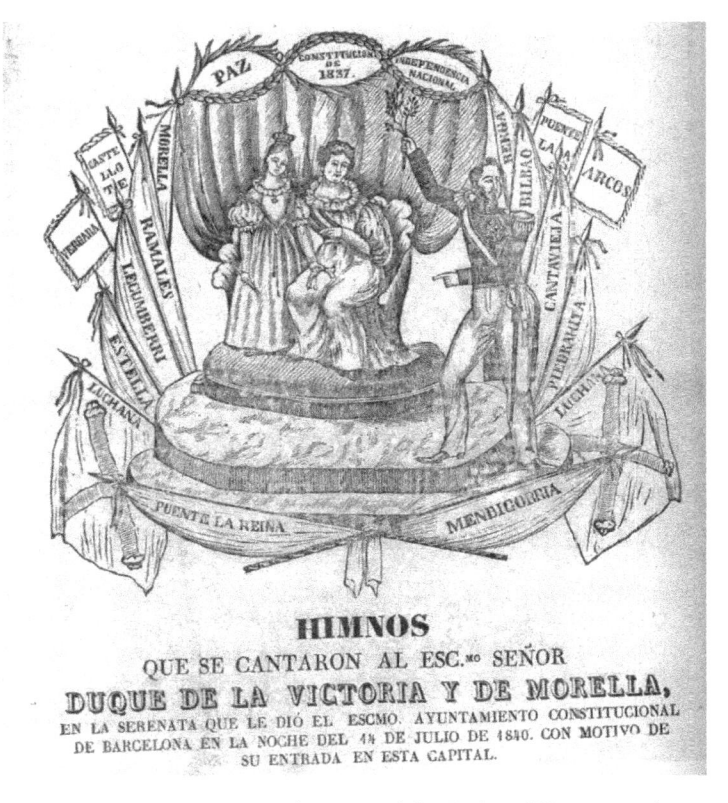

Figure 7 "Songs sung in honour of the Duke of Victory at the serenade on 14 July 1840." Historical Archive, City of Barcelona (Arxiu Històric de la Ciutat de Barcelona).

the Espartero cult and a further stimulus for it. Vergara was celebrated in *Coblas nuevas patrióticas al Convenio celebrado entre los Generales Españoles Espartero y Maroto*. He had to share top billing with the Carlist general, but Espartero – "You will be called Peacemaker" – was the star.[116] He was also the central figure of *Morella rendida a la fuerza del bombec y sitio al día 30 de mayo de 1840*, which described him as "*Spanish Bonaparte*."[117] The excitement of Espartero's entry into Barcelona and the next night's serenade generated no less than three separate *romances*.[118] The events of the night of 18 July were celebrated in another,[119] as was the sumptuous celebration of the first anniversary of Vergara.[120]

These *romances* were all illustrated, and many had images of Espartero. The number of such publications and their large, popular audiences gave Spaniards a rare degree of familiarity with Espartero's appearance. (The ubiquity of Espartero images made other leading generals jealous. O'Donnell convinced the *Diario Mercantil Valenciano* to commission his own portrait and distribute it with the paper.)[121] Espartero's face was probably the best known in the country and led to other aspects of the Espartero cult in daily life: men copied his signature facial hair, known as a *luchana*; more affluent men could own silver cigar cases with his image on them; and children would be dressed "Espartero style" for special occasions.[122] Together, the *romances* powerfully identified Espartero with the throne, the constitution, liberty, and peace.

Espartero and his ministers reached Valencia on 8 October. The city council had prepared a reception "on the style of ancient Rome." A huge crowd endured the "suffocating heat," waiting along the designated route hours before Espartero's expected arrival. At one point, the crowd "threw itself upon the horse and rider and tried to carry him to the coach" that the city council had prepared, but he convinced them to desist. Then the aldermen arrived, bearing "a magnificent crown of silver leaf painted green to imitate laurel," which Espartero "hung from his arm." Almost as soon as he got into the coach, the militia "unhitched the horses and pulled it" into the city, "despite the tightly packed multitude that blocked the road ... their uninterrupted cheers mixed with the pealing of the bells, the playing of the bands, and the applause of the spectators who released doves and threw flowers and sweets from their balconies as he passed."[123]

Before his audience with María Cristina, Espartero met with Arthur Aston, the British attaché. Their conversation provides the best sense of what Espartero was thinking as he prepared to take his new cabinet to meet the queen regent. He "was desirous that no change should take place in the Regency [and] vehemently disclaimed any ambitious designs." This was a matter for the Cortes, but "he feared that unless a promise, or at least expectation, were held out that it should be submitted to the Cortes, the Juntas would not consent to dissolve." That said, "it would not be urged as a condition by the Ministry. He should oppose any such proposal." Aston next asked about demands from the juntas that María Cristina issue a manifesto denouncing the Pérez de Castro government. Espartero replied that he "had no intention of making such a ... proposal offensive to the feelings of the Queen Regent or derogatory to Her Majesty's dignity."[124]

Espartero and his ministers met with María Cristina at 11:30 that night. They were expecting simply to take their oath of office, but she caused them "considerable embarrassment" by demanding that they present a program and made it impossible for them to avoid raising the question of the co-regency, something they had hoped to avoid.[125] This was enough to drive even these men to take up the radical positions they had resisted until then. Cortina drafted a program, which Espartero read to María Cristina when they met again on the night of 10 October. The situation was dire: "a complete dissolution of the State" was a possibility. María Cristina needed to hear straight talk from her ministers. First, she must issue a manifesto stating that the mistakes of the past were the fault of previous ministers, who might be subject to legal charges, and that the Constitution would be "faithfully respected and executed." Second, the Law of Municipalities would be suspended and revisited by the Cortes. Third, the dissolution of the current Cortes had to be accompanied by a co-regency. According to Cortina, this was a step too far for Espartero, who "fought strongly" and accepted it only when faced with "unanimous opinion of his colleagues." He did, however, insist that "the possibility of his becoming co-regent be excluded so that he could not be accused of provoking or accepting this change out of personal ambition."[126] Finally, until the new Cortes was in session, the provincial juntas should be allowed to exist as adjuncts to the government. This was a "bitter truth" but a necessary one if they were to avoid joining the list of ministers who "have deceived Your Majesty."[127]

The ministers then swore their oaths and were dismissed, but María Cristina kept Espartero back. She told him that she was going to resign the regency altogether and quit the country, leaving the queen and her sister in his hands.[128] "Terror-stricken," on the verge of tears according to some, Espartero spent more than an hour vainly trying to persuade her to change her mind.[129] He then took his ministers to his house and "with much agitation acquainted them … that the Queen Regent had declared … her determination to abdicate immediately the Regency … [the ministers] and *entrusted*" Espartero to "take charge" of the position. Despite his using "every argument," he could not convince her to change her mind. "Nothing should induce him," he told her, to take up the regency, "or be the means of affording any facility for carrying into effect a measure he considered, under present circumstances, would prove injurious to Queen Isabella and to Spain."[130] The next night, the full cabinet spent four fruitless hours trying to persuade the queen regent to change her mind. At one point, Espartero threatened to resign as well and leave Valencia immediately, using his oft-repeated expression, "because he was ambitious for nothing," to which she replied with a threat to issue a public manifesto explaining what had really happened. Espartero was "enraged," but Cortina managed to calm him down and make him see that his resignation would throw the country into the arms of the revolution.[131]

On 12 October, before the cabinet and a crowd of officials, María Cristina read the act of resignation that Cortina had drafted. The next day the government explained what had transpired since their arrival in Valencia and announced the new situation to the country. They would serve as a provisional regency "until the Cortes appoints new people to the position."[132]

Espartero had always felt respect, admiration, and even affection for "la Señora," as he called her. None of this had been reciprocated, certainly not towards the end. "*Don Valdomero, pig, swine*," she spat out in one of the letters she sent to her husband as "Baltasara."[133] Now she was going into exile, leaving him as the most powerful person in the country. María Cristina left Valencia on 17 October. (The day before her departure she told Astor that she "considered that the Duke of Victory had sufficient influence to overcome the difficulties of the present situation.")[134] Jacinta was in María Cristina's carriage; Espartero two carriages behind. They arrived at the dock a little after 7 in the morning. As the queen regent and Espartero said farewell, "they both cried a little ... [She] told him 'Espartero, care for my daughters,' but the general who had won so many battles was speechless, seeing only a mother." Foreign Minister Ferrer and Jacinta accompanied her on the lighter which took her from the dock to her ship and "did not take their farewell until the steamer got underway."[135]

María Cristina had pushed Espartero into the role of a reluctant revolutionary, but he was determined that as president-regent, his new title, he would be a man of order. In his first conversation with Aston in his new role, he emphasized that the government was going to adhere to its stated program, that it would resist any attempt "by any Party" to go further and that if necessary "force would be used." He expected that "extreme measures" would not be required, but "he had entire confidence in the subordination and fidelity to the constitution of the army under his command."[136] The initial measures of the new administration bore this out. On 18 October, the government addressed the question of the juntas. Those in provincial capitals would continue to exist, but only as "auxiliaries" with no authority beyond "whatever the government considers opportune to entrust to them." All the others would resign immediately. Five weeks later, the juntas were extinguished completely.[137] The decision to dissolve the juntas was, according to Marliani, an Espartero advocate, a grave mistake, the political equivalent of "sending your troops home on the eve of a battle with the enemy in sight."[138]

Accompanied by the queen and her sister, the court, and the cabinet, Espartero left Valencia at dawn on 20 October. While not as frenetic as the greeting he had received twelve days earlier, "an immense crowd" braved the early hour to see him off.[139] At 1:00 p.m. on a cold and rainy 28 October, after a journey of eight days, Isabel II entered the capital she had last seen on 11 June. The city government had banned the use of private carriages in the main streets for the day. Dressed in a "luxurious uniform," Espartero rode to the right of the queen's carriage as the procession, led by "two dance troupes of young people of both sexes accompanied by bands," wound its way from the Puerta de Atocha along the Calle Duque de la Victoria and through the Puerta del Sol before arriving at the Royal Palace, where a stage had been set up for dances. Soldiers and militiamen lined the entire route. Along the way, doves wearing pink ribbons were released. The unseasonably poor weather kept the crowds down. The weather was no better the next day, but the scheduled events, including "the descent of a balloon in front of the royal box," went ahead as scheduled. The final day's events, however, were rained out.[140]

Even before Espartero returned to Madrid, the question of who would serve as guardian to Isabel and her sister had arisen. María Cristina's sister Luisa Carlotta had pushed her husband, the Infante don Francisco, to publish a manifesto in Paris on 25 October requesting the guardianship. María Cristina reacted immediately, sending a blistering letter in which she insisted that she would remain her daughters' guardian and demanding that a five-man committee chosen by her fill the role while she was out of the country. She also demanded that the government publish her declaration, in which "she appeared as an offended queen and a mother cruelly separated from her daughter."[141] It appeared in the *Gaceta* on 16 November with a reply in which, citing the program they had presented her in Valencia, the cabinet rebutted a number of her assertions.[142] This was far from the last word in the struggle over control of the child queen.

With Isabel safely established in the capital, on 3 November the *Gaceta* published Espartero's first address to the Spanish people. His government was the "necessary product" of the movement of 1 September but it was also the servant of "the Constitution rigorously observed and religious respect for the law." This meant, for example, replacing only one-third of the senators, disappointing the juntas that had demanded the whole chamber be dissolved. The Ávila junta denounced the government's decision as nothing less than "repugnant."[143] During the debate in cabinet, Espartero had been a "decided adversary" of dissolution.[144] Here again he was advocating the least revolutionary option.

Jacinta had gone home to Logroño to recover from her travails in Valencia. As always, she and Baldomero kept up a steady correspondence. She was soon working on placing her protégés. Baldomero had already spoken to Finance Minister Agustín Fernández de Gamboa about one of them, but he would speak with Cortina if the young man preferred to be in his ministry.[145] After only a week in Madrid, Baldomero was "bored with this inferno," but "things are returning to their place and spirits have calmed down."[146] In what was the most revealing statement of his political thinking at this time, and probably in his entire life, he expressed optimism about the future. "With the Constitution in hand one commands as with military regulations. When he who commands is just and firm, nothing should frighten him and nothing will stop his march towards the peace and well-being of the fatherland. You may say I have rose-coloured glasses but we will get there." Just like military regulations, the Constitution was a text to be followed literally and unquestioningly. There was no place for interpretation or for differing opinions, for politics in other words. But he was more than simply a just and firm leader; he was the very embodiment of the unity of Spain. "I am the Spanish flag and all Spaniards will rally around it." The few who remained outside this national communion "mean nothing." Few would have been able to resist the tsunami of adulation that had crashed down on him since Vergara and which became more powerful with every step he took, but for a supremely self-confident, even arrogant, man like Espartero it was impossible. Madrid wasn't all political drudgery, however. "Despite their governess," the night before he had taken Isabel and Luisa Fernanda to the Circo Olímpico, where they saw gymnastics, jugglers, and clowns. He planned to take them on further outings every other Sunday. If God granted him "some years of life" after that, he was going to spend them "planting trees in la Fombrera and improving Logroño as a simple citizen," the Cincinnatus – or George Washington – of the Rioja.[147]

Baldomero was missing Jacinta badly and was thrilled when she decided to go to Madrid at the end of the year. In the last letter of their voluminous correspondence, he described the celebration of the fourth anniversary of Luchana, which had taken place the day before. He had addressed his "comrades of glories, privations, and dangers," recalling those who had died and praising them for their conduct under difficult circumstances. He signed it, as he had always signed such declarations, "Your general, Espartero." There had been a "magnificent" service at San Isidro church with a "numerous and splendid ... attendance," followed by a military parade, and, at 9:00 in the evening, three hundred musicians gave "a grand serenade" outside his house. He concluded,

"I imagine that on the 1st your Baldomero will embrace you."[148] Jacinta did indeed arrive on New Year's Day 1841, "in a coach escorted by a large squadron of cavalry."[149]

Baldomero and Jacinta had been married for six years when the war started. Other than occasional, brief interludes in Logroño, he spent the entire conflict on campaign, and this was the first occasion in their married life that they were apart for any length of time. This separation gave rise to a remarkable correspondence. Between March 1834 and December 1840, Baldomero wrote Jacinta 570 letters. Her letters appear not to have survived, but he makes specific reference to 211 he received from her. As a result, we cannot hear Jacinta's voice directly and can only guess at what she said from the nature of his responses. Even this one-sided conversation provides a unique window into a Spanish marriage at a moment in which the liberal revolution was bringing about a profound and meaningful rupture from the Ancien Régime, one which included concepts of gender and the place of women in society.[150]

The letters cover topics from family and household affairs to military and political matters. The first observation is that they, particularly he, needed to communicate frequently. He wrote an average of one letter every four days, but this covers over those periods in which there were no letters because they were together, those during which the letters were less frequent because he was campaigning in isolated places, or those in which the letters are simply missing. If he anticipated that he would not be able to write, as when he set off after the Gómez expedition, he would warn her. There were long stretches of time in which he wrote daily or almost daily; there were even days when he wrote more than once. He wrote first thing in the morning and late at night before going to bed; occasionally, he even wrote from horseback.[151]

Baldomero was emotionally dependent upon Jacinta and needed to hear from her. If the time between her letters was too long, it would leave him "in a very bad mood." When three mail deliveries passed without a letter, he didn't "know to what to attribute your silence. Write, by God, and don't make me so anxious." If her letters were not up to his expectations, he complained: "You write as if you were bored … so carelessly your handwriting is illegible."[152]

A major reason for Baldomero's concern was Jacinta's health and safety: cholera outbreaks, more normal illnesses, bouts of "melancholy," and the dangers of war all produced numerous statements of worry. Word of cholera in 1834 prompted him to write that "May God spare you … this scourge because without you I don't want to live." When she was in Madrid during the winter he was worried because it was the season for pneumonia, and when she was sick again in 1836 he recommenced "in good weather walk a lot morning and afternoon, and drink a lot of cow's milk."[153] In March 1837 Jacinta was thinking of going to Montpellier to take the waters, but Baldomero thought that the "universal hospital" was an awful choice. "Remember how badly the climate and food there were for you. I think Madrid, Sonsigala, Sevilla, Cameros somewhere else in the peninsula would be better, and outside it, I'd choose Italy if I were you."[154]

Baldomero's love for Jacinta and his open expression of it shine through immediately. Almost every letter begins "My beloved Chiquita." He signed off with a variety of phrases, most frequently "your Baldomero is all yours," but also "I adore you deliriously," and "never forget your very tanned, charred Baldomero."[155] At times he used nicknames, especially "Chuchumeca" or the diminutive "Chuchumeguilla," although this became much less frequent as time went on.[156] Occasionally Baldomero would indulge in longer, more poetic flights, such as this one the day before her birthday in 1835: If not in the field "I will celebrate with my friends, offering a thousand toasts to the joy of my soul, the beautiful *riojana* I adore, the only thing that makes me want to live."[157] Or this, after his victory at Orduña in March 1836: "In the midst of bloody combat, of whom did I think? Of my adored owner, yes, I thought of you, because my heart is always the same, always yours."[158] He often complained about the war separating them so much: "when this infernal war is over, when I am at home … do you know what I promise you? Kiss you a million times every minute, not get out of bed for a month and sleep more than Morpheus … that is the sum of my happiness, that and adoring more every day the soul of my life, the most beautiful flower of the Rioja, the most enchanting *chuchumeca*."[159]

He worried about her being lonely. They had no children at this point, and they never would. This was something he mentioned only rarely. In November 1835, he sent her a relic of Saint Baldomero that he had received from Rome. It was "specially for sterile women; if they 'come together' after being away from their husbands for a long time, twins are the infallible result."[160] He suggested that two different nieces of his live with them to keep her company. Eventually Eladia did, even though "I don't know how old she is, but she will be a virtuous village girl who, educated at your side, will be useful to you." Eladia made a good first impression. "I can see that you will love her as if she were your own daughter … You have no children and [she] will be your idol and your recreation."[161]

Only twice did Baldomero comment on Jacinta's physical appearance, both times about her putting on weight: "I am happy you are getting fat because I am somewhat oriental in this, but do not get too round."[162] In contrast, he talked about his own appearance frequently. He was "an Ethiopian burned by the sun, but with a beautiful moustache I know you will love ... I look like an African, like Othello himself ... you will be frightened to see me burned like a little black from Angola but as strong as a Patagonian."[163] In Vitoria "the women" told him that "I am interesting in my sash, which doesn't surprise me because not only do I have a woman's foot but my waist is made on a lathe, but none of this has the value of my moustache."[164]

When he wasn't concerned for Jacinta's health, Baldomero's letters often had a playful, teasing tone. After mentioning that the people of Bilbao called him their "young general," he added, "I don't know if you consider me old."[165] Portraits were a particular topic of such banter. "At the first opportunity," he wrote in October 1835, "I will send you my portrait so you can get one done the same size. They say it's a true likeness and I believe it. I have sideburns as you like and a goatee that's worth a silver mine [potosí]. You'll like it although less than the original."[166] Jacinta's failure to have her own portrait done produced a mock lecture on wifely obedience. "You mean you have disobeyed your husband? You have forgotten the epistle of Saint Paul? ... I will absolve you if you comply with my command."[167]

Baldomero found time to do errands for Jacinta. The day after he arrived in Bilbao in March 1834, he went shopping. "Very modern earrings ... a beautiful fan ... an exquisite and delicate shawl with an embroidered dress and white veil."[168] He sent her frequent gifts, including clothes he ordered from Paris, such as a "chinchilla cape and tippet ... like those of the ladies in Louis Philippe's palace." He even sent a piano. Baldomero actually appears to have been interested in the things he bought. He made a point of telling Jacinta that "I chose them all; you know that I proved my good taste at the Pamplona fair." He paid attention to detail. The sewing table he ordered from Paris was "very pretty, with a beautiful selection of everything needed to sew, embroider, and draw and as it forms a dresser with its mirror, it also has all you need for la toilette. All the pieces are ivory." To go with it, he sent "a gold and silver filigreed Chinese comb."[169] He even hired a maid. "She is not pretty, but not ugly either; she is graceful and above all, skilled," but when she turned out to be a "dud," he found another: "she comes well recommended and at least she is not a hick [provinciana]."[170]

Such interest in women's clothes and other accoutrements seems discordant in a soldier, but Baldomero could indulge because he was absolutely confident in his masculinity. Perhaps because he was that much older, or perhaps because he was a professional soldier, his model of masculinity was very different from that of liberals like Joaquín María López and Salustiano Olózaga, for whom being a man involved what María Cruz Romeo describes as "making a show of an aggressive masculinity that did not include prudish morals."[171] In Baldomero's view, valour was what made a man a man, and he had proven his repeatedly. Only a real soldier was capable of truly loving a woman: "she who doesn't love a son of Mars doesn't know true love."[172]

All this was private or domestic, but Baldomero also filled his letters with discussions of matters belonging to the most unquestionably masculine areas of the public sphere. He shared his ideas about military strategy, his frustrations with the way the war was going, his complaints about his superiors and their failure to provide him the troops or resources to prosecute the war, and his views on politics and politicians. He certainly didn't bite his tongue, lashing out at the "knaves" around María Cristina and the "Strategists" designing military operations in Madrid.[173] As he became more important and his political involvement mounted, especially in 1839 and 1840, his letters got longer and more detailed. As the burdens of command and influence became greater, the letters became less light-hearted. The more he had to deal with, the more he needed to share with Jacinta, and to engage her help.

Jacinta was not just a passive recipient of her husband's views. She had her own ideas and she expressed them. And he took her opinions, and her judgments of people, seriously. In August 1839 he wrote, "Convince yourself, my dear, you know men and things well, and you work with this knowledge."[174] This did not mean he always agreed with her: for example, Jacinta thought well of General Federico Roncali, but Baldomero called him a "scatterbrain like so many others."[175] Jacinta repeatedly challenged her husband's optimism about the outcome of his military and political endeavours, and he was quick to anticipate the charge of "seeing things through rose-coloured glasses."[176]

Jacinta acted as a patron in her own right, asking Baldomero to use his influence on behalf of her clients. In May 1836 he instructed her to "tell your protégé who wants a promotion to consider it done, but he needs to send me a request." In March 1839, Jacinta received a much more important favour: at her request, Baldomero pardoned a godson of hers, a soldier who had been sentenced to death. And in November 1840, when Baldomero was president-regent, she was busy trying to place her protégés in various ministries in Madrid.[177] But Jacinta did not always get what she wanted. In July 1839, he said simply that "I cannot send the person you recommend to Madrid."[178]

Jacinta was also Baldomero's collaborator, and here she played a directly political part. He would often ask her to pass letters or other documents along to his friends and political allies.[179] As Baldomero's political role became more central, Jacinta's services as his intermediary took on much greater importance. Her presence at court meant made her "a living letter" to the queen regent. Jacinta was present at a number of the most decisive moments in July 1840 and she accompanied the court to Valencia even though he was deeply concerned that she was suffering "body and soul in such an unhealthy atmosphere."[180] Along with letter writing, this represented "the highest level of politics to which a woman could aspire" at the time.[181]

Baldomero and Jacinta's marriage developed in a number of ways during these years. While he was off engaging in what he called his "dominant passion,"[182] Jacinta, who was only twenty-two when the war started and had lived almost all her life in small provincial towns like Logroño and Palma, was having major new experiences. She was effectively in charge of their household. She went to Madrid and moved among politicians, and even the court. She took on a crucial new role in furthering Baldomero's career. They became a team with a unity of interests which operated in the public sphere as much as in the private one. At the same time, if their marriage was a partnership, in public affairs she was a silent partner, and this was a role with which she was not entirely happy. In the days following Luchana, Baldomero sent various letters in which he described the battle. Answering one of her replies, he said that "you should not feel bad about not being a man because my glories are your glories; at least that is how I would think if I were in your position."[183]

On 21 December, the government announced elections for 1 February 1841, with the new legislature to meet on 19 March, the anniversary of the promulgation of the Constitution of 1812. It wanted the election to be as clean as possible, sending a number of circulars to the provincial and local authorities urging them not to intervene. There were more than half a million eligible voters, a significant increase over the previous election, but the actual turnout was lower, owing to the Moderates' decision to abstain and to the negative campaign undertaken by their press and that of the republicans. Unsurprisingly, the Progressives won a massive victory, with 236 seats to only 5 for the Moderates. The vast majority of the deputies were new faces; only 29 had sat in the previous legislature. The Progressives also took a majority of the 69 available Senate seats.[184] Espartero was elected as a deputy in Valencia and Logroño and as a senator for Segovia. He chose to sit as deputy for his adopted home.[185]

The most serious issue facing the new Cortes was the selection of María Cristina's successor. Or successors: the constitution allowed for a one-, three-, or five-person regency. And while all three combinations would be proposed, the real question was a much starker one: would Espartero be the sole regent or not?

The key moment in the public debate came in late March. On the 26th, *El Eco del Comercio* published an article in which it claimed to know Espartero's private thoughts on the regency issue. He was furious, and if the paper was trying to get him to clarify his position publicly, it succeeded. He had Linaje send a letter stating that he would respect the decision of the Cortes but would not join a three-person regency. Before publishing it, the paper's owner and editor showed the letter to Cortina, who tried, unsuccessfully, to persuade Espartero to withdraw it.[186] The letter, which appeared on 28 March, confirmed that Espartero's desire was "to withdraw from public affairs and rest in the domestic hearth." He was "ready to obey the resolution of the Cortes" on the size of the regency but "not to participate in it if what the Cortes decides does not conform to his opinion ... on what is needed to save the country in the current circumstances. In this case, he would have an honourable occasion to retire as he desires."[187] The paper made the best of a bad situation, arguing that Linaje's letter and its article had much in common.[188] Aston felt that it certainly would have been "more judicious if [Espartero] had abstained from stating his intentions in so public a manner."[189]

This was Espartero's only public statement of his views on the regency, but he did discuss the question frequently in his private conversations with Aston, and he held to a consistent position: a sole regency was the best solution, but he was reluctant to serve as regent. Before the publication of Linaje's letter, Espartero had "on several occasions expressed to me [Aston] his wish not to be named Regent ... if it became a question between becoming Regent or retaining the command of the Army, he should not hesitate to prefer the latter ... The Duke has abstained from all interference in respect to the election of the Regency." And after the letter came out, Espartero held to the same positions. Three regents "could not direct affairs with benefit to the country, and that if he were to join it, he would only increase the difficulties of the situation, that he considered he should more effectively serve his country by withdrawing from the government ... should the Cortes determine for three regents he would willingly obey their decision and cause it to be obeyed." He categorically rejected reports that as sole regent he would dissolve the Cortes if the cabinet he appointed did not get support. He would always "form a government in accordance with the sentiments of the majority of the Cortes and composed of men whose ability and energy would ... enable them to conduct with advantage the affairs of the country ... he was surprised that any party should think him capable of attempting to impose upon the country any Ministry at variance with the sentiments of the majority of the Cortes and the People."[190]

The capital was seized by "great anxiety,"[191] and "public business [was] almost entirely suspended" as people awaited the decision of the Cortes on the burning question of the day.[192] After the two chambers spent two weeks determining the procedures to be followed, the debates finally got underway on 28 April.

The debate in the Senate lasted only three days and only fifteen senators spoke, eight in favour of a sole regent, six in favour of the three-person option, and one in favour of a five-person regency. The main argument in favour of a one-man regency was the need for "unity, action and brevity," especially in the dangerous circumstances the country was facing. The main arguments for the multiple-person regency were that it would help prevent what Martín de los Heros called the "usurpations" deriving from ambition and, through the "reasoning" of three people debating, provide more effective government.[193]

The debate in the Congress took much longer and featured many more speakers, with Progressives on both sides of the question. Antonio González defended the sole regency, Mendizábal a multiple one. The two last major speeches were given by party heavyweights: Salustiano Olózaga, a *unitario*, as the advocates of one-man regency were known, and Joaquín María López, a *trinitario*, a defender of the three-man option.[194]

The debate was wide ranging. Speakers invoked political theory and constitutional practice in such diverse places as Great Britain, France, the United States, Belgium, Portugal, Brazil, Haiti, Andorra, and San Marino. They invoked history, from ancient Greece and Rome to medieval Spain to the French Revolution to the war against Napoleon and more recent events at home. They invoked the spirit of the Constitution of 1837 and the meaning of the revolution of 1 September. They invoked public opinion. And they invoked the existing circumstances and the (real or imagined) dangers facing Spain. In the end, though, the actual arguments were few, and not much different from those advanced in the Senate. Advocates of a multi-person regency spoke of the limitations of one person – "there has never been a man completely informed about the multiple, diverse aspects of a State, with the ability to reconcile such seemingly opposed interests" – and the benefits of the "discussions" among multiple regents.[195] Above all, they spoke of the "possible abuse of power" by a sole regent.[196] *Unitarios* spoke of the need for "firm ... stable ... energetic [government] capable of resisting any possible enemy." They warned that in the past multiple regencies had been "calamitous" and that in the future they could become "the asylum for party wars ... perhaps even insurrections."[197]

The real heart of the question, though, was always Espartero, and during the last three days, he was at the centre of a debate which Aston characterized as having "degenerated into a personal question [with] some direct and offensive allusions" against him.[198] In the most provocative speech of the entire debate, Luis González Bravo passed from allusion to mentioning Espartero by name. The publication of Linaje's letter had changed many deputies' minds. Some might be afraid that Espartero would use force against a three-man regency, which meant that "we are debating under the influence of ... fear." It was, González Bravo concluded, unlikely that "General Espartero" would act in this way. If the Cortes decided on this option, then Espartero would be left with only two choices, to oppose it "constitutionally or unconstitutionally." The former would mean "the duty ... of participating in the power that the Cortes delegates to him." The latter would depend on the fear of the elected representatives, but they had to yield before "what we have heard and seen in the towns that elected us ... It is time that we vote openly."[199]

As the debate became more personalized, parliamentary decorum began to fray despite the speaker's best efforts. Jacinto Felix Domenech expressed his "complete disgust" at the "slanderous imputations" that González Bravo and others had made about the motives of the *unitarios*, and Olózaga denounced the "horrifying tone" that the discussions had assumed. Coming after Olózaga, Joaquín María López changed the register from accusation to irony. The man whose speech in January 1837 had done so much to help build Espartero's stature as a hero now expressed (mock) concern for the damage a sole regency might do to that reputation, destroying the "magic enthusiasm" that Spaniards felt for him.[200] Finally, after almost thirty-eight hours, the debate came to a ragged conclusion with the speaker repeatedly denying the floor to a deputy who was demanding it on a question of privilege because the chamber had already decided that there had been sufficient discussion.[201]

While the debate was still going on, the *trinitarios* sent a delegation to persuade Espartero to accept the presidency of a three-man regency, even allowing him the possibility of choosing his two colleagues himself. The proposal was, he said *"contrary to the spirit of the Constitution."* He had no doubts that a "regency composed of more than one man, whoever the individuals might be, would prove a source of serious embarrassments and detriments to the interests of Spain," and he would not be party to an arrangement which would be "injurious to his country." If they were convinced that this was the best solution, then they should go ahead and vote for it, without being influenced by his opinions. Aston subsequently heard that "this frank declaration had produced considerable effect upon the deputation."[202]

The Senate and Congress had deliberated separately but they voted together in a "grand and solemn act" on Saturday, 8 May. The public and reserved galleries were filled, while a large crowd of those who had been unable to get in congregated in the square outside. "The general anxiety was at its peak" as the deputies and senators gathered in the Senate chamber precisely at noon. There were some theatrics beforehand. Some *unitarios* had arrived as early as 10:00, but the occasional *trinitario* who came early "immediately left the chamber on seeing so many of the enemy and so few colleagues." A few minutes before noon, "large groups of *trinitarios* entered through various doors and took their seats in the places the others had left empty."[203]

The first item of business was procedural: would the vote on the composition of the regency be secret or "by voice"? The latter won by 254 to 36. Next came the vote itself: the one-man regency received 153 votes, only 7 more than the required majority, the three-man 136, and the five-man one. Finally, it was time for the culminating act, the vote on who would be the sole regent. Parliamentarians voted by paper ballot "in the order in which they were sitting," with the question to be decided by "absolute majority." The list of senators and deputies would be read out before the vote started, and no one would be allowed to leave the chamber while it was proceeding. When all the ballots had been cast, they were read out one by one and the total tallied. Espartero received 179 votes, Agustín Argüelles 103, María Cristina 5, and the Count of Almodóvar and Tomás García Vicente 1 each. There was one blank ballot. The president announced that "the Cortes declares it has elected the Duke of Victory as sole regent of the realm." Four hours and ten minutes after it had begun, he declared the session over.[204]

This was far from a resounding triumph, and certainly not the repeat of the session of 7 October 1839 that Espartero undoubtedly desired. The nation, or at least its representatives, had not rallied round the self-proclaimed "Spanish flag." Not only had he been challenged by many from the party to which he supposedly belonged, but also the narrow majority for the sole regency was due to the votes of Moderate members of the Cortes who considered Espartero the least bad choice. This was the view of both *El Eco del Comercio*, which had been the unabashed voice of the three-person option, and *El Corresponsal*, which had supported the sole regency.[205] On the other hand, he had not been elected as a purely partisan figure, which might have been worth something if the Moderates had been prepared to act as a *loyal* opposition. Manuel Marliani, one of Espartero's most ardent supporters, later admitted that his regency "emerged from the Cortes debate and vote fatally wounded by the lack of unity in the Progressive party."[206] It was not a propitious start.

6

Regent of the Realm, May 1841–July 1843

Espartero was sworn in as regent on 10 May 1841. The sunny spring morning brought *madrileños* out in force. The public gallery in the Congress chamber was full long before Argüelles called the joint session of deputies and senators to order at 12:45 p.m. Jacinta, "whose natural charms and celestial beauty were highlighted by the aura of satisfaction and glory that, without any vanity, filled her modest countenance," sat in one of the last rows with members of her family.[1] The senators and deputies arrived in groups, some in uniform, others in formal wear.[2]

Dressed in his captain general's uniform, Espartero left his residence at 1:00 p.m. and, accompanied by his general staff, rode on horseback along the Prado, which was lined with soldiers and militiamen. He arrived at the Congress just before 1:30. As he entered the chamber, accompanied by a delegation of two senators and two deputies, everyone present except the president got to their feet. Espartero stood to the right of Argüelles, who rose, Bible in hand, and asked: "Do you swear by God and the Holy Bible that you will protect the Constitution of the Spanish Monarchy of 1837 and the laws of the kingdom, and that you will be loyal to the August Isabel II, Queen of the Spains, delivering command of the kingdom to her as soon as she reaches her majority?" To which, in a "strong and sonorous voice," Espartero replied "I so swear, and if I contravene any or all of what I have sworn, I should not be obeyed and the contravention be considered null and void." After Argüelles replied, "If you so act, may God reward you and if not, may he hold you to account," Espartero took the seat placed before the throne.

After everyone sat down, the new regent requested permission to address the chamber. Speaking "with great emphasis,"[3] he said:

> Every citizen's life belongs to his fatherland. The Spanish people want me to continue devoting my life to it ... and I submit to its will. In giving

me this great demonstration of confidence, it imposes on me the duty to preserve the law, the Constitution, and the throne of a child, the Second Isabel ...

On campaign I always considered myself the soldier in the army, most ready to give his life for the fatherland. NOW, AS FIRST MAGISTRATE, I WILL NEVER FORGET THAT CONTEMPT FOR THE LAW AND DISRUPTION OF THE SOCIAL ORDER ARE ALWAYS THE RESULT OF THE WEAKNESS AND INDECISIVENESS OF GOVERNMENTS.

Senators and deputies, count on me always to uphold all the acts inherent in representative government. I expect the representatives of the nation will also be the councillors of the constitutional throne, on which the glory and prosperity of the nation rest. (Extraordinary applause)[4]

After a brief reply by Argüelles, Espartero left the chamber accompanied by the delegation of deputies and senators. Shouts of "viva!" came from the gallery, but "few members of the Cortes" echoed them. When the delegation returned to the chamber, Argüelles closed the session. It had lasted fifteen minutes.[5]

Then, along streets lined with soldiers and militiamen, Espartero rode to the Royal Palace. He was, Aston noted, "much cheered" both en route to the Royal Palace and on returning to the regent's official residence, Buenavista.[6] Shortly after arriving at the palace, the new regent appeared on a balcony with the queen and her sister to preside over a march past of the troops which had lined the streets. Overall, "there was not the same enthusiasm as on other occasions when [he] was received by the people of Madrid."[7]

So began the regency of Baldomero Espartero. As crucial as it is little known, it would last not much more than two years and would turn out to be the Progressives' great lost opportunity. It was a moment whose promise of change was undone by political disunity among its nominal supporters and, above all, by the determined and unrelenting assault of its enemies, which culminated in a successful military rebellion. It was a moment whose fate would set the terms of the country's history for decades. It was also a moment marked by the personality and actions of the regent himself. The prevailing image, derived mainly from accounts written at the time and propagated afterwards by Espartero's enemies, is one of incompetence, favouritism, subservience to British interests, and lack of due deference to constitutional norms; of a man who was in over his head and chose to rely on a small circle of mediocrities and longstanding friends, many of them soldiers like himself, the so-called *ayacuchos*. Such charges, and there is some truth behind them, do not convey the entire story, however. Espartero started his regency with

Figure 8 Portrait of Espartero as regent
by Antonio María Esquivel, 1841. Courtesy of Wikimedia.

clear ideas about the need to respect the Constitution and parliament, but as regent he had to work with the political materials at hand, and these were far from optimum. The actions of the major Progressive leaders, and especially Salustiano Olózaga, must be part of any assessment, and these were, for the most part, obstructive and self-serving. In the end, these leaders made the disastrous decision, of which many soon repented to go with the devil they didn't know. In many ways, the regency of Espartero can be seen as a nineteenth-century analogue to the Second Republic of the 1930s. And like the Second Republic, to quote Santos Juliá, "it didn't fail, it was made to fail."[8]

Under the Constitution of 1837, ministers were responsible to parliament, but the monarch, or in this case the regent, had the power to call, suspend, and dissolve the Cortes as well as to "freely name and dismiss ministers."[9] Appointing his first cabinet took twelve days of conversations and arguments with leading Progressives, which revealed the lack of solidarity that would eventually lead the party into what Carlos Dardé calls "a suicidal vertigo."[10]

After taking the oath, the regent summoned Antonio González, Vicente Sancho, and Salustiano Olózaga for consultations. They put forward two opposing positions. González thought it necessary to include some leading "Trinitarians," those who had supported a three-person regency, in the cabinet, and, if it did not win the confidence of the Cortes, it should resign and a new one should be named. Dissolving parliament "in the present situation of affairs and state of the parties" would be an "extremely imprudent and dangerous" step, as well as contradicting what the regent had said in his speech. Sancho and Olózaga argued for dissolution on the grounds that no ministry would command a majority.[11] Espartero, who had already told Aston that he was determined to avoid a dissolution, even if "the ministry appointed by him fails in obtaining the support of the majority," then charged González with forming a government, although it took four hours of "quite heated" discussion to convince him to accept.[12]

González spent "several days" fruitlessly negotiating with leading "Trinitarians" who refused to "join any Ministry formed by the Duke of Victory." Espartero then invited Olózaga to try, but González refused to join because of their disagreement over the question of dissolution. Even Olózaga's statement that he would dissolve the Cortes "only in the event of the government being in a minority upon the first ministerial question" could not change González's mind, and on 17 May Olázaga told the regent that he had failed. The next morning, an "angry, impassioned" regent "overflowing with wrath and rancour" convinced González to try again.[13] On 22 May, González finally presented his ministry and its "ambitious program [of] political, economic, administrative, and judicial reforms" to parliament.[14]

In Aston's view, Espartero had "acted with frankness" towards Olózaga and González and "shewn good judgement in not imposing conditions which might impede the successful termination of their efforts." He was also pleased that Espartero still "considered the dissolution of the Cortes as an extreme measure to be resorted to only in case of absolute necessity."[15] Among the political class, however, the regent's respect for parliament only earned him criticism over the long delay in forming a government and then for its representing only "a small fraction" of the legislature.[16] This was the beginning of the charges that Espartero favoured, or was even the captive of, a small, unrepresentative faction and that he was a tyrant who ignored parliament. Despite a rocky beginning, the González government retained the support of the Cortes for almost a year, and even a critic had to admit that it was productive.[17]

Another important challenge confronting the new regency was establishing control over the royal children, Isabel and her sister, Luisa Fernanda. Appointing a tutor for the princesses was at the heart of "a political struggle that took place in the liberal public sphere [and] the shadowy halls of the palace, from Madrid to Paris, passing through Rome and the Vatican."[18]

María Cristina made her case in a letter delivered to Espartero by her agent in Madrid, Juan Donoso Cortés. There was no clash between her willingness to yield on the regency and her insistence on having a powerful say on the raising of her daughters. She had first proposed the creation of a tutorship committee "under my authority" and then promised to renounce it if she received guarantees that the new tutor was "someone who merits my confidence." She also questioned Espartero's protestations of loyalty, something which she knew would hurt.[19] The government sent the question to the Supreme Court, which ruled that María Cristina had abandoned the tutorship and that it fell to the Cortes to select a new one. On 10 July 1841, a joint session of both chambers voted 203 to 36 to declare the tutorship vacant and then to elect Agustín Argüelles, the grand old man of liberalism, as tutor.[20] He was sworn in two weeks later, but even the nature of the ceremony proved to be a source of division between the cabinet and Progressives who opposed it.[21]

All this time, Donoso Cortés had been working behind the scenes to organize parliamentary opposition to removing María Cristina as tutor, even meeting with newly appointed prime minister Antonio González. Having got nowhere with him, he met with Espartero, who received him "more affectionately than ever and spoke of you [María Cristina] with such tender solicitude that anyone would have wondered whether [he] or I love Your Majesty more." In the end, however, he hadn't "advanced a single step."[22] A second meeting did not go at all well. At one point

Espartero "began to rant and rave," claiming that "there are cliques that want to discredit me but the army and the people are with me. I am like the sleeping lion, be sure of it ... And it seems [María Cristina] has only her enemies advising her."[23] The next day Donoso Cortés received a summons to return to Buenavista. Espartero received him "as if nothing had happened" and showed him the "most respectful letter" he was about to send to María Cristina. The tutorship, he wrote, was "the exclusive responsibility of the Cortes and I have to accept its decision." His sole goal had been to "avoid that the question would cause Your Majesty bitterness." As the five-man committee that María Cristina had proposed would not be accepted by the Cortes, the time had come "to bring these negotiations to an end" and let the Cortes make a decision.[24] Espartero would repeat this argument about having to defer to the Cortes on many occasions.

A week after the election of Argüelles, María Cristina issued a manifesto denouncing the decision and insisting on her right to continue as tutor. It was accompanied by a letter addressed to Espartero himself which was nothing less than a declaration of war against his regency. The Cortes had overstepped its authority in replacing her as tutor, and, in putting the question to the Cortes at all, Espartero and the government had overstepped theirs. Even worse, they had ignored "the sentiments of nature." She had made "every posssible sacrifice compatible with my dignity and my maternal duties [but] in vain."[25] At María Cristina's request, the government published her manifesto in the *Gaceta* but also appended a letter signed by Espartero and Prime Minister González that denounced the "men unworthy of calling themselves Spaniards" who were influencing María Cristina. The well-being of Isabel and her sister, it said, were "intimately tied to the constitutional political system," which was why the government and Cortes had acted as they did. Far from being "a violent usurpation of her authority," the Cortes' actions were "the legal exercise of the authority granted by the constitution."[26]

While all this was going on, the Marquise of Santa Cruz, Isabel's chief lady in waiting, kept María Cristina informed of life in the Royal Palace and served as her vehicle for attempting to retain control over her daughters. The marquise did her best to prevent Isabel and her sister from receiving visits from Progressive politicians; she had even tried to keep them from receiving Espartero the day he was sworn in as regent. He and Jacinta genuinely enjoyed spending time with the young girls, who were eleven and nine when the regency began. They visited every Sunday – Jacinta came by herself if Baldomero was unavailable – and, just like a kindly aunt and uncle, they took them out to "the theatre or the circus," ignoring the marquise's complaints that "it was too hot or cold or too late." The vivacious thirty-year-old consort and her down-to-earth husband, who dressed in civilian clothes except on formal occasions, must have seemed like a breath of fresh air after the protocol-ridden atmosphere of the palace. When the girls appeared to return their affection, the marquise was beside herself: on 3 July, Baldomero and Jacinta "succeeded on entering Her Majesty's chamber and the girls themselves invited them to see some flowerpots they were tending."[27] It would be hard to imagine anything that would have made the avid gardener happier.

The marquise's "suffering" ended when Argüelles appointed Juana de la Vega, Countess of Mina, as the princesses' governess, although it took him several conversations to persuade her to accept. Juana de Vega was a commoner who had been given a noble title by the Cortes only a few years before; she was also a true liberal, and it is not clear which of the two upset the marquise more. She and all the other ladies but one resigned, a decision which left María Cristina "furious."[28] After the walkout by the ladies in waiting, the countess reluctantly decided that she had to live in the palace even though this meant that she "completely ... renounced my liberty and independence."[29]

While Espartero had had "political relations" with her late husband, she had not met him before becoming governess. In this role, she would see him and Jacinta on their weekly visits to the royal sisters. It was Jacinta who corresponded with the countess, and the two women developed a close personal relationship. In the last of the letters, written to her "great friend" just before she left Madrid in the summer of 1843, Jacinta sent her "a small memoir which, although of little value .. you will be able to use when you write." She signed it "your impassioned, Jacinta."[30]

As regent, Espartero had to deal with a wide range of issues. In the absence of any evidence left by the regent himself, the best sources for his thoughts about these matters are the reports of the British minister, Arthur Aston, who met with him so frequently that some said he was actually running the country. The British embassy was across from the regent's residence, and one day a piece of graffiti appeared, saying: "The regent lives in this palace / but the guy who governs lives across the street."[31]

Espartero's views on foreign policy were quite simple. So long as he was regent, the principles underlying foreign policy would be "to cultivate relations of friendship with all Powers in alliance with Spain. To abstain from all interference in the affairs of Foreign States and, at the same time, not to permit any interference on their part in the internal affairs of Spain." There would be no tolerance for attempts at revolutionary propagandism.[32]

Some issues combined domestic and foreign affairs, none more powerfully than ecclesiastical policy. Since the revolution of September 1840, Church-state relations had become increasingly strained, especially after a prohibition on monks wearing clerical garb in public. On 29 December, the government expelled the vice-regent of the Nunciatura and closed the Tribunal de la Rota, the ecclesiastical appeals court, whose activities were taken over by the Supreme Court of Justice. Two months later, Pope Gregory XVI condemned the government's ecclesiastical policies and threatened to excommunicate those responsible for them.[33] The pope's attack was spread widely by Spanish clergy, some of whom even preached sermons directly denouncing Espartero.[34] (The regency's ecclesiastical policies also sparked a controversy in Great Britain.)[35] The González government was not deterred and quickly introduced a bill which amounted to a "plan to create a 'national Catholic Church.'"[36] The pope responded with a bull, "On the situation in Spain," in which he denounced "the execrable law" that would impose state control over communications with Rome and called on Spain's bishops to offer "full indulgences" to all Spaniards who participated in "public rogations."[37] The pope didn't name any names, but the Catholic and conservative press did. The *Revista Católica*, for example, called Espartero worse than Nero and Tiberius, and claimed that nuns were going hungry so that money could be sent to the regent, "to pay for his Asiatic luxury."[38]

Always concerned about threats to "national independence," Espartero blamed the problems on the Vatican, especially the pope's "most hostile disposition towards the Constitutional Government" ever since the Carlist War. The government insisted on a very clear distinction between "spiritual matters [and] the temporal affairs of Spain" and could not allow "writings signed by a foreign Sovereign to be circulated in Spain in which the Government was designated illegal and the people incited to revolt." On the other hand, the pope's refusal to confirm bishops nominated by the government was to blame for the "deplorable" state of the Spanish Church, including "a feeling of indifference towards the clergy [that] was rapidly increasing amongst the people which threatened the worst results to religion and to the morality of the country … If the Pope perservered in his present course, the Government would probably before long be compelled by public opinion to declare *Queen Isabella II the Head of the Church in Spain*."[39]

A second issue which combined the domestic and the diplomatic was the future marriage of the queen. Isabel was not yet eleven when

Espartero became regent, but speculation and intrigue over whom she would marry were already well underway and had reached the chancelleries of the European powers, especially France and Britain, where it became another site in their ongoing struggle for influence in Spain. Three names were in play: the Count of Montemolín, the eldest son of the Carlist Pretender; Francisco de Asís, the eldest son of Isabel's uncle, Francisco de Paula; and Louis Philippe's son the Duc d'Aumale.[40] Espartero rejected all three. A Carlist connection would trigger a new civil war, and "if it were accepted by any foreign power to impose it upon Spain, he would not hesitate to have recourse to arms to prevent it, and he was convinced he should be supported by the nation."[41] Marrying Isabel to Francisco de Asís was "almost equally objectionable and he should decidedly resist such a project." (Marrying the queen to anyone from the Bourbon family was "repugnant.") A son of Louis Philippe would be "worse and even more unpopular than ... a son of Don Carlos."[42]

Espartero's preference was for the son of a minor German prince.[43] Impatient with González's position of waiting until the queen reached the age of majority and fearing that delay would leave Isabel subject to the intrigues of her mother and to "French influence," in September 1842 Espartero surprised Aston with a plan of his own that not even the cabinet knew about: to marry Isabel to a son of the King of Holland. The king had been educated in England and was "an enlightened and liberal sovereign" who had "fought for the cause of Spanish independence." Holland was not powerful enough to cause any worries about undue influence in Spain, and the Dutch royal family was connected by marriage to the royal families of Prussia and Russia, which should lead them to support the marriage. And, of course, Holland and Britain had long and very close ties. "The prejudices of the people" and the objections of the pope would require the prince to convert, but Espartero had no doubt that "the crown of Spain would be an object of ambition sufficiently great to induce the Prince to become a Catholic."[44] In the end, this plan went nowhere, and by April 1843 Aston was despairing of the matter ever being settled. Espartero had been unable to get his ministers "even to take into serious consideration this vital question to the future independence of the country."[45]

The third issue, and the most damaging for Espartero, was relations between Spain and Great Britain, and specifically the question of a commercial treaty which would seriously reduce the tariff protection enjoyed by Catalan textiles. The British had been seeking such a treaty for years: Mendizábal and Clarendon had been discussing it back in 1836,[46] and William Wylde raised the question with Espartero repeatedly. (Wylde even recommended that if Great Britain awarded Espartero the Grand Cross of the Bath "it would have the happiest effect.")[47] There can be no doubt that Espartero was strongly pro-British: he had expressed his admiration for them during the Carlist War, and he certainly considered Britain the guarantor of Spanish "independence" and constitutional government in the face of French scheming.[48] He also favoured freer trade and considered the existing "exclusive commercial privilege" enjoyed by Catalonia "injurious to the rest of Spain."[49] Following a contretemps with the newly appointed French ambassador over the presentation of his credentials, Espartero became "more convinced that the only security for the prosperity and independence of Spain is a close alliance with England."[50] He pushed his ministers to propose what he told Aston was "the great measure of his Regency," but there was a line he refused to cross. He would not make the treaty "a question of a dissolution of a Ministry."[51]

Espartero saw the uprising in Barcelona in November 1842 as an opportunity. Before leaving Madrid, "[h]e said he had always foreseen that he should have to give battle to the Catalonian Republicans and Monopolists, and that it was well that it should be fought at the present moment [rather] than later, when perhaps the Government might be under greater difficulties."[52] It did not work out this way. When he did return, Espartero was "extremely disappointed and annoyed" at the government's failure to come to a decision despite "strongly pressing" it to do so and had "commented severely upon their want of capacity and courage." He had even offered to ratify and implement a treaty before the Cortes met. Aston believed that the only thing holding Espartero back from changing the cabinet was "the extreme difficulty of finding ... successors, and of the uncertainty that the new men would act with more decision than the present. The want of practical and able men constitutes the real difficulty of Espartero's position."[53] In the end, Espartero was unable to "coerce the Ministry," as Aston put it, and no commercial treaty was ever signed.[54]

María Cristina's residence in Paris quickly became ground zero for politicians, military and civilian, who opposed Espartero's regency and who hoped to use her as a "political flag." Even though she was no real fan of the Moderates, the manoeuvres of her sister, the appointment of Argüelles as tutor, and the elimination of her agents in the palace pushed her into "a reluctant alliance" with them. The loss of control over her daughters was the catalyst for the October 1841 rebellion, which marked a turning point in the regency. The goal of the conspiracy was to restore María Cristina as regent. Donoso Cortés was the point man in Madrid, and the main supporters there were the most right-wing elements of the Moderates. The plan was for a series of military uprisings starting in the Basque Provinces, spreading through Aragón and the south, and culminating in the capital. If Madrid could not be taken, then they would kidnap the queen and her sister and spirit them to Vitoria, or even to France if necessary.[55]

In August, the British embassy in Paris picked up rumours of a plot to assassinate the regent, but when he was told about it, Espartero refused any additional security, "as he was directly opposed to any measures which might lead it to be supposed that he entertained any apprehensions, and more especially to any arbitrary interference on the part of the police." Prime Minister González had his own information about large sums of money having been distributed in Madrid, and without the regent's knowledge, he took measures to prevent any assassination attempt.[56] At the beginning of October, the government discovered a plot involving Moderate officers, "the highest nobility ... the personal female attendants of the Queen and several of the Officers of the Palace" to kidnap the princesses. And "[a]s it was expected that the Regent would put himself at the head of the troops to quell the disturbance, an attempt would be made to assassinate him which, if successful, would of course paralyze the efforts of the government." For his part, Espartero was both incredulous that "such an attempt was really in contemplation" and determined, if it were, "to make an example of the guilty."[57]

With the government aware of the conspiracy, the movement began earlier than anticipated and in a haphazard manner. On 3 October, Leopoldo O'Donnell took control of the fortress in Pamplona and proclaimed María Cristina as the regent. (When the city refused to support him, he bombarded it repeatedly between 5 and 11 October.)[58] This was followed by risings in Vitoria, Bilbao, and Zaragoza, but, lacking popular support, the movement in the north quickly fell apart. O'Donnell abandoned Pamplona on 13 October, and, after a week trying to rally troops, fled to France. General Zurbano took back Vitora on the 19th and Bilbao two days later, bringing the revolt to an end. General Borso di Carminati, who had rebelled in Zaragoza, was captured by the National Militia while trying to join up with O'Donnell and executed after a court martial. The uprising that Narváez was to have led in Andalucía never even started.

In Madrid, the conspirators, led by Manuel de la Concha, moved into action on the evening of 7 October. Espartero was outraged by Concha's participation; his brother had recently married Jacinta's half-sister. "A few days ago in this very room," Espartero yelled, "I took his brother's hand and put it in the hand of my wife's sister and today he conspires against me?"[59] Concha took control of his former regiment and marched it to the Royal Palace. Inside contacts allowed them to enter the grounds without any problem, but when they advanced on the royal apartments, they faced armed resistance from a small group of the halberdiers commanded by Lieutenant Colonel Domingo Dulce, which was able to hold a strategic staircase. Diego de León, the other key figure, arrived only hours later because he thought that the uprising would take place the next day. He failed to raise a Guards regiment, and the officers who had tried to support the plan, "finding the aspect of things in the Regiment so different from what they had hoped, *actually sought refuge and protection in the house of the Regent, where they were arrested.*"[60] Around 5:00 in the morning, the rebels gave up.[61] The leaders hid or escaped, but de Leon was captured on the outskirts of Madrid. The assault had left 234 bullet holes "in the doors of the royal apartments and elsewhere."[62] The two British officers who were at the palace the next morning found "stairs and passages covered with blood."[63]

Despite having advance information, the authorities were taken by surprise. The government insisted that Espartero remain in his residence, and, "much against his will," he directed operations from there. According to Argüelles, "wearing his spurs, he gave orders serenely and with respect for the law." He rejected advice to use artillery to drive the attackers from the palace, "[f]earful of increasing the danger to the queen and the princess." This decision was in part based on the belief that Dulce had a full contingent of forty guards, but these were posted only at 8:00 p.m., by which time the rebels were already in the palace. As the British military attachés put it, "There was without doubt, a general want of precaution."[64]

The Countess of Mina was with Isabel and Luisa Fernanda throughout the attack. A little before 8:00 in the evening, she heard shouting and ran to their room. As soon as she arrived, Isabel "threw herself in my arms and, deeply alarmed and in tears, asked, 'Are they rebels?'" As gunfire rang out in the principal staircase, the countess heard "the sound of picks in the mezzanine": the attackers were trying to find another way onto the main floor, where the only defence was locked doors. At 10:30, with gunfire continuing, she managed to get the girls to bed, although fully dressed and in the same room, a cot having been brought to the queen's bedroom for her sister. A half-hour later a bullet shattered a window and Mina decided to move the girls somewhere safer. The only place available was "a passageway whose location and thick walls offered reasonable safety for the Ladies and I put two mattresses there." Just before Isabel dozed off, she said "I am going to send a message to the Duke of Victory so he will come." The shooting stopped around 6:15 the next morning, but because the rebels were still in the palace, the countess decided not to open the doors to allow the staff arriving for the morning shift to enter. When the superintendant of the palace arrived a few minutes later and told her that everything was over, Mina opened the doors. The girls woke up then. When Espartero arrived, he explained to Isabel and her sister what had happened and "begged them ... to go to the Ambassadors' Room so that the many people who were there would see that they were well." After having some breakfast, Isabel thanked Dulce and his guards and then accompanied the regent onto a balcony.[65]

The question now became how to deal with those involved. Diego de Leon was brought before a court martial on 13 October, where he was defended by General Federico Roncali, assisted by Progressive deputy Luis González Bravo. The key piece of evidence was a letter addressed to "Sr. D. Baldomero Espartero" that de Leon was carrying when arrested, which said that María Cristina had ordered him to "restore my authority, which has been usurped and trampled upon."[66] In light of this letter and de Leon's undeniable involvement in the attempt on the queen, Roncali's defence strategy was to avoid the death penalty by demanding that his client be tried for a political crime, something of which many were guilty. In a question undoubtedly directed at Espartero himself, he asked who "[i]n this age of continual disorder and conflict can claim to be free of the crime of sedition ... exempt from the responsibility that weighs on those who at any time, and for any cause, have provoked disorders in their fatherland?"[67] De Leon was convicted, but the court split three to three on the death penalty, with the president casting the deciding vote in favour. After the sentence was confirmed by the Military Supreme Court, Espartero was besieged by requests for leniency. General Francisco Javier Castaños, who had defeated the French at Bailén in 1808, appealed to Jacinta, but Espartero refused to be swayed.[68] Roncali went to Espartero personally to beg him to pardon de Leon, but the regent, "tears in his eyes," said only, "I cannot save Diego." As Roncali left, his parting words made it clear that this decision would have major consequences.[69] The British also pushed for clemency. Foreign Secretary Lord Aberdeen felt that leniency would demonstrate the strength of the regime and encourage the "Northern Powers" to recognize Isabel.[70] In his meeting with Aston, Espartero displayed an "especially anxious desire to act leniently towards the accused," but he also "deplored to [Aston] the cruel necessity imposed upon him of deciding on the fate of men who had, most of the time, served with distinction in the last civil war, and in whom he had hitherto placed entire confidence – but the criminality of the parties was, he feared, too well proved and the disastrous consequences which would have resulted to the country if the attempt had succeeded too evident to admit of palliation before the Tribunal." Beyond this, "the mass of the publick demand street justice."[71]

With "reluctance and sincere regret," the regent allowed the sentence to stand, and Diego de León went before a firing squad on 15 October.[72] The Moderates used his trial and execution to create a martyr cult in which de Leon, and the uprising in which he had taken part, were turned into "a milestone in the struggle for liberty against the despotism" represented by Espartero.[73]

Three days after de Leon's execution, Espartero headed north with thirty-two thousand men. His entourage included two British military officers, Lieutenants Lynn and Askwith, who enjoyed unusual access to Espartero and whose reports are a unique source on his conduct at the time. The journey to Vitoria was a triumphal procession. "In the two Castiles nothing could have exceeded the enthusiasm of the inhabitants of the towns and villages as the Regent passed. All the National Guards within a great distance of the road were formed to receive him, and the inhabitants of every small village came out in a body to meet him, offering their persons and property to secure the suppression of the rebellion and *preserve peace*." Espartero revelled in this sort of adulation, but by the time he reached Álava his mood had soured. The municipal authorities of Vitoria, "who had been active in favour of the revolt," were received "coldly, merely intimating that he should proceed with calmness to investigate their conduct and to punish the guilty." The execution of Diego de León had "contributed not a little to keeping up the discipline of the army and stifle the revolt."[74]

During his stay in Vitoria, Espartero took one of the most important decisions of his regency. At Vergara, just under two years before, he had promised to recommend that parliament respect the Basque *fueros*. Now, as punishment for the Basque Deputations having supported the revolt, he was abolishing what had been left in place by the law of 25 October 1839, bringing the Basque Provinces into line with the rest of the country and ordering the customs posts moved to the country's coasts and borders.[75]

En route to San Sebastián, the regent "was received in a most flattering manner by the inhabitants … The only wish expressed by the people throughout the provinces has been … for peace." In San Sebastián, a city known for its liberalism, "his reception was most enthusiastic." Espartero spent only a day there before leaving for Pamplona, where he arrived on 5 November. He left for Zaragoza two days later, his procession through Navarra and Aragón "marked throughout …

by even more enthusiasm than before, and in the capital, nothing could exceed it."[76]

In Zaragoza, Espartero waited to get word of developments in Barcelona. There, on 9 October, the city council and provincial Deputation had decided to create a Junta Suprema de Vigilancia y Seguridad Pública despite the opposition of Captain General Van Halen and the civil governor. After Van Halen left the city to deal with the uprising in Pamplona, the junta, which included some republicans, undertook a series of radical measures, including the destruction of the Ciudadela, the fortress which Philip V had built overlooking the city and which they saw as a symbol of tyranny. When Van Halen returned to Barcelona on 15 November, he declared a state of siege and had local authorities replaced and three battalions of militia disarmed. A delegation from the junta that visited Espartero in Zaragoza heard that the government "would not hesitate to punish the instigators in so criminal an attempt to set the laws at defiance at a moment when the army was occupied in putting down a revolt."[77]

The triumph continued when the regent returned to the capital on 23 November. The provincial Deputation met him at the border with the province of Guadalajara, and the city council, accompanied by a sizeable crowd, greeted him at the city limits. Despite the cold and damp weather, "an immense crowd composed of all classes of society" lined the streets to cheer as Espartero rode in an open carriage with coachmen in ceremonial uniform. The buildings along the route were decorated, and on the Calle del Duque de la Victoria the city council had erected a triumphal arch which was illuminated with coloured lights after dark.[78]

The joy was short-lived. On 26 December, Espartero reopened the Cortes, which had been closed the day before the October revolt. His lengthy speech devoted only three short paragraphs to the dramatic events of October and one more to the changes in the Basque Provinces. *El Eco del Comercio* condemned it as "lacking the "dignity and loftiness" the circumstances demanded.[79] The parliamentary reaction was even more critical. The debate over the speech lasted a month, at the end of which the government survived by only a narrow margin. The Progressive factions led by Olózaga, Joaquín María López, and Manuel Cortina presented a joint motion of non-confidence in the González ministry, which passed by a vote of 85 to 78 after a debate which lasted thirteen and a half hours. González presented his resignation to the regent, who accepted it. For the first time in Spain's history, a government had been brought down by a parliamentary vote.[80]

The regent now had to appoint a new cabinet. The anti-González groups had shown that they had the support of the Cortes, so, following parliamentary logic, Espartero invited Olózaga to form a government. He refused because, "as he should carry on the Government upon the same principles as M. González," he would not get the confidence of the Cortes. Espartero then rightly asked Olózaga how he could vote against a government whose policies he supported and "reflected severely" on his having acted from "factious and personal motives." Olózaga backtracked, offering to "designate persons who would be able to form a Government." Espartero was not mollified. He had summoned him to form a ministry, not "to receive advice as to the appointment of other persons." In light of Olózaga's refusal "for reasons which did not appear to be very sound or very honourable," he should apply elsewhere, and the conference ended.[81]

The anti-González coalition existed, in fact, for no reason beyond bringing down the government. The faction leaders had even specifically discounted taking up the burden of office should their non-confidence vote succeed.[82] This was irresponsible, particularly on Olózaga's part. As ambassador to France, and still drawing his salary, one of his principal tasks was to keep an eye on the machinations of María Cristina and the other exiles; he more than anyone should have known the danger of creating a political crisis.

Cortina had already made it clear that "he would neither undertake to form a Ministry nor belong to any that at present might be constituted," and Olózaga rejected an offer of "unconditional powers." Unable to find a Progressive deputy to head a cabinet, Espartero summoned the presidents of the Congress and the Senate and asked them to provide him with a list of three names. General Rodil, a senator, was at the head of their list. Difficulties in finding ministers meant that Rodil could not complete a cabinet until 17 June and then only two of the five ministers were elected deputies.[83] The Cortes was closed on 23 June. When sittings resumed on 14 November, the political situation had deteriorated significantly and the challenges facing Espartero had grown more daunting.

By the fall, the regency was facing a new kind of opposition from the press. On 2 October, a Royal Decree announced the creation of a committee charged with revising the press law to close a loophole that had allowed papers to skirt prohibitions by changing the definition of a newspaper to include flysheets. An initiative by the *Eco del Comercio* led to the creation of an "Independent Press Association" that brought together Madrid-based papers from a wide variety of political positions and soon came to include papers in provincial cities such as Valencia and Málaga.[84] The campaign against the commercial treaty brought new members, including the Republican *La Guindilla*, a one-man show created by Wenceslao Ayguals de Izco.[85]

The commercial treaty moved to the forefront in the autumn after Finance Minister Ramón Calatrava announced that he was going to introduce a new law on cotton imports. By the end of the year, even the *Eco del Comercio* had abandoned its support for freer trade, and some dissident Progressives were spreading rumours that the government had signed a treaty that was manifestly unfavourable to national interests.[86] On 2 January, the press coalition published a joint statement denouncing "the apparent state of dependence of the Spanish government on the government of Great Britain" and warning against any treaties that "were not ratified by the Cortes after full and free discussion."[37] More significantly, Moderates thought they had found the issue they could use to damage Espartero's personal reputation, something one leader admitted "could not be done any other way."[88] Almost immediately, the Moderate press began to paint Espartero as a tyrant and a traitor, a trope also used by the left-wing *Guindilla*.[89]

The Cortes reopened on 14 November and almost immediately found itself debating a new and unexpected crisis coming from Barcelona.

Criticisms of the regent had been circulating through the city for some time. One manifestation was the great popularity of a violently anti-Espartero poem, *The Campaign of King Wamba*, written by Antonio Ribot i Fontseré. (Wamba was a Visigothic king who, in the early nineteenth century, appeared frequently in oral culture a vehicle for commenting on contemporary politics and was appropriated by "written culture when it wanted to appear popular").[90] The poem had spread through the city by word of mouth, in pamphlets, and in the republican press well before it was published officially. Even the Progressive paper *El Constitucional* printed a version in August 1841.[91] The poem appeared in press accounts of politically motivated street incidents as early as October 1841.[92]

Early in 1842 a new anti-Espartero periodical, *El Papagayo*, appeared in Barcelona. Funded by the Moderates and published in both Spanish and Catalan, the latter to ensure that it was reaching the city's working class, the paper skewered the regent mercilessly in both words and images. He was "El Perdigón," the corrupt one sacrificing Catalan industry to "English cottons."[93] He was the lazy one who spent his time playing cards with his cronies in the Buenavista palace. (Laziness, or "indolence," was a criticism even such a staunch supporter as Aston accepted.)[94] And when he went to bed he was the one haunted by the ghost of Diego de León.[95]

Such propaganda helps explain the "accidental and almost laughable" catalyst for what happened.[96] The 13th of November was a

Sunday, and, as was customary, many Barcelona residents had gone on outings and were returning to the city with unfinished bottles of wine they had purchased outside the city walls. When customs agents at the gates tried to collect duties, scuffles broke out. These soon escalated into riots in the city centre and, two days later, into a conflict between the National Militia and the army garrison which left some five hundred dead and wounded and a number of stores ransacked by soldiers. The next day, a Provisional Popular Junta appeared. Its members were largely unknown men, and its president, Juan Manuel Carsi, who had until days before been an editor of the Republican paper *El Huracán*, was quite possibly a double agent. The rebels made three failed attempts to take the Ciudadela fortress, where Van Halen had taken refuge. Meanwhile, the French consul general, Ferdinand de Lesseps, was evacuating people, Van Halen's wife and daughters among them, to a French vessel in the harbour. (Lesseps' conduct would later be the centre of a major diplomatic dispute, with the Spanish government claiming that Lesseps had been involved in the uprising.) On 17 November, Van Halen withdrew from the city, leaving only the symbolic Montjuich fortress in government hands. *El Papagayo* proclaimed this popular uprising "a holy revolution of salvation."[97] The Junta Popular issued its demands on 19 November: the dismissal of Espartero and the government, a Constituent Cortes, a collective regency, the marriage of Isabel to a Spaniard, and protection for "national industry."[98] Two days later it named a Consultative Junta composed of members of the city's middle and upper classes, but this never met as the members either refused to take part or had already fled the city. The Popular Junta also announced the creation of a new armed force, the Tiradores de la Patria.

Word of the events reached Madrid late on 18 November. As he had done with the Basque Provinces in October 1841, Espartero now decided to go to Barcelona to deal with the situation personally.[99] The Cortes addressed the crisis on 20 November. After the minister of war read the dispatches he had received from Van Halen, he announced that the regent would leave for Barcelona the following day. Fearing that it would be defeated, the government failed to request extraordinary powers, which meant that its ability to deal with the uprising was severely constrained. On 22 November, parliament was prorogued until Espartero's return.[100]

Before leaving the capital, Espartero visited Isabel and once again repeated "his desire to see the moment arrive when he would be free of the responsibilities that overwhelmed him."[101] Washington Irving, the US minister and an admirer, was among the crowds who witnessed the regent's departure from the capital on 21 November and he described it with his writer's eye.

> All the uniform companies or national guard of Madrid, consisting of several thousand men, well-armed, equipped and disciplined, paraded in the grand esplanade of the Prado in the neighbourhood of the Regent's palace of Buena Vista ... [T]he air resounded with military music, several of the regiments having complete bands. It was a bright sunshiny day. About two o'clock the Regent sallied forth from Buena Vista at the head of his staff. He is a fine martial figure, and was arrayed in full uniform, with towering feathers, and mounted on a noble grey charger with a flowing mane and a long silken tail that almost swept the ground. He rode along the heads of the columns, saluting them with gauntleted hand, and receiving cheers wherever he went. He stopped to speak particularly with some of the troops of horse men; then returning to the centre of the Esplanade, he drew his sword, made a signal as if about to speak, and in an instant a profound silence prevailed over that vast body of troops and the thousands of spectators ... The Regent then moved slowly backwards and forwards with his horse, about a space of thirty yards, waving his sword and addressing the troops in a voice so loud and clear that every word could be distinctly heard to a great distance. The purport of his speech was to proclaim his determination to protect the constitution and the liberties of Spain against despotism on the one hand and anarchy on the other; and that as on a former occasion, when summoned away by distant insurrection, he confided to the loyalty of the national guards the protection of the peace of the capital and the safeguard of their young and innocent Queen. His speech was responded to by enthusiastic acclamations from the troops and multitude; and he sallied forth in martial style from the great gate of Alcalá.

As Espartero began his slow ride, "a solitary Raven came sailing down the course of the public promenade; passed immediately above him and over the whole line of troops, and so flitted heavily out of sight."[102]

Espartero arrived at Van Halen's headquarters at Sarrià outside Barcelona on 29 November, determined to use the uprising as the opportunity to crush what he saw as combined Moderate and Republican opposition to the commercial treaty with Britain. Three days earlier, he had ordered a maritime blockade of the city. As the situation became more threatening, the National Militia stormed into a meeting of the Popular Junta, dissolved it at gunpoint, and imposed a new twenty-one-person Governing Junta, which included the Bishop of Barcelona as well as Carsi. The militia also took up positions across the city, forcing the Tiradores to take refuge in one of the barracks. After the new junta proved unable to muster a quorum, it was replaced on 30 November by yet another committee, the Junta of Conciliation, which, as its name indicates, was created to negotiate with Van Halen and the regent. That evening, a delegation went to his headquarters, but Prime Minister Rodil, who had arrived with Espartero, refused to meet them. The next day another delegation, this one including the Bishop of Barcelona, returned; Rodil received them, but they were denied access to Espartero, although the bishop was told he could meet him the following day. With the government demanding unconditional surrender and the disarming of the militia, the radicals made one last stand: creating a new Provisional Junta on 2 December.[103]

The bombs began falling on the city at 11:30 the next morning. Manuel Crespi, a shoemaker, left a detailed description of the bombardment in his diary. "The confusion and disorder were so great that ... people ran devastated through the streets without knowing where to hide ... wherever one looked there was only the spectacle of horrible death and the horrific din of the houses as they collapsed ... Five bombs fell on the Santa Cruz hospital causing great damage and terrifying the patients ... The gorgeous chamber of the city hall ... has been reduced to a pile of ruins, turning many of the old documents of the province and principality to ashes, its walls blackened with smoke offering the most horrifying scene."[104] The bombardment continued for thirteen hours until a citizens' delegation offered complete surrender. By then, the army had fired 1,014 projectiles; twenty people were wounded, and 464 buildings damaged.

The regent never entered Barcelona itself, but he did remain in Sarrià long enough to oversee the beginnings of a harsh repression. An indefinite state of siege was declared. Thirteen people were shot, seventy-four condemned to ten years in prison, and seven others to six years. Many more, mostly workers and servants, fled to France. Beyond this, the National Militia was disarmed, the Barcelona city government was to pay for the rebuilding of the Ciudadela, and the residents were to pay twelve million *reales* for the costs of the military operation and as indemnity to the widows and families of the soldiers who had been killed. Finally, the most important trade union, the Asociación de Tejedores, was dissolved.

On New Year's Day, 1843, Espartero returned to a very different Madrid. His reception "was cold, and little or no enthusiasm was manifested by the troops or the national guards."[105] The events in Barcelona had exacerbated the serious problems the regency already had with the press, and by the end of 1842, Espartero could count on the support of only *El Espectador* and *La Iberia*.[106] And he was unwell. It was not a good start to what Isabel Burdiel has called "the decisive year ... in the history of Spanish liberalism in the second third of the nineteenth century."[107] Espartero dissolved the Cortes on 3 January and announced that, following elections on 27 February, it would reopen three months later, the last possible moment allowed by the Constitution. According to Marliani, this served only "to further inflame spirits."[108]

The Progressives entered the election campaign still riven into three factions: one led by González, one by Olózaga, and the "puros" or "Pure Progressives" headed by Manuel Cortina and Joaquín María López. The latter two groups opposed the government, but, unlike the Moderates, for the time being they continued to respect the regent. Some, supported by *El Eco del Comercio*, even accepted a Moderate invitation to join an anti-government electoral coalition,[109] although in the end there was no single opposition slate and the electoral landscape was varied and complex.

The Moderates had abstained from the previous elections, but María Cristina and her advisers had decided in October 1842 that they should take part in the next one.[110] Their platform for the election was simple, boiling down to getting Espartero out of the regency as soon as possible, ending British influence, and rejecting any commercial treaty.[111] The Moderate campaign was also simple: "all-out defamation" of Espartero as regent and as a man.[112] To attack the head of state in this way was unprecedented at the time and was possible only because of Espartero's "patience with newspapers less dedicated to criticism or opposition than to ridicule of his person."[113] He was accused of misuse of public funds, of starving the army to pay for "magnificent parties," and of wanting to sell out Spain, and particularly the Catalan textile industry, to the British.[114] The Moderates also claimed that Espartero was planning to make himself dictator, or even king. And some of them at least actually appeared to believe these fantasies.[115]

Espartero's enemies used Jacinta as a weapon against him. She was criticized for taking on airs, "wanting to imitate the actions of royalty," and for being an "expensive wife," with her spending habits allegedly funded by the British House of Commons.[116]

As she had during the Carlist War and its aftermath, Jacinta continued to play a behind-the-scenes role in public affairs. It was Jacinta who communicated Espartero's messages to Arthur Aston when he was not in Madrid. At times, she knew things the government did not. From Vitoria, Baldomero sent a message *"in a letter to the Duchess"* explaining how "recent events in Catalonia, and the presence in consequence of a large force" could be used to eliminate "the exclusive commercial privilege so injurious to the rest of Spain," something he had not yet discussed with the cabinet.[117] From Barcelona in November 1842 he sent "several messages ... through the Duchess ... that the treaty is advancing towards a satisfactory termination."[118]

Jacinta also had a more public role. She was patroness of the longstanding Junta de Damas de la Económica de Madrid, a position held by María Cristina until October 1840. When the women's section of the Instituto Español, a philanthropic organization of women with Progressive sympathies, was created, she became its honorary patron. These women advocated a model of "female public respectability" which was markedly distinct from that of more conservative liberals and which focused on the education of women. In July 1842, she toured the Instituto's school for girls, "visiting all the classes, attentively examining the girls' work and happily listening to their lessons."[119] (Spain's leading educational theorist, Pablo Montesino, had an important role, and his son, Cipriano, would marry Espartero's niece Eladia. During the regency, he was named to the Public Education Council. Perhaps Jacinta knew him and they discussed his ideas.)[120] The Countess of Mina was a key figure in this world, and Mónica Burguera's description of her could apply equally to Jacinta: "a rational, religious and protected middle-class woman, a faithful lifelong wife but also committed to a civic project of social action."[121]

Jacinta was a few months short of her thirtieth birthday when Espartero became regent. The most extended and intimate descriptions of her during these years come in the letters that Washington Irving, who took up his post as US minister to Spain in July 1842, wrote to his sister and niece. Irving was much taken with Jacinta, by both her beauty and her character. After his first visit, he described her as "one of the handsomest women I have seen in Spain ... a fine brunette, with black hair, fine dark eyes; her person well shaped though a little inclining to embonpoint [stoutness]; her manners extremely affable, graceful and engaging." She carried off her role "with native dignity and propriety ... one of the most pleasing and easy and graceful modes of receiving company I have ever witnessed at any court."[122] Irving's appreciation for Jacinta only increased as the fortunes of her husband fell. Her soirée on 21 June 1843 was the first he had been able to attend in months; it was the last before Espartero left Madrid to confront the military uprising that would overthrow him. It was "thinly attended," and Irving found her "pale, [with] a dejected air, complaining of a headache." He thought it rather a "heart ache" for the dangerous situation facing her husband. "She is an amiable and lovely woman: and her dejected air rather heightened her beauty in my eyes."[123]

On 10 February, the *Gaceta* published an address to the nation signed by the regent and the members of the cabinet. (It had already been published as a flyer and distributed to the provinces.) Speaking in the first person, Espartero began by pointing out the "cruel Machiavellian plan [that] our enemies" had been carrying out, first with the attempt to kidnap the queen in October 1841 and then the attempt to start "another civil war" that lay behind the events of Barcelona. These events had moved him to call elections. There then followed a remarkable statement that demonstrated how much his ideas on political parties had evolved. They were no longer necessarily the source of division and conflict: "all parties, all opinions, so long as they respect the limits of the Constitution, can be useful to the State. There are knowledgeable and experienced people you can trust in all of them. For me, they are all respectable and, for the current purpose, equally necessary and useful. What is most important is to elect men who are smart and prudent, sufficiently informed about the country's needs and possibilities, of recognized virtue and probity, opposed to intrigue, impenetrable to corruption and free from fear." The attacks directed at him by "the bitter enemies" of the Constitution would fail. His only goal was to hand over power to Isabel "at the moment established by the Constitution" and he would do so.[124] Aston felt that Espartero's manifesto "produced in Madrid a good effect,"[125] but many others saw it as a major mistake.[126] Most ominously, the *Eco del Comercio* now saw Espartero as disposable.[127]

Despite the press freedom, the government did not refrain from using tried and true methods to shape the outcome. It changed civil governors, manipulated electoral registers, put pressure on mayors, and even sought to get the clergy to use its influence.[128] The heated campaign produced a massive turnout: 71 per cent of those eligible cast their vote and the number of voters was the highest of any of the six elections that took place under the Constitution of 1837.[129] The result was a fragmented parliament, with pro- and anti-government Progressives, the latter divided into factions, as well as Moderates.[130] The political atmosphere was so tense that a number of the results were contested: even the election of Agustín de Arguelles, the greatest living liberal icon, was challenged on the grounds that as the queen's tutor he was ineligible. And to the extent that it had been a plebiscite on the regent himself, Espartero was a loser.[131] In Aston's view, he was now in a situation "of extreme difficulty."[132]

The new Cortes opened on 3 April. The regent's speech was surprisingly upbeat, given the circumstances, and he concluded by calling on the Cortes to pass the laws which would consolidate the institutions of the state and promote prosperity so that "when Her Majesty, *at the fortunate moment that is approaching,* will take over the reins of government, she finds no obstacles to the benefits her generous spirit will confer."[133] The press savaged the speech. For *El Eco del Comercio,* ignoring "the dissolution of the Cortes, the state of siege, the ... attacks on the press" was a display of "profound contempt" for parliament.[134] The Senate gave the throne speech a relatively easy ride, but the lower house was scathing in its response. It congratulated the army and the militia for putting down the Barcelona insurrection but then demanded an investigation of the officials "responsible for public peace, for the state of siege in Barcelona and the imposition of an unconstitutional tax or fine." The reply also criticized some of the government's fiscal measures, denounced the proposed press law, and called for an amnesty for those who had been forced into exile since the end of the Carlist War.[135]

On 30 April, Manuel Cortina was elected president of the Chamber of Deputies by a large majority. The regent immediately invited him to form a government. Both he and then Olózaga proved unable to put together a ministry, and they failed for reasons that demonstrated the sad calibre of political life. The two men were quarrelling over "the apparent breach of the engagement concluded with the old majority respecting the appointment of the officers of the Chamber." Cortina had used the votes of the party "previously his political opponents" and then been "reproached" by Olózaga "with a violation of his promise ... of one of the first Vice-Presidents falling on a member of the coalition ... and a coldness had ensued between them which was calculated to prevent a junction of the friends of these two chiefs of the opposition." Attempts "by mutual friends" to heal the breach failed.[136] Rather than call new elections, Espartero charged the other Progressive leader, Joaquín María López, with forming a government.

According to the self-justification he wrote at the end of 1844, López went into the interview inclined to refuse, but his meeting with Espartero changed his mind. López was surprised by the regent, whom he barely knew. Rather than the "man who flaunted the opulence and ostentation of his office" which so many people ridiculed, he found "a plain-speaking soldier and son of the people with a burning desire for the common happiness." By the end of the short meeting, the man who had become famous for swaying others with his oratory was wavering: "his every word weakened my resistance." López's friends finished the job, emphasizing the consequences for the party and for the country if he refused. At their next meeting, he found Espartero "in one of those outbursts of patriotism it is impossible to fake and which are contagious."[137] Putting together a cabinet was not easy, and when he finally succeeded it was at the price of violating parliamentary practice: three of the four other ministers were neither deputies nor senators.[138]

The López government was finally announced on 10 May. Its program was short and, seemingly, innocuous: "religiously observe constitutional principles and practices" and "grow the seed of well-being." To achieve the first, the program proposed a number of measures, most of which were undoubtedly aimed at Espartero: working for reconciliation, including a sweeping amnesty for political crimes "after the Civil War"; respecting the "electoral prerogative" and freedom of the press; and strengthening the National Militia. For the new prime minister, this was a "binding contract" between the regent and the cabinet.[139]

López had built his reputation as a spellbinding speaker, but this turned out to do him little good once he was in power.[140] One of the government's key pieces of legislation was a bill offering "broad amnesty" to anyone who had been or might be charged for their involvement in "political events ... between 4 July, 1840 and 15 May, 1843," the main beneficiaries of which would be those involved in the events of October 1841 and November 1842. Espartero had wanted an even broader amnesty, including "the Carlists, or a portion of them who are still expatriated, but to that the minority objected," and he did not insist.[141]

The bill never came before the Cortes as the government resigned the next day, after only ten days in office. The issue was Espartero's confidant General Linaje. According to López, the problem was that Linaje was inspector general of both the Infantry and the National Militia, and the government had decided to divide them into two separate positions. However, rather than allow Linaje to retain one of the new posts, it planned to appoint him captain general, which would have removed him from Madrid. The regent immediately registered "the most open and stubborn resistance." López claimed to have suspected that there were "hidden manoeuvres" at work against his government. Marliani also felt that there was an "invisible hand," but he saw different agents, the "counter-revolutionary party that had already enveloped the poor López ministry."[142] The Linaje question was virtually the only topic at a crucial cabinet meeting chaired by Espartero on 16 May. He opposed the proposed changes "heatedly"; it was, among other things, a matter of loyalty to the man who had saved his life in 1836 and long served as his secretary. López made it a question of principal, a violation of the "contract" of 9 May. The meeting ended with each side entrenched its position.[143]

Aston's reports give us some of Espartero's perspective. General Fransciso Serrano, the war minister, had already pushed for the dismissal of General Villalonga, a divisional commander in Barcelona, on the grounds that he had played a major role in putting down the recent insurrection there and that his remaining in the city was "prejudicial to the feeling of reconciliation which they wished to promote." Espartero refused: dismissing a subordinate officer "who had done his duty faithfully for a long period" would be an attack on military discipline.[144] The dismissal of Linaje was only one of several that had been proposed, and others, including Gerónimo Valdés, the Captain General of Cuba, were in the works. Espartero's argument that these changes "were founded upon unjust and frivolous grounds" was so compelling that Serrano refused to sign the decrees. The regent then invited the cabinet to reconsider and said that if they could "show good cause ... for the dismissal of four officers of such distinguished services and merit ... he would be ready to sign the decrees for their removal." The cabinet responded with arguments that were "vague in the extreme," and the regent "observed that such measures ill agreed with the programme and professed intentions of the Ministry, which were amnesty and oblivion for all past political offences, and they now insisted in turning out men who had made themselves conspicuous by their service in the cause of Liberty, and that he feared that the true reason was that they were his personal friends." The cabinet also announced that they wanted to relieve the entire Madrid garrison immediately, a politically sensitive move, even though Espartero pointed out that most of it had been rotated in only recently.[145]

The ministry sent the regent its resignation the next day, and he accepted it on 19 May.[146] In between, Fermín Caballero, the interior minister, arrived at Buenavista with a sheaf of dismissals. Espartero signed them all except for those of Linaje and Zurbano, and when he asked for an explanation, Caballero "remained ... completely silent." Persuaded by an article in the 18 May issue of the *Heraldo* that some of the ministers were in direct contact with the "counter-revolutionary party," Espartero contemplated resigning the regency that night. He felt he had to take advice before deciding, and the people he invited to the palace succeeded in dissuading him. At 6:00 a.m. on 19 May he called on the seventy-two-year-old president of the Senate, Álvaro Gómez Becerra, to form a cabinet.[147]

News of the resignation of the López cabinet and the appointment of a new one, even if it included the Progressive icon Mendizábal, ignited a parliamentary storm. Following a "most violent speech" by Olózaga, the Chamber of Deputies sent a message to the regent expressing the deputies' "certain expectation of seeing [him] directing the destiny of Spain" until the queen came of age "so long as the good of the country demands it and always in keeping with the basic conditions of parliamentary government." A committee headed by Olózaga was chosen to deliver the message and presented itself at Buenavista without any advance notice. Despite being "in a housecoat and without any ministers present," as established practice required, Espartero received the delegation "with great graciousness" and told them "that taking the message into consideration, he would act as he thought best for the good of the country."[148] After Olózaga reported back, the Chamber took another shot at the regent by passing a motion stating that the Lopez government had enjoyed its confidence "until its final moment in power."[149]

Gómez Becerra presented his cabinet the next day during a "very turbulent" session that would become one of the most famous in Spain's parliamentary history. "The public galleries were crowded and a considerable assemblage was collected outside the [Congress] building." Gómez Becerra's arrival met with "great confusion and violence." When he and his war minister, General Hoyos, neither of whom was a deputy, entered the chamber, they were greeted with shouts of "out, out." Before Gómez Becerra was allowed to speak, Olózaga took the floor and accused Espartero of endangering Spain's freedoms before concluding, "God save the country. God save the queen." Gómez Becerra then announced the suspension of the two chambers for a week; when he left to go to the Senate, he "was assailed by the crowd and his carriage pursued to the door of the Senate House."[150] The anti-Espartero press responded with one voice, publishing the same headline: "Open and unyielding war against the *anglo-ayacuchos*. God save country and queen!" (The two Republican papers dropped the reference to the queen for one to "the sovereign people.")[151]

On 26 May, the government dissolved the Cortes and convoked a new one for 26 August. By this time, revolts protesting the fall of the López government, but not attacking the regency itself, had broken out in a number of southern cities. Espartero considered going to Andalucía to deal with the situation himself, but the cabinet dissuaded him and decided to send Van Halen, who had been in command in Barcelona in November 1842.

Far from the parliamentary precincts of Madrid, much more dangerous enemies had long been preparing. The Orden Militar Española [Spanish Military Order], a secret society of military officers, was created in Paris in October 1842. Members included officers with a range of political views held together only by a burning desire to bring down Espartero.[152] In January 1843, the Order took control of the periodical *Archivo Militar*, using it to attack the regent and "spread the idea that the army is independent of Espartero." By mid-March, according to a report to the supreme commander, it believed that a political crisis was inevitable. Espartero had every reason to hang on to power as long as he could, because once he lost it he would lose "not only his position but most likely his very existence." If María Cristina wanted to take up the regency again, the Order would be happy. If she didn't, then the best solution was to proclaim Isabel queen at the outset, even if that meant violating the Constitution. In either case, a provisional government should be named from the outset with the program: "Majority of Isabel II ... the Constitution understood in a monarchist spirit ... severe punishments for those who continue fighting ... the just cause, rewards for its zealous defenders."[153]

The military revolt began on 27 May when Juan Prim and Lorenzo Milans del Bosch rose in Reus, declaring "Down with Espartero! The queen's majority!" On 4 June, Zurbano was passing through Barcelona on his way to confront Prim, which provoked an uprising there and the proclamation of a junta. To avoid another possible bombardment of the city, the junta moved to Sabadell, where, on 8 June, it issued a proclamation demanding the creation of a Junta Central. The pattern which had started with the resistance to Napoleon in 1808 was repeating itself yet again. Zurbano managed to take Reus, but not before Prim fled to Barcelona, where the junta put him in charge of organizing a volunteer unit. An uprising in Zaragoza on 9 June was quickly defeated, but one in Valencia the next day succeeded, and a junta was created. From there, the insurrection quickly spread to Alicante, Cartagena, and Murcia. On 18 June, it was Seville's turn. Where revolts succeeded, the support of the army was crucial.

Back in Paris, María Cristina hesitated before committing herself to the uprising. It was only in mid-June that she provided money, but it was money that paid for the ships that carried Narváez and his supporters to Spain. (There were also one hundred thousand francs for Narváez, O'Donnell, and Córdova "personally.")[154] Only on 27 June, a month after Prim's uprising in Reus, did Narváez, Concha, and the other generals who had been in exile arrive in Spain. Landing near Valencia, they quickly issued a proclamation supporting the juntas. The Valencia junta appointed Narváez commander in chief. With the struggle for power clearly underway, Serrano, war minister in López's cabinet, who had arrived in Barcelona, convinced the city's junta to name him universal minister by promising to call a Junta Central once the revolution was successful. On 28 June, he issued a decree deposing Espartero as regent.[155]

Initially the government seemed paralysed. It took no action as the opposition press made the most outrageous charges against the regent and openly called for revolution. It even had to deny claims that "the Regent entertains the design of clandestinely removing the Queen and her sister from Madrid ... in order ... to place Her Majesty under the protection of Great Britain" so that Espartero could extend the regency and have the queen married "without the previous consent of the Cortes."[156] Only on 1 July did the government prohibit the distribution of newspapers through the mail.

Espartero responded publicly with a series of manifestos in which he defended his record in respecting the Constitution, denying any Napoleonic ambition, and promising to defend the queen and the Constitution "as a soldier."[157] According to Aston, the early reactions to his "patriotic and manly language" were positive.[158] Later, Espartero announced his decision to take the field against "the enemies of the fatherland" who were determined to undo the fruits of the revolution of September 1840.[159] In the final manifesto, issued on the day Espartero marched out of Madrid, he charged the National Militia with protecting "the person of our beloved queen, the laws, and public order."[160]

On 20 June, as he prepared to take the field against the rebels, Espartero, accompanied by Jacinta, went to the palace to take his leave of Isabel and her sister. He would be going to Albacete to "try to quiet down those deserters" whose goal was to do away with the "institutions." His time as regent was nearly over; she well knew that he was impatient for it to end, but "under no circumstances would he deliver her into anarchy."[161] The next morning the diplomatic corps heard the regent make "a frank and manly address" in which he expressed "his determination to resist every attempt to throw the country into a state of anarchy; and to defend the throne of Isabella and the constitution of 1837 like a good soldier."[162] He then left the capital amidst the theatrical scenes that had become his trademark. "Surrounded by the National Guard and the people, stunned by the vivas and the frenzied applause, Espartero ... arrived at the Prado where he reviewed the armed citizens in a way impossible to describe. Holding the battalions' banners to his chest, embracing some commanders, barely capable of breaking through the waves of people drunk with enthusiasm that surrounded him ... the Duke of Victory left Madrid."[163] He would not return for four and a half years.

As General Francisco Javier Azpiroz approached Madrid on 11 July, Evaristo San Miguel, who had been left in charge of the defence of the capital, declared a state of siege and deployed the National Militia, his major armed force.[164] While San Miguel and Azpiroz exchanged manifestos, "barricades and trenches appeared in the main avenues" of the city. Rumours were rife: Narváez was approaching and had threatened to cut the water supply; Espartero was headed back to the capital, or was on his way to Cádiz. By the 18th, the militia were "tired out" after eight straight days on duty, although work on the defences continued.[165] Aston was observing from his vantage point at the British embassy.

> Battalions and barricades were erected in all the principal streets, and the houses commanding the different approaches were occupied by the National Guards. Above all, measures were taken for the protection of the Palace and for the personal security of the Queen and the Infanta.
>
> Frequent and sharp skirmishes took place between the National Guards and the advance posts of the besiegers. The inhabitants have been kept in constant alarm during the last four days and nights, expecting every moment an assault ...
>
> The absence of all intelligence respecting the movements of the Regent and of General Seoane increase greatly the public anxiety and the difficulties of the Government, whilst the most alarming reports were spread by the emissaries of the Insurgents of Madrid being abandoned by the Regent's forces and every means resorted to produce defection and discourage the National Guards.
>
> Under these trying circumstances, the behaviour of the Militia has been beyond all praise. The most perfect order has been maintained within the city, and the military service has been performed with the greatest of zeal and intrepidity.[166]

On 19 July, Seoane reached Guadalajara, about sixty kilometres from Madrid. When the long-awaited battle took place at Torrejón de Ardóz three days later, it was little more than a skirmish in which Seoane himself was captured, although Zurbano managed to escape.[167] After learning of Seoane's defeat, the Madrid authorities decided to negotiate, and at 5:00 p.m. on 23 July, General Azpiroz led the rebel troops into the capital and to the Royal Palace to greet the queen, who, accompanied by the Countess of Mina, watched the parade from a balcony. As he left, the troops called out, "Death to the regent, who they sometimes called the Cartmaker of Granátula."[168] Narváez entered Madrid at the head of his troops at 11:00 that night. The Countess of Mina resigned as governess a few days later. "In what may be the last time I can speak with Your Majesty," she said in what proved to be her final conversation with the queen, "I beg you not to forget that it was General Espartero who had the good fortune to end the civil war and consolidate Your Majesty on the throne."[169]

The victorious rebels quickly got down to business. Serrano, who had been declared "universal minister" in Barcelona, proclaimed a provisional government headed by López, with himself as war minister. (Progressives like López and Olózaga, who had been critics of Espartero as regent, whether for his support for a commercial treaty with Great Britain or for what they saw as his "despotic" behaviour, supported the uprising. Both would lead short-lived post-Espartero governments but would come to rue their decision to throw their hand in with Moderate and reactionary officers.) The militia was disarmed, even though this was not part of the terms of surrender. Serrano published a letter to Espartero in the *Gaceta* on 28 July threatening that, if his resistance continued, he "and all who support him will be declared traitors, deprived of your honours ... and delivered to the public execration of Spaniards and all humanity."[170] This was the only effort the new government made to communicate with Espartero, and Aston was shocked by both this "reprehensible silence" and the "spirit of personal vengeance" that seemed to be driving the movement's military leaders. Their conduct "gives [the rebellion] a character of vindictiveness which must leave a lasting stigma upon them."[171]

During the siege, Jacinta moved from the Buenavista, which was in an exposed position, to the safer confines of the Royal Palace. After it ended, she went to live with an aunt in the city centre. Washington Irving continued to visit, and "her great reverse of fortune" only increased his admiration for her. She was "calm, self-possessed and free from all useless repining or weak lamentation," better in fact than before. "She said her conscience was clear; she had never been excited by her elevation as the wife of the Regent, and trusted her conduct had always been the same as when the wife of a simple general. She felt no humiliation in her downfall." Baldomero, "whose habits were so simple; whose desires so limited; who cared not for State and less for money; whose great pleasure was to be in his garden planting trees and cultivating flowers," could not be further from the power-crazed figure his enemies claimed. She was particularly proud that they left the Regency poorer than when they entered it. She showed "no acrimony" towards the rivals who had brought down her husband, but the betrayal by former supporters and protégés was "the severest blow of all." Both Narváez and O'Donnell had offered her an escort and other services, but she took these offers very differently. The former "has always been the avowed enemy of my husband," she said, "but an open and frank one; he practiced nothing but what he professed; I accept his offers with gratitude and thanks." O'Donnell, on the other hand, had been Espartero's friend, but a "faithless" one. "I will accept nothing at his hands and beg his name not be mentioned again to me. 'Oh' said she, drawing a long breath, 'how glad I shall be to find myself once more at complete liberty; where I can breathe freer air, and be out of this atmosphere of politics, trouble and anxiety.'"[172]

While all this was going on, Espartero was essentially missing in action. During the siege of Madrid, "nothing is known about the Duke of Victory,"[173] and after the capital had fallen there were "many conflicting reports in circulation" but no solid information.[174] He had arrived in Albacete on 22 June and spent thirteen days there without engaging the enemy, even though Narváez was not far away. As he lingered in Albacete and received word of the reverses suffered by his forces in Catalonia, Espartero grew more concerned about the morale of his own troops. Finally, on 7 July, he left Albacete at the head of almost six thousand men.

The best sources for Espartero's thinking after he left Madrid are notes prepared by Van Halen shortly after the events. The purpose of going to Albacete was "to connect with Seoane's troops to defeat the rebels of Valencia," but news of growing desertions scuttled that plan. With his own troops "showing soon signs of defecting," the only available alternatives were to return to Madrid or join up with Van Halen. The former would have produced "demoralization or desertion, or both at the same time," so he ordered Seoane to move to Madrid while he would meet Van Halen in Seville and, after defeating the rebels there, return to Madrid, where he would unite his troops with Seoane's and "go to the most useful place."[175]

On 23 July Espartero reached Seville, where Van Halen had been bombarding the city for two days, and ordered him to stop, "and only respond to its cannon shot by shot." The bombardment continued a day later when the city refused to surrender.[176] (Inside the city, crowds stormed the city hall demanding to be given the portrait of Espartero which hung there so they could destroy it. As the famous painting by Esquivel had already been removed, they were given a lithograph which had been used in public processions.)[177] When he learned about the events at Torrejon de Ardóz, Espartero decided to head for Cádiz; by the time they reached Utrera, news of Seoane's defeat had spread to the troops and "many deserted that night." From Utrera they continued towards Jeréz de la Frontera. Van Halen soon found that his soldiers refused to continue and he joined Espartero, accompanied by only seven senior officers. Bypassing Jeréz, which they heard had rebelled, the small contingent arrived in Puerto de Santa María at 10:00 on the night of 29 July.[178] Manuel de la Concha was in close pursuit. He arrived in Puerto de Santa María "resolved to capture Espartero at any price" but missed him by "a few minutes": Espartero had already boarded a boat, "taking a Treasury chest with him."[179] (This claim would be widely repeated, although it would be formally repudiated by the government in 1851.) Frustrated by his failure to take Espartero, Concha ordered that "[f]our horses belonging to the Duke, which with others were in the stable of an inn at Cádiz[,] were taken out and sold to officers of [his] division."[180]

At 3:30 in the morning of 30 July, accompanied by only a handful of loyal followers, the regent boarded the steamship *Betis*. The elements at least were on his side. The strong swell prevented warships supporting the rebels from approaching, allowing Espartero to reach the Royal Navy vessel *Malabar*.[181] His regency was over and his exile was about to begin.

7

Exile and Return, July 1843–July 1854

As the sun rose on 30 July, the Spanish steamer *Betis* approached the Royal Navy vessel HMS *Malabar* carrying Espartero and his clutch of diehard followers. Captain George Sartorius greeted Espartero, still legally the regent, and the others who came on board at 10:00 with a twenty-one-gun salute.[1] Espartero's last act before leaving the Spanish ship for the British one was to address the Spanish people. A formal document, notarized by the minister of justice, in which he refused to resign the regency "to those who have made themselves an anti-constitutional government," was followed by a more personal "Protest" addressed to the "Nation." He had never violated his oath to uphold the Constitution, and this "blind respect" had brought the triumph of its enemies. Now he was going into exile.[2] Lacking orders, Captain Sartorius offered to take Espartero to Gibraltar or Lisbon; he chose the latter. As always, Espartero had Jacinta's safety at the top of his mind. Lisbon, wrote Lord Howard de Walden, the British ambassador there, was "the place to which the Duchess of Victoria would endeavour to escape, with a view to joining the Duke, the way through France being too evidently objectionable, and no port in Spain being open to her."[3]

The *Malabar* anchored in the Tagus on the night of 6 August. Espartero's presence created an immediate political and diplomatic problem for the Portuguese government, one which the conduct of Ambassador de Walden, who was pushing the government to receive Espartero with full honours, only exacerbated. As *A Revolução de Septembro* put it, "Lord Howard wants a satellite";[4] to preserve its dignity, the cabinet refused Espartero's request to live in Lisbon while he waited for Jacinta and granted him permission only "to land, as a private individual, for exercise, and where he may not attract remark, in company with Sir George Sartorius."[5]

Espartero's presence was "the news of the day ... there was much curiosity to see the regent."[6] There was a lot of coverage in the press, but it was primarily driven by domestic politics, as events in Spain were being interpreted in a Portuguese key.[7] Both pro- and anti-government newspapers saw the changes in Spain as a good thing. Where the former saw a comforting end to revolution, the latter saw an encouraging end to tyranny. Reaction to Espartero's presence was also connected to Portugal's relations with Britain. Espartero was a tyrant and an executioner; he was also in the pocket of the British.[8] There was even speculation that Espartero's presence on board a British ship in the Tagus had less to do with waiting for his wife than with a demonstration that "the Tagus is English."[9]

Stuck on board ship, Espartero wasn't receiving visitors. Even one of the Portuguese officers who had served under him during the Carlist War "was condemned to see him from afar."[10] Faced with the position of the Portuguese government, Espartero decided to head to London. He would make the trip on the HMS *Prometheus*. In his log, the ship's commander, Lieutenant Frederick Lowe, noted Espartero's arrival on board in the laconic language of those documents.

> Saturday, 12 August 1843: moored in the River Tagus
> (a.m.) Carpenter employed altering the cabins abaft for the reception of His Highness the Regent of Spain and suite.
> (p.m.) 4.50 embarked His Highness the Regent of Spain and suite.[11]

As the *Prometheus* set sail, the British ships in the harbour gave Espartero a twenty-one-gun salute, but they did not fly the Spanish flag.[12]

Meanwhile, the new government lost no time in punishing Espartero and his supporters. On 16 August, it issued a decree that stripped him, and everyone who had signed the "Protest" of 30 July, of "all their titles ... positions, honours and decorations."[13] It also accused him of "stealing public funds."[14] The *Prometheus* reached Bayonne, where Espartero hoped to meet Jacinta, on 18 August, but she was not there. The next day it stopped at Falmouth to take on supplies. The *Cornwall Royal Gazette* reported an episode from Espartero's brief stay in nearby St Just Pool that illustrates his down-to-earth nature and his easy way with children. He and his entourage disembarked and walked through the churchyard and the rectory gardens. The rector arrived only after they had left but set off in a steamer with his family to greet them. As they approached the *Prometheus*,

> Espartero himself came to the vessel's side, returned Mr. Carlyon's salute by taking off his hat, and ... inviting him on board ... received him with a

hearty shake of the hand, kissed the children, asked their ages, etc. and as Mrs. Carlyon had preferred remaining in the boat he pressed her to come on board, and stood himself at the gangway to receive her ... Mr. Carlyon was invited below to the cabin set apart for the Regent, and the Spanish Officers assisted the children down.[15]

Word soon arrived that Jacinta was waiting in Le Havre, and husband and wife were finally reunited there on the morning of 22 August. According to the local press, "during the short time he was visible, [Espartero] kept his eyes fixed on the part of the quay where his wife was to appear, only taking them off occasionally to look at the picturesque and animated scene" of the harbour. As soon as she boarded the ship, the duchess "threw herself into her husband's arms."[16] After the *Prometheus* moored at Woolwich the next afternoon, Lieutenant Lowe recorded "(p.m.) Disembarked HH the Duke of Victorion [sic] and suite and George Rose passenger."[17] There Espartero was greeted by Sir Francis Collier, the superintendent of the dockyard, with whom he spoke in French, and later by Lord Bloomfield, the commander of the Royal Arsenal. He refused their offer of official help, having already made his own arrangements.[18]

Espartero said that "he wished his visit to be as private as possible," but his presence in England had already been raised in parliament. While he and the *Malabar* were still in the Tagus, the Marquess of Londonderry asked Foreign Minister Lord Aberdeen whether "such a man, the deserter of his duty, would be received on the part of the Government of this country." Aberdeen replied that rather than "refusing to receive the Regent on board of a British ship, he had no hesitation in saying that that eminent person ought to be received with every honour and distinction."[19] Two weeks later, Conservative MP Peter Borthwick asked Prime Minister Robert Peel whether the government planned to receive Espartero "as a person of distinction in distress, or in his official capacity as Regent of Spain?" He did not get a straight answer. "General Espartero had arrived in the country suddenly and unexpectedly – but there could not be a doubt that de jure he was Regent of Spain, although de facto he did not exercise the functions of Regent ... He would therefore receive from her Majesty's Government the reception which his position and character deserved."[20] For his part, the Spanish ambassador, Vicente Sancho, lodged a protest that the Royal Navy had treated Espartero with inappropriate honours.[21]

For the first few weeks, Espartero's daily activities were news. He and his entourage initially took rooms at Mivarts Hotel, which a few years later became Claridge's, although he, Jacinta, and Eladia soon moved to a private residence, Abbey Lodge, on Regent's Park. On the first day, "the hotel was literally besieged with visitors of all ranks. The Duke of Wellington was among the early calls upon His Excellency and the noble and gallant Duke subscribed his name as follows in the visitors' book: 'Field Marshal the Duke of Wellington and Captain General Duque de Ciudad Rodrigo.'" The other visitors included Lord Aberdeen, Sir Robert Peel, the Earl of Clarendon, and Colonel William Wylde, who was now equerry to Prince Albert.[22] The following day, Espartero took a walk while Jacinta and Eladia attended mass at the chapel in Spanish Place. There were even more visitors than the day before, including Viscount Canning and the Marquis of Westminster, and "a considerable crowd of persons assembled in front of [the] hotel at various times during the day anxious to catch a glimpse of His Excellency."[23] Drawn by a crowd at the door of an art gallery and noticing Espartero's carriage, nineteen-year-old *Punch* illustrator Richard Doyle "waited for a quarter of an hour, at which time he appeared together with his lady and niece, was loudly cheered, stood up and waved his hat as he drove off."[24]

Over the next few days Espartero had a two-hour visit from Lord Clarendon and a long meeting with Lord Palmerston. De Lacy Evans, who had commanded the British Legion, called. He "took airings" with Jacinta and Eladia in Hyde Park and Kensington Gardens as well as visiting some of the city's public buildings, including the Mint and the Bank of England, and a special showing of an exhibition of cartoons at Westminster Hall; visited Windsor Castle, the Royal Infirmary at Greenwich, and Woolwich, where, dressed in civilian clothes, he reviewed troops on horseback; and the London Docks, where he, Jacinta, and Eladia saw the Spanish wool warehouse and the vaults which held twenty thousand hogsheads of Spanish wine.[25] He was made an honorary member of the Reform Club.[26] He also dined at the Palmerstons'. Lady Palmerston described the occasion as a "Great dinner to Espartero which went off beautifully. We collected a party of eighteen, all people of note and who suited him. The Duchess de la Victoria and Donna Eladia did not come."[27]

Queen Victoria granted Espartero an audience at Windsor Castle on 27 August, although on condition that there be no discussion of Spanish affairs.[28] On this occasion, he wore full military uniform with decorations, "the star of the Order of the Bath placed conspicuously in the centre." After being presented by the Earl of Aberdeen, "he met with the queen and Prince Albert for about a half an hour."[29] Ambassador Sancho was pleased to report that Espartero had not been invited to dine or to spend the night, even though there was a party for Prince Albert's birthday.[30]

After his audience with Queen Victoria, the high point of Espartero's first weeks in Britain was the banquet given in his honour by the Lord Mayor of London on 26 September. Before the banquet, the Court of Common Council approved an address to Espartero; in moving the motion, Deputy Peacock described Espartero as matched only by Washington, "who had drawn his sword only in support of the liberties of his country"; as a "friend to free trade and to civil and religious liberty"; and as an honest man who "had come to England without a shilling except for his own private property and that of his wife." The motion passed, but only after "a very long discussion" which centred on the question of whether the address constituted interference in Spanish domestic affairs.[31]

When Espartero, wearing civilian clothes and his two British decorations, arrived at the Mansion House at a quarter to 6, he was "cheered loudly by the multitude" that had gathered outside. After the lord mayor read the address, Espartero gave a short speech. He spoke in Spanish, but "with such an earnestness of manner and such a grace of emphasis and action ... [that he] produced a very great effect" on the audience. The lord mayor then read an English version of the speech: "As a citizen, as a soldier and as Regent of Spain, my efforts have ever been directed to obtain the independence, the liberty and welfare of my country, and to consolidate the constitutional throne of my Queen. Spain, unfortunate at present, will one day be as prosperous as she deserves to be and intimately connected with England, and with all civilized nations will contribute her share to the general happiness of mankind." After these formalities, the three hundred guests moved to the Egyptian room for the meal. Jacinta watched some of the proceedings from the balcony. Dinner was followed by toasts. In introducing Espartero, the lord mayor emphasized that he had been the victim of prejudice against his humble birth, that Espartero, like most of those present, "had sprung from the people." Next came a song specially written for the occasion. Then, "amidst loud cheers which were prolonged for some time," Espartero rose to deliver a toast of his own in which he emphasized his role as citizen soldier, champion of liberty and constitutional monarchy, his respect for the law, and his desire to return to private life once his task was completed. "Preserving the constitutional throne of Isabel II undamaged and handing her the authority that had been entrusted to me at the precise time the law dictated, in order to immediately retire to private life and lose myself among my compatriots was always my desire but the spirit of evil has prevented it and I have had to abandon my beloved fatherland."[32] This was greeted by renewed cheering, which "kept up for several minutes." The evening concluded with a series of additional toasts, including one by Viscount Canning and another by General van Halen.[33]

Once the initial enthusiasm over his arrival had died down, how did Espartero pass his time in London? For the most part, quietly and discreetly, and certainly without much mention in the press. (He did remain an attraction, his likeness going on display at Madame Tussaud's wax museum in the spring of 1844.)[34] The day after the banquet, he sat for a bust by the artist J.E. Jones, which was later entered in the 1844 exhibition of the Royal Academy and which the *Art Union* described as "full of vigour and life with just the character we should attribute to one of the most remarkable men of the age."[35] A few days after that, he, Jacinta, Eladia, and Van Halen had a daguerreotype taken.[36] The society columns noted that he and his wife were spending the season "in comparative retirement" at Abbey Lodge, and in December 1844 his illness made the papers. Until falling ill, he had been "daily out" with Jacinta, Eladia, and Ignacio Gurrea.[37]

Espartero also was a guest at the homes of British acquaintances. He dined a number of times with Lord Palmerston. In October 1846, he was at Dale Park, the Sussex home of merchant and member of Parliament John Abel Smith. Olózaga was there at the same time, and, according to Richard Ford, the two enemies "smoked the calumet of peace together."[38] And in the fall of 1847 he spent time at the Cheshire home of Arthur Aston, who had been British minister during his regency.[39]

This lack of public attention was broken in February 1845 when the *Examiner* reported on a contretemps between Jacinta and the new Spanish ambassador, the Duke of Sotomayor. Ever since their arrival in London, Jacinta had rented a pew in in the Spanish Chapel, but the ambassador demanded she abandon it on the grounds that it was reserved for embassy personnel.[40] According to one report, Jacinta told the ambassador off: "The whole world will know about this episode and impartial public opinion will judge the Spanish ambassador; the Duchess of Victory has never offended anybody and will not allow anyone to offend her." Espartero then sent Gurrea to deliver a note: his wife had been "grossly mistreated" and the ambassador had acted as a "poor gentleman." The ambassador's response was to send Jacinta a letter which *El Clamor Público* described as "comic" and then another to Espartero.[41] Of course, the incident was widely covered in the Spanish press, with opinions on the ambassador's behaviour following political leanings. The ambassador even felt compelled to send a letter to the editor of *El Clamor Público* justifying his conduct.[42]

One rare glimpse of what Espartero thought about the events that had carried him to London or how he saw his future comes from a letter he wrote to his friend, agent, and senator for Logroño, José Segundo Ruiz, on 29 November 1843, just three months into his English exile. Unusually long for him, it reveals Espartero's pride in his tenure as regent, his bitterness over what had happened, and especially the assaults on his personal reputation, his belief in his eventual vindication, his (justified) concern for the throne, and his view of himself as Cincinnatus.

> As a Spaniard I am consoled by reading history, which teaches me that ... *every redeemer is sacrificed in the end*. I endure recent events with an unchangeable calm and here in exile, forgotten by everyone, I feel happier than when, much to my regret, I was regent.
>
> Every day the nation spends making comparisons, it will do me more justice, and when I can return to my fatherland, *in my domestic corner like Cincinatus*, I will be greater than at Luchana, at Vergara, or in the Buenavista Palace.
>
> Amidst such ingratitude, calumny, and injustice, *what saddens me most is to see how in the Congress they say I wanted to betray the minority and in the Senate that I dreamed of having a throne* ... and of the 209 people present not a single one had the love of truth or a trace of Castilian nobility to get up and refute these claims that not even those who made them believed.[43]

Espartero broke his public silence only on the occasion of the proclamation of Isabel II as queen on 10 October 1844. This took place eleven months before Isabel's fourteenth birthday, which was the date the Constitution of 1837 set for her accession, but bringing Isabel to the throne quickly had been one of the conspirators' key goals. Once Espartero was gone, the alliance of convenience between Progressives and Moderates began to break down, and the two groups engaged in a struggle for control of the queen. Prime Minister Joaquín María López thought that advancing the age of majority would help the Progressives, but it ended up benefiting their enemies, and especially those who belonged to María Cristina's circle, not to mention María Cristina herself.[44] Olózaga replaced López as prime minister but he was soon done in by "one of the darkest scandals" of Isabel's reign. In brief, Moderates in the palace persuaded Isabel to claim that Olózaga had coerced her into signing a law. They then carried out what Isabel Burdiel has called a "political lynching" that led to Olózaga going into exile. By March 1844, María Cristina was back in Madrid, again a centre of power; by May, Narváez was prime minister, and the construction of system designed by the Moderates, and based on their constitution of 1845, was underway.[45]

The heart of Espartero's proclamation "To the Spaniards" was a defence of his conduct as regent. He had been, he said, a "faithful observer of the laws" and always respected judicial independence. His protest before leaving the country was made, not in the name of "an ambition I have never felt," but in defence of "the dignity of the Nation and the Throne." If he were allowed to return home, he would "lose myself in the ranks of the people" and enjoy the benefits of the liberty he had helped give the country. However, if those institutions were endangered, the fatherland, "to whose voice I have never been deaf," could count on him "to sacrifice myself in its name."[46]

Shortly after this, in November 1844, Espartero's loyal lieutenant, Martín Zurbano, led a failed uprising demanding the restoration of the Constitution of 1837 and the return of Espartero.[47] Fearful that Espartero himself would take charge of the revolt, Narváez sent a confidential document informing the captains general that, according to "reliable, semi-official warnings," Espartero was heading for Spain on a foreign ship. When arrested, "HE SHOULD BE PUT BEFORE A FIRING SQUAD AS SOON AS HE IS IDENTIFIED." The government's supposed information was amazingly detailed: Espartero was carrying two passports "and the same number of disguises: one as an officer of the Royal Navy, the other a merchant from Martinique wearing a leather hat, a blue jacket, olive green trousers, boots, and glasses."[48] It was a total invention, but the Spanish embassy in London did keep an eye on Espartero's comings and goings as best it could, given what its ambassador called "the limited means available for this purpose in this country … Nothing in the capital can prevent [him] from leaving clandestinely at any time, with or without a passport, since one is not required to board ship in any English port."[49]

Was Espartero actually involved in political plotting? The announcement at the end of August 1846 that on 10 October, her sixteenth birthday, the queen would marry her cousin, Francisco de Asís, and that her sister would marry the Duke of Montpensier, the youngest son of Louis Philippe, led to some discussions about an alliance between Progressives and Carlists against the common enemy.[50] Espartero was involved – at least at one remove. There were two approaches from Carlists to which Espartero, speaking through his confidant, Francisco Linaje, replied that any "sacrifice in [my] political principle" was out of the question.[51] At the same time, Pedro Tacón reported that Espartero had rejected attempts by Cabrera and Montemolín, who were in London, to establish an alliance.[52] In early October, Espartero and Olózaga met with Palmerston to discuss the situation. Espartero urged patience. "[A]ny movement … should be for the Queen and the Constitution of 1837 and the exclusion of the offspring of Montpensier's marriage. All that would be perfectly consistent with loyalty to the Queen ... [T]hey ought all to keep quiet and wait for better times unless they have a clear and manifest chance of success."[53]

That these initiatives coincided with the outbreak of the Guerra dels Matiners, or Second Carlist War, terrified the authorities.[54] Back in April, Sotomayor had reported that the events in Galicia had galvanized the émigrés. He had been assured that Espartero "had given his word to come to Spain if the news is good"[55] and he had heard that Espartero had chartered a ship to "take him to whatever place in the Peninsula he believes his presence would strengthen the insurrection."[56] There were all kinds of rumours in Madrid: Cabrera and the Carlist Pretender were heading for Spain; Espartero had arrived in Lisbon; there was an "monstrous alliance" between the two.[57] *El Imparcial* ran a letter from its London correspondent claiming that Montemolín was going to raise a one-hundred-thousand-man army and divide its command among Espartero, Cabrera, and two other generals.[58] The anxious authorities had little tolerance for the slightest public expression of sympathy for Espartero: on 31 July 1846, three people were arrested in Zaragoza for "singing songs alluding to Espartero."[59]

Throughout 1847 and into 1848, the consulate in Perpignan was informing Madrid about what it called the "Carlist-Progressive alliance," in which *Esparterismo* was always present.[60] Confidential Progressive correspondence intercepted in November indicated that "*ayacuchos* and Carlism" had reached a tacit agreement that the former rebel in the cities and the latter in towns and rual areas.[61] Espartero was "fully" involved in the "mysteries" of the alliance, which "of course already had the support of republicans and communists."[62] Jacinta was supposedly even running her own political activities: "manoeuvring in Paris with emissaries of the French opposition ... she has flaunted her power and with her husband in Madrid will have the future of the State in her hands."[63]

In the summer of 1847, a political crisis engulfed Madrid. The indiscreet conduct of the queen, who had been married for less than a year, and especially her dalliance with General Fransciso Serrano, were used as weapons by the hardline Moderates around María Cristina against the government, which was seeking some sort of reconciliation with the Progressives. There were even rumours that the queen might be forced to abdicate and be replaced by a regency.[64] As the crisis peaked in August and September, the "Espartero question" became an important part of the equation.[65]

Rumours about his return had been swirling since at least July,[66] and *El Clamor Público* reported that Espartero had rejected an offer from the government to restore his honours on the condition that he remain out of the country for ten months.[67] Espartero was also on the minds of ordinary Spaniards. In August 1847, Eugenio Aviraneta, who was keeping tabs on public opinion for María Cristina, reported that "in the taverns, on the streets, and the poor neighbourhoods … men and women dressed in rags argue about the queen, the king, Montpensier … *Espartero* and the tax system."[68] It was not just Madrid. Late-night crowds ran through the streets of Granada shouting "vivas" to Espartero; a local festival in Valencia ended with "cries of Long live Espartero and the Republic, and other subversive things"; while in Tarragona, "a flyer proclaiming Espartero and the Republic" had appeared.[69]

At the end of August, Isabel appointed Florencio García Goyena to head a grand liberal coalition. The new government moved quickly to show that its talk of reconciliation was real: On 3 September, it announced an amnesty for all political exiles, and the next day a separate decree restored all the "titles, honours, and decorations" that had been taken from Espartero in August 1843. Isabel also appointed Espartero to the Senate.[70] In his reply, Espartero expressed his gratitude for the appointment, congratulated Isabel for her decision to overcome the "divisions" caused by "political oscillations," and assured her that he and others who "had so doggedly fought to defend her throne supported by the Constitution, even before she was able to understand their sacrifices," would not abandon her.[71] If the government's motive was to win support, both for itself and for the queen, it was certainly successful. The Progressive mouthpiece *El Clamor Público* published the decree on 5 September beneath a declaration of "Long Live Isabel II" in big bold print.[72] *El Tío Camorra* reported that blind people were selling the decree appointing Espartero to the Senate in the streets of the capital.[73] There were reports that the government had met with friends of Espartero's and sent a letter giving him permission to return.[74] The joy reached into the provinces. In Albacete three hundred people signed a statement thanking the queen for granting the amnesty, as did a large group of "liberals" from Cuenca.[75] In Logroño, the local government ordered city hall to be lit up, and "there were fireworks, bands playing the Hymn of Riego, cheers for the queen."[76]

Not everyone was happy. *El Heraldo* declared that the government had committed suicide: letting Espartero back into the country might even lead to civil war.[77] The government certainly did not want him to return. In a confidential communiqué, Minister of State Modesto de Cortázar told Ambassador Istúriz that, to keep him from returning to Spain, the government had decided to name Espartero ambassador to London. And if he did not accept the position, it "will look for other ways of keeping him away, such as permission to travel for as long as he wants."[78] The García Goyena government fell days later, but its successor, headed by Narváez, followed the same policy.[79]

Istúriz personally delivered the ambassadorial appointment to Espartero's house. "He immediately said he would not accept," and he repeated his refusal "many times" during the hour-long meeting. His long stay in London had left him without the "financial means" to do the job properly; he lacked the "diplomatic skills" for the role; and his "broken health" required that he return home and remain "distant from public affairs." Espartero was also adamant that his refusal was not political. Istúriz then suggested that he accept the job and resign after a few months, but Espartero was having none of it. A few days later, Espartero brought his written response, which repeated the same arguments. When Istúriz saw that Espartero was "immovable," he communicated, "word for word," the government's position that it was "indispensable that he wait in London" until the government had decided what to do. Espartero replied that "would obey," an answer "given with the tone of a resigned spirit" but one which also betrayed "profound regret."[80]

Palmerston, whom Espartero had kept apprised of these developments, thought the Spanish government was overestimating the danger he posed. Espartero lacked the "inordinate ambition" attributed to him.[81] While his "undaunted physical courage, inflexible integrity, unflinching patriotism, devoted loyalty and remarkable good plain sense" were undeniable, he did not possess the "commanding talents and overreaching qualities of mind which give one man moral ascendancy over his fellows and enable him to sway the destinies of a nation."[82] In the existing circumstances, "I fear that he has not activity or energy enough to make his honesty a match for the roguery of Narváez."[83] He would, however, be useful in providing advice to the queen, and that "*very superior woman,*" Jacinta, even more so.[84]

Jacinta was also an important factor in Ambassador Henry Bulwer's thinking. "If Espartero, *and especially his wife,*" were willing to side with Serrano in the power struggles in Madrid, then all would go well. If, however, "the Duke and the Duchess think they can come here and, relying on *their* own weight and popularity, set up an independent banner," it would be a disaster. Bulwer was also frustrated with the squabbling among the Progressives, but "if the Duke and *especially* the Duchess de la Victoria will enter frankly into a common plan with them we have a good chance of success."[85]

Espartero returned to the embassy on 15 November, and this time he was less resigned. He made it clear that he couldn't stay in London any longer and that if he were not allowed to return home "he would move to Belgium or some other place better suited to his health and interests" – and let the Senate know the reasons for his absence. Istúriz pleaded for clear instructions, as the issue had become "widely reported" in the national and international press.[86] In August, there was speculation about Espartero having to leave London, perhaps for Belgium, because of money troubles. (Indeed, in April 1847 he had asked Palmerston "to obtain permission from the Belgian government for me.")[87] At a dinner attended by Lady Palmerston, "the Esparteros talk[ed] of going to live at Brussels. They find everything here so dear. Palmerston offered him secret *Tesorie* money but he would not accept."[88] He also reportedly turned down the offer of a pension from Queen Victoria.[89]

In the meantime, the queen had sent him a "royal licence" for six months' travel and asked that he delay his return, "to prevent the disagreeable possibility of people attempting to abuse Your Excellency's name to create a conflict which your loyalty and great patriotism would wish to avoid."[90] Espartero remained adamant, informing the government that he had decided to "leave for Madrid immediately." He refused the British government's offer of a Royal Navy vessel, insisting on travelling on a Spanish ship. He also asked Istúriz to inform the government, "as his tact did not allow him to do so directly," that he would keep his return discreet and do everything he could "to avoid any kind of demonstration," including arriving in the capital "after eleven at night, if possible, and through a different gate than usual."[91]

Just before leaving England, Espartero and Jacinta, accompanied by Colonel Wylde, dined with Queen Victoria at Windsor Castle. Espartero was "wretchedly ill, suffering one of his attacks of stones. He looked yellow and pale."[92] Victoria liked Jacinta, and in her *Journal* she provides a rare glimpse of what was on Jacinta's mind and Baldomero's on the eve of their departure. "The Duchess," who was only thirty-six, "must once have been very handsome and has still great remains of good looks."

> She is pleasing and very talkative, talking French fluently, though very imperfectly. She is full of anxiety at the Duke's return, fearing that it will be of no use in any way. They have been quiet here, and after three year's war, three year's Regency and nearly five years exile, she dreads new vicissitudes. It is more than nine years [since] they have been at their own home. The poor Duke spoke to me for some time in very broken French, but he made himself understood and understood all I said. He is also fearful of being of no use – indignant at the way in which the poor Queen had been sacrificed by the French, and *determined that her marriage should be*

dissolved, it having been accomplished by force, and he said it could be. He is full of gratitude for the hospitality shown him in England.[93]

On 31 December 1847, Espartero boarded the Spanish steamer *M.A. Heredia* at Southampton. (Jacinta travelled separately to Le Havre and then to Paris.) He arrived at San Sebastián on 4 January. The military authorities had ordered all troops to remain in barracks "so that no soldier would be seen cheering the illustrious Peacemaker of Spain," but once his ship came into sight, crowds thronged the docks; "the women waving their beautiful handkerchiefs were particularly noticeable."[94] He remained only a few hours, leaving at midnight for Vitoria, where he was greeted by members of Jacinta's family. Then, travelling incognito, he proceeded to Madrid, where he arrived at 4:00 a.m. on 7 January.

The Progressive press was ecstatic. *El Espectador* put out a special front page, decorated "as is done on a national holiday or a great event or the birthday of a monarch," as the conservative paper *El Español* put it.[95] *El Eco del Comercio* reported that the city's butchers celebrated Espartero's return by selling their meat "with the bones removed but withour raising the price," testimony to "sympathies that all classes of the Spanish people feel for General Espartero."[96] The reaction of *El Clamor Público* was initially restrained but became more fulsome after it was called out by some conservative papers for being only lukewarm. Using language that sounded as if the regency had never happened, it presented Espartero as "a leader, a point of unity, a symbol of reconciliation."[97] Even *El Tío Camorra*, the satirical paper put out by Juan Martínez Villergas, who had so cruelly attacked him as regent, greeted Espartero with a lengthy poem that praised him as the "muse of hope" and "the joy of the Iberian people."[98]

Once word of Espartero's presence in Madrid got out, crowds thronged to his residence on the Calle Montera, even though he had asked his supporters to tone things down, so as not "to provoke the government's suspicions."[99] During Manuel Cortina's visit, "a group of men and women of the people entered the Duke's room and crowded around him, crying and hugging his knees. Their extreme demonstrations upset the General's sensitivities; he had strongly urged the friends who visited him to free him from scenes like these and prevent cheers and loud demonstrations, otherwise he was ready to abandon [Madrid]." By late that night, the crowds had dispersed, but soldiers, "including some cavalry," were patrolling the nearby streets.[100] Publisher Benito Hortelano came five days after Espartero's arrival and found the house still surrounded by "an immense crowd that waited day and night to see the leader of the people should he go out on the balcony. A single glimpse would have electrified them."[101] On 21 January, Evaristo San Miguel brought greetings from the city of Oviedo, one of the "many delegations representing different towns."[102] Even members of the government went, including Narváez himself.[103]

In addition to the personal visits, "written greetings" arrived from across the country, such as one signed by eight hundred "liberals" from La Coruña. The Progressives of Villamalea (Albacete) expressed their repentance for having turned against him: "Our errors have brought us the evil of fevered and pitiless reaction. *Your Excellency left us free men and has found a nation of slaves*." And in a rare public pronouncement on politics, 35 "ladies" and 25 "young women" of Guadix sent greetings "born from the most intimate part of their hearts, and as the weak class cannot serve to invigorate the pedestal of the true cause, it can at least have the satisfaction of expressing the sincere thought that animates it."[104] By the time Espartero left Madrid, 120,000 people had signed such documents.[105]

Espartero's first act was to write to Narváez to request an audience with the queen. He was given one for 5:30 that afternoon. Unusually, it was to be private, without any ministers present. Isabel greeted him warmly, expressing her sadness that he had for so long been "banished from the fatherland." Espartero replied that, through all the bitterness of exile, his only thought had been for "the happiness of the queen and his country." As the audience was ending, Isabel expressed her wish to see him "at the palace frequently," but his reply, that he "would come instantly whenever you need and summon me," led her to demand an explanation.[106] There was no meeting with María Cristina, however. As a result, Espartero was not invited to a ball at the Royal Palace, a slight which led Progressive senators to boycott the event. It also provoked an extended controversy in the press, with the two parties' papers exchanging long articles which quickly moved from this particular incident to a discussion of Espartero's political role.[107]

Only two days after Espartero arrived in Madrid, Francisco Linaje, his long-time comrade and confidant, died. Sick with a cold and "deeply saddened," Espartero did not attend the funeral.[108] By the next day he was sufficiently recovered to take the oath as senator. When Espartero arrived at the Senate "wearing a black suit," the public galleries were packed, and many people were unable to get in. When the session ended, many senators congratulated Espartero, and crowds gathered at the door to catch a glimpse of him and, if possible, shake his hand. Those who couldn't "waved their hats and handkerchiefs, maintaining a silence as eloquent as it was profound."[109]

Espartero did not linger in the capital. On 24 January, he informed the Senate that he had to leave Madrid "to attend to domestic business." His last act was to pay another visit to the queen.[110] Accompanied by Ignacio Gurrea and Luciano Murrieta, Espartero left Madrid before midnight on 5 February. As they entered the Rioja, some villages received him "with bells, fireworks, and cheers," but his reception in Logroño recalled the glorious days after Vergara. "The inhabitants insisted on unhitching the horses and pulling his carriage around the town to enter by the main street, although they eventually gave in to his requests and those of his friends and relatives in the crowd to let him enter his house through a side street and as quietly as possible given all the confusion." The entire city council came to visit, and in response to the mayor's welcome, Espartero made it clear that "he desired to live retired from public affairs to attend to his private ones" as well as to join in "promoting the agriculture and industry of the province." He asked that "political questions not be discussed in his presence."[111] The next day large numbers of people from all social classes visited his house, and Espartero greeted each one individually. He told one young boy, "Come, come, child, and give me those hands because you too are Spanish."[112]

Travelling separately from France, Jacinta arrived two weeks later. Finally, Baldomero could realize the goal he had shared with her while campaigning against the Carlists – to be at home together – as well as the goal he had been repeating more recently: to get their financial affairs in order. Espartero's favourite self-image was that of Cincinnatus; now he had the chance to realize it.

A little over a month after his return, the *Eco del Comercio* described Espartero's "system of life" in Logroño: "On holidays he attends mass and goes for a walk; the rest of the week he stays at home," attending to private affairs. For her part, Jacinta took frequent walks, especially on Friday afternoons. "Accompanied by relatives and Col. Gurrea," she often went to church at the Cristo del Humilladero hermitage. She also hosted a salon.[113] Four years later, little had changed. Much of Espartero's time was spent with "relatives," but the Casa-Palacio, as it was called, was "open to anyone who wanted to visit, irrespective of political opinions." With politics off limits, conversation "focused on general matters, and occasionally on the Duke's feats of arms, which he still discusses enthusiastically." His favourite activity was working on La Fombera, his farm on the outskirts of the city. In the evenings, he read the papers.[114] In spite of this quiet life, the British were worried for Espartero's safety. Following the February Revolution in Paris, Palmerston wrote Bulwer that Espartero would be better off outside Spain. "for if any outbreak were to happen Narváez would immediately take Espartero up, on the same principle on which the Irish schoolmaster flogged his boys all round in the morning because he was convinced they would want it before nightfall. You had better advise him to retire."[115]

Espartero's return to Spain had not stopped Progressives and others from conspiring against the regime, and while it appears that he himself was not directly involved, he figured prominently in their plans. The Perpingnan consulate reported on a meeting at the Clarendon Hotel in London on 25 June 1848 involving Olózaga, José de Salamanca, and Patricio de la Escosura in which they agreed to make Espartero head of a provisional government and "lieutenant general of the Realm until the crisis had passed." (The documents do not say so explicitly, but the creation of this new title makes it appear that one of the goals was to replace Isabel II as head of state.) In the meantime, "we name him head of the Committee." The action points at the end of the meeting included having Olózaga invite Espartero "to come and occupy his position,"[116] which suggests that they hadn't discussed the plan with him. They certainly didn't know their man if they expected him to abandon Logroño for a new exile.

Espartero was by far the most famous and most prestigious, if not the richest, resident of the small provincial capital of some eleven thousand people. He and Jacinta would certainly have been at the centre of local social life.[117] One rare glimpse of this comes from an account of the ceremony held on 6 January 1852 to celebrate the birth of the queen's daughter. "Three poor orphans" each received four ounces of gold as a dowry, the money donated by the resident "military class, with the illustrious Duke of Victory," who gave 600 of the 3,840 *reales* donated, "at their head." For her part, Jacinta was reported to have given "a full trousseau." During the ceremony, Espartero, wearing his captain general's uniform with all his medals, gave "an eloquent if laconic speech."[118] Espartero also supported worthy local initiatives. In May 1849, he donated 500 *reales* to pay the membership fees for fifty people to the newly created Mutual Aid Society for Proletarian Artisans.[119] His generosity was not limited to Logroño: in 1850 he donated 1,000 *reales* towards the construction of a primary school in the Villa de Plencia (Vizcaya).[120] On the other hand, he stayed far away from Madrid, refusing all invitations to attend events at court, including ceremonies surrounding the births of Isabel's children, usually on grounds of ill health. In June 1850 he added the cryptic "and the well-known reasons that keep me away from the Court."[121]

Espartero's most significant economic activity, and one in which he showed himself open to innovation, was his collaboration with Luciano

Murrieta, the future Marqués de Murrieta, in launching the modern Rioja wine industry. Espartero had known Murrieta since he was infant in Arequipa, and the younger man had tied his career to his, serving as Espartero's aide-de-camp and going into exile with him. He remained Espartero's aide-de-camp after returning from exile and held the position into the 1850s. While in exile he observed the prestige of "great wine" in Britain. Back in Logroño he realized that local wines suffered from "horrible preparation" and went to Bordeaux to learn about winemaking. When he returned, he faced resistance from grape growers, but determined to carry on and, "supported by the Duke and Duchesss, *who loaned me their vineyards and cellar,*" Murrieta started to apply the lessons he had learned in France.[122] Espartero's contribution to the enterprise was far from insignificant: he and Jacinta had ten hectares of vineyard with thirty thousand vines as well as fully equipped production facilities with storage capacity for forty thousand litres.[123] After an initial success producing "an excellent wine" that did not go off quickly, as local wines did, Murrieta decided to export his wine, sending fifty barrels to each of Havana and Vera Cruz, Mexico. In March 1851, *La Marina de la Habana* reported the arrival of wine from "the cellars of General ESPARTERO." The reviews were positive: the wine's "purity and the security against adulteration it offers the consumer" would make it a "strong competitor to the French product."[124] Espartero's winemaking activities quickly produced another testament to his incredible popularity. By April 1852, stores in Madrid were reportedly selling fraudulent "wines from the cellars of General Espartero."[125]

Shortly after he was forced into exile, biographies, novels, and books of other kinds about Espartero, often sold on subscription, poured onto the market. In many respects, this was the perfect combination of subject and context. The early 1840s were a significant period of change for Spanish publishing as greater press freedom, new technologies, new readers, and a much more commercial approach produced "a new type of cultural market."[126] These years also saw the appearance of what Raquel Sánchez García describes as "the Romantic book ... full of all sorts of decorations."[127] In this context, Espartero became a publishing phenomenon that combined political motives with commercial opportunism.[128]

The best example was the *Vida militar y política de Espartero* published by Benito Hortelano in 1845. While Hortelano was an *esparterista*, he saw this as primarily a commercial operation. He hired Carlos Massa y Sanguinitti, author of a recent book on Diego de León, to write the biography on commission, but Massa's name did not appear on the title page. Instead, Hortelano chose to emphasize the serial's popular appeal by listing the author as "A Society of Former Militiamen." Hortelano had been a member of the militia; he was also acutely aware of Espartero's popularity among the lower classes of the capital. "General Espartero was in exile in London. The people of Madrid placed their hopes in him, he was their saviour, their idol ... the Messiah of the People. When he was regent a few bad and rachitic portraits had been put out and the people sought them as if they were relics and put them over their beds; some even put candles as if it were the effigy of a saint. The name of this beloved man was uttered with veneration in families and in the workshops."[129] Hortelano also offered subscribers a "full-length portrait" as well as bringing out the instalments on Saturday afternoons when the "artisans" got paid and had money in their pockets. As distributors, he hired militia company messengers, who went right into the workshops, which had the important political side effect of escaping "police vigilance."[130] The strategy worked: Hortelano sold eight thousand subscriptions and made the astounding profit of twenty-eight thousand *duros*. He had had to pawn a cape to buy the paper for the project, but within three months he was able to set up his own press.[131]

Hortelano quickly brought out another Espartero product, the *Synoptic Portrait of the Life of General Espartero*, which he advertised as a "biographical summary of the life and military and political deeds of this celebrated personage who has had such an important role in our recent history." In addition to a portrait of Espartero, it included "the flags of the National Militia and the Army ... and sixteen beautiful lithographs of the actions where he most distinguished himself, with coats of arms and other decorations that allude to the subject that will excite the curiosity of the public, of his countless friends and anyone who wants to have a souvenir of the most notable feats of arms of our last civil war at hand."[132] This too was a success, although it brought Hortelano "persecutions." It also brought him into direct communication with Espartero: he sent the author to London to hand-deliver a deluxe edition and received a thank you letter, which was "everything I desired."[133]

Hortelano was soon approached by the aspiring writer Ildefonso Antonio Bermejo, who proposed a novelized version of Espartero's life. He was too busy, but another publisher took it on and it was published in instalments starting in December 1845 under the title *Espartero, o las profecias de una gitana* [Espartero, or a gypsy woman's prophecies].[134] Bermejo begins by declaring Espartero to be "champion of our time." He also makes it clear that the book is a novel, not a biography. While the book follows the broad outlines of Espartero's life, these take second place to a creaky plot featuring invented characters such as his boyhood friend Eduardo Torres, the Marqués de Mayol, who is a *pícaro*, or trickster figure, and Laura, the daughter of a local noble, with whom he is in love and who appears in Peru and Logroño. There she turns up at Jacinta's house and dies in her arms, her final words being that she should become her successor in Espartero's heart. Espartero is always a liberal and always the strict servant of the law. A gypsy who had told Espartero's fortune in 1814 reappears at the very end of the book. As Jacinta prepares to join her husband in exile, the gypsy predicts Espartero's triumphant return. The novel concludes with Bermejo asking his readers if they believe the gypsy's prediction as he does: "because the Spanish people cannot long endure the yoke of such odious slavery."[135]

Hortelano's was not the first laudatory biography of Espartero. That honour belonged to José Segundo Florez and Wenceslao Ayguals de Izco, republicans who had been staunch critics of Espartero's regency and supported the coup against him.[136] Ayguals was the founder of the Sociedad Literaria publishing house, a leader in producing serialized novels, one of the most significant – and lucrative – innovations of the 1840s.[137] Ayguals's biography of Espartero also came out in instalments, and was promoted as enjoying the collaboration of both Espartero and his wife. It would include a lithograph "copied from the best likeness his lady wife owns" as well as a large number of documents, "unknown to the public, that Espartero himself has promised to send from London." The book itself, "a deluxe, large-format four-volume edition ... with lithographs and engravings," was more expensive than the Sociedad Literaria's usual publications. Ayguals was clearly aiming at an affluent market, and, according to Benito Hortelano, there were not a lot of subscribers. Sales were not helped by the publishers' past hostility to Espartero, which led people to expect that it would be a critical work. The book was also far too expensive for the "artisans" who were the obvious market.[138] Ayguals later brought out a less expensive edition, which sold better.[139]

Whether it was a matter of a guilty conscience or simply profit, Ayguals de Izco came back to Espartero repeatedly. In addition to producing portraits, he published two more books in 1848, the year Espartero returned from exile. The thirty-four-page *Reseña histórica del heróico comportamiento del Pacificador de España, el invicto Espartero durante su emigración en Londres y su regreso a la Corte* claimed to be written by an ex-miliciano and described itself as a "complement" to the existing biographies, something no *esparterista* could do without. It was primarily a compilation of texts framed by an introduction that described Espartero's ability to "show a pure and serene front surrounded by the aureole of holy virtue" in the face of his enemies' insults, and a conclusion congratulating the Spanish people on its enthusiasm over Espartero's return.[140] Ayguals also reflected at length and positively on Espartero in his novel *La Marquesa de Bellaflor, o el niño de la Inclusa*.[141]

Florez and Ayguals were not the only leftists who had serious second thoughts about what had happened in 1843. In 1846, Eduardo Chao, a Democrat who had written for *El Huracán* and *La Guindilla* and who would become development minister during the First Republic, brought out a collection of documents with a brief prologue in which he claims that Espartero was as important to Spain as Washington to the United States and Napoleon to France. It also contains an image of Espartero in London with a warning that some readers might find it "notably disfigured" but that it was an exact copy of the daguerreotype he had had made in London.[142]

Espartero. Su pasado, su presente, su porvenir [Espartero. His Past, Present and Future] was the work of the editors of *El Espectador* and *El Tío Camorra*, the latter of which was also the pseudonym of Juan Martínez Villergas, the most fearsome satirist of the day.[143] It was dedicated to Espartero as a sign of the "support and respect" of the authors, one of whom, Antonio Ribot y Fontseré, had published two viciously satirical poems about Espartero in 1842. This book could not have been more laudatory, repeatedly comparing Espartero to George Washington and Napoleon.[144] Only Espartero could reconcile the differences among Progressives, who had taken him to be their symbol, just as Christians "take the cross as the symbol of our religious beliefs."[145]

Martinez Villergas wrote a second book about Espartero in 1851: *Paralelo entre la vida militar de Espartero y la de Narváez* [Parallel between the military careers of Espartero and Narváez], which would earn him several months in prison for libel, and then exile. The prospectus described the two men as "the head and tail of the Spanish army."[146] The chapter titles made the point clear; for example, "Narváez's expedition to Zaragoza. His boasting ... His manoeuvres to avoid encountering the enemy."[147] While in prison, Martinez Villergas put out feelers to Narváez about a possible pardon. This led to his writing a complete retraction of what he had said in the *Paralelo*, which Narváez insisted he include as the final instalment of the *Desenlace de la Guerra civil*.

Benito Hortelano may have directed his Espartero biography at Madrid's artisans, but the completed book was a massive seventeen hundred pages and ended up being far from cheap. There was another category of Espartero book directed at an audience unable to invest that amount of time and money: a thirty-two-page, anonymously written *Historia del General Baldomero Espartero* published by José María Marés in 1851. This was part of a much bigger phenomenon: the series of contemporary histories and biographies dealing with the period between the Napoleonic invasion and the Moroccan War of the early twentieth century which formed part of the Spanish "bibliothèque bleu." Between sixteen and forty pages in length, these books were often adapted from longer volumes intended for elite audiences. With numerous versions published in Barcelona, Madrid, Palma, and Reus, Espartero was the most popular individual subject, with editions published in 1847, 1851, 1858, 1866, 1874, and 1879.[148]

As the prologue to the 1851 edition explained, it was written "in a simple style [for] the real people, those who lack the means to acquire more voluminous books," and was intended to use the lives of "outstanding men ... to educate the Spanish people."[149] Espartero had made mistakes, but this was inevitable in a "such a dangerous and treacherous career" as politics. Espartero "has a great and magnanimous heart and we are sure his desire has been to make his country happy, and he might have achieved it had he not been surrounded by bad advisers and had there not been a powerful party ready to use the most extraordinary means to overthrow him."[150] The vast majority of the book dealt with the Carlist War; it even included the full text of the Agreement of Vergara. The Revolution of September 1840, the regency, and Espartero's fall take up only a single page. The book ends with Espartero in Logroño, "completely retired from politics," spending his time on gardening and improving grape cultivation, and "talking with people who know about how to strengthen the agriculture of the place where he resides."[151]

Even less expensive, and less demanding on readers, was the *aleluya*. This was a long-established genre that originated in Catalonia, where it was known as an *auca*, in the seventeenth or eighteenth century. It was commercialized nationally in the 1840s, after Joan María Marés moved from Barcelona to Madrid and began to produce what would be the most important series. *Aleluyas* continued to be produced until the 1930s, but they were particularly important between 1850 and 1900. In its commercial form, the *aleluya* measured thirty by forty-two centimetres, was printed on cheap paper, and consisted of eight rows of six crudely drawn images, each accompanied by a small amount of rhyming text in a metre easily committed to memory. (In a country with very high illiteracy rates, keeping text to a minimum was important.) The subject matter included literary works, such foreign ones as *Robinson Crusoe*, *The Count of Monte Cristo*, and *The Wandering Jew* among them, although recent history and biography predominated. With a "strong didactic nature" and sold "by the same blind people who sold popular literature hung from poles during bullfights and festivals ... in small bookstores or in street stalls," *aleluyas* were clearly intended for a lower-class public, precisely the kind of people who were reported to have Espartero "altars" in their homes.[152] In addition, they appealed to children, who would often cut out the images and use them as an early kind of card for collecting and trading. They might even have been used in schools to compensate for the scarcity of books.[153]

The *Historia del General Espartero* was number 58 in the Marés series, but there was at least one other, produced by a Barcelona publisher.[154] After an introduction, "Famous in History will be / the Duke of Victory," the *aleluya* told the story of Espartero's life: there was one square devoted to his service against Napoleon and four to his years in America. With twenty-three, including Luchana and Vergara, the Carlist War received the most attention: "In peace, in outstretched arms / the agreement is made." His involvement in politics to the end of his regency received thirteen, including the bombarding of Barcelona in 1842: "The Duke marches to Barcelona / which is rebelling again." His exile in England, return to Spain in 1848, and retirement in Logroño – "He returns to Spain as a citizen / and lives as a villager" – received four images and the revolution of 1854 two: "With a sincere heart Espartero / returns to govern" and "Facing another reaction / he presents his resignation."[155] The overall impression is of a valiant and victorious soldier, a simple man who does not lust for power and sides with the people.

Other types of Espartero product were available as well. At least two different statues of Espartero were on sale in the summer and fall of 1846.[156] In addition to these commercial products, there were others produced at home by Espartero's admirers. After his return he received letters, poems, and, in one case, even a hand-drawn copy of his portrait.[157]

Espartero had long protested that his great desire was to retire from politics, but given the expectations expressed by so many opponents of the new regime, it is not the least bit surprising that politics would make this difficult. Did he cling to his retirement? Or did he find the lure of public life and political engagement too strong to resist? In the spring of 1851, the Progressives came calling. The events revealed Espartero's continued prestige in the party as well as his willingness to assume only a symbolic role in its activities.

Now shorn of their most radical elements, who had left in 1849 to create the Democratic Party, and facing the increasingly reactionary realities of the post-1848 world, in 1851 Progressives took the decision to rebrand themselves as reformists under the Constitution of 1845. On 13 April 1851, they held a giant meeting in Madrid's Teatro Circo.

Figure 9 A fan writes to Espartero on his return from exile, 1850. Image from Espartero family papers.

The statement accompanying the public announcement of the meeting declared that its goal was for it and "any other opposition party" to come to power "by legal means."[158] After voting unanimously to contest the next election, the delegates turned to choosing the new Electoral Committee. The highlight of the discussion came when Olózaga, the man who had called on the Cortes to save the country from Espartero in 1843, declared that Espartero was "the leader of the Progressive Party … who, after having given his country peace, saving representative institutions and the constitutional throne, would again know how to defend them at all times against all their enemies." This provoked a standing ovation that lasted fifteen minutes. Espartero was then acclaimed honorary party president, despite an agreement that only people present at the meeting would be appointed to the Committee. The "Address" the Committee issued the following day invoked Espartero as the "personification of our party."[159]

Espartero was thrilled, and in his letter to the Committee, which was published in the press, he stated that "it has been many years since I have had such a happy day." To Pascual Madoz, who had chaired the meeting, he wrote that "those spontaneous cheers speak right to my heart," and to his "esteemed friend" Olózaga he stated that he was "fully in support of the manifesto."[160] In an even stronger sign of the rapprochement between the two men, Espartero wrote to the party's Zaragoza committee urging it make Olózaga a candidate.[161]

Figure 10 A fan's drawing of Espartero, 1850. Image from Espartero family papers.

News of Espartero's acceptance of the honorary presidency triggered a flood of letters from local committees, their language testimony to the immense esteem in which he continued to be held by the party's rank and file. They were also helping create the new public image of Espartero as the virtuous and selfless defender of liberty. From Pradoluengo (Burgos): "the born leader of Progress." From Cuenca: "the fortunate mortal whom Providence aided in its grand designs." From Asturias: "the personification of our party ... as head of state he did not violate liberal institutions, preferring ostracism and retirement to perjury." From Huesca, the committee, composed of "five landowners, one lawyer and landowner, one surgeon and landowner, one merchant and landowner, and one doctor and landowner," described Espartero as "rising on the wings of sublime self-denial and virtues ... [to] rekindle Spain's enthusiasm and revive its faith." From Burgos: he was "Great in misfortune and as illustrious exile; greater still in domestic retirement."[162]

Late in 1852, Prime Minister Juan Bravo Murillo attempted to push through a series of measures intended to "eliminate all restraints on the government" and to do so without any debate in parliament. This "institutional coup" brought Moderates and Progressives together, and on 10 December the two groups issued separate but similar manifestos which bore the signatures of most significant political figures.[163] There was nothing in the Progressive manifesto that Espartero could not endorse, but his name does not appear, nor is there any indication he was asked to sign.[164] After failing to force his reforms through, Bravo Murillo resigned, opening a crucial two-year period which saw the ongoing "internal disintegration" of the Moderates, greater freedom of action for the Crown, and a series of "clearly anti-parliamentary cabinets" which also failed to carry through Bravo Murillo's reforms. The queen herself fell into increasing disrepute, with talk of her private immorality and its connection to the reactionary political situation. Her position was further weakened by the criticism of her mother's involvement in shady business dealings, including such politically sensitive ones as railway concessions.[165]

After the government won elections in February 1853, *The Times* reported that the opposition was "grievously disappointed at Espartero not taking advantage of the split in the [Moderate] party and coming forward as a leader. To all advances made him on that subject he invariably replied that ... he would not quit his retreat until the Queen and the country called him from it."[166] In June, British ambassador Lord Howden asserted that in the desolate landscape produced by the extreme fragmentation of the parties, Espartero stood out as "absolutely the only man whose name in an emergency can unite his party for good, reclaiming those who are falling off, curbing those most likely to go further than Espartero ever dreamt of in the time of his political existence."[167]

By the fall of 1853, Moderate and Progressive officers were discussing a coup, and there was increasing talk of forcing Isabel to abdicate. In this context, Espartero's name appeared again. On 26 October, *The Times* reported that the government had decided to pay him twenty-five thousand *duros* in government bonds for the salary he had not collected as regent. Espartero had not asked for the payment and he refused it when it was offered. Was this an attempt by the government to discredit Espartero, whose reputation for honesty and disinterestedness was one of the cornerstones of his popularity? He told his "esteemed friend" Olózaga: "I believe I have fulfilled a sacred duty without making any sacrifice, for I have never aspired to be rich, and in this corner, where I will remain until God disposes otherwise, my needs are few."[168]

The Cortes opened on 29 November but was closed only ten days later after the Senate turned down a government bill on railroad contracts. When the government issued a long list of topics that the press could not discuss, more than two hundred journalists and politicians met at the house of Manuel Gutiérrez de la Concha and produced a joint manifesto. Prime Minister Luis Sartorius responded by ordering suspect generals out of Madrid. O'Donnell refused to go to the Canary Islands, the most remote posting possible, and hid out in Madrid, part of the time in the storeroom of the Progressive paper *Las Novedades*. In Logroño, Espartero was "closely watched."[169] A failed uprising in Zaragoza on 20 February led to more generals being banished and opposition journalists arrested.

In the spring of 1854, the Progressive press was running lengthy accounts of articles in *The Times* and the Paris paper *Le Siècle* about Espartero's possible role in resolving the crisis. According to *Times* correspondent Frederick Hardman, who had served as an officer in the British Legion, he was "the man in Spain most generally respected ... his popularity daily increases, not only with the mob of Madrid ... but with the higher classes and ... with men of most political shades the majority of whom have been at one time or other opposed to him ... At the present time, no man in Spain could form so strong and popular a government as the Duque de la Victoria." And it was precisely his retirement in Logroño that was the basis for this popularity. According to Espartero's friends, this was "part of a system." Participating in partisan politics and "contend[ing] for power with ... the common herd ... who seek to fill their pockets" would have been beneath his dignity and "beneath the high character for probity and independence he has ever enjoyed ... Instead of running after the wheel he waits until it comes around to him." Where foreigners saw "apathy and blamable inactivity," Spaniards saw something very different. For them, Espartero was not a "man of genius or even commanding talent, but an infinitely rarer thing among them, an honest man, sincerely desirous of his country's good and free from personal aims."[170] Espartero was "a haven of refuge" for the queen,[171] but, by May, Hardman was wondering whether Isabel II had waited too long.[172]

After numerous delays and various false starts, the uprising finally came on 28 June. Initially it was strictly a military affair, with the Madrid cavalry under General Domingo Dulce the rebels' only significant force. They were undoubtedly expecting the government to capitulate, but it chose to fight instead. On 30 June, there was a small and inconclusive battle at Vicálvaro, just outside Madrid, after which the rebels marched south. At Manzanares, they were joined by Serrano, who convinced them to issue a more stirring manifesto. Drafted by the twenty-six-year-old future Conservative prime minister Antonio Cánovas del Castillo, the Manifesto of Manzanares demanded the formation of local juntas and offered, among other things, lower taxes, greater press freedom, and the restoration of that Progressive talisman, the National Militia.

As these events were unfurling, on 13 July Espartero received a visit from Antonio de Riego, a nephew of liberal martyr Rafael de Riego, who came as an emissary for Pierre Soulé, the US minister. Soulé was an ardent expansionist whose driving goal in Madrid was to find a way to make Cuba American.[173] He was a supporter of Spain's republicans, but as the political situation became ever tenser, he came to see revolution as the quickest way to realize his Cuban ambition. There were rumours that Soulé had helped bankroll the failed uprisings in Zaragoza in February and Barcelona in April 1854, as well as provoking discontent among the population of Madrid. He had certainly put the sale of Cuba to his republican friends. Getting "the Great Manitou of Liberalism," as he called Espartero, on side was a key objective.[174] The message Riego carried to Logroño said that the United States, "desirous of seeing a truly constitutional government established in Spain, was willing to help the D[uke] with funds from the extent of from ten to twelve millions of *reales* to obtain the above object." Cuba was not mentioned, and there is no evidence that Espartero was aware of Soulé's ulterior motive, but he was not prepared to mortgage himself to the Americans and "refused, saying that dear as liberty was to him, [he] would not have it for his country with foreign aid."[175]

The government was prepared to face down O'Donnell, but it soon found itself dealing with a much more dangerous situation. The rebels had always feared triggering a popular revolution, but now this was what happened, first in Barcelona on 14 July, followed by Valladolid, Valencia, Zaragoza, and other cities. In Madrid, events began on the evening of 17 July, as crowds were leaving a bullfight. News that the government had resigned had the effect of "exploding fireworks in a powder-magazine," and a popular revolt was well under way before Progressive leaders decided to act. Crowds freed prisoners from the Saladero prison, took control of city hall, where they found a large number of guns; and headed for the residences of the most despised public figures, including María Cristina, which were sacked and their contents set on fire. Fernández de los Ríos, whose paper appeared around 11:00 p.m. calling for the revolution to continue, wrote to O'Donnell urging him to come to Madrid and take charge, but he was not prepared to take the risk.[176]

Throughout 18 July, insurgents, some armed with the muskets taken from city hall, most with much older ones or even just stones, fought with soldiers and police. Barricades "like small fortresses" were built across many streets and gamely defended by "café owners, bullfighters, artisans and shop clerks."[177] That night, Fanny Calderón de la Barca heard "shouts of 'Death to Cristina, Death to the Thief, Long Live Espartero'. Pictures of Espartero crown the barricades, and men and women are dancing and singing round them."[178] The next day, two juntas were established, one composed of Progressives and Moderates and a second, more radical one of Democrats and republicans.

With the Royal Palace under virtual siege, Isabel II announced she was going to invite Espartero to form a government.[179] Isabel Burdiel considers this a clever call, combining the available information with "the type of political cunning" characteristic of the queen and her advisors.[180] O'Donnell was in open revolt and had raised the idea of replacing Isabel as ruler, whereas Espartero had never moved from his oft-repeated loyalty. Not that the queen had any respect for him. Three years before, in May 1851, when he wrote her to express his concern over the accident in which María Cristina broke her leg, she passed the letter on to her mother so she could see that "the dead return to life … what a shame it's not he who broke a leg."[181] Now, a desperate Isabel appealed to this "dead man," scribbling a few lines on a small piece of plain paper:

> Espartero: I have never forgotten the good and loyal services you provided during my childhood, and everything you have contributed to supporting my throne. Now that circumstances are difficult, I have not hesitated for a moment to call you to form a new cabinet so that your advice can help me bring this country the happiness my heart so desires. I believe that you will come immediately to offer this service to the nation and to your queen. Isabel.[182]

At mid-afternoon, a messenger set off for Logroño.

8

"The Personification of Liberty," July 1854–July 1856

By the time Isabel's messenger left Madrid bearing the note begging him to save her throne, Espartero had left Logroño for Zaragoza. Following a failed military uprising in that city in February, there had been a number of conspiracies involving Espartero's "personal and political friends," especially Ignacio Gurrea.[1] Since 7 July, Gurrea had been hiding out near Zaragoza on the estate of the financier Juan Bruil, firming up support among the more liberal segments of the garrison by invoking "the immaculate name of the Duke of Victory."[2] When news of the uprising in Barcelona reached Zaragoza early in the morning of 17 July, it sparked immense enthusiasm. After convincing a reluctant Captain General Rivero to call for the creation of a junta, Gurrea went to city hall, where he made a speech in which he offered the participation of Espartero. This calmed the waters and allowed representatives of the city government, the Deputation, and "the people" to select the junta. Espartero was chosen as president – and "Supreme General of the Armies" – with Gurrea as vice-president.[3]

News of events in Zaragoza reached Logroño on 18 July and provoked an uprising there. The revolutionary junta was led by Jacinta's relative José Santa Cruz, whose mission was to carry out the "Duke's main charge .. that we preserve order."[4] Just before he left, Espartero issued a proclamation enjoining *riojanos* to obey the junta and "maintain order, the sure guarantee of our triumph."[5]

The Zaragoza Junta soon found itself in a tense standoff with General Rivero, who had reneged on his initial offer to resign as captain general. On 18 July it sent one of its members, Benito Bernardin, to meet Espartero, who was on his way from Logroño. When he learned of the situation he was furious, and when it was suggested he wait in the village of Ainzón until the situation had been settled, he replied testily: "You mean that the Duke of Victory will have to cross mountains as if he were lost, to hole up in a village because the doors of Zaragoza are shut?" Bernardin eventually persuaded Espartero, who set off for Ainzón while Bernardin returned to Zaragoza. News that Espartero was close to the city led Rivero to resign, and Gurrea replaced him as captain general.[6] The junta now set about preparing for Espartero's triumphal entry. The public announcement of his imminent arrival illustrated his new public image. In addition to the great soldier who had brought peace, he was now "the man who has always been a model of abnegation and purity, the man who has known how to be an obscure citizen in Logroño."[7]

Early on the morning of 20 July, Espartero set out from Alagón, about thirty kilometres from Zaragoza. The town had filled with people from the capital who milled through the streets, "drunk with happiness ... all the façades were decorated with beautiful tapestries and garlands of flowers ... the fair sex competed in showing its joy."[8] Zaragoza itself hummed with preparations for the big day. Mariano Gracia Albacar, who was seven years old at the time, recounted that "some days before 20 July, everything in my house was about washing and starching immaculate white pants and brushing down jackets, some faded by the passing of the years." Could they greet the "Messiah of the Fatherland" in anything else? His father wanted young Mariano "to greet Espartero dressed in uniform, like a man," so the women of the house quickly whipped up a uniform of the militia fire brigade.[9]

Dressed in a black frock coat, Espartero made his much-awaited entry into Zaragoza at 8:00 a.m. on 20 July. Soldiers lined the route through the city centre, and when Espartero dismounted at the house of the Marquis of Nibbiano, he was greeted by an honour guard of soldiers and armed civilians. There he and the mayor got into an open carriage, followed by a cavalry unit and preceded by "an escort of brave and elegant citizens." As the procession passed, people launched "a rain of flowers, candies, crowns, and their own verses" from their balconies. The façade of the house facing Espartero's residence featured "a beautiful placard that was illuminated at night on which one could read 'Long live the first citizen of the Nation / Baldomero Espartero / idol and hope of the people.'"[10] ("[T]rue triumphal arches" were also erected in other parts of the city.)[11] The members of the junta and the city council greeted Espartero at the door. The house was soon overrun by visitors: "above all innumerable citizens of all classes and both sexes, some of whom gave him humble but estimable gifts." Outside, bands played political songs praising Espartero to the skies.[12]

When he finally got a moment's quiet, Espartero drafted two short proclamations. The first was addressed to the people of Zaragoza "You have summoned me to help recover our lost liberty and my heart bursts with joy at being among you again. May the national will be fulfilled; you can always count on the sword of Luchana and the life and reputation of your compatriot for this sacred goal." It was signed simply "Baldomero Espartero." The second, briefer still and without the emotional flourishes of the first, was to the army: "Comrades. The nation is counting on you to recover its lost liberty. We will all do our duty and the fatherland will not forget its own – Espartero."[13] These documents increased the general enthusiasm even further.

The celebrations continued into the night. Much of the city was illuminated and there were improvised dances in a number of squares as bands played patriotic songs mixed with *habaneras*. Small groups of musicians roamed the streets playing *jotas* and a new *copla* was repeated everywhere: "If in Madrid you suspect / a small betrayal / Come, Duke, to Zaragoza / We will make you king of Aragón."[14]

The next morning Espartero attended a service in the Pilar cathedral before heading to the city hall. As he got to his feet, the crowd, which had squeezed into every corner of the building, burst out into a "delirious and touching ovation." Espartero's remarks were brief, but when he said, "in his magnificent tribune's voice," that he "would *not sheathe my sword until we have recovered our lost liberty*," the crowd shuddered "as if hit by an electric current." When a voice shouted that they wanted the same National Militia as in 1843, Espartero replied that "You will have the militia," and the crowd again broke out into cheers and *vivas*.[15]

Isabel's messenger finally caught up with Espartero in Zaragoza on 22 July. At 4:30 the following morning, José Allende Salazar left for Madrid. Those hours in between were undoubtedly filled with lengthy and heated conversations, but about what was said, and by whom, we know nothing. Allende Salazar carried Espartero's written reply as well as a verbal explanation for Espartero's silence and the request that the queen issue "a decree convoking a Constituent Cortes and that the juntas would continue functioning until the Cortes had revealed the national will." That same day, Alfonso Escalante arrived from Madrid, representing the "junta formed ... on the barricades in the midst of gunfire."[16]

The news that Isabel had summoned Espartero initially produced cheers on the barricades, but these soon gave way to "days of much anxiety and even apprehension."[17] Delegations from the various juntas went to the palace, and they were dominated by suspicion that "Espartero had not actually been summoned and that it was all a ruse" to win time for O'Donnell to arrive.[18] As a mark of her good faith, Isabel appointed the popular Evaristo San Miguel as "universal minister."

He did everything he could to calm the waters with the people on the barricades, where Espartero's "portrait, surrounded by the appropriate mottoes," was ubiquitous.[19] Seventeen-year-old Julio Nombela read his poems on the barricades, and when he mentioned Espartero's name, "everyone broke out in frenetic cheers for the great chieftain of liberty."[20] San Miguel urged Espartero to "[c]ut the speeches and fly here because the situation won't last long, and I even less." The notes on Espartero's activities summarized the message as "everything was hanging by a thread."[21]

Allende Salazar arrived in Madrid on 24 July and went directly to the palace. His manner left the people present "frightened by such disrespect." After delivering the letter, Allende Salazar told the queen that Espartero could not receive power from her "'impure' hands … he spoke of the blood of the people, of divine and human vengeance … that [she] had no choice but to turn to universal suffrage so the nation could decide the government it wanted. Until then, Espartero would only receive power from the juntas and he advised [her] to issue a manifesto to the nation, to summon a Constituent Cortes and leave the juntas in place until it had met." San Miguel found himself taking the queen's side, and after "a long debate," he convinced her to accept a modified version of Espartero's demands.[22] According to Fanny Calderón de la Barca, Espartero's letter also demanded that Isabel "dismiss all the individuals of her household, without exception." When she refused, Allende Salazar "broke out into a series of abusive charges against the queen's private conduct," which left her almost speechless. (He later described it as using "severe, very severe language … the kind of language rarely heard in palaces.")[23] Isabel then "burst into tears" and after Allende Salazar left "she impetuously resolved to abdicate rather than submit to the conditions of Espartero or to the insolence of his emissary," although she was convinced to change her mind.[24]

After leaving the palace, Allende Salazar went to the barricades and to the Junta de Salvación. He also went to the Círculo de la Unión, the recently created club of Progressives, Democrats, and some republicans, to ensure that they knew that "today's Espartero is not the Espartero of 1843" and that he was determined to be "the Washington of Spain." The Círculo responded by electing Espartero its honorary president.[25]

After her encounter with Allende Salazar, Isabel sought advice from the French ambassador. Given the situation, with the palace surrounded by barricades, he told her she had no choice but to give in: she should summon Allende Salazar, tell him to write out, in San Miguel's presence, Espartero's demands, and accept them. Resistance would only provide an excuse to dethrone her. The queen agreed, but she made it clear that "anything she signed from now on will be the product of moral violence."[26] She then summoned Allende Salazar to tell him her decision.[27]

After Allende Salazar left for Zaragoza, Isabel issued what came to be known as "the manifesto of deplorable mistakes" after its opening sentence: "Spaniards, a series of deplorable mistakes has … [brought] absurd mistrust between the people and the throne." But now, "a new era" was about to start, with Espartero in power as "the most secure token that your noble aspirations will be realized."[28] It was, Isabel Burdiel says, a white flag of surrender.[29]

Meanwhile, with the situation in Madrid getting increasingly fraught, the Junta de Salvación felt it necessary to invoke Espartero's name, announcing that "very soon they would see at the heart of the capital the illustrious leader to whom the reins of the state will be given."[30] According to the US minister, news of these developments "spread like wildfire throughout the city and created emotions of joy which I would in vain attempt to describe … The confidence of the people in the integrity of General Espartero is so absolute that not the least doubt is entertained but that everything is right and that the national liberties are well secured."[31] That night on the barricades there were concerts and even dances.[32] The barricades around the palace came down, and Isabel was cheered when she appeared on a balcony.

Allende Salazar arrived back in Zaragoza on the 26th, and Espartero and his entourage left Zaragoza for Madrid the following day. We don't know much about what Espartero was doing during these tense days, but his one extant letter, sent on 26 July to General Juan de Zavala in Pamplona, shows him working to consolidate the revolution in the north. Guns were clearly top of mind. Zavala should move "as many as possible" of the "excessive" number of guns in Logroño to Zaragoza, which needed them more. He should also organize and arm a battalion of volunteers, arm the Pamplona National Militia, establish the militia in Guipúzcoa and San Sebastián, and name an officer to carry out the same tasks in Álava and Vizacaya. It was also "essential," he warned, "to be careful of the intrigues of the Jesuits of Loyola."[33]

Espartero and his entourage spent the night of the 28th in Alcalá, where they were met by an emissary of O'Donnell's with the message that he was at Tembleque (Toledo) awaiting orders. This was a key moment. O'Donnell was about one hundred kilometres south of Madrid, and if Espartero had indicated that he would not welcome his presence in the capital he would have had to decide whether he was prepared to fight his way into power. Instead, Espartero replied that he was heading to Madrid "and there I will want to embrace you."[34] It was the first of a number of bad decisions.

Espartero finally entered Madrid at 8 in the morning on 29 July. The reception was ecstatic, frenzied, delirious. The descriptions of the event are all similar. Here is the correspondent for *Blackwood's*, an admirer:

> The road was lined with people for miles without the town ... The garrison was formed up on the right hand outside the Alcalá gate and the National Guard on the left. His approach was announced by a general peal of all the church bells of Madrid. There were triumphal arches, and every balcony in the town was draped with coloured hangings. But the glorious part of the ovation was the unmistakable and irrepressible joy of the people and their demonstrations of affection ... His carriage could hardly proceed for the people that thronged around it, eager to touch his hand or even the skirt of his garment. This continued the whole of the way to the palace, which is at the opposite extremity of the town to that at which he entered, and all the way back to Espartero's temporary residence near the Puerta del Sol. The Duke de la Victoria is far too warm-hearted a man not to be deeply moved by such a reception, and I saw him more than once wipe the tears from his eyes.[35]

Fanny Calderón de la Barca, the wife of a Moderate, took a more jaundiced view. "Several officers ... and a company of unwashed patriots, the defenders of the barricades," surrounded Espartero's carriage. "He opened his paternal arms as if he would gladly have taken the whole population to his heart in one embrace."[36] Karl Marx devoted one of his articles for the *New York Tribune* to Espartero, whom he described as "one of those traditional men whom the people are wont to take upon their backs at moments of social crises, and whom, like the ill-natured old fellow that obstinately clasped his legs about the neck of Sindbad the sailor, they afterward find it difficult to get rid of ... The Espartero who, on the 29th of July, held his triumphant entrance into Madrid, was no real man; he was a ghost, a name, a reminiscence."[37]

Marx could not hear the cheers of the crowds that thronged the streets, but even those who could did not know what motivated them. Fortunately, many Spaniards wrote to Espartero during the revolution, and these letters give us a clear look at what was behind the enthusiasm. Many saw the events of 1854 in the context of those of 1843 and the subsequent repression, which they had often suffered directly. For them, Espartero was not the tyrant excoriated by the political elites and the press. And to the extent that they might have ever believed that, the

Figure 11 Espartero enters Madrid, July 1854.
Image from the personal collection of the author.

rapid repentance of people like Pascual Madoz and Wenceslao Ayguals de Izco both confirmed popular faith in the "Peacemaker" and built it anew. Espartero was the man of peace and the symbol of freedom, but, as the Zaragoza proclamation had made clear, he was now also the embodiment of honesty and disinterestedness, the man who had given up power, endured exile, and withdrawn to private life in a small, provincial city.

For the new city government of the Puerto de Santa María, which was the same one that had seen Espartero off when he went into exile, Espartero was the vehicle for a renewed contract between the Crown and the people. Calling on "the foremost champion of Spanish Liberty, the token that … symbolizes the institutions for which the Spanish people yearn" was proof of the queen's "maternal solicitude."[38] For the municipal government of Calatayud, Espartero was "unvanquished leader and peacemaker" whose presence would guarantee the victory of the movement against the "immoral and insatiable clique" that had been ruling the country.[39] And in offering Espartero command of their battalion, the National Militia of Jaen described how he was known to young and old alike. While the latter remembered the victories of the Carlist War, the former "have read about your name always connected to an honourable or glorious action and have become accustomed to blessing it."[40]

For some, all of this was intensely personal. Cristobal de ____ from Granada lost "my fortune and my position in the ill-fated year of '43, my posting in '44," as well as suffering "prison in '48 and my confinement in the Cádiz jail awaiting transportation to the Philippines, all the horrible persecution I have suffered constantly and the misery to which my family has been reduced." But now, the fate of the country was in the hands of the "Castilian Cincinnatus who ... had known how to voluntarily relegate himself to a corner of the peninsula and deliver himself to the simple pleasures of private life."[41] José María Puig y Salazar, from Adra (Almería), claimed to have been hit in the leg by the last shot fired against the Militia of Madrid by the "traitorous coalition in 1843" and then to have "left his sickbed, dragging his leg to console the Duchess in those critical days." For him, Espartero was "the most Spanish, the most eminent, the purest of Spaniards ... a modest man of sublime self-denial."[42] The lifelong liberal and sixty-five-year-old parish priest of the village of Calzadilla de los Barros (Badajoz), Vicente Pardo y Mendoza, was another. His political ideas had been "public since 1812," and in 1842 he had received a diploma from Espartero for his role in "the glorious rising of September 1840." He also suffered for his liberalism, having lost his savings "due to the many, ongoing persecutions and intrigues in both the ecclesiastical and civil courts." The recent revolution, and especially Espartero's having been called to power, had inaugurated "a new era of happiness"; all he needed in order to live out his days happily was to see Spaniards "enjoying forever a rational, just, and holy liberty."[43]

Even people on the left saw in Espartero the symbol of the revolution and of liberty. For Fernando Garrido, Espartero was nothing less than a providential figure, "called to personify the revolution, to save it and to consolidate it." He had the chance to be Spain's George Washington. Garrido's was a revolutionary program: push Isabel II from the throne and have the National Assembly install Espartero as the head of an "an executive power that accepts its mission of regeneration with all its consequences."[44]

Espartero reached the palace at 9, where he met briefly with Isabel and her husband. According to a confidential report sent to Alejandro

Figure 12 "Let the national will be done," 1854. Original in the library of the Fundación Sancho el Sabio Fundazioa (Vitoria-Gasteiz)

Franchi, the chargé of the Holy See, "the dynastic question was completely resolved ... the news about the ecclesiastical or religious question is not so good." He also spent a half hour with the princess, who was in bed. Espartero returned to the palace that night to take the oath as prime minister but left without kissing the king's hand.[45] Between these two visits, he was at the house of Manuel Matheu, just off the Puerta del Sol. There he was joined by O'Donnell, who had arrived in Madrid discreetly, by train. What they discussed is unknown, but the two men embraced in the main salon and then did so again on a balcony. As Espartero repeated his famous slogan, "Let the national will be done," the crowd in the street "erupted into frenzied cheers for the idolized champion of liberty."[46]

Espartero returned to the palace at 9:00 the next evening to present his ministers, a mixture of Progressives and "Puritans," a group on the left of the Moderates who wanted a more open political system. O'Donnell got the War Ministry. He was also promoted to captain general. Isabel balked on hearing that Allende Salazar would be the navy minister, but soon backed down. Before the ministers arrived, Espartero reminded Isabel of his affection for her: "he loved her like a daughter, she was a little fat but *pretty*, he would do whatever he could to make her happy, and was sorry there was one thing he could not do for her ... *I am sorry you are married to the king*." The ministers arrived at 10:30; Allende Salazar again scandalized those present by adding that he swore to defend the rights of the people and then telling the queen that he was part of the cabinet for Espartero, not for her.[47]

With Espartero at the head of the government, albeit in coalition with O'Donnell, the question became whether the revolution was over or whether it was really just beginning. What would he do with the tremendous popularity he enjoyed and the power he held in his hands? Did he even know himself?

Unfortunately, we have no sources that can help answer these questions. As always, Espartero left no explanations of his behaviour, and his public pronouncements were short on detail. Unlike the years of the regency, when Arthur Aston was a trusted confidant, Lord Howden, who had been British ambassador since 1850, did not have a close relationship with Espartero, nor did he hold him in much esteem.[48] On the other hand, Isabel relied on Howden for advice, and this put him in a position to learn about the relationship between the queen and her prime minister.

With the new government in place, it fell to Espartero to bring normality to the capital. On 31 July, Casimiro Rufino Ruiz, head of the Junta de Salvación for the Pontejos and Plaza Mayor districts, informed

Espartero that following his appointment as prime minister, he had ordered forty-four barricades taken down and "sent the citizens manning them, mostly waiters and shop clerks, to their homes."[49] Espartero toured the barricades on 31 July and 1 August. His presence was magical. No sooner did he appear at a barricade than the people there "left for their homes, as if Espartero's mere presence among them were enough to make them believe that liberty was guaranteed."[50] On 2 August, accompanied by the Junta de Salvación, he presided over a parade from the balcony of the main post office. The junta issued a proclamation telling the people of Madrid that it was time to return to their homes. Espartero's brief speech received "an immense acclamation."[51]

Almost immediately, the cabinet was divided over a crucial question: should the Constituent Cortes be elected using the 1837 or the 1845 electoral law? The more conservative members wanted the latter, the more left-wing ones the former. The result was a compromise: the 1837 electoral law was chosen, but O'Donnell's price was guaranteeing Isabel's future. The decree convoking the Cortes made it clear that the dynasty was something "that cannot be questioned and about which the government will admit no ... debate."[52] During the controversy, Howden went to see Espartero at the request of one of his ministers and found him "so excited, so elated and so confident of the support of the People as to pay little attention to what may appear to him as the minor details of government." He was adamant that the Cortes would not have a senate and that under no circumstances would he fire on the people; if it came to that, "he would retire to unconquered Aragón where he would raise his standard and there do what ... his ardent love of his country enjoined him to do."[53]

The decree gave Espartero his first experience of having the "people" protest rather than cheer him on. A delegation from the Círculo de la Unión visited him to complain and received "a weak and evasive answer." A few days later, a delegation from another club went to protest the exclusion of the dynastic question. Espartero *"immediately"* broke off a cabinet meeting to receive them and gave them "the incredible answer that there was no occasion to take the matter to heart, as it was of little consequence, *it being only the opinion of the government.*"[54] He proved far stronger in his dealings with the queen. When he went to the palace to demand wholesale changes in her household, he faced down her objections with "the greatest coldness ... reminding her that when he came to Madrid, the Throne was on its last legs."[55]

As symbol of the corruption of the former regime, María Cristina was also a major issue. She wanted to leave Spain, but many revolutionaries, especially the Democrats, wanted her put on trial. At her request, Lord Howden agreed to intervene with Espartero, who told him that while he personally wanted to allow her to depart, María Cristina's demands, that she have a coach for her and her family and a separate one for her household, "would attract dangerous attention," and "he could not answer for what might happen to her in leaving Madrid."[56] In the end, the government agreed to arrange a dignified departure on 28 August. The French ambassador attributed Espartero's change of heart to having his house invaded by radicals demanding that María Cristina be put on trial. The next day, Espartero issued a proclamation addressed to the "people of Madrid" and the militia, defending the decision, which bore his name alone. The government "had done what it had promised: that *María Cristina would not leave furtively by day or by night*; it had also wanted to spare the Cortes"[57] from dealing with the issue. The decision triggered a return to the barricades accompanied by cries of "death" to O'Donnell and to Espartero, but the militia remained loyal and did its job of containing radicalism. Within four days, the political clubs, including the Círculo de la Unión, which had made Espartero its president, were banned and the Junta de la Salvación dissolved.

Fernando Garrido undoubtedly spoke for many radicals when he called the departure of María Cristina the defeat of the revolution. (Rico y Amat, a conservative, said exactly the same.) He still refused to question Espartero's intentions, but "everyone saw in that act the complete abdication of this man and his party."[58] As for Espartero himself, his deep-seated royalism and dynastic loyalty had won out over the intoxication of being a revolutionary idol.

Elections for the Constituent Cortes took place on 4 to 6 October, although in some places they were delayed by cholera outbreaks. The most significant development was the appearance of candidacies headed by Espartero or O'Donnell bearing the name Liberal Union. This itself was a reflection of the strong internal divisions among Moderates and Progressives, and especially the latter, who were not even able to put out a common manifesto. Carried out against a backdrop of food shortages, cholera, and social conflict in urban and rural areas, including riots against the consumption tax, and unionization drives, especially in Barcelona, the campaign was. "intense and hard fought." It also saw relatively little government interference, and turnout was high, as some 70 per cent of the eligible voters cast their ballot.[59] Making sense of the results was not easy. *La Iberia* divided the deputies into five "factions," although it did not dare suggest how many belonged to each.[60] Isabel Burdiel interprets the results as a handful of Moderates and some twenty Democrats, with Unionists and Progressives making up the rest, "with unclear boundaries and a certain Progressive majority."[61]

Espartero was selected as a candidate in a number of provinces. In Ciudad Real he headed the ticket for the Liberal Union, which included the neo-Catholic Cándido Nocedal, while in Seville he headed the Progressive-Democratic list.[62] He was elected in six provinces: Cádiz, Ciudad Real, Logroño, Málaga, Murcia, and Zaragoza. In Cádiz and Zaragoza, he received an astonishing 98 per cent of the votes cast. He chose to represent Zaragoza. His letter to the voters, which appeared in the city's newspapers as well as the *Boletín Oficial*, stuck to his tried and true slogans and avoided even hinting at any specific policies. "As deputy for this province I will demand and vote for the national will to be done ... that is the only way we will succeed in cementing the durable foundation of liberty, order, and public happiness."[63]

Between the elections and the opening of the Cortes, there was much discussion of Espartero's intentions, especially regarding the future of the monarchy, something only encouraged by what Howden considered the "remarkable" fact that "neither in speeches, toasts or his innumerable communications with Deputations" had Espartero "ever committed himself directly or personally to the conservation of the monarchy."[64] After the elections, conservative papers like *La Nación* and *El Diario Español* revived charges from the regency about Espartero's ambitions: this time that he wanted to become regent again, or even president of a republic, and the *Times of London* published a report by Hardman, whom the British ambassador called "the bosom friend" of Ignacio Gurrea, that people were placing bets over what Espartero really had in mind.[65]

The Cortes began its sessions on 8 November. They opened with a speech from the queen, although there had been speculation about whether or not this tradition would be maintained. On the whole, she was well received. Espartero's continued silence on the queen's future led the conservative press to demand that he clarify his position. The clearest statement, and it wasn't particularly clear, came in an interview with the deputy from Valencia, Fermín Gonzalo Morón, in which Espartero merely repeated the government's program: "consolidate liberty ... fulfil the program of the throne and the people ... never to pass laws only by royal order and govern with the majority of the Cortes so the national will may be done."[66] Concerned observers were left looking for "auguries," and one came on 17 November, when Allende Salazar made an important speech in which he declared himself a supporter of the Crown. Coming from "the intimate friend of Marshal Espartero, *the Linage of the present day,"* as Howden called him, this was truly consequential.[67]

Four days later, however, Espartero suddenly and unexpectedly announced his resignation as prime minister. There had been rumours that he might do so, but the actual act took everyone by surprise. His explanation was that he had accepted the queen's request to take power on condition that he be able to step down once the Cortes were in session. Now he was leaving her "with full freedom to choose her responsible councillors, in conformity with parliamentary practice."[68] As he left, he received "a complete ovation from the Galleries and the Entrances of the Chamber, though the Chamber itself seemed struck with surprise."[69] When the vote for president of the Cortes came on 28 November, Espartero won a massive majority, with 238 of the 255 votes cast, and the next day he formed a new cabinet, which was almost identical to its predecessor.[70]

On 30 November, Moderates and some Progressives introduced a motion declaring "the constitutional throne of Isabel II ... one of the foundations" of the new political order. The subsequent debate revealed what Isabel Burdiel calls the Progressives' "monarchist illusion": the belief that Spain and the Bourbon monarchy were inseparable and that an enduring constitutional system could be realized by "surrounding the monarchy with the nation: an elected Congress and Senate, popular municipal and provincial governments, the militia, etc." This would force the Crown to "submit to the representative powers which, under free elections, they believed, would always return a Progressive majority."[71] After San Miguel gave a major speech supporting the motion, Espartero rose to make his long-awaited public statement. It was all of eleven words long: "Gentlemen, the government agrees with the motion that has been presented." The motion passed 194 to 19.[72] That night, the cabinet called on the queen. She expressed her unhappiness that Espartero had waited so long to state his support, which earned her a strong reply: "the Marshal, with a degree of address – I will not use the stronger word employed to me – which astonished the Ministers replied, 'the reason, Madam ... is I thought there never could be any question in the mind of anybody on the matter.'"[73]

On 2 December, the government was defeated on a minor question, but it was enough for Espartero to submit his resignation. The next day, he and Howden had a lengthy meeting, and the conversation gives a rare insight into Espartero's thoughts. He had always planned to return to Logroño once "the monarchical principle had been consigned as an article in the constitution," and the recent Cortes vote had settled the question earlier than anticipated. Having served as regent, he was not prepared to "submit to the insults of the Chamber"; the defeat was only the first "of a series of humiliations"; "the vote against him ... was a shame, an injustice, a gross indecency"; and this repeated lack of respect would "destroy all his power of good." He repeated three times that "it was impossible to govern" with the Cortes that had been elected and that the only solution was one "to which he would never have recourse as it would mean violating the law." In the end, Espartero did revoke his resignation, although he repeated "his intention of 'returning to his garden at Logroño' once the Constitution is voted."[74]

During one of these conversations, Espartero surprised Howden by talking about money: "the post of Minister was not only hateful to his nature but ruinous to his pocket, and his tastes were so entirely opposed to his destiny that he was the most unhappy man alive." Shortly afterwards, Howden suggested to the finance minister that Espartero be given some land belonging to the Crown or the nation. Such a measure, he said, would please both Espartero and his wife: *"a Lady of remarkable intelligence in the management of pecuniary matters and who has great influence over her husband."*[75] This was a serious misreading of both their characters. Espartero's comment about the conflict between his tastes and his destiny spoke to his preference for a quiet life over the stresses and obligations of power. Some of this comes through in Fanny de la Barca's description of Espartero at a banquet given by the French ambassador in late August.

> Divested of his uniform and multitudinous crosses, he would appear an ordinary looking individual, rather in feeble health, devoid of strength either moral or physical. His manners are grave, his features in no way remarkable: his hair dyed dark, and rather closely cropped. In conversation, he is far from brilliant, and except that he is himself a man of the people, one looks in vain for the qualities which have made him the hero of the popular cause ... Espartero spoke little, and ate less, and looked sleepy and suffering.[76]

One area where Espartero did try to take the initiative was doing away with conscription. (In exile, he had talked about "disbanding [the army] in mass, and at once and replacing it with 40 or 50,000 men in a modern army.")[77] He had a plan to replace conscription with voluntary enlistment, including "some fund or provision for the soldier after his time of enlistment" as an inducement. And to make up for an anticipated shortfall, there would be a Provincial Militia that would not take men away from their jobs.[78] In the end, Espartero abandoned his plan, and the bill that was presented to the Cortes, and passed, called for twenty-five thousand men to be drafted in 1855.[79]

Jacinta did not arrive in Madrid until the end of November. (Baldomero skipped a banquet for the general staff of the militia to receive her.)[80] She was immediately visited by "all classes of Madrid society" and the militia provided "a magnificent serenade."[81] She also returned to her position as lady of honour to the queen.[82] Jacinta's most prominent activities were philanthropic. Even before arriving in the capital, she sent a letter to the press announcing that she was contributing four thousand *reales* to the subscription to relieve "misfortunes that have filled this heroic city with mourning."[83] She returned to assisting the Inclusa and the Colegio de la Paz as she had during the regency. She was part of the organizing committee for the 1855 raffle,[84] and, along with the Marquise of Malpica and the Countess of Montijo, sold tickets for a masked ball fundraiser. She also auctioned "fruits from her land and wine from her harvest."[85] At Easter she was "begging" in the San José church, raising twelve thousand *reales* for "residents of charitable establishments."[86] She also became the "protector" of the bandurria teacher Miguyel Echevarria, who had lost his sight, and arranged for an audience with the queen, who promised to support him and his family.[87] In June, she went north the take the waters.[88] Back in Madrid in the fall, she was one of the patrons of an event to raise money for the victims of the cholera outbreak and "the wounded at Sebastopol,"[89] and took two government ministers on a tour of the Lancastrian school.[90] She again sold tickets for the fundraiser for the Inclusa in 1856.[91] Then, on 2 July, she left for Logroño to escape Madrid's summer heat.[92] She would never return to the capital.

The government had yet to deliver on most of the major demands of the revolution, and unhappiness among Espartero's supporters was growing. An excellent example of this rising disappointment came in a petition sent at the end of December 1854 by 124 "Spanish citizens" from Tarragona who asked what they had gained since the revolution. The militia "was being organized slowly and had few arms; the country is holding its breath to hear the finance minister confirm the consumption tax remains suspended … a draft is looming … the country is disgusted by this so-called Liberal Union, which it sees as nothing more than the liberticide coalition of 1843." Espartero should follow his "patriotic impulses" and not fear that "exalted liberals like them would produce anarchy,"[93] but this was precisely something Espartero did fear. Fernández de los Ríos was much closer to the mark when he wrote that

Espartero "wanted liberty because he loved the people, but the noise of liberty repelled him because, above all, he was a soldier who loved discipline, and was also proud of being a loyal monarchist."[94]

These questions affected the entire country, but in Catalonia there was the additional issue of labour unrest. Despite this, the region's industrial working class were particularly persistent *esparteristas*. Whatever discredit the events of November 1842 had brought was long forgotten, and well into 1855 support for Espartero and demands for the right to organize coexisted easily.

In July 1854, workers in Sallent issued a proclamation criticizing their employers' "egotism and greed and neglect for what is most sacred, the good salary of the worker, the real producer." It concluded with "vivas" to the Duke of Victory, "liberty properly understood," and "the organization of labour." Pascual Madoz, who was named civil governor of Barcelona at the beginning of August, held a meeting with some eight hundred workers, where he was struck by "the influence of the magic name of the Duke of Victory."[95] The popular songs collected by Josep Termes, including *coplas* such as "Because they deceive us / two pillars have been erected / one is Espartero / the other is the union," demonstrate that Espartero's popularity persisted until at least the end of 1854.[96]

Other evidence demonstrates that this support remained strong in 1855. In February, a group of women in Barcelona were arrested for supposed political activity, and while they were being taken to jail one shouted that they were being jailed "for having said 'Long live Espartero!'" Even the general strike in Barcelona and surrounding towns which started on 2 July in response to Captain General Zapatero's banning of unions began with the slogan "Espartero, Liberty, Association or Death, Bread and Work." In Vic, strikers appeared in the main square with a flag and a portrait of Espartero.[97]

Gurrea and Madoz convinced a reluctant Espartero to meet with a delegation of strikers. While they were waiting for news of the meeting, on 5 July the strike commission told their followers not to take any action until the delegation had convinced the government and the "always beloved Duke of Victory" of the need to establish a joint committee to resolve the issues.[98] At the meeting, Espartero reportedly "demonstrat[ed] his disgust at the events [in Barcelona] and that he had nothing to say to the representatives of a city in revolt. His last words were: 'When the workers return to work I will do them justice because the sons of the people have always been my favourite children.'"[99] This encounter became the subject of a *romance* which portrayed the workers as humble supplicants before an Espartero whom "the workers trust," although he does not reply when they state their demands: "only to live ... like honest artisans from the sweat of their brows" and a law establishing arbitration committees with representatives of workers and employers with "a third person, different from both."[100]

Believing that Espartero's "word would have an effect on the Catalans," the cabinet decided to send Colonel Sarabia, one of his aides-de-camp, with a letter which had been written for Espartero. Sarabia got the strikers to return to work in return for a promise that the Cortes would discuss a law legalizing unions.[101] Espartero also sent a letter to the captain general to be published in the press. It was full of the paternalist language he used when speaking of workers. They must heed his "paternal voice." Until the government proposed legislation to improve "the workers' lot," they must "quietly await the decision of the Cortes in their homes." He would hear "respectful complaints of all classes and all citizens" but he would also "severely punish all who break the law, conspire against liberty and public order, or ignore the authority of the Cortes and the constitutional throne of our queen."[102]

As legislation that satisfied the workers did not materialize, their confidence in Espartero began to dim. One manifesto in January 1856 denounced him, along with O'Donnell, as "so-called defenders of the people."[103] Yet, when news of Espartero's resignation in July 1856 reached Catalonia, it provoked popular uprisings in Barcelona and other industrial towns.[104]

Work on the new constitution began on 11 December 1854 when a seven-man committee was appointed to create a set of principles. The list it presented on 13 January, especially the proposal leaving the Crown with the power to veto laws passed by parliament, proved another major disappointment from the perspective of the July days. This was passed by a slim majority of 130 to 107. In contrast, the opening declaration, that sovereignty resided "essentially" in the nation, received overwhelming support.[105]

On 21 January, Pascual Madoz was named finance minister. Madoz, who represented Barcelona, was one of those Progressives who had turned against Espartero in 1843 only to repent soon thereafter; he accepted this crucial cabinet position largely as a way of atoning "for the error I made in 1843."[106] Determined to confront the government's dire financial position, he quickly announced his major initiative: a new law that would extend the 1837 Mendizábal disentailment by selling the properties still owned by the Church, but also go beyond it by proposing to sell lands belonging to the country's towns and cities.[107] The renewed attack on Church lands ran into the queen's religious scruples, and she signed the bill that was going to be sent to the Cortes only after some very tough talk from Espartero. According to the papal chargé, "he grabbed the pen and shouted, 'I am not going to force your hand as you said others did'" – an allusion to the claim that toppled Olózaga in 1843 – "'but you will sign anyway because if you do not I will abandon you.'" When Isabel said that she feared eternal damnation, he said she was crazy.[108]

That same day, the Cortes began debating Article 2 of the Constitution: "The nation obligates itself to maintaining the practice and ministers of the Catholic religion, which Spaniards profess, but no foreigner may be prosecuted (civilly) for his beliefs so long as he commits no public acts against the [Catholic] religion." Isabel wasted little time in making her opposition clear, keeping cabinet papers and passing them on to her *camarilla*. The cabinet sent Espartero to tell her that her behaviour was unacceptable. He performed his task, in Howden's words, "as an honourable man and a constitutional statesman, telling Her Majesty that ... for the future" her ministers would not be able "to leave with Her any papers on which they came to take Her Majesty's orders." The only exception would be the draft of the Constitution: since that document might well determine the fate of the throne, they felt she was entitled to seek advice.[109]

The debates on Article 2 were long and heated. Outside the Cortes, Catholics mobilized to bring pressure on the queen. The final vote came early on the morning of 1 March, and the article passed 200 to 52.[110] Espartero did not speak during the debate and, if he was still in the chamber when the vote was taken, he voted neither for nor against. He had met with Franchi in August and "showed a strong desire to protect the Catholic religion ... that the religion prosper among the Spanish people and that required a full agreement with the Holy See."[111]

The year 1855 was the first time since the revolution that Spaniards had the opportunity to celebrate 27 February: San Baldomero, Espartero's birthday and saint's day. And celebrate it they did, especially in Catalonia. In Barcelona, there were special performances in two theatres; at one a "large number of specially written poems dedicated to the illustrious General ESPARTERO" were distributed.[112] In Tortosa (Tarragona), the Círculo Popular held its inaugural meeting on 27 February and decided that, as no one but Espartero "could symbolize the[ir] great ideals of liberty, tolerance, unity, and enlightenment," to name him honorary president.[113]

In Huelva, San Baldomero was a "day of enthusiastic celebration." The militia paraded through the streets and the band played "happy and martial hymns ... that opened hearts which had lived the most horrific oppression of eleven consecutive years. Espartero's portrait was paraded through the illuminated streets of the city."[114] In Salamanca, in addition to marching bands, illuminations, and fireworks, the flag was raised over city hall, "as if it were a national holiday [or] the queen's birthday," *La España*'s correspondent wrote indignantly.[115] Verín (Orense) began its celebrations with fireworks at dawn; there was a *besamanos* for the militia with more fireworks at noon, and at 8:00 in the evening the band of the Second Battalion "paraded through the streets playing patriotic hymns" as still more fireworks went off. Wenceslao Suárez Ponte, who sent this account to Espartero, also requested he send "a few lines to animate this battalion ... which is burning with desire to see Your Excellency's autograph," testimony to the reverence he inspired in so many Spaniards.[116]

The militia became the centre of political concern in March. On the 27th, a delegation of militia commanders called on Espartero to demand he dismiss four of his ministers, but he cut them off immediately. Speaking "energetically," he told them that "the Cortes alone" could suggest that the monarch change the government. The cabinet then agreed with Madoz's proposal to present a bill prohibiting the militia from "discussing or making public statements about politics or anything else not directly related to that organization."[117] The debates dragged on until 11 April, with the large crowds outside the parliament building adding to the tension.[118] Espartero spoke on 4 April. It was one of his longer speeches and was marked by his passionate defence of, and identification with, the militia. It was, he said, "my product," and he loved it "as a tender father." He would support the bill to defend the militia, and Spain's freedoms, "from the claws of our enemies."[119] The bill passed by 165 to 28.

On 28 April, Espartero had a "long conversation" with Isabel about the newly passed disentailment law. She chose to follow the advice the papal chargé had given her earlier that day and refused to sign. An angry Espartero returned to Madrid and summoned the cabinet, which decided to resign. The next day, the entire cabinet, accompanied by the speaker and vice-presidents of the Cortes, went to Aranjuez to convince the monarch to change her mind. (The ministers travelled *"with their resignations duly drawn out and signed in their pockets."*) Isabel held out gamely but finally signed after being advised by the French ambassador to do so. She later complained that her ministers, *"especially Espartero ... tell me nothing about matters of state; they told me I am crazy and that's how they treat me."*[120] Espartero would have another showdown with Isabel in September, when the government issued decrees giving the government control of appointments to the staff of the Royal Palace. After O'Donnell failed to get the queen to sign, Espartero went to Aranjuez himself and "chastised the queen for yielding to influences that constantly put her in conflict with her responsible councillors and could compromise her throne and her person." Isabel signed the decrees the next day.[121]

In June, Madoz's plan to collect taxes in advance and his decrees announcing major changes to the militia provoked serious protests among the capital's *milicianos* that led to a number of ministers resigning and the controversial decrees being dropped.[122] The names of the new ministers, including Espartero's admirer the Zaragoza financier Juan Bruil at Finance, were announced on 8 June. Howden was shocked by the way the changes were made, putting "the Throne ... out of the question altogether. The resignations of the Ministers were made in the most unvarnished manner to the Duke of Victory alone, the Duke of Victory accepted them in precisely the same manner and formed his new ministry almost openly at his house ... he then went by train to Aranjuez and returned with the decree signed."[123] There were demands in the Cortes that Espartero explain what had happened; he replied with what was undoubtedly the longest speech of his parliamentary career. (Howden described it as "not over wise.")[124] He began by denying that the cabinet had fallen: the five ministers who left had done so because "they were fed up with ... the harsh and unjust attacks directed at them." The new appointments were made strictly by the book, and, even with the changes in personnel, the government's program remained unchanged. "As a result, there has been no offence to parliament." Then Espartero looked into the past. Undoubtedly intended as a call to Progressive unity, this part of his speech reflected his self-importance and self-image as the true voice and guardian of Spanish constitutionalism. Unlike a real parliamentarian, "I speak from the heart, not the head," his only eloquence "the art of moving soldiers' hearts." During the civil war, "I imagined myself as more than a man, I imagined myself protected by the angel of liberty; I imagined myself the exterminating angel of tyranny." Then he was "condemned to ostracism," but his enemies, "who are the enemies of liberty," ordered he be shot on sight if he returned. Spain had suffered "the worst of despotisms" because of "our disunity, our ambitions, our resentments and ... the anarchy of the Cortes of 1843 ... [that] anarchy was the reason liberty died in Spain. I pray to heaven that ... the Cortes of 1855 are not a second edition of the Cortes of 1843." After José Olózaga criticized his remarks about the Cortes of 1843, Espartero rose again to explain that he had invoked the past only as a warning against disunity, "so that we will all try to avoid the same pitfalls."[125]

After the Cortes approved the final article of the new constitution on 30 June, Espartero announced his resignation as head of the government without consulting his cabinet or even Jacinta. He was, he said, unwell, and, in any case, he had completed the mission he had assumed the previous year. "[S]urprised and affected at this totally unexpected proceeding," Isabel vainly tried to convince him to remain. She then sent for O'Donnell, who, after "a long conference," got Espartero to withdraw his resignation. Meanwhile, the news had created "an impression of surprise and alarm throughout Madrid impossible to describe." Espartero frequently threatened to resign, but on previous occasions these threats had come after a crisis or what he took to be a personal insult. Not this time. Loftus Charles Otway, the British chargé, felt that the real reason was a combination of frustration caused by the obstructionism of the Cortes, "the feeling of being both morally and physically totally unfit for the situation in which accident has placed him," and his "inherent apathy and love of ease."[126] A few weeks later, Otway learned "from the very best authority" that "there is nothing he more ardently desires than to retire from public life and return to his domestic concerns at Logroño."[127]

Espartero and O'Donnell were now the only two survivors from the cabinet of 29 July 1854, but their relative positions had changed since the heady atmosphere of Espartero's triumphant return to Madrid. O'Donnell had added the foreign affairs portfolio to that of war, but more importantly, Espartero was becoming increasingly deferential, even when it meant undercutting his own supporters.

As an institution symbolic of revolution, the militia was a prime battlefield. Defanging it had been a goal of O'Donnell's from the outset. When the government ordered expulsions from the militia in August, there were rumblings over Espartero's lack of response.[128] On 7 November, during the debate on the constitutional provision of civil equality and the eligibility of all Spaniards for public employment, a republican deputy moved an amendment to include positions in the Royal Palace. O'Donnell spoke against it, and Espartero backed him, denouncing the amendment as "contrary to the monarchy and declaring that nobody had the the right to doubt his fidelity to Queen Isabel II."[129] And in December, when the opposition proposed to censure O'Donnell for the repression of an uprising in Zaragoza, Espartero, who was not in the chamber, rushed to the Cortes so that he could "declare his support generously and frankly."[130] O'Donnell even felt himself strong enough to dismiss Ignacio Gurrea as Captain General of Zaragoza.[131]

Tensions over the *consumos* tax rose again in January 1856. On 7 January, some members of the militia unit guarding the Cortes fired shots in the air outside the building, and one *miliciano* prevented deputies from entering or leaving the chamber, even pointing his rifle at Espartero when he arrived. Espartero responded to the situation with one of his grandiloquent speeches: he would "restore the public tranquillity that was disturbed a few minutes ago or die in the attempt. (Great applause) The Cortes may work in peace because, whether on these benches or in the streets, this citizen soldier will do his duty ... Goodbye gentlemen."[132] When he returned to the chamber, he assured the deputies that the incident had been nothing more than "one or two drunken men" in the unit on duty, who would be punished. Should the Cortes be threatened again, "I will fly here to ... die in its defence."[133] In a few months, he would have the chance to put those words to the test.

These events were quickly followed by yet another cabinet shuffle. The most important change would be the elevation of Patricio de la Escosura, a former Moderate who had served in one of Narváez's ministries before switching to the Progressives, to the Interior Ministry. Espartero introduced his new cabinet to parliament in a statement which was both characteristically short and full of generalities, although now the maintenance of order was added to the usual list.[134] Práxedes Mateo Sagasta moved a motion rejecting Espartero's statement, but Espartero left it to O'Donnell and Escosura to speak for the government.[135] A few weeks later Howden told London that Espartero "is practically absorbed by Marshall O'Donnell [who] is the person who really rules and resumes government in himself."[136]

There were still many true believers across Spain, and San Baldomero continued to be celebrated. In Barcelona, "everything indictates that San Baldomero will be celebrated more enthusiastically than last year."[137] There were "public celebrations" in Almadén. The Teruel Militia sent a congratulatory letter to "the Peacemaker of Spain, the symbol of its liberties and the leader of the people," as did their counterparts from Igualada.[138] In Madrid, there was a *besamanos* which caught Ambassador Howden's attention. Those present included Espartero's aides de camp, dressed in "the same uniform they wear going to the court of the Sovereign," as well as the heads of government departments, the army, and the militia, who went to his house "with 'loyal' addresses in pretty much the same manner as things are done on similar occasions at the Palace." Howden had no doubt that Espartero was incapable of any "wickedness," but "I believe him to be capable of any folly from vanity. Unfortunately, in politics folly is evil."[139]

On 9 March, an immense and enthusiastic crowd gathered to watch Espartero, wearing a militia uniform, ride out at the head of the militia's lancers. When he spoke, "holy ardour filled peoples' breasts," the "religious silence" broken only when the crowd echoed his hurrahs to the "constitutional queen" and to liberty. One line would be remembered, although not in the way he would have wanted. If freedom were to be threatened, he assured them, "The white feather of my helmet will be your guide and with this veteran sword I will show you the road to glory."[140] This immediately became fodder for his critics, especially the satirical paper *El Padre Cobos*, which had been launched two months after the July revolution with the Moderate, and later neo-Catholic, politician Cándido Nocedal as its editor.[141] To give just one example: on 30 March, it advertised a company called La Baldomera, "a Progressive financial company on the road to bankruptcy ... To avoid getting lost on this road one only has to follow the white feather on General Espartero's helmet."[142]

Many on the left continued to see Espartero as their hero. Only a few weeks after this episode, *La Democracia* explained what "the true Espartero" meant to its readers. For them he was not a "man" but an aspiration that included a smaller army, universal male suffrage in all elections, complete freedom of the press, jury trials, and freedom of religion, assembly, and association. This was the "true Espartero; he should be the only idol of the people."[143] This was a long way from the flesh and blood Espartero. Two days later, before a large and adoring crowd of up to forty thousand, Espartero presided over the ceremonial delivery of flags to the militia of the province of Madrid. His speech set out where his thinking on the meaning of the revolution then stood. He called for the preservation of "public order, obedience to the laws and the constitutional throne of our queen" so that "industry, agriculture, and commerce progress and open the roads to civilization and public wealth," which was the only real way of ensuring "the liberty and well-being of peoples."[144]

Espartero's continued popularity explains why political elites clung to him so strongly. Early in March, a group of conservatives joined by some Progressives created the Centro Parlamentario, intending it as the nucleus of a more centrist government that would stand up to "the dangers of reaction as well as of anarchy."[145] One of its first acts was to send a delegation to seek Espartero's blessing. He expressed his "surprise" and urged instead "the unity of the Progressive Party, the great national party to which I have always belonged, and always will."¹⁴⁶ This initiative prompted a response from some ninety Progressives, Espartero intimates like Allende Salazar and Gurrea among them, who created the Centro Progresista to clearly distance themselves from other parliamentary fragments and end the coalition with O'Donnell. Their manifesto, written by Olózaga, proclaimed that they "recognized the Duke of Victory as their only leader, and their principal goal is to promote and maintain unity among good liberals."¹⁴⁷ They were, as Kiernan puts it, "even more loyal to Espartero than the other camp."¹⁴⁸

Espartero insisted he was still a Progressive, but his actions continued to belie his words. He blocked all initiatives undertaken by the Centro Progresista and defended O'Donnell against them. Espartero certainly proved not the leader the Progressives needed. Isabel Burdiel calls him a "dead weight," but also points out that the reason Espartero appeared so indispensable and the key to the ultimate failure of the revolution of 1854 (the *Bienio*) was "the enormous fragmentation of all the political parties." The Progressives in particular found themselves under pressure from O'Donnell's emerging Liberal Union on the right and the Democrats on the left. Combined with "the strong fear of revolution or reaction" that hung over the period, this made them cling to Espartero even as they saw him drifting away, preventing them from building a "solid parliamentary party" which could govern on its own.¹⁴⁹ For all Espartero's failings, the real problem lay less with him than with them.

In the spring, Espartero went north, on what the Duke of Rivas described as a "triumphal march under the pretext of inaugurating the railroad."¹⁵⁰ His first stop was Valladolid. The city was packed with as many as forty thousand visitors, including three thousand *milicianos* from across the province. There was a general illumination at 9:00 and then fireworks, which went on until after midnight. The next day, harsh weather forced the inauguration ceremony and the bullfight to be rescheduled.¹⁵¹ When Espartero addressed the troops and *milicianos*, the veterans who had served under him broke down in tears.¹⁵² His speech talked as much about the past as the present, but he did emphasize economics. "This is the moment, Castilians, to make our material interests prosper. For this I count on the morality of all and on order upheld by the army and the militia."¹⁵³ At the banquet that evening, he responded to a question from the president of the Audiencia, emphasizing the role God had played in his life. "God," he said, "has made Man to progress and we will progress step by step in a suitable way, because liberty exists so that, under its protection, all the great principles of science and reason will be developed. That is why I am a Progressive, and I hope God helps me along the road."¹⁵⁴

In Burgos, the city was decorated for the celebration, including a triumphal arch praising Espartero and recalling his "principal victories and feats of arms." Events included a mass, bullfights, fireworks, and an illumination of the city.[155] After Burgos came Logroño. From the moment Espartero entered the province, there was "an uninterrupted ovation." At Haro, where he spent the night, "so many people had gathered from all over that the general and his party could barely move through the streets."[156] When he reached Logroño, he was unwell; there were reports that he had suffered a "nervous convulsion" after having a flaming row with Gurrea over the ongoing alliance with O'Donnell.[157]

The next stop was Pamplona. The city was not on the new rail line, but the municipal government had requested he visit because his name "has been popular in this city since 1839, when he achieved for it, for all Navarra, and for the entire Nation the greatest gift a mortal can give, the end of the cruel and horrific civil war." To demonstrate their gratitude, the city government prepared an elaborate program of events. In addition to the usual triumphal arch, illumination, fireworks, parades, and banquets, they built a "slim obelisk" in front of the Deputation. One face was inscribed "The city of Pamplona to the Peacemaker of Spain"; a second, "Commander in Chief, 1836. Agreement of Vergara 1839. Regent of the Realm 1841"; the third, "Unity, Tolerance, Respect for the Law"; and the last, "Liberty, Order and Progress." On top, there was a "beautiful globe on which was written 'Isabel II. Constitutional Monarchy.'" The heavy rains forced the bullfight to be cancelled, but even this did not extinguish the festive atmosphere, especially around Espartero's lodgings, where crowds congregated continuously. As always, he was gracious with the ordinary Spaniards, "a large number of youths and militia men who called to show their affection."[158]

The zenith of the tour came in Zaragoza. It was Espartero's first visit since the heady days of July 1854, and to receive him the city built a new gate that was also a triumphal arch. It also organized a series of events, including a parade of soldiers and *milicianos*, two bullfights, a special mass, a gala in the Teatro Principal, fireworks, and illuminations. The Casino distributed four thousand vouchers to the poor while the Junta de Comercio held a lottery to raise money for poor orphans. The ceremony inaugurating the construction of the railway took place at 1:00 in the afternoon on 13 May. The atmosphere was like a fair: all around the specially built pavilion, "a multitude of stalls ... selling knickknacks and candies" had sprouted up. The cheers of the huge and excited crowds for Espartero and Isabel II mixed with "martial sounds of trumpets and drums." After breaking the ground using a specially designed shovel, Espartero gave a short speech in which he emphasized the importance of economic progress and the figure of the queen.[159] He then mounted a "magnificent white horse" to head to the bullfight. The plaza was absolutely packed; one witness described it as a scene worthy of a Goya painting. When Espartero made his appearance in the presidential box, "a thunderous cheer greeted him as the Messiah of liberty and the idol of the people." That evening there was a banquet at the university, but even after Espartero returned to his residence at 11:00 he was followed by a militia band. The outstanding singer of the day performed some *coplas* which began: "There are two things in the world that / All Aragon adores / Our Virgin of the Pillar / and the Duke of Victory." For many in Zaragoza, at least, Espartero remained "a demigod. Some militiamen even kneeled in his presence."[160]

This triumphal tour sent Espartero back to Madrid convinced that he had been following the right path in sticking with O'Donnell. Early in June, the Captain General of Barcelona, General Zapatero, closed down the network of Progressive organizations in Catalonia. Progressive deputies introduced a motion of censure, signed by Allende Salazar among others, which O'Donnell declared a question of confidence. Espartero said nothing during the debate and then voted against the motion, approving the attack on his own party.[161] Ninety-six deputies, including many of Espartero's friends, supported the motion. He took this as a public rebuke and a personal betrayal and, according to one pro-O'Donnell paper, he even forbade "old friends from entering his house."[162]

Espartero tried to explain himself in a statement which appeared in the *Gaceta* on 16 June. He denied that he had banned his friends from his house or abandoned Progressive ideals. That there were divisions within the party was a sad reality and would not prevent him from doing his duty. Had he come to power under normal circumstances, he would have made his program perfectly clear, but this was not the case, and he had made himself the willing prisoner of the national will. "*So long as I am president of the Council of Ministers, I will always govern with the majority of the Cortes, whatever the ideas it represents, as the legal expression of the national will.*"[163]

The events that would finally lead to the break between Espartero and O'Donnell began in Valladolid. On 19 June, serious riots broke out there and in other parts of Castile and were met with fierce repression, including the execution of women by garrotte.[164] The government claimed it was fighting communism; the "Puritans" approved, as did some Democrats. Interior Minister Escosura was sent to Valladolid on 25 June to investigate. A week later, the Cortes adjourned. With the conservative press becoming increasingly aggressive and Progressives and Democrats fearing that a military coup was in the works, a delegation was sent to share their concerns with Espartero. One of its members, Ángel Fernández de los Ríos, editor of *Las Novedades*, described the meeting in a book written twenty years after the events.

They entered Espartero's house by "the secret staircase." This was the first time Fernández de los Ríos had met the famous man, whom he described as:

> Short, sturdy without being fat. His head was small and nor its shape, nor his forehead nor his eyes, which were also small but lively, revealed a great intelligence. His face, however, contained a certain dignity and animation that produced a good effect: military campaigns, physical ailments, and age had left his countenance with premature signs of age ... without having any distinguishing characteristics beyond his customary moustache and sideburns, his was still a noble head that inspired a degree of sympathy and respect.

Calvo Asensio explained that they were worried about a possible military coup, but Espartero's reply was not what they were expecting. He turned to Fernández de los Ríos and "began to discuss intimate details from periods of his military career." The man reputed to be an atheist turned out to be "almost superstitious." The man who had been accused of abandoning María Cristina in September 1840 said, "with the accent of truth," that the regent had forced him to become prime minister; that he insisted "she not abandon her daughter, that she not orphan her daughter and the government of the country"; that he had even threatened to resign if she left. He had nothing to say about the regency but talked at length about his exile in London and then about his "isolation" in Logroño, his "unwavering faith" that he would be called back to public life, and his "firm decision" to refuse. Then came the call from Zaragoza "with such requests" that he did return. He talked about the summons from the queen and showed Fernández de los Ríos her letter.

After about an hour, Fernández de los Ríos was finally able to interrupt him and ask the question they had come to ask: danger was close, "would he be with them or those who surrounded him?" It was a question guaranteed to anger him. "He slapped his thigh" and replied "heatedly": "Is there anyone who doubts my conduct? ... If anyone dreamed of attacking the Cortes in any way I would not need the army or the militia to ruin their plans; with a single company, I'd teach them a lesson; I'd need only ten, five men to triumph, because having justice on my side, God will help me ... This will never happen because no one would be so foolish." Aware of what many generals had been saying and doing for the past year, neither Fernández de los Ríos nor Calvo Asensio found Espartero's bravado reassuring, so they told him what they knew and warned him of the dangers of resigning. They didn't know him at all, he said. How many times had he talked about resigning and returning home, and how many times had he stayed at his post? And there he would stay "until the Cortes has completed its mission," but if he should be thrown out of office, as had happened in 1843, "not even then would I go to Logroño. I'd take a small room in any old house and live there modestly, but in Madrid ready to fight for the prerogatives of the Assembly or the liberty of my country." They left Espartero's house after three hours, and the next day Fernández de los Ríos published an article, although one which hid his real impressions, in which he made it clear that Espartero would defend the Cortes at all costs.[165]

Shortly afterwards, Escosura returned from Valladolid, went to Espartero with news that he had discovered a military conspiracy, and advised him to dismiss O'Donnell and all the military commanders he had appointed. Espartero refused. The crucial moment finally arrived at a cabinet meeting over which Isabel presided. For hours Escosura and O'Donnell went head to head over the question of how to deal with the events in Castile. Escosura finally announced that either he or O'Donnell had to go. Espartero asked for their resignations; the former tendered his, the latter did not. When Escosura got up from the cabinet table, Espartero stood beside him and challenged the queen to choose between himself and O'Donnell. With tears in her eyes, "as was customary for her at such moments," she asked him to stay on. But with O'Donnell she pleaded, "You won't abandon me, will you?"[166] Espartero had threatened to resign many times over the previous two years, but only now, at the decisive moment, did he follow through. By 1:00 a.m., all the ministers except O'Donnell had resigned. Espartero's resignation, dated 14 July, read simply, "My broken health prohibits me from continuing as president of the Council of Ministers. Relieve me of this charge and I will thank you for the greatest favour Your Majesty could do for me."[167] On the morning of 14 July, O'Donnell was sworn in as prime minister.

News of these events triggered a popular reaction, with barricades soon appearing across the capital. Would Espartero put himself at the head of the resistance to what many on the left saw as a military coup? Would he defend the Cortes and the revolution as he had so often promised?

On 14 July, as O'Donnell declared martial law, some ninety Progressive and Democratic deputies declared the Cortes in session again. Madoz, who was presiding wearing his militia uniform, proposed a motion of no confidence in the new government. It passed, but O'Donnell refused to recognize it on the grounds that there had not been a quorum. There were reports that Espartero had visited the barricades but disappeared without commiting to joining the resistance.[168] With clashes between the army and the militia taking place across the city, the rump Cortes remained in session overnight. According to Democratic deputy Eugenio García Ruíz, there was a motion to give Espartero command of the forces needed to defend the Congress and other motions offering a discharge to any soldiers who put themselves under Espartero's orders and a pension to the families of those who died fighting. When asked if he would accept command, "if he did not refuse, he did not formally accept either." When Espartero arrived in the Cortes very early on the morning of 15 July, he was received by both deputies and the public "with a delirious enthusiasm." On entering the chamber, he "gave cheers to liberty and national independence" before moving to the speaker's office "along with others who looked askance at the revolution." Shortly afterwards he simply disappeared, "without even mentioning the famous sword of Luchana he had offered every day only to leave it sheathed at the supreme moment."[169] He was cheered in the streets but neither put himself at the head of the resistance nor urged the *milicianos* to put down their weapons. He then holed up in Venancio Gurrea's house.

The fighting continued throughout the day, with the *milicianos*, lacking overall leadership, very much on the defensive. The Cortes remained in session, but with a dwindling number of deputies present. Then Serrano, the new captain general of Madrid, fired cannon at the parliament building, with one ball hitting the roof and another decapitating one of the lions guarding the main stairway. At 4:00 p.m. on 16 July, the few remaining deputies voted to suspend the sitting.[170] The street fighting also ended that day. More than one thousand people had been killed.

Outside the capital, there was little serious resistance to the coup. Even the *esparterista* stronghold of Zaragoza succumbed quickly. The only exception was Catalonia: in Barcelona, there were barricades and four days of street fighting, with the militia in the forefront. Their defeat was followed by a severe repression that Espartero was in no position to resist, even if he had been so inclined.[171]

This was the lowest point of Espartero's public life. Court and Cortes were not his milieus and he had not excelled as a politician, but now he had had the chance to act on a stage with which he was much more familiar and much more comfortable: armed combat. His physical courage had never been in question, so what happened?

Unusually, Espartero offered a lengthy public account of these events a year later. After his resignation, he had counselled everyone to remain "in the strictest legality"; he would rather die than have his name become "the flag of discord and civil war."[172] When it came to defending the Cortes, he was facing an impossible choice and hoped that his "complete disappearance from the stage would calm spirits," so he took refuge in a friend's house.[173] The "always loyal National Militia of Madrid took up arms, legally," to preserve public order and defend the Cortes. The bloodshed was down to those who had "violated the solemn alliance to which we liberals were excessively loyal for two years."[174] Then, the key question: "Why, why that absolute inertia?" The answer: the situation was not as clear cut as it seemed in retrospect. It might appear that the conflict was between "liberty" and "reaction," but "events and circumstances had placed me in a desperate position" because "for a moment it appeared as if the fighting was for one cabinet and against another ... How could I take part in that fratricidal war ... when it was clear to me that the recklessness of those who provoked it meant the only possible outcome was the immediate, if transitory, ruin of one of the institutions to which I had devoted my whole life?" Doing nothing was "a thousand times more cruel than death," but this "harsh sacrifice" was the latest he had been forced to make "for the inflexibility of my principles and the clarity of my conscience." And what had it got him? "The throne calls me a demagogue and the people paint me as a deserter from the holy cause!"[175]

How can we assess this explanation? Is it a cover for cowardice? Putting his life on the line would have been nothing new. But for what? If by the possible ruin of "one of the institutions to which I had devoted my whole life" he meant the monarchy, then there is a ring of truth. Loyalty to the Crown, after all, had been the guiding principle of Espartero's politics far longer than liberalism or constitutionalism. He had been a monarchist well before he became a Progressive, although he had tried to weld the two together. If taking up arms against O'Donnell also meant putting the throne of Isabel II at risk, then this was a step too far. And would be in the years ahead.

Whether this explanation would convince anyone remained to be seen, but for the moment Espartero's prestige was gone. What would have hurt him most was taking place in the streets of Madrid, where his portrait, which two years earlier had been "displayed in all the principal streets surrounded with flowers and lamps, as would be that of a Madonna," was being burned.[176]

9

The Retiree of Logroño, July 1856–September 1868

Once again, Espartero had been forced from power, the victim of his former allies. This time, however, they would leave him in peace, and his request for a passport for Logroño was quickly granted. Before leaving the capital, Espartero met with the queen one last time. According to press reports, the conversation lasted only five minutes. "Duke, how has it gone since we last saw each other?" she asked. "Where have you been that neither I nor anyone else has seen you?" To which he could reply only, "My lady, I am retiring to private life. I can no longer serve my queen or my country but in Logroño I will pray for both … If they leave me alone, which I doubt, in Logroño they will be able to wound my body but not my soul."[1]

Espartero's departure from Madrid on 6 August could not have been more different from his triumphal entry two years earlier. As French ambassador Turgot observed, he "boarded a carriage as alone as the most obscure citizen," accompanied by only the ever-faithful Ignacio Gurrea and two aides de camp.[2] Yet, twelve years later, Isabel was in exile in France and Espartero was a popular choice to replace her on the throne. The first of these developments is not that surprising. After all, if it had not been for Espartero, she might well have lost her throne in 1854, and it would soon become clear that she had learned little from the experience. But the second? Espartero's second experience of power was, if anything, a greater failure than the first, and most leading Progressives were writing him off as a political force. He was also sixty-three years old. How was such a reversal of fortune possible?

What was Espartero thinking as he returned once more to private life? Three months into what would come to be widely known as his "modest retirement," he described his state of mind in a letter to Victor Balaguer and Lluís Cutchet, two of his most ardent defenders. Some of the phrasing, such as "freedom and well-being of my fatherland," were tropes of his, but his use of religious language such as "the faith of the apostles and the hope of the martyrs" to describe himself was new.[3] A year later, he told his old friend Baldomero Goicoechea that "every day his faith in the principles that emanate from God, who gave man his intellectual faculties and the means to develop them so that he would progess, were becoming stronger. Unfortunately, the road of progress is littered with the rubble of absolutism, the reefs of anarchy, and the mire of corruption, but these obstacles must disappear so that man, despite his mortal sins, will comply with the will of God."[4] By the summer of 1858, God had become "the Great Progressive of the Universe."[5] Two years later, "damned time" had transformed "the man of Luchana" into "the loner of Logroño," but he remained firm in his principles because "I trust that God is in the heavens."[6] In fact, Espartero was far from maintaining such equanimity.

Whatever his innermost thoughts, Espartero and Jacinta returned to the life they had lived between 1848 and 1854. Logroño remained a small place. The first modern census, in 1857, put its population at 11,475 people. Their own household was a large one. The municipal *Padrón* done on 25 and 26 December 1860 showed that he and Jacinta had seven servants to help them with their immense Casa-Palacio. They also had two guests in residence, his aide-de-camp, Luciano Murrieta, thirty-seven years old and still a bachelor, and Jacinta's god-daughter, Jacinta Gurrea Arrieta, the seventeen-year-old daughter of Espartero's longtime secretary, Ignacio Gurrea.[7]

Espartero and Murrieta continued their wine-making collaboration, and at the 1857 Madrid Agricultural Fair they won a silver medal for a champagne-style wine. Espartero also won two gold medals, one for introducing "Australian barley" and the other for his olive oil.[8] He was involved in other important local economic initiatives. He bought thirty-one shares in the Tudela-Bilbao railroad, which was built between 1858 and 1863,[9] and six shares in the subscription launched in late 1858 to build a new theatre. In 1860, the provincial Junta de Agricultura, Industria y Comercio appealed to him to use his influence on behalf of its petition to the minister of development to finance a canal to cross the province,[10] and in 1864, he was one of a group of "political friends" behind an unsuccessful attempt to establish an issuing bank in the city.[11] Espartero continued to participate in philanthropic activities as well. As the city feared a cholera epidemic in 1865, the newly created Friends of the Poor made him its honorary president.[12] He and Jacinta also practised their own, private philanthropy. The winter of 1857 was a hard one, and, as

Jacinta told Cipriano Montesino, they provided some help by taking on additional workers.[13]

Jacinta ran a regular salon where topics like the progress in building the railroad were discussed.[14] They went to the theatre occasionally, but turned down invitations to balls.[15] In the early years, at least, Jacinta would spend six weeks or so in August and September taking the waters in Bagnères-de-Luchon. Baldomero himself stayed put in Logroño, although in June 1860 he received permission from the civil governor of Logroño to accompany Jacinta and Murrieta "to take the waters."[16] While he and Jacinta were happy to stand godparents to Goicoechea's newest child in January 1858, he was not prepared to travel to Valladolid for the baptism.[17] By July 1864, Jacinta was also too tired to travel: "I would like to go to Zaragoza but, to tell the truth, to do so, taking baggage, a maid, etc, would require the energy neither I nor the Duke have."[18]

On the other hand, they were happy to receive company, and Baldomero invited friends to visit. In March 1857, it was Baldomero Goicoechea, who had recently suffered the death of a daughter, and three months later it was Balaguer and Cutchet from Barcelona. Other people asked to visit, like José Deura, a high school teacher from Tudela. He went in June 1864 and was "received … in such a dignified way. I told all my friends in Girona and Olot all about it during the holidays."[19]

There were also illness and ill humour, and Jacinta had to manage both. She dreaded Baldomero getting sick, especially if it meant calling a doctor, since it "makes me suffer a lot."[20] A few days after she wrote this, on his sixty-fourth birthday, he was "a bit ill, or rather *with the Blue Devils*, and he stayed in bed until four."[21] The best thing for his frame of mind was to go to his beloved Fombera. On days he couldn't go, "he is in a terrible mood and you can't talk to him about anything … Yesterday and today he has been pruning trees and been in better humour."[22]

Public criticism affected Baldomero profoundly and gave Jacinta something else to handle. "It is necessary to deal with [him] as with a child who is going to have a tooth extracted. There are some things he cannot take philosophically … *It is a pity all that has happened*." It didn't help that Baldomero dwelled on the negatives. He copied out newspaper articles, "and especially the bad ones."[23] Jacinta read the papers first and carefully controlled what she allowed him to see. *La Discusión* was a particular bugbear; its articles "do nothing more than make him throw tantrums. I don't want him to see it."[24] When Montesino sent her some newspapers with articles about Espartero, she gave him verbal summaries but hid the articles themselves. And there was additional fallout for her: "conversations in which I cannot avoid telling him the truth, which no one has done more than I. He doesn't like it and gets angry with me."[25]

Espartero also discussed current affairs with his friends. He had a lot to say on the so-called War of Africa that Spain fought against Morocco, which began in October 1859. The war was immensely popular, including among people on the left such as Emilio Castelar,[26] and it would turn Juan Prim into a national hero. But Espartero was not a big fan. He did not feel the sacrifice of men or money was justified. "It's easy to start but the compensation for so much expense and sacrifice is difficult, perhaps impossible," he told Cutchet. "We will win but I don't see what we will gain. I only know that if something is bad by nature, no one can turn it into something good. Some illnesses are incurable. This is the century of reason, not of miracles."[27] Nor did he seem to share the "civilizing" impulse that justified imperialism: even if successful, the "Moors will remain Moors and the Christians, Christians and they will never be friends."[28] His experiences in America had led him to realize "how hard is . . the sad fate of those who suffer the empire of a stranger. Trade among people who exchange their goods has made more conquests than all the warriors and conquistadors put together."[29]

Espartero also discussed the Second Italian War of Independence, in which France and Piedmont fought the Habsburg Empire. He told Cutchet, to whom he had given a letter of introduction to the Piedmontese general Gioacomo Durando, who had served with Espartero during the Carlist War, that he was not surprised that Napoleon III had unilaterally signed the peace of Villafranca with the Habsburgs. His experience and his reading of history left the situation clear.[30] In an undated draft, he expressed his admiration for Victor Emmanuel and his sympathy for the Italian cause. The Piedmontese king would "unite all of ... the Italian peninsula in a single great nation" and he would do so "counting only on the Italians," since the French and Austrians would do everything possible to avoid having "such a large new nation" on their borders.[31]

There is no evidence of what Espartero made of Garibaldi, nor of his views on the US Civil War. This is surely something he would have followed, as a military man and one with his own experience of fighting a civil war. Did he and Jacinta discuss it as she read coverage in the *Illustrated London News*?[32] Did he consider the Union cause, especially after the Emancipation Proclamation, to embody the march of progress and the spirit of the century he invoked so often?

Then there was the correspondence. Espartero received a huge number of letters, especially on his birthday and the anniversary of Luchana. They came from from cities and small towns, from people of all social classes, from personal acquaintances and from supporters and admirers who had never met him. This correspondence "revealed the importance [Espartero] had assumed in the mental worlds of a great many [Spanish] men and women," to paraphrase Edward Berenson's comment about the late nineteenth- and early twentieth-century French colonial hero Hubert Lyautey.[33] And Espartero made an effort to reply to each one, as Jacinta told Montesino, and as the pile of drafts in his papers, more painfully written as he got older, demonstrates.[34]

Many people sent simple birthday wishes. At times the language could be over the top, as when Mariano Gil y Alcayde proclaimed that "Loving you is like winning the lottery. (May you live 1000000000000 years, and the Duchess too.)"[35] Some wrote year after year, treating it as almost a religious obligation. In 1863, Carolina González Llanos wrote from Madrid on behalf of her father, who was too sick to do it himself, but who "does not forget you and asks me to write for him."[36] Occasionally someone would send food, like José Carabia (Burgos), who sent a suckling lamb "so that it would be one of the delights on your table on Saint Baldomero day."[37]

Most letters came from individuals, although some came from organizations, usually local Progressive committees. There were occasional collective letters. Santiago García Santa Olalla, a priest from Seville, organized one each year which would carry hundreds of signatures: 698 in 1862 and more than 1,800 in 1865.[38] The letters Espartero received for his birthday also revealed what he meant to Spaniards and, as we shall see later, can tell us a lot about the persistent and powerful Espartero cult.

Many correspondents sent poems. Carlos Galofre, a "volunteer soldier during the civil war, now a poor and modest worker," wrote to the "sublime father of liberty of our beloved fatherland" for the first time in 1864 with a "poor composition," a sonnet written in Catalan.[39] Some of these creations came from women. Catalina Rando de Boussignault sent two poems. Her admiration for Espartero was a product of oral tradition: in Madrid she had lived with her brother-in-law, one of Espartero's aides de camp, from whom "at all hours I heard the story of Your Excellency's heroism and great deeds which filled my spirit with his enthusiasm. Although I am a woman my heart is very impressionable when it comes to the great and heroic." Her sonnet, "To the undefeated Duke of Victory," had been published a in newspaper called *La Unión*. She did not hide her consciousness of writing as a woman. The poem begins: "To judge acts of valour / Some people say / Is fit not for women / who flee the fervour of war / But we who converse with the muses / although badly / always have excuses." The bulk is devoted to celebrating the "shining sun of / the Duke of Victory / Peacemaker of Spain."[40] Pascuala Fuentes y Altafago from Zaragoza, whose mother was "always an enthusiast for Your Excellency," was more prolific still. Her third poem, written in 1864, concludes by making Espartero the reincarnation of the greatest military figures in Spain's history: "Pelayo and the Cid are not dead ... while the great soldier who bears the blessed name of Espartero remains alive."[41] Twice she included a poem for Jacinta on her birthday. These emphasized Jacinta's philanthropy: "Such an angel of goodness, a thousand times you gave your hand to the needy."[42]

Jacinta was often mentioned in Espartero's correspondence. Most of the letters he received included a greeting of some kind for her, although it is difficult to know to what extent this was merely formulaic. Many clearly demonstrated a real interest in her. Manuel de Entrambuagas, the son of a cavalry officer who was a "frenzied" admirer of Espartero, already owned a portrait of Espartero, and he had "no other ambition in my humble retirement than to own a portrait of your wife" to match it.[43] In its birthday greeting for 1863, the Casino Industrial Catalán of Sabadell wished Espartero many years of health and happiness "at the side of the Lady Duchess whom we also love well because she has suffered much, sharing the upsets and disruption our Nation has caused Your Excellency."[44]

Jacinta had her own extensive correspondence. Her extant letters are all to Cipriano Montesino, but she complained to him that "thinking of all the letters I have to answer frightens me." She rarely named specific correspondents, but she did mention the Zaragoza financier and ardent *esparterista* Juan Bruil: "He writes long letters but says nothing important."[45] She sent off a subscription to the statue of Mendizábal. She received poems that people wrote in her honour, such as the Republican Mariano Álvarez Robles's "The Last Word spoken on the Cross by the Redeemer of the World, offered to the Duchess of Victory and Morella, out of respect for her virtues."[46]

Jacinta received requests for charity. One that arrived on Espartero's birthday in 1868 tells a particularly heart-rending story that illuminates what liberal politics could mean for anonymous militants. After serving in the Cristino forces from 1834 until 1841, Domingo Vigues went into the book trade, "travelling continuously through the interior of the kingdom." Things went well until 1856 when he went to Buenos Aires and then "the Pacific," where he "went broke." He returned to Barcelona in 1860, and Victor Balaguer and other "political friends" placed him as the doorman and archivist at the Casino del Porvenir, of which Espartero was the honorary president. The government shut the Casino down two years later, but Vigues's friends soon found him a job as secretary in the Sants town hall. That ended when the captain general suspended the city council and had him fired. In the five months since then, he and his daughters had gone hungry, "wearing summer clothes through the rigours of the winter, without beds ... absolutely everything has been sold," their only income the twelve *reales* his thirteen-year-old daughter earned working from 5:00 a.m. to 8:00 p.m. in a factory belonging to the Guells. The friends who might have helped him out had themselves all suffered "hardships and misfortunes," and now he was forced to turn to Jacinta, "the Mother of Charity." In the past, wherever he had been, he had celebrated Espartero's birthday by giving alms, and in 1864 and 1865, "the last two times we could display our political beliefs openly," poems of his had been read in the Barcelona San Baldomero celebrations. Whether Jacinta sent him help, or even replied, is unknown.[47]

Jacinta wrote on political issues on behalf of Baldomero, something that "makes me uncomfortable; I wish he'd ask someone else."[48] Her most significant intervention of this sort was to commission Patricio de la Escosura, who was in exile in Paris, to write a "defence" of Baldomero's conduct during the crucial final days of the *Bienio*. On 20 March 1857, Escosura wrote that he had received a visit from Luciano Murrieta bearing a letter from Jacinta. "The Duchess first mentioned the latest attacks in the press ... I asked that they send me from Logroño a kind of program, an indication of the main points they want me to address." There was really only one serious problem: "How do we explain the complete inaction of the D[uke] from when we left the palace the morning of 13 July until all the places that defended the liberal cause fell or surrendered?" Escosura saw only one explanation. "O'Donnell had left a choice only between reaction and revolution," which meant that Espartero either had to lead the revolution, which would have put the monarchy in danger and "overthrown the dynasty at least," or abstain from taking part. Given the choice of "contradicting a long and glorious career in a single day, overthrowing that which his victories had affirmed and his popularity sustained [and] appearing timid and reluctant with his party," Espartero chose the second, "and it cost him dear."[49]

For many, Espartero's failure to defend the Revolution of 1854 represented the end of his political career. On 5 November 1856, Fernando Corradi, the editor of *El Clamor Público*, wrote a long editorial in which he proclaimed Espartero to be one of "the *political dead* who must be judged severely. The story of his resurrection in 1854 and *his death as a public man in* 1856" was a lesson to "the people not trust their salvation to a single individual."⁵⁰ The next day it was O'Donnell's turn, and Corradi ended that piece with a line that became famous: "For Espartero oblivion, for O'Donnell atonement."⁵¹ This proclamation of Espartero's political death may have reflected the view of the Madrid-based leadership, but for many Progressives, especially among the rank and file, and above all in Catalonia, Espartero remained their real leader. His role would be one of the central issues the party would have to face over the next decade as it navigated the difficult new conditions of the post-*Bienio* period.

The overthrow of Espartero and the Progressives did not bring political stability to Spain. In the two years after the July events, there were four cabinets. This marked what Isabel Burdiel has called "a key turning point in Isabel's reign," as the queen endeavoured to escape the influence of her mother and her husband.⁵² She dumped O'Donnell after only two months because he was too liberal, particularly on an issue that she considered one of personal conscience, the disentailment of Church lands. She then turned to Narváez, but he had to deal with a Moderate party that he no longer controlled as before, as well as a monarch intent on asserting her own power. Narváez lasted a year, during which he oversaw the gutting of the legislation of the *Bienio* and a revision of the Constitution of 1845 in an even more conservative direction.

Narváez also called elections for March 1857, which forced the Progressives to decide whether or not to participate. At a meeting in Olózaga's house in January 1857, they decided that they would, even though they complained repeatedly about the voters' lists, which excluded "most of the men of our political communion." Overall, just under 150,000 people were eligible to vote, compared to the almost 700,000 who had voted in 1854; in addition, the "government controlled them closely."⁵³ Espartero strongly agreed that the party should take part, assuming that were possible "amidst so much misery and perfidy," but he was in a very different position from Montesino and other Progressives. As prime minister of a system that had been "blown away by cannon," he could do nothing that would "contribute to legitimizing such a barbarous and illegal assault."⁵⁴

In February, Espartero resigned his seat as senator for life, to which Isabel had appointed him in 1847, "for reasons Your Majesty knows better than anyone."⁵⁵ When news of his resignation appeared in the Madrid press, *La Época* asked whether Espartero really was abandoning politics or whether he was preparing to run for the Cortes for Zaragoza. While it discounted this as unlikely, the paper did say that he should appear in the next parliament to explain his conduct.⁵⁶

Espartero did agree to stand as Progressive candidate in Logroño's second district, but he would lose to the government candidate, who also had the backing of Olózaga, a sign of the major fault line in the party. As Jacinta put it, "D. S[alustiano] manages everything ... He recommended his friends ... Of course the Government candidate won."[57]

Espartero did stand in the first and second districts of Barcelona, something that angered the Democratic paper *La Discusión*. After "the terrible and bitter disillusionment of 14 July," how could anyone support the man who was "prime motive ... of everything that is happening in Spain"?[58] Espartero was not elected, but this is hardly surprising given the extremely reduced electorate, as well as the active intervention of government officials. Even so, he did surprisingly well In the first district, he lost to Juan Guell by 308 to 211 votes; in the second he received 165 votes against Juan Agell's 251. Other Progressive candidates did little better: Juan Prim received only 211 votes in the third district and Pascual Madoz 228 in the fourth, although he lost by only 20 votes.[59]

As always, Jacinta had her own thoughts on politics. The death of poet and liberal Manuel José Quintana – "How sorry his death makes me. The blessed old liberals keep disappearing" – provided her with the occasion to criticize how Spain treated the people who had served it. "I have seen the magnificent funerals for the patricians. In Spain you have to die before you get justice." She approved of the placement of some of Quintana's poems in the Cortes, but she was not pleased that they would be going up with ones by Larra and Espronceda. They were "good poets," but as men they could not compare, "and Larra's unmoral end" – he committed suicide – "is another problem. If I were [Quintana's] relative I would oppose strongly."[60] And when it came to Baldomero, she did not bite her tongue: "I am so disillusioned with everything that is going on in this crazy country ... The thought that the D[uke] may get involved in certain things again makes me sick. I am not surprised that [Olózaga and O'Donnell] are getting together again; you men are much worse than women with your loose tongues ... What goes on in this country is disgusting."[61]

Ever since his fall, there had been rumours in the press that Espartero was going to publish an explanation of his actions. He did so after the 1857 election, issuing a manifesto to the liberal voters of Barcelona on 1 April.[62] It had little public impact. The full text did not appear in the in the press until mid-May;[63] until then, only small fragments were printed, even though at least one paper claimed to have a copy of the full text.[64] Those extracts provoked limited, and almost entirely negative, comment. *El Occidente* commented that "his sympathies were with the rebels but his duty put him on the queen's side. He ignored the former and did nothing about the latter."[65]

The publication of the full text also led some rank-and-file Progressives to write to Espartero. José Roger, a young man from Lorca (Murcia), said that reading it had made him "cry tears of joy and sadness at the same time." His admiration for Espartero was, he explained, a family tradition: "After God's, yours was the first name my parents taught me to say with respect and veneration." Could Espartero please answer him, so he could pass on his *esparterista* faith to the next generation, carrying out "the duties of fatherhood, showing my children the signature of the illustrious man who gave our nation so many days of glory"?[66]

Isabel dismissed Narváez in October 1857. He was followed, in quick succession, by two other prime ministers, but their weakness made it clear that the queen's goal of realizing "some kind of personal government based on the Moderates" was an illusion. Facing the exhaustion of the Moderates, a growing fear of a revived Carlism, and the efforts of the British and French ambassadors to encourage her to move in a more liberal direction, on 30 June 1858 Isabel again called O'Donnell to power.[67] O'Donnell's approach was to fuse what he described as "the best of the politics of the *Bienio* and the best of the [Moderate] decade" into a party which could provide stable, constitutional government.[68] Many Progressives were tempted. By 1858, even Fernando Corradi and *El Clamor Público*, which in November 1856 had excoriated those Progressives who had gone over to O'Donnell, were supporting the new Liberal Union. And it was an approach that worked: O'Donnell's "Long Government" remained in place until March 1863.

As the first election under O'Donnell's control approached, the Progressives split into two factions, the *resellados*, who were prepared to work with O'Donnell even though they continued to call themselves Progressives, and the "Pure Ones," who were not.[69] Even before these events, Espartero was looking ahead to a moment when the party factions would both turn to him. Until then, as he told Victor Balaguer, "prudence dictates I observe the most absolute neutrality and quietly wait my turn."[70]

For someone who was supposedly a political cadaver, Espartero received considerable attention in the summer of 1858. In June, Balaguer led a movement to send Espartero a mass petition of support. After getting the civil governor's permission, the document was circulated and more than five thousand signatures collected in Barcelona and in towns across the province.[71] After the handwritten documents were sent to Espartero, Balaguer had them published, along with some letters between Espartero and the organizers.[72] In his desire to "unite virtue and enlightenment," Espartero resembled "the first [Queen] Isabel and Charles III." He had done more than anyone else to build the "new edifice" of liberal Spain.[73] The organizing committee then sent Balaguer to Logroño to deliver the text to Espartero, who sent back an expression of gratitude to the liberals of Catalonia. "Modern civilization cannot be stopped," he wrote. "The spirit of the century will say 'onward' and mankind will continue improving its condition. The destiny of societies is Progress." He himself had a clear conscience, confident that, "in the end, justice will be done to my honourable intentions."[74]

The publication of the Barcelona document inspired the Progressives of Lérida to send Espartero their own message, signed by more than four thousand people. The attacks from right and left would not destroy "the cult the country offers you." They shared Espartero's goals of "prudent, progressive liberty," praising him as the symbol of Progressive unity.[75]

The preparation of the petition revealed the growing tensions between Progressives and Democrats in Barcelona as well as the growing distance of the former from the lower classes. *La Discusión*, the Democrats' paper in Madrid, devoted much attention, and much invective, to Espartero and his Catalan supporters. In July it responded to rumours that Espartero was going to issue a manifesto by stating that "since '56 he had lost the right to address a people whom he miserably abandoned at the hour of greatest danger." It also ran a satirical poem that dusted off old charges about Espartero being in the pocket of the British.[76] In August, it entered into a dispute with *El Clamor Público* over who was to blame for the bombardment of Barcelona in 1842 and the coming to power of the Moderates in 1843. A long article by Francisco Pi i Margall put the blame squarely on the Progressives and "stupidity and weakness of their leader."[77] And when the Barcelona petition became public, *La Discusión* devoted one of its *folletines* to a send-up by the well-known satirist Manuel del Palacio: "it saddens someone who was born here that there can be twelve thousand idiots in such an enlightened country."[78]

The collapse of O'Donnell's "Long Government" and his resignation at the end of February 1863 was a turning point.[79] Isabel's reflex was to recall Narváez, but she was persuaded that this was not a good idea. She then invited a number of men to try and form a government, but none was able to put together the necessary support. During these days of uncertainty and rumour, the Progressives presented themselves as a viable option, "a respectable liberalism capable of blocking both the growing democratic wave and the threatening clouds of reaction," and the possibility that they would be given a chance to govern was widely discussed in the press.[80] The call never came, and finally, on 2 March, the Marquis of Miraflores managed to put together a cabinet. This led Prim, who had had expectations of succeeding O'Donnell, to publicly return to the Progressives. As these events were taking place, Espartero asked Balaguer to make it known that he had "written nothing recommending General Prim."[81]

Elections were called for October. On 20 August, the interior minister sent out a circular in which he urged the civil governors to exercise tight control over the electoral process, including imposing serious limitations on the right of assembly, restricting attendance at electoral meetings to local residents, and asserting the right to chair all meetings. The Progressives responded by boycotting the elections, a decision Espartero endorsed.[82] This *retraimiento* [withdrawal] was a tactic largely imposed by Sagasta, Calvo Asensio, and others of the younger generation who controlled the party press in Madrid. Among its strongest opponents were Pascual Madoz and the Barcelona Progressives he represented, for whom its potentially revolutionary implications were a danger best avoided. Out of party loyalty, however, Madoz put his name to the document and withdrew as a candidate for Barcelona.[83] Victor Balaguer, who was standing in Sabadell, also withdrew, a decision Espartero applauded as "proof of the unaninimity and discipline ... of our great party."[84] The government certainly considered Espartero sufficiently important to keep his house under surveillance. In October 1863, Narváez received a telegram from Logroño reporting that Espartero "with great severity has refused to receive Olózaga and go to [Madrid]."[85]

The elections produced a "chaotic political situation."[86] The new government lasted only until January 1864, and the situation deteriorated even further in the following months. In response, the Progressives, led by Olózaga and Prim, became more aggressive in their opposition to the regime, and Espartero would be drawn back into the political limelight.

The unity achieved around *retraimiento* was soon destroyed. The occasion was a massive banquet in Madrid's Campos Eliseos on 3 May 1864, organized as part of the celebrations surrounding the return of the remains of the Progressive hero Diego Muñoz Torrero to Madrid. (Holding banquets was a way of getting around legal restrictions on political meetings.) The celebration of Muñoz Torrero was part of a campaign to create a party pantheon, but one which did not include Espartero.[87]

After many others had spoken, Olózaga rose before a crowd of 2,500 militants to offer a toast that became the catalyst for a debilitating internal conflict. After stating that rumours about any disagreement between him and Espartero were untrue and proclaiming his respect for what Espartero had achieved during the Carlist War, as well as his belief that this had never been sufficiently recognized, Olózaga suggested that Espartero should be allowed to retain the title of "Highness" he had enjoyed as regent. He then concluded with some ill-fated words: Espartero had no desire to "govern the nation by himself. I do not think it would be good for him and I declare in the strongest possible terms that it would not be good for either the Progressive party or the nation."[88]

It was a provocation, and a needless one at that. Anyone who knew Espartero could predict that he would take it very badly. So why did Olózaga do it? Was he carried away by the excitement of the moment? Or might he have been carried away by something else? His toast came at the end of a long evening during which prodigious amounts of alcohol had been consumed. The official total was 3,120 bottles of wine, including sherry, Valdepeñas, and champagne, for the 2,500 attendees, as well as liqueur, probably cognac or *aguardiente*.[89] The effect was immediate. Carlos Rubio, who had spoken just before Olózaga, called the speech "a new '43."[90] The subsequent furore derailed plans for a revolution that the Progressives and Democrats had scheduled for eight days after the banquet, which included sending Prim, Sagasta, and Olózaga to Logroño to convince Espartero to serve "as a unifying symbol and attract public support."[91] The aftershocks would roil the party for many months and make it clear that Espartero was far from politically dead.

Relations between Espartero and the party were difficult even before the banquet. The leadership had invited him only at the last minute, and then only after his backers raised a fuss.[92] When Olózaga read Espartero's refusal to the organizing committee, "everyone was shocked." On the other hand, "for the government and the Moderates it was a relief, as his presence frightened them."[93]

Jacinta, who was a privileged, if far from objective, observer, provided Cipriano Montesino with an extended – and often caustic – commentary on the events. The invitation to attend was "a little late," but "the Duke" would not have attended in any case. "Those who advise the D. to attend are either bad friends or idiots."[94] Manuel Gómez, for example, was "more of a party man than a friend." Her own view was that Baldomero should do "as the English say, he must abide his time." Baldomero had decided not to send even a written toast that could be read for him. "If they send him a greeting he will answer by telegram, and this is only for you, since he is not going to say anything about this to anyone!"[95]

When she next wrote, on 4 May, sketchy news of the banquet had reached Logroño. A brief telegram, sent while the banquet was still going on, had arrived at 2:00 in the morning. "A shame it woke him up." Diego Martínez de Tejada, one of Espartero's friends who had left Madrid at 4:00 in the afternoon and thus missed the banquet, had arrived in Logroño with details of the infighting around Espartero's invitation. "Imagine the effect this had on the D., who is already peevish."[96] By 6 May, they had received detailed news of the banquet, which "will keep us entertained for a few days." By acting as an "ambitious and jealous little man," Olózaga had undermined the political impact of the banquet. For his part, Prim had demonstrated his usual two-facedness: "as easily drawn to the Palace as throwing himself in the arms of the people." If she were Baldomero, "The only part of D. Salustiano's toast I would answer would be that about compensation." Now there was talk among "the hotheads" in Logroño of organizing a banquet there, but Baldomero wouldn't attend, and she certainly didn't want any part of it. "Let them have the Leadership but leave us our peace and quiet." In the end, she was happy about the whole affair "because the Duke has won."[97]

The anger at Olózaga's speech spread through the party rank and file across the country, for many of whom the anti-Espartero coup of 1843 remained an open wound.

Many letters came from Madrid. Bernardo Tomé, a "businessman," was moved to write to Espartero for the first time: "Since I was a child I was taught to respect and love Your Excellency; today this profound affection I feel for you is a deeply held conviction."[98] The day after the banquet, Juan Antonio Zanne, director of a construction company, wrote that "any liberal who is worth anything knows how to judge those who choose an honourable retirement over becoming an apostate."[99] José Antonio Pérez advised Espartero not to worry: the country at large and the party in particular knew both Espartero and Olózaga well and had made up their mind. "Let both walk down the street and we'll see who attracts more and better people: the victor of Luchana and Peacemaker of Spain or the one whose famous 'Salve' [a reference to Olózaga's famous parliamentary speech in May 1843] still echoes in my ears."[100]

Espartero also received letters from the provinces. They praised his character as well as his accomplishments, and they demonstrated widespread repugnance for other Progressive leaders, especially Olózaga. Francisco Gispert from Pamplona denounced Olózaga as "the executioner of our party."[101] José Puig y Salazar wrote on behalf of a number of

Progressives from Cádiz affirming their view that Espartero remained the party's leader. Under him, it was the "great national party" which had defended Spain's liberties and the constitutional monarchy "with great loyalty and sacrifices." Without him, "delivering itself blindfolded to the mercy of the Olózagas and Prims, it is the perfect image of the sheep licking the hand of the butcher who is about to slit its throat."[102] Carlos Botello wrote from Badajoz. From a Progressive family, he had inherited a portrait of Espartero from his father. Only a child in 1843, he remembered the "sad events" of that year and saw them as an attack on the great liberal tradition that Espartero symbolized: "with Your Excellency also fell the Arguelles, Calatrava, Gómez Becerra, San Miguel ... all of whom have been the glory of Spain, for this century and many others."[103] Finally, from Zaragoza, José Ugarte described Olózaga's remarks as nothing less than "a political crime." Espartero's supporters now had to prevent "the schism [his enemies] were trying to introduce into the great liberal Church."[104]

The support for Espartero in Catalonia could not have been stronger. That Catalan Progressives were, for the most part, opposed to the electoral *retraimiento* of which Olózaga was the leading advocate was an additional reason for them to line up so solidly behind Espartero. Ponciano Masadas denounced Olózaga as "the ruin of the party, which is still lamenting the consequences of his well-known errors."[105] Balaguer was adamantly pro-Espartero. He and Agustín Aymar "already demonstrated in Madrid our disgust at what happened at the banquet," and Madoz had seconded them. "Opinion here is unanimous: Without you nothing, with you everything."[106] On the other hand, Juan Vilardell, who was in Madrid, was more ambivalent. Everyone he spoke with was advising against the Catalan branch of the party supporting Espartero. More significantly, the situation was heating up, and even he, an "admirer of the Duke," was leaning towards the Olózaga faction: "Have no doubts: the revolution will come very soon."[107]

Balaguer drafted the official statement of the Barcelona committee. It was a balanced one, praising both the "Catonian example" of Olózaga as well as the "noble and *vasingtoniana*" figure of Espartero.[108] In a cover letter, Balaguer told Espartero that he had written it "measuring every word," while Aymar explained that a lot of people were unhappy with the text but that it had been essential to prevent "any disagreements on the committee from becoming public," since this would have been additional ammunition for their enemies, who were already putting about that Espartero was "an admirer of the Constitution of 1845."[109]

Balaguer, Aymar, and Masadas were part of the Barcelona party leadership; Antonio Rodríguez was not. He assured Espartero that for "true Progressives, especially in Barcelona," he embodied "the politics of constancy and honesty," in contrast to Olózaga's "politics of convenience and bastard ambition."[110] A large number of "pure Progressives" from Tàrrega (Lleida) asked whether "the political conduct of Salustiano Olózaga or any other politician could compare to that of the illustrious General Espartero? Never!"[111] Eleven Progressives from the village of Artés, near Manresa, "more used to wielding a hoe than a pen, and possessed of a righteous indignation," wrote to denounce Olózaga's remarks. These "honest citizens" valued all Espartero had done for the country; in contrast, Olózaga had demonstrated "his unlimited ambition and unequalled pride," even at the cost of "fragmenting the party."[112]

The next stage in the controversy came on 19 May. Sagasta, Ruiz Zorrilla, and Aguirre went to Logroño to get Espartero to agree to some face-saving measure, but before the meeting could take place the Central Committee issued a circular to the provincial committees and Olózaga put out a statement of his own declaring his agreement with it.[113] Espartero's supporters in Madrid were far from happy about all this and on tenterhooks to learn the outcome.[114]

Jacinta was certainly not impressed: "yesterday we saw the famous document of the Committee and that of the *Leader* ... The best of all is that his friends, the delegates, came to implicate the Duke without even bringing him a copy of the document, that is with the pious intention of making him look ridiculous ... To put it in English, one must say they are <u>Rascals</u>, and forgive the strength of my words." Baldomero, she continued, had held his own in the conversations, and his three guests were "*very much disappointed.*" All in all not a bad outcome: Baldomero "should be happy about not having to say any more. Let the *Leader* or the guides sort it out. What's terrible is the number of letters he has to answer."[115] Jacinta left the letter open in case there was anything to report later. There was, but it came from Baldomero himself: the second session with the delegation had lasted another three hours and was basically a repetition of the first.[116]

The Committee met on the evening of 21 May to discuss the outcome. It was a larger gathering than usual, testimony to the importance of the issue. Aguirre reported on the delegation's trip to Logroño. After a lengthy, and at times heated, debate, the Committee decided not to reconvene until the commissions had finished their work. Madoz, who chaired the meeting, said he would go to Logroño to convince Espartero to be conciliatory. Espartero was having none of it: "I'll say it a thousand times, I don't want, and will never want, a deal with Mr Olózaga."[117] Madoz was disappointed at Espartero's intransigence, which he blamed on the bad advice he was getting from his supporters in the capital, who had "convinced him that this was a replay of '40 to '43 and '54 to '56, and that those who love him but don't flatter him are his enemies."[118]

On 3 June, Espartero's friend Rafael Saravia had a private conversation with Prim which he had promised not to divulge to "a living soul." Prim wanted to go to Logroño, "not to talk about Olózaga ... but to discuss more important questions."[119] Espartero was adamant in refusing to receive Prim, whatever the subject. "I don't want my name mixed up in anything he might be planning."[120] By the end of June, Espartero was finding it all a bit much to take. As Jacinta told Montesino, "Tejada and Gomez write frequently with all the gossip on the Olózaga question and every day there is some new invention in the papers ... I really wish they would leave us in peace since the Duke is exasperated."[121]

Espartero wouldn't have much time to rest. In October, the question of *retraimiento* emerged again. Narváez had returned to power on 16 September and he set about trying to coax the Progressives back into the system with a policy that included an amnesty for all press offences since 1857 and allowing military officers to return from exile, something which benefited Prim: he had been sent to Oviedo after a badly botched attempt at an uprising, which was presumably what he had so urgently wanted to discuss with Espartero.

Narváez also called elections for 22 October. To deal with this situation, a meeting of representatives from across the country to elect a new Central Committee was called. Representatives of the Madrid and Zaragoza committees travelled to Logroño on 14 October to invite Espartero to preside over the meeting. He refused, but they returned the next day to say that Olózaga "wished to embrace [Espartero] in [his] home" and then travel with him to Madrid. He refused, "indignantly." Jacinta, who had been unwell, added her own, characteristically forceful thoughts at the bottom of the letter. The delegation was "as insolent as it is stupid ... I must say how shocked I was by the announcement that D. Salustiano ... was hoping the Duke would receive him. All Europe would have laughed its head off if he had accepted this farce!"[122] At the same time, the Barcelona Junta Provincial urged him to "make the sacrifice" and become president of the new Central Committee. This would "totally revive the spirit of the party, especially in Aragón and Cataloria," as well as bringing "many men who have withdrawn back into the political fray."[123] Espartero rejected all these approaches: "When a public man had been the subject of discussion in his party he must stand aside ... because, now more than ever, the party must be united ... I will always respect the will of the party when it is properly represented and do my best to support its decisions."[124]

At the meeting, Espartero was elected to the Central Committee, and, much to his delight, his name came ahead of Olózaga's. Even before he received official notification, he was planning to refuse.[125] When the official letter arrived, it provoked another blast from Jacinta: "After not writing since the famous toast [Sagasta] now says that all Progressives, except the fortunately small number of Olozaguistas, will be happy ... [The Duke] is convinced that in rejecting the presidency he is doing a great service for the party and the country ... He wants his refusal to be published in full. He doesn't write to you because, as you can imagine, he is alone, with so many letters in such a labyrinth."[126] Espartero's refusal appeared in *La Iberia* on the 27th. "I cannot accept this important responsibility due to powerful reasons everyone knows and I needn't set out here." His loyalty to the party should never be doubted, nor his lack of ambition ever be questioned. Then came the part which he had described to Montesino as the party's real program. "Liberty! Constitutional Monarchy! That was my cry in the days of combat and this will be my motto because it is the motto of the national will."[127]

The Central Committee met at Olózaga's house between 23 and 28 October to debate the question of *retraimiento*. These discussions ended with an overwhelming 66 to 4 vote in favour, with Madoz abstaining. Of course, the party leadership wanted Espartero to endorse this position, to which his answer was that he had been practising *retraimiento* since 1856 and "will not quit until the just and legal reasons that motivate me have disappeared ... Liberty and constitutional monarchy, the former prudent but without disguises, the latter in all its purity ... That is what I desire."[128] The party's manifesto appeared on the front page of *La Iberia* on 3 November, followed immediately by Espartero's endorsement. The current regime was "dangerous for the constitutional monarchy and the people ... We sincere lovers of liberty and constitutional monarchy ... can only deplore with deep sadness the dangers both face today; but as our saving voices have been ignored, we will grievingly withdraw and not be accomplices in their sad ruin. But if Providence gave us the opportunity to avoid it, who among us would not extend his arms to save such beloved objects?"[129] The party leadership was thrilled. Unity had been restored, and the Moderate press, "which so praised [Espartero] two weeks ago[,] is now attacking him violently."[130]

The publication of Espartero's letter prompted a flood of endorsements from party committees across the country. In Chinchilla (Albacete) it produced "indescribable enthusiasm," especially as it put to rest rumours that he had distanced himself from the party.[131] Alicante Progressives who "venerated his voice with uninterrupted religiosity" applauded his letter unreservedly,[132] while in Avilés (Asturias) his "magic voice has filled [us] with the most ardent enthusiasm."[133] In Granada, Espartero's letter put a stop to "the factions" who had been creating divisions in the party.[134] After expressing their pride that Espartero's ancestors hailed from the town, the Progressives of Daimiel, only forty kilometres from Espartero's birthplace, congratulated him on his letter and denounced "those fair weather politicians … who don't want to understand that the Duke of Victory tied himself to liberty on the battlefield and liberty is incompatible with that sort of politician."[135]

In two instances, Espartero's replies were more expansive than usual. To the Barcelona committee he emphasized the tight connection between the throne and liberty. The real reason Spaniards had defended their child queen "so steadfastly and heroically" was that she embodied "our hopes for liberty and the new future of the country."[136] In its letter, the Zaragoza committee had complained at length about the disastrous state of the country, and especially "ominous theocratic influence." Espartero did not disagree, but he made some – for him – unusual remarks about Catholicism. For too long Progressives had let themselves be attacked as enemies of religion, and this had to stop. The party "detests and combats superstition, but it loves the faith of our parents, the true faith. Our party knows that Religion and Liberty are two rays of the same sun, two glimmerings of the same divinity, in whose dual splendour peoples will advance along the path of happiness."[137] In this he was in line with many leading Progressives whose thinking on religious matters was evolving towards "identifying the discourse of nation with Catholicism."[138]

The crisis of 1864 left absolutely no doubt that Espartero continued to be immensely popular among many ordinary Spaniards. The Espartero cult that had been created following Luchana had survived the fall of the regency and retained its vitality after the events of the *Bienio*, and not just among adults who had fought with Espartero or experienced the Carlist War in other ways. If anything, his "retirement" in Logroño had reinforced it. His was a new kind of popularity, unprecedented in Spain and extremely rare anywhere else in Europe, one which other politicians of the day were unable to comprehend. Operating in the world of small-scale parties of notables made it easy for them to dismiss Espartero as a political force.

Espartero's "retirement" in Logroño was similar to that of Garibaldi on his island of Caprera at the same time, and it had similar effects. For Garibaldi, it "secured … the identification of Cincinnatus already achieved by George Washington" while "preserv[ing] the more archaic and rural overtones of the Cincinnatus myth." And if Garibaldi was "indirectly compared" to Washington, "the antithesis of Napoleon, the military leader who surrendered his exceptional powers and returned to civil life,"[139] in Espartero's case the comparisons were frequent and direct. For both, retirement may have acted as "inspired separateness," a technique of "enhancing their stature by making themselves scarce" used by some European "celebrities and charismatic leaders."[140] Ildefonso Antonio Bermejo, who wrote a novelized life of Espartero in 1847, pointed to this in his history of the revolutionary years 1868 to 1874: "The greater Espartero's isolation, the more his popularity has grown. The less he allowed his name to be used, the greater its importance became. The greater his modesty, the greater his fame, and the less his ambition, the more he has been sought after."[141] Bermejo was right, but Espartero was not using distance as a deliberate strategy. He revelled in recognition, but he had no intention of abandoning his quiet life with Jacinta in Logroño.

Images continued to be important to the Espartero cult. They appeared during popular demonstrations. In July 1861, the town of Iznajar (Córdoba) was the scene of a republican revolt, known locally as the "War of Bread and Cheese." One of the leaders, Joaquín Narváez, a distant relative of the Moderate politician Ramón María Narváez, was executed, and as part of the protest by the townspeople, "the portrait of Espartero … competed with the saints for occupying the pre-eminent place of devotion in their homes."[142] On the other side, a portrait of Espartero got Ramón de Oliver into trouble when he was on business in Burgos in November 1856. An inveterate smoker, when he took out his cigarette case, which had a portrait of Espartero on the cover, he was accosted by three men who threatened to tear it up. When he dared them to try, they pulled out knives, "but I am calm and was smarter than them and in less than five minutes two of them were badly hurt and the third had disappeared … I will defend the conduct and honour of the Duke of Victory with my life."[143]

The Espartero cult was bolstered by a new technology: photography, especially the *carte de visite*, the small photographic portrait invented by the French photographer Disderi in 1854. Spain soon had a "real industry" producing them, and Madrid was experiencing what Antonio Flores called "photomania … No one escapes being photographed and being sold."[144] Espartero's portrait was one of the many that found their way onto a *carte de visite*, although the few that remain appear to have been taken after 1860, when he was twenty years older, and stouter, than the Romantic icon in Antonio María Esquivel's widely reproduced painting.

Espartero received numerous requests for his "portrait," and this was usually about much more than adding it to an album. Such mass-produced objects could contribute to constituting the self-identity of their owners, insofar as they identified themselves with the principles of the figures they represented. Objects and images "told stories not only about the figures they depicted but also those who owned, displayed, or used them."[145] Showing Espartero's image or autograph to friends and family and passing it on to the next generation were as important as the simple act of ownership.

As the 1863 celebration of Espartero's birthday approached, Francisco de A. Planas requested "a photo-card of Your Exellency that I will give to my fellow believers in Badalona when we celebrate your birthday with a splendid banquet."[146] Antonio Álvarez Penalta, a homoepathic pharmacist from Málaga, requested, as a special favour, "a card with your portrait because I want the satisfaction of having Your Excellency among my family, as you always occupy a special place in my heart."[147] And Catalina Rando de Boussignault, who sent Espartero poems, conveyed a favour her husband had requested: "a photograph of you, which my brother-in-law already has; this would be the most precious gift anyone could give us."[148]

Espartero's autograph was also a desirable object. Francisco Boada from Barcelona said that if Espartero replied to his letter, "I would feel as if I owned a treasure." Both his parents had been Progressives, his father in the National Militia and his mother "having been wounded," and he asked Espartero to imagine "the joy it would give my aged mother to read your reply."[149] A group of admirers from San Andrés del Palomar (Barcelona) included a particularly emotional anecdote in a letter congratulating Espartero on his birthday. As they were writing, a friend who lived nearby dropped in and said:

> Look, it's been more than twenty years since I've been able to walk and I'm twice as old as you are. One day you'll go to Logroño to visit Espartero and I won't be able to see him. If only he would send us his autograph and every time I look at it my heart would brighten. Having said this, he started to cry and after his tears came the tears of his friends. What a blessed moment! Those tears strengthened the loyalty of those hearts.[150]

The thousands of letters Espartero received every year, and especially on his birthday, reveal why he remained so important for so many Spaniards. Most of the themes were longstanding. First there was his military prowess in the Carlist War, but transcending his victories on the battlefield was his status as the "Peacemaker." The Progressive

Figure 13 *Carte de visite*, Espartero in civilian clothes, c. 1860.
Museo del Ejército.

committee in the village of Algarinejo (Granada) captured what this meant for many families: "today many husbands embrace their wives, many mothers their sons."[151] He was also the embodiment of Spanish liberalism. Marcos González, a retired soldier living in Teverga (Asturias), expressed this idea with simple eloquence: "we were slaves and he made us citizens."[152] Occasionally this was expressed in familial terms with Espartero as a father figure. For Jose Manuel López y López from Écija (Sevilla), he had shown "the intense and selfless love of a father for his children," and Spaniards had responded with "truly filial love."[153]

What was most striking about the Espartero cult in these years, however, was the emphasis on his personal virtues: his honesty, his disinterestedness, and his lack of ambition. Seen in this light, Espartero's losses of power in 1843 and 1856 were not failures to be criticized but signs of his selflessness. He had preferred to sacrifice himself rather than "compromise liberal principles or national interests." Rather than "shed a drop of citizens' blood for his personal cause," wrote the Murcia Progressive Club, "like another Cincinnatus he left the palace for his modest home until his country called on him to save it from the abyss where false prophets had lured it."[154] In the opinion of Enrique Rodríguez Cortés and a group of friends from Lugo, this put him in the company of "the illustrious George Washington [who] made no greater contribution to his country's independence and liberty than his retirement to Mt. Vernon."[155] The conservative domination and prevailing corruption of public life made Espartero's virtues stand out in full relief, as *El Peninsular* of Cádiz explained in a statement, signed by more than 2,500 people, congratulating him on the failure of an assassination attempt in February 1865. "The contrast between the Peacemaker of Spain, retired in a small town, far from public life, while those who were the soldiers of despotism occupy the leading positions of the State and enjoy the luxuries of the Court ... speaks volumes."[156]

Nowhere was the Espartero cult stronger than in Catalonia. This was a varied and widespread phenomenon. It was located in Barcelona and in towns and villages across the principality. It was individual and collective, and embraced by elites and by ordinary people both. It was expressed in Catalan as well as Spanish and took a number of forms, from poems and newspaper articles to San Baldomero Day celebrations featuring almsgiving, banquets, speeches, plays, and bands.

It was not a centralized movement, but its central figure was Victor Balaguer, assisted by his "literary mentor," Lluís Cutchet.[157] A proud Catalan – he was the first best-selling author to write in Catalan – as well as a Progressive, Balaguer was also a devoted follower of Espartero, and even abandoned *La Corona de Aragón*, the paper he had helped found in 1854, after a disagreement with the editor over his position on O'Donnell's coup in July 1856. In the years following the *Bienio* he was at the heart of Progressive politics in Barcelona. In September 1856, he founded a new paper, *El Conceller*, which in addition to following his particular political line would be a vehicle for publishing his own Catalan-language literary works.[158] It would also be one of the many vehicles in which he expressed his "special admiration" and political support for Espartero.[159] After *El Conceller* closed down in June 1857, Balaguer considered starting a new paper to be called *Progress and Espartero*, although Espartero himself urged him to drop his name from the title.[160]

El Conceller was *esparterista* from the outset.[161] On 27 February 1857, the first time it had the opportunity of celebrating Espartero's birthday, the paper dedicated its front page to a long poem in which Balaguer makes it clear that in addressing and praising the "saviour of Spain," he does so as a Catalan. This was followed, on page 2, by an article signed by "The Editors." They highlighted less the public man, "the Peacemaker, the liberator," than the private one, the embodiment of "probity [and] morality ... the source of all political virtues."[162]

Balaguer's adulation of Espartero went even further in his long Catalan-language poem, *Homenatje y Recort al Excm. Senyor D. Baldomero Espartero*, written the same year that he helped launch the modern *Jocs Florals*, the poetry competitions that had been celebrated in the late fourteenth and fifteenth centuries. Liberty had had a series of "apostles": the Athenians at Thermopylae, William Tell, Pau Claris, George Washington, and the Greeks at Missolonghi. Now it was Spain's turn, and its great hero was a Christ-like Espartero, whose greatest feat took place "the very same night that God / Gave a Saviour to the world."[163] The poem also addressed Espartero's personal qualities: "Your probity ... virtue and prudence ... you have always sown virtue while preaching freedom."[164]

This was part of a broader phenomenon, in both Catalonia and Spain as a whole, which Balaguer did much to help create. In the years after the *Bienio*, Espartero's "modest retirement in Logroño" came to be seen as a symbol of virtue, in stark contrast to the corruption of the political elite in Madrid.[165] (We can catch a glimpse of the reasons for this in a letter to his close friend Baldomero Goicoechea about having received a case of razor blades as a present: "I accepted it with great repugnance; you know that neither in power nor out have I wanted presents of any type, and I do not need them in order to offer protection to those, like Sr. del Olmo, who so justly deserve it.")[166] Was Espartero, with Jacinta beside him, providing the moral leadership that the queen and the rest of the royal family had abdicated?

Nobody praised Espartero's personal qualities more fully, nor tied them more closely to public life, than Balaguer, especially in his 1858 book *La Libertad Constitucional. Estudios Políticos* [Constitutional Liberty, Political Studies].[167] One of Balaguer's key themes was that the nature of a politician's private life was a crucial indicator of his behaviour in public life.[168] Whether as regent, in exile, or in Logroño, Espartero had displayed "the same strict conduct and the same moral principles. Modest and upright, tolerant and just, good and simple, accessible to everyone ... Espartero was born to be a leader, not of a political party but of a party of law-abiding, just and good men."[169]

Other Barcelona-based Progressives echoed Balaguer's rhetoric. Agustín Aymar emphasized Espartero's "almost Spartan simplicity, a contrast to the colossal fortunes that those who pretend to be his rivals have created."[170] For Román de Lacunza, the celebration of Espartero's birthday was a symbol of the virtues of the Progressive party, virtues which their opponents lacked and itself a display of virtue in the face of its reigning absence. "The Progressive party, which represents the true country which wants nothing for itself, must protest against corruption, first of the political faith and then as an inevitable consequence, of social life ... and that is what it does by celebrating General Espartero's birthday."[171]

It is precisely the celebration of San Baldomero, both Espartero's birthday and his saint's day, that demonstrates the reach of *esparterismo* in Catalonia. This celebration was an invented tradition, a kind of Progressive "civic holiday," as the party's Barcelona junta described it.[172]

The day quickly became associated with philanthropy: giving money and especially loaves of bread to the poor, a kind of liberal charity, was one of its defining features. In 1860, at the height of the War of Africa, the organizers decided to direct this philanthropy to Catalan soldiers wounded there, and to give the festivities a more formal and public presence by organizing a "theatrical function" as a fundraiser. They strove to make the connection between Espartero's battles and the current war: Espartero fought for "liberty ... civilization ... progress ... the greatness of dignity of the country," and O'Donnell was fighting for those same causes.[173] That Espartero himself disapproved of the war was irrelevant. The following year, the proceeds went to "the needy of Barcelona." For the first time, the program included Anselmo Clavé's choir, and all members of the audience received a forty-eight-page edition of Espartero's service record.[174] The 1864 event began with the *Himno de Luchana* and included an orchestral version of Daniel Aubert's opera about national liberty, *La Muette de Portici*.[175] The full house cheered Espartero with "true frenzy ... When the orchestra and choirs began the Hymn of

Luchana, the shouts to liberty and Espartero filled the magnificent hall, and that ardent enthusiasm continued throughout the show."[176] After 1865, the San Baldomero celebrations fell victim to government repression. By 1868, the organizers weren't even able to meet.[177]

San Baldomero was also celebrated in numerous towns and villages across Catalonia. These celebrations varied in form and scale. In some places, as in Reus, they were "family affairs," but elsewhere they were more public. In Cardona, local Progressives met for a banquet in an inn before heading to a private room in a café where they and their friends enjoyed music.[178] The Progressives of Palafrugell, who boasted of "not having risen against Your Excellency's government in '43," celebrated with a banquet which was lubricated with wine from Espartero's own production. They also sent a poem which had been read by a "young enthusiast."[179] In San Sadurni de Noya, "a parade made up of almost all party members" went through the town on 26 February collecting some five hundred *reales*, which were used to purchase two hundred "pound-and-a-half loaves of the best bread" to distribute to the poor. In the evening, there was a masked ball.[180]

The festivities in San Andrés de Palomar, an industrial town on the outskirts of Barcelona, were more elaborate still. At 2:00 p.m. on 26 February, "a general pealing of bells" announced the upcoming celebration, and that evening the town band "marched through the streets, followed by an immense crowd." The next morning, a committee distributed small amounts of money to poor families recommended by the town's doctors, after which there was a mass in memory of Saint Baldomero. Then a large crowd, including "more than one hundred and seventy poor people of both sexes, preceded by the band and the designated officials, went to the large room of the Estrella, where the well-known innkeeper Joaquín Mas, alias Xabana, served them a wonderful meal ... which was animated by the orchestra playing joyous and patriotic songs." This "edifying scene" was watched by more than eight hundred people "from all classes of the population." There were other celebratory meals, and that evening the band marched through the streets followed by "hundreds of people, seventy of whom carried large candles."[181]

Other places had additional elements. In Caldas de Monbui, the festivities included the quintessential Catalan activity, choral singing. "At eleven in the morning, the Euterpe caldense choral society arrived in the Constitution Square to the sound of Mr Clavé's celebrated song *Nets dels Almuçavers*." After the distrubution of bread to the poor, "an immense crowd" listened and "applauded frantically" as the choir performed a number of songs, including the Catalan anthem *Los segadors*.

After the performance, there was a reception for the choir at a private home, where Espartero's portrait was displayed in the living room and before which more songs were played.[182]

The 1864 celebrations in Sabadell lasted a full twenty-four hours. "The dance started at 1 in the morning and went on until 7:00. At 8:30 the Moxins orchestra went through the streets of the town playing the Hymn of Riego." That was followed by the distribution of food to the poor in the Duke of Victory Square and then by banquets and, at 3:00 pm, "music and toasts" in the Casino Industrial Catalán. "At 8:00 in the evening, in the Duke's Square and *with his portrait presiding*, the orchestra played three pieces, concluding with the Hymn of Riego before going to play a waltz in front of the Casino Catalán and three other places, where people pledged money for charity." Then there were speeches recalling "the Duke's immense services to the liberal cause" and urging "unity and concord" among Progressives. The events concluded with more music.[183]

The celebrations almost always included sending a birthday message to Espartero himself. In 1864, the town government of Torrellas de Foix (Barcelona) wrote that not celebrating Espartero's saint's day "would be to fail the duty of every Catalan."[184] *Esparteristas* in Lérida did not have "words to show our love for the Peacemaker of Spain, who is living in undeserved retirement in Logroño."[185] Some who sent messages identified themselves as workers. From Reus came a message from "working-class veterans" who had served in the Carlist War. Miguel Planas and a group of "poor workers" from San Andrés de Palomar sent a poem to show him "what love is, what enthusiasm is"; and the "workers" of the Sabadell Círculo Instructivo congratulated "the protecting star of freedom and peace."[186]

One document from Manresa opens a unique window onto Progressive sentiment and political culture in small-town Catalonia in this period and deserves to be explored at length. The 1864 celebration was special, as it was the occasion for the inauguration of the local Progressive club, of which Espartero was honorary president. There was a banquet in the main hall, with Espartero's portrait hung among "rich tapestries in the national colours." An empty chair at the centre of the head table was reserved for Espartero, who presided *in absentia*. After a few words from the president, the secretary reminded those present that the banquet was dedicated to "the foremost Leader of the time, the unyielding defender of our liberties ... the most worthy and leading representative of our political opinions ... liberty together with order that never turns into licence, progress in the laws and administration to find savings that can rescue our unfortunate Treasury from its predicament and which, at the same time, allow us the free use of our individual faculties."

When lunch came, the dishes intended for Espartero's place were sent, in his name, to "poorest liberal family of the city." Coffee was next, accompanied by numerous toasts: to liberty and progress, to the eminent men of the party, to the Central Committee and the Provincial Junta, and to the recent amnesty. And, of course, there were multiple toasts to Espartero. The final one called Espartero "another Vasington [sic] ... [who] after making his people happy, descended to inhabit a modest farm where he quietly lived out his days, blessed by his fellow citizens." Similarly, after uniting Spaniards at Vergara, Espartero was made regent and faithfully upheld the Constitution of 1837 until "the enemies of freedom managed to besmirch his name, but, to refute them, he retired to his home in Logroño where lives quietly, thinking only of the happiness of all liberals."

The "fraternity and good humour" of the occasion peaked with dessert. The bowls carried small skewers, each one with an inscription which was read aloud. "Platter for independence = To the loyalty and glory acquired defending liberty on the battlefield, His Excellency, the Duke of Victory, D. Baldomero Espartero = Manresa's Progressives in the name of all free citizens of [Catalonia]." Others were dedicated to the "sublime oratory" of Salustiano de Olózaga, who had visited them shortly before; to "civil and ecclesiastical disentailments" represented by Pascual Madoz; to Prim and "the glory Spain acquired in Africa"; and to the Spanish soldiers who had died fighting in Santo Domingo, "the fatal legacy the Liberal Union has left our unfortunate fatherland." After the banquet concluded, the Committee distributed a one-and-a-half-pound loaf of bread and one *real* each to three hundred poor people while the president and vice-president took the "leftovers" from the banquet to the prisoners in the town jail.[187]

Espartero took particular pleasure in the continuing esteem that came from Catalonia and repeatedly expressed his affection and admiration for the Catalans. In a letter to the organizers of his 1861 birthday celebrations, he described Barcelona as "a great city that, through its civilization, its industry, and its commerce has since times long past been among the first in the world."[188] Thanking Balaguer for having been unanimously elected honorary president of the Círculo de Barcelona, he recognized that "the indominitable, noble, free Catalan people ... have always done justice to my honest intentions ... have always shown profound affection for me, especially in times of hardship." He also gave it a special role in Spain's future: Catalonia "marches at the head of our political, moral, and material reorganization."[189]

In January 1865, while the congratulatory letters were still arriving at the Casa-Palacio, Espartero had a special guest: María Cristina, who had briefly returned to the country. It was a miserable night and the streets were nearly impassable, but Espartero, wearing his captain general's uniform, and Jacinta, "elegantly dressed all in blue," were at the station waiting with local dignitaries and a large crowd of onlookers when her train arrived at 9:45. After Jacinta and María Cristina embraced and Espartero kissed her hand, the three of them had a private conversation in the royal coach, which lasted twelve minutes. They then waited on the platform until the train was out of sight.[190] The topic of their conversation became the subject of repeated conjecture.[191]

Concerned about the fragility of the throne following the fall of the Bourbons in Sicily, as well as about finding a way to be allowed to return to Spain, María Cristina had sent a representative to Logroño early in 1861 to discuss the possibility of Espartero returning to active politics. Jacinta described the conversation in her customarily frank way.

> It is true that the Señora's messenger told the D[uke] that she was convinced that he alone, leading the Progressives in power, could save the throne of her daughter. To which the D[uke] replied that *he could not, nor should not, nor wanted to take part in such a matter* ... The messenger asked if he would agree if [María Cristina and her family] were allowed to return to Spain. When he answered NO! the man was speechless. With his characteristic honesty and frankness, [Espartero] added that not only should they not call on him but that [María Cristina] should not come. He had saved her once, putting his life on the line, he could not do it again ... Monarchs need many disappointments to learn their duties ... It is some small satisfaction for the D[uke] that everyone recognizes his honesty and loyalty and that, at moments of danger, even his enemies remember the man they have so condemned.[192]

As the political crisis was about to enter its terminal phase, Espartero's rupture with Isabel and her mother was now complete.

On 10 June 1865, Prim attempted to lead the Bourbon regiment in Valencia against the government. He failed, in large part because the troops "refused to support the movement if it were not headed by Espartero, as they had been promised."[193] This was the first in a series of conspiracies and attempted revolutions which would culminate in the

"Glorious Revolution" of September 1868. As in this instance, Espartero's support remained a crucial factor throughout.

Eleven days after these events, Isabel replaced Narváez with O'Donnell, who was determined to bring the Progressives back into the game and thereby create a stable political system. He announced a series of very liberal measures; some, like recognizing the kingdom of Italy, were symbolic; others, especially an amnesty for people convicted of press offences and a new electoral law which tripled the electorate by reducing the property qualifications and promised to eliminate "excessive" government intervention, were very tangible. O'Donnell also spoke directly with key Progressive leaders to try to reach some sort of agreement. Prim, ever hungry for a shot at power, was on board, but the party was deeply divided.[194]

Sagasta understood that Espartero remained immensely popular and that this was an important asset, while Olózaga's intransigence was "more an element of discord than of unity."[195] In August, Sagasta told Prim, Aguirre, and Ruiz Zorrilla that Espartero refused to be involved in anything that "might bring down the dynasty, but he is convinced that the party should only accept power if it could bring back the Constitution of 1856 ... I believe he would be *inclined to accept power under these conditions*." But the internal problems remained: Espartero continued to believe that the real obstacles were "not in the Palace but in [Olózaga]" and that the party must choose between them.[196] Progressives met on 25 October to elect a new Central Committee; the gathering proved to be "especially tumultuous." Madoz and Prim spoke against continuing the *retraimiento* but were shouted down. The new Committee then spent several days discussing whether or not to participate in the election O'Donnell had called for 1 December before voting 71 to 12 in favour of *retraimiento*. The new manifesto was ready by 20 November but it was not made public until six days later, after Espartero's approval had been assured.[197] Then, with Espartero's approval in hand, the Committee ordered the manifesto to be published in *La Iberia*. In a powerful tribute to the magic of his name among the party rank and file, his endorsement appeared immediately beneath the manifesto on the front page. "Why would I not endorse it if it echoes the national will; if its principles are those which constitute the sacred dogma of our great party and the ones I have always proclaimed and am prepared to sacrifice myself for? This frank and spontaneous display will show our adversaries that they are wasting their time looking for any disagreement amongst us."[198]

An explosion of conspiracies followed. Prim led a failed uprising on 3 January, only a month after the election and a week after the new parliament opened. "The movement's slogan," the French ambassador reported, "was Long live the Queen, Long live Marshall Espartero, Long live General Prim."[199] In June, sergeants at the San Gil barracks in Madrid led a revolt which was met with a fearsome display of force: more than two hundred killed, more than six hundred wounded, and hundreds arrested. There were also worrisome rumblings lower down. A judge in Daimiel was investigating the appearance of "a number of alarming posters with the motto *long live Espartero and down with the consumption tax.*"[200]

Two attempted revolutions in six months spelled the end of O'Donnell's time in power; on 10 July Isabel once more turned to that proven shield against revolution, Narváez. Some Progressives had already been working with Democrats and Republicans, and these plans intensified in the summer of 1866, culminating on 16 August in the Pact of Ostend. The agreement contained only two points: "1°, destroy the existing power structure; 2°, under the direction of a provisional government, have a constititent assembly elected by direct, universal [male] suffrage decide the future of the country."[201] Prim would be the leader of the movement.

The monarchy had entered into a death spiral. Spain was hit by its worst financial crisis of the century. The figure of the queen lost whatever vestigial respect remained, as a flood of satires and scurrilous publications – of which *The Bourbons in Their Underwear* was the most notorious – left her "reduced to a compendium of all possible depravities."[202] There was generalized abstention from the elections of March 1867, which were tightly managed by the government anyway. In mid-August, there was another failed military coup. The sudden death of the fifty-eight-year-old General O'Donnell on 5 November 1867 removed the only obstacle preventing the Liberal Union from adhering to the Pact of Ostend, and the death of Narváez on 23 April 1868 deprived Isabel of her last reliable defender. His successor, González Bravo, blithely dismissed multiple warnings about planned uprisings.

Earning Espartero's endorsement of their activities mattered seriously to Prim and his fellow conspirators, but Espartero had decided on his position: Under no circumstances would he support "armed revolution ... since I could not fight against the principles that I so steadfastly defended during the Seven Years War without losing my dignity."[203] On the other hand, he would not publicly denounce any conspiracy. To do so, as he told one leading Barcelona Progressive in September 1866, would be "to say that our enemies are right and sow new seeds of division in the Progressive party when now more than ever we need concord and unity to overcome the immense misfortunes that overwhelm our country and threaten to destroy it."[204] Progressive leaders spent much time and effort trying to win Espartero's support. In January 1867, Madoz wrote to Prim, who was in exile, that "there is great anxiety … Everyone asks about Florence, Brussels, Paris, Logroño."[205] For his part, Sagasta had been "writing and writing again, talking and talking again," to get clarity on Espartero's position, and it was that "Espartero will not do anything."[206]

Many years later, Justo Tomás Delgado, Espartero's longtime secretary, described a visit that Sagasta, Prim, Aguirre, and Madoz paid Espartero to request his permission to "tell the army and the people that the glorious sword of Luchana was with us." After Prim whispered something in his ear and showed him some documents, Espartero gave his answer. The "ideas and methods" that Prim had shown him were "not those of the Progressive party nor mine. You are going down the wrong road and it is impossible for me to accompany you." His great concern was the monarchy, which was synonymous with Spain as well as being the system of government in the most advanced countries of Europe. What would happen if they lost control of events and the revolution threw Isabel from the throne? Prim's answer was an Iberian union ruled by the king of Portugal. For Espartero this was "a beautiful dream, but an impossible one!" Did they have any other plans? No, but getting rid of the current reality was what mattered. This was a big mistake: "Destroying without having a plan for building something new is crazy, and you will regret it." In his view, the problem was that the queen was in thrall to "a clique of men without convictions and not affiliated to any party … to save the queen from this kidnapping, I am prepared to conspire and do what is asked of me, but under no circumstances will I draw my sword against the queen."[207]

The Progressive press made a bigger deal than usual out of Espartero's birthday in February 1868, his seventy-fifth. *La Nueva Iberia* led with its congratulations; *Gil Blas* connected him to liberal unity; *El Eco Nacional* even devoted its entire 27 February issue to his life.[208] As 1868 wore on, there were rumours about Isabel again turning to Espartero. *La España* reprinted an article from a Paris paper claiming that Espartero had been offered the prime ministership, a claim which it dismissed out of hand.[209] And the *Manchester Guardian* reported that "the few partisans of the dynasty which still cherish the hopes of not seeing it sink, have come to speak of the abdication of the Queen in favour of her son with Espartero as Regent, and it is asserted that overtures have already been made to the old Progressive chief."[210]

On 16 September 1868 two young artists from Barcelona informed Espartero that their entry in the upcoming Aragonese Exhibition was "your figure ... symbol of Spanish glories ... the flag of all hearts that love peace ... the Peacemaker of the Iberian people."[211] Two days later, there was yet another military revolt. This one would succeed, thrusting Espartero into the political limelight in unprecedented ways.

10

"King or President?" September 1868–December 1870

Revolution finally arrived on 17 September 1868. That day Admiral Juan Bautista Topete issued a manifesto denouncing the "most horrible dictatorship" that had destroyed the country's institutions and broken the bonds contained in the officers' oath. He and his supporters aspired to giving Spain "a true constitutional monarchy" that respected the rights of citizens and was not corrupt. The next day, with thirteen of the naval vessels in Cádiz harbour behind him, Topete fired a salvo to announce the revolt. Prim was quickly brought from Gibraltar to Cádiz, where he issued a more truculent proclamation of his own, calling on the "great liberal communion" to destroy the existing system. Many of the leaders of the conspiracy arrived only on the 19th, when they published the most famous document of the revolution, "Long Live Spain with Honour!"[1] So began what came to be known as the Revolutionary Six Years.[2]

The outbreak of the revolution found Queen Isabel and the government escaping the Madrid summer heat in San Sebastián. Prime Minister González Bravo, who had ignored warnings of an imminent revolution, resigned the day after learning of the events in Cádiz and advised the queen to appoint a general to deal with the situation. The role fell to José de la Concha, who immediately left for the capital. Meanwhile, Isabel found herself in the middle of a "feverish atmosphere," receiving conflicting advice about what to do, including abdicating in favour of her son, the ten-year-old Prince Alfonso.[3] On 21 September, Concha requested that the queen return to Madrid, but shortly before her train was to leave, the trip was cancelled because the rail line was insecure. Isabel was, the French ambassador reported, "despondent and cried frequently."[4]

The revolution of 1868 was much more than a simple *pronunciamiento*. In Cádiz and across Andalucía, the military revolt was accompanied by armed civilian uprisings, and it was this combination that brought the revolutionaries success "without bloodshed." And it was this relative bloodlessness that led to the revolution being called "La Gloriosa," echoing the English "Glorious Revolution" of 1688.[5] The turning point came on 28 September, when an army loyal to Isabel and commanded by the Marquis of Novaliches engaged with one under the command of Serrano, reinforced by some two thousand armed civilians, at the bridge at Alcolea that crossed the Guadalquivir River near Córdoba. After a brief but intense battle, the royalists withdrew. When news of the rebel victory reached Madrid, Concha resigned and was replaced by his brother, Manuel, who ordered the loyalist forces to stand down before transferring power to Pascual Madoz and General Joaquín Jovellar as interim civil and military governor of Madrid respectively. Madoz immediately transferred power to the junta, which included Democrats and even republicans, as well as members of the Liberal Union and his own Progressives.[6]

The morning of 29 September, the streets of the capital were more animated than usual and offered such definitely unusual sights as "a welldressed young man who walked happily along Montera Street, rifle in hand, without anyone in authority saying anything." There was also no shortage of rumours, among them that the queen had "summoned Espartero."[7] The Madrid Junta was concerned about emerging disorder. Nicolás Estevánez recounts how his friend and junta member Nicolás Calvo was worried because "Things were going badly ... Espartero has not answered the junta's telegrams or mine."[8]

Following the defeat of her supporters at Alcolea, Isabel left for France; on 30 September she arrived in Biarritz, where she was received with full honours by Napoleon III. The French emperor suggested – or rather demanded – that Isabel and her entourage move to Paris; he didn't want them anywhere near the border where they could more easily stir up trouble. Before leaving Biarritz, Isabel issued a manifesto which was so politically inept that the Junta Revolucionaria in Madrid quickly printed and distributed one hundred thousand copies. In defending her right to the throne, Isabel talked about religion and the long history of the monarchy, but of liberalism or constitutions she said not a word.[9]

News of the Battle of Alcolea and events in Madrid triggered similar developments across the country. By 1 October, revolutionary juntas had replaced existing government authorities in every provincial capital. In many places, there was an orderly transfer of power, but in some the civil governors simply fled, leaving the revolutionary committees to assume power. Logroño was one of these. There, the governor had defeated an earlier attempted uprising in the nearby towns of Calahorra and Haro. When he marched the prisoners through the streets of Logroño, it nearly set off a riot. When a junta was appointed, it proved unable to prevent a crowd from attacking the governor's house.[10] The junta proclaimed Espartero its honorary president. In accepting, he called on people to "preserve order." The announcement that Espartero was the honorary president, along with the full text of his letter, appeared as the first item in the next issue of the official *Boletín*.[11]

The fall of the queen and the transfer of power to the juntas provoked a "revolutionary holiday" across the country.[12] Portraits of Isabel II were destroyed in public, often after having been dragged through the streets, and military officers even tore the royal insignia off their uniforms. Streets named after royalty had their signs removed, replaced by ones honouring the heroes of the hour: the Plaza Isabel II in Madrid became the Plaza de Prim. Businesses also changed their names: Madrid's Café de la Princesa became the Café Prin, while newspapers *La Corona de Aragón* and *El Principado* became *La Crónica de Cataluña* and *El Telégrafo*. The town of Morales del Rey in the province of Zamora became Morales del Progreso.[13]

This spontaneous phase was quickly replaced by a more organized one, as the new authorities sought to channel popular enthusiasm into institutionalized – and less potentially radical – forms. For example, on 20 September, the new city government of Huelva announced three days of festivities consisting of the typical activities for public celebrations: fireworks, band concerts, illumination of the main streets, distribution of bread to the poor, and a bullfight. During the evenings, as if to preside over things, a portrait of Espartero would be exhibited on the balcony of the town hall.[14] And Huelva was far from unique: Espartero mattered to many of the newly installed revolutionary juntas. In Barcelona, his bust graced the Deputation building while a huge portrait was placed on the façade of the city hall.[15] In Valladolid, where the first day of celebrations was dedicated to him, his portrait was paraded through the streets accompanied by a military band that played the Hymns of Riego, Garibaldi, and Luchana.[16] Nor was it just the new authorities who found Espartero's name useful. Along with sheet music for *Prim. Himno nacional para canto y piano* and the liberal classic, the *Himno de Riego*, music stores were advertising music for the *Himno de Espartero*.[17] Clearly, below the level of Madrid-based politicians, Espartero was not seen as guilty for the failure of the *Bienio* or for his failure to resist O'Donnell's coup.

On 4 October, Madrid's Junta Provisional Revolucionaria took the unilateral decision of recognizing Serrano as the head of the Provisional

Government. (Many provincial juntas protested, but to no avail.) Serrano's choice of ministers marked the first significant crack in the revolutionary coalition. They were all Progressives or members of the Liberal Union; the Democrats were shut out, although their leader, Nicolás Rivero, had refused a post in favour of becoming mayor of Madrid. One of the Provisional Government's priorities was to dissolve the juntas and end the period of dual power, and on 13 October it issued a circular ordering that new town councils be established and that the juntas could name their members. With conventional town halls in place, there was no longer any need for the juntas to exist; the Madrid Junta announced it was dissolving itself on the 19th, and the next day the government decreed that all others follow suit.[18]

Before the revolution, one of the strengths of the rebel coalition was that, beyond getting rid of Isabel II, its aims were undefined. Once the revolutionaries were in power, this vagueness became a weakness: the battle over the meaning of the revolution remained to be fought, and the primary battleground would be whether Spain was to remain a monarchy or become a republic. Answering this question would quickly lead to the fracturing of the revolutionary coalition. The matter was settled, at least temporarily, with the proclamation of a new constitution in 1869 and the selection of a new monarch in November 1870. Throughout these dramatic events, Espartero remained in Logroño, consistently rebuffing calls to return to public life. Even so, his name would be invoked repeatedly.

With the juntas out of the way, on 25 October the Provisional Government issued a "Manifesto to the Nation" in which it spoke to the burning question of the new form of government, promising that it "would respect the vote of the sovereign nation, appropriately consulted," while making absolutely clear its preference for a monarchy.[19] Two weeks later, it issued its decree on universal suffrage, granting the vote to all males twenty-five years or older. This increased the number of eligible voters from the 418,271 who qualified for the elections of 1865 to a little over 3.8 million. The decree also stated that the electoral districts would be provinces, not more local units, thus fulfilling a long-held Progressive demand. (In theory, this would make it more difficult for local notables to manipulate the results.) The elections were called on 6 December, with voting days set for 15 to 18 January 1869. That decree also left no question as to the government's preferred outcome: "a monarchy elected by those to whom the Spanish people grants its power."[20]

The irreparable split between monarchists and republicans had already been made public in the so-called *Conciliation Manifesto* that the governing parties issued on 12 November. In return for the Democrats' supporting a constitutional monarchy, the Progressives and Unionists agreed to maintain the expansive rights that the Provisional Government had already acknowledged. This would be a new type of monarchy, one "surrounded by democratic institutions, a popular monarchy."[21] This manifesto divided the Democrats, with most leaving to form the Federal Republican Party.[22] These questions dominated what turned out to be an "explosive" election campaign.[23] Would Spain be a monarchy or a republic? And if it were to be a monarchy, would this be traditional one or a new kind of "democratic" monarchy?

The revolution did away with the strict censorship regime of the final years of Isabel's reign, creating an unprecedented degree of freedom to publish newspapers and pamphlets and to perform plays.[24] Politics could be discussed as never before, and Espartero immediately became an important part of the broad public debate over the future form of government.

Spanish governments had always been particularly wary of the theatre, and the 1849 Organic Decree for the Theatres of the Realm established close censorship because of the influence theatre had "on the morality, the politics, the education, and everything to do with private and public behavior." Theatre could also reach a largely illiterate population in ways that published material could not. The Revolution of 1868 produced a brief period of unprecedented freedom for Spanish theatres, establishing "the freedom of the theatre in its widest possible form."[25] This decree was issued in January 1869, but writers and theatre owners had already begun creating and putting on plays that dealt with the political issues of the day, including ones in Catalan, something that had been prohibited by a Royal Decree of January 1867 on the grounds that it undermined "the most effective means through which the use of the national language is generalized."[26]

Either Espartero was a character or his name was prominently mentioned in at least three plays that were performed before the end of 1868.[27] Given his popularity in Catalonia, it is not surprising that the first such play, *Lo pronunciament*, was written in Catalan and presented in Barcelona. Set there on the day of the revolution, the plot revolves around Rufino enlisting his fiancée, Carmeta, to convince her father, Senyo Lleó, that the revolution is a good thing. Rufino is also a supporter of Espartero, who is frequently referred to as "the Grandfather." Espartero is never seen, but his name and shouts of "Long live Espartero" punctuate the play. In one scene towards the end, Carmeta tells her father that shouting "Long live Espartero" and "Long live Liberty ... is the same!"[28]

Starting on 11 December 1868, the Novedades theatre in Madrid put on *¿Qién sera el rey?, o Los petendientes* [Who will be king? Or the Pretenders] by José María Gutiérrez de Alba, one of the pioneers of explicitly political theatre in Spain.[29] A metaphorical Mother Spain brings together her children, the various provinces, to decide what the new form of government should be. Spaniards, she says, are not ready for a republic, so Spain must be a monarchy, and the new ruler must be Spanish. A Frenchmen, a Portuguese, an Italian, two Germans, and an Englishman appear in consecutive scenes and are dismissed. They are followed by a young boy – the Carlist Pretender – and a Basque who announces that a ten-year-old boy has come from France, Isabel's son Alfonso, who is not allowed even to appear. Finally, Mother Spain tells her children that the decision is theirs, warns them against hidden ambitions, and then recalls that there is one man who deserves to be king: "An honest man / who has given a thousand proofs / of not having ambition … A man full of glory / without children … A venerable old man / who can even be accepted / as a bridge to a stable republic." And to ensure that no one in the audience missed this endorsement of Espartero for king, there appeared "a rainbow with stars spelling out in brilliant letters: "Let the national will be done!" With this the orchestra strikes up the *Himno de Bilbao* as the curtain descends.[30] French radical Elie Reclus was in the theatre on 12 December and observed that the play "was much applauded by the petty bourgeois audience."[31] A few days later, Reclus saw Salvador Granés's comic zarzuela *Así en la tierra como en el cielo* [On earth as in heaven]. Jupiter, who represents Espartero, descends from Olympus in disguise to visit revolutionary Madrid. Juno takes advantage of his absence to establish a dictatorship, but Jupiter appears later wearing the uniform of a captain general to announce his program: "Unlimited freedom … to a certain point, you understand."[32] Reclus was not impressed by the Espartero character: "you can't tell if he is an honest man, an old idiot, or a braggart."[33]

Public manifestos proposing Espartero as head of state had appeared even before the election was called. Again, Barcelona led the way. On 29 October, José Yglesias Veguer sent Espartero a manifesto entitled "The Candidacy of General Espartero to Be King of Spain," which was circulating in the city "frantically." Years of reactionary government had left Spain unprepared for a republic, so the best solution was "a democratic monarchy" with a Spaniard on the throne as a transitional measure. And Espartero, "the sentinel of our liberties, this veteran who symbolizes the sovereignty of the people," was the best possible monarch.[34] Similar arguments were made in a number of other pamphlets that appeared before the election. Francisco Sicilia de Arenzana, who would be a Republican candidate for the Cortes in Logroño, published *Un Monarca ... y la República, o Espartero Rey* [A Monarch ... and the Republic, o Espartero for King], in which he argued that making Espartero, "an old man without children but with a brilliant record in private and public life," king was the best way to achieve a successful republic. Spain lacked suffient "popular education" for a republic; the way to square the circle was to find a monarch who would serve as a transitional figure. Fortunately, just such a person existed and everyone knew who it was.[35] Three pamphlets and at least one flyer published in Madrid at about the same time made similar points. Spain was not ready for a republic; a "democratic monarchy" with a Spaniard on the throne was the best transitional regime, and the only viable candidate was Espartero: a man with "a sublime love of liberty, a Spartan disinterestedness ... a magnificent loyalty and an inviolable respect for the law,"[36] someone who had remained apart from the corruption of Isabel's reign, living "in obscurity during the most immoral times of the fallen dynasty."[37]

The new political context gave rise to a new phenomenon: newspapers created specifically to promote the cause of one or other of the potential candidates for the crown. There were thirty papers backing the Duke of Montpensier, including the influential *Correspondencia de España*.[38] Far fewer papers backed Espartero; they also had less financial backing and were more short-lived. Three of them, *El Madrileño*, *La Humanidad*, and *El Cronista*, appeared late in 1868. Only the last survived into the following year.

La Humanidad began publication on 15 November 1868, but only one issue, a special edition dated 18 November, remains in existence. It advocated a "transitional elective and popular monarchy" with very limited powers. The monarch had to be "identified with freedom" in order to serve as a bulwark against reaction, and "Providence" had given Spain just such a person: "one who embodies the liberal glories of the century; an exemplary citizen ... who knows how to live modestly and with resignation ... the hero who loves his fatherland deliriously." The Constituent Assembly should proclaim Espartero "the popular and transitional king of Spain, a king for Spain without equal."[39] The paper also published a manifesto, "Espartero, head of State," which, it said, was "circulating widely" in Madrid.[40]

El Cronista functioned, in many respects, as a typical Spanish newspaper of the time, but by far the bulk of its efforts went into promoting Espartero as a candidate for king of an elective monarchy and, increasingly, denouncing his principal rival, the Duke of Montpensier, and the politicians of the former Liberal Union who supported him. Whenever it mentioned Espartero by name or as Duke of Victory, it used capital letters, and starting on 24 December 1868, the anniversary of the Battle of Luchana, "Let the national will be done!" and "Espartero, Head of State" appeared immediately below the masthead. It regularly reported on meetings and demonstrations in favour of Espartero in places across Spain, as well as pro-Espartero statements that appeared in other newspapers. In the first issue, it reported on a meeting in Salamanca and printed a flyer that had been distributed there denouncing the idea of a "foreign yoke" and proclaiming Espartero "supreme leader of the Nation."[41] It also reprinted pro-Espartero manifestos like that proposing an "Espartero monarchy without a dynasty" as a "transitional solution" that would preserve domestic peace, preserve Spanish neutrality, and provide the order and liberty needed to make reforms.[42]

The paper also promoted Espartero's candidacy directly. He was for Spain "what Cincinatus was for Rome, Aristides for Greece."[43] In the lead article in its 24 December issue, "the night of Luchana," the paper even compared Espartero to Christ.[44] The contrast between Espartero and Montpensier could not be starker. Espartero was a man of the people, a new Cincinnatus, who had held the highest posts but then gone into quiet and obscure retirement while Montpensier came from a family that was concerned only with becoming kings. Espartero was a military hero while Montpensier played with fireworks. Espartero gloried in the title of "Peacemaker of Spain" while Montpensier would bring another civil war. Espartero could bring together all liberals while Montpensier would be a king only for the Liberal Union. Finally, Espartero was a Spaniard, a born democrat, and a loyal defender of the law while Montpensier, a Frenchman, was closely tied to the discredited Bourbons.[45]

El Eco del Progreso also backed Espartero. The moving spirit there was Francisco Salmerón, a lawyer from Almería and brother of future President of the Republic Nicolás Salmerón. He was a defender of advanced liberal positions such as freedom of religion, played an active role in the revolution of 1854, and was a deputy in the Constituent Cortes. He was also an ardent advocate for making Espartero king. As he told his father shortly before the election, it would be "either the Duke of Victory or ignominy."[46]

Republicans invoked Espartero repeatedly. More in touch with public opinion than politicians belonging to the traditional parties of notables, they were very aware that he remained immensely popular and that his name was a powerful political asset.

In the Rioja, the Republicans included him on their ticket, but he refused the offer.[47] The Republicans also hoped to attract "Progressives who love Espartero."[48] José María Orense, one of the most important republican leaders, made a similar pitch in his pamphlet *Advantages of the Federal Republic*, published in January 1869. As king, he wrote, Espartero "would pass like a summer storm," but as president he would recover "the cheers of 1854." And when Emilio Castelar made his triumphal entry into Zaragoza, the greeting included five bands playing the Marseillaise and the marches of Riego, Garibaldi, and Espartero. In December, the city saw separate demonstrations demanding Espartero as king and president.[49] Late in the year, a flyer, *Espartero King or President*, appeared in Barcelona. Beneath a crude drawing of a seated Espartero being offered a scroll that reads "FEDERAL REPUBLIC" from one side and a crown from the other, there is a dialogue in which "Monarchists" and "Republicans" take turns explaining why they want him as head of state. For the former, he was not a foreigner but a Spaniard, and one who "gave us liberty on the battlefield" and was "good, upright and just." The latter wanted someone who was "pure and clean as the sun," and Espartero had shown himself to be "upright, brave and loyal." He had been the first to proclaim "the national will," and "the Iberian people should trust" that he would "embrace our slogan": the Federal Republic.[50]

In December, *El Federal*, a republican paper in Palencia, predicted that Espartero would be President of the Republic while Salamanca's Sociedad Obrera, "republican at heart," sent him a letter comparing him to George Washington and Cincinnatus and saying that they wanted him as president or king.[51] Local republicans also campaigned in favour of Espartero. On 19 December, *El Cronista* included a report from a republican paper in Valencia that a republican campaign meeting had ended with "cheers for the Federal Republic, the sovereign people, and the unvanquished general ESPARTERO as President of the Republic."[52] The manifesto of Juan Pablo Soler, who wound up getting elected in Zaragoza, included a promise to propose Espartero to become president: "the victor of Luchana deserves an even greater glory, that of becoming *the first president of the Spanish Republic.*"[53] More surprising was a campaign speech that veteran republican Fernando Garrido delivered in Valencia in November in which he called on Democrats and Progressives to unite in support of a republic with Espartero as president. Espartero had disappointed Garrido after 1854, but that was, he said, the fruit of Espartero's own monarchical illusion.[54] In another speech, Garrido said that Espartero was too good for the throne: "the only thing worthy of him we have to offer, and for him to accept, is the great mission of being a [George] Washington."[55]

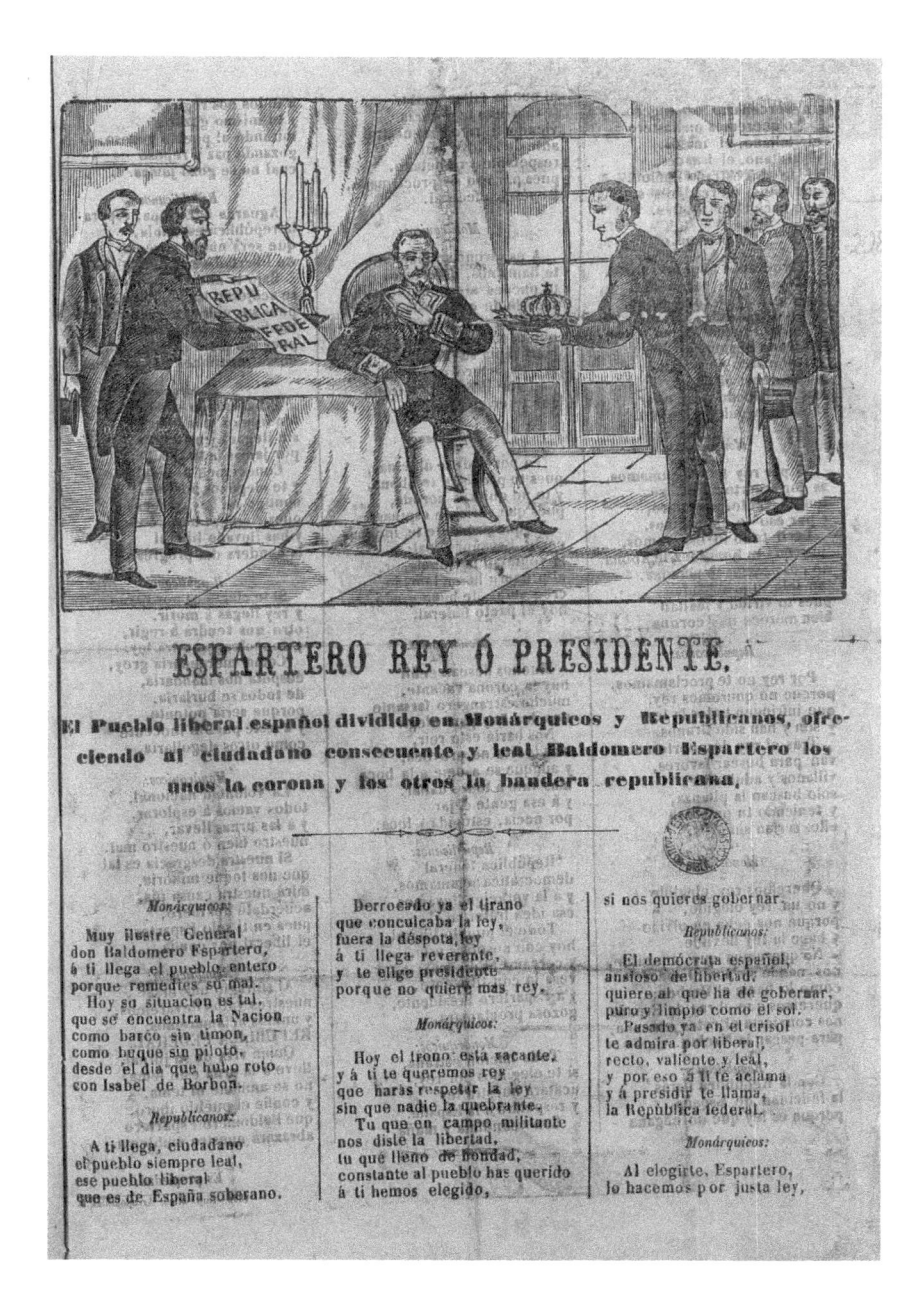

Figure 14 "Espartero: King or President?," 1868. Biblioteca de Catalunya.

With a turnout of about 70 per cent of eligible voters, the elections produced a strong majority for the three parties supporting a constitutional monarchy: 159 Progressives, 69 Unionists, and 20 Democrats. On the left, the Federal Republicans won 85 and the Unitary Republicans only 2, while on the right, the Carlists took 20 seats and the supporters of a Bourbon monarchy in the person of Prince Alfonso won 14.

Espartero topped the polls in Longroño with a stunning 96.3 per cent of the votes. The other three deputies, all from the same list, Sagasta, Dulce, and Olózaga, came far behind.[56] In Zaragoza, he took 21,654 votes of a total 44,268. Espartero's ticket lost in Barcelona, but trailed the victorious Republicans by only 18,233 to 15,844 votes. One of his supporters claimed that the defeat was due to intimidation by the Republicans.[57] Espartero refused to serve and so informed the civil governors of both provinces in identical letters that were relayed to the Cortes, letters which reveal his view of the influence he felt he wielded: "I do not want anyone to imagine that my personal views might influence the balance of opinion [or] the spirit of the people's representatives, whose votes should be informed only by considerations of the greatest patriotism."[58]

Espartero's ability to attract votes in an unprecedentedly democratic context is not at all surprising in light of the letters that he had been receiving since the very first days of the revolution. Much of this "chorus of voices" came from small towns and villages; many were written on cheap paper with handwriting and spelling that suggest correspondents who did not write that often. For large numbers of ordinary Spaniards, he remained the hero who could resolve the country's problems.

Some just wanted to hear the "authoritative voice of the modern Cincinnatus."[59] Antón Gómez Carmona, who described himself as an active liberal since 1820 and lifelong Progressive, asked if he "should vote for the Democratic Party."[60] Many others called on Espartero to return to public life. The Junta Revolucionaria de Alar del Rey (Palencia) called on the "Symbol of the Spanish People" to go to Madrid so that his presence would "consolidate the triumph of the Glorious Revolution."[61] There were many different ideas about what his role should be. Some wanted him to be a candidate for the new Cortes. The electoral committee of Quintanar de la Orden (Toledo) chose him, along with Federal Republican theorist Francisco Pi i Margall, a most unusual combination, but one which testified to Espartero's broad appeal. He was also chosen as a candidate by the Democratic-Monarchist Committee of Almagro, the town where he had gone to university, and the Monarchist Party in Ronda (Málaga) and in Lanestosa (Vizcaya).[62]

Many more saw Espartero in a far more exalted role: head of state. What is most striking about these proposals is that they came from both monarchists and republicans, and even from people who seemed not to have a preference for one form or the other, so long as Espartero had the job.

A number of Republicans wanted Espartero to become the president of a Spanish Republic. In January 1869, the Republicans of Argamasilla de Alba (Ciudad Real) paraded, "adorning our banners with Your Excellency's illustrious name as President of the Republic."[63] In a letter that addressed him simply as "Mr Baldomero Espartero, Citizen," the Republican Committee of Novelda (Alicante) wrote that they had issued a manifesto calling on the Constituent Cortes to name him "President for Life of the Federal Republic."[64] Similarly, the Republican Committee of Calatorao (Zaragoza) told "Citizen Espartero" that more than one thousand of their members wanted him to be head of state.[65]

Others wanted to see Espartero on the throne. On 24 November, 170 "landowners, manufacturers, artisans, and residents" from the town of Villatobas (Toledo), describing themselves as liberal monarchists and "men of order," sent a handwritten manifesto to the government requesting that Espartero be made king. Their ideal monarch would be "A popular king who protected and helped the people who suffer wasteful and corrupt administrations ... a simple king, without a court or show ... a son of the people who rules by and for the people, reducing the number of public jobs and increasing revenue ... in a word, one with less politics and more and better administration directed at improving agriculture ... protecting commerce and industry and whose beneficent hand protects property, society and families." Who better than the "Peacemaker of Spain, simple, hardworking, and economical," who had already done the job "honestly and patriotically"?[66]

Still others were indifferent to the form of government so long as Espartero was at its head. Gregorio Rodríguez, the president of the electoral committee of Quintanar de la Orden, was one: "with the son of Granátula as king or president ... Liberty is assured ... please accept, by God."[67] From the newly renamed Morales del Progreso, a large number of liberals, including twenty-six "who cannot write but who want their name to appear," expressed their wish that "you and no other" should head the new regime: "President of the Republic, King of the Monarchy."[68] Antonio Quintana, a member of the Murcia Progressive committee, even expressed it in verse. The refrain of his "Improvisation dedicated to the Duke of Victory" went: "Everyone wants / Espartero KING of Spain / even the children demand / President Espartero."[69]

Through these letters echo the ways in which Spaniards remembered Espartero, the aspects of his career that were alive in the popular memory, things that monarchists and republicans could value equally. The letters also reveal what Spaniards desired for the future and what they most feared about the current moment.

The most common by far was that Espartero was the "Peacemaker of Spain," "the greatest title a nation could give." He was the "symbol of peace for all Spaniards," the man who ended "the fratricidal seven year war." Only "yesterday's Peacemaker [could be] the cord of unity and fraternity today."[70] Espartero was also the unflagging champion of liberty, of what many referred to as the "holy cause," the "Liberator of the Nation," as one old soldier put it, the "lighthouse of our liberties," in the words of the Republican Committee of Calatorao (Zaragoza).[71]

Many admired his personal qualities, particularly his honesty, modesty, and lack of ambition. Good in themselves, they also made Espartero stand out in contrast to other politicians, both those of the old regime and those of the new. "Tired of being ... the prey of vultures and other raptors," Spaniards wanted his "honesty, consistency, and talent." They admired his "modest retirement from a corrupt court" and saw him as someone without ambition, "whose only desires are for the well-being of his fatherland," someone uniquely placed to "control the race of political passions, because he was a martyr to them." Republicans saw him as "another modest Washington ... the best legacy we can leave our children."[72]

Espartero's responses to all this varied little. On the one hand, he told his correspondents that he gave the men who had carried out the revolution his full support.[73] On the other, he made it clear that he had no interest in taking an active role in events. To Mariano Acevedo Álvarez's question of whether he wanted to be king or president, he replied, "I wish only that we all support the Provisional Government so that the Constituent Cortes use their sovereignty to create as soon as possible [a constitution] we should all accept and defend."[74] He even refused to allow the "young republican" author of a pamphlet arguing that he should be king to dedicate it to him because he thought it might influence the Cortes' decision.[75]

The Constituent Cortes began its sessions on 11 February 1869. After Serrano tendered the resignation of the Provisional Government, the Cortes immediately named him to head the new government. That done, the legislature confronted its principal task: drafting a new constitution. The job was given to a fifteen-member committee, five members from each of the revolutionary coalition parties, with Espartero's old nemesis, Olózaga, as its chair. The Federal Republicans were not offered a place, even though they were the second largest party in the Cortes. The committee worked quickly, presenting its handiwork on 30 March.

The debates were lengthy and impassioned. Two articles – number 32, "National sovereignty resides essentially in the nation, from which all power emanates," and number 33, "The form of government of the Spanish nation is monarchy" – were debated together over eight full days. The Republicans fought them with great determination. The highlight was a long speech by Emilio Castelar, who had been a professor of history before entering parliament. In his arguments against the monarchy, Castelar invoked Espartero and placed him in some very select company. Trying to join monarchy and democracy was, he said, "demented, the greatest possible error ... In Europe only three generals have been able to do it: Lafayette, Garibaldi, and Espartero."[76] Despite Castelar's spellbinding oratory, the Republicans lost by a vote of 214 to 71. Spain was once again a constitutional monarchy.[77] The Constitution was approved on 1 June 1869, with 214 votes in favour and 55 against; it was proclaimed five days later.

A few days after the Constitution had been proclaimed, Serrano was appointed regent and Prim succeeded him as prime minister. With Spain now officially a constitutional monarchy, the country had to find a monarch. This was not unprecedented in nineteenth-century Europe. Both Greece and Belgium had been in this situation when they emerged as independent countries after their respective wars of independence. Both cases made it clear that going abroad for a monarch quickly enmeshed a country in the diplomacy of the great powers, and Spain's revolutionary rulers would soon find themselves in just this situation. International complications combined with internal political machinations to delay the decision until November 1870, a full eighteen months after the Constitution had been proclaimed.

On the opening day of the Cortes, Prim had made one thing absolutely clear: the Bourbons "will never, ever, ever return."[78] In early 1869 this certainly didn't seem at all likely: only fourteen conservative deputies led by Antonio Cánovas del Castillo advocated the cause of Isabel's son, Prince Alfonso. The problem was that each group in the revolutionary coalition had its own candidate. The Liberal Unionists supported the Duke of Montpensier, the youngest son of Louis Philippe of France and the husband of Isabel II's sister, Princess Luisa Fernanda. Many Progressives and Democrats looked to Fernando of Saxe-Coburg and Gotha, the widower of Queen María II of Portugal, although he was soon out of the running. Concerned that many of the people backing his candidacy were also proponents of an Iberian union, the Portuguese government informed its ambassador in Madrid that Fernando would not be a candidate.[79] Others wanted a member of the House of Savoy, which ruled the newly united Kingdom of Italy. A member of the Hohenzollern family was briefly in the mix.

There was also a campaign in favour of Espartero. Led by Pascual Madoz, Francisco Salmerón, and other Progressives based primarily in Barcelona and Madrid, the campaign to make Espartero king mobilized the immense popularity that the old man still enjoyed across the country. According to historian and contemporary Antonio Pirala, it was "without doubt the most popular [candidacy]. No other was proclaimed in as many pamphlets and articles, nor generated as many or as spontaneous demonstrations in Madrid and other [provincial] capitals."[80] Emilio Castelar claimed that had the outcome depended on a plebiscite rather than a parliamentary vote, the result would "surely have been the Republic or the monarchy of General Espartero."[81]

The competition for the crown took a dramatic turn in March 1870. Just before the election, Prince Enrique de Borbón, a cousin of Isabel II and a bitter rival of the Duke of Montpensier, sent a letter to the regent, General Serrano, in which he proclaimed his liberal beliefs, praised Espartero, and launched a violent diatribe against Montpensier, which concluded by comparing the "puffed-up French pastry chef" to "the object of national veneration" that was Espartero.[82] Montpensier responded by challenging Enrique to a duel. The two met outside Madrid on 12 March and Montpensier killed Enrique on the second shot. A military court sentenced him to a month's exile from Madrid and an indemnity to be paid to Enrique's family.[83]

In the spring of 1870, the pro-Espartero campaign became more organized. On 26 April, Madoz and Salmerón called a meeting of Progressive deputies who were willing to back Espartero for king; some thirty attended.[84] This campaign forced Prim to act. On 13 May he wrote a letter to Espartero which he gave to Madoz to deliver personally. "It is well known," he wrote, "that your friends and supporters have recalled the services of the Peacemaker of Spain to the constitutional cause. Authorized by the government, and as was the case with all other candidacies, I would like to know *if you would agree to become King of Spain should the sovereign Constituent Cortes decide to elect you.*" The government was neutral, "leaving the Assembly the most total freedom," but it did have the responsibility "to prevent passions from becoming unnecessarily agitated if the person chosen should refuse to accept."[85]

Justo Tomás Delgado, later Espartero's secretary, was a member of the delegation that carried the letter to Logroño and provided the only eyewitness account of the meeting, although it was made public thirty-three years after the event. Unaware of the reason for the visit, Espartero received them "with his habitual kindness because he saw in us loyal and affectionate friends and unconditional supporters." After Salmerón told him why they were there, "Espartero's expressive face reflected his surprise that a matter of such transcendant importance was being treated in this manner." He was "nothing more than a simple soldier ready to sacrifice everything for his country [and] deeply embarrassed" by all the praise. "I beg you to excuse me from going to the bottom of the mission that has been entrusted to you. Let us not dream, my friends … When you transmit my gratitude to General Prim and the other friends who thought of me so well, *tell them from me to forget it completely* … That they should forget about bringing a foreign prince to Spanish soil because that would risk prolonging the dangerous period in which we find ourselves." Espartero then invited them to accompany him to La Fombera, where "we spent a wonderful afternoon entertained by "Espartero and his wife." At one point Espartero took Delgado aside and told him that "in Madrid they are overwhelmed by the smoke and dust of the ruins of what they have burned and destroyed and they want me to pull their chestnuts out of the fire."[86]

Espartero's formal reply to Prim was clear and, as always, brief. It also repeated what he had said many times already: while he was ready to sacrifice everything for his country, "an obligation of conscience" prevented him from "accepting such a lofty position, because my age and poor health would not allow me to do a good job."[87] He also told Cipriano Montesino that "if in spite of my absolute refusal" his name continued to be mentioned, he should publish his "firm determination" to refuse the throne because he was "not in a condition to carry it out."[88]

This is often referred to as Prim offering the throne to Espartero, but it was, in Pere Anguera's words, a trap: if Espartero said no, then Prim could stop worrying about him; if he said yes, then he could be criticized for overweening ambition.[89] Espartero did give the "resounding no" that Prim wanted, but that did not mean that his supporters would abandon the cause or that Prim could stop worrying about him. If anything, in the following weeks, the campaign in favour of Espartero grew more vociferous.

On its return to Madrid, the delegation that had carried Prim's letter to Logroño was met by a large and enthusiastic throng. Salmerón clambered onto an omnibus to address the crowd. While not describing the details of the meeting, he made it clear that Espartero had refused the offer. He also made it clear that this was not the last word: "We will spread our opinion and make it the majority one."[90] Espartero's supporters sent their own delegation to try and get him to change his mind, but he told them "not to present me as a candidate, because I wouldn't be elected, and even if I were an obligation of conscience would require me to turn it down because my advanced age and bad health would not allow me to fulfil my duties."[91]

Espartero himself continued to receive letters of support. From Vitoria, Andrés G. Navarro, "a republican by background, principles, and belief," expressed his disgust at the way Prim had dealt with Espartero. By now, he said, the choice facing Spain was Espartero "or the Republic." Only he could prevent a war that could even be worse than that of the 1830s.[92] And from Badajoz, Carlos Botello del Castillo called on him to accept the throne. He was a committed *esparterista*, having fought for him in 1843, and he had been publicly threatened with being shot for having distributed Espartero's portrait in the town the day the victory at Tetuan was announced in February 1860. There was, he wrote, no other choice, unless Espartero wanted to see the country descend into civil war.[93]

With the Cortes debating a law on how the new monarch would be elected, the Espartero campaign turned up the pressure. The pro-Espartero deputies published a manifesto on 30 May. With the "great monarchist party divided into three tendencies: Espartero, Montepensier, Limbo," Espartero was the only acceptable choice. He was a military hero "shaped in the camp of victory," but it was his personal qualities that stood out. "[H]is rectitude honours our liberal patriarchs ... In his modesty, the fatherland sees the coming of longed-for economies, the people await his unflinching virtue, the triumph of good ... victim of Bourbon ingratitude, he is freedom's martyr; having sacrificed his fortune for the sake of the country." He was, in sum, "a hero of selflessness." That he had already said no was not a concern. Indeed, wasn't this refusal itself "the most sublime example of honesty"? They concluded by calling on Spaniards to create "the majestic surge of public opinion" to get Espartero elected because, "KING ESPARTERO IS SPAIN WITH HONOUR."[94] From Logroño, Espartero sent his by now habitual refusal, in exactly the same words he had used with the Progressive delegation.[95]

The *esparterista* deputies also organized a mass demonstration in Madrid for 5 June. Ten groups from the different districts of the city plus another group of students were to gather in the Plaza de la Villa at 6:00 in the afternoon. Led by a band and bearing their respective flags, they would escort a carriage carrying the petition – supposedly signed by forty thousand people – through the old heart of the city to the Puerta de Alcalá. The petition, "To Our Fellow Citizens," emphasized the usual combination of Espartero's personal virtues and his public accomplishments: "the consistent patrician, the proven liberal, the conscientious politician ... who with an unmatched abnegation and love for the Spanish people, always obeyed his principles, fulfilling his motto, 'Let the national will be done!'"[96] Camilo Mojén, who was there representing the Liberal Circle of the Ciudadela de Menorca, was impressed by "the enthusiasm of the people of Madrid" but also troubled by "certain defections ... it's impossible to know what will be the outcome of everything those who call themselves liberals are plotting these days."[97]

There were also pro-Espartero rallies in the provinces. The one in Cuenca took place on 29 May. Organized on short notice by "ardent young enthuasiasts of that national glory," a large crowd carrying a "profusion of flags, banners, and pennants bearing slogans and allegorical verses" took part. Even some republicans and members of the Catholic Youth chose to miss meetings of their own organizations to join in. There was a demonstration in Villar del Saz de Arcas the same day: "they improvised an orchestra, triumphal arches, and banners, and carried the portrait of the distinguished Peacemaker" through the town. At nightfall, the Plaza de la Constitución was the site of a "public dance lit by the large bonfires the residents had prepared."[93] There were also demonstrations in Burgos, one of which was described in the French paper *Le Monde Illustré*.[99]

Progressives in Catalonia, and especially in Barcelona, were deeply divided by the question of the new head of state. Support for Espartero was strong, even in the face of pressure from Victor Balaguer, who had become a backer of Prim, to rally support for the government. While the form of the new regime remained undecided, the group involved in organizing the San Baldomero Day celebrations promoted Espartero as head of state, "whatever the form of government the Cortes chooses."[100] Once the new constitution had been proclaimed, it launched a petition signed by "many thousands of citizens – two thousand in Manresa alone,"[101] that Espartero become king with the Duke of Genoa, the government's candidate, as his heir with the title Prince of Asturias.[102] Balaguer's efforts to impose discipline only earned him criticism from some of his friends. One lamented that he had been seduced by "the courtesan atmosphere of Madrid" while another denounced his armtwisting as "a sordid way of destroying [the] sacred right" to express one's opinion.[103] As always, Pascual Madoz spoke his mind. Balaguer could be the Italian prince's "herald everywhere, except in Barcelona. Someone who used to be such a solid *esparterista* cannot lend himself to the propaganda against [him] today. I predict that this will cause you more than a little trouble." Madoz would vote for Espartero on the first ballot; if there were a second he would vote for the Duke of Genoa, "although with great repugnance."[104]

The publication of the manifesto of the pro-Espartero deputies in May 1870 reignited the conflicts within the party. According to Prim's informants, the party leaders were agitating on their behalf, and Espartero's candidacy was "growing greatly in the public's spirit."[105] Even though news that Prim was not one of the signatories "fell like a bomb,"[106] this did nothing to narrow the gap. At a meeting on 5 June, Espartero's advocates even created their own party, the Partido Liberal Esparterista, and issued a manifesto calling on "all citizens who belong to the great liberal family … convinced liberals and not party men" to back Espartero as king "as a symbol of our nationality." Membership was open to anyone, even republicans, who upheld the new constitution, rejected extra-legal means of advancing their cause, and, most importantly, agreed to support Espartero's candidacy.[107] In a letter to Espartero, one of its leaders decried the goals of the new party as "uniting all the liberal forces in the face of the growing wave of political passion … and guaranteeing the conquests of the revolution under the motto Fatherland, Liberty and Independence."[108] Not even Prim's name could dent Espartero's prestige, wrote another. "We laugh at his former authority and stale ideas."[109]

The most concrete products of the pro-Espartero campaign were the 268 petitions, signed by a minimum of one hundred thousand people, which flooded into the parliamentary mail room between October 1869 and June 1870.[110] Produced over a period of eight months, the petitions peaked at two moments: in mid-May, following the meeting at which thirty deputies agreed to back Espartero's candidacy, and especially between 4 and 7 June, after Espartero had rejected Prim's invitation to put his name forward and Madoz's group published its manifesto, when the pro- Espartero campaign was at its most active.[111]

The signatures betray every possible level of familiarity with writing, and a number of petitions include multiple signatures by the same hand with a note that they were done "At the request of those who cannot sign themselves" or something similar.[112] The petitions came from forty of the fifty provinces, but they were far from evenly distributed. Cuenca, with twenty-two, produced the most followed by Castellón (seventeen), Murcia (fourteen), Huelva and La Coruña (thirteen), Alicante, Badajoz, and Cáceres (ten), Almería and Valencia (nine), Granada and Toledo (eight), Albacete, Ciudad Real, and Sevilla (seven), Logroño, Madrid, Palencia, and Valladolid (six), Guadalajara, Cádiz, and Córdoba (five),

Burgos, Leon, Salamanca, Santander, and Zaragoza (three), Gerona, Lérida, Lugo, and Málaga (two), and Avila, Barcelona, Jaén, Navarra, Orense, Oviedo, Segovia, Teruel, and Zamora (one). These numbers can be misleading; in some cases, Salamanca for example, a single petition contains pages of signatures from a number of different towns and villages which "adhered" to the petition from the capital, while in Cuenca these appear as separate petitions. Also, the numbers of signatories varied enormously, from one single individual to many thousands.

The petitions demonstrate that the pro-Espartero campaign was able to get its supporters to repeat a standard message. In a number of cases, multiple petitions used the same language or were even copied verbatim in multiple locations. The most striking example is a series of ten petitions from towns in the province of Murcia between 6 and 13 June 1870, when the campaign was at its height.[113] There are even examples of multiple petitions using the same, prepared signature pages.[114]

All the petitions asked the Constituent Cortes to name Espartero king of the monarchy created by the Constitution of 1869. (The petition from Tarazona de la Mancha [Albacete] includes a note that there would have been more signatures but "some people wanted him to be named President of the Republic.")[115] Almost all explained what it was about Espartero that made him the best, or indeed the only, person for the job.

Eighty petitions referred to the personal qualities that made Espartero a worthy monarch: honesty, modesty, disinterestedness, abnegation, and lack of ambition, virtues which had been sorely lacking in the politicians who had ruled Spain before the revolution. He was the "Great Colossus of virtue, abnegation, and patriotism," "the perfect model of self-denial, modesty, honesty, and proven patriotism." Past virtues ensured his future good conduct: as the residents of San Vicente de Alcántara (Badajoz) asked, "if he has lived so long remaining incorruptible and without a stain on his honour, will he, in the future, become ambitious, corrupt, or dishonourable?"[116]

Espartero's humble origins were mentioned thirty-three times. Most often he is described simply as "a son of the people," although there are also references to "being born to humble parents" and his "eminently popular origin." The massive petition from Salamanca called him "the apotheosis of the People, glorified in one of its children."[117]

Twenty-six petitions refer to the fact that Espartero was living in Logroño. In some cases this was connected to his personal qualities: he was the "modest retiree of Logrono" or, more elaborately, he had moved "to a third-rate provincial capital where he thought only of the well-being of its inhabitants. He lived there modestly, loved by all, protector of the honest worker, of the virtuous head of family."[118] Others connected this to his rejection of the "miserable intrigues of the political gangs" or his desire not to "witness the disappearance of the freedoms that he conquered for the fatherland at such cost."[119] In still others, his residence in Logroño was an exile; Espartero was the victim of a queen who "repaid the blood he shed for her with ingratitude."[120] From here it was only a small step to invoking the name of Cincinnatus, as eighteen of the petitions did.

Espartero's public achievements were dominated by his role in the Carlist War, and above all by his bringing of peace. Seventy referred to him as the "Peacemaker of Spain," usually capitalized as if it were as official as his noble titles. Others called him the "rainbow of peace" or noted that he "put an end to the fratricidal seven-year war, giving Spain peace."[121] Occasionally, his peacemaking in the past was seen as essential to overcoming the difficult circumstances of the present. For a second time he would be "our peacemaker and with his modesty and goodness oblige us put aside the political differences that divide us for the Good of all and the honour of Spain ... Today as at Luchana we must again bring an end to our conflicts."[122]

Thirty-nine petitions presented him as the embodiment of liberalism and constitutional government. The most common phrasing, which was used fourteen times, was to call him the "Patriarch of Freedom," although he was also described as the "radiant star of our freedoms," the "glorious torch of liberty," the "living personification of our liberties," and the "consecration of the dogma of National Sovereignty." It was Espartero who had "Crown[ed] the liberal army with glory, raising the constitutional throne on the ruins of absolutism."[123]

The phrase most associated with Espartero, "Let the national will be done!," appeared in only fourteen petitions, usually as part of broader praise, such as "the simple and modest resident of Logroño ... the honest citizen who was always faithful to the motto 'Let the national will be done!'"[124] In one case, however, petitioners used it against him: Commenting on a letter that appeared in the press in which Espartero said he would not accept the crown, the residents of San Vicente de Alcántara (Badaloz) wrote, "You have repeated 'Let the national will be done!' so many times; accepting the will of the Nation if the Cortes elect you king would be to do so, even if it means your sacrificing tranquillity."[125]

Thirteen petitions argued that Espartero would unify the squabbling political factions. For some he was the "knot of unity among all the liberal factions." Others saw him bringing a more expansive unity. For the people from Salamanca, an Espartero monarchy would produce "a truce" that would extend to "many sensible republicans," while petitioners from Dolores (Alicante) called for a plebiscite to discover "the aspiration of all ... even the Carlists, who are excited when they speak the magic name of the modern Cincinnatus."[126]

There was no "typical" petition, but perhaps the one that touched the most bases came from the municipal government and residents of Dalías (Almería). After strongly rejecting the idea of a monarch from a foreign dynasty, it continued:

> The Decalogue of the liberal church is written in the blood of its martyrs and needs only to be defended by a man of the People, one who has known his own martyrdom ... and has contributed to breaking the chains of its oppressive enslavement and loves its glories and its prosperity.
>
> Behold this man in the Cincinnatus of Logroño, the Hero of Luchana, the rainbow of the peace of Vergara, the Patriarch of Freedom, General Espartero. There is no need to worry that he who shed his blood for liberal institutions will not love them enthusiastically or defend them valiantly. There is no need to worry that he, who with his victorious sword and the popular halo that surrounded him, could have easily trampled on the law but was its chief guardian, will abuse his power. There is no need to worry that the honest Patrician who left [the regency] and whose virtue shone greater in his modest retirement will stain it with venality and lies. It is only just and merited, patriotic and honourable that he who built our greatest glories and conquered the Crown of Spain for an unjust girl have this same Crown rest on a head adorned with so many and such great virtues.[127]

On 11 June, before a packed Cortes, Prim delivered a major speech on the search for a new king. This had proven "harder than it looks at first glance." After assuring them that the government shared the deputies' "real impatience" to bring the *interinidad* to an end, he forcefully refuted rumours that he wanted to prolong it in order to impose the Prince Alfonso, repeating his famous "not ever, never, never!" He then described the road that had taken the government from Fernando of Portugal to two princes of the House of Savoy to a fourth candidate whom he could not name. All had fallen through, leaving the government with "no candidate to present to you." Unless the Cortes came to a consensus, "it will be impossible to escape from this limbo."[128]

The session ended on 23 June, but within two days Prim's hoped-for solution collapsed when word that Leopold of Hohenzollern Sigmaringen might be the new king was inadvertently leaked. A desperate Prim wrote to Olózaga, again ambassador in Paris, that the government was at risk of "being overwhelmed by the Duke of Victory, the Duke of Montpensier and the Republic" and that Olózaga must convince

Napoleon III to accept Leopold. On 4 July, the cabinet voted in favour of the German and made the decision public. The French ambassador expressed his government's unhappiness on the 11th, and the next day Leopold's father withdrew his son's name. A few days later, France and Prussia were at war.[129]

These dramatic events led one of the Duke of Montpensier's supporters, Manuel Cantero, to contact Cipriano Montesino. Speaking for the Duke, he proposed that Montpensier withdraw his candidacy and Espartero take the throne, so that the Cortes could "later name a son of Montpensier heir to the throne." Espartero was not interested. Recent events had not changed "my firm decision not to accept the Crown if it were offered to me, as my advanced age and poor health prevent me from occupying such an elevated position."[130]

These developments had a major impact on the exiled Isabel, who, under pressure from Napoleon III, abdicated on 25 June.[131] This was something she had been considering since late 1868, and she had twice turned to Espartero for advice and assistance.

After the revolution, most conservatives who hoped to save the throne for the Bourbons had urged the queen to abdicate in favour of her son, Alfonso. This would require a new regency, but who could be regent? Why not Espartero? In December 1868, Isabel had her chief advisor, the Count of Cheste, draft a decree naming the old man, who almost thirty years earlier had taken her and her sister to the circus and who had saved her throne twice before, regent. The decree was accompanied by a long personal letter in which "your fondest" poured out her soul, and which deserves to be quoted at length.

> You see the disunity among those three gangs which claim to comprise the national will. They can only get along in order to destroy, and my legitimate and constitutional authority, which I inherited from one hundred kings, with the consent of one hundred generations, is obliged to do what it can to repair these great disasters that threaten the complete ruin of religion, the monarchy, and even the unity of Spain.
>
> But vilified and mocked as I am ... until the power of truth, which will come sooner or later, restores the brilliance that I need to inspire the general respect only under whose shadow can such an ancient and Catholic monarchy provide the precious fruits of peace, good, government, and strong administration that is the foundation of public well-being, I cannot be among you.
>
> For these reasons, until these clouds dissipate ... until I am called by the very people who dismissed me and who have no idea what it means for the daughter of kings to eat this bitter bread of emigration and mount

the steps of someone else's house ... I want you exercise the royal power as regent, briefly or for a long time, since, if I do not receive the demonstration of affection that my heart requires ... I will know how to put my crown on the head of the Prince of Asturias ... I want everything for my son, better said for my children since Alfonso is only the first of them, ungrateful Spaniards ...

Espartero, forgive this baring of my soul. By God, help stop them tearing down the temples of Jesus Christ, so that it won't be said that we left the holy religion we received from our fathers to our grandchildren debased and profaned.[132]

Jaime de Andreu, the president of Barcelona's Instituto Industrial and Espartero's friend, took the letter to Logroño. Espartero was not interested. He didn't want people to think he was seeking another regency; the memory of 1843 and his subsequent exile was still strong, and he did not want to ruin the time that remained to him "fighting with a fickle people and with political parties sunk into prostitution and driven by ambition."[133]

After the constitution had been proclaimed, Isabel once again turned to her "esteemed and beloved" Espartero. Abdication was a "grave decision," and she needed help from people such as he who "never denied me counsel nor lost my esteem." She needed him to answer two questions. "First: Will it be convenient for Spain first and my dynasty second if I abdicate the Crown in the current circumstances? Second: If I were to abdicate today in favour of the Prince of Asturias, my legitimate heir, who would have to confirm it?"[134] Espartero was not prepared to help. His papers contain an intriguing document which relates a conversation the unidentified author had with Espartero on 18 July. Two days earlier, someone called Calleja had arrived from Paris bearing a letter from Isabel. Espartero handed it back unopened, "stating that he couldn't accept it, something that should not surprise that Lady, if she recalled the last words he spoke to her when he left the prime ministership in 1856. Since then I have remained in my home, saying only that the national will should be done." The next day Espartero got a telegram asking for a reply, which "he didn't answer either."[135]

Isabel then approached Jacinta. According to a document headed "– a letter from the Duchess of Victory, 3 August 1869," Jacinta had received a telegram from the Conde de Ezpeleta on the queen's behalf asking about Espartero's health. "Of course I didn't reply, and *we* decided to hold onto it until we saw if the papers wrote about it." You can imagine, she continued, "how indignant *we* were; the Duke has been ill various times since '56 and not once did it occur to that Lady to write; now she comes up with this to compromise and endanger *us*. They can go to hell."[136]

"Espartero" returned to the stage during 1870. In January, *Don Baldomero*, by a republican named José Mariano Vallejo, used the selection of a doctor by a local government as a metaphor to comment on the election of a new monarch, and to advocate for Espartero over Montpensier. Set in "a small town in Castile in the present day," the play finds the town councillors, each of whom represents a major politician, divided on whom to appoint after their original choice has fallen through or, as in the case of the "youngsters," whether to appoint anyone at all. After one of the candidates is rejected for being a "frog," a crowd of youths representing the republican people enter the room. At first, they don't want to bother with a new doctor; their leader, Justo, convinces them to respect the wishes of their elders to have a doctor, but one who was "purely popular, born of the people," none other than Don Baldomero. When the councillors protest, Justo invokes Espartero's motto and announces "it's the people who proclaim him and we will impose him on you." Brought to the meeting room, Don Baldomero proffers his excuses – "I am old, tired, and weak" – but finally gives in. To his cry of "Long live the people!" one of the characters replies: "Long live Don Baldomero," and the curtain falls to "liveliness and joy."[137]

Espartero also appeared in *La Passió Política*, which debuted in Barcelona on 30 June. The play uses the passion of Christ as a motif to criticize the government's betrayal of the popular revolution, with biblical characters representing contemporary political figures. Espartero appears in the guise of Baldomero Pere – Peter – whose first speech is accompanied by the Hymn of Luchana. Three times during the play he says he does not recognize the Christ figure, Salvador Espanyol [Spanish Saviour], but eventually, and while the orchestra plays the Hymn of Luchana, he repents, leaving a suggestion that he might become the leader of "the new popular faith."[138]

In August, with the Cortes in recess and France and Prussia at war, a short satirical play called *Viva – la muerte: contrasentido inmoral e impolítico de julio de 1870* [Long live – death: an immoral and impolitic piece of nonsense from July 1870] was published under the pseudonym "A rogue of this court." The widow Espadaña is to be remarried but rejects her foreign suitors. Finally given the right to choose her own husband, she goes to the front of the stage, tells the orchestra conductor,

"Young man. Play the Espartero hymn!" The curtain falls as the hymn is played.[139]

The Cortes renewed its sittings on 31 October. Three days later Prim reported on the events that had transpired since the last session: the acceptance of Leopoldo of Hohenzollern that had led to war between France and Prussia and his subsequent withdrawal. The government then turned once again to Amadeo, the Duke of Aosta and second son of King Victor Emmanuel II of Italy, who, with the support of his father, had accepted on condition that the Cortes vote for him.[140] This provoked a long and impassioned speech from Emilio Castelar in which he compared Amadeo and Espartero. The former was "one of those royal adventurers who will abandon their own country to satisfy their hunger for power." In contrast, Espartero was "a disinterested old man" who enjoyed an "inextinguishable popularity" and for whom the people "maintain a respectful cult." Espartero "could carve the names of Luchana and Morella on the walls of his palace"; Amadeo could offer only "Lizza and Custoza."[141]

The law required that the Cortes close for eight days before the final vote. The forces opposed to Amadeo used this hiatus to unleash a propaganda barrage. On 4 November, a flyer entitled ¡Rey Español! [Spanish King!], arguing in favour of the Duke of Montpensier or Espartero, was distributed in the streets of Madrid. Probably put out by Montpensier's supporters, it claimed that the men in power were neglecting obvious Spanish candidates for the throne and "inventing" foreign ones as a way to extend the period of *interinidad* for their own benefit.[142] On the 12th, the streets of the capital were plastered with large yellow posters demanding that the Cortes elect Espartero. "With him we will have stature, freedom and work … [Espartero] is the honoured son of the people, whom the majority want for the second time as the Peacemaker of Spain … All with him, nothing for foreigners."[143]

This was a futile last gasp by the *esparterista* forces. On 11 November, *La Época* had published a letter in which Espartero expressed in no uncertain terms what he had been saying ever since his name had first been broached as a possible head of state. It was his "irrevocable decision" not to accept the throne, and he called on his supporters to "abandon all personal affection and, inspired by the purest patriotism that the current circumstances demand, put my name aside and vote for the candidate they judge most worthy of occupying the throne."[144] The *esparterista* deputies still refused to take no for an answer. The next day, a delegation travelled to Logroño in a final, futile attempt to persuade Espartero to change his mind. With this they finally abandoned the cause, dissolving their caucus and leaving each deputy to vote his conscience.

Esparteristas in places like Sabadell were unable to understand "how a Cortes in which the majority call themselves Progressives does not vote for the man who has always been the head of the party," while others begged Espartero to accept the throne, for the sake of "all true Spaniards."[145] So did the clerks at Madrid's Gran Bazar de la Unión, men who had heard "our parents bless your name."[146] Other *esparteristas* took their hero at his word. The city government of Tafalla, and the town's Voluntarios de la Libertad, applauded Espartero's "abnegation [and] patrician sentiments," as did the Tertulia Monárquico-Democrática of Pamplona. Its counterpart from Palencia, which had sent a petition to make Espartero king, accepted his refusal, although "the reasons for it are beyond our comprehension," and sent a telegram to Prim expressing their support for the Duke of Aosta.[147]

The 16th of November 1870 was the decisive day. The parliamentary session was tumultuous: "a total circus" was Pérez Galdós's judgment.[148] The debate lasted eight hours, but when the vote was finally taken it was not even close: of the 311 votes cast, the Duke of Aosta received 191, the Duke of Montpensier 27, the Duchess of Montpensier 1, and Isabel's son Alfonso 2. Sixty deputies voted for the federal republic, and 19 cast a blank vote. Espartero got 8 votes. Even Pascual Madoz abandoned him for Amadeo, who was proclaimed "king of the Spaniards." The *esparterista* deputies who voted for Amadeo sent Espartero a letter explaining their decision. There was some rancour: they had been persistent, but Espartero's refusals had neutralized their efforts, "and if we never lost our enthusiasm, we were discouraged more than once."[149] Given that he had rebuffed every effort to promote his candidacy, the tone and content of Espartero's reply is no surprise: "As it is my opinion that, in matters concerning the fatherland, deputies should be guided by their conscience and their patriotism alone, these are also the only judges of actions which I believe are intended to achieve the country's happiness, which is and has always been my only desire."[150]

Not long after Amadeo's election, historian Antonio Pirala sent Espartero congratulations on the anniversary of Luchana. He also expressed his disgust at the political scene. Things in Madrid were "getting worse every day," with the "neo-Progressives" abandoning their political principles as well as their "religious and even moral ones." Espartero, "the father of the party," would recognize nothing of what was going on as truly Progressive. "What children!"[151]

11

The Necessary Man, January 1871–March 1876

The ship carrying Amadeo of Savoy and his entourage from Italy arrived at Cartagena on 28 December. That same evening, as Prim was riding in his carriage through the streets of Madrid, he was shot. He died of his wounds two days later. Suspicion fell first on the Republicans, then on Serrano and Montpensier, but the assassin was never found. More important than the identity of the perpetrator were the consequences of the act: the new king was deprived of his most powerful advocate and the one person who might have provided some stability amidst the turbulence of an unsettled political scene.[1]

Amadeo was determined to be a truly constitutional monarch and not be prisoner of any one party, as Isabel had been, but his good intentions were insufficient to overcome an increasingly fractious political situation. Without Prim to hold them together, the two main wings of the Progressives descended into increased factionalism, divided between a radical group led by Manuel Ruiz Zorrilla, which tilted towards the Democrats, and a more conservative one led by Sagasta, which was prepared to work with Serrano and the Unionists. Moreover, both Progressives and Unionisists "attacked and insulted the monarch depending on the circumstances."[2] Amadeo's parliaments also included sizeable contingents of Republicans and Carlists as well as a smaller group of *Alfonsistas*, all of whom wanted to replace his monarchy with something else. The result was a permanent instability which produced six cabinets and three elections in two years.

In the first elections held under the new regime, Espartero was elected to the Senate for Madrid and Logroño. Surprisingly, he accepted, choosing to represent the latter.[3] Without consulting him, the members of the government majority selected Espartero to be president of the Senate, a decision which highlighted his position as the only figure everyone could agree on. Naturally, he turned it down.[4]

Amadeo was on the throne, but Espartero remained very much on people's minds, starting with the backers of the new monarchy. In the fall of 1871, the king was sent on a tour of the north. Monarchs had always travelled around their realms; Isabel II had used such excursions, as well as the still-new medium of photography, to good effect,[5] but as Antonio Pirala, the trip's chronicler, explained, this was especially important for constitutional rulers, for whom "the people's love" was crucial.[6] However, Ildefonso Antonio Bermejo believed that the whole trip was an excuse to get the king to Logroño to visit Espartero as a way of benefiting the government and as a weapon in the internal struggle for control of the Progressives.[7]

Amadeo was confronted with the old man's popularity even before he arrived in Logroño. As his train pulled out of Zaragoza station, the crowd cheered him, his wife, their children – and Espartero; something similar happened in Tarrassa.[8] When the king arrived, Logroño was packed, as the authorities had made every effort "to generate enthusiasm."[9] After the two men embraced on the platform, Espartero addressed the king and the crowd, pledging his loyalty to the monarch, "whose supreme dignity has been conferred by the national will." He could offer no greater praise. Espartero then invited Amadeo to stay at his home. As soon as Espartero finished speaking, the crowd burst into an "explosion of joy" that drowned out Amadeo's reply. On their way through the city, "flowers, doves and poems rained upon them from every balcony," and when they reached Espartero's home, Jacinta met the party at the door. That evening, Espartero escorted the king to a performance at the Liceo Artístico Literario. The next day he accompanied him on his ceremonial visits, to a bullfight, and to an official reception before seeing Amadeo off at the station at 8:30 in the evening.[10] According to the official municipal account, as the king's train left the station, the crowd surrounded Espartero, "cheering and embracing him with such enthusiasm that it took him a long time and much effort to return home."[11] *La Iberia* described Espartero's embrace of Amadeo as nothing less than a "consecration of the king." For their part, some republican papers claimed that Espartero had not sworn allegiance to Amadeo, a claim which, however false, demonstrated that they considered Espartero's attitude to carry considerable weight with their readers.[12]

Only days after Amadeo left Logroño, another cabinet crisis exploded, and Espartero's name again appeared as a possible solution. At the beginning of October, Sagasta brought down Ruiz Zorrilla's government. In the ensuing stalemate, he suggested that Amadeo call on Espartero to form a government in the belief that no one calling himself a Progressive could refuse to serve under the party's patriarch. News that the king had invited Espartero to form a ministry created some optimism in a very difficult situation, but when his refusal arrived around noon the next day, it only added to "the general concern." After Ruiz Zorrilla again refused to form a government, Amadeo again appealed to Espartero to overcome the "essentially personal divisions" between the warring Progressive groups.[13] Although it meant it as an insult, the satirical paper *Gil Blas* was not far off the mark when it compared Espartero to a well-known patent medicine, good for "chilblains, hernias, migraines, for any ailment."[14]

All this produced intense controversy among Progressives and eventually led to a schism. The two new parties, the Radical Progressive Democratic and the Democratic Conservative, both sought Espartero's blessing, but he refused to be drawn in.[15] Local groups of Progressives also wrote to Espartero. From Calders, near Manresa, the Centro monárquico-liberal called on him to intercede to overcome the differences between the two factions so that they could "consolidate liberty," while the Tertulia Progresista-democrática of San Fernando warned that only his great prestige could provide the "powerful stimulant that will resolve this most grave conflict."[16] With the two factions publicly disputing his approval, Espartero finally broke his silence to make clear that he would not take sides. Given the state of the party, he said, his duty was "to remain neutral, always hoping with all my soul that it becomes reconciled and powerful so we can sustain the institutions that the Nation has created by using its sovereignty."[17]

As he marked his first anniversary on the throne, Amadeo was still struggling to consolidate his legitimacy. Once again, he sought to benefit from Espartero's prestige and popularity: On 2 January 1872, for only the second time in Spain's history, a man who was not the son of the monarch was given the title of prince.[18] Reaching back to the birth of constitutional government in Spain and associating himself with the moment of their recent history that many Spaniards considered both the most trying and the most glorious, Amadeo issued a decree that touched on the aspects of Espartero's reputation that most resonated with ordinary Spaniards, above all his role as peacemaker. "Wishing to reward appropriately his virtues and his eminent services to the country, which have done so much to consolidate our public freedoms, and *especially his services on the fields of Vergara, bringing to an end the Civil War that caused so much noble Spanish blood to flow and restoring the peace that everyone longed for and joyfully accepted,*" Amadeo bestowed on him the title of Prince of Vergara.[19]

On 7 January, General José Rossell called on Espartero to deliver the decree and a personal letter from the king. "Few military leaders have had the great honour of ending a fratricidal war in a way that satisfied both sides," and Amadeo wanted to associate himself with that great moment, one that transcended political differences, since "everyone applauds the Bringer of Peace."[20] Astonishingly, Espartero refused the title: "because ... my only ambition has been the well-being of the fatherland." The news was made public on 9 January, and enemies of the regime, like the Catholic paper *Altar y Trono*, called Espartero's refusal "a slap in the face" to the king. Two days later Amadeo sent another letter, this time delivered by Cipriano Montesino, in which he used Espartero's well-known slogan against him: allowing Espartero to refuse the title would "amount to contradicting the national will." There is no record of what Montesino said to Espartero, but this time he accepted. In a letter which was published in the press on 12 January, Espartero said that the king was the "true expression of the national will, which has been a constant law for me" and this was what "induced me to accept such a great honour." He concluded by repeating his "most sincere support" for the king.[21]

As Sagasta and Ruiz Zorrilla continued to contend for Espartero's blessing, the struggle reached into the grass roots. "All the committees, all the political groups belonging to the two factions invoke your name to legitimize their actions," the owners and editor of the *Eco del Progreso*, a paper which had supported the campaign to make Espartero king, informed him. "And cabinet ministers boast of deserving your approval."[22] In February, Sagasta created a new party and included Espartero on the list for Madrid.[23] At the same time, Ruiz Zorrilla asked him to run for the Radicals. As he had done before, Espartero responded using Cipriano Montesino as his mouthpiece. In a letter published in the press, Montesino announced that Espartero "strongly deplored" the split, refused to be a candidate for any group, and urged "all self-respecting liberals" to embrace unity while he remained outside the political fray, "so that his voice could be heard."[24] This did not stop Sagasta's group from proclaiming Espartero as its candidate for the important Centro district of Madrid, on the grounds that only by his forming a government could the Progressive factions be reunited.[25]

Following the elections on 2 April, Espartero was chosen as a senator for both Madrid and Logroño. In the latter, he received 138 votes, one more than his eternal rival Olózaga, which must have been gratifying. However, he declined to take up his seat on grounds of ill health.[26] Even so, when yet another political crisis exploded in June, "the same thing happened as always happened: there was talk of the Radicals, of the conservatives, and of General Espartero." *Gil Blas* had no doubts about where this last option would lead: asking Espartero to assume office was "like asking a nun if she smoked."[27]

The political situation continued to deteriorate through the rest of 1872. Another Carlist war began in April and was followed by a series of Republican revolts. In June, yet another political crisis led to Ruiz Zorrilla being named prime minister. Serrano and his Liberal Union followers essentially went on strike. The election of a Radical majority in August led to further tensions, including a mass resignation of artillery officers to protest the appointment of a new captain general in the Basque Provinces. Ruiz Zorrilla ultimately won his standoff with the officers, but the political cost was astronomical: on 11 February Amadeo announced that he was abdicating.[28] Later that day, a joint sitting of Cortes and Senate proclaimed the First Republic with Estanislao Figueras as president of the Executive Power.

Even though he had been a lifelong monarchist, Espartero immediately announced his loyalty to the "Government of the Republic." "Let the national will be done," he wrote in a letter that was published in the Republican press, "has always been and will remain my motto. Using their sovereignty, the legislative bodies have proclaimed the Republic; I obey and thank the gentlemen who form the government the consideration they have shown this Veteran of Liberty."[29] In Logroño, the crowd celebrating the creation of the Republic went to Espartero's house, where "he announced to the crowd his complete adherence to the national will."[30]

Espartero's public support for the Republic came even as he was being asked support a military coup to bring Isabel's son Alfonso to the throne. On the day the Republic was proclaimed, General Domingo Moriones, who had been commanding the Army of the North against the Carlists, declared himself an *alfonsista* and was replaced by General Manuel Pavía. Moriones immediately went to see Espartero and told him that he was prepared to march on Madrid and bring down the Republic, but only on one condition: "I must be able to tell the troops that General Espartero will lead the new government and proclaim Alfonso as king." Espartero supposedly agreed with bringing back Alfonso but not to leading the government: Alfonso's youth would require a regency, and at this point in his life he did not want to be tainted with the label of ambition. To Moriones's claim that this was the only way to save Spain, Espartero allegedly replied, "The country will not be saved; it is already completely lost." Moriones appealed to Jacinta but without success; her husband's involvement, she said, would only hasten his death without achieving anything useful.[31]

This was not the first time that supporters of the Bourbons had tried to enlist Espartero. Just four days after Amadeo had been formally proclaimed king of Spain, Isabel herself sent Espartero a letter from Geneva, where she had fled after Napoleon III's defeat in the Franco-Prussian War. She pleaded with Espartero to use his influence to save the throne for her son. She could not believe that he would lend his support to "a foreigner and a usurper ... standing beside those who have not worried about humiliating Spain ... subjecting it to the horrors of a fratricidal war that will destroy it and drag its glorious Crown which, with your sword, you kept on the head of a little girl, begging from door to door in search of a borrowed king." She was ready to hand her son over to the "custody ... of the loyal and honourable man who, victorious in the name of the mother, can easily raise the son to the throne ... and guide him to serve the Spanish people."[32] There is no indication that Espartero replied, or even read the letter.

On 21 April 1872, the Carlists launched a new uprising. It was essentially a failure, but a second one in December was not, and during the first six months of 1873 the Carlists were able to take control of most of the Basque Country and Navarra. By the end of the year they had established "a real counter-state." As it had been in the 1830s, Bilbao was a major goal for the Carlists, who put it under siege in late December and were forced to withdraw only at the start of May 1874.[33]

Unsurprisingly, Espartero was an important reference for both sides. For the government, he was the victor of the first Carlist war and the "Bringer of Peace," and two generals commanding the Army of the North, Manuel Pavía and Ramón Novaliches, sent Espartero their addresses to the troops for his approval.[34] For the Carlists, Espartero was close to the Antichrist. After capturing Vergara on 13 August, the Carlist commander ordered that the "stone that contains the ignominious Agreement of Vergara" be destroyed and the document be "reduced to ashes and thrown to the winds so that this work of Masonic impiety disappear."[35]

As it had ever since the revolution, Espartero's name continued to hold varying political meanings. Even federal republicans could celebrate him: A flyer distributed in 1873 contained the *Himno al Duque de la Victoria y de Morella* [Hymn of the Duke of Victory and Morella] at the top, followed by *Gozos a la Reública Federal* [Verses for the Federal Republic] at the bottom.[36] Many continued to see Espartero as the answer to the country's problems, especially as the military situation in the north worsened. In June, with the fight against the Carlists going badly and the army in disarray, there were rumours that Espartero would be given command of the Army of the North. If this were to happen, *El Federal Salmantino* proclaimed, "not one of the Volunteers for the Republic should remain at home."[37] The rumours were fed by the visit to Logroño of the president of the Cortes, Nicolás Salmerón, and emerged again in September, shortly after Emilio Castelar had assumed the presidency.[38] On both occasions, the press emphasized the need for someone to impose discipline on the army as Espartero had done during the First Carlist War.

On 18 July, the day after the new draft constitution had been presented to the Assembly, two days after the Carlist Pretender had entered the country, and six days after the start of the Cantonalist Revolt in which a number of municipalities proclaimed their status as independent cantons, a group of seven deputies presented a bill to "name Espartero president of the Federal Republic as well as commander in chief of the army and navy" until the new system had been created and a president elected.[39] *El Federal Salmantino*, whose title page carried the slogan "Long Live the Democratic Federal Republic!," commented that in normal times "remembering Espartero" would have been "nothing more than a pleasant thought," but with Carlism threatening the survival of the Republic, this was something that "all good republicans, long-time liberals, and true patriots should support."[40] *El Diario Español* called on the Cortes to name Espartero, "with whose ideas we have never agreed," president. There were still Carlists to be vanquished, and "General Espartero cannot ignore this summons. If today there is not a throne to save there is a society that is dying and that must be stopped from going into the abyss."[41] The idea of Espartero for president emerged again when a group of deputies met to discuss it in August.[42] As had happened during the search for a king, there was now an *esparterista* caucus in the Cortes whose goal was to make Espartero president immediately "so that all liberals will unite within his shadow to fight the Carlist insurrection."[43]

It was at this time that a correspondent for the *Manchester Guardian* made his way to Logroño to interview Espartero. Published under the title "Marshall Espartero on Spanish Politics," the interview constituted one of his most extensive public statements on political affairs. The journalist arrived at Espartero's house after lunch and found him and Jacinta "in a long saloon in the centre of which stood a billiard table of colossal proportions." Espartero did not look more than sixty-five, while his wife, "tall [and] stout," was reading the most recent issue of the *Illustrated London News* and greeted the journalist in English. Asked if a republic were possible in Spain, Espartero replied sarcastically, "under two conditions. First of all, if the nobility and wealthy classes become absentee landlords and choose to live in perpetual exile; and secondly, if all the Intransigents are drowned in their own blood. Then a Republic might be possible, in so far that Spain would split up into little municipalities who would eat other up or be devoured by the first adventurer who could command a homogeneous army." Spaniards were so attached to their individual independence that "a voluntary unity of action is impossible" and the Republic was left without any troops "worthy of the name." Certainly not the Volunteers, who fell into two groups, "the respectable citizens" motivated only by the desire to defend their property, and the "canaille [who] have taken to arms for possible plunder and diurnal rations and pesetas." As for "what is by courtesy called the army," none of the officers were convinced republicans, and "the few officers who are in command do not resign because they have no private means and are forced to remain." The enlisted men were interested only in their pay "and possible pillage, and would just as like shoot their own officers as the Carlists." Espartero, who described himself as "Liberal as the most Liberal man in England," believed that Spain could be governed "only by the stick. Wield it justly and Spain would be as quiet as England." The Carlists had done brilliantly on their home ground but would never escape it; "first of all the men object to leaving their own province and secondly, because they know they would be beaten in the plains where the people are against them ... Carlism has as much its natural limits as the vine or the palm. It cannot go beyond. For besides personal antipathy, Don Carlos has to fight against the conviction which has steadily been gaining strength that the Jesuits are making Spain their stronghold." As to the alternatives, Espartero would "welcome any regent who would give peace to Spain," but this would have to be a Spaniard; a foreign ruler "would never find a resting place in Spain." But now he had changed his mind on who this might be. Prince Alfonso was the most likely and the most desirable solution. "His party is certainly the most widely diffused, as it is also the most influential: but it is a party that will only use constitutional means to gain power ... I cannot betray any confidences placed in me, but read the signs of the times. With your experience of Spain, you cannot but have remarked the hopefulness of his party; you must have admired their patience; you must have honoured their patriotism in refusing to add to the woes of their country by a premature interference."[44]

Two months later, the *alfonsista* paper *La Época* printed what it claimed to be an interview Espartero had given in early August to a journalist for a British paper called the *Herald*. This one was significantly different from the one he gave to the *Guardian*. Espartero said less about the weaknesses of a republic, and said it less scathingly. He also spoke more, and much more favourably, about the *alfonistsas*. Monarchism, he said, was stronger in Spain than republicanism, and he considered Alfonso, "the only prince who does not have agreements with the ultra-conservatives … its saviour."[45]

Alfonso's supporters certainly had their eyes on Espartero. On 16 August, just a few days after the interview with the *Guardian*, Count Foxà wrote to Isabel that it would be very valuable for her son's cause "if the Duke of Victory took an active part in working for the restoration." The former queen agreed. Forgetting or ignoring his refusal to answer her previous letters, she wrote to Espartero that he "would not want to see his country destroyed." For her part, she remembered that when she was "a young orphan he defended my crown and many times risked his life for me. Having seen what has happened these last five years, he will know who is responsible for the suffering of the fatherland … Tell him for me that, with all his prestige, the greatest service he can do for our beloved country is to act before it is too late." She then sent Foxà a letter to be delivered to Espartero. Foxà met with Juan Domingo de Santa Cruz, who conveyed Espartero's reply that "he didn't want to get involved in politics and that he would accept whatever the national will decided."[46] From a lifelong monarchist such as Espartero, this was a resounding rebuff.

On 3 January 1874, the very same day that *El Bien Público* pronounced that "everything appears to smile on the government," the chaotic course of the Republic took another dramatic turn. With the National Assembly deliberating on a new president following Castelar's defeat in a key vote, General Pavía, the captain general of Madrid, dissolved it at gunpoint. Before deciding on a republican dictatorship under General Serrano, the men behind the coup had turned to Espartero. Addressing the Cortes two years later, Pavía explained that at the time he considered Espartero the only person "with the moral and material force to dominate the country," but he had long refused to take part in active political life. With no other alternative in sight, Pavía agreed to ask the leaders of the political parties to form a "national government that would save the country and society."[47]

Pavía certainly kept Espartero in the loop as events unfolded. At 9:15 a.m. he sent a telegram to the captains general, provincial military and civil governors, admiral of the navy, and the "Duke of Victory" explaining the motivation behind the coup.[48] At 3:00 that afternoon he sent another telegram, this one to Espartero alone: "Complete tranquillity reigns. All the provinces adhere unanimously to the movement I launched. The parties have named General Zavala minister of war; he will inform you of the rest of the cabinet."[49] Among the first acts of the new president, General Serrano, was to send a telegram to Espartero, whom he addressed as "the patriarch of liberty and the great peacemaker of this poor country once again afflicted by Carlist sectarians." His government expected to enjoy the support of what Espartero had always called for, "the close union of the liberal country." In reply, Espartero expressed his confidence that, backed by "all self-respecting liberals," the government would succeed in giving Spain the "freedom and well-being it deserves."[50]

The military authorities also kept Espartero abreast of important developments. On 5 January, the captain general of Aragón wired that he had had to use force in Zaragoza, since the city and provincial governments, "along with the Volunteers, refused to obey the orders of the established government." Espartero thanked him for the report and applauded his "energy in putting down the insurrection," although he was saddened that because "part of this heroic city" – one of the greatest strongholds of *esparterismo* – "had ignored the voice of reason you have been obliged to shed blood."[51] In March, the minister of war, General Juan de Zavala, who had once been Espartero's aide-de-camp, began sending him copies of the telegrams he received from the commander of the Army of the North.[52]

Shortly after the coup, Manuel Vera y Ramos wrote on behalf of a Madrid battalion of the "former militiamen" to let him know that they were planning to place a monument to the Constitution in the Plaza Mayor to replace the one that had been ripped out and to dedicate the ceremony to Espartero "as the most genuine representation of true liberty connected with order." Espartero was grateful but also urged them not to use his name in any event "which might be the cause of some disorder at precisely the time the government needs to give all its attention and energy to dominating the moral and material anarchy that is devouring our country."[53]

When government forces finally broke the siege of Bilbao on 1 May 1874, the victory was immediately compared to Espartero's legendary relief of the Carlist siege on Christmas Eve 1836, and the hero of the hour, Serrano, was described in the official announcement sent out by the minister of the interior as "the rival of Espartero."[54] The capture of Bilbao would be the prelude to the complete defeat of Carlism in 1874, just as "in the last civil war when Espartero defeated the Carlists, forcing them to lift their siege."[55] The rumours about Espartero continued. *La Correspondencia de España* reported that he was so exasperated by the length of the war that "it would require only the voice of public opinion" to bring him out of retirement.[56] In November, the same paper reported that, once again, Espartero was being touted as a possible king.[57] And in December, there was a story that "military circles" were discussing holding "a council of generals" in Logroño to which Espartero would be invited.[58]

Serrano arrived in Logroño on 10 December. From the station, he went to Espartero's house but did not meet with him as the old man was reportedly suffering from "an illness that, while not grave, demands complete rest." Instead, he was received by Jacinta, and the two spent "a long time" talking about the first Carlist War.[59] Clearly, she had forgiven, if not forgotten, his earlier betrayals. Interestingly, the government took the trouble to deny that Espartero had refused to meet Serrano. However, two weeks later, and in the final days of Serrano's presidency, when Espartero was allowed by his doctors to get out of bed and receive visitors, Serrano "did not waste a minute in rushing" to his house, where the two "caudillos hugged each other as brothers ... The meeting was so cordial and affectionate that those present were deeply touched."[60]

As the thirty-eighth anniversary of Luchana approached, the press accorded Espartero an unusual degree of prominence. On 24 December, *La Iberia* led with a long article describing the battle, which concluded with the hope that "soon we will be able to celebrate a new victory." In its 22 December issue, *La Ilustración Española y Americana* ran a lengthy story on the first Carlist War as well as a full-page portrait of Espartero. The next issue, which came out on 30 December, had an engraving of his house on the front page and a small article about the meeting between Espartero and Serrano, which had taken place a few days before. "On undertaking his new campaign, General Serrano will be strengthened by the opinion and suggestions of the illustrious patrician who ended the first Carlist insurrection *in an honourable and humane* manner."[61]

Serrano would not get the opportunity to undertake that campaign. On 29 December 1874, a coup led by General Arsenio Martínez Campos brought the Republic to an end and announced the restoration of the Bourbons under Isabel's seventeen-year-old son, Alfonso XII. Espartero quickly pledged his allegiance to the new monarch. On 10 January 1875, mere days after Alfonso was proclaimed king, Espartero sent him a letter offering his support and his wishes that "all liberals will unite around Your Majesty so that we can restore peace and good fortune to our fatherland."[62]

The architects of the new regime known as the Restoration wasted no time in associating the seventeen-year-old monarch with the eighty-two-year-old icon.[63] According to José Allende Salazar, Espartero's old collaborator from 1854, Alfonso liked the letter so much that he had it published in the *Gaceta* before his entry into Madrid. Alfonso's reply, that "no congratulations please me more than those from the victor of Luchana and the Peacemaker of Spain," was also published.[64] Espartero's letter had also pleased the government, "since what comes from you is always very important. What we need now," Allendesalazar wrote, "is that the men around the adolescent king don't do to him what was done to his mother: turn him into the leader of a party and not the ruler of a nation."[65]

On 9 February, only six weeks after coming to the throne, Alfonso was in Logroño. *La Época*, the principal *Alfonsista* paper, had a correspondent, "L," travelling with the royal party; his telegraphic report appeared in the paper on the 12th and was later reprinted in numerous provincial papers. The royal train was met at the station by the civil and military authorities. The military governor gave the king the symbolic keys to the fortress and explained that Espartero's health had prevented him from coming to the station. The king then rode through the city on horseback, passing through three specially constructed arches, one of which had been paid for in part by Espartero. After hearing a Te Deum, Alfonso went to Espartero's home, "where a meeting worthy of the start of a great reign" would take place. The rest of the king's stay was taken up with a military parade, a visit to the military hospitals, and a banquet. He left for Burgos the next morning.[66]

Cánovas considered the king's meeting with Espartero so important that, in order not to "deprive the Nation of the interesting details," he had a supposedly confidential letter from the navy minister, the Marquis of Molins, describing the visit published in the official *Gaceta de Madrid* and then reprinted in other papers. Espartero's house was, Molins wrote, "comfortable, but with an air of severe modesty" which reflected the owner's character. There were no guards or doormen, only a "spacious doorway and a clean and comfortable staircase," testimony to the "quiet life and domestic tranquillity" that Espartero and Jacinta enjoyed. It also meant that the king could "reach the Duke's own rooms without being announced by doormen or servants." Jacinta greeted Alfonso at the door, but, "with a natural and youthful impatience," the king went up to the main floor alone, where he found Espartero "wearing an overcoat and Greek hat." At first, Espartero thought the "young general with his kepis held respectfully in his hand, a plain jacket without braid and only a modest decoration on his chest" was one of Alfonso's aides. When he realized who it was, however, he got up "as quickly as he could," but when he went to remove his hat the

Figure 15 King Alfonso XII visits Espartero, 1875.
Biblioteca Virtual La Rioja (CC-BY-4.0).

king stopped him and "affectionately gave him his hand." This was how Jacinta, Molins, and the rest of Alfonso's retinue found them, and at this point the conversation took on such gravity that "it imprinted itself deeply" in Molins's memory.

Espartero began by congratulating the king on his victories against the Carlists. "Your Majesty will return to Madrid with your glory and valour proven and will continue directing the constitutional monarchy which, with a prudent liberty, will ensure the prosperity and happiness of the fatherland." The king, "with the simplicity and dignity of youth," replied by praising his troops and, in a very *esparterista* vein, stated that he had "shared their suffering" and hoped that this had "earned me their love." As for constitutional monarchy, he knew it well, having "spent the early years of my life in Austria and England, where I learned the advantages of that prudent liberty you mention." At this point, Molins decided to intervene, "speaking to the king but raising my voice so that the Duke could hear." A number of generals, he said, had been urging the king to wear the Cross of San Fernando, Spain's highest military decoration, and the government agreed, but the king had refused. Espartero now spoke up. "You, sire, deserve to wear the cross of the brave as much as anyone ... Where are my crosses? Bring me my Grand Cross of San Fernando." When he had it in his hands, Espartero, "in a tone in which age and pain add dignity to dignity itself," addressed the king. "You are the first monarch since Phillip V to have led our troops in battle, exposing yourself to the bullets of the absolutists. You may legitimately wear th[is] symbol of valour and strength. Allow me the honour of placing on your chest the sash that that this veteran of a hundred battles won shedding his blood for the integrity of the fatherland, for its independence, for your ancestors, for public liberties." After the consecration came a lesson in government. "Remember that, more than brave, a constitutional monarch must be the faithful custodian of public liberties. In this way, you will ensure the happiness of the people and win their love, which today is the only guarantee of the stability of the throne." Having refused the decoration from others, Alfonso accepted it from the man who "alone represents the entire army." What followed was, Molins said, "difficult to explain but easy to understand. His wounds barely allowed the old warrior to raise his arms to put on the young king the sash that he had worn for so many years ... Don Alfonso, less composed on this occasion than he had been on the battlefield, let the joy that was in his heart show on his face."[67]

A tremendous scene, brilliantly choreographed, but one which spoke, above all, to the recognition by the new political elite of the astonishing prestige that Espartero continued to enjoy. Monarchs, even constitutional ones, inherit their thrones, as they decorate their soldiers, but here it is Espartero's blessing which confers full legitimacy as he pins Spain's most prestigious military medal on the king's uniform. And in case anyone missed the message, Molins spelled it out himself: "let all Spain say what the embrace between the oldest and greatest leader of our freedom and the youngest and spirited trustee of the legitimate monarchy signifies for its future."[68]

The account soon appeared in newspapers across the country, and the *Ilustración Española y Americana* commissioned a drawing of the historic encounter. This media strategy was successful: One of the congratulatory letters Espartero received on his saint's day in 1875, which fell a few days after the king's visit, noted "how much the story of Your Excellency decorating the king has circulated." Another said that his interview with the king, in which Espartero had given "the sanction of your recognition," would be "a page for the history books." A third congratulated him on his decision to "embrace the young monarch" and then asked Espartero to send him a reply, which would he would "bequeath to my heirs as an everlasting memory."[69]

The press served as an echo chamber, repeating and magnifying the importance of the blessing Espartero had bestowed on the new regime. On 16 February, *La Época* reported at length on an article in *El Diario de España* describing the restored monarchy's good start. Spaniards who had wanted Espartero as head of state or who had accepted "the new conditions that are emerging" could see that the meeting between the two men had been much more than pure protocol and was the signal for all liberals to join "the common project of the new monarchy ... all those who remain loyal to the monarchist flag must not forget the cordial embrace His Majesty gave to General Espartero."[70] The visit was also noticed by the foreign press, and its reaction was then relayed back to Spain. *La Época* and other papers commented on the editorial in the London *Times* on 12 February, which said that Alfonso had done well in receiving "a kind of patriotic blessing" from "the patriarch of Spanish liberty ... [T]he cause of the young king could not have a more revered patron."[71] Espartero, *The Times* proclaimed, "stands out in favourable contrast with the men of his generation – the ferocious military chiefs, the unscrupulous politicians, the mendacious courtiers, who surrounded the throne of the youthful Queen and dragged constitutional government through the dirt ... [He] might long ago have secured Spain against another [Carlist] war had he been able to make his principles of government take root in the country. At least, we now see these principles brought out once more."[72]

Espartero had given Alfonso the Gran Cruz of San Fernando, *his* Gran Cruz, but there was one more thing he could do for the new king. What Spaniards most revered about Espartero was that he had brought peace after a brutal civil war; he was the Peacemaker. This was the supreme title and it was the title that his political backers sought for Alfonso. When the war was over, they undertook an "unmatched propaganda campaign" around "the Peacemaker."[73] Here too Espartero had a role.

The end of the war came in February 1876. On 19 February, government forces took the Carlist stronghold of Montejurra. When news reached Logroño, the celebrating crowds, "with that instinct that comes from the heart," quickly moved to the square in front of Espartero's home, although he was too ill to come to the window to acknowledge them.[74] On 28 February, the day after Espartero's birthday and as Carlos VII fled the country, Alfonso entered Pamplona. Espartero immediately wired Alfonso, whom he hailed as the "peacemaker of the Basque Provinces and Navarra." To which the king replied that "it pleases me as much to congratulate the Peacemaker of Vergara, illustrious exmaple of valour and skill."[75]

For many of the people who sent birthday congratulations that year, the timing was more than appropriate. Tomás Lletgel from Barcelona considered it 'providential that the current war ended at the precise moment at which all good liberals celebrate the birthday of the great general who so happily ended the last one." Santiago García Santa Olalla, an eighty-four-year-old priest who had served as a canon of Seville cathedral for twenty-one years, wrote that Spain should be grateful for having military leaders who, "imitating Your Highness, bring to an end this unjustified rebellion." The Sociedad de Milicianos Nacionales Veteranos de 1820 a 1823 (Society of 1820 to 1823 Veterans of the National Militia) of Barcelona celebrated Espartero's birthday even more enthusiastically than usual, "seeing that the longed-for moment when civilization triumphs over obscurantist fanaticism is near," while the city's First Battalion of Volunteers of Liberty saw "the coming complete triumph of the holy cause of liberty over absolutism, which has always been Your Highness's longed-for desire."[76]

A few days after the war had ended, Alfonso was again in Logroño and he again visited Espartero. This time, however, the meeting received little coverage La Iberia said only that soon after entering the city the king met with Espartero, "with whom he spoke affectionately," and that the next morning the two men spoke "at length."[77] Beyond that, there were rumours that Espartero and Ramón Cabrera, his old Carlist antagonist who had abandoned Carlism for Alfonso in 1875, would ride alongside the king when he entered Madrid and "renew through an embrace the tie of peace formed at Vergara."[78] The lower key was only to be expected. Alfonso was now a peacemaker in his own right and no longer needed second-hand prestige. The troubled times were over and the old hero could finally be retired.[79]

Epilogue:
Death and Afterlife, March 1876–

After Alfonso's visit, Espartero finally fell out of the public eye. His last years passed quietly. Miguel Salvador, a senator from Logroño who knew Espartero well, described his quiet, orderly daily routine.

> He would wake up early and after washing and having his breakfast, go down to the billiard room where the Duchess dealt with her correspondence; at noon he received visitors and the continual flow of intimate friends who came to his house until lunch time. In the afternoons, he took his coach to La Fombera where he stayed until evening. Then his usual *tertulia* would gather in the billiard room and stay until precisely 10:00, when he withdrew. The only exceptions were his saint's day and that of the Duchess when the members of the *tertulia* were invited to dine. Occasionally, he would take them to La Fombera to taste the strawberries [1]

His health, though frail, was steady. "No news about the Duke," Jacinta told a friend in November 1877, "beyond his usual aches and pains."[2]

Then on 3 June 1878, Jacinta died suddenly. Two days earlier, after attending mass at San Agustín church as she did every day, she suffered a stroke. She was put to her bed immediately and never left it.[3] She was only sixty-six; they had been married for fifty-one years. Given the difference in their ages and his own poor health, Baldomero surely never imagined he would outlive her. He was devastated. Six weeks after her death he ended a note to his executors: "On 3 June 1878 the wife whom I idolized died, leaving me in the deepest sorrow."[4]

Jacinta died intestate, which brought another kind of misery. As she lay dying, with her servants and Damiana Olloqui, a cousin on her father's side, caring for her, her maternal relatives were doing everything they could to gain access while Baldomero was doing everything he could to keep them away. Then, on 11 June, José Gutiérrez de Concha, husband of Jacinta's half-sister, Vicenta Fernández de Luco, took the matter to court and won. On 21 September, the courts declared Vicenta to be Jacinta's sole heir.[5]

Espartero's only reaction to these manoeuvres was to prepare his own will. It began with an invocation of God, the Virgin Mary, and the Holy Trinity, a statement of having lived "as a faithful Catholic Christian," and a request for a Christian burial. Luciano Murrieta received some symbolic items; each of the children of his sister Antonia and his brother Francisco received a bequest of 1,250 pesetas, and each of their grandchildren a bequest of 1,000 pesetas. Jacinta's goddaughter, Jacinta Gurrea de Bellsolá, and her daughter, Teresa Bellsolá y Gurrea, received 2,000 and 1,000 pesetas respectively. Then there were his servants: 650 pesetas for his butler and chambermaid and 500 for the others, "including the coachman." Everything else went to his "beloved niece Eladia Fernández Espartero y Blanco, legitimate wife of Cipriano Segundo Montesino y Estrada." Eladia would also inherit his titles.[6]

Jacinta's death was reported in the press. On 3 June 1878, *La Academia* magazine published a portrait of her on its front page. A week later, *La Ilustración Española y Americana*, the most widely read publication among Spain's middle classes, did the same.[7] This was public recognition of her importance, that she and Baldomero had been, to use a phrase from our own day, a "power couple."

King Alfonso XII, who himself had been widowed in June, paid a visit of condolence on 21 October. It was a much lower-key visit than the two previous ones, but accounts of the meeting still made it into the papers. According to the minister of war, who was accompanying the king, their conversation was "both affectionate and moving." Espartero told the king that he had "only sought the well-being of his fatherland ... that he was a loyal subject ... and hoped that the union of all Spaniards would happen during his reign." He then asked the king for permission to embrace him. As Alfonso left, Espartero had tears in his eyes.[8] For the authorities of the still-young Restoration, this was another opportunity to bask in Espartero's aura. *La Época*, the mouthpiece of Cánovas's Conservative Party, hailed him as "the living example of the monarchist tradition ... fathers teach their sons that [he] is an exemplary citizen ... a model of political honesty."[9]

The Restoration continued to use Espartero and his most significant exploit into the twentieth century. The statue to María Cristina de Borbón which was erected in 1893 included inscriptions to the Agreement of Vergara, and one of the two reliefs on the pedestal showed the Embrace of Vergara. (The other was the signing of the Royal Statute of

Figure 16 Portrait of Jacinta, 1878. Biblioteca Virtual de Prensa Histórica.

1834.)[10] It also appropriated the title of Peacemaker, first giving Alfonso XII the title for ending the Third Carlist War and then dedicating the massive monument in the Retiro to that achievement. Indeed, peace became "a central part" of the regime's monuments.[11]

Life without his "querida Chiquita" must have been miserable, and Baldomero survived her by only seven months. At 7:00 in the morning on 8 January 1879, Baldomero Espartero, Viscount of Banderas, Count of Luchana, Duke of Morella, Duke of Victory and Prince of Vergara, former president of the Council of Ministers, and former Regent of the Realm, died in his home in Logroño. He was a few weeks short of his eighty-sixth birthday.

Baldomero and Jacinta left a substantial estate, valued at 1,549,435.76 pesetas. More than half, 845,784.10, consisted of cash and investments of which the bulk, 712,833.32, was his French bonds. The next largest category, 401,298.07 pesetas, was the "arrears" owed on his salary, including 119,585.58 from his time as regent. The rest, 302,352.80, was made up of fifteen urban properties in Logroño and just under sixty-five hectares of land, stocks in the Bilbao-Tudela railway, and various personal effects. Of the total, 283,326.22 pesetas were declared as Jacinta's "exclusive property," 306,244.81 as Baldomero's, and the remainder, 959.864.73, as "joint property." Espartero's niece Eladia inherited half of the last and all of his private assets, while Jacinta's half-sister Vicenta inherited all of her private assets plus half of the joint property. The remainder went to Damiana Olloqui.[12]

Wearing the dress uniform of a captain general, a "tortoiseshell cane" in his hand and a general's hat by his side, Espartero's body was laid out in the salon of the Casa-Palacio for the people of Logroño to view. There was an honour guard on both sides of the body as well as at the entrance to the salon and at the door to the house, which, along with the surrounding streets, "are packed with people at all hours."[13]

How would the most famous and revered Spaniard of his time be remembered, if at all? Would this "glorious anachronism," as one writer described him just a week after his death, quickly be forgotten? Or would he be made into the centre of one of the official hero cults which were "an almost universal phenomenon" in the age of nationalism?[14] Would there be one single memory of Espartero or many competing ones? Would the way(s) in which he was remembered change over time and, if so, how?

The day after Espartero's death, a royal decree announced that the government would pay for a state funeral.[15] As soon as the news reached the Philippines, the governor general ordered a special mass, which took place on 5 March "with all civil and military officials as well as the religious orders attending."[16] Espartero's death and funeral were big news and a unique moment of near unanimity in the press. The *Ilustración Española y Americana* gave them lots of coverage, even delaying its 8 January issue so that it could include a notice and a full-page portrait under the title "The Glories of the Fatherland." The following week, it published an entire page of drawings as well as a full-page article.[17]

The news hit the rest of the press the following day. On 9 January, *La Iberia*, the mouthpiece of Sagasta's Liberal Party, appeared with a black border on its front page. It also carried a lead article entitled simply "Espartero," which described him as a "national glory ... bringer of peace and the chieftan of our modern liberties." The next day it recalled that Espartero had never claimed the eighty thousand pesetas that he was owed by the government, an example which, "unfortunately, too few imitate."[18] The Conservative *La Época* published Espartero's service record on its front page, followed by an article which highlighted Espartero's public and private virtues: "the model of all virtues and all heroisms. [He] loved God, the Fatherland, the Law, the King, Liberty, and the family."[19]

Papers outside the two main parties were even more laudatory. The highly influential independent liberal daily *El Imparcial* appeared with a black border on its front page, which included Espartero's service record and a fulsome assessment. Espartero was the "embodiment of patriotism and liberty," and when he was unable to achieve his goal of reconciling liberty and the monarchy, he chose "political death" over "wielding his sword against one of the two principles to which he had devoted his life." For all his achievements, it was his personal virtues, his honesty, disinterestedness, the simplicity of his way of life, which were most praiseworthy. Espartero was as close as Spain could come to producing a George Washington.[20]

Further left, Alicante's pro-Republican *El Graduador* published a black-ringed "affectionate memory" to this "lover of public liberties, terror of the unyielding partisans of absolutism, and model of virtue, honesty, and patriotism," beside an article glorying in the recent electoral victory of the French Republicans.[21] In Barcelona, *La Campanya de Gracia*, the Catalan-language, politically republican paper directed primarily to artisans and workers, praised him using the affectionate nickname many Catalans applied to Espartero, "l'Avi." Without "the victorious sword of Luchana," their own ideas would not have been able to flourish. Without this "hero of liberty ... the sun of liberty would not have shone on our fatherland."[22] No paper devoted more space to

Espartero's death than Emilio Castelar's *El Globo*. For these republicans, Espartero was part of their heritage. On 9 January it described him as one of the "beacons that has long directed Spain along its difficult but heroic march along the path of liberty." Beginning 11 January, when the paper appeared with a black border and an engraving of Espartero on its front page, it ran a biography in three long instalments written by its editor, the Republican politician Joaquín Martín de Olías. While not uncritical, its overall assessment of Espartero's political career was positive. Even his greatest failure, his fatal decision not to fight for power in 1856, was, in the judgment of history, "patriotic ... liberal ... prudent ... noble and worthy."[23]

The state funeral took place in Logroño on 11 January. The king did not attend, although out of respect he cancelled a scheduled evening at the opera, his first public appearance since the death of his wife. The procession route was lined with soldiers, and residents "spontaneously" hung black banners from their balconies. The church service took place in Santa María la Redonda at 10:00, and at 12:45 Espartero was buried in the cemetery mausoleum where Jacinta's remains already rested.[24]

Memorial services were held in places large and small across the country. In Zaragoza, city hall paid for the service after the government turned down the civil governor's request for the state funding. Services in Madrid and Valencia were organized by local branches of the Militia Veterans Philanthropic Society. In Ibros (Jaén), the ceremony was paid for by former senator Antonio Manuel Garrido.[25] In Morella, the scene of one of Espartero's greatest military victories, local liberals organized the event and ordered a "magnificent crown" from Valencia, which they sent to Logroño after the ceremony to be placed on Espartero's grave.[26] In Alicante, local liberals put on a particularly elaborate event in the nave of Saint Nicolás church, which featured a pyramid draped in black velvet with gold edging and the words "Morality, Patriotism, Consistency." Hanging from the pyramid was "a most precious crown of extraordinary proportions."[27]

The event in Barcelona did not take place until 10 June. The invitations showed a mausoleum with a crowned bust of Espartero and the Embrace of Vergara in the background. In the days before the ceremony, two magnificent floral wreaths, one from the Centro Constitucional and one from the Batallón de Veteranos, were displayed in the windows of one of the city's florists. On the day, the church of San Agustín was "full to the rafters." Continuing the local tradition of philanthropy in Espartero's name, 1,500 pesetas' worth of clothing was redeemed from two Monte Píos, and 500 pesetas donated to the Sociedad Económica

Amigos del País to be given to two local men who had served under him during the Carlist War.[28]

Espartero's death came at an important moment in the history of public commemoration in Europe, what the French historian Maurice Agulhon has called "statuemania." For Agulhon this was part of the history of urban expansion as well as of the political project which, beginning with the French Revolution, reached its zenith under the Third Republic.[29] More recently, Joep Leerssen has presented this as part of the continent-wide phenomenon of "Romantic Nationalism," which included, among many other things, making public spaces "increasingly nationalized and historicized by architectural, pictorial and sculptural means."[30] Spain had its own "monument mania," although, as Carolyn Boyd noted, it started later – with the Restoration – and was less vigorous than in France. The Spanish phenomenon also lacked any "centralized guidance or funding," gave great weight to honouring local people as a way of connecting "local memory with the history of the nation," and was "another arena in which the most disparate groups competed to define the cultural foundations of Spanish political life."[31] Carlos Reyero and Ignacio Peiró Martín see the efforts of this "Golden Age of the public monument" more positively, as contributing to the creation of a "landscape of official memory," one which initially privileged the heroes of the fight against Carlism, including, of course, Espartero, as part of a larger effort to glorify their recent past.[32] Based on his study of Barcelona between 1830 and 1930, Stéphane Michonneau has drawn attention to the primacy of local rather than state initiative in Spanish memory politics before the Primo de Rivera dictatorship.[33]

The first proposal for a monument to Espartero actually came from the municipal government of Logroño at the end of 1840. The project was stillborn, even though the National Militia undertook to raise funds through a subscription.[34] The next attempt came during the *Bienio Progresista*, and its story illustrates the way in which the failure of Isabel II, the Moderates, and the Progressives to create a functional liberal political system impeded the creation of a politics of memory. The proposal was for a monument to the Agreement of Vergara to be erected in Vergara itself "to perpetuate the glorious memory of the Agreement that brought the horrors of the civil war to an end." The parliamentary commission designated to prepare the bill quickly received a submission from historian Antonio Pirala, who described Vergara as a "national glory." By the time it came before the Constituent Cortes, the project had turned into a multifaceted attempt to create a national memory: in addition to the monument, which would include a bust of

Espartero, there would be a commemorative medal, public competitions for a "lyric composition" and a work of history, and an annual "civic-religious festival" on 31 August. The only debate came over the project's financing, specifically whether the proposal violated the special financial status contained in the Basque *fueros*. The queen signed the bill into law on 26 January, but the end of the *Bienio* meant that the project was never realized.[35]

There was yet another failed attempt in Logroño in 1871. The initiative came from the municipal architect as part of the conversion of one of the city's streets into "a beautiful square." In order to provide it with "something to adorn the centre," he proposed a monument to Espartero. When approached by the mayor, Espartero's first response was that it was "too much of an honour," but he later changed his mind and was present when the site was inaugurated on 27 February 1872, his seventy-ninth birthday.[36] Espartero gave one of his characteristically brief speeches, including one of his signature statements: "this veteran of Liberty ... will always be ready to defend the constitutional monarchy and the institutions the Nation, using its sovereignty, has given itself."[37] The only monument that was actually built while Espartero was still alive was in the Plaza de Espartero in Sabadell in 1877. Very little is known about it other than that it was designed by Pere Moxí and Buenaventura Llauradó and constructed of bricks and terracotta with terracotta reliefs.[38]

A number of monuments to Espartero were built after his death. Three were funded by the national government: two in Logroño and one in Madrid. Two of these were approved in a law that quickly passed through the Senate and the Congress of Deputies in June 1882. The first was an equestrian statue honouring him as "one of the country's worthy champions of the constitutional regime," to be located in "one of the best squares" of the capital. The law budgeted 150,000 pesetas for the statue, which was to be the subject of an open competition. Espartero was to be on horseback – something extremely rare in nineteenth-century Spain – and the pedestal was to include reliefs showing Luchana and Vergara, his "greatest achievements." The overall goal was to show Espartero less as the "heroic soldier" than as the "Bringer of Peace ... the title that explains [his] fervent and enduring recognition."[39]

Nine sculptors presented projects, which were put on display in the patio of the Colonial Ministry at the beginning of June 1884.[40] The winner was Pau Gibert i Roig, the Catalan sculptor who had already earned the commission for the statue of the Marques of the Duero and would later do the statues to Sagasta and Espartero in Logroño.[41] It showed Espartero's entrance into Madrid after having signed the Agreement of Vergara, "carrying the document in his left hand ... the Bringer of Peace rather than a man of war."[42] The inauguration of the statue was originally planned for the anniversary of Vergara but delayed because of the absence of politicians and the court from the capital during the summer heat, and then again because of the first anniversary of the death of Alfonso XII on 25 November 1885. In the end, there was no ceremony at all. In late December, the tarp which had covered the statue for a number of months was removed without any word.[43]

The second part of the 1882 law was more interesting. In what may well be the only example in Spain of the state recognizing the wife of a public figure, sixty thousand pesetas were approved to build a mausoleum in the church of Santa María la Redonda in Logroño to house Espartero's remains and "those of his illustrious wife."[44] The transfer of Baldomero's and Jacinta's remains took place on 30 August 1889, the day before the fiftieth anniversary of the Embrace of Vergara. The ceremony began at 9:00 in the morning as each coffin was placed on a pair of cannon which served as a carriage and General Concha gave a speech. Soldiers lined the route from the cemetery to the church. Jacinta's casket went first, covered with wreaths, preceded by the civil governor and mayor, accompanied by the president of the Audiencia and two deputy mayors and followed by a detachment from the city's garrison. Then came the "magnificent gun carriage" bearing Baldomero, with members of the Mausoleum Commission and "an old man" walking alongside. As the procession reached the church, "the crowd invaded it almost squeezing out the officials." After a "solemn but modest" religious service which included neither eulogy nor music, the two caskets were placed side by side in the mausoleum, which bore the inscription "To General Espartero, Bringer of Peace to Spain, and his wife, Doña Jacinta Martínez de Sicilia, the nation erects this monument."[45]

The transfer of the remains provided an opportunity for new assessments of Espartero's importance a decade after his death. *La Iberia* called him the father of modern Spain. He had been more popular than anyone in Spain's history and in retirement showed himself to be "the just man who had done his duty."[46] *El Imparcial* ran a front-page article entitled "The Soldier of Liberty" but which highlighted his honesty and his modesty, qualities which earned him "the respect of his contemporaries." Espartero was a figure who "grew larger as he recedes in time," one who appears to the younger generations as "surrounded by the luminous halo of legendary epic."[47] The Conservative *La Época* was less fulsome but still respectful. Although his political career included

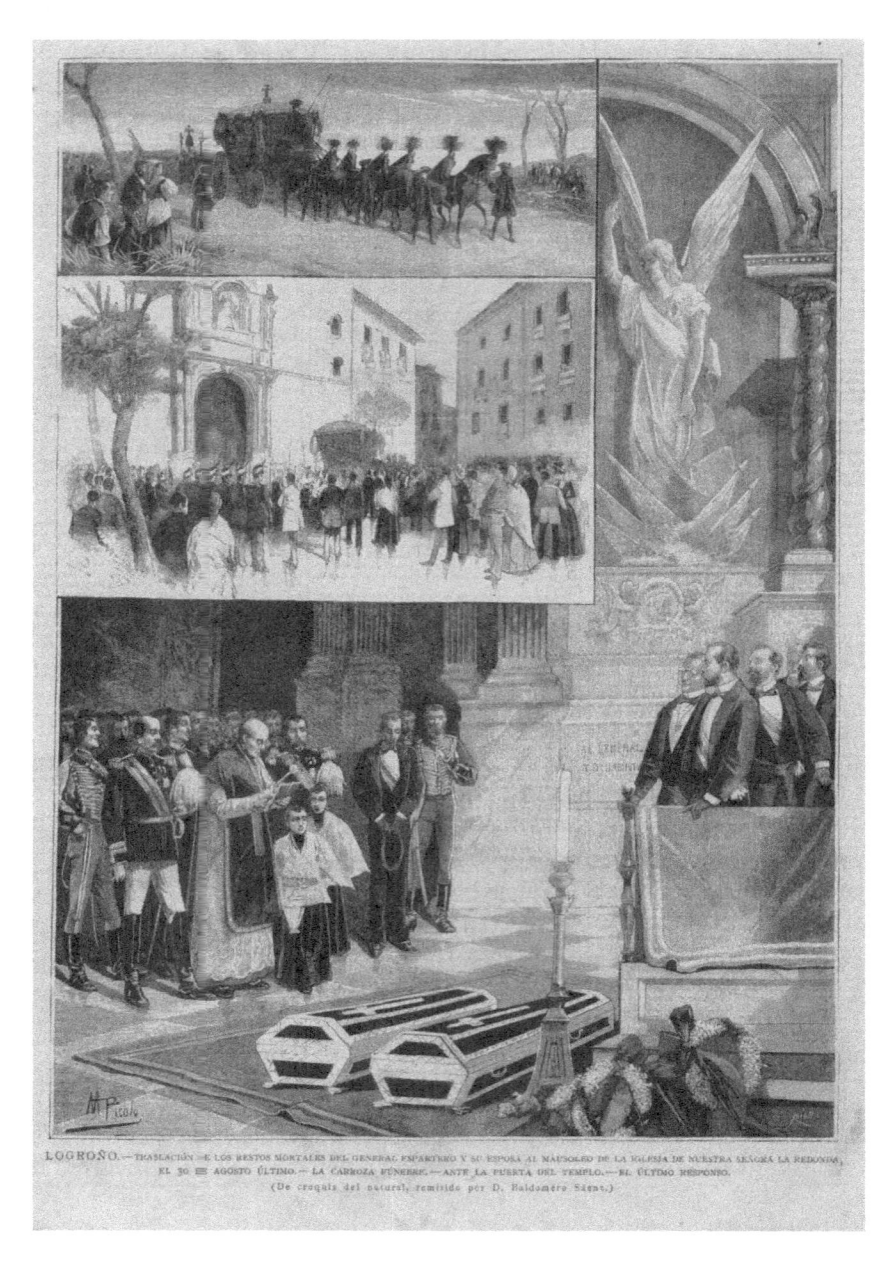

Figure 17 Transfer of the remains of Espartero and his wife, 1889. Biblioteca Virtual La Rioja (CC-BY-4.0).

"some reverses," he enjoyed geater popularity than "any person in Spain had achieved in this century." Though he was widely admired in his old age, his home in Logroño never became his Saint Helena; instead, it was a "Mecca" where the revolutionary government and two kings "travelled to pay homage."[48] *El Liberal* in Mahón, a democratic paper which a few years later would become the mouthpiece of the Unión Republicana, found a profoundly anti-monarchical lesson in the life of this convinced monarchist, especially the pilgrimages of the two kings to Logroño. "The royalty of birth bending its knees before the grandeur of personal merit, does such a spectacle not demolish the ancient prestige of monarchy? ... The people have learned that strength does not come from birth, that only he to whom the people gives its affection is truly strong."[49]

The reaction of the Catholic press showed that even ten years after his death, Espartero remained a controversial figure and a lightning rod for current conflicts. *La Unión Católica*, organ of Alejandro Pidal y Mon's Catholic wing of the Conservative party, had nothing positive to say about him. On the day of the transfer ceremony, it ran an editorial entitled "The Fusionist *Kulturkampf* " attacking the religious policies of the Sagasta government, which, it said, resembled those undertaken by "its forefathers, Espartero's radical Progressives."[50] The *Diario de Barcelona* was even fiercer, launching a vicious attack on the man it denounced as "average in every way" and the "incarnation of all the popular errors" of the times. Even his great military victories, Luchana included, were much less than advertised.[51] This provoked responses from a number of papers, led by the Madrid's *El Liberal*, which described the "vicious attack" on the man who had vanquished Carlism as "a warning of the dangers that surround us." Thanks to the weakness of the government, the influence of Carlism was on the rise once again.[52] *La Antorcha*, the Republican paper of Teruel, reprinted *El Liberal*'s article, which, it said, captured perfectly what was going on locally. As bad as the inaction of the government might be, the behaviour of Teruel's republicans, who simply looked on passively, was "ignominious!"[53]

The third monument funded by the national government was a version of the Madrid equestrian statue for Logroño. The 1872 fundraising campaign had allowed the city to build a pedestal but nothing more. In May 1890, Amos Salvador, a nephew of Sagasta's who sat as deputy for Logroño between 1886 and 1899, presented a bill calling on the government to provide the bronze and pay the costs of casting, transport, and assembly for a copy of Gibert's statue of Espartero. The sculptor had agreed to provide the moulds for free. Both the government and the opposition leaders were supportive, and by 29 June it had received royal assent. The following July, a bill to allocate sixty thousand pesetas for the project also became law.⁵⁴ It would be five years before the statue was inaugurated. The ceremony was more understated than the one which had marked the beginning of the project twenty-three years earlier.⁵⁵

Even sixteen years after his death, Espartero still had things to say to Spaniards, although now it was Conservatives who were finding them. Writing in *La Época* at a moment when Spain was fighting to retain control of Cuba, deputy and future minister Julio Burrell found that there was something "enduring" about this figure from a very different time. "For Spaniards who are fighting in Cuba, and for us who enjoy peace and political progress, Espartero is above all 'that man' ... who fought for the name of Spain in America to the last minute and who, in the name of liberty, vanquished the bloody demands of absolutism."⁵⁶ The Logroño statue also provoked an interesting comment in the Catalan-language weekly, *La Tomasa*. In an article entitled "The Statue of the 'Grandfather,'" someone writing under the pseudonym Pepet del Hort said that Espartero's story was as well known among Spaniards as Napoleon's was among the French: older people have their memories and younger ones learned about it in school or "in the comfortable living rooms of well-off houses on long winter nights."⁵⁷

There was also an abortive effort to erect a statue to Espartero in Bilbao, part of a failed project to commemorate the generals who had saved the city from two Carlist sieges, Espartero in 1836 and Manuel Gutiérrez de la Concha in 1874. As well as the importance of local initiative in commemoration, this incident reveals the obstacles facing celebrations of the country's liberal, constitutional heritage.

The question came before the council in September 1887 in the form of a motion presented by eight councillors calling on the municipal government to open a subscription for the two statues, which would "commemorate the raising of the Carlist sieges in 1836 and 1874 by these two generals." There was immediate dissent. One councillor absolutely refused to support the motion even though he had fought to defend Bilbao because the proposed statues "will recall political events intimately connected with the loss of the country's dearest rights and freedoms." When the vote was taken, four councillors voted against.⁵⁸ The special committee elected to study the project reported back to council three weeks later with a proposal to include a number of important local figures in the steering committee, but even after the presidents of the Sociedad Euskal-erria and the Círculo Católico as well as the editors of six local newspapers were added, the same four councillors voted against, as they later voted against a proposal that the city contribute twenty thousand pesetas to the fund. In the end, the public subscription failed to raise sufficient funds to go ahead with the project, "which caused great joy among the Carlists."[59]

This is the official and political memory. How was Espartero remembered in other, more popular spheres?

In a cartoon from 1884, *Madrid Cómico* painted people nostalgic for Espartero as harmless but sad, even pathetic.[60] Yet Espartero retained a place in the hearts of many, especially among Madrid's lower classes, as this description of the preparations for the Cruz de Mayo celebrations in 1880 illustrates. "The doorways of many houses in the dark and dirty outlying neighbourhoods of the capital were transformed into eye-catching scenes with more colour than a Fortuny painting … Alongside holy cards portraying the life and miracles of some saint were portraits of Espartero and Prim."[61] Fernando Chueca's wildly popular zarzuela *La Gran Vía*, which premiered in Madrid in July 1886, suggests the same thing. The third scene finds the "Gentleman" and the "Stroller" in a down-market dance hall catering to "servants [and] cooks" soon to fall victim to urban redevelopment. There they join Eliseo and the chorus in singing "El Chotis del Eliseo madrileño," which recalls that there was an Espartero before the superstar bullfighter of the moment.

ELISEO
Not the bullfighter!
The valiant general,
The great patriot,
The constant liberal.
ALL
Liberal?
ELISEO
Liberal.
ALL
They don't make them like that any more.[62]

Espartero also had a place in the greatest written monument to Spain's nineteenth century, the *Episodios Nacionales* [National Episodes], Benito Pérez Galdós's epic cycle of novels. His presence there is striking in two respects. First, although there are volumes named after individuals such as Zumalacárregi, Mendizábal, Narváez, O'Donnell, Prim, Amadeo I, and Cánovas, no volume bears the title *Espartero*. Even in *Luchana* he is more an absence than a presence, appearing only at the end of the book. That said, Espartero hovers over much of the epic, as Raúl Martín Arranz has shown.[63]

After almost three decades in which he was essentially forgotten, there was something of a revival of interest in Espartero in the 1930s. It began with a book by Álvaro de Albornoz, who would be a signatory to the Pact of San Sebastián, a member of the Revolutionary Committee, and minister during the first two years of the Second Republic, which he wrote in Madrid's Carcel Modelo while serving time for his political activities against the Primo de Rivera regime.[64] *El gobierno de los caudillos militares* [The Government of the Military Chiefs] was a comparison of the four great military-political figures of the nineteenth century: Narváez, O'Donnell, Prim, and Espartero. Albornoz saw very clear differences, "gradations in their authoritarianism," among them. Espartero was a "great patriot and a great liberal" who sought to govern "scrupulosuly respecting the rule of law and the constitution," but who lacked the skills to do so. Even for this convinced republican, however, there was greatness in Espartero's loyalty to the throne: not fighting to keep power was "the most heroic sacrifice in the interest of public peace and the greatest example of loyalty in our history."[65] What he did not much value was Espartero's greatest achievement, the negotiated conclusion to a civil war. With the complacency of someone who had never experienced one, Albornoz wrote elsewhere that civil wars "were necessary for a people to grow" and that they should end in victory, not compromise. "No more Agreements of Vergara ... no more deals with an enemy irreconciliably opposed to our ideas and our sentiments." It was an attitude that both sides in the Civil War of the 1930s would embrace.[66]

Two biographies were published in 1932. The first was written by the Count of Romanones, one of Spain's predominant political figures in the first two decades of the twentieth century, who twice served as prime minister. During the Second Republic, he continued to sit as deputy for Guadalajara, the seat he had held without interruption since 1886, but, far removed from office, he had more time for other activities. One of these was writing biographies, and during the 1930s he would produce six in which he "covered the trajectory of nineteenth-century liberals."[67]

Romanones' Espartero is not a great man. He warns his readers that other than personal valour, they were unlikely to find "any qualities of extraordinary intelligence or character nor any other greatness." Espartero's political life was guided by "simplistic ideas," a "complete lack of understanding of civilians," and a "simple spirit always ready to trust the good faith of others." Both on the battlefield and in political life he was hard-hearted and "placed no importance on human life."

Yet, despite his overall mediocrity, Espartero was a "representative person" who was able to "embody the sentiments, the desires and the conscience of his era."[68] Having himself suffered at the hands of the Primo de Rivera dictatorship (1923–30), Romanones found an important lesson in Espartero's life. While Espartero deserved Spain's gratitude for having ended the Carlist War, he had something serious to answer for: "after him, and even during his lifetime, other generals, liberals and conservatives, took such control over the governing of the country that even in our own times we remain subjected to them, suffering from an excessive fear which has no real basis."[69]

The second biographer, Carlos Fernández Cuenca, was forty years younger and a poet, movie director, and film historian.[70] His Espartero shares some characteristics with Romanones's, although his overall assessment is less negative. For example, he does not blame Espartero for Spain's ongoing history of praetorian politics. He was "valiant rather than thoughtful," lacked the intelligence to be in the same league as Napoleon or Cromwell, and was much more effective on the battlefield than in the corridors of power. Even so, he was "the key figure" of Spain's nineteenth-century history.[71]

In the context of the new civil war of the 1930s, Espartero, and especially the achievement that had been the basis of his enduring popularity in the nineteenth century, the negotiated Agreement of Vergara, were almost unanimously seen on both sides as negative.

The best-known reference to Vergara came less than a month after the start of the war. General Emilio Mola, the commander of the military uprising in the north, gave a speech over the radio in which he described its leaders' determination to fight until they had achieved all their goals. Negotiation, like surrender, was out of the question, and he concluded the speech with a phrase that would become notorious: "neither surrender nor Embraces of Vergara ... Nothing but overwhelming and definitive victory."[72] Thereafter, Nationalist references to Vergara were infrequent and, with only one exception, critical. This came in April 1937, with the Nationalist offensive in the Basque Country in full swing. In a radio talk, which the press reported under the headline "The New Embrace of Vergara," Nationalist propaganda chief Vicente Gay called on the Basques fighting with the Republic to change sides, and in doing so he invoked Vergara and the two generals who had embraced there: "They were patriots, men of honour and deeply held religious beliefs."[73]

All the remaining references were negative, and usually featured the word "betrayal." Responding to rumours that the "red camp" was interested in international mediation, *El Diario Palentino* said that the only possible reconciliation was surrender and punishment: "The tragedy of Spain cannot end with a new and traitorous embrace of Vergara."[74] The Carlist paper *El Requeté* published a poem, "No More Embraces!", which began "No more embraces of Vergara, brothers / no more traitorous Iscariot kisses."[75]

There was one place in Nationalist Spain where Espartero and Vergara were more than just afterthoughts. For *El Pensamiento alavés*, the anti-Basque nationalist paper set up in 1932 by the team which put out the Catholic paper *El Siglo Futuro*, the First Carlist War and the Embrace of Vergara were local events which were still alive, and it discussed Espartero or Vergara on five occasions during the war.[76] On 31 August 1939, the centenary of the Embrace, it ran an editorial comparing Vergara to the recent Hitler-Stalin Pact, an unnatural union produced by "an Iscariot." Any pact with evil, even "the lesser evil," was unacceptable: "That is why we reject the so-called Embrace of Vergara as we reject any pact with Communism." Basque nationalists had not done so, for which "they will be perpetually execrated."[77]

Republicans referred to Vergara more frequently than the Nationalists, but no more positively. Throughout the war, and especially during the crisis of spring 1937, groups in the Republican zone from across the political spectrum used Vergara as a pejorative. In August 1936, *La Voz* responded to reports that Alejandro Lerroux had offered his services as a mediator with the comment that "They don't have a Maroto nor we an Espartero. We need a complete, permanent and perfect victory." Vergara had actually been a victory for Carlism and that was why Republicans were fighting them now. In October, a POUM militia commander told a crowd in Barcelona that "we will not allow any embraces of Vergara in our house,"[78] and in January 1937, the anarcosyndicalist union CNT issued a statement commenting on the international context of the war: "Whoever intervenes and however they do it, the CNT will not agree to a new embrace of Vergara."[79] The next month, Prime Minister Francisco Largo Caballero issued a manifesto in which he said that "The arms of the man who is currently head of Spain's government will never be open to the men who betrayed their country." The next day, *La Libertad* proclaimed on its front page "We are with the prime minister. The anti-fascist Spanish people prefers to die before acceptiong a new and humiliating embrace of Vergara."[80]

The May 1937 events in Barcelona and the replacement of Largo Caballero by Juan Negrín as head of the Republican government produced a flurry of references to Vergara as the government and Republican political organizations competed to proclaim their steadfastness in the fight

Figure 18 Spanish Civil War cartoon satirizing a Luchana-style negotiated peace, March 1937. Biblioteca Virtual de Prensa Histórica.

against Franco. On 21 May, Negrín made it clear that his policy was to fight to the end. Echoing Mola, he proclaimed: "Neither mediation nor Embraces of Vergara." A few days later, the Politbureau of the Communist Party announced its support for the new government, which would "lead the Spanish people to the total destruction of its enemies without any 'embrace of Vergara' with those inside the country or outside." The CNT paper *Solidadridad Obrera* attributed the government's backbone to popular pressure: "THE ATMOSPHERE FOR AN EMBRACE OF VERGARA HAS BEEN MADE IMPOSSIBLE BY PRESSURE FROM THE MASSES AND THE COMBATANTS."[81] Even the moderate Izquierda Republicana party joined in, with one of its deputies telling a meeting in Madrid that his party had been "The most authentic enemy of this embrace of Vergara" that was being mentioned.[82] In addition, the publications of at least two units of the Republican army also rejected Vergara. In April 1937, *Camarada* wrote that it would not accept any "Embrace of Vergara while a single foreigner remained in Spain," while in September, *Victoria*, the organ of the Twenty-Fourth Mixed Brigade, declared there was no room for a Vergara in the "war of independence but also a class war" it was fighting.[83]

Franco detested Spain's liberal heritage, and in a speech in February 1940 in Ciudad Real, not far from Espartero's birthplace, he said he wanted to "banish liberalism." When it came to historical memory, however, his regime did not "totally eradicate liberalism from public spaces." Rather, it took active measures only against figures, such as Riego, who were "most clearly linked with the Republic, socialism, and communism," who had "recent historical significance," and who were not simply figures from "the distant past."[84]

The treatment of Espartero bears this out. In Barcelona and Valencia, where there was a "systematic purge" of the street names, Espartero was one of a host of nineteenth-century liberals who had their streets eliminated.[85] In Madrid, he lost two streets and the subway station named Príncipe de Vergara to General Mola. He did keep his statue, despite an early suggestion by the Nationalist mayor that it and the statue of Pablo Iglesias, founder of the Socialist Party, "people who were ... opposed to the ideals of the National Movement," should be removed, an unusual pairing if there ever was one.[86] The only statue actually taken down in the capital was that to Progressive hero Mendizábal.

Bilbao retained its Espartero Street and Duke of Victory Street despite "intensive political action designed to saturate public space with the values of the new regime," of which street names were a central element. Unlike names connected to Basque nationalism, socialism, or the Second Republic, Espartero's met the test of being consonant with the "public decorum needed in a city of the New Spain." Agreement of Vergara was replaced by Alzamiento Nacional [National Uprising], but was changed back after only three years.[87]

In the Spain of the "Leader by the grace of God," where biography became a propaganda tool "exalting the heroism and exemplary Christian nature of people whose lives fit the profile demanded by the regime," Espartero was also excluded from the Francoist "gallery of national myths."[88] It is not surprising, then, that the one biography which appeared during the regime, Antonio Espina's *Espartero, o ¡Cúmplase la voluntad nacional!*, was written from exile.[89]

Espina was a novelist, poet, and essayist and a significant member of the Madrid intellectual scene in the 1920s. He was also, according to Anna Caballé, "the most professional biographer of the period."[90] Jailed during the Primo de Rivera dictatorship, he joined Manuel Azaña's Izquierda Republicana and served briefly as civil governor of León at the beginning of the Republic. His journalism sent him to jail in 1935, but immediately after the elections of February 1936 he was named civil governor of Ávila and then, in May 1936, civil governor of Mallorca. He was arrested immediately after the military uprising of 18 July 1936 and spent the entire Civil War in prison, being released only in 1940. He was able to sneak into France in 1946 and two years later he moved to Mexico, where he remained until 1956, when he was allowed to return to Spain. Even though it was published in Madrid and received "some enthusiastic reviews," his *Espartero* went largely unnoticed.[91]

While positive overall, Espina's was a balanced portrait: Espartero was neither an unblemished hero nor a villain. Espina did not hesitate to point out Espartero's shortcomings. He did not minimize his military defeats during the Carlist War and he laughed at the "ridiculous hyperbole" of those who compared him to George Washington, let alone to Napoleon.[92] As a politician, Espartero was weak and out of his element: "he got depressed in the halls of the palace ... he turned out to be a mediocre leader of his ministers and deputies."[93] But if Espartero made mistakes, he always acted in good faith. He was a "man of action" with "real military talent" and "astonishing luck."[94] He was unfailingly honest and, despite all the "sinister stories" which were spread about him, he was "the least sinister man in the world."[95] A book which begins with the famous phrase "In a place in La Mancha" – the opening words of *Don Quixote* – concludes referring to Espartero's "grandeur of spirit."[96]

Given Espina's politics and his experiences after 18 July 1936, the question arises whether he used his biography of Espartero to comment on the Civil War and the *Caudillo* of his own time. Having the book published in Madrid of course precluded any direct comment, but there is one point at which one can discern some coded criticism. In describing the Embrace of Vergara, which essentially ended the Carlist War, he wrote: "the drama was not a lie. Six years of pain and blood cast their shadow over the life of the country. The general ovation given to the Agreement of Vergara was, therefore, fully justified because the agreement signalled the end of the war, the awakening from a macabre nightmare."[97] Was this a contrast to the "macabre nightmare" so many Spaniards were still living in a post–Civil War Spain beset by repression, fear, hunger, and even starvation?[98]

Despite the regime's overall rejection of Espartero, fleeting fragments of positive memory could emerge in odd corners. After the Civil War, the regime imposed a rationing system which provided ample opportunity for corruption while doing little to alleviate the "years of hunger" during which a large number of Spaniards died from the effects of malnutrition.[99] While the amounts of food to which Spaniards were limited were determined centrally, the actual coupons were printed locally. In at least one case, in the village of Villuercas (Cáceres), local authorities were clearly not on the same page as Madrid. The sheets of coupons printed in 1942 bore the image of Espartero with the title, "Baldomero

Espartero. 1793–1879. Valiant Spanish general *who contributed to the triumph of liberalism.*"[100]

Franco and many of his supporters may have reviled the liberal tradition, but post-Franco democrats did not embrace it as part of their inheritance. As Peyrou and Cruz Romeo have written, Spanish democracy "was born suffering from ... a notable indifference towards Spain's liberal tradition," an indifference they attribute to its having been "eroded, deactivated, killed," and not only by the actions of the Franco regime. By 1975, some saw liberalism as "synonymous with the fragmentation of the whole, a partisan struggle that resulted in violent conflict," while others saw it as the tool of an oligarchy that had stood in the way of democracy. For "many progressives, nineteenth-century liberalism was identified with an idea of failure."[101]

Espartero did not escape, and, in some respects, post-Franco Spain has been no friendlier to him than was the dictatorship. Madrid restored his street and his subway station in 1981 and 1983.[102] The smaller Duke of Victory Lane, which had become General Mola Passage, was not changed until 2017, when it was named after Enrique Ruano, a student who was killed while in police custody in 1969.[103] In two other of the country's most important cities, Bilbao and Barcelona, as well as a number of smaller places, however, municipal governments renamed the streets that had borne his name.

Bilbao took the lead in what José Varela Ortega has called a "paradoxical settling of scores with liberal and democratic history."[104] In August 1979, the municipal government controlled by the PNV [Basque Nationalist Party] changed the name of the street which, since May 1879, had been called Calle Espartero to Calle Juan Ajuriaguerra, after a Basque nationalist politician whom the city's mayor described as "a complete patriot who struggled ceaselessly for his fatherland, Euskadi."[105] (In contrast, Carlist hero Tomás Zumalacarrégi kept his street even though it had been given to him by the Franco regime.) Council approved the change by a vote of 23 in favour and 2 abstentions, but only after considerable debate. While none of the speakers was against naming a street after Ajuriaguerra, a number argued that doing so at Espartero's expense was "ripping a page out of the history of Bilbao." However, the remarks of Xabier Martín-González of the radical nationalist LAIA party made it clear that, for some in post-Franco Spain, constitutional government in itself had little value. "At the end of the day," he said, Espartero was ' someone who defended Bilbao ... against the Carlists, *who were the real Basques*, and then was the protagonist of something more historically dubious, the embrace of Vergara."[106]

It would be almost another thirty years before Espartero lost his two streets in Barcelona. The delay is surprising, since, from the nationalist perspective, there was more reason there to remove the name of the man who bombarded the city in 1842 than there was in Bilbao. This may reflect the city's focus on the legacies of the Second Republic, the Civil War, and the Franco regime, which began to change only after the passage of the national Law on Historical Memory and the analogous Catalan law in 2007.[107] Completing an initiative which had started two years earlier, in October 2008 the city council voted to change the name of the Calle Duc de la Victoria and the Pasaje Duc de la Victoria in the Gothic Quarter to Calle del Duc and Pasaje Francesc Pujols. This was part of what mayor Jordi Hereu described as the "normalization" of the city's streetscape to eliminate references to "times of dictatorship." For some cultural organizations, especially the nationalist Òmnium Cultural and Memorial 1714, these changes were insufficient: even the title "Duc" encouraged "bad memories as it invokes the [seventeenth-century] Count-Duke of Olivares, the [eighteenth-century] Duke of Berwick, and the Duke of Victory."[108]

The attack on Espartero's name was not limited to the Catalan capital. In 2011, the municipal government of the spa town of Caldes de Montbui held a referendum on whether or not to retain Espartero's name on a street there. Of the 2,047 people who voted, 810 favoured keeping the existing name, 302 wanted to change the name to "Esparter," while, largely as the result of a social media campaign led by the Evangelical church, 935 voted for George Lawrence Davis (1830–1894), a Protestant missionary from Wales who founded a school for the poor and an Evangelical church in the town. The street was renamed after Davis in February 2012.[109] In 2013, the far-left Candidatura Unitat Popular in the town of El Vendrell (Tarragona) demanded – unsuccessfully – that a nineteenth-century fountain called the Fuente del Duque de la Victoria be renamed, since it was "a disgrace" to have something honour this "protagonist of the dark chronicle of Catalonia."[110] Finally, in December 2014 the municipal council of Vilanova stripped Espartero and two other nineteenth-century generals, the Duke of Ahumada, founder of the Guardia Civil, and Manuel Gutiérrez de la Concha, who served as captain general of Catalonia during the Second Carlist War and put down the Guerra dels Matiners, of their streets in the city.[111]

Some Catalans seem unable to free themselves of a certain image of Espartero, that of November 1842. When I was interviewed on TV3 in November 2016, one of the first questions was about the remark, which Espartero never actually made, that it is necessary to bombard Barcelona every fifty years.[112] And in the run-up to the independence "referendum" of 1 October 2017, *La Vanguardia* published an opinion piece entitled ' The Ghost of General Espartero."[113]

The "indifference" to the liberal tradition that led to Espartero being ignored also affected his female contemporaries, but to a much greater degree. Even the emergence of women's history did not help much so long as the gender system of nineteenth-century liberal societies was understood to have been based on a strict and impermeable separation between a female private sphere and a male public one, and political activity was narrowly defined. The recent replacement of this simplistic vision by a more complex and textured one has allowed the contribution of women to public life in the period of the liberal revolution to be discovered. Juana de la Vega, Countess of Mina is the best-known individual, but her role as governess to the royal princesses during Espartero's regency gave her an unusual degree of visibility. As I hope to have shown, a forgotten woman such as María Jacinta Guadalupe Martínez de Sicilia y Santa Cruz – Jacinta – also played a role in the construction of Spain's liberal political order.

Espartero remains both contentious and essentially orphaned. He has critics but no advocates, but he is far from unique. The same can be said for the other leading figures of Spain's nineteenth-century liberal tradition and, indeed, for that tradition itself. Forty years of Francoist denigration of what they liked to call "false, outmoded liberalism," among other things, did their work.

One attempt to turn that history into legacy was Ikusager's "Colección Memoria de la Libertad," directed by Antonio Rivera, which sought to use history, and the nineteenth century in particular, as a tool "for building civic values." The two first volumes in the series were re-editions of the Conde de Romanones' books on Olózaga and Espartero.[114] But that was a private initiative. Spain's post-Franco political leaders have shown virtually no interest in trying to make the nineteenth century into a usable past. There were some invocations of Cánovas, the architect of the Restoration, as a figure of conciliation during the Transition itself, but essentially nothing since.[115] One very rare example came in 1997 when Prime Minister José María Aznar took advantage of the centenary of Cánovas's assassination to locate the origins of his own conservative Popular Party in the liberalism of the Restoration.[116] Another was the postage stamp issued in 2014 to commemorate the bicentennial of the birth of Juan Prim, who, in the words of the Popular Party deputy who proposed it, was "a constitutional monarchist who valued order and liberty as the most valuable assets of civic co-existence." For the Partido Socialista de Catalunya, which unsuccessfully proposed creating a research prize named after him, Prim was a "defender of liberty and democracy."[117]

There has been no shortage of commemorations, and in 2002 the government even created a State Society for Cultural Commemoration. During its lifetime, the Society organized a number of centenary celebrations, but the vast majority were for cultural figures such as Isaac Albéniz, or for works of culture such as *Don Quixote* or the *Cantar de mío Cid*. The only celebrations of political figures or events were the centenary of the death of Isabel II in 2004 and the bicentenaries of the War of Independence (2008) and the Constitución de Cádiz (2012). None of the other anniversaries celebrated involved the great liberal figures of the nineteenth century.

Baldomero Espartero was an unprecedented phenomenon in the history of Spain. He was the country's first modern public figure, and Spaniards made him the object of a unique cult, one matched in Europe only by those of Napoleon and Garibaldi. Never before had so many identified so closely or invested so many hopes for so long in a single individual. And it is arguable that they have not done so since. Yet the most famous and revered Spaniard of his time, the person many saw as the embodiment of peace and constitutional government, has been completely forgotten. Only in May 2020, and prompted by the publication of the Spanish edition of this book, was he accorded even the modest recognition of a postage stamp.

Notes

Introduction

1. Pirala, *Historia*, 3:478; Bacon, *Six Years in Biscay*, 416; *Reseña historica del último sitio*. Unless otherwise indicated, all translations from Spanish are the author's.
2. Bacon, *Six Years*, 436.
3. Duncan, *The English in Spain*, 104–5; Oráa, *Memoria*, cited in Pirala, *Historia*, 3:496; Wylde to Palmerston, 25 December 1836, FO 72/464, NA.
4. Lieut. Vicars' Report on the Relief of Bilbao, 24 December 1836, WO 396/74, NA.
5. Rivas, "Un asistente de Espartero." His orderly claimed that he "grabbed hold of the horse's tail and in this way I had the honour of crossing the Luchana bridge."
6. Espartero to Jacinta, 7 January 1837, AE.
7. Pirala, *Historia*, 2:501; Poco Mas, *Scenes and Adventures in Spain*, 1:276–84.
8. Pedro ? to Espartero, 25 December 1868, AE.
9. Pirala, *Historia*, 3:501–2; *Galería Militar Contemporánea*, 2:230–4; Poco Mas, *Scenes and Adventures in Spain*, 1:276–84; Pedro ? to Espartero, 25 December 1868, AE; Wylde to Palmerston, 25 December 1836, FO 72/464, NA: Espartero to Jacinta, 30, 31 December 1836, AE.
10. *Reseña historica del último sitio*, 28.
11. Lieut. Vicars' Report on the Relief of Bilbao, 24 December 1836, WO 396/74, NA.
12. Garrido Muro, *Guerra y paz*, 119–25.
13. *Gaceta Extraordinaria de Madrid*, 1 January 1837. It appeared in the press the next day.
14. *El Eco del Comercio*, 2, 3 January 1837; Pirala, *Historia*, 2:510.
15. Estevánez, *Mis memorias*, 53; *DSC*, 2 January 1837, 851–2.
16. Pirala, *Historia*, 2:1138–42.

17 Garrido Muro, *Guerra y paz*, 124; Pirala, *Historia*, 2:1139.
18 *Elogio fúnebre que ... en sufragio; Oración fúnebre ... que dijo el Dr. D. Miguel Moragues.*
19 *Sucinta relación de las honras fúnebres.*
20 *Elogio fúnebre que en las solemnes exeqias* [sic].
21 *Diario Oficial de Avisos de Madrid*, 25 March 1837.
22 Pirala, *Historia*, 2:512; *Glorias de Azara en el Siglo XIX*, 926; Garrido Muro, *Guerra y paz*, 123.
23 de la Fuente Monge, "La figura del general Espartero" 107–8; García Gutiérrez, *El Sitio de Bilbao*.
24 Espartero to Jacinta, 28, 30 December 1836, AE.
25 Barbara Caine, *Biography and History* (London, 2010), 1, 3; Jo Burr Margadant, *The New Biography: Performing Femininity in Nineteenth-Century France* (Berkeley and Los Angeles, 2000); Birgitte Possing, *Understanding Biographies: On Biographies in History and Stories in Biography* (Copenhagen, 2016); *Biography, Gender and History: Nordic Perspectives* (Turku, 2016); Burdiel and Foster, eds., *La historia biográfica en Europa*.
26 Linda Colley, *The Ordeal of Elizabeth Marsh: A Woman in World History* (New York, 2007); Martha Hodes, *The Sea Captain's Wife: A True Story of Love, Race, and War in the Nineteenth Century* (New York, 2006); Natalie Zemon Davis, *Trickster Travels: A Sixteenth-Century Muslim between Worlds* (New York, 2006).
27 Riall, *Garibaldi*; Cazorla-Sánchez, *Franco*.
28 Burdiel and Foster, eds., *La historia biográfica en Europa*, 9–11.
29 Burdiel, "Historia política y biografía," 61.
30 de Riquer i Permanyer, "La débil nacionalización española del siglo XIX"; Álvarez Junco, *Mater dolorosa*; Archilés i Cardona, "Hacer región es hacer patria"; Santirso Rodríguez, *España en la Europa liberal (1830–1870)*; Romeo Mateo, "¿Y estos en medio de la nación soberana son por ventura esclavos?"; "La tradición progresista"; Lario, "La monarquía de Isabel II y el liberalismo post-revolucionario."
31 Moreno Luzón and Núñez Seixas, *Los colores de la patria*, 83–4; Molina and Cabo Villaverde, "An Inconvenient Nation," 66–8.
32 Burdiel, "Historia política y biografía," 65.
33 Shubert, "Being – and Staying – Famous in 19th-Century Spain."
34 Lilti, *Figures publiques*.
35 Leonore Davidoff and Catherine Hall, *Family Fortunes: Men and Women of the English Middle Class, 1750–1850*, revised edition (London, 2002); Joan Landes, *Women and the Public Sphere in the Age of the French Revolution* (Ithaca, 1988); Joan Scott, *Only Paradoxes to Offer: French Feminists and the Rights of Man* (Cambridge, 1996); Mary Beth Norton, *Mothers and*

Fathers: Gendered Power and the Forming of an American Society (New York, 1996); Dena Goodman, "Public Sphere and Private Life: Toward a Synthesis of Current Historiographical Approaches to the Old Regime," *History and Theory* (February 1992): 1–20. Davidoff and Hall expressed the permeability of these spheres pithily: "Public was not really public and private not really private despite the potent imagery of 'separate spheres'" (33).

36 Burguera, "Mujeres y revolución liberal en perspectiva," is an excellent overview of this new literature. See also Burguera, *Las Damas del Liberalismo Respetable*, and Romeo Mateo, "Domesticidad y Política." Spain was also in the unusual position of having a woman in the most important position of political power: Queen Isabel II, who ruled from 1833 to 1868. Her mother, María Cristina, was also politically powerful for much of her reign – whether as regent from 1833 to 1840 or without any formal role after that – and was recognized as such. Luengo, *Una sociedad conyugal*; "Las élites liberales en la España del siglo XIX."

37 Burguera, "Mujeres y revolución liberal en perspectiva."

38 Romeo Mateo, "Domesticidad y política"; Aresti, "El ángel del hogar y sus demonios."

39 When discussing the interactions between the two, I will refer to him as Baldomero in order to treat them as equals.

40 Palmerston to Bulwer, 23 September 1847, GC/BU/560, BP.

41 The literature is extensive. For an excellent recent overview and analysis, see Aguilar and Ramírez-Barat, "Reparations without Truth or Justice in the Spanish Case."

42 Martín Arranz, "Espartero: Figuras de legitimidad"; Bermejo Martín, *Espartero*; Díaz Marín, "Espartero: el regente plebeyo," "La construcción política de Espartero antes de su Regencia, 1837–1840," and "Espartero en entredicho"; de la Fuente Monge, "La figura del general Espartero"; Inarejos Muñóz, "El aura del general Espartero"; Cañas de Pablo, "Espartero y Prim" and "Personificando la Revolución de 1840"; Garrido Muro, *Guerra y paz*; Pérez Núñez, "Los amigos de Espartero"; Aquillué Domínguez, "El liberalismo en la encrucijada."

43 http://www.bne.es/es/Catalogos/HemerotecaDigital/; http://prensahistorica.mcu.es/es/estaticos/contenido.cmd?pagina=estaticos/presentacion.

44 *Dichos y opiniones de Espartero en conversación con sus amigos.*

45 David W. Blight, "The Silent Type," *New York Review of Books*, 24 May 2018.

46 Garry Wills, *Cincinnatus: George Washington and the Enlightenment* (New York, 1984), 3.

47 Andreu Miralles, "Nación, emoción y fantasía."

1. From Gránatula to America, February 1793–February 1815

1 Donoso García, *Iglesia Parroquial de Santa Ana*, http://oretum.es/iglesia/iglesia.pdf.
2 *Censo de Floridablanca*, 17:1281, 1290, 1304.
3 Cited in Lanza Ruedas, ed., *Baldomero Espartero*, 9.
4 AGS_CE_RG_L473_295.jpg, http://pares.mcu.es/Catastro/servlets/ImageServlet. The *Catastro* was compiled between 1750 and 1754.
5 AGS_CE_RG_L469_051.jpg, 076.jpg, http://pares.mcu.es/Catastro/servlets/ImageServlet.
6 *Vida militar y politica de Espartero*, 1:2.
7 Espartero to his father, 30 January 1818, AE; Lanza Ruedas, ed., *Baldomero Espartero*, 37.
8 Espartero to Francisco Espartero, 17 January 1837, AE.
9 A. Álvarez de Morales, *La Ilustración y la Reforma de la Universidad en la España del siglo XVIII* (Madrid, 1985); Sánchez de la Nieta Santos, *La Universidad de Almagro*; Fernández García, "Universidad de Almagro."
10 Espartero to Antonio Fernández Espartero, 30 January 1818, AE.
11 La Parra, *Manuel Godoy*.
12 La Parra, *Fernando VII*.
13 Artola, *Los afrancesados*; López Alós, "Ensayo sobre los afrancesados"; Fuentes Aragonés, "Afrancesados y liberales."
14 Cited in Pérez Garzón, *Las Cortes de Cádiz*, 103.
15 Álvarez Junco, *Mater Dolorosa*, 120–5. See also Fraser, *Napoleon's Cursed War*.
16 On the guerrilla war, see Tone, *The Fatal Knot*.
17 Artola, ed., *Las Cortes de Cádiz*; Pérez Garzón, *Las Cortes de Cádiz*.
18 Vidal Delgado, "Espartero," 4.
19 D.M.H. y D.J.T., *Espartero, su vida militar, política, descriptiva y anecdótica*, 2:910.
20 Napier, *History of the War in the Peninsula*, 2:241.
21 Ibid., 242.
22 Cited in Oman, *A History of the Peninsular War*, 3:84.
23 Napier, *History*, 2:249; Esdaile, *The Peninsular War*, 216.
24 Ibid., 217.
25 Napier, *History*, 2:251.
26 D.M.H. y D.J.T., *Espartero, su vida militar, política, descriptiva y anecdótica*, 1:20.
27 Oman, *A History*, 3:97.
28 Esdaile, *Outpost of Empire*.
29 Izquierdo Navarrete et al., *La Academia General Militar*, 24.
30 Solís, *El Cádiz de las Cortes*, 116–17.

31 Ibid., 63–4.
32 On Trafalgar, and especially the Spanish role in the battle, see John D. Harbron, *Trafalgar and the Spanish Navy* (Annapolis, 1988).
33 Solís, *El Cádiz*, 91.
34 Ibid., 189.
35 Alcalá Galiano, *Memorias*; Toreno, *Historia del levantamiento, guerra y revolución de España*, 1112.
36 Solís, *El Cádiz*, 145.
37 Alcalá Galiano, *Memorias*.
38 Pérez Galdós, *Cádiz*, 124–5.
39 http://www.cervantesvirtual.com/obra-visor/diario-de-sesiones-de-las-cortes-generales-y-extraordinarias-6/html/0299914e-82b2-11df-acc7-002185ce6064_3.htm.
40 http://www.cervantesvirtual.com/obra-visor/coleccion-de-los-decretos-y-ordenes-que-han-expedido-las-cortes-generales-y-extraordinarias-desde-su-instalacion-en-24-de-septiembre-de-1810-hasta-igual-fecha-de-1811-0/html/0027b5e4-82b2-11df-acc7-002185ce6064_19.html.
41 Miranda Calvo, "La Universidad de Toledo en 1808."
42 Cited in Clonard, *Memoria histórica de las academias militares de España*, 179.
43 According to Eric Christiansen, about a third of all commissions had gone to NCOs (*The Origins of Military Power in Spain, 1800–1854*, 3).
44 http://www.cervantesvirtual.com/obra-visor/coleccion-de-los-decretos-y-ordenes-que-han-expedido-las-cortes-generales-y-extraordinarias-desde-su-instalacion-en-24-de-septiembre-de-1810-hasta-igual-fecha-de-1811-0/html/0027b5e4-82b2-11df-acc7-002185ce6064_218.html.
45 Clonard, *Memoria*, 194–5.
46 Florez, *Espartero*, 1:11. See also D.M.H. y D.J.T., *Espartero, su vida militar, política, descriptiva y anecdótica*, 1:18.
47 Napier, *History*, 2:281–4; Esdaile, *The Peninsular War*, 335–6.
48 Florez, *Espartero*, 1:11; *Vida militar y política de Espartero*, 1:4.
49 Pérez Garzón, *Las Cortes de Cádiz*, 217.
50 Agustín Arguelles, *Exámen histórico de la reforma constitucional que hicieron las Cortes Generales y Extraordinarias* (London, 1835), 478; Antonio Alcalá Galiano, *Orígenes del liberalismo español* (Madrid, 1955), 440.
51 Jaime Rodríguez O, "Las instituciones gaditanas en Nueva España, 1812–1824," in Rodríguez O, ed., *Las Nuevas Naciones*, 101; Breña, *El primer liberalismo español y los procesos de emancipación de América, 1808–1824*.
52 http://www.cervantesvirtual.com/obra-visor/the-political-constitution-of-the-spanish-monarchy-promulgated-in-cadiz-the-nineteenth-day-of-march-0/html/ffd04084-82b1-11df-acc7-002185ce6064_1.html. Not everything was new: Article 12 proclaimed that "The religion of the Spanish nation is, and ever shall be, the Catholic Apostolic Roman and

only true faith; the State shall, by wise and just laws, protect it and prevent the exercise of any other."
53 Berbel, "A Constitucao Espanhola no Mundo Luso-Americano (1820–1823)," 227.
54 Alcalá Galiano, *Memorias*.
55 Florez, *Espartero*, 1:15.
56 Ibid., 16n; also *Vida militar y política*, 2:911.
57 D.M.H. y D.J T., *Espartero, su vida militar, política, descriptiva y anecdótica*, 1:20.
58 Baldomero Espartero, Carpeta 3, Expediente Personal, Servicio Histórico Militar, Madrid.
59 Oman, *A History of the Peninsular War*, 7:406.
60 La Parra, "La restauración de Fernando VII en 1814."
61 http://www.cervantesvirtual.com/obra/real-decreto-de-fernando-vii-derogando-la-constitucion-valencia-4-mayo-1814/.
62 Chasteen, *Americanos*, 47.
63 Albí, *Banderas olvidadas*, 149.
64 *Vida militar y política*, 1:8; Apuntes biográficos de Espartero, AE.
65 D.M.H. y D.J.T., *Espartero, su vida militar, política, descriptiva y anecdótica*, 2:912.
66 Florez, *Espartero*, 1:22–3.

2. Defender of the Empire, February 1815–November 1825

1 Sevilla, *Memorias de un oficial del Ejército*, 24.
2 Cited in Lynch, *Spanish American Revolutions*, 203. On Bolívar, see Lynch, *Simon Bolivar*, and Araña, *Bolívar*.
3 Stoat, *Pablo Morillo and Venezuela*, 67–9.
4 Claudia Rosas Lauro and Manuel Chust, eds., *El Perú en Revolución, independencia y guerra: un proceso* (Castellón, 2017); Anna, *The Fall of the Royal Government in Peru*.
5 García Camba, *Memorias para la historia de las armas españolas en el Perú*, 1:258.
6 Fisher, "The Royalist Regime in the Viceroyalty of Peru, 1820–1824," 76; Albi, *El ultimo virrey*, 129, 135.
7 Ibid., 121–2.
8 García Camba, *Memorias*, 1:314–15, 326.
9 Espartero to his father, 30 January 1818, AE; emphasis added.
10 *Hoja de servicios del Excmo. Sr. Capitán General D. Baldomero Espartero, Duque de la Victoria y de Morella*, 8.
11 Roca, *Ni con Lima, ni con Buenos Aires*, 361.
12 Albi, *Banderas olvidadas*, 191–4.
13 *Hoja de servicios*, 8.
14 de la Pezuela, *Memoria de gobierno*, 636; *Hoja de servicios*, 11.

15 On San Martín, see Lynch, *San Martín*.
16 Gil Novales, *El trieno liberal*.
17 Martínez Riaza, "'Para Reintegrar la Nación'"; Salvador Broseta, *Autonomismo, insurgencia, independencia. América en las Cortes del Trieno Liberal, 1820–1823* (Cádiz, 2012).
18 Romanones, *Espartero*, 48.
19 Cited in Lynch, *Spanish American Revolutions*, 174, 177.
20 On the "free trade dispute," see Marks, *Deconstructing Legitimacy*, 219–64.
21 Anna, *The Fall of the Royal Government in Peru*, 166; Marks, *Deconstructing Legitimacy*, 301.
22 Torata, *Documentos para la historia de la guerra separatista del Perú*, 2:305–10.
23 Ibid., 2:305–10; Marks, *Deconstructing Legitimacy*, 303–5.
24 *Hoja de servicios*, 11.
25 *Estado Mayor General del Ejército Español*, 116; "Espartero – D. Baldomero," in Mendiburu, *Diccionario histórico-biográfico del Perú*, 3:55–6.
26 Garcia Camba, *Memorias*, 1:371–2; *Rebelión de Aznapuquio por varios jefes del ejército español*.
27 *Hoja de servicios*, 4.
28 Chambers, *From Subjects to Citizens*, 1–30; Haigh, *Sketches of Buenos Ayres, Chile, and Peru*, 362.
29 "Diálogo entre Lisipo y Tolomeo," Mi pasatiempo, AE.
30 Chambers, *From Subjects to Citizens*, 48–9; Condori, "Guerra y economía en Arequipa," 836.
31 Borrell Merlín, "Historia y Cultura del Rioja," 169–71.
32 Cited in Albi, *El ultimo virrey*, 446.
33 *Boletín Extraordinario del Ejército Nacional de Operaciones al Sur de Arequipa*, 16 February 1823, AE.
34 García Camba, *Memorias*, 2:48; Alexandro González Villalobos, 29 March 1824, AE.
35 Sobrevilla Perea, *The Caudillo of the Andes*.
36 *Hoja de servicios*, 11.
37 Cited in Albi, *El ultimo virrey*, 468.
38 Martínez Riaza, "'Para Reintegrar la Nación,'" 684.
39 Caillet-Bois, *La mission Pereyra-La Robla al Rio de la Plata y la convención preliminar de paz del 4 de Julio de 1823*, 14, 16–17, 20.
40 Martínez Baeza, *Vida del General Juan Gregorio de las Heras*.
41 Cited in Roca, *Ni con Lima*, 513; La Serna to Espartero, 13, 19 October 1823. AE. For the assessment of one Argentine officer, see J.M. Calderón y Belgrano to Bernardino Rivadavia, 19 February 1824, S. 10.C. 1.A 10 #1, AGN.
42 La Serna to Espartero, 13, 19 October 1823, AE.
43 Las Heras to Espartero, 15 November 1823, AE; Espartero Las Heras, 21 November 1823, AE.

44 Las Heras to Espartero, 25 November 1823, S. 10.C. 1.A10 #1, AGN.
45 Las Heras to Espartero, 28 November 1823, AE.
46 Espartero Las Heras, 28 November 1823, AE. Las Heras immediately reported this to Buenos Aires. Las Heras to Rivadavia, 4 December 1823, S. 10.C. 1.A10 #1, AGN.
47 Las Heras to Rivadavia, 20 December 1823, S. 10.C. 1.A10 #1, AGN.
48 Espartero to Las Heras, 10 December 1823, Correspondencia con Barias Autoridades, AE.
49 Las Heras to Espartero, 14 December 1823, AE.
50 Espartero to Las Heras, 16 December 1823, AE.
51 Las Heras to Espartero, 19 December 1823, Correspondencia con Barias Autoridades, AE; Las Heras to Rivadavia, 3, 17 January 1824, S. 10.C. 1.A10 #1, AGN.
52 Espartero to La Serna, 15 December 1823, Correspondencia con Barias Autoridades, AE.
53 Espartero to La Serna, 23 December 1823, Correspondencia con Barias Autoridades, AE.
54 Las Heras to Rivadavia, 23 February 1824, S. 10.C. 1.A10 #1, AGN.
55 La Serna to Espartero, 19 January 1824, AE.
56 Las Heras to Espartero, 12 February 1824, AE; Las Heras to Rivadavia, 20 February 1824, S. 10.C. 1.A10 #1, AGN.
57 Cited in Piñeiro, *Las Heras, Espartero y la Paz con España*, 40.
58 Cited in Roca, *Ni con Lima*, 519. For their part, regular army officers, and especially Valdés, looked down on the man they considered only an amateur soldier, and a corrupt one at that. Valdés to La Serna, 21 December 1823, 7182, 7192, Colección Torata, RAH.
59 Espartero to La Serna, 24 March 1824, Correspondencia con Barias Autoridades, AE; Valdés, *Exposición*, 1:145–6. See also Espartero to La Serna, 26 December 1823, Correspondencia con Barias Autoridades, AE.
60 La Serna to Olañeta, 4 February 1824, 7192, Colección Torata, RAH; Valdés, *Exposición*, 1:156–7, 4:358. See also Las Heras to Rivadavia, 20, 23 February, 5 March 1824, S. 10.C. 1.A10 #1, AGN.
61 Martínez Baeza, *Vida del General Juan Gregorio de las Heras*, 284–5.
62 Chao, *Espartero*, 1–2.
63 Albi, *Banderas olvidadas*, 313.
64 For the full text, see Valdés, *Exposición*, 1:184–5.
65 La Parra, *Los Cien Mil Hijos de San Luis*.
66 *Real cedula de S.M. y señores del Consejo, por la cual se declaran nulos y de ningún valor todos los actos del Gobierno llamado Constitucional, de cualquiera clase y condición que sean, y se aprueba interinamente todo cuanto se ha decretado y ordenado por la Junta Provisional de Gobierno y por la Regencia del Reino, con lo demás que en ella se expresa* (Madrid, 1823).

67 7194, Colección Torata, RAH, Madrid.
68 Cited in Anna, *The Fall*, 214.
69 Ibid., 229.
70 La Serna to Canterac, 27 March 1824, 7182, #21, Colección Torata, RAH.
71 La Serna to minister of state, 24 March 1824, AE.
72 Condori, "Lucas de Cotera."
73 Durston, "Quechua Political Literature in Early Republican Peru (1810–1876)."
74 Florez, *Espartero*, 1:105. See also Romanones, *Espartero*, 44–5.
75 In *La Campaña del Maestrazgo*, Pérez Galdós, whose portayal of Espartero in his *Episodios Nacionales* is positive overall, also has him described as a card sharp.
76 Gárate Ojanguren, "Financial Circuits in Spain," 81; Juan de Arrache to Espartero, 8 November 1822, AE.
77 Arrache to Espartero, 23 May 1823, AE.
78 Arrache to Espartero, 21 December 1824, AE.
79 Espartero to Arrache, 21 December 1824; Arrache to Espartero, 21 December 1824, AE.
80 Patsy Richards, *Inflation: The Value of the Pound 1750–2001*, Research Paper 02/44, July 2002, House of Commons Library. I want to thank my colleague Nicholas Rogers for the reference to this source.
81 Donoso García, *Baldomero Espartero*, 11.
82 Mendiburu, *Diccionario historico-biografico del Peru*, 7:399–400.
83 Passport, 28 December 1824, AE.
84 Chao, *Espartero*, 4.
85 Romanones, *Espartero*, 55–6.
86 Alegría, "Entre Bolívar, Espartero y un Extra."
87 Antonio García, 10 December 1824, José Montenegro, 15 December 1824, José Vidart, 15 December 1825, AE; Florez, *Espartero*, 1:102–4. On Infante, see López, *El General Infante*.
88 José Vidart, 15 December 1825, AE.
89 *Dichos y opiniones de Espartero en conversación con sus amigos*, 2–3; emphasis in original.
90 Arrache to Espartero, 7 January 1826, AE.
91 Expediente Personal, #27, Archivo General Militar, Segovia.

3. Defender of the Throne, November 1825–September 1836

1 Christiansen, *The Origins of Military Power in Spain*, 28–31; Puell de la Villa, *Historia del ejército en España*; Cepeda Gómez, *Los pronunciamientos en la España del siglo xix*, 17–27.
2 Pérez Núñez, "Los amigos de Espartero"; Sobrevilla Perea, "From Europe to the Americas and Back."

3 Gerónimo Valdés, 11 November 1826; Carpeta Azul 3, AE. See also Valentín Ferraz, 11 November 1826, Carpeta Azul 3, AE, and José Santos de la Hera, 16 November 1826, Carpeta Azul 3, AE.
4 7192, Colección Torata, RAH.
5 Pedro Tedde de Lorca, *El Banco de San Carlos (1782–1829)* (Madrid 1988), 58, 359; José María de Francisco Olmos, *Los miembros del Consejo de Hacienda (1722–1838) y organismos económicos-monetarios* (Madrid, 1997), 345–8.
6 Pérez Alonso to Espartero, 2 January 1825, AE; Pérez Alonso to Espartero, 12, 16, 23 January 1826, AE; Pérez Alonso suggested he wait a couple of months before requesting leave to take the waters at Bañeras. Pérez Alonso to Espartero, 23 March 1826, AE.
7 Expediente Personal, #27, Archivo General Militar, Segovia. On this incident, see Cepeda Gómez, "El general Espartero durante la 'década ominosa.'"
8 Pérez Alonso to Espartero, 20 September 1826, AE.
9 Expediente Personal, Carpeta 7, AE; Bermejo Martín, *Espartero*, 83.
10 Pérez Alonso to Espartero, 20 September 1827, AE..
11 Jesús Javier Alonso, "La formación de la elite liberal burguesa."
12 Romeo Mateo, "Juana María de la Vega."
13 Fernández de Córdova, *Mis memorias íntimas*, 1:119–20.
14 Jesús Javier Alonso, "La formación de la elite," 217.
15 Carpeta 27, AE.
16 Bermejo Martín, *Espartero*, 73–5.
17 Ibid., 271–2. This role brought Espartero almost immediately into conflict with local farmers (87–8).
18 Ibid., 273–6. The letters of Francisco Pérez Alonso contain much detail about Espartero's financial arrangements and investments.
19 Koontz, *Marriage*, 6–7; Muñoz López, *Sangre, amor e interés*, 70.
20 Bermejo Martín, *Espartero*, 58.
21 Ibid., 81; *Visit to Paris, or the Stranger's Guide* (London, 1830), 17–20.
22 Bermejo Martín, *Espartero*, 81–2; Condori, "Lucas de Cotera," 123n74.
23 Carpeta 23, AE.
24 Bermejo Martín, *Espartero*, 84–6.
25 Ibid., 87.
26 Pérez Alonso to Espartero, 21 September, 29 October 1829, AE. Baldomero and Jacinta did not return to Logroño until March. Pérez Alonso to Espartero, 11 March 1830, AE.
27 Pérez Alonso to Espartero, 31 March 1828, 18 May 1829, AE.
28 Carpeta 9, Expediente Personal, Archivo General Militar.
29 Santirso Rodríguez, "Revolución liberal y guerra civil en Cataluña (1833–1840)," 25–6.
30 Florez, *Espartero*, 1:113–15; Jacinto Vilardaga y Cañellas, *Efemérides bergadanas* (Manresa, 1919), 211; Cardeñosa y Mir, *Vida militar y política de Espartero*, 1:88–9; Vidal Delgado, *Entre Logroño*, 111.

31 *Hoja de Servicios del Duque de la Victoria y Morella* (1852); Carpetas 7, 8, Expediente Personal, Archivo General Militar; Florez, *Espartero*, 118–19.
32 Florez, *Espartero*, 1:117–18; Carpeta 1, Expediente Personal, Archivo General Militar.
33 Torras Elías, *La Guerra de los Agraviados*.
34 Coverdale, *The Basque Phase of Spain's First Carlist War*, 114–15.
35 ficus.pntic.mec.es/jals0026/documentos/textos/abrantes.pdf
36 Coverdale, *The Basque Phase*, 125–63; *Vida y hechos de don Tomás Zumalacárregi*.
37 Pirala, *Historia*; Canal, *El Carlismo. Dos siglos de contrarrevolución en España*; Aróstegui, Canal, and González Calleja, *El Carlismo y las guerras carlistas*; Bullón de Mendoza, *La primera guerra carlista*; Lawrence, *Spain's First Carlist War*.
38 Garrido Muro, *Guerra y paz*, 45–6. The 200,000 deaths out of a population of around 12.5 million in the First Carlist War were, in per capita terms, many more than the 300,000 out of 23.7 million of the Spanish Civil War. For a comparative study of the two wars, see Lawrence, *The Spanish Civil Wars*.
39 Gueniffey, *Bonaparte*, 49–50; emphasis in original.
40 Espartero to Ayuntamiento de Logroño, 6 June 1834, AE.
41 Boix, *Xátiva*, 388–9; Millán, "Els militants carlins del País Valencià central"; José Muñóz San Martin to Espartero, 7 January 1834, AE.
42 Conde de Cuba to Espartero, 23 December 1833, AE; Manuel Frepe to Espartero, 30 January 1834; Valdés to Espartero, 13 January 1834, AE.
43 Carpeta 11, Expediente Personal, Archivo General Militar.
44 *Hoja de servicios*, 19–23. See Fernández de Córdova, *Mis memorias íntimas*, 1:149; Vidal Delgado, *Entre Logroño*, 134n35.
45 Espartero to Valdés, 12 April 1834, AE.
46 Espartero to Jacinta, 6, 10 March 1834, AE.
47 Espartero to Jacinta, 17 March 1834, AE.
48 Espartero to Jacinta, 27, 29 April 1834, AE.
49 Espartero to Jacinta, 6 May, 11 June 1834, AE.
50 Espartero to Jacinta, 25 March 1834, AE.
51 Ayuntamiento de Bilbao to Joaquín de Osma, 1, 16 April 1834; Ayuntamiento de Bilbao to Espartero, 15 April 1834, AE.
52 Espartero to Jacinta, 16 May 1834, AE.
53 Vidal Delgado, *Entre Logroño*, 154–5.
54 Espartero to Jacinta, 2 July 1834, AE.
55 Espartero to Jacinta, 10, 15, July 1834, AE.
56 Espartero to Jacinta, 15, 20 September 1834, AE.
57 AE.
58 Espartero to Jacinta, 8 October 1834, AE; Espartero to minister of war, 20 September 1834, ACM; emphasis added.

59 Carpeta 11, Expediente Personal, Archivo General Militar.
60 Espartero to Diputación de Vizcaya, 7, 14 November 1834; José Alonso to Espartero, 10 November 1834, AE.
61 Espartero to Jacinta, 11, 15, November 1834, AE.
62 Espartero to Osma, 22 December 1834, AE.
63 Espartero to Jacinta, 24, 30 November, 23 December 1834, AE; *Hoja de servicios*, 23.
64 Espartero to Jacinta, 17 January 1835, AE.
65 Espartero to Jacinta, 17, 21, 24 February 1835, AE.
66 Espartero to Jacinta, 6 April 1835, AE.
67 Bacon, *Six Years*, 181, 187–90.
68 Espartero to Jacinta, 31 March, 4, 14 April 1835, AE; *Hoja de servicios*, 24.
69 Villiers to Palmerston, 23 May 1834, FO 72/423, NA.
70 William Doyle, *The Oxford History of the French Revolution* (Oxford, 2002), 257.
71 Garrido Muro, *Guerra y paz*, 36–8; Vidal Delgado, *Entre Logroño*, 186; *Galería Militar contemporánea*, 279.
72 Pirala, *Historia*, 1:396–8.
73 Espartero to Osma, 11 May 1834, AE. The order itself is not in his papers.
74 F.C. Mather, "Achilles or Nestor? The Duke of Wellington in British Politics," in N. Gash, ed., *Wellington: Studies in the Military and Political Career of the First Duke of Wellington* (Manchester, 1990), 185.
75 *Papers Relating to Lord Eliot's Mission to Spain in the Spring of 1835*, 91.
76 *El Gobierno y las Cortes del Estatuto: materiales para su historia* (Madrid, 1837), 170–2.
77 Coverdale, *The Basque Phase*, 216–17; Fernández de Córdova, *Mis memorias íntimas*, 1:210–23.
78 Espartero to Ramón Solano, nd, in *Epistolario militar de la primera guerra civil carlista*, 1:25–6; Espartero to Jacinta, 5 May 1835, AE; Pirala, *Historia*, 1:492–4; *Hoja de servicios*, 24. For this action, he was awarded the Gran Cruz de San Fernando.
79 *Epistolario militar*, 1:26.
80 Espartero to Jacinta, 6 June 1835, AE.
81 *Estado Mayor General del Ejército Español*, 129–30. For a Carlist account, see Ferrer, *Historia del tradicionalismo español*, 6:217–22.
82 Canal, "La primera guerra carlista," 55–6.
83 Espartero to Jacinta, 4 July 1835, AE.
84 *Hoja de servicios*, 24; *Estado Mayor General del Ejército Español*, 131; Espartero to Jacinta, 8, 10 July 1835, AE.
85 Espartero to Jacinta, 8, 10, 21 July 1835, AE.
86 *El Eco del Comercio*, 14, 15 July 1835; Espartero to Jacinta, 25 July 1835, AE.
87 Full text in Douglas M. Gibler, *International Military Alliances, 1648–2008* (Washington, 2009), 134–5. See Bullen, "France and the Problem of Intervention in Spain, 1834–1836."

88 Douglas Porch, *The French Foreign Legion: A Complete History of the Legendary Fighting Force* (New York, 2010), 22–49.
89 Espartero to Jacinta, 15 January 1836, AE.
90 Espartero to Jacinta, 4, 30 April 183, AE.
91 Brett, *The British Auxiliary Legion in the First Carlist War 1835–1838*; Moises Rodriguez, *Under the Flags of Freedom*.
92 http://www.historyofparliamentonline.org/volume/1820-1832/member/evans-george-1787-1870; Spiers, *Radical General*; Somerville, *History of the British Legion, and War in Spain*, 276.
93 Espartero to Jacinta, 23, 30 September 1835, AE.
94 Espartero to Jacinta, 15 January, 20, 29 February 1836, AE.
95 Espartero to Jacinta, 14 May 1836, AE.
96 Wylde to Villiers, 11 June 1836, WYL 1/1–48, WP.
97 Canal, "La primera guerra carlista," 50.
98 Pirala, *Historia*, 1:675–80; Fernández de Córdova, *Mis memorias íntimas*, 1:242–6; *Estado Mayor General del Ejército Español*, 131–2.
99 Espartero to Jacinta, 17, 20, 21 July 1835, AE.
100 Espartero to Jacinta, 30 July, 18 August 1835, AE. For Fernández de Córdova's explanation, see *Memoria justificativa*, 94.
101 Espartero to Jacinta, 10 August, 4 September 1835, AE.
102 Espartero to Jacinta, 2, 8, 10 August 1835, AE.
103 *La Revista Española*, 11 August 1835; Espartero to Jacinta, 13 August 1835, AE.
104 Espartero to Jacinta, 22 August 1835, AE.
105 Espartero to Jacinta, 31 August 1835, AE. Luis Fernández de Córdova, 6 September 1835, AE.
106 Fernández de Córdova, *Mis memorias íntimas*, 1:276–7; Pirala, *Historia*, 1:202–4.
107 Espartero to Jacinta, 15 September 1835, AE. See also Bacon, *Six Years*, 279–81.
108 Richardson, *Journal of the Movements of the British Legion*, 31–2.
109 *Hoja de servicios*, 25; Espartero to Jacinta, ?, 16, 23 September 1835, AE.
110 Espartero to Jacinta, ? September 1835, AE.
111 Espartero to Jacinta, 28 October 1835, AE; Espartero to María Cristina, ? November 1835, AE.
112 Espartero to Jacinta, 2, 14, 18 November 1835, AE.
113 Richardson, *Journal*, 51, 71–2.
114 Espartero to Jacinta, 13 December 1835, AE.
115 Espartero to Fernández de Córdova, 13 December 1835, AE; Pirala, *Historia*, 2:242–3.
116 Diversos-Colecciones, 161, N.59/2, AHN.
117 Richardson, *Journal*, 137–8. See also Pirala, *Historia* (Madrid, 1868), 2:242.
118 Espartero to Jacinta, 16, 29 December 1835, AE.

119 *DSC*, 28 December 1835, 156.
120 Pirala, *Historia* (Madrid, 1868), 2:596–8. On 16 December, the commander in chief had praised Espartero's actions in his general order for the day. Diversos-Colecciones, 161, N.59/1, AHN.
121 Espartero to Jacinta, 5 January 1836, AE.
122 Espartero to Jacinta, 12, 15 January 1836, AE.
123 *Contestacion a un papel que circula impreso bajo el titulo de Dictamen que dió el Exemo Sr. D. Baldomero Espartero, comandante general de las provincias Vascongadas al Excmo. Sr. general en gefe de los ejércitos de operaciones y de reserva.*
124 General Order, 2 February 1836, 6/1, AE.
125 Espartero to Jacinta, 15, 18 January 1836, AE.
126 Espartero to Jacinta, 30 January 1836, AE.
127 Espartero to Jacinta, 2, 3, 5, 8, ?, 13 February 1836, AE. For the enmity between the two men, see Pirala, *Historia*, 2:482–3.
128 Espartero to editors of *La Revista Mensajera*, nd, AE.
129 Espartero to Jacinta, 3 March 1836, AE.
130 *Hoja de servicios*, 26; Espartero de Jacinta, 5, 9 March 1836, AE.
131 Fernández de Córdova to minister of war, 18 March 1836, Diversos-Colecciones, 189, N.1/2–5, AHN; *Hoja de servicios*, 26; Vidal Delgado, *Entre Logroño*, 308–9.
132 Espartero to Jacinta, 22, 15, 26, 29 March 1836, AE.
133 Espartero to Jacinta, 17 March 1836, AE.
134 Espartero to Jacinta, 29 March 1836, AE; Facundo Infante, 27 April 1836, Diversos-Colecciones, 189, N.1/79, AHN; Oráa to Espartero, 15 May 1836, AE.
135 Espartero to Jacinta, 3 May 1836, AE.
136 Espartero to Jacinta, ? May 1836, AE; *Hoja de servicios*, 26; Pirala, *Historia*, 2:417–27.
137 *Epistolario militar*, 1:44; Fernández de Córdova to Espartero, 26 May 1836, AE. See also Wylde to Palmerston, 22 June 1836, WYL 1, WP.
138 Espartero to Jacinta, 26, 29 May, 3 June 1836, AE.
139 Espartero to Jacinta, 22 May, 1, 6 June 1836, AE.
140 Espartero to Jacinta, 14, 19 June 1836; Fernández de Córdova to Espartero, 10 June 1836, AE.
141 Espartero to María Cristina, nd, 1836, AE. In a letter of thanks to María Cristina, he called her "the mother of the Spaniards ... of their political regeneration." Espartero to María Cristina, 20 June 1836, Diversos. Títulos y familias, 3514, L.42-149-50, AHN.
142 Burdiel, *Isabel II: Una biografía*, 33–4.
143 Pro Ruiz, *El Estatuto Real y la Constitución de 1837*, 19–51, 199–208; Burdiel, *La Política de los Notables*; Monerri Molina, "Las Cortes del Estatuto Real (1834–1836)."

144 Espartero to Jacinta, 8 June 1834, AE. Reproduced in Romanones, *Espartero*, 151.
145 Espartero to Jacinta, 30 April, 3, 4 May 1836, AE.
146 Espartero to Jacinta, 10 August 1835, AE. García Rovira, *La revolucic liberal a Espanya i les classes populars*; Moliner Prada, "Anticlericalismo y revolución liberal."
147 Espartero to Jacinta, 4 September 1835, AE.
148 Espartero to Jacinta, 15 January 1836, AE.
149 Espartero to Jacinta, 14 May 1836, AE; emphasis added.
150 Espartero to Jacinta, 29 May, 16 June 1836, AE.
151 Burdiel, *Isabel II: Una biografía*, 43–9.
152 Espartero to Jacinta, 22 August 1836, AE.
153 Bullón de Mendoza, *La Expedición de Gómez*; Pirala, *Historia*, 3:179–276, 461–8. For an account by an officer in Espartero's division, see Evans, *Memorias sobre la Guerra de Navarra*.
154 Wylde to Palmerston, 7, 28 July 1836, WYL/2, WP.
155 AE.
156 Espartero to Jacinta, 29 June 1836, AE.
157 Espartero to Jacinta, 3, 5, 7 July 1836, AE.
158 General Order, 4 July, AE.
159 Evans, *Memorias*, 48–9
160 Espartero to Jacinta, 9, 11 July 1836, AE.
161 General Order, 12 July 1836, AE; *Gaceta de Madrid*, 29 July 1836.
162 Pirala, *Historia*, 3:186–7.
163 Nicolás López Ballestero to Espartero, 20 July 1836, AE.
164 José de Baino y Alba to Espartero, 6 August 1836, AE.
165 Benito Losada to Espartero, 23 August 1836, AE.
166 Espartero to interventor, 1 July 1836; interventor to Espartero, 2 August 1836, AE.
167 Diversos-Colecciones, 161, N.26/1, AHN; Pirala, *Historia*, 3:189.
168 *Epistolario militar*, 1:51; Espartero to Jacinta, 24, 25 July 1836, AE.
169 Espartero to Jacinta, 30 July 1836, AE.
170 Delgado, *Relato oficial de la meritísima expedición carlista dirigida por el general andaluz Don Miguel Gómez*, 35. No other source mentions this.
171 *Hoja de servicios*, 27; Espartero to Jacinta, 8 August 1836, AE; Pirala, *Historia*, 3:192–3; Bullón de Mendoza, *Expedición de Gómez*, 68–72; *Gaceta de Madrid. Suplemento*, 12 August 1836.
172 Delgado, *Relato oficial*, 38.
173 *El Español*, 27 August 1836.
174 Pirala, *Historia*, 3:195; Proclamation, 21 August 1836, AE; General Order, 23 August 1836, AE; Bullón de Mendoza, *Expedición de Gómez*, 257–63.

175 Linaje to minister of war, 31 August 1836, Fondo Pirala, Leg 9-6800-12, RAH.
176 Espartero to Jacinta, 2, 3, 4, 5 September 1836, AE.
177 Espartero to Jacinta, 21 April, 14 May 1836, AE; Wylde to Villiers, FO 72/185, NA.
178 Villiers to Palmerston, 24, 31 July 1836, in Bullen and Strong, eds., *Palmerston*, 476–82. Fernández de Córdova fled to France following the revolt at La Granja. His account in his *Memoria justificativa*.
179 *Gaceta de Madrid*, 19 September 1836.
180 Villiers to Palmerston, 13 September, 24 December 1836, in Bullen and Strong, eds., *Palmerston*, 514, 576–7.
181 Duncan, *The English in Spain*, 95; Evans to Villiers, 5 September 1836, MS Clar 461.

4. Commander in Chief, September 1836–August 1839

1 Villiers to Palmerston, in Bullen and Strong, eds., *Palmerston*, 477.
2 Vidal Delgado, *Entre Logroño*, 355–6.
3 *Gaceta de Madrid*, 29 September 1836.
4 Espartero to Jacinta, 13 October 1836, AE.
5 Pirala, *Historia*, 3:464–70, 482–92; Vidal Delgado, *Entre Logroño*, 385–425.
6 Espartero to Jacinta, 28, 30 October, 4, 11, 16, 18, 21 November 1836, AE.
7 Espartero to Evans, 15 November 1836, MS Clar 461.
8 Evans to Villiers, ?, MS Clar 461; Evans to Espartero, 18 November 1836, MS Clar 461.
9 Villiers to Palmerston, 24 December 1836, in Bullen and Strong, eds., *Palmerston*, 568, 570, 576–7.
10 Espartero to Jacinta, 23 November 1836, AE.
11 Wylde to Palmerston, 29 November 1836, FO 72/464, NA.
12 Vidal Delgado, *Entre Logroño*, 474–5; Espartero to Jacinta, 30 November 1836, AE.
13 Wylde to Palmerston, 8 December 1836, FO 72/464, NA.
14 Ibid.
15 De la Saussaye to Villiers, ? November, 15 December 1836, MS Clar, c463.
16 Wylde to Palmerston, 22 December 1836, FO 72/464, NA.
17 Vidal Delgado, *Entre Logroño*, 480.
18 Pirala, *Historia*, 3:490.
19 Vidal Delgado, *Entre Logroño*, 409.
20 Espartero to Jacinta, 22 December 1836, AE.
21 See pages 4–6 of the introduction.
22 Pirala, *Historia*, 3:506–7.
23 Ibid., 3:507–8.

24 Espartero to Jacinta, 7, 10 January 1837, AE.
25 Garrido Muro, *Guerra y paz*, 135.
26 Espartero to Jacinta, 21 January, 12 February 1837, AE.
27 Villiers to Palmerston, 4 January, 11 March 1837, in Bullen and Strong, eds., *Palmerston*, 583, 614.
28 Villiers to Palmerston, 21 January 1837, FO 72/477, in Bullen and Strong, eds., *Palmerston*, 590–1, 604, 636.
29 Espartero to Jacinta, 1 June 1836, AE.
30 Bullen and Strong, eds., *Palmerston*, 598.
31 Ibid., 585, 592, 587.
32 Wylde to Evans, 16 January 1837, Evans to ?, 20, 28 January 1837, MS Clar 461.
33 Evans to ?, 31 January, 30 March 1837, MS Clar 461.
34 Espartero to Jacinta, 25 March 1837, AE.
35 Espartero to Jacinta, 28 March 1837, AE.
36 Espartero to Jacinta, 1, 11, 21 April 1837, AE.
37 Villiers to Palmerston, 1 April 1837, FO 72/479, NA.
38 Espartero to Jacinta, 21 April 1837, AE.
39 Diversos-Colecciones, 161, N.41/1, AHN; Evans, *Memories*, 98.
40 Diversos-Colecciones, 161, N.41/3, AHN.
41 Diversos-Colecciones, 161, N.41/5, AHN. Even Villiers was impressed these proclamations "do him infinite credit." Villiers to Palmerston, 28 May 1837, FO 72/480, NA.
42 Full text at http://www.senado.es/web/conocersenado/senadohistoria/senado18341923/Constitucion1837/index.html.
43 http://www.congreso.es/portal/page/portal/Congreso/Congreso/SDocum/ArchCon/SDHistoDipu/SDBuscHisDip?_piref73_1340033_73_1340032_1340032.next_page=/wc/servidorCGI&CMD=VERLST&BASE=DIPH&FMT=DIPHXDSP.fmt&DOCS=1-1&DOCORDER=FIFO&OPDEF=Y&QUERY=%28ESPARTERO%29.DIPU.
44 Pro Ruiz, *El Estatuto Real y la Constitucion de 1837*, 112–14.
45 http://www.mecd.gob.es/mnceramica/colecciones/seleccion-piezas/ceramica/plato-duque-victoria.html.
46 Bullón de Mendoza, *La Expedición Real*.
47 Pirala, *Historia*, 3:677–85; Espartero to Jacinta, 8, 17 July 1837, AE.
48 Poco Mas, *Scenes and Adventures*, 363–4. See also Turner to Villiers, 1 August 1837, FO 185/167, NA.
49 Turner to Villiers, 28 July 1837, FO 185/167, NA.
50 Cited in Garrido Muro, *Guerra y paz*, 152.
51 *Gaceta de Madrid*, 31 July 1837; Espartero to Jacinta, 5 August 1837, AE.
52 Pirala, *Historia*, 3:718–19.
53 Cepeda Gómez, "Don Manuel de Mazarredo y Mazzaredo," 96–7.
54 Villiers to Palmerston, 19 August 1837, FO 72/482, NA.

55 *El Eco del Comercio*, 14 August 1837.
56 Espartero to Jacinta, 21 January 1837, AE.
57 Florez, *Espartero*, 2:190–200; Cepeda Gómez, "Don Manuel de Mazarredo y Mazzaredo"; Garrido Muro, *Guerra y paz*, 148–1.
58 Espartero to María Cristina, 19 August 1837, AGP.RF7-28/14, 1, AHPR.
59 Espartero to Jacinta, 19 August 1837, AE.
60 Villiers to Palmerston, 19 August 1837, FO 72/482, NA.
61 Espartero to Jacinta, 19 August 1837, AE.
62 Espartero to María Cristina, 19 August 1837, AGP.RF7-28/14, 1, AHPR.
63 *El Eco del Comercio*, 1 September 1837; Espartero to Jacinta, 28 August, 1 September 1337, AE.
64 Garrido Muro, *Guerra y paz*, 151–6, 175–6.
65 Espartero to Jacinta, 24, 27 August 1837, AE.
66 Espartero to Jacinta, 8 September 1837, AE.
67 Espartero to Jacinta, 20 September 1837, AE; Pirala, *Historia*, 3:718–46; von Rahden, *Andanzas de un veterano de la guerra de España (1833–1840)*.
68 Turner to Villiers, 9 March 1838, FO 72/504, NA.
69 Pirala, *Historia*, 3:899–906, 912–19; Garrido Muro, *Guerra y paz*, 164–5.
70 Lynn to Villiers, 17 August 1837, FO 185/167, NA.
71 Río Aldaz, "Peseteros y radicales, el asesinato de Sarsfield en agosto de 1837 en Pamplona."
72 Pirala, *Historia*, 3:920–2, 1208.
73 Ibid., 3:922–3, 1219.
74 Espartero to Jacinta, 19 November 1837, AE.
75 Espartero to María Cristina, 21 November 1837, AGP.RF7-28/14, 2, AHPR.
76 Wylde to Palmerston, 1 November 1837, FO 72/486, NA.
77 Pirala, *Historia*, 3:744.
78 Espartero to Jacinta, 21, 24, 27 November 1837, AE.
79 Espartero to minister of war, 27 November 1837, AE.
80 *Gaceta de Madrid*, 19 December 1837, Espartero to Frías, 1 January 1838; Espartero to Jacinta, 14 January 1838, AE.
81 Espartero to Someruelos, 1, 4 January 1838, Someruelos, C. 26, D.40, AHN-N.
82 Espartero to Someruelos, 1 January 1838, Someruelos, C. 26, D.40, AHN-N. See also Espartero to Someruelos, 4 January 1838, Someruelos, C. 26, D.40, AHN-N.
83 Espartero to Someruelos, 1 January 1838, Someruelos, C. 26, D.40, AHN-N.
84 Espartero to Someruelos, 20 February 1838, Someruelos, C. 26, D.40, AHN-N.
85 Espartero to Someruelos, 22 February 1838, Someruelos, C. 26, D.40, AHN-N.
86 Espartero to Someruelos, 4 January 1838, Someruelos, C. 26, D.40, AHN-N.
87 Minister of war to Espartero, 9 February 1838, AE.
88 Espartero to Someruelos, 20 February 1838, Someruelos, C. 26, D.40, AHN-N.
89 Espartero to minister of war, 14 February 1838, AE.

90 Espartero to Latre, 26 February 1838, AGP 28/18; emphasis in original.
91 Espartero to Someruelos, 20 February 1838, Someruelos, C. 26, D.40, AHN-N.
92 Espartero to Latre, 26 February 1838, AGP 28/18.
93 Espartero to María Cristina, 27 February 1838, AGP 14/5; Espartero to Someruelos, 9 March 1838, Someruelos C.26 D40, AHN-N.
94 Espartero to María Cristina, March 1838, AGP 14/7.
95 Garrido Muro, *Guerra y paz*, 189; María Cristina to Espartero, 3 March 1838, AGP 14/8.
96 Espartero to the Congreso de los Diputados, 23 February 1838, AGP 28/15; Espartero to minister of war, 23 February 1838, AGP 28/16.
97 Barrio Ayuso to Espartero, 8 March 1838, AE.
98 Diversos-Colecciones, 161, N.41/38, AHN; *El Eco del Comercio*, 10 March 1838; *DSC*, 12 March 1838.
99 Pirala, *Historia*, 2:981–98.
100 *Hoja de servicios*, 33–4; Pirala, *Historia*, 2:997.
101 Duncan, *The English in Spain*, 201–2; emphasis in original.
102 Espartero to María Cristina, 6 April 1838, AGP 28/14-13.
103 Espartero to Jacinta, 9 April 1838, AE.
104 Espartero to Jacinta, 21 June 1838, AE.
105 Espartero to Jacinta, 21 June 1838, AE; Lynn to Palmerston, 23 June 1838, FO 72/514, NA.
106 Espartero to Jacinta, 22 June 1838, AE; Pirala, *Historia*, 2:1011–20; *Hoja de servicios*, 34–5.
107 Espartero to Jacinta, 21 ?, 3 July 1838, AE.
108 Espartero to Jacinta, 4 July 1838, AE.
109 Wylde to Palmerston, 8 September 1838, FO 72/514, NA; Espartero to Someruelos, 8 September 1838, C. 26, D.40, AHN-N.
110 Diversos-Colecciones, 161, N27/2, 6, 12, AHN; Espartero to Alaix, 13 February 1839, AE.
111 Villiers to Ofalía, 17 April 1838, MS Clar 456.
112 Great Britain, *Foreign and State Papers* (1838), 1101–9.
113 Diversos-Colecciones, 161, N.41/15, AHN; Wylde to Villiers, 13 November 1838, FO 72/514, NA.
114 Espartero to María Cristina, 26 June 1838, AGP 28/14-18.
115 Wylde to Palmerston, 6 August 1837, FO 72/514, NA.
116 Espartero to María Cristina, 23 July 1838, AGP 28/14-9.
117 María Cristina to Espartero, 29 July 1838, AGP 28/14-20.
118 Espartero to Latre, 24 July 1838, AGP 28/18-3; Garrido Muro, *Guerra y paz*, 191–2. See also Espartero to Oraá, 20 August 1838, RAH.
119 *El Correo Nacional*, 5 August 1838.
120 Ofalía to Espartero, 8 August 1838, ES28079, Archivo Regional Madrid.

121 Espartero to Ofalía, 14 August 1838, AGP 28/14-22, Espartero to María Cristina, 14 August 1838, AGP 28/14-21.
122 Títulos y familias 3363, 35/2, 7, AHN.
123 Espartero to María Cristina, 1 September 1838, AGP 28/14-24.
124 Espartero to Frías, 14 September 1838, AGP 28/18-4; María Cristina to Espartero, nd, AGP 28/14-26; Espartero to María Cristina, 15 September 1838, AGP 28/14-27; Espartero to María Cristina, 6 October 1838, AGP 28/14-27.
125 Garrido Muro, *Guerra y paz*, 223.
126 Salcedo Olid, *Ramón María Narváez (1799–1868)*, 46–141; Narváez, D. *Ramon María Narvaez, Ex-comandante General de la division de vanguardia del ejercito de operaciones, al Congreso Nacional y al público* (Madrid, 1837).
127 Cepeda Gómez, "Don Manuel de Mazarredo," 86.
128 Garrido Muro, *Guerra y paz*, 206.
129 *Gaceta de Madrid*, 25 October 1838.
130 Espartero to María Cristina, 31 October 1838, AGP.RF7-28/14-20.
131 *Esposicion que el Ecmo. Señor Conde de Luchana, capitan general de los ejércitos nacionales, general en gefe [sic] del de operaciones del norte y comandante general de los reunidos ha dirigido a S.M. con motivo del Real Decreto de 23 de octubre ultimo por el que se manda la organizacion de un Ejército de reserva de cuarenta mil hombres* (Madrid, 1838); Fernández de Córdova, *Mis memorias intimas*, 1:358.
132 *Esposicion que el Ecmo. Señor Conde de Luchana*. See also Espartero to María Cristina, 2 November 1838, AGP.RF7-28/14-31.
133 Garrido Muro, *Guerra y paz*, 211–13.
134 Salcedo Olid, *Narváez*, 180–8; Fernández de Córdova, *Mis memorias intimas*, 1:366–86; José Velásquez y Sánchez, *Anales de Sevilla: reseña histórica de los sucesos políticos, hechos notables y particulares intereses de la tercera capital de la monarquía, metrópoli andaluza: de 1800 a 1850* (Seville, 1872), 487–93.
135 *Exposicion dirigida a S.M. la Augusta Reina gobernadora sobre los sucesos de Sevilla* (Madrid, 1838).
136 Ibid.
137 *Manifiesto del mariscal de campo Ramón María Narváez: en contestacion á las las acusaciones del Capitan general Conde Luchana* (Madrid, 1839). Narváez's defence included criticisms of Alaix, who fought back with his own pamphlet. *Impugnación al manifiesto del fugitivo Mariscal de campo Don Ramón María Narváez* (Madrid, 1839).
138 Narváez to Saavedra, nd, AE; Narváez to ?, 2 January 1839, 9/8144, 85/6, Archivo Narváez, RAH; Garrido Muro, *Guerra y paz*, 233; Cepeda Gómez, "Don Manuel de Mazarredo," 89.
139 Villiers to Palmerston, 8 December 1838, FO 72/510, NA.

140 Garrido Muro, *Guerra y paz*, 229–31; Espartero to María Cristina, 12, 18 December 1838, AGP, 28/14-35; Villiers to Palmerston, 15 December 1838, FO 72/510, NA.
141 Garrido Muro, *Guerra y paz*, 229–31.
142 Espartero to Jacinta, 27 February 1839, AE.
143 Letras giradas por el General en Gefe Conde de Luchana para proveer a las necesidades del Ejército de Operaciones, AE 30/172-92.
144 Alaix to Espartero, 17 July 1839, Títulos y familias, 161, AHN.
145 Espartero to María Cristina, 12 December 1838, AGP, 28/14-35; Garrido Muro, *Guerra y paz*, 236–8.
146 Espartero to Alaix, 13 February 1839, AE.
147 Maroto, *Vindicación del general Maroto, y manifiesto razonado de las causas del Convenio de Vergara, de los fusilamientos de Estella y demás sucesos notables que les precedieron* (Madrid, 1846), 133–40
148 Ibid., 144–6; Canal, "La primera guerra Carlista," 61–3; Manuel de la Concha to Espartero, 19 February 1839, AE.
149 Espartero to Jacinta, 28 February 1839; Espartero to Alaix, 25 February 1839, AE.
150 Espartero to Jacinta, 14 March 1839, AE.
151 Espartero to Jacinta, 24, 14 March 1839, AE.
152 Pirala, *Historia*, 3:1046–9.
153 Espartero to Alaix, 4 April 1839, 14/2-2, AGP; Fernández de Gamboa to Espartero, Títulos y familias, 161, AHN.
154 Espartero to Jacinta, 21, 24, 27 April 1839, AE; Espartero to Alaix, 18, 23 April 1839, AE.
155 Espartero to Jacinta, 28 April, 3, 5, 6 May 1839, AE.
156 Espartero to Alaix, 8 May 1839, AE.
157 Espartero to Alaix, 13 May 1839, AE; Poco Mas, *Scenes and Adventures*, 2:7–8.
158 Espartero to Jacinta, 13, 16, 21 May 1839, AE.
159 *Gaceta de Madrid*, 8 June 1839.
160 Espartero to Jacinta, 27 May, 2, 5, 9 June 1839, AE.
161 Espartero to Jacinta, 11 June 1839, AE.
162 Espartero to Alaix, 25 May, 6 June 1839, AE.
163 Espartero to Jacinta, 13, 17 June 1839, AE; Espartero to Alaix, 13, 16 June 1839, AE.
164 Wylde to Palmerston, 19 June 1839, GC/WY/12, BP.
165 Espartero to Jacinta, 1 July 1839, AE.
166 Poco Mas, *Scenes and Adventures*, 2:28.
167 Espartero to Jacinta, 17, 18 July 1839, AE.
168 Espartero to Jacinta, 14, 23, 25 June 1839, AE; emphasis added.
169 Espartero to Jacinta, 25 March 1839, AE.
170 Espartero to Pérez de Castro and Alaix, 28 March 1839, AE.

171 de Torija y Carresse, *El guirigay, los ministros y Espartero*.
172 *El Correo Nacional*, 30 July 1839.
173 Pío Pita to Jacinta, 1 July 1839; AE; Wylde to Palmerston, 6 August 1838, FO 72/514, NA.
174 Espartero to Jacinta, 16 August 1839, AE.
175 Pirala, *Historia*, 3:361.
176 Espartero to Jacinta, 10 August 1839; Espartero to Alaix, 9 August 1839, AE.
177 Wylde to Palmerston, 15 August 1839, Great Britain, *Foreign and State Papers, 1839–1840* (1857), 28:166.
178 Espartero to Jacinta, 10, 13, 15 August 1839, AE.
179 Poco Mas, *Scenes and Adventures*, 2:51.
180 Espartero to Jacinta, 24 August 1839, AE.
181 Espartero to Alaix, 22 August 1839, AE; Diversos-Colecciones, 161, N.41/12, AHN.
182 Wylde to Palmerston, 28 August 1839, Great Britain, *Foreign and State Papers, 1839–1840*, 28:170.
183 Cited in Santirso Rodríguez, "El Convenio de Vergara y otras paces descartadas," 1077.
184 Pirala, *Historia*, 3:152–60.
185 Ibid., 3:335–7; Santirso Rodríguez, "El Convenio de Vergara," 1079–80. See also Alaix to Espartero, 25 July 1839, Títulos y familias, 161, AHN.
186 Aviraneta, *Memoria dirigida al Gobierno español*; Pirala, *Historia del Convenio de Vergara*; Miraflores, *Memorias para escribir la historia contemporánea de los siete primeros años del reinado de Isabel II*, 2:171; García Rovira, "Eugenio de Aviraneta e Ibargoyen (1792–1872)."
187 Espartero to Alaix, 4 April 1839, 14/2-2, AGP; Maroto, *Vindicación*, 166; Echaide, *Reseña histórica sobre los preliminaries del Convenio de Vergara*.
188 Burdiel, *Isabel II. Una biografía*, 55–6.
189 Miraflores, *Memorias*, 1:161–2, 2:22–6; Espartero to Miraflores, 5 April 1839, 14/3, AGP.
190 Wylde to Palmerston, 1 September 1839, Great Britain, *Foreign and State Papers, 1839–1840*, 28:174.
191 Turner to ?, 2 May 1838, MS Clar 464.
192 Maroto, *Vindicación*, 112–13.
193 Wylde to Palmerston, 29 July 1839, Great Britain, *Foreign and State Papers, 1839–1840*, 28:181–200.
194 Espartero to Alaix, 2 August 1839, AE.
195 Hay to Minto, 29 December 1839, Great Britain, *Foreign and State Papers, 1839–1840*, 28:178–9.
196 Maroto, *Vindicación*, 175–8. See also Palmerston to Wylde, 10 August 1839, Great Britain, *Foreign and State Papers, 1839–1840*, 28:161–2.

197 Wylde to Palmerston, 19 August 1839, Great Britain, *Foreign and State Papers, 1839–1840*, 28:167–70; Espartero to Alaix, 19 August 1839, AE: Alaix to Espartero, 21 August, 1839, AE.
198 Espartero to Alaix, 24 August 1839, AE.
199 Wylde to Palmerston, 26 August 1839, Great Britain, *Foreign and State Papers, 1839–1840*, 28:167–70.
200 Wylde to Palmerston, 26 August 1839, Great Britain, *Foreign and State Papers, 1839–1840*, 28:167–70; Espartero to Alaix, 27 August 1839, AE: Urbitzondo y Eguía, *Apuntes sobre la guerra de Navarra en su última época*, 15–18.
201 Espartero to Maroto, 28 August 1839; Maroto to Espartero, 28 August 1839, AE.
202 Urbitzondo, *Apuntes*, 23–4.
203 *Convenio de Vergara y confirmación y modificación de los fueros de Navarra decretadas por las Cortes.*
204 Maroto, *Vindicación*, 187, 191.
205 Wylde to Palmerston, 1 September 1839, Great Britain, *Foreign and State Papers, 1839–1840*, 28:173.
206 Poco Mas, *Scenes and Adventures*, 2:93–8.
207 Espartero to Alaix, 31 August 1839, AE.
208 Poco Mas, *Scenes and Adventures*, 2:93–8.
209 Maroto, *Vindicación*, 230.
210 Urbitzondo, *Apuntes*, 35.
211 Espartero to Jacinta, 31 August 1839, AE.

5. The Reluctant Revolutionary, August 1839–May 1841

1 Diversos-Colecciones, 161, N41/16, AHN; emphasis added.
2 Espartero to Jacinta, 3, September 1839, AE.
3 Espartero to Jacinta, 3, 11, 14 September 1839, AE; emphasis added.
4 Wylde to Palmerston, 21 September 1839, Great Britain, *Foreign and State Papers, 1839–1840*, 28:179.
5 Espartero to Jacinta, 21 September 1839, AE.
6 *El Castellano*, 1 October 1839.
7 Wylde to Palmerston, 21 September 1839, Great Britain, *Foreign and State Papers, 1839–1840*, 28:179–80.
8 *El Piloto*, 2 October 1839.
9 *El Correo Nacional*, 28 September 1839.
10 Wylde to Palmerston, 21 September 1839, Great Britain, *Foreign and State Papers, 1839–1840*, 28:179–80; Espartero to Jacinta, 2 October 1839, AE.
11 Espartero to Jacinta, 6 October 1839, AE.

12 Diversos-Colecciones, 161, N.41/21-23, AHN.
13 Wylde to Palmerston, 2 November 1839, FO 97/379, NA.
14 Espartero to Narváez, 29 November 1839, AE.
15 Garrido Muro, *Guerra y paz*, 246–70.
16 Congreso de los Diputados, *DSC*, 7 October 1839, 698.
17 Wylde to Palmerston, 29 September 1839, GC/WY/13, BP; emphasis in original.
18 Espartero to Jacinta, 16 August 1839, AE.
19 Extract from a letter from Mas de las Matas, 20 November 1839, RF 7, 31/48, AGP. For other statements of Espartero's political ideas at this time, see Espartero to Narváez, 18, 25 November 1839, AE; and Pirala, *Historia*, 3:472–4.
20 *El Eco del Comercio*, 2 December 1839.
21 *El Eco del Comercio*, 16 December 1839; emphasis in original.
22 Garrido Muro, *Guerra y paz*, 352–3.
23 Response to a statement published in *El Eco de Aragón*, 499306/0003, ARCM, Pérez de Castro, Arrazola, Santillán, Montes de Oca, Calderón Collantes and Narváez to María Cristina, 15 December 1839, RF7, 14/10, AGP.
24 Espartero to María Cristina, 19 December 1839, RF7, 28/14, 55, AGP. In addition to writing herself, she used Jacinta as an intermediary. Instruction for my aide-de-camp Salvador Valdés, 20 December 1839, RF7, 14/12, AGP; Espartero to María Cristina, 11 December 1839, RF 7, 28/14, 54, AGP; María Cristina to Espartero, 23 December 1839, RF7, 28/14, 57, AGP.
25 *Epistolario*, 2:51. Baldomero was also deeply concerned that María Cristina had been "ofended" by the letter.
26 Ibid., 2:62–3.
27 Ibid., 2:64, 67.
28 Ibid., 2:69.
29 Espartero to Narváez, 15 January 1840, AE.
30 Description of the forces, 29 January 1840, AE.
31 *Epistolario*, 2:58.
32 Poco Mas, *Scenes and Adventures*, 2:164; Pirala, *Historia*, 3:506–11.
33 Mitchell to Palmerston, 31 May 1840, FO 72/560B, NA.
34 Pirala, *Historia*, 3:524–32; *Gaceta de Madrid*, 3 June 1840.
35 Mitchell to Palmerston, 31 May 1840, FO 72/560B, NA.
36 *Gaceta de Madrid*, 5 June 1840.
37 Poco Mas, *Scenes and Adventures*, 2:231–2.
38 Diversos-Colecciones, 161, N. 28/1, AHN.
39 Espartero to Jacinta, 2 July 1840, AE; Poco Mas, *Scenes and Adventures*, 2:275.
40 Diversos-Colecciones, 161, N. 28/6, AHN.
41 Poco Mas, *Scenes and Adventures*, 2:280–6; Espartero to Jacinta, 8 July 1840, AE; Pirala, *Historia*, 3:569–72.
42 9/6947, Legajo VII, #17, Col. Isabel II, RAH; Pirala, *Historia*, 3:573–4.

43 Aquillué Domínguez, "El liberalismo en la encrucijada," 72; Pareja de Alarcón, *El abrazo de Vergara*, 5.
44 Pirala, *Historia*, 3:480–2.
45 Romeo Mateo, "De patricios y nación."
46 Garrido Muro, *Guerra y paz*, 271–88, 357–62; Tomás Villaroyo, "La Ley de Ayuntamientos y la Renuncia de María Cristina de Borbón a la Regencia," 459–61.
47 Burdiel, *Isabel II. Una biografía*, 56–7; María Cristina to Espartero, 8 April 1840, Espartero to María Cristina, 11 April 1840, RF7, 14/19, 3, 4, AGP
48 Cited in Garrido Muro, *Guerra y paz*, 398.
49 María Cristina to Espartero, 3 May 1840, Espartero to María Cristina, 11 May 1840, RF7, 14/19, 6, 7, AGP; Garrido Muro, *Guerra y paz*, 399–400.
50 *El Constitucional*, 16 June 1840.
51 *Descripción de los obsequios que a su MM y A ha hecho la Ciudad de Zaragoza* (Zaragoza, 1840), 91; Espartero to Jacinta, 23 June 1840, AE.
52 ? to Espartero, 8 June 1840, AE.
53 ? to Espartero, 20 June 1840, AE.
54 Burdiel, *Isabel II. Una biografía*, 58.
55 Poco Mas, *Scenes and Adventures*, 2:248–9.
56 Burdiel, *Isabel II. Una biografía*, 58–9; Garrido Muro, *Guerra y paz*, 407–8; Diversos. Títulos y familias, 3479, LEG.379, Exp.1, AHN.
57 Poco Mas, *Scenes and Adventures*, 2:254–63.
58 Espartero's speech, 27 June 1840, AE.
59 Garrido Muro, *Guerra y paz*, 451.
60 Diversos. Títulos y familias, 3479, LEG.379, Exp.1, AHN; Garrido Muro, *Guerra y paz*, 409–11. See also Gaviria to María Cristina, 29 June 1840, RF 7, 17/5, AGP.
61 Espartero to Jacinta, 8 July 1840, AE; emphasis added.
62 *Epistolario*, 3:22.
63 Garrido Muro, *Guerra y paz*, 361.
64 Bishop of Barcelona to Espartero, 23 June 1840, AE.
65 *El Eco del Comercio*, 11 July 1840; Corrales, "L'estampa i la primera guerra carlina a Catalunya (1833–1840)," 576–85; Roca Vernet, "Fiestas cívicas en la Revolución Liberal."
66 Coroleu, *Memorias de un menestral de Barcelona, 1792–1854*, 195; *El Eco del Comercio*, 22 July 1840; RF 7, 15/28-1, AGP; Buxeres, *Barcelona en julio de 1840*, 17; the last is cited in Garrido Muro, *Guerra y paz*, 413n8.
67 Corrales, "L'estampa," 597–8.
68 Cited in Burdiel, *Isabel II. No se puede reinar*, 107.
69 Burdiel, *Isabel II. Una biografía*, 60–1.
70 Garrido Muro, *Guerra y paz*, 415–16; Castillo de Ayensa to Isturiz, 17 July 1840, 9/6279, Colección Isturiz-Bauer, RAH; RF7, 15/12, 2.

71 Espartero to María Cristina, 16 July 1840, AE.
72 Garrido Muro, *Guerra y paz*, 416–17; Burdiel, *Isabel II. Una biografía*, 61–2.
73 Ibid., 61; Garrido Muro, *Guerra y paz*, 417–18.
74 Historia de los sucesos de Barcelona en 1840, RF 7, 15/28, 1, AGP.
75 Pages of an incomplete diary, ES 28079 ARM DC/03/03.02/03.02.06/49930 8/0023, ACM; Diversos. Títulos y familias, 3480, 384/4, 9, AHN.
76 Pages of an incomplete diary, ES 28079 ARM DC/03/03.02/03.02.06/49930 8/0023, ACM; cited in Burdiel, *Isabel II. No se puede reinar*, 109; emphasis in original; Garrido Muro, *Guerra y paz*, 419–20; RF 7, 15/28, 1, AGP.
77 María Sierra, "Nación de un solo hemisferio: Las fronteras americanas de la representación a través de la vida de un exiliado," *Journal of Iberian and Latin American Research* 20, no. 1 (2014): 111–25; Juan Antonio González Caballero, "Biografía de Antonio González González," in José M. Lama, ed., *Los primeros liberales españoles. La aportación de Extremadura, 1810–1854 (Biografías)* (Badajoz, 2010), 535–52.
78 Pages of an incomplete diary, ES 28079 ACM; *El Eco del Comercio*, 27 July 1840, Diversos-Colecciones, 161, N. 28/8; Burdiel, *Isabel II. No se puede reinar*, 111; Aquillué Domínguez, "La Violencia desde el liberalismo, 1833–1840," 363–4; RF7, 15/11, AGP.
79 Burdiel, *Isabel II. Una biografía*, 66; Garrido Muro, *Guerra y paz*, 426–7.
80 Corrales, "L'estampa," 601–4; Roca Vernet, "Fiestas cívicas," 83.
81 Espartero to Jacinta, 30, 26 August 1840, AE.
82 Espartero to Jacinta, 26 August 1840; Espartero to Azpiroz, 29 August 1840, AE.
83 Espartero to Jacinta, 26, 30 August 1840, AE; *Epistolario*, 3:31.
84 Espartero to Jacinta, 26, 28, 30 August 1840, AE.
85 Espartero to Jacinta, 26, 30 August 1840, AE.
86 Espartero to Jacinta, 30 August 1840, AE.
87 Pérez Núñez, "La revolución de 1840"; cited in Garrido Muro, *Guerra y paz*, 429–30.
88 *Epistolario*, 3:43. A scurrilous biography of Espartero in *El Correo Nacional* added to the anger. *El Correo Nacional*, 1 September 1840.
89 Pérez Núñez, "La revolución de 1840," 155–6; Garrido Muro, *Guerra y paz*, 433–4.
90 "Zaragozanos," 3 September 1840, AE.
91 *Epistolario*, 3:44; Espartero to Jacinta, 18 September 1840, AE.
92 Espartero to Jacinta, 18 September 1840, AE.
93 Espartero to Jacinta, 8 September 1840, AE.
94 Espartero to Jacinta, 8, 18 September 1840, AE.
95 *Epistolario*, 3:39, 36; María Cristina to Muñóz, 13 September 1840, ES 28079, ACM; Aston to Palmerston, 21 September 1840, FO 72/554, NA.
96 Espartero to Jacinta, 24 September 1840, AE.

Notes to pages 144–6   381

97 *DSC*, 5 December 1843, 393; Ferrer to Espartero, 19 September 1840, AE; Pirala, *Historia*, 3:652; Pérez Núñez, "La revolución de 1840," 157–8.
98 Cited in Garrido Muro, *Guerra y paz*, 470; *El Eco del Comercio*, 30 September 1840.
99 *El Correo Nacional*, 2 October 1840; *Diario de Madrid*, 2 October 1840; Pérez Núñez, "La revolución de 1840," 160–1.
100 Manuel Bretón de los Herreros, *La Ponchada, improvisación cómica en un acto* (Madrid, 1840), 31–2.
101 Scott to Palmerston, 3, 5 October 1840, FO 72/554, NA; emphasis in Scott's letter; Garrido Muro, *Guerra y paz*, 439–40.
102 Pérez Núñez, "1839: Madrid ante los Fueros Vascos," 211–13; Garrido Muro, "El Nuevo Cid," 16–18.
103 Aquillué Domínguez, "El liberalismo en la encrucijada," 298n724.
104 *Programa de las funciones públicas con que el Ayuntmiento e Jerez de la Frontera ha dispuesto celebrar los faustos sucesos de Vergara* (Jerez de la Frontera, 1839).
105 *El Guardia Nacional*, 8 June 1840; *El Ayuntamiento Constitucional de Valencia al … Duque de la Victoria y de Morella* (Valencia, 1840); *El Ayuntamiento Constitucional de Valencia al invicto Duque de la Victoria: himno* (Valencia, 1840); *El Ayuntamiento constitucional de Valencia al invicto duque de la Victoria: soneto* (Valencia, 1840); *Himno dedicado al … Duque de la Victoria y de Morella por el Ayuntamiento Constitucional de esta capital, cantado en el Teatro de Valencia* (Valencia, 1840).
106 *Oda en loor del Excelentísimo Sr. D. Baldomero Espartero* (Zaragoza, 1839).
107 *El Constitucional*, 30 August 1840; de la Fuente Monge, "La figura del general Espartero," 111.
108 Ibid., 111–12.
109 Cited in Alberto Castilla, *Carolina Coronado de Perry: biografía, poesía e historia en la España del siglo XIX* (Madrid, 1987), 28. See also *Canción nueba de la gloriosa función que pasó en la Toma de la Plaza y Castillo de Segura por el Exmo. Señor Duque de la Victoria el día 27 de febrero de 1840* (Lérida, 1840); *Morella vencida por las virtudes heróicas del ejército español, conducido al triunfo por el fidelísimo y escelso [sic] Duque de la Victoria en 30 de mayo de 1840* (Granada, 1840); Francisco Navarro Villoslada, *Luchana: ensayo épico dividido en tres cantos, 1º Los Carlistas, 2º Bilbao, 3º Espartero* (Madrid, 1840).
110 Castelar, *Discursos parlamentarios*, 1:235.
111 Pascual M. Estan … to Espartero, 30 April 1869, AE.
112 María Antonia Piños to Espartero, 2 July 1840, AE.
113 Baldomero Martinez to Espartero, 23 January 1869, AE.
114 Romualdo Nogués y Milagro, *Memorias y reflexiones de un general erudito* (Pamplona, 2013), 36.

115 On the *romance*, see Andrew M. Beresford, "The Poetry of Medieval Spain," in *The Cambridge History of Spanish Literature* (Cambridge, 2005), 87–8; Joaquín Alvarez Barrientos, "Eighteenth-Century Poetry," in ibid., 324–5.
116 *Coblas nuevas patrióticas al Convenio celebrado entre los Generales Españoles Espartero y Maroto* (Barcelona, 1839), AHCB.
117 *Morella rendida a la fuerza del bombeo y sitio al día 30 de mayo de 1840* (Barcelona, 1840), AHCB.
118 *Himnos cantados al Exmo. Sr. Duque de la Victoria, en la noche siguiente de su llegada a Barcelona, en la serenata que le dio el Exmo Ayuntamiento Constitucional* (Barcelona, 1840); *Himnos que se cantaron al Exmo. Sr. Duque de la Victoria y de Morella, en la serenata que le dio el Exmo Ayuntamiento Constitucional de Barcelona la noche del 14 de julio* (Barcelona, 1840); *Himnos que se cantaron en la brillante serenata con que las Compañías de Artillería y Zapadores de la M.N.V. de Barcelona obsequiaron en la noche del 14 del corriente mes al Exmo. Sr. Duque de la Victoria y de Morella* (Barcelona, 1840), AHCB.
119 *El Pueblo de Barcelona, esucdado en la Constitución, en la Noche del Sábado 18 de Julio* (Barcelona, 1840), AHCB.
120 *Barcelona agradecida en el día de 30 de Agosto de 1840* (Barcelona, 1840), AHCB.
121 Chust, "Héroes para la nación," 109.
122 Garrido Muro, "El Nuevo Cid," 564–5.
123 Chust, "Héroes para la nación," 94; Boix, *Historia de la ciudad y reino de Valencia*, 3:472–3.
124 Burdiel, *Isabel II. Una biografía*, 70; Aston to Palmerston, 9 October 1840, FO 72/554, RA.
125 Aston to Palmerston, 9 October 1840, FO 72/554, RA.
126 Marliani, *La Regencia de Espartero, conde Luchana, duque de la Victoria y de Morella, y sucesos que la prepararon*, 218.
127 RF 7, 17/12, AGP.
128 Burdiel, *Isabel II. No se puede reinar*, 124–6.
129 For a reconstruction of the conversation see Marliani, *La Regencia*, 212–13.
130 Aston to Palmerston, 10 October 1840, FO 72/554, NA.
131 Aston to Palmerston, 10, 11 October 1840, FO 72/554, NA; Marliani, *La Regencia*, 213–15; Garrido Muro, *Guerra y paz*, 442–3.
132 Morayta, *Historia general de España, desde los tiempos antehistóricos hasta nuestros días*, 6:663–4; *Epistolario*, 3:59–60.
133 María Cristina to Muñóz, 17 June 1840, ES28079, ACM; emphasis in original.
134 Aston to Palmerston, 19 October 1840, FO 72/555, NA.
135 *El Corresponsal*, 23 October 1840; Marliani, *La Regencia*, 220. Months later, the former Reina Gobernadora would send gifts to her ladies in waiting.

The Marquises of Santa Cruz and Torrejón each got a "rich bracelet"; as "a slight," Jacinta got *"some costume jewellery."* Títulos y familas 3376. 59.1, 6, AHN.
136 Aston to Palmerston, 19 October 1840, FO 72/555, NA.
137 *Gaceta de Madrid*, 20 October, 28 November 1840.
138 Marliani, *La Regencia*, 227.
139 *El Corresponsal*, 23 October 1840; Boix, *Historia*, 3:477; Garrido Muro, *Guerra y paz*, 460.
140 *Gaceta de Madrid*, 28 October 1840; *Diario de Madrid*, 28 October 1840; *El Católico*, 28 October 1840.
141 Burdiel, *Isabel II. Una biografía*, 75–7.
142 *Gaceta de Madrid*, 16 November 1840.
143 *El Eco del Comercio*, 28, 31 October 1840.
144 *Gaceta de Madrid*, 3 November 1840; Pirala, *Historia*, 3:677.
145 Espartero to Jacinta, 17 November 1840, AE.
146 Espartero to Jacinta, 5 November 1840, AE.
147 Espartero to Jacinta, 9 November 1840, AE; *El Correo Nacional*, 10 November 1840.
148 Espartero to Jacinta, 24 December 1840, AE; General Order, 24 December 1840, AE.
149 *El Católico*, 2 January 1841.
150 Shubert, "Baldomero and Jacinta."
151 Espartero to Jacinta, 20, 28 January 1836, AE.
152 Espartero to Jacinta, 14 October 1836.
153 Espartero to Jacinta, 20 December 1835, 4 April 1836, AE.
154 Espartero to Jacinta, 28 March 1837, AE.
155 Espartero to Jacinta, 5 September 1834, 5 January 1836, ? August 1839, 2 July 1834, AE.
156 Espartero to Jacinta, 24 April 1834, 1 June 1834, 13 January 1836, AE.
157 Espartero to Jacinta, 15 August 1835, AE.
158 Espartero to Jacinta, 15 March 1836, AE.
159 Espartero to Jacinta, 14 January 1835, AE.
160 Espartero to Jacinta, 28 November, 9 December 1835, AE.
161 Espartero to Jacinta, 30 May 1836, AE.
162 Espartero to Jacinta, 28 February 1839, AE.
163 Espartero to Jacinta, 26 April, 8, 15 July 1834, 9 July 1836, AE.
164 Espartero to Jacinta, 13 August 1834, AE.
165 Espartero to Jacinta, 24, 29 April, 6 May 1834.
166 Espartero to Jacinta, 7 October, 27 November, 9 December 1835. AE.
167 Espartero to Jacinta, 25 December 1835, AE.
168 Espartero to Jacinta, 15 March 1834, AE.

169 Espartero to Jacinta, 28 October, 6 December 1835; 8 July, 24 October, 15 November 1834, AE.
170 Espartero to Jacinta, 28 January, 31 March, 1835, 28 February, 7 June 1836, AE.
171 Romeo Mateo, "Domesticidad y Política," 124.
172 Espartero to Jacinta, 15 March 1836, AE.
173 Espartero to Jacinta, 30 May 1836, 9 April 1838, AE.
174 Espartero to Jacinta, 16 August 1839, AE.
175 Espartero to Jacinta, 21 January 1837, 14 June 1839, AE.
176 Espartero to Jacinta, 8, 16 November 1836, 9 November 1840, AE.
177 Espartero to Jacinta, ? May 1836, 29 March 1839, 17 November 1840, AE.
178 Espartero to Jacinta, 13 October 1836, 31 July 1839, AE.
179 Espartero to Jacinta, 4 September 1835, 30 January, 26 February 1836, 26 February 1835, nd [October] 1835, AE.
180 Espartero to Jacinta, 7, 8 July, 30 August, 24 September 1840, AE.
181 Romeo Mateo, "Juana de la Vega, Condesa de Espoz y Mina," 400.
182 Espartero to Jacinta, 17 March 1834, AE.
183 Espartero to Jacinta, 21 January 1837, AE.
184 Díaz Marín, *La Monarquía tutelada*, 109–18.
185 Laureano Marzo Muñóz to Espartero, 8 February 1841, AE.
186 Pirala, *Historia*, 3:717–18; Díaz Marín, *La Monarquía tutelada*, 120.
187 *El Eco del Comercio*, 28 March 1841.
188 *El Eco del Comercio*, 29 March 1841.
189 Aston to Palmerston, 4 April 1841, FO72/554, NA.
190 Aston to Palmerston, 20 March 1841, FO72/574, 4 April 1841, FO72/554, NA.
191 Guizot to María Cristina, 18 April 1841, RF7, 31/11, AGP.
192 Aston to Palmerston, 18 April 1841, FO 72/554, NA.
193 *DSC-Senado*, 28 April 1841, 177–91, 29 April 1841, 196–208.
194 Díaz Marín, *La Monarquía tutelada*, 125–6; *DSC-Senado*, 6 May 1841.
195 *DSC-Senado*, 30 April 1841, 658; 1 May 1841, 691; 30 April 1841, 672.
196 *DSC-Senado*, 29 April 1841.
197 *DSC-Senado*, 28, 29, 30 April 1841.
198 Aston to Palmerston, 5 May 1841, FO 72/555, NA.
199 *DSC-Senado*, 5 May 1841, 78–88.
200 *DSC-Senado*, 6 May 1841, 801, 819, 827.
201 *DSC-Senado*, 6 May 1841, 833.
202 Aston to Palmerston, 5 May 1841, FO 72/555, NA; emphasis added.
203 *El Eco del Comercio, El Correo Nacional*, 9 May 1841.
204 *DSC-Senado*, 8 May 1841, 241–9.
205 *El Eco del Comercio*, 9 May 1840; *El Corresponsal*, 9 May 1840.
206 Marliani, *La Regencia*, 256.

6. Regent of the Realm, May 1841–July 1843

1. Florez, *Espartero*, 4:83.
2. *El Correo Nacional*, 11 May 1841.
3. Aston to Palmerston, 11 May 1841, FO 72, 575, NA.
4. *DSC*, 10 May 1841, 859–60. Espartero's enemies would later claim, with some reason, that the speech plagiarized the one Napoleon gave on becoming Consul for Life in 1802. *Espartero. Études biographiques*, 143–5.
5. *DSC*, 10 May 1841, 859–60; *El Correo Nacional*, 9 May 1841; *El Católico*, 11 May 1841; *El Eco del Comercio*, 9 May 1841.
6. Aston to Palmerston, 11 May 1841, FO 72, 575, NA.
7. *El Eco del Comercio*, 11 May 1841.
8. Santos Juliá, "El fracaso de la República," *Revista de Occidente* (November 1981): 200.
9. http://www.congreso.es/portal/page/portal/Congreso/Congreso/Hist_Normas/ConstEsp1812_1978/Const1837. On the Constitution of 1837, see Pro Ruiz, *El Estatuto Real y la Constitución de 1837*, and Varela Suanzes-Carpegna, "La Constitución española de 1837."
10. Dardé, "Los partidos y la vida política, 1836–1868."
11. Aston to Palmerston, 18 May, 5 May 1841, FO 72, 525, NA.
12. Florez, *Espartero*, 4:105.
13. Aston to Palmerston, 18 May 1841, FO 72, 575, NA; Florez, *Espartero*, 4:109.
14. Díaz Marín, *La Monarquía tutelada*, p. 146.
15. Aston to Palmerston, 18 May 1841, FO 72, 575, NA.
16. *El Eco del Comercio*, 22 May 1841.
17. Fernández de los Ríos, *1808– 1863. Olózaga*, 335. For details, see Díaz Marín, *La Monarquía tutelada*.
18. Burdiel, *Isabel II. Una biografía*, 76–7.
19. María Cristina to Espartero, 23 April 1841, 499306/0005, ACM.
20. The documents are in *Discusión de las Cortes sobre la tutela de S.M. la Reina Doña Isabel II y su Augusta Hermana, con otros discursos y documentos que la esclarecen / publicase a espensas de algunos ciudadanos en homenaje de amor y gratitud a S.M. la Reina Viuda* (Madrid, 1842); *DSC*, 10 July 1841.
21. Aston to Palmerston, 24 July 1841, FO 72, 577, NA.
22. Donoso Cortes to María Cristina, 30 May 1841, 499306/0005, ACM.
23. Juan Donoso Cortés to Duque de Riansares, 10 June 1841, AHN, Diversos. Títulos y familias, Caja 3376/60, 134.
24. Espartero to María Cristina, 8 June 1841, 499312/0012, ACM. There was an additional exchange of letters between the two: Espartero to María Cristina, 9 June 1841; María Cristina to Espartero, 26 June 1841, 499312/0012, ACM.
25. *El Eco del Comercio*, 31 July 1841.

26 *El Eco del Comercio*, 6 August 1841.
27 Burdiel, *Isabel II. Una biografía*, 89; Mina, *Apuntes para la historia*, 37–8.
28 Burdiel, *Isabel II. Una biografía*, 94.
29 Mina, *Apuntes*, 5–17.
30 Diversos. Títulos y familias, 3757-32-4, AHN.
31 Haverty, *Wanderings in Spain*, 2:130.
32 Aston to Palmerston, 10 July 1841, FO 72, 577, NA.
33 Gregorio Alonso, *La Nación en capilla. Ciudadanía católica y cuestión religiosa en España (1793–1874)* (Granada, 2014), 156–76.
34 Text of the pope's speech in Pirala, *Historia*, 3:1133–6.
35 Daniel O'Connell, *Morning Chronicle*, 8 December 1841; *Espartero. Sir De Lacy Evans' Reply to Mr. O'Connell's Attacks on the Regent of Spain* (London, 1842); *A Letter to Daniel O'Connell, Esq., M.P., Lord Mayor of Dublin, in reply to his attack upon General Espartero, Regent of Spain* (London, 1842).
36 Gregorio Alonso, *La Nación en capilla*, 180.
37 *Bula de Nuestro Santísimo Padre el Sr. Gregorio XVI sobre los asuntos de España* (Mexico City, 1842).
38 Callahan, *Church, Politics and Society in Spain, 1750–1874*, 176–9. See also M. Saez de Ocariz, "El cumplimiento pascual en la Ciudad de Logroño a lo largo del siglo XIX," *Berceo* (1965): 282.
39 Aston to Palmerston, 10 July 1841, FO 72, 576, NA; emphasis added.
40 The best single study of this question remains Parry, *The Spanish Marriages, 1841–1846*.
41 Aston to Palmerston, 3 January 1842, FO 72, 598, NA.
42 Aston to Aberdeen, 28 November 1841, *Selections from the Correspondence of the Earl of Aberdeen*, 140, 147, 330. Aston to Aberdeen, 20 November 1841; 24 April 1842.
43 Aston to Aberdeen, 28 November 1841; Aberdeen to Aston, 23 December 1841; Aston to Aberdeen 29 January 1842, *Selections*, 148, 208, 289.
44 Aston to Aberdeen, 5 September, 17 October 1842, *Selections*, 380–1, 430–1.
45 Aston to Aberdeen, 27 June 1843, *Selections*, 628.
46 Díaz Marín, *La Monarquía tutelada*, 269–79.
47 Wylde to Palmerston, 29 September 1839, GC/WY/13, BP.
48 Aston to Aberdeen, 23 October 1841, FO 72, 580, NA.
49 Aston to Aberdeen, 28 November 1841, *Selections*, 146.
50 Aston to Aberdeen, 23 December 1841, 3 January 1842, *Selections*, 225, 238.
51 Aston to Aberdeen, 24 April 1842, FO 72, 600, NA; Aston to Aberdeen, 24 April 1842, *Selections*, 332. On his frustrations, see, for example, Aston to Aberdeen, 24 May 1842, FO 72, 601, NA; 21 December 1842, FO 72, 605, NA; 17 October 1842, *Selections*, 433.
52 Aston to Aberdeen, 21 November 1842, *Selections*, 469.
53 Aston to Aberdeen, 23 January 1843, *Selections*, 560–1.

54 Aston to Aberdeen, 23 January 1843, *Selections*, 563. For a detailed account of British efforts to secure such a treaty, including an assessment that Espartero did not sell out Spanish interests, see Alonso Rodríguez, "Espartero y las relaciones comerciales hispano-británicos, 1840–1843."
55 Burdiel, *Isabel II. Una biografía*, 98–9.
56 Aston to Palmerston, 24 August, 4 September 1841, FO 72, 578, NA.
57 Aston to Palmerston, 3 October 1841, FO 72, 579, NA.
58 Fernando Mikelarena Peña, "La sublevación de O'Donnell de octubre de 1841 en Navarra," *Historia Contemporánea* 38 (2010): 239–75.
59 Marliani, *La Regencia*, 310.
60 Lynn and Askwith to Aston, 9 October 1841, FO 72, 579, NA; emphasis in original.
61 Joaquín Buxó de Abaigar, *Domingo Dulce, general isabelino. Vida y época* (Barcelona, 1962).
62 Caja 130 – Histórica, Archivo Palacio Real.
63 Lynn and Askwith to Aston, 9 October 1841, FO 72, 579, NA.
64 Aston to Aberdeen, 8 October 1841, FO 72, 579, NA; *Vida militar y política de Espartero*, 3:626. For other plots to kill Espartero, see Aston to Aberdeen, 15 October 1841, FO 72, 579, NA and Aston to Aberdeen, 12 December 1841, *Selections*, 185.
65 Mina, *Apuntes*, 62–74.
66 Marliani, *La Regencia*, 295–6.
67 *Causas formadas á consecuencia de la sedición militar que tuvo lugar en esta córte en la noche del 7 de octubre de 1841* (Madrid, 1841). See also Raquel Sánchez, *Románticos españoles* (Madrid, 2005), 129–46.
68 Nicomedes Pastor Díaz, *Biografía de don Diego de León* (Madrid, 1868), 78.
69 Carlos Masa y Sanguineti, *Vida militar y política de Diego León* (Madrid, 1843), 293.
70 Aberdeen to Aston, 5 November 1841, *Selections*, 96.
71 Aston to Aberdeen, 14 October 1841, FO 72, 579, NA.
72 Aston to Aberdeen, 26 October 1841, FO 72, 580, NA.
73 Sánchez García, "Héroe y Martir," 267; María Zozaya, *El Casino de Madrid, orígenes y primera andadura* (Madrid, 2002), 161–70.
74 Lynn to Aberdeen, 23 October 1841, FO 72, 581A, NA.
75 *Gaceta de Madrid*, 3 November 1841.
76 Lynn to Aberdeen, 23 October, 1841, FO 72, 581A, NA.
77 Lynn to Aberdeen, 9 November 1841, FO 72, 581A, NA.
78 *El Eco del Comercio*, 24 November 1841.
79 *El Eco del Comercio*, 27 December 1841.
80 Marcuello Benedicto, *La Práctica Parlamentaria en el reinado de Isabel II*, 180–2, 212–13.
81 Aston to Aberdeen, 8 June 1842, *Selections*, 340–1.

82 Marcuello Benedicto, *La Práctica Parlamentaria*, 216–21.
83 Aston to Aberdeen, 8 June 1842, FO 72, 601, NA.
84 Castro, *Los anales de la imprenta*, 53–4; *El Eco del Comercio*, 25 October 1842.
85 Cecilio Alonso, "Notas sobre prensa satírica e ilustración gráfica." See also Dérozier, "La caricatura en la prensa satírica ilustrada de la regencia de Espartero."
86 *El Eco del Comercio*, 21 December 1842.
87 *El Eco del Comercio*, 2 January 1843.
88 Suárez, *Donoso Cortés y la fundación de El Heraldo y El Sol*, 299.
89 Cecilio Alonso, "Notas sobre prensa"; Díaz Marin, *La Monarquía tutelada*, 320–3.
90 José Manuel Pedrosa, "Wamba, Ramiro II, Enrique III y Carlos I: relecturas políticas de leyendas medievales en la Edad Moderna (siglos XVIII–XX)," *Memorabilia* 14 (2012): 99–143; Luis F. Díaz Larios, "Notas sobre Antonio Ribot y Fontseré," *Anales de Literatura Española* 20 (2008): 119–37. Ribot y Fontseré also wrote the satirical "*El romancero del conde-Duque, o la Nueva Regencia* (Barcelona, 1842).
91 *El Constitucional*, 7 August 1841. It also published other variants on 8 August and 8 and 11 September. Pedrosa, "Wamba, Ramiro II, Enrique III y Carlos I," 130–2.
92 *El Católico*, 18 October 1841; *El Eco del Comercio*, 3 July 1842. In the first incident, a militia battalion commanded by the Republican Abdón Terradas sang the poem and then shouted "Long live the Republic!"
93 Romea Castro, *Barcelona romántica y revolucionaria*, 43, 68, 116–27; *Vida militar y política*, 3:684.
94 Aston to Aberdeen, 24 April 1842, *Selections*, 331.
95 Romea Castro, *Barcelona romántica*, 43, 68, 116–27.
96 Santirso Rodríguez, "Barcelona. Rueda del progreso (1840–1843)," 116. Two major primary sources, from differing sides of the conflict, are Adriano, *Sucesos de Barcelona, desde 13 de noviembre de 1842 hasta 19 de febrero de 1843*, and Van Halen, *Diario razonado de los acontecimientos que tuvieron lugar en Barcelona desde el 13 de noviembre 1842, con reflexiones que sirven para dilucidar su naturaleza*.
97 Cited in Risques, "La insurreció de Barcelona pel novembre de 1842," 103.
98 Adriano, *Sucesos*, 29.
99 *Vida militar y política*, 3:696.
100 Marliani, *La Regencia*, 387–91. The message from the Senate was much more supportive.
101 Mina, *Apuntes*, 198. Earlier in her memoir she notes that Espartero often said that he was looking forward to Isabel's coming of age (58).
102 Irving to Catherine Paris, 20 November 1842, *Letters*, 409–10.
103 Risques, "La insurreció de Barcelona pel novembre de 1842," 111.

104 Manuel Crespi, *Diario de Memorias de Barcelona*, AHCB, MS.A-116.
105 *The Times*, 12 January 1843. See also Irving to Catherine Paris, 12 January 1843, *Letters*, 463.
106 Castro, *Los males de la imprenta*, 53–4.
107 Aston to Aberdeen, 6 January 1843, FO 72/623, NA; Burdiel, *Isabel II. Una biografía*, 119.
108 Marliani, *La Regencia*, 489–90.
109 Díaz Marín, *La Monarquía tutelada*, 354–5.
110 Donoso Cortes to Ríos Rosas, 8 October 1842, in Suárez, *Donoso Cortes*, 265.
111 *El Heraldo*, 18 January 1843.
112 Díaz Marín, "Espartero en entredicho," 191, 205.
113 Castro, *Los males de la imprenta*, 51.
114 *El Heraldo*, 22 February 1843; Rios Rosas to Donoso Cortés, 28 October 1842 in Suárez, *Donoso Cortés*, 269.
115 Donoso Cortes to Rios Rosas, 30 December 1842, 25 February 1843. in Suárez, *Donoso Cortes*, 311, 369.
116 *El Heraldo*, 5 August 1842, 8 April 1843. This charge relates to a trip she made to the south in October 1841. *Espectador*, 12 October 1841; *El Corresponsal*, 13 October 1841.
117 Arthur Aston to Lord Aberdeen, 28 November 1841, *Selections*, 146; emphasis added.
118 Arthur Aston to Lord Aberdeen, 21 December 1841, *Selections*, 522.
119 Burguera, *Las Damas del Liberalismo Respetable*, 270–1.
120 Carmen Massa Hortigüela, *Pablo Montesino (1781–1849), la perseverancia de un educador liberal* (Salamanca, 2014).
121 Burguera, "Mujeres y revolución liberal en perspectiva," 290.
122 Irving to Sarah Storrow, 12 August 1842, *Letters*, 281.
123 Irving to Catherine Paris, 21 June 1843, *Letters*, 543–4.
124 *El Regente del Reino a los Españoles* (Madrid, 1843).
125 Aston to Aberdeen, 11 February 1843, FO 72-623, NA.
126 Marliani, *La Regencia*, 492; Díaz Marín, "Espartero en entredicho," 197.
127 *El Eco del Comercio*, 13 February 1843.
128 Florez, *Espartero*, 4:807–8; Díaz Marín, "Espartero en entredicho," 207.
129 Díaz Marín, "Espartero en entredicho," 207–8.
130 Marliani, *La Regencia*, 500, *Vida militar y política*, 3:732.
131 Díaz Marín, *La Monarquía tutelada*, 373.
132 Aston to Aberdeen, 13 April 1843, FO 72-624, NA.
133 *Discurso pronunciado* … (Madrid, 1843); emphasis added.
134 *El Eco del Comercio*, 5 April 1843. See also Díaz Marín, *La Monarquía tutelada*, 375–6.
135 *DSC*, 11 May 1843, Apéndice Segundo, 363–4.

136 Aston to Aberdeen, 6 May 1843, FO 72-625, NA; López, *Exposicion razonada de los principales sucesos políticos que tuvieron lugar*, 149.
137 López, *Exposicion razonada*, 4–6. See also *Vida de Joaquín María López*, 120.
138 Marliani, *La Regencia*, 504; Aston to Aberdeen, 10 May 1843, FO 72-625, NA; López, *Exposicion razonada*, 6–7.
139 José María López 2/4, Archivo Municipal de Villena; López, *Exposicion razonada*, 11.
140 Romeo Mateo, "Joaquín María López," 88.
141 Aston to Aberdeen, 19 May 1843, FO 72-625, NA.
142 López, *Exposicion razonada*, 22; Marliani, *La Regencia*, 513. There were even rumours that López had had contacts with agents of María Cristina. Flórez, *Espartero*, 835.
143 López, *Exposicion razonada*, 18–24.
144 Aston to Aberdeen, 19 May 1843, FO 72-625, NA. Espartero was "not acquainted with Villalonga."
145 Aston to Aberdeen, 19 May 1843, FO 72-625, NA.
146 López, *Exposicion razonada*, 24–5.
147 Marliani, *La Regencia*, 517–20.
148 Aston to Aberdeen, 21 May 1843, FO 72-625, NA.
149 Florez, *Espartero*, 4:875.
150 Aston to Aberdeen, 21 May 1843, FO 72-625, NA. This usual quotation is incorrect; according to the *DSC*, Olózaga actually said, "Dios la salve, señores, y salve a nuestra Reina." Legislatura de 1843, *DSC*, 510.
151 Castro, *Los males de la imprenta*, 54.
152 Even Prim, who was a *Progresista*, joined. Anguera, *El General Prim*, 100–3.
153 "De reunion de la Asociación Orden Militar Española," ES 28079 ARCM ES. 28079 ARCM / DC/05/05.01/499312/0010.
154 Burdiel, *Isabel II. Una biografía*, 121–2.
155 Marliani, *La Regencia*, 619–23. For Aston's defence of Espartero against the rebels' charges, see Aston to Aberdeen, 27 June 1843, FO 72/626, NA.
156 Aston to Aberdeen, 8 June 1843, FO 72-625, NA.
157 Marliani, *La Regencia*, 598–601.
158 Aston to Aberdeen, 14 June 1843, FO 72-626, NA.
159 Marliani, *La Regencia*, 601.
160 Ibid., 601–3.
161 Mina, *Apuntes*, 217.
162 Irving to Catherine Paris, 21 June 1843, *Letters*, 542. For Aston's account, see Aston to Aberdeen, 21 June 1843, FO 72-626, NA.
163 Fernández de los Ríos, *Olózaga*, 374.
164 For events in Madrid, see San Miguel, *Sobre las ocurrencias de Madrid desde principios hasta el 23 de julio del presente año*, and the more detailed, anonymous account, *Acontcemientos de Madrid: Diario de los sucesos ocurridos desde el día 11 de julio de 1843 hasta el 23 del mismo*.

165 Ibid.
166 Aston to Aberdeen, 18 July 1843, FO 72, 627, NA.
167 Florez, *Espartero*, 4:960–4.
168 Mina, *Apuntes*, 237.
169 Ibid., 242.
170 *Gaceta de Madrid*, 28 July 1843; Aston to Aberdeen, 25, 29 July 1843, FO 72–627, NA.
171 Aston to Aberdeen, 6 August 1843, FO 72-627, NA.
172 Irving to Catherine Paris, 10 August 1843, *Letters*, 585–6.
173 *Acontecemientos de Madrid: Diario*.
174 Aston to Aberdeen, 6 August 1843, FO 72-627, NA.
175 AE, 12-1842-7. See also Aston to Aberdeen, 6 August 1843, FO 72-627, NA, and Florez, *Espartero*, 4:932–3.
176 AE, 12-1842-7.
177 Reyero, "Sevilla y las políticas," 711.
178 AE, 12-1842-7.
179 *Gaceta de Madrid*, 3 August 1843.
180 Aston to Aberdeen, 26 August 1843, FO 72, 627, NA.
181 AE, 12-1842-7.

7. Exile and Return, July 1843–July 1854

1 ADM 51/3630, NA.
2 D.M.H. y D.J.T., *Espartero, su vida militar, política, descriptiva y anecdótica*, 721–3. There is a handwritten copy in Espartero's papers.
3 Howard de Walden to Ashton, 8 August 1843, FO 355/6, Box 1, NA.
4 *A Revolução de Septembro*, 8 August 1847.
5 M.A. Vaz de Carvalho, *Vida do Duque del Palmella* (Lisbon, 1903), 3:242–4; Howard de Walden to Ashton, 8 August 1843, FO 355/6, Box 1, NA.
6 José Trazimundo Mascarenhas Barreto, *Memorias do Marques de Fronteira e d'Alorna* (Lisbon, 1930), 7–8:13.
7 Maria de Fátima Bonifácio, "1834–42: A Inglaterra perante a evolução política portuguesa (hipóteses para a revisão de versões correntes)," *Análise Social* 20, no. 83 (1984): 467–88; Maria Manuela Tavares Ribeiro, "A restauração da Carta Constitucional: cabralismo e anticabralismo," in José Mattoso, ed., *História de Portugal. O Liberalismo: 1807–1890*, vol. 5, coordinated by Luís Reis Torgal and João Lourenço Roque (Lisbon, 1993), 106–19.
8 *A Revolucão de Septembro*, 10 August 1847.
9 *A Revoucão de Septembro*, 11 August 1847.
10 Mascarenhas Barreto, *Memorias do Marques de Fronteira e d'Alorna*, 7–8:13.
11 ADM 51/3734, NA.
12 Vaz de Carvalho, *Vida do Duque del Palmella*, 244.

13 *Panorama Español, crónica contemporánea* (Madrid, 1845), 3:443. The others stripped of their titles were Agustín Nogueras, Pedro Gómez de la Serna, Conde de Peracamps, Francisco Linaje, Facundo Infante, Francisco Osorio, Juan Lacarte, Salvador Valdés, Cipriano Segundo Montesino, Ignacio Gurrea, Pedro Falcón, and Ventuta Barcástegui.
14 *Gaceta de Madrid*, 16 August 1843.
15 *Cornwall Royal Gazette*, 25 August 1843.
16 *The Times*, 21, 22 August 1843.
17 ADM 51/3734, NA.
18 *The Times*, 24 August 1843; *Spectator*, 26 August 1843.
19 House of Lords Debates, 7 August 1843, vol. 71, c. 314.
20 House of Commons Debates, 21 August 1843, vol. 71, c. 986. In Ireland, nationalist leader Daniel O'Connell, who had been a severe critic of Espartero's regency, revelled in the fall of the "tyrant" at one of his mass meetings for the Repeal of the Act of Union. *Observer*, 13 August 1843.
21 Ministerio de Exteriores, 1553, AHN.
22 *The Times*, 25 August 1843.
23 *The Times*, 26 August 1843.
24 *The Illustrated Letters of Richard Doyle to His Father, 1842–1843*, 289.
25 *The Times*, 28, 29, 30 August, 6, 13, 19 September 1843; *Illustrated London News*, 30 September 1843.
26 This annoyed Lord Aberdeen because the club was a Whig bastion. Sancho to minister of state, 10 September 1843, Exteriores, 1553, AHN.
27 Lady Palmerston's Diaries, Hatfield House, 29 August 1843. A dinner in July 1847 was also attended by the Duke of Palmela, something that Ambassador Istúriz considered worth reporting to Madrid. Istúriz to minister of state, 14 July 1847, Exteriores, 1555, AHN.
28 Sancho to minister of state, 26 August 1843, Exteriores, 1553, AHN.
29 *Spectator*, 2 September 1843; *Examiner*, 2 September 1843.
30 Sancho to minister of state, 28 August 1843, Exteriores 1553, AHN.
31 *Spectator*, 2 September 1843; *Morning Post*, 2 September 1843.
32 AE, 12-1842-9d.
33 *Standard*, 27 September 1843, *Morning Post*, 27 September 1843.
34 *Illustrated London News*, 18 May 1844; *Madame Tussaud's Catalogue*, (London, 1844), 22.
35 *The Times*, 28 September 1843; *Art Union* (1844): 171.
36 *The Times*, 30 September 1843.
37 *Living Age* (1844): 288; *Spectator*, 21 December 1844; *The Times*, 17 December 1844.
38 Ford, *Letters to Gayangos*, 74.
39 *The Times*, 26 November 1847; *Illustrated London News*, 27 November 1847.
40 *Examiner*, 22 February 1845.

41 *El Clamor Público*, 11 February 1845.
42 *El Clamor Público*, 2, 4 March 1845. See also Sotomayor to minister of state, 24 February 1845, Exteriores, 1554, AHN.
43 AHN, Diversos-Colecciones Autógrafos, 12, N. 905; emphasis added.
44 Burdiel, *Isabel II. Una biografía*, 118–58.
45 Ibid., 143, 147, 158.
46 *Reseña histórica del heroico comportamiento del Pacificador de España, el invicto Espartero, durante su emigración en Londres y su regreso a la Corte* (Madrid, 1848).
47 Marcelino Izquierdo and Pablo Saez, *Zurbano, vida y mito de un héroe del liberalismo español* (Logroño, 2007). Zurbano and his two sons were captured and executed.
48 Confidential memo, 25 November 1844, Expediente Personal Espartero, Carpeta 20, 129; emphasis in original.
49 Sotomayor to minister of state, 21 July 1847, Exteriores, 1554, AHN.
50 Burdiel, *Isabel II. Una biografía*, 160–81; Parry, *The Spanish Marriages, 1841–1846*.
51 AE, 12-1846-2c; *El Espectador*, 13 September 1846; AE, 12-1846-2e.
52 Tacón to minister of state, 22 September 1846, Exteriores, 1554, AHN.
53 Palmerston to Bulwer, 8 October 1846, GC/BU/518, BP.
54 García de Paso García, "El 1848 español"; Robert Vallverdú i Martí, *La guerra dels Matiners a Catalunya (1846–1849). Una crisi econòmica i una revolta popular* (Abadia de Montserrat, 2002); Josep M. Ollé Romeu, *Matiners* (Barcelona, 2007).
55 Sotomayor to minister of state, 21 April 1846, Exteriores, 1554, AHN.
56 Sotomayor to minister of state, 28 April 1846, Exteriores, 1554, AHN.
57 *El Heraldo*, 22 September 1846.
58 *El Espectador*, 1 October 1846.
59 *El Espanol*, 6 August 1846.
60 3 March 1847, Legajo 8362 (Perpiñan), Estado, AHN.
61 11 November 1847, Legajo 8362 (Perpiñan), Estado, AHN.
62 7 January 1848, Legajo 8362 (Perpiñan), Estado, AHN.
63 7 January 1848, Legajo 8362 (Perpiñan), Estado, AHN.
64 Burdiel, *Isabel II. Una biografía*, 208.
65 *El Español*, 19 September 1847.
66 *El Católico*, 12 July 1847; *La Esperanza*, 16 July 1847.
67 *El Clamor Público*, 31 July 1847.
68 Cited in Burdiel, *Isabel II. Una biografía*, 202; emphasis added.
69 *El Español*, 15, 31 August 1831; *El Espectador*, 25 August 1847.
70 *Gaceta de Madrid*, 3 September 1847.
71 *Espartero. Su pasado, su presente, su porvenir*, 44.
72 *El Clamor Público*, 5 September 1847.
73 *El Tío Camorra*, 9 September 1847.
74 *El Español*, 5 September 1847.

75 *El Clamor Público*, 10, 11 September 1847.
76 *El Espectador*, 10 September 1847.
77 *El Eco del Comercio*, 5 September 1847.
78 Cortázar to Istúriz, 1 October 1847, Colección Istúriz-Bauer, RAH.
79 Narváez to Istúriz, 12 October 1847, Colección Istúriz-Bauer, RAH.
80 Istúriz to minister of state, 25 October 1847, Colección Istúriz-Bauer, RAH. On 26 October, Espartero sent Lord Palmerston a copy of the decree and his reply to Narváez. GC/VI/5, BP.
81 Palmerston to Bulwer, 23 September 1847, BR GC/BU/560, BP.
82 Ibid.
83 Palmerston to Bulwer, 28 October 1847, BR GC/BU/565, BP.
84 Palmerston to Bulwer, 23 September 1847, BR GC/BU/560, BP; emphasis added.
85 Bulwer to Palmerston, 3 October 1847, GC/BU/403, BP; emphasis added.
86 Istúriz to minister of state, 15 November 1847, Colección Istúriz-Bauer, RAH.
87 Espartero to Palmerston, 31 April 1847, CG/VI/3, BP.
88 Lady Palmerston to Frederick Lamb, nd August 1847, BR 29/16/1, BP.
89 *Illustrated London News*, 21 August 1847; *Observer*, 22 August 1847; *Examiner*, 21 August 1847.
90 Minister of state to Espartero, 14 November 1847, Colección Istúriz-Bauer, RAH.
91 Espartero de Istúriz, 23 November 1847, Colección Istúriz-Bauer, RAH; Istúriz to minister of state, 21 December 1847, Exteriores, 1555, AHN.
92 Palmerston to Lady Palmerston, 29 December 1847, BR 23 AA/1/11, BP.
93 *Queen Victoria's Journals*, 24:192–4, http://www.queenvictoriasjournals.org; emphasis added.
94 *El Clamor Público*, 8 January 1848.
95 *El Español*, 12 January 1848.
96 *El Eco del Comercio*, 8 January 1848.
97 *El Clamor Público*, 11 January 1848.
98 *El Tío Camorra*, 12 January 1848.
99 Bermejo, *La Estafeta de Palacio, historia del último reinado*, 3:74.
100 *El Católico*, 8 and 9 January 1848.
101 Hortelano, *Memorias*, 128–9.
102 *El Correo salmantino*, 26, 23 January 1848.
103 *El Correo salmantino*, 19, 23 January 1848.
104 *El Clamor Público*, 6 February 1848; *El Correo salmantino*, 23 January, 11 February 1848; *El Eco del Comercio*, 13 February 1848; *El Espectador*, 8 March 1848. For a manifesto from Málaga, see *El Eco del Comercio*, 6 February 1848, from Jaén, *El Espectador*, 6 February 1848, and from Úbeda, *El Eco del Comercio*, 10 February 1848; emphasis added. The press claimed

that the greeting from Seville was signed by more than 2,500 people. *El Genio de la Libertad*, 9 February 1848.
105 *El Correo salmantino*, 11 February 1848.
106 *El Correo salmantino*, 14 January 1848.
107 Bermejo, *Estafeta*, 3:80. For press comment, see *El Popular*, 7 February 1848; *El Espectador*, 12 February 1848; *El Popular*, 12, 15 February 1848.
108 *El Correo salmantino*, 16 January 1848; *La Carta*, 11 January 1848.
109 *El Correo salmantino*, 19 January 1848, Bermejo, *Estafeta*, 3:77.
110 *DSC*-Senado, 24 January 1848, 352; Bermejo, *Estafeta*, 3:79.
111 *El Eco del Comercio*, 10 February 1848.
112 *El Espectador*, 12 February 1848.
113 *El Eco del Comercio*, 25 March 1851.
114 *La Época*, 11 March 1852.
115 Palmerston to Bulwer, 18 April 1848, GC/BU/579, BP.
116 11 July 1848, Perpiñán, 5265, Estado, AHN.
117 Bermejo Martín, *Espartero*, 169.
118 *El Zurrón del Pueblo*, 8 January 1852.
119 Antonio Samaniego to Espartero, 29 May 1849; Espartero to Samaniego, 30 May 1849, AE, 12-1846-09.
120 Juan Antonio de ? to Espartero, 14 August 1850, AE.
121 Espartero to minister of state, 15 June 1850, AE, Asuntos de Palacio.
122 Francisco Javier Gómez, *Logroño histórico* (Logroño, 1893), 158–60; emphasis added. See also Hugh Johnson, *Vintage: The Story of Wine* (New York, 1989), 427–8.
123 Bermejo Martín, *Espartero*, 172.
124 *El Zurrón del Pueblo*, 27 March 1851; *El Genio de la Libertad*, 8 April 1851.
125 *El Clamor Público*, 13 April 1852.
126 Jesús Martínez Martín, "La edición artisanal y la construcción del Mercado," in Jesús Martínez Martín, ed., *Historia de la edición en España, 1836–1936* (Madrid, 2001), 55. Lucy Riall describes a contemporaneous phenomenon in Italy where it was key to the spreading of the cult of Garibaldi (Riall, *Garibaldi*).
127 Raquel Sánchez García, "Las formas del libro. Textos. Imágenes y Formatos," in Martínez Martín, *Historia de la edición*, 122.
128 Of course, not all the work about Espartero was laudatory, and some of the earliest published assessments were all-out attacks written by his conservative enemies. See, for example, Balmes, "Espartero," and Pastor Díaz, *Galería de Españoles Célebres*, vol. 5.
129 Hortelano, *Memorias*, 97. Such veneration was not limited to the lower classes. Nicolás Estevánez, who was born in 1838, recalled that his father, a retired military officer and a Progressive, had no decoration in his study

other than portraits of Voltaire, Quintana, Zurbano, Espartero, Mazzini, and Garibaldi. *Fragmentos de mis memorias*, 14.
130 Hortelano, *Memorias*, 95–8.
131 Ibid., 95–8.
132 *Diario Oficial de Avisos de Madrid*, 10 January 1848.
133 Ibid., 128.
134 *El Clamor Público*, 10 December 1845.
135 Antonio Ildefonso Bermejo, *Espartero, novela historica contemporanea por un admirador de sus hechos, y dedicada a sus verdaderos amigos* (Madrid, 1847), 2:310.
136 Andreu Miralles, "El pueblo y sus opresores."
137 Martínez Gallego, "Democracia y república en la España isabelina." On Ayguals, see Andreu Miralles, *El descubrimiento de España*, and on the Sociedad Literaria, see Victor Carrillo, "Marketing et edition au XIXe siècle."
138 *El Espectador*, 13 February 1845; *El Clamor Público*, 14 February 1845.
139 Carrillo, "Marketing," 21; *El Clamor Público*, 3 September 1846.
140 *Reseña histórica del heróico comportamiento del Pacificador de España*.
141 Ayguals de Izco, *La Marquesa de Bellaflor, o el niño de la Inclusa*.
142 Chao, *Espartero*, vii–ix.
143 Alberto Gil Novales, "Martínez Villergas, el gran satírico," *Trienio. Ilustración y Liberalismo* 20 (1992): 101–36.
144 *Espartero. Su pasado, su presente, su porvenir*, 7–22.
145 Ibid., 63–82. Subscribers were promised a portrait of Espartero. *El Tío Camorra*, 28 April 1848.
146 Cortés, *Juan Martínez Villergas: bosquejo biográfico-crítico*, 54–5. For an advertisement, see *Diario Oficial de Avisos de Madrid*, 29 March 1851.
147 Ibid., 310–14. Martínez Villergas was charged with libel by Mariano Narváez and defended by Francisco Salmerón, brother of the future president of the First Republic. *Escritos que en defensa del autor del Paralelo han presentado* (Madrid, 1851).
148 The following is based on Botrel, "Las historias de cordel y la historia del tiempo presente en la España del siglo XIX," and "Les 'Historias de Colportage.'"
149 *Historia del General Baldomero Espartero, Duque de la Victoria y de Morella*, 1.
150 Ibid.
151 Ibid., 32.
152 On *aleluyas* see Angela Birner, "Los pliegos de aleluyas," *Anthropos* 166/7 (1995): 117–20; Jean-François Botrel, "La serie de aleluyas Marés, Minuesa, Hernando," http://www.cervantesvirtual.com/obra-visor/la-serie-de-aleluyas-mars-minuesa-hernando-0/html/0133c1ee-82b2-11df-acc7-002185ce6064_7.html; and "Aleluyas," in Joaquín Alvarez Barrientos, ed., *Diccionario de la literature popular española* (Salamanca, 1977), 24–6.

153 Pedro C. Cerrillo Torremocha and Jesús María Martínez González, eds., *Aleluyas: juegos y literatura infantil en los pliegos de aleluyas españoles y europeos del S. XIX* (Toledo, 2012), 39–44; Antonio Martín, "Las Aleluyas, primera lectura y primeras imágenes para niños en los siglos XVIII–XIX. Un antecedente de la literatura y la prensa infantil en España," http://pendientedemigracion.ucm.es/info/especulo/numero47/aleluya.html.
154 Both can be found on the website of the Fundación José Díaz: http://www.funjdiaz.net/aleluyas1.php?t=Espartero. Marés, in fact, produced at least two, one of them serving almost as a news flash about Espartero's resignation from government in 1856.
155 *Historia del General Espartero* (Madrid, 1856).
156 *El Clamor Público*, *El Espectador*, 13 August, 15 October 1846.
157 Cánidido de la Rosa Poriano (Monterrubio, Badajoz), 26 October 1850, AE.
158 *El Clamor Público*, 13 April 1851.
159 *El Clamor Público*, 15 April 1851.
160 *El Genio de la Libertad*, 27 April 1851; Espartero to Junta Directiva de Elecciones, 18 April 1851; Espartero to Madoz, 18 April 1851; Espartero to Olózaga, 18 April 1851, AE.
161 Espartero to Lasala, 17 April 1851, AE; Junta Electoral progresista de Zaragoza to Espartero, 24 April 1851, AE.
162 AE, 13-1851-4, 5, 6, 9, 12, 13, 14, 15, 16.
163 Pro Ruiz, *Bravo Murillo*, 377–402; Burdiel, *Isabel II. Una biografía*, 341.
164 *El Clamor Público*, 18 December 1852.
165 Burdiel, *Isabel II. Una biografía*, p. 247, 261.
166 *The Times*, 2 March 1853.
167 Cited in Burdiel, *Isabel II. Una biografía*, 256.
168 Espartero to Olózaga, 26 October 1853, AE, 13-1851-24.
169 Soulé to Department of State, 5 July 1854, NS 1273, Reel 38, NA.
170 *The Times*, 14 March 1854. *Le Siècle* had many similar things to say. *El Genio de la Libertad*, 19 April 1854. Hardman had dedicated his 1846 book, *Peninsular scenes and sketches, by the author of "The student of Salamanca"*, "To an illustrious exile, Don Baldomero Espartero."
171 *The Times*, 25 April 1854.
172 *The Times*, 26 May 1854.
173 Jennifer R. Green and Patricia Kirkwood, "Reframing the Antebellum Democratic Mainstream Transatlantic Diplomacy and the Career of Pierre Soulé," *Civil War History* (September 2015): 212–51; and A. Ettinger, *The Mission to Spain of Pierre Soulé* (New Haven, 1932).
174 Ibid., 299, 456.
175 AE, 13-1851-42.
176 *Blackwood's Magazine* (September 1854): 356; Burdiel, *Isabel II. Una biografía*, 313.

398   Notes to pages 222–7

177 Nombela, *Impresiones y recuerdos*, 2:21–2; Fernández de los Ríos, *Estudio histórico de las luchas políticas*, 405; Calderón de la Barca, *The Attaché in Madrid*, 321
178 Ibid.
179 There are differing accounts of why she came to this decision. See Bermejo, *Estafeta*, 3:429; Miraflores, *Memorias*, 3:48–9, 61; Fernández de Córdova, *Mis memorias íntimas*, 3:404.
180 Burdiel, *Isabel II. Una biografía*, 318.
181 Cited in ibid., 234. Espartero's letter: Espartero to Isabel II, 8 May 1851. AE, Asuntos de Palacio.
182 AE, Asuntos de Palacio.

8. "The Personification of Liberty," July 1854–July 1856

1 Borao, *Historia del Alzamiento de Zaragoza en 1854*, 17.
2 Ibid., 23–5.
3 Ibid., 25–37, 54.
4 Junta de Gobierno de la Provincia de Logroño to Gurrea, 21 July 1854, AE, 13-1851-33c.
5 AE, 13-1851-31; AE, 13-1851-33c.
6 Borao, *Historia*, 55–60.
7 Ibid., 121–2.
8 Ibid., 66.
9 Gracia Albacar, *Memorias de un zaragozano*, 68.
10 Borao, *Historia*, 66–7.
11 Gracia Albacar, *Memorias*, 70.
12 Borao, *Historia*, 68. On 8 August, Ramón Leon, the owner of the newspaper *El Avisador* and a devoted follower of Espartero, renamed it *El Esparterista*. http://www.enciclopedia-aragonesa.com/voz.asp?voz_id=5214.
13 Borao, *Historia*, 69.
14 Gracia Albacar, *Memorias*, 72.
15 Ibid.; emphasis in original.
16 Apuntes, AE, 13-1851-42.
17 "The Spanish Revolution," *Blackwood's Magazine* (September 1854): 363.
18 Diversos. Títulos y familias, 3460, LEG.304, Exp.1, AHN.
19 Soulé to Department of State, 22, 25 July 1854, M31, Reel 38, NARA.
20 Nombela, *Impresiones y recuerdos*, 2:37.
21 Cited in Burdiel, *Isabel II. Una biografía*, 321; Apuntes, AE, 13-1851-42.
22 Burdiel, *Isabel II. Una biografía*, 324.
23 *DSCC*, 1854, 439.
24 Calderón de la Barca, *The Attaché*, 328. *DSCC*, 1854, 439.

25 Garrido, *Espartero y la revolución*, 25; Jordi Roca Vernet, "Del liberalismo exaltado al democrático a través de las sociedades patrióticas (1820–1854), una forma de sociabilidad liberal popular," in Montserrat Arnabat and Ramon i Duch, eds., *Sociabilidades en la Historia Contemporánea de España* (Valencia, 2014), 106.
26 Burdiel, *Isabel II. Una biografía*, 325–6.
27 Diversos. Títulos y familias, 3460, LEG.304, Exp.1, AHN.
28 *Gaceta de Madrid*, 26 July 1854.
29 Burdiel, *Isabel II. Una biografía*, 326–7.
30 Urquijo y Goitia, *La Revolución de 1854 en Madrid*, 179.
31 Otway to secretary of state, 28 July 1854, NS 1273, Reel 38, NARA.
32 Nombela, *Impresiones y recuerdos*, 50–1.
33 Espartero to Zavala, 26 July 1854, AE.
34 Apuntes, AE, 13-1851-42; Borao, *Historia*, 72–3.
35 *Blackwood's Magazine* (September 1854): 364–5.
36 Calderón de la Barca, *The Attaché*, 339–42. For another description, Nombela, *Impresiones y recuerdos*, 55–8.
37 Karl Marx, "Eszpartero," http://marxengels.public-archive.net/en/ME0800en.html.
38 Ayuntamiento de Puerto de Santa María to Espartero, 1 August 1854, AE.
39 Calatayud to Espartero, 20 July 1854, AE.
40 Milicia Nacional de Jaen to Espartero, 17 September 1854, AE.
41 Cristobal de ? to Espartero, 24 July 1854, AE.
42 José María Puig y Salazar to Espartero, 25 July 1854, AE.
43 Vicente Pardo y Mendoza to Espartero, 21 July 1854, AE.
44 Garrido, *El Pueblo y el trono*.
45 Diversos. Títulos y familias, 3460, LEG.304, Exp.1, AHN. Núñez Muñoz, *El Bienio progresista y la ruptura de relaciones de Roma con España*, 70.
46 Nombela, *Impresiones y recuerdos*, 56.
47 Diversos. Títulos y familias, 3460, LEG.304, Exp.1, AHN.
48 See Howden to Clarendon, 25, 28 November 1854, FO 72, 847, NA; 25 April 1856, FO 72, 892, NA.
49 Casimiro Rufino Ruiz to Espartero, 31 July 1854, AE.
50 *Las Novdedades*, 1, 3 August 1854; Ruiz de Morales, *Historia de la Milicia Nacional*, 676.
51 *Las Novedades*, 3 August 1854.
52 *El Clamor Público*, 13 August 1854.
53 Howden to Clarendon, 8 August 1854, FO 72/845, NA.
54 Howden to Clarendon, 14, 17 August 1854, FO 72/845, NA; emphasis in original.
55 Diversos. Títulos y familias, 3460, LEG.304, Exp.1, AHN.
56 Howden to Clarendon, 5 August 1854, FO 72/845, NA.
57 Cited in Burdiel, *Isabel II. Una biografía*, 342.

58 Garrido, *Historia del reinado del último Borbón de España*, 3:237; Bermejo, *Estafeta*, 3:437.
59 Burdiel, *Isabel II. Una biografía*, 348–52.
60 *La Iberia*, 24 November 1854.
61 Burdiel, *Isabel II. Una biografía*, 353–4.
62 Iñarejos Muñoz, *La revolución de 1854 en la España rural*, 78; Comisión Electoral Progresista y Demócrata to Espartero, 7 October 1854, AE, 1851-66a.
63 Espartero to Electors of Zaragoza, 31 October 1854, AE, 13-1851-66e.
64 Howden to Clarendon, 13 September 1854, FO 72, 846, NA.
65 Burdiel, *Isabel II. Una biografía*, 355–6; Howden to Clarendon, 6 April 1855, FO 72/866, NA.
66 Azagra, *El bienio, progresista en Valencia*, 104.
67 Howden to Clarendon, 18 November 1854, FO 72, 847, NA; emphasis in original.
68 *DSC*, 21 November 1854, 132.
69 Howden to Clarendon, 21 November 1854, FO 72, 847, NA.
70 *DSC*, 28 November 1854, 250.
71 Burdiel, *Isabel II. Una biografía*, 376, 388–93. See also Burdiel, "Monarquía y nación en la cultura política progresista."
72 *DSC*, 30 November 1854, 269–93.
73 Howden to Clarendon, 1 December 1854, FO 72, 848, NA.
74 Howden to Clarendon, 4 December 1854, FO 72, 848, NA.
75 Howden to Clarendon, 9 December 1854, FO 72, 848, NA; emphasis added.
76 Calderón de la Barca, *The Attaché*, 364–5.
77 Palmerston to Bulwer, 19 August 1847, GC/BU/558, BP.
78 Howden to Clarendon, 1 November 1854, FO 72, 847, NA.
79 Colección Legislativa, vol. 44 (Madrid, 1855), 194–7.
80 *La Época*, 28 November 1854.
81 *La Iberia*, 28 November 1854.
82 *El Católico*, 28 December 1854.
83 *El Genio de la Libertad*, 4 August 1854.
84 *Diario Oficial de Avisos de Madrid*, 1 January 1855.
85 *Diario Oficial de Avisos de Madrid*, 12 February 1855; *El Clamor Público*, 22 February 1855.
86 *La Época*, 10 April 1855.
87 *La Iberia*, 28 June 1855. Also *Gaceta Musical de Madrid*, 10 June 1855.
88 *El Clamor Público*, 23 June 1855.
89 *La Época*, 29 September 1855.
90 *El Clamor Público*, 6 December 1855.
91 *La Época*, 19 February 1856.
92 *El Clamor Público*, 2 July 1856.
93 José Montaldo and others to Espartero, 26 December 1854, AE, 23-78.

94 Fernández de los Ríos, *Estudio histórico de las luchas*, 430.
95 *DSC*, 19 May 1855, 4930.
96 Benet and Martí, *Barcelona a mitjan segle XIX*, 1:365–6, 575–7. See also de Felipe, *Trabajadores, lenguaje y experiencia en la formación del movimiento obrero español*, 223–4.
97 De Felipe, "La orientación del movimiento obrero: hacia el republicanismo en España en el siglo XIX," *Historia y Política* (June 2011): 132–4; Benet and Martí, *Barcelona*, 2:29–33, 61.
98 *El Clamor Público*, 10 July 1855.
99 Cited in Benet and Martí, *Barcelona*, 2:80. See also *La España*, 10 July 1854.
100 *Memorial que unos operarios de Barcelona dirigen al Excelentísimo señor don BALDOMERO ESPARTERO* (Barcelona, 1855).
101 *Actas del Consejo de Ministros* (Madrid, 1989), 10:258; Benet and Martí, *Barcelona*, 2:98.
102 *El Clamor Público*, 13 July 1855.
103 Benet and Martí, *Barcelona*, 2:350, 390.
104 García Balañà, "Patria, plebe y política en la España isabelina," 31–2, and *La Fabricació de la fábrica*, 446–8.
105 Kiernan, *The Revolution of 1854*, 121–2.
106 *DSC*, 9 June 1855, 5518; Paredes Alonso, *Pascual Madoz, 1805–1870*, 257. See also *Actas del Consejo de Ministros* 10:193–4.
107 On the disentailment, see F. Simón Segura, *La desamortización Española del Siglo XIX* (Madrid, 1980); José María Moro Barreñada, "Una medida liberal: la desamortización de Madoz," in *Homenaje a Juan Uría Ríu* (Oviedo, 1997), 1:573–98.
108 Burdiel, *Isabel II. Una biografía*, 422–3.
109 Howden to Clarendon, 8 February 1855, FO 72/864, NA.
110 *DSC*, 28 February 1855. On the place of the Church, see Callahan, *Church, Politics and Society in Spain, 1750–1874*; Gregorio Alonso, *La Nación en capilla*; Millán and Cruz Romero, "Iglesia y religión en el liberalismo anterior a la sociedad de masaas"; and Mínguez, *Evas, Marías y Magdalenas*.
111 Núñez Muñoz, *El Bienio progresista*, 250.
112 *El Áncora*, 27 February 1855.
113 Felipe Ascot to Espartero, 1 March 1855, AE.
114 *La España*, 7 March 1855; Gerónimo Quintana to Espartero, 4 March 1855, AE, 23-82.
115 *La España*, 7 March 1855.
116 Wenceslao Suárez Ponte to Espartero, 28 February 1855, AE, 23-81.
117 *La Época*, 29 March 1855; *Actas del Consejo de Ministros*, 10:225–6.
118 *El Clamor Público*, 11 April 1854.
119 *DSC*, 4 April 1855, 3565.

120 Howden to Clarendon, 30 April 1855, FO 72/866, NA; cited in Burdiel, *Isabel II. Una biografía*, 442; emphasis added.
121 Lafuente, *Historia general*, 23:210; Burdiel, *Isabel II. Una biografía*, 450.
122 The cabinet discussion is in *Actas de Consejo de Ministros*, 10:252–3.
123 Howden to Clarendon, 10 June 1855, FO 72/867, NA.
124 Ibid.
125 *DSC*, 8 June 1855, 5474–5.
126 *Gaceta de Madrid*, 1 July 1855; Otway to Clarendon, 1, 3 July 1855, FO 72/868, NA.
127 Otway to Clarendon, 7 August 1855, FO 72/868, NA.
128 *Las Novedades*, 21 August 1855.
129 Lafuente, *Historia general*, 23:215.
130 Ibid., 23:216.
131 Burdiel, *Isabel II. Una biografía*, 472.
132 ? to Victor Balaguer, 8 January 1855, Epist. 1855–67, BMVB; *DSC*, 7 January 1856, 9653.
133 *DSC*, 7 January 1856, 9655.
134 *DSC*, 16 January 1856, 9910.
135 *DSC*, 17 January 1856, 9939–61.
136 Howden to Clarendon, 6 February 1856, FO 72, 891, NA.
137 *La Iberia*, 1 March 1856; Tomas Maria Quintana to Espartero, 9 February 1856, AE.
138 Lorenzo Cebrian et al to Espartero, 25 February 1856; Juan Antonio Bartroli et al. to Espartero, 21 Fenruary 1856, AE.
139 Howden to Clarendon, 1 March 1856, FO/72, 991, NA.
140 *La Iberia*, 10 March 1856.
141 Angel Luis Rubio Moraga and Lucía Berruga Sánchez, "El Padre Cobos o la prensa satítica al servicio de la contrarrevolución (1854–1856)," in Antonio Laguna Platero and José Reig Cruañes, eds., *El humor en la historia de la comunicación en Europa y América* (Cuenca, 2015), 153–70.
142 *El Padre Cobos*, 30 March 1856. See also 25 April, 5, 10, 30 May, 15 June 1856, among others.
143 *La Democracia*, 18 April 1856.
144 *La Época*, 21 April 1856. See also Pérez Garzón, *Milicia Nacional y Revolución Burguesa*, 480.
145 *La Época*, 12 March 1856.
146 *La Iberia*, 17 March 1856.
147 *La Iberia*, 17 March 1856.
148 Kiernan, *The Revolution of 1854*, 197.
149 Burdiel, *Isabel II. Una biografía*, 466, 470.
150 Rivas to Narváez, 20 May 1856, 9/8113, 51, Archivo Narváez, RAH.
151 *La Época*, 28 April 1856; *La España*, 29 April 1856.

152 Bellogín, "Historia Contemporánea. La Gloriosa de Valladolid," 329.
153 *La Época*, 3 May 1856.
154 *El Clamor Público*, 17 May 1856.
155 *La Época*, 3 May 1856.
156 *La Iberia*, 9 May 1856.
157 *La Época*, 9, 10 May 1856; *La Esperanza*, 10 May 1856.
158 *Relación de los festejos hechos en la Ciudad de Pamplona en Mayo del presente año con motive de la visita del Exmo Sr. Duque de la Victoria a su paso para Zaragoza* (Pamplona, 1856).
159 *La Época*, 17 May 1856.
160 Gracia Albacar, *Memorias*, 97–9.
161 *DSC*, 6 June 1856, 13785–91.
162 *La Iberia*, 17 June 1856.
163 *Gaceta de Madrid*, 16 June 1856; emphasis in original.
164 Kiernan, *The Revolution of 1854*, 213–17.
165 Fernández de los Ríos, *Estudio histórico de las luchas políticas*, 2:425–9.
166 Burdiel, *Isabel II. Una biografía*, 481. O'Donnell gave his account to the Cortes on 18 May 1857.
167 Espartero to Isabel, 14 July 1856, Exp. 137, Leg. 13, Archivo de la Presidencia del Gobierno.
168 Otway to Clarendon, 18 July 1856, FO 72/894, NA.
169 García Ruiz, *Historias*, 2:595–6.
170 Lafuente, *Historia general*, 23:223–5.
171 Kiernan, *La revolución de 1854 en España*, 234–8.
172 A los Electores liberales de Barcelona, in *El Partido Progresista, o Espartero, y Olózaga* (Madrid, 1864), 60–1.
173 Ibid., 61.
174 Ibid.
175 Ibid., 62–4.
176 Otway to Clarendon, 22 July 1854, FO 72/844, NA; *La Época*, 20 July 1856.

9. The Retiree of Logroño, July 1856–September 1868

1 *El Genio de la libertad*, 14 August 1856.
2 Cited in Burdiel, *Isabel II. Una biografía*, 495.
3 Espartero to Balaguer and Cutchet, 9 November 1856, MS 359, BMVB.
4 Espartero to Baldomero Goicoechea, 6 December 1857, #7, Fundación Dinastía Vivanco, Diversos, AHN.
5 Espartero to Cutchet, ? July 1858, MS 358, BMVB.
6 Espartero to Manuel Gil de Santivánez, 26 January 1858; 24 December 1860, AE, 14-36.
7 *Doña Jacinta y Sinforosa. La Mujer en el S. XIX*.

8 *Boletín Oficia de la Provincia de Logroño*, 11 March 1858.
9 He also agreed to lend his moral support to the railway project. Charles de Villerdeuil to Espartero, 25 October 1861, AE, 15-6; Espartero to Villerdeuil, 30 October 1861, AE, 15-6.
10 Junta de Agricultura, Industria y Comercio to Espartero, 3 September 1860, AE, 14-66. The petition is in 14-67.
11 Bermejo Martín, *Espartero*, 174–5.
12 Francisco Javier Gómez, *Logroño histórico*, 190.
13 Jacinta to Montesino, 19, 28 February, 17 March 1857, AE.
14 Jacinta to Montesino, 20 February 1861, AE, 15-4.
15 Jacinta to Montesino, 23 March 1857, AE.
16 Espartero to Baldomero Goicoechea, 25 July, 10 September 1859, #10–11, Fundación Dinastía Vivanco, Diversos, AHN; Expediente Personal, Carpeta 30.
17 Espartero to Baldomero Goicoechea, 27 December 1859 #12, Fundación Dinastía Vivanco, Diversos, AHN.
18 Jacinta to Montesino, 1 July 1864, AE.
19 José Deura to Espartero, 27 February 1865; Antonio Trias to Espartero, 28 March 1863, AE.
20 Jacinta to Montesino, 15 February 1857, AE.
21 Jacinta to Montesino, 28 February 1857, AE. Italicized words are in English in the original.
22 Jacinta to Montesino, 15, 17 March 1857, AE.
23 Jacinta to Montesino, 9, 23 March 1857. Italicized words are in English in the original
24 Jacinta to Montesino, 9 March 1857, AE.
25 Jacinta to Montesino, 21 March 1857, AE.
26 Garcia Balaña, "Patria, plebe y política."
27 Espartero to Cutchet, 27 January 1859, AE, 14-54.
28 *Dichos y opiniones de Espartero en conversación con sus amigos* (Madrid, 1868), 15.
29 Ibid., 3.
30 Espartero to Cutchet, 21 July 1859, AE, 14-59
31 Undated draft, AE, 14-60.
32 Jacinta to Montesino, 15 March 1857, AE.
33 Berenson, "Charisma and the Making of Imperial Heroes in Britain and France, 1880–1914," 39.
34 Jacinta to Montesino, 9 March 1857, AE.
35 Gil y Alcalde to Espartero, 29 February 1864, AE.
36 Carolina González Llanos to Espartero, 24 February 1863, AE.
37 José Carabia to Espartero, AE, 23-230, 24-76.
38 Santiago García Santa Olalla to Espartero, 21 February 1862; 22 February 1864, AE.

Notes to pages 259–65

39 Carlos Galofre to Espartero, 26 February 1864, AE.
40 Catalina Rando de Boussignault to Espartero, 23 February 1865, AE.
41 Pascuala Fuentes y Altafago to Espartero, 25 February 1864, AE.
42 AE, 27-13, 27-12.
43 Manuel de Entrambuagas to Espartero, 1 March 1864, AE.
44 Casino Industrial Catalán to Espartero, 24 February 1863, AE.
45 Jacinta to Montesino, 28 February, 15, 23 March 1857, AE.
46 AE, 27-48
47 Domingo Vigues to Jacinta, 26 February 1868, AE.
48 Jacinta to Montesino, 9 March 1857; from a letter from Escosura in Paris, 20 March 1857, AE.
49 From a letter from Escosura in Paris, 20 March 1857, AE.
50 *El Clamor Público*, 5 November 1856; emphasis added.
51 *El Clamor Público*, 6 November 1856.
52 Burdiel, *Isabel II. Una biografía*, 489, 541–2.
53 Ollero Vallés, *Sagasta, de conspirador a gobernante*, 214; Burdiel, *Isabel II. Una biografía*, 526.
54 Espartero to Montesino, 23 March 1857, AE, 14-29.
55 Espartero to Isabel, 1 February 1857, AE, 1856-17.
56 *La Epoca*, 7 February 1857.
57 Espartero to Antonio Mota y Arguemi, 20 March 1857, AE, 14-28. Jacinta to Montesino, 16 February 1857, AE.
58 *La Discusión*, 6 March 1857.
59 *La España*, 29 March 1857.
60 Jacinta to Montesino, 15, 17 March 1857, AE.
61 Jacinta to Montesino, 9, 17 March 1857, AE.
62 See chapter 8.
63 *El Genio de la Libertad*, 18 May 1857.
64 *La Discusión*, 21 April 1857.
65 *La Epoca*, 9 April 1857; *La Esperanza*, 20 April 1857. For a positive comment, see *El Genio de la Libertad*, 18 May 1857.
66 José Roger to Espartero, 13 May 1857, AE, 14-33.
67 Burdiel, *Isabel II. Una biografía*, 560, 562–9.
68 Ibid., 568.
69 *La Iberia*, *La Epoca*, 2 October 1858.
70 Espartero to Balaguer, 19 July 1858, MS358, BMVB.
71 Cutchet to Espartero, 28 July 1858, AE, 16-40.
72 *Felicitación dirigida por un Gran Número de Liberales de la Provincia de Barcelona*, (Barcelona, 1858).
73 Ibid.
74 Ibid.
75 Liberales de Lérida to Espartero, 26 September 1858, AE.

76 *La Discusión*, 22 July, 2 September 1858.
77 *La Discusión*, 5, 12, 15 August 1858.
78 *La Discusión*, 2 September 1858.
79 Burdiel, *Isabel II. Una biografía*, 692. This section follows her analysis on 692–727.
80 Ibid., 706.
81 Espartero to Balaguer, 19 March 1863, MS358, BMVB.
82 The full manifesto appeared on the front page of *El Clamor Público*, 11 September 1863; Espartero to Joaquín Aguirre, 8 September 1863, AE, Legajo 15, 1861-24.
83 Paredes Alonso, *Pascual Madoz, 1805–1870*, 338–9.
84 Espartero to Balaguer, 19 September 1863, MS358, BMVB.
85 9/8103, 247, Archivo Narváez, RAH, Madrid.
86 Burdiel, *Isabel II. Una biografía*, 725.
87 Zurita Aldeguer, "El Progresismo," 333–4; Fernández de los Ríos's *Historia de las luchas* was highly critical of Espartero.
88 Rubio, *Historia filosófica de la revolución española de 1868*, Madrid, 1:118.
89 *El Clamor Público*, 4 May 1864.
90 Rubio, *Historia filosófica*, 1:118, 120.
91 Millán García, *Sagasta, o el arte de hacer la política*, 130. See also Pirala, *Historia contemporánea: Anales*, 3:54.
92 Martínez de Tejada to Espartero, 26 April 1864; Manuel Gómez to Espartero, 26 April 1864, AE.
93 Manuel Gómez to Espartero, 29 April 1864, AE.
94 Jacinta to Montesino, 27 April 1864, AE.
95 Jacinta to Montesino, 1 May 1864, AE.
96 Jacinta to Montesino, 4 May 1864, AE.
97 Jacinta to Montesino, 6 May 1864, AE.
98 Bernardo Tomé to Espartero, 10 May 1864, AE.
99 Juan Antonio Zanne to Espartero, 4, 16 May 1864, AE.
100 Juan Antonio Perez to Espartero, 12 May 1864, AE.
101 Francisco Gispert to Espartero, 14 May 1864, AE.
102 José Puig y Salazar to Espartero, 13 May 1864, AE.
103 Carlos Botello to Espartero, 24 May 1864, AE.
104 José Ugarte to Espartero, 12 May 1864, AE.
105 Ponciano Masadas to Espartero, 11 May 1864, AE.
106 Balaguer to Espartero, 14 May 1864, AE.
107 Vilardell to Balaguer, nd, BMVB 258.
108 Junta Provincial de Barcelona al Comité Central de Madrid, 31 May 1864, AE.
109 Aymar to Espartero, 4 June 1864, AE.
110 Antonio Rodríguez to Espartero, 16 May 1864, AE.
111 Progresistas de Tárrega to Espartero, 16 May 1864, AE.

112 Progresistas de Arlés to Espartero, 11 June 1864, AE.
113 Both in *El Clamor Público*, 19 May 1864.
114 Saravia and Seaone to Espartero, 19 May 1864, AE.
115 Jacinta to Montesino, 20 May 1864, AE. Jacinta's use of the English word "leader" was taken from Olózaga's letter, in which he tried to distinguish between the terms *jefe* and *guía*.
116 Jacinta to Montesino, 20 May 1864, AE.
117 Saravia to Espartero, 22 May 1864; Espartero to Saravia, 23 May 1864, AE.
118 Madoz to Balaguer, 30 May 1864, BMVB, MS 472.
119 Saravia to Espartero, 3 June 1864, AE.
120 Espartero to Allende Salazar, 8 June 1864, AE. See also Murrieta to Montesino, 4 June 1864; Espartero to Montesino 6 June 1864, AE.
121 Jacinta to Montesino, 1 July 1864, AE.
122 Jacinta to Montesino, 15 October 1864, AE.
123 Aymar to Espartero, 15 October 1864, AE.
124 Espartero to Madoz, 13 October 1864, AE.
125 Espartero to Montesino, 21 October 1864, AE.
126 Jacinta to Montesino, 25 October 1864, AE.
127 *La Iberia*, 27 October 1864. Original in AE.
128 Lasala to Espartero, 27 October 1864, AE; Espartero to Aguirre, 27 October 1864, AE. See also Espartero to Calatrava, nd, AE.
129 *La Iberia*, 3 November 1864, AE.
130 Madoz to Balaguer, 5 November 1864, BMVB, MS 472.
131 Comité Progresista de Chinchilla to Espartero, 9 November 1864, AE.
132 Comité Progresista de Alicante to Espartero, 15 November 1864, AE.
133 Comité Progresista de Avilés to Espartero, 19 November 1864, AE.
134 Comité Progresista de Granada to Espartero, 18 December 1864, AE.
135 Comité Progresista de Daimiel to Espartero, 2 January 1865, AE.
136 Espartero to Junta Progresista de Barcelona, 14 November 1864, AE.
137 Comité Progresista de Zaragoza to Espartero, 22 December 1864; Espartero to Comité Progresista de Zaragoza, AE.
138 Millán and Cruz Romeo, "La Nación Católica en el Liberalismo," 196. This was one thing on which Espartero and Olózaga could agree. See ibid., 203.
139 Lyttleton, "The Hero and the People," 43–4. See also Riall, "Travel, Migration, Exile: Garibaldi's Global Fame."
140 Berenson and Giloi, Introduction to *Constructing Charisma*, 12.
141 Bermejo, *Historia de la interinidad y guerra civil de España desde 1868*, 178–9.
142 Cited in Thompson, *The Birth of Modern Politics in Spain*, 159–60.
143 Ramón de Oliver to Espartero, 20 December 1856, AE, 14-2p.
144 Publio López Mondejar, *Historia de la fotografía es España* (Barcelona, 2005), 51–6.

145 Simon Morgan, "Academic 'Pseudo-Event' or a Useful Concept for Historians?' *Cultural and Social History* 8, no. 1 (2011): 95–114.
146 Francisco de A. Planas to Espartero, 8 February 1863, AE.
147 Antonio Alvarez Penalta to Espartero, 17 February 1865.
148 Catalina Rando de Boussignault to Espartero, 23 February 1865, AE.
149 Francisco Boada to Espartero, 13 May 1864, AE.
150 Miguel Planas y amigos to Espartero, nd, AE. The letter also contained a poem.
151 Progresistas of Algarinejo to Espartero, 10 March 1865, AE.
152 Marcos González to Espartero, 27 February 1865, AE.
153 Jose Manuel López y López to Espartero, 17 February 1865, AE.
154 Casino Catalán Industrial to Espartero, 25 February 1858; Comité Progresista de Palafrugell, 23 February 1859; Gerónimo Torres to Espartero, = March 1865, AE.
155 Enrique Rodríguez Cortes to Espartero, 24 February 1864, AE.
156 *El Peninsular* to Espartero, 17 February 1865, AE.
157 Fradera, *Cultura nacional en una sociedad dividida*, 166. On Balaguer, see García Balañà, "El primer Balaguer o la temptativa populista a la Catalunya iberal (1859–1869)," and Palomas i Moncholí, *Victor Balaguer*.
158 A. Elías de Molíns, *Diccionario biográfico y bibliográfico de escritores y artistas catalanes del siglo XIX* (Barcelona, 1889), 1:512.
159 Palomas i Moncholí, *Victor Balaguer*, 92–4, 155–6, 168.
160 Espartero to Balaguer, 4 October 1858, MS 358, BMVB.
161 *El Conceller*, 11 October, 2 November 1856.
162 *El Conceller*, 27 February 1857, MS 312, BMVB.
163 V. Balaguer, "Homenatje y Recort al Excm. Senyor D. Baldomero Espartero," in F.P. Briz, ed., *Los trovadors moderns* (Barcelona, 1859), 178–85. For other poetic tributes, see *Al General Espartero, pacificador de España, CAMPEON DE LA PATRIA LIBERTAD* (Barcelona, 1862); *La Corona*, 27 February 1863; and Francisco de Mas y Otzet, 27 February 1866, AE.
164 Balaguer, "Homenatje y Recort."
165 *Progresistas* in general emphasized the honesty, disinterestedness, and even poverty of their heroes. See Zurita Aldeguer, "El Progresismo," 327–8.
166 Espartero to Baldomero Goicoechea, 11 November 1856, #5, Dinastía Vivanco, Diversos, AHN.
167 Balaguer, *La Libertad Constitucional. Estudios Políticos*.
168 Ibid., 49. These ideas were also shared by Democrats. See Peyrou, "Familia y Política."
169 Balaguer, *La Libertad Constitucional*, 252–3.
170 *La Corona*, 27 February 1865.
171 *La Corona*, 27 February 1860, 1 March 1864.
172 Junta Provincial de Barcelona al Comité Central de Madrid, 31 May 1864, AE.
173 *La Corona*, 27 February 1860.

174 *La Corona*, 27 February, 1 March 1861. The organizers distributed 2,945 loaves of bread valued at 9,475 *reales*. Aymar to Espartero, 31 January 1861, AE, 15-2.
175 *La Corona*, 26 February 1864.
176 Jaime Rafecas to Espartero, 13 March 1864, AE.
177 Aymar to Espartero, 25 February 1868, AE, 25-51; Comisión de Festejos to Espartero, nd, AE, 25-60; Espartero to Agustín Aymar, 23 March 1868, Agustí Aymar, Papers personals i correspondencia politica, Biblioteca de Catalunya, MS 1260.
178 *La Corona*, 3, 6 March 1859; 5, 6 March 1865.
179 Martín Puig to Espartero, 28 February 1864, AE.
180 *La Corona*, 5 March 1865.
181 *La Corona*, 2 March 1862.
182 *La Corona*, 2 March 1864.
183 Carlos Llopis to Espartero, nd, AE; emphasis added.
184 *La Corona*, 27 February 1864.
185 Juan B. Romeu et al to Espartero, 26 February 1864, Epist. 1855–68, BMVB.
186 Bernardo Fusté to Espartero, 22 February 1864, AE; Miguel Planas to Espartero, 25 February 1864, AE.
187 Comisión Local to Junta Provincial, 29 February 1864, Epist. 1855–68, BMVB.
188 Espartero to Agustín Aymar, Manuel Torrents, Victor Balaguer, and others, 6 May 1861, Agustí Aymar, Papers personals i correspondencia politica, Biblioteca de Catalunya, MS 1260; Espartero to Balaguer, 9 June 1861, MS 358, BMVB.
189 Espartero to Balaguer, 1 December 1862, MS 312, BMVB.
190 *La Época*, 7 January 1865. See also *La Iberia*, 21 January 1865.
191 *La Correspondencia de España*, 5, 8 January 1865; *La Iberia*, 9 January 1865; *La Libertad*, 10, 22 January 1865.
192 Jacinta to Montesino, 20 February 1861, AE, 15-4; emphasis in original.
193 Anguera, *El General Prim*, 425.
194 Burdiel, *Isabel II. Una biografía*, 767–73.
195 Millán García, *Sagasta*, 139.
196 Ollero Vallés, *Sagasta*, 304.
197 Espartero to Comité Central, 30 November 1865, AE.
198 *La Iberia*, 26 November 1865.
199 French ambassador to minister of foreign affairs, 3 January 1866, 107, Exp. 1, Leg. 284, Diversos y Familias 3455, AHN.
200 F. Fuster Ruiz and J. Cano Valero, *Agitaciones sociales y políticas en la Mancha y Murcia, 1858–1927* (Albacete, 1985), 39.
201 Jorge Vilches, *Progreso y Libertad. El Partido Progresista en la Revolución Liberal Española* (Madrid, 2001), 71.
202 Burdiel, *Isabel II. Una biografía*, 795.

203 Espartero to Balaguer, 21 March 1865, MS 358, BMVB.
204 Both in Álvarez Villamil, *Cartas de conspiradores*, 267–8.
205 Madoz to Prim, 12 January 1867, ibid., 274.
206 Sagasta to Prim, 9 February 1867, ibid., 290–1.
207 *La Correspondencia de España*, 29 September 1903. Delgado claimed that the letter was published in *La Correspondencia de España*.
208 *Gil Blas*, 1 March 1868; *La Época*, 28 February 1868.
209 *La España*, 5 August 1868.
210 *Manchester Guardian*, 26 August 1868.
211 Francisco Vilar and Francisco Esplug to Espartero, 16 September 1868, AE.

10. "King or President?" September 1868–December 1870

1 Full texts in Valeriano Bozal, *Juntas revolucionarias. Manifiestos y proclamas de 1868* (Madrid, 1968), 67–76.
2 On the history of the concept of *sexenio revolucionario*, see García Balañà, "À la recherche du *Sexenio Democrático* (1868–1874) dans l'Espagne contemporaine."
3 Burdiel, *Isabel II. Una biografía*, 808–9.
4 Ibid., 810.
5 de la Fuente Monge, *Los revolucionarios de 1868*, 17.
6 Ibid., 90–2.
7 Estevánez, *Fragmentos de mis memorias*, 255–6.
8 Ibid., 262, 264.
9 Burdiel, *Isabel II. Una biografía*, 815.
10 *La Iberia*, 30 September 1868; de la Fuente Monge, *Los revolucionarios*, 79.
11 Junta Revolucionario de Logroño to Espartero, 1 October 1868; Espartero to Junta Revolucionario, 1 October 1868, AE, 16-1868-25; *Boletín Oficial de la Provincia de Logroño*, 3 October 1868.
12 de la Fuente Monge, *Los revolucionarios*, 92–3.
13 Liberals of Morales del Progreso (antes del Rey) to Espartero, 14 January 1869, AE, 17-34.
14 de la Fuente Monge, *Los revolucionarios*, 94.
15 Ibid., 103.
16 Bellogín, "Historia Contemporánea," 329.
17 *La Correspondencia de España*, 8 October 1868; *La Iberia*, 6 October 1868.
18 de la Fuente Monge, *Los revolucionarios*, 148–63.
19 Bozal, *Juntas revolucionarias*, 109–19.
20 *Gaceta de Madrid*, 7 December 1868.
21 García Ruiz, *Historias*, 2:788.
22 On the Democrats, see Peyrou, *Tribunos del pueblo* and "A Great Family of Sovereign Men."

23 Rosa Monlleó Perís, "Republicanos contra monárquicos: Del enfrentamiento electoral y parlamentaria a la insurrección federal de 1869," *Ayer* 44 (2001): 60.
24 On censorship, see Adrian Shubert, "Spain," in Robert Justin Goldstein, ed., *The War for the Public Mind: Political Censorship in Nineteenth-Century Europe* (Westport, 2000), 175–210. For the hurdles facing political theatre before 1868, see Rubio Jiménez, "José María Gutiérrez de Alba y los inicios de la revista política en el teatro."
25 Cited in Shubert, "Spain," 189, 195.
26 Cited in ibid., 195.
27 de la Fuente Monge, "La figura del general Espartero."
28 Jaume Piquet, *Lo pronunciament* (Barcelona, 1868).
29 Rubio Jiménez, "José María Gutiérrez de Alba y los inicios de la revista política en el teatro."
30 José María Gutiérrez de Alba, *¿Qién sera el rey?, o Los petendientes*, MS 34-17, Biblioteca Nacional, Madrid.
31 Reclus, *Impresiones, de un viaje por España en tiempos de Revolución*, 147–8.
32 Salvador Granés, *Así en la tierra como en el cielo* (Madrid, 1869).
33 Reclus, *Impresiones*, 163.
34 José Yglesias Veguer to Espartero, 29 October 1868, AE, 16-1868-52.
35 Sicilia de Arenzana, *Un Monarca … y la República, o Espartero Rey*, 9–10.
36 Fernando de Tschudy y Cornejo, *Espartero rey. Carta a S.A. El Duque de la Victoria* (Madrid, 1868).
37 Adolfo Serullo, *España por Espartero* (Madrid, 1868). See also José Ruiz y Campos, *Baldomero I Rey de España* (Madrid, 1868). Other pamphlets: T.H.M, *Las verdades del varquero que apoyan la conveniencia y la nacional tendencia de que, REY SEA ESPARTERO* (Madrid, 1869). The title comes from a popular saying meaning "the plain truth." See also Ibo Alfaro, *Historia de la interinidad española*, 2:390. The full Manifesto is on 414–16.
38 Antonio Checa Godoy, *El Ejercicio de la libertad. La prensa española en el Sexenio Revolucionario* (Madrid, 2006), 73–4.
39 *La Humanidad*, 18 November 1868.
40 Ibid.
41 *El Cronista*, 18 November 1868.
42 *El Cronista*, 5 January 1869.
43 *El Cronista*, 1 December 1868, 5, 9 January 1869.
44 *El Cronista*, 24 December 1868.
45 *El Cronista*, 8 December 1868.
46 Francisco Salmerón to his father, 7 January 1869, MS 1747, Biblioteca de Catalunya.
47 Sáez Miguel, "Política y políticos en La Rioja: sexenio democrático (1868–1874)," *Brocar: Cuadernos de investigación histórica* 26 (2002): 237–8.
48 Cited in Ollero Vallés, *Sagasta*, 346.

Notes to pages 296–300

49 Bermejo, *Historia de la interinidad*, 654; Josê María Orense, *Ventajas de la República Federal* (Madrid, 1869), 38–53; *La Época*, 4 December 1868.
50 *Espartero. Rey o presidente?*, F. Bon. 2085, Biblioteca de Catalunya.
51 *El Cronista*, 8 18 December 1868.
52 *El Cronista*, 19 December 1868.
53 *El Cronista*, 13 January 1869; emphasis in original.
54 *Las Provincias*, 21 November 1868.
55 *El Cronista*, 31 December 1868.
56 *Boletín Oficial de la Provincia de Logroño*, 28 January 1869.
57 Manuel Rodríguez y Benaders to Espartero, 20 January 1869, AE, 17-42.
58 Espartero to civil governor of Logroño, 31 January 1869, AE, 17-48a; Espartero to civil governor of Zaragoza, 7 February 1869, AE, 17-51; *Crónica de las Cortes constituyentes de 1869 y de los acontecimientos políticos de España durante el periodo legislativo* (Madrid, 1869), 1:163.
59 Villa-Robledo to Espartero, 8 October 1868, AE, 16-1868-29.
60 Junta Revolucionaria, Mérida, to Espartero, 10 October 1868, AE, 16-1868-32; Anton Gomez Carmona to Espartero, 8 January 1869, AE, 17-18.
61 Junta Revolucionaria de Alar del Rey to Espartero, 11 October 1868, AE, 16-1868-39.
62 Comité Electoral, Quintanar de la Orden, to Espartero, 28 November 1868, AE, 16-1868-87; Democratic-Monarchist Committee of Almagro to Espartero, 7 January 1869, AE, 17-16; Rebollado de Otero to Espartero, 11 January 1869, AE, 17-24; Acta de elección, Villa de Lanestosa, Balmaseda, Vizcaya, 18 January 1869, AE, 17-37.
63 Republican Committee, Argamasilla de Alba, to Espartero, 8 January 1869, AE, 17-17.
64 Republican Committee, Novelda, to Espartero, 24 December 1868, AE, 16-1868-128
65 Republican Committee, Calatorao, to Espartero, 9 January 1869, AE, 17-22.
66 Various, Villatobas (Toledo), to Espartero, 28 November 1868, AE, 16-1868-88.
67 Democratic Republican Committee, Almagro, to Espartero, 30 November 1868, AE, 16-1868-96.
68 Liberals of Morales del Progreso (antes del Rey) to Espartero, 14 January 1869, AE, 17-34.
69 Antonio Quintana to Espartero, 6 December 1868, AE.
70 Junta Revolucionaria de Alar del Rey to Espartero, 11 October 1868, AE, 16-1868-39; Pedro Campos to Espartero, 28 October 1868, AE, 16-1868-53; Comité Electoral Liberal-Monarquico de Zaragoza to Espartero, 12 December 1868, AE, 16-1868-116; Domingo Ruiz Plana to Espartero, 31 December 1868, AE, 16-1868-136; Comité Electoral Liberal-Monárquico de Zaragoza to Espartero, 12 December 1868, AE, 16-1868-116; Juan Angel to Espartero, 11 January 1868, AE, 17-23; Casino Democratico de Morón de la Frontera to Espartero, 13 January 1869, AE, 17-32.

71 Pedro Campos to Espartero, 28 October 1868, AE, 16-1868-53, Republican Committee, Calatorao, to Espartero, 9 January 1869, AE, 17-22.
72 Gregorio Rodríguez to Espartero, 20 November 1869, AE, 16-1868-93; José Iglesias Vejer to Espartero, 29 October 1868, AE, 16-1868-57; Liberals of Ceviso de la Torre (Palencia) to Espartero, 12 January 1869, AE, 17-28; Democratic Republican Committee, Almagro, to Espartero, 30 November 1868, AE, 16-1868-96; Gerónimo Torres to Espartero, 24 December 1868, AE, 16-1868-129; ? to Espartero, 4 November 1868, AE, 16-1868-63; Republican Committee, Novelda, to Espartero, 24 December 1868AE, 16-1868-128.
73 ? to Luciano de Murrieta, 6 October 1868, AE, 16-1868-28.
74 Espartero to Mariano Acevedo Alvarez, 26 November 1868, AE, 16-1868-80.
75 Espartero to Gregorio Barragan, 26 November 1868, AE, 16-1868-82.
76 Castelar, *Discursos parlamentarios*, 1:237.
77 The text of the Constitution of 1869 is at: http://www.congreso.es/docu/constituciones/1869/1869_cd.pdf.
78 *DSCC*, 11 February 1869.
79 Rosa Monlleó Perís, *La Gloriosa en Valencia* (Valencia, 1996), 321. On the idea of an Iberian federation, see María Victoria López-Cordón, *El pensamiento político-internacional del federalismo español (1868–1874)* (Barcelona, 1975).
80 Pirala, *Historia contemporánea. Anales*, 3:402.
81 Castelar, *Discursos parlamentarios*, 253–5.
82 Bermejo, *Historia de la interinidad*, 860–5.
83 Ibid., 898–909, 932–3; Alberto José Esperón Fernández, "Honor y escándalo en la encrucijada del Sexenio Democrático. La opinión pública ante el duelo entre Montpensier y Enrique de Borbón," in Raquel Sánchez García, ed., *La cultura de la espada. De honor, duelos y otros lances* (Madrid, 2019), 245–86.
84 Bermejo, *Historia de la interinidad*, 1:940.
85 Ibid., 1:944; emphasis added.
86 *La Correspondencia de España*, 29 September 1903.
87 Bermejo, *Historia de la interinidad*, 1:944.
88 AE, 18-38.
89 Anguera, *El General Prim*, 588.
90 AE, 18-60; cited in Bermejo, *Historia de la interinidad*, 950–1.
91 AE, 18-54.
92 AE, 18-43.
93 AE, 18-50.
94 *La Iberia*, 2 June 1870.
95 AE, 18-73.
96 *A Nuestros Conciudadanos*, Hemeroteca Municipal de Madrid, A695.
97 AE, 18-82, 80.
98 *El Eco de Cuenca*, 1, 4 June 1870.

99 AE, 18-65, 18-66; *Le Monde Illustré*, 11 June 1870.
100 Daniel Carbonell y Jover to Círculo Liberal de Barcelona, nd, Epist. 1869, BMVB.
101 ? to Balaguer, 15 November 1869, Epist. 1869, BMVB.
102 Miguel to Balaguer, 25 October 1869, Epist. 1869, BMVB.
103 Jaime Ráfecas y Bonastre to Balaguer, 22 November 1869, Epist. 1869, BMVB.
104 Madoz to Balaguer, 20 October 1869, Epist. 1869, BMVB.
105 Daniel Carbonell y Jover to Balaguer, 30 May 1870, Epist. 1870, BMVB.
106 Daniel Carbonell y Jover to Balaguer, 30 May, 4 June 1870, Epist. 1870, BMVB.
107 *El Telégrafo*, 5 June 1870; *Diario de Barcelona*, 24 June 1870, AE, 18-97.
108 AE, 18-93.
109 Federico Pons to Balaguer, 2 August 1870, Epist. 1870, BMVB.
110 Legajo 229, Archivo del Congreso de los Diputados.
111 *La Iberia*, 2 June 1870. See also Paredes Alonso, *Pascual Madoz, 1805–1870*, 393.
112 Valencia de Alcántara, 28 May 1870, #86; Motilla del Palancar, 28 February 1870; Alcira, 1 January 1870, #133.
113 Calasparra, 5 June 1870, Celugín, 6 June 1870, Bullas, 8 June 1870, Paduco, 8 June 1870, Picote, 8 June 1870, Alaran, 8 June 1870, Mazaron, 13 June 1870.
114 ?, 29 May 1870, #107, Torrijos, 4 June 1870, #266, Manzanares, 4 June 1870, #285. There was even a debate in the Cortes between supporters of Espartero and Montpensier over the legitimacy of petitions in favour of the two candidates. *DSC*, 14:8980–1, 9005–12.
115 Tarazona de la Mancha, 16 January 1870, #150.
116 Valdepeñas de la Mancha, 6 January 1870, #151; Moeche, 14 March 1870, #152; Cuenca, ? February 1870; San Vicente de Alcántara, 5 June 1870, #217.
117 Caravaca, 8 January 1870, #131; ?, 29 March 1870, #142; Piedrabuena, 15 May 1870, #92; Majar, 26 May 1870, #274; Gibraleon, 12 May 1870, #7; Salamanca, 24 April 1870, #105.
118 Alcira, 1 January 1870, #133; Alhama, 1 May 1870, #20; Caravaca, 8 January 1870, #131.
119 Dolores, 3 June 1870, #211; Aroche, 15 May 1870, #116.
120 Badajoz, 15 May 1870, #74; Montanchez, 5 June 1870, #113.
121 Villanueva de la Jara, 20 March 1870, #135.
122 Guadalupe, 8 June 1870, #272.
123 Tarazona, 9 June 1870, #236; Calaña, 1 June 1870, #279; Moral de la Frontera, 7 May 1870, #125; Valdepeñas de la Mancha, 6 January 1870, #151; ?, 20 November 1869, #210; Guadix, 11 May 1870; Nombela, 22 May 1870, #228; Astorga, 19 May 1870, #189.
124 Alcira, 1 June 1870, #133.
125 San Vicente de Alcántara, 5 June 1870, #198.
126 Burgos, 31 December 1869, #117; Salamanca, 24 April 1870, #105; Olivenza, 3 June 1870, #90.

127 Dalías, 1 February 1870, #148.
128 *DSC*, 8784–7.
129 Anguera, *General Prim*, 593–4; Jonathan Steinberg, *Bismarck: A Life* (Oxford, 2013).
130 AE, 18-100, 101, 102.
131 Burdiel, *Isabel II. Una biografía*, 826–7.
132 Colección Isabel II, Legajo XVII, #106, RAH, Madrid.
133 Bermejo, *Historia de la interinidad*, 1:587. Espartero's papers contain no trace of this question.
134 Isabel II to Espartero, 21 June 1869, Colección Isabel II, Legajo XVIII, #44, RAH.
135 AE, 17-108.
136 AE, 17-107; emphasis added.
137 José Mariano Vallejo, *Don Baldomero* (Madrid 1870); de la Fuente Monge, "La figura del general Espartero," 130–1.
138 Marie Pierre Caire Merida, "La revolución de 1868 en el teatro representado en Barcelona," *Dioniso* 3 (2006): 11–19; de la Fuente Monge, "La figura del general Espartero," 131–2.
139 "A rogue of this court," *Viva – la muerte: contrasentido inmoral e impolítico de julio de 1870* (Madrid, 1870).
140 Cited in Anguera, *El General Prim*, 602.
141 Castelar, *Discursos parlamentarios*, 3:414–16, 435.
142 Ibo Alfaro, *Historia de la interinidad española*, 2:838–43. Another pro-Montpensier tract published earlier in 1870 had devoted an entire chapter to why Espartero should *not* be king. *¿Quién será el Rey de España?* (Madrid, 1870), 27–34.
143 Ibo Alfaro, *Historia de la interinidad española*, 820.
144 The handwritten original is in AE, 18-100. *La Época*, 11 November 1870.
145 AE, 18-113, 114.
146 AE, 18-119.
147 AE, 18-120, 121, 116, 117.
148 Cited in Higueras Castañeda, *Con los Borbones, jamás*, 183. See also Victor Balaguer, *Memorías de un constituyente: estudios históricos y políticos* (Madrid, 1872), 92–4.
149 *La Iberia*, 24 November 1870.
150 Pirala, *Historia contemporánea. Anales*, 405n1; AE, 18-133.
151 AE, 18-138, 136.

11. The Necessary Man, January 1871–March 1876

1 Anguera, *El General Prim*, 613–22. For a recent fictionalized version, see Ian Gibson, *La Berlina de Prim* (Madrid, 2012).

2 Bolaños Mejías, *El Reinado de Amadeo*, 185.
3 AE, 19-13.
4 Bermejo, *Historia de la interinidad*, 2:204.
5 Bernardo Riego, "Imágenes fotográficas y estrategias de opinión públicalos viajes de la Reina Isabel II por España (1858–1866)," *Reales Sitios: Revista del Patrimonio Nacional* 139 (1999): 2–15.
6 Pirala, *El Rey en Madrid*, 3–7.
7 Bermejo, *Historia de la interinidad*, 2:420–1; Bolaños Mejías, *El Reinado de Amadeo*, 211. Ruiz Zorrilla even tried to get Espartero to visit the king in Madrid. Higueras Castañeda, *Con los Borbones, jamás*, 212.
8 *El Eco de Alicante*, 3 October 1871; *El Constitucional*, 1 October 1871.
9 Bermejo, *Historia de la interinidad*, 2:431.
10 Pirala, *El Rey en Madrid*, 380–4. A handwritten copy of Espartero's speech is in his papers, AE, 19-2.
11 Bermejo Martín, *Espartero*, Appendix II, 295–9.
12 *El Imparcial*, 17 February 1871.
13 Bermejo, *Historia de la interinidad*, 2:444, 449–51; Bolaños Mejías, *El Reinado de Amadeo*, 213; Ollero Vallés, *Sagasta*, 390–1.
14 *Gil Blas*, 8 October 1871.
15 AE, 19-60; *La Correspondencia de España*, 15 October 1871; AE, 19-65a.
16 AE, 19-68, 64.
17 AE, 19-71.
18 The first was Charles IV's favourite, Manuel Godoy, who was named Prince of Peace in 1795.
19 *Gaceta de Madrid*, 2 January 1872; emphasis added.
20 Pirala, *El Rey en Madrid*, 123–4.
21 Ibid., 125; *Altar y Trono*, 13 January 1872; *La Correspondencia de España*, 12 January 1872.
22 AE, 19-1872-2.
23 Millán García, *Sagasta*, 232.
24 *La Epoca*, 18 March 1872.
25 *La América*, 28 March 1872.
26 Expediente Personal, Archivo, Senado de España; AE, 19-1872-17, 18.
27 *La Correspondencia de España*, 12 June 1872; *El Imparcial*, 13 June 1872; *Gil Blas*, 16 June 1872.
28 *Gaceta de Madrid*, 12 February 1873.
29 AE, 19-1873-4; *El Federal Salmantino*, 16 February 1873.
30 *La Correspondencia de España*, 13 February 1873.
31 Bermejo, *Historia de la interinidad*, 3:317–18.
32 Isabel II to Espartero, 6 January 1871, 9/6957, Legajo XVIII, no. 45, RAH.
33 Canal, *El Carlismo*, 176–7, 185.
34 AE, 19-1873-6, 7, 12.

35 Canal, *El Carlismo*, 188.
36 Biblioteca de Cataluyna, Ro. 135 B.
37 *El Bien Público*, 18 June 1873, *El Federal Salmantino*, 8 June 1873.
38 *La Lucha*, 11 September 1873.
39 Archivo del Congreso de los Diputados, Madrid.
40 *El Federal Salmantino*, 20 July 1873.
41 *La Iberia, La Época*, 18 July 1873.
42 *La Iberia*, 21 August 1873.
43 *La Epoca*, 25, 30 August 1873.
44 *Manchester Guardian*, 15 August 1873.
45 *La Epoca*, 21 October 1873.
46 Bermejo, *Historia de la interinidad*, 3:145–6.
47 *DSC*, Legislatura 1876–7, 476.
48 Pavía to captains general and Espartero, 3 January 1874, AE.
49 Pavía to Espartero, 3 January 1874, AE.
50 *La Iberia*, 6 January 1874.
51 AE, 20-1874-4.
52 AE, 20-1874-13.
53 AE, 20-1874-8, 9f.
54 *Boletín Oficial de Segovia*, 4 May 1874.
55 *Crónica Meridional*, 5 May 1874.
56 *El Constitucional*, 12 August 1874.
57 *La Correspondencia de España*, 3 November 1874.
58 *El Constitucional*, 13 December 1874.
59 *La Epoca, El Imparcial*, 12 December 1874.
60 *La Epoca*, 13 December 1874, *La Correspondencia de España*, 26 December 1874.
61 *La Ilustración Española y Americana*, 22, 30 December 1874; emphasis added.
62 AE, 20-1875-08.
63 On the intense propaganda in favour of Alfonso XII, see Fernández Miret, "La forja del rey conciliador."
64 *La Epoca*, 21 January 1875, *La Iberia*, 23 January 1875.
65 Allende Salazar to Espartero, 18 January 1875, AE, 20-1875-12.
66 *El Bien Público*, 19 February 1875.
67 *Gaceta de Madrid*, 14 February 1875.
68 *El Bien Público*, 23 February 1875.
69 AE, 26-1871-486, 461, 20-187523.
70 *La Epoca*, 16 February 1875.
71 Ibid.; *La Correspondencia de España*, 17 February 1875.
72 *The Times*, 12 February 1875.
73 Fernández Miret, "La forja del rey conciliador," 368.
74 *La Iberia*, 23 February 1876.

75 *La Iberia*, 3 March 1876; AE, 21-1876-03.
76 AE, 26-510, 515, 524, 526.
77 *La Iberia*, 7 March 1876.
78 *El Imparcial*, 27 March 1875.
79 Even so, Alfonso commissioned Ramón Padró y Pedret to paint the moment in which Espartero had given him the Gran Cruz de San Fernando. *La Epoca*, 28 November 1876.

Epilogue: Death and Afterlife, March 1876–

1 Nido y Segalerva, *Historia política y parlamentaria de S.A. D. Baldomero Fernández Espartero*, 829–30.
2 Jacinta to Pepa, 5 November 1877, Diversos-Colecciones, 7, N.616, AHN.
3 Manuel Hiraldez de Acosta, *Espartero: su vida militar, política, descriptiva y anecdótica* (Barcelona, 1869), 2:971–2.
4 Apuntes, 10 July 1878, AE.
5 Bermejo Martín, *Espartero*, 236. The full inventory is in Bermejo Martín, 300–9.
6 http://www.bermemar.com/ESPARTERO/doctesta.htm; amounts fulfilling the Duke's bequests, AE.
7 *La Academia* 7 July 1878; *La Ilustración Española y Americana*, 15 July 1878.
8 *La Iberia*, 22, 23 October 1878.
9 *La Época*, 22 October 1878.
10 Carlos Reyero, "Monumentalizar la capital: la escultura conmemorativa en Madrid durante el siglo XIX," in María del Carmen Lacarra Ducay and Cristina Giménez Navarro, eds., *Historia y política a través de la Escultura pública, 1820–1920* (Zaragoza, 2003), 49–50; and Carlos Reyero, *La Escultura Conmemorativa en España* (Madrid, 2004), 406, 511.
11 Carlos Serrano, *El Nacimiento de Carmen:símbolos, mitos, nación* (Madrid, 1999), 197.
12 Bermejo Martin, *Espartero*, 153–62, 243–5. For a description of the house, see Rosa Maria Lazaro Torres, "La fortuna de Espartero," *Aportes* (March 1996): 75–6.
13 *La Iberia*, 12 January 1879.
14 *Ilustración Española y Americana*, 15 January 1879; Robert Gewarth, "Introduction," *European History Quarterly* (July 2009): 382.
15 These costs came to 8,654 pesetas. Archivo Congreso, P-01-00202-005.
16 Governor general of the Philippines to colonies minister, 8 March 1879, AHN Ultramar, 5237, Exp. 2, #2; Report to Council, 8 May 1879, AHN Ultramar, 5237, Exp. 2, #3.
17 *Ilustración Española y Americana*, 8, 15 January 1879.
18 *La Iberia*, 9, 10 January 1879.

19 *La Época*, 9 January 1879.
20 *El Imparcial*, 9 January 1879.
21 *El Graduador*, 10 January 1879.
22 *La Campanya de Gracia*, 11 January 1879.
23 *El Globo*, 9, 11, 12, 13 January 1879. The one discordant note came from the Catholic press, particularly *La Fe*. *El Globo*, 10 January 1879; *La Unión*, 10 January 1879.
24 *La Ilustración Española y Americana*, 22 January 1879; *Gaceta de Madrid*, 22 January 1879.
25 *La Unión*, 21 January 1879; *El Imparcial*, 19 January 1879.
26 *La Iberia*, 12, 15, 19, 30 January 1879.
27 *El Graduador*, 26 January 1879. For a contemporary Italian comparison, see Banti, "The Remembrance of Heroes."
28 *Diari Catalá*, 5, 6, 7, 9, 10, 11 June 1879.
29 Agulhon, "La 'statuemanie' et l'histoire," 149
30 Leerssen, "When Was Romantic Nationalism?" 13.
31 Carolyn Boyd, "Statue-Mania in 19th-Century Spain," paper delivered at the annual meeting of the Society for Spanish and Portuguese Historical Studies, April 1997. See also Castells, "Celebremos lo local, celebremos lo nacional."
32 Reyero, "El reconocimiento de la nación en la historia," 1206; Peiró Martín, *En los altares de la patria*; Reyero, "Monumentalizar la capital"; *La Escultura Conmemorativa*, 393.
33 Michonneau, *Barcelone*, 13.
34 AE, Estátuas 24, 25.
35 Archivo del Congreso de los Diputados, P01-00102-0020. *El Clamor Público*, 10 January 1856. See Romeo Mateo, "Memoria y política en el liberalismo progresista," 76; *La Iberia*, 3 January 1856.
36 Archivo Congreso, A-02-000035-0003-0004.
37 *La Rioja*, 23 September 1895; AE, Estátuas 26, 28.
38 Reyero, *La Escultura Conmenorativa*, 481; Subirachs i Burgaya, *L'escultura del segle XIX a Catalunya*, 226.
39 Archivo Congreso, P-01-00209-009.
40 AE, Carpeta 0, Estátuas 7.
41 Gibert was a protégé of Liberal politician Gaspar Nuñéz de Arce. On Gibert, see Puigdollers, "Pau Gibert I Roig, un escultor oblidat."
42 *Estatua del General Espartero*, AE, Carpeta 0, Estátuas 1.
43 This earned a withering comment from *La Época* on 31 December 1886. The Madrid statue later became a *lieux de mémoire* as the site of the annual 7 July celebration of the creation of the Milicia Nacional in 1822 which continued into the Second Republic. *Luz*, 7 July 1932. See also *La Voz*, 7 July 1929.

44 Archivo Congreso, P-01-00209-009. AE, Estátuas, 31, 32
45 *La Ilustración Española y Americana*, 8 September 1889; *El Correo Militar*, 30, 31 August 1889.
46 *La Iberia*, 30 August 1889.
47 *El Imparcial*, 31 August 1889.
48 *La Época*, 30 August 1889.
49 *El Liberal*, 6 September 1889.
50 *La Unión Católica*, 30, 31 August 1889.
51 *Diario de Barcelona*, 5 September 1889.
52 *El Liberal*, 8 September 1889.
53 *La Antorcha*, 12 September 1889.
54 Archivo Congreso, P-01-000255-0056, P01-000262-030. In fact, the Logroño statue was not a copy, although it did use some of the elements of the original. Puigdollers, "Pau Gibert i Roig," 111–12.
55 *La Rioja*, 23 September 1895.
56 *La Época*, 22 September 1895.
57 *La Tomasa*, 9 August 1894.
58 Archivo Municipal, Bilbao, ES 48020 AMB-BUA520943.
59 Ibid., ES 48020 AMB-BUA520991, ES 48020 AMB-BUA521421; Castells, "Celebremos lo local, celebremos lo nacional," 363, 377.
60 *Madrid Cómico*, 20 January 1884.
61 *La América*, 3 May 1880.
62 http://atodezarzuela.blogspot.ca/2014/01/la-gran-via-libreto.html.
63 Martín Arranz, *Galdós y Espartero*.
64 Albornoz, *El gobierno de los caudillos militares*; Alvarez Tardío, "Historia y revolución."
65 Ibid., 50, 35–6, 190, 196.
66 *ABC*, 10 October 1931.
67 Moreno Luzón, *Romanones, caciquismo y política liberal*, especially pages 434–6.
68 Romanones, *Espartero*, 140, 109, 110, 114, 130.
69 Ibid., 35.
70 Augusto M. Torres, *Directores Españoles Malditos* (Madrid, 2004), 127–8.
71 Fernández Cuenca, *Espartero*, 5–17.
72 Emilio Mola, *Obras completas* (Valladolid, 1940), 117. The speech was reported widely in the Nationalist press. See, for example, *El Heraldo de Zamora* and *El Diario Palentino*, 17 August 1936. It was also reprinted in a number of Nationalist papers in October 1938 when rumours of an attempted international mediation were circulating; for example, *El Día de Palencia*, 19 October 1938; *El Noticiero de Soria*, 20 October 1938.
73 *El Día de Palencia*, 13 April 1937.
74 *El Diario Palentino*, 13 September 1938.

75 *El Requeté*, February 1939.
76 http://www.euskomedia.org/aunamendi/123544.
77 *El Pensamiento alavés*, 31 August 1939.
78 *La Voz*, 8 August 1936. See also *El Luchador*, 18 August 1936, *La Voz de Menorca*, 26 August 1936. *Full oficial del dilluns de Barcelona*, 26 October 1936.
79 *La Libertad*, 24 January 1937. "Abrazo de Vergara" became a pejorative term to describe supposed attempts at international mediation in the war. *La Voz*, 1, 15 April 1937, *La Verdad*, 23 April 1937.
80 *La Libertad*, 27, 28 February 1937.
81 *La Libertad*, 21, 27 May 1937; *La Voz*, 21 May 1937; *Solidadridad Obrera*, 29 May 1937.
82 *Hoja oficial de la provincia de Barcelona*, 14 June 1937.
83 Xosé Manoel Núñez Seixas, *Fuera el invasor: nacionalismos y movilización bélica durante la Guerra civil Española*, (Madrid, 2006), pp. 148, 169.
84 Peyrou and Cruz Romeo, "Mitos, símbolos y monumentos de la memoria de la españa liberal en el Siglo XX," 82–92.
85 Ibid., 86.
86 *Azul*, 3 May 1939.
87 *Nomenclator Municipal* (Bilbao, 1945), Carballés, "La evolución de la memoria de la Guerra Civil en el espacio urbano de Bilbao."
88 Caballé, "La biografía en España," 110.
89 Espina, *Espartero*.
90 Caballé, "La biografía en España," 108.
91 Jaime Más Ferrer, *Antonio Espina: del modernismo a la vanguardia* (Alicante, 2001); Caballé, "La biografía en España," 113.
92 Espina, *Espartero*, 67.
93 Ibid., 205.
94 Ibid., 26, 53, 29.
95 Ibid., 96, 153–4, 161.
96 Ibid., 229.
97 Ibid., 111.
98 Antonio Cazorla-Sánchez, *Fear and Progress: Ordinary Lives in Franco's Spain (1936–1975)* (Oxford, 2009).
99 Cazorla-Sanchez, *Las Políticas de la Victoria*.
100 Coupons owned by the author.
101 Peyrou and Cruz Romeo, "Mitos, símbolos y monumentos," 96–8.
102 The street was one of twenty-eight whose Francoist names were changed in 1981. http://elpais.com/diario/1983/06/22/madrid/425129061_850215.html.
103 Luis Miguel Aparisi Laporta, "Toponimia Madrileña. Proceso evolutivo," Ayuntamiento de Madrid (2001), 7; https://www.elmundo.es/madrid/2017/04/27/5901db7ae2704e52608b45c3.html.

104 José Varela Ortega, "Políticas de la Memoria: Desde la Transición y con la Reqapública," Fundación José Ortega y Gasset, Documento de Trabajo 2011/7, 9.
105 *El País*, 25 August 1979. This was one of almost 130 changes in street names in the city between 1979 and 1983. Of these, only 58 were directly related to the Civil War. Carballés, "La evolución de la memoria."
106 Archivo Municipal, Bilbao, http://www.bilbao.net/cs/Satellite/archivosMunicipales/Informacion-ampliada-de-la-busqueda/es/100123558,Contenido?asuntoBuscarGeneral=Espartero&cidPaginaPadre=100121284&codigoRef=462318&fechaDesde=1978&fechaHasta=2008; emphasis added.
107 Remesar Betlloch and Ricart Ulldemolins, "Estrategias de la Memoria."
108 http://www.lavanguardia.com/vida/20070307/51312223859/el-cambio-de-nombre-de-la-calle-del-duc-de-la-victoria-de-barcelona-enfrenta-a-vecinos-institucione.html,http://elpais.com/diario/2008/10/19/catalunya/1224378444_850215.html. On the concept of "heritage-scape," see Viejo-Rose, *Reconstructing Spain*.
109 http://www.aravalles.cat/noticia/64885/el-carrer-espartero-de-caldes-es-rebateja-a-com-a-george-lawrence-davis;http://protestantedigital.com/ciudades/27105/Pueblo_catalan_con_calle_para_misionero_protestante_gales.
110 *Diari de Tarragona*, 12 June 2013, http://diaridetarragona.com/noticia.php?id=14540.
111 http://mas-ediciones.e-noticies.es/garraf/vilanova-retira-el-nombre-de-tres-militares-espanoles-90471.html.
112 http://www.ccma.cat/tv3/alacarta/mes-324/entrevista-a-adrian-shubert/video/5632328/.
113 Francesc-Marc Alvaró, "El fantasma de Espartero," *La Vanguardia*, 28 September 2017.
114 https://www.abebooks.com/ikusager-ediciones%2C-s.a-vitoria-gasteiz/52914482/sf; Romanones, *Espartero*, editor's note.
115 Peyrou and Romeo, "Mitos, símbolos y monumentos," 99.
116 Boyd, "The Politics of History and Memory in Democratic Spain," 141; Ruiz Torres, "Political Uses of History in Spain."
117 http://www.pp.es/actualidad-noticia/pp-insta-al-gobierno-colaborar-difusion-figura-militar-politico-catalan-juan-prim;http://www.elconfidencialdigital.com/defensa/socialistas-catalanes-Defensa-General-Prim_0_2372762712.html.

Bibliography

Abbreviations

ACM	Archivos de la Comunidad de Madrid
AE	Espartero Archive, property of the Duque de la Victoria
AGN	Archivo General de la Nación, Buenos Aires
AGP	Archivo General, Palacio Real, Madrid
AGS	Archivo General de Simancas
AHCB	Arxiu Històric de la Ciutat de Barcelona
AHN	Archivo Histórico Nacional, Madrid
AHN-N	Archivo Histórico Nacional, Sección de Nobleza, Toledo
AHPR	Archivo Histórico de Protocolos de La Rioja
ARCM	Archivo Regional de la Comunodad de Madrid
BMVB	Biblioteca Museo Victor Balaguer
BP	Broadlands Papers, University of Southampton
DSC	*Diario de Sesiones de las Cortes*
DSCC	*Diario de Sesiones de las Cortes Constituyentes*
MS Clar	Clarendon Papers, Bodleian Library, University of Oxford
NA	National Archives, London
NARA	National Archives and Records Administration, Washington. DC
RAH	Real Academia de la Historia
WP	Wylde Papers, Durham University

Periodicals

ABC
La Academia
Altar y Trono
La América
La Antorcha

El Bien Público
Boletín Oficial de la Provincia de Logroño
Boletín Oficial de Segovia
La Campanya de Gracia
El Católico
El Clamor Público
El Conceller
El Constitucional
La Corona
El Correo Militar
La Correspondencia de España
El Corresponsal
La Crónica de Mallorca
Crónica Meridional
El Cronista
La Democracia
Diari Catalá
Diario Oficial de Avisos de Madrid
Diario de Barcelona
Diario de Madrid
Diario de Palencia
Diario de Sesiones de las Cortes
El Eco de Alicante
Eco del Comercio
La Época
El Español
La Esquella de Torratxa
El Federal Salmantino
Gaceta de Madrid
Gaceta Extraordinaria de Madrid
Gil Blas
El Globo
El Graduador
El Heraldo de Zamora
La Iberia
Illustrated London News
La Ilustración Española y Americana
El Imparcial
El Liberal
La Libertad
El Liberal
La Lucha

Madrid Cómico
Manchester Guardian
El Noticiero de Soria
Las Novedades
El Pabellón Nacional
El Padre Cobos
El País
El Pensamiento Alavés
El Requeté
La Rioja
El Sol
Solidadridad Obrera
The Times of London
El Tío Camorra
La Unión Católica
La Vanguardia
La Voz
El Zurrón del Pueblo

Books and Articles

Acontecimientos de Madrid: Diario de los sucesos ocurridos desde el día 11 de julio de 1843 hasta el 23 del mismo. Madrid, 1843.

Adriano. *Sucesos de Barcelona, desde 13 de noviembre de 1842 hasta 19 de febrero de 1843*. Barcelona, 1843.

Aguilar, P., and C. Ramírez-Barat. "Reparations without Truth or Justice in the Spanish Case." In N. Wouters, ed., *Transitional Justice after War and Dictatorship: Learning from European Experiences (1945–2000)*. Antwerp-Oxford, 2014.

Agulhon, Maurice. "La 'statuemanie' et l'histoire." *Ethnologie française* (1978): 145–72.

Albí, Julio. *Banderas olvidadas: el ejército realista en América*. Madrid, 1990.
— *El ultimo virrey*. Madrid, 2009.

Albornoz, Álvaro de. *El gobierno de los caudillos militares*. Madrid, 1930.

Alcalá Galiano, Antonio. *Memorias*. http://www.cervantesvirtual.com/obra/memorias-de-d-antonio-alcala-galiano-0.

Alegría, Ciro. "Entre Bolívar, Espartero y un Extra." In Estuardo Núñez, ed., *Bolívar, Ayacucho y los tradicionalistas peruanos*. Lima, 1974. 21–30.

Alonso, Cecilio. "Notas sobre prensa satírica e ilustración gráfica." *IC – Revista Científica de Información y Comunicación* (2015): 50–4.

Alonso, Gregorio. "Imaginando a Fernando VII, rey católico y felon." *Pasado y Memoria. Revista de Historia Contemporánea* 14 (2015): 57–77.

Alonso, Jesús Javier. "La formación de la elite liberal burguesa. Alianzas matrimoniales y desamortizaciones." *Brocar* 19 (1995): 211–32.
Alonso Rodríguez, Manuel. "Espartero y las relaciones comerciales hispano-británicos, 1840–1843." *Hispania* 165 (1985): 323–61.
Álvarez Junco, José. *Mater Dolorosa; la idea de España en el siglo XIX*. Madrid, 2001.
Alvarez Tardío, Manuel. "Historia y revolución en la cultura política de la izquierda republicana. El caso de Álvaro de Albornoz y los radical-socialistas." *Historia y Política* (2008): 175–200.
Álvarez Villamil, V. *Cartas de conspiradores. La Revolución de septiembre*. Madrid, 1929.
Andreu Miralles, Xavier. *El descubrimiento de Espana. Mito romántico e identidad nacional*. Madrid, 2016.
– "Nación, emoción y fantasía. La España melodramática de Ayguals de Izco." *Espacio Tiempo y Forma. Serie V, Historia Contemporánea* 29 (2017): 65–92.
– "El pueblo y sus opresores: populismo y nacionalismo en la cultura política del radicalismo democrático, 1844–1848." *Historia y Política* 25 (November 2015): 65–91.
Anguera, Pere. *El General Prim: Biografía de un conspirador*. Barcelona, 2003.
Anna, Timothy. *The Fall of the Royal Government in Peru*. Lincoln, 1979.
Aquillué Domínguez, Daniel. "El liberalismo en la encrucijada: Entre la revolución y la respetabilidad 1833–1843." PhD thesis, Universidad de Zaragoza, 2017.
– "La Violencia desde el liberalismo, 1833–1840." Ch. 5 in *Temas y Perspectivas de la Historia*. Salamanca, 2016.
Araña, Marie. *Bolívar: American Liberator*. New York, 2014.
Archilés i Cardona, Ferrán. "Hacer región es hacer patria. La región en el imaginario de la nación española de la Restauración." *Ayer* 64 (2006): 121–47.
Aresti, Nerea. "El ángel del hogar y sus demonios. Ciencia, religion y género en la España del siglo XIX." *Historia Contemporánea* (2000): 363–94.
Aróstegui, Julio, Jordi Canal, and Eduardo González Calleja. *El Carlismo y las guerras carlistas*. Madrid, 2003.
Artola, Miguel. *Los afrancesados*. Madrid, 1989.
Artola, Miguel, ed. *Las Cortes de Cádiz*. Madrid, 2003.
Aviraneta, Eugenio de. *Memoria dirigida al Gobierno español, sobre los planes y operaciones puestos en ejecución, para aniquilar la rebelión en las provincias del norte de España*. Toulouse, 1841.
Ayguals de Izco, Wenceslao. *La Marquesa de Bellaflor, o el niño de la Inclusa*. Madrid, 1847.
Azagra, Joaquín. *El bienio, progresista en Valencia: análisis de una situación revolucionaria a mediados del siglo XIX (1854-1856)*. Valencia, 1978.
Bacon, John Francis. *Six Years in Biscay: Comprising a Personal Narrative of the Sieges of Bilbao, in June 1835, and Oct. to Dec., 1836*. London, 1838.

Balaguer, Victor. *La Libertad Constitucional. Estudios Políticos*. Barcelona, 1858.
Balmes, Jaime. "Espartero." In *Biografías. Obras completas*. Barcelona, 1925.
Banti, Alberto Maria. "The Remembrance of Heroes." In Silvana Patriarca and Lucy Riall, eds., *The Risorgimento Revisited*. London, 2012. 171–90.
Bellogín, Angel. "Historia Contemporánea. La Gloriosa de Valladolid." In Rafael Serrano García, ed., *La Revolución Liberal en Valladolid (1808–1868)*. Valladolid, 1993.
Benet, J., and C. Martí. *Barcelona a mitjan segle XIX*. Barcelona, 1976.
Berbel, Marcia Regina. "A Constitucicao Espanhola no Mundo Luso-Americano (1820–1823)." *Revista de Indias* (2008): 225–54.
Berenson, Edward. "Charisma and the Making of Imperial Heroes in Britain and France, 1880–1914." In Berenson and Giloi, *Constructing Charisma: Celebrity, Fame, and Power in Nineteenth-Century Europe*. New York, 2010.
Berenson, Edward, and Eva Giloi. Introduction. *Constructing Charisma: Celebrity, Fame, and Power in Nineteenth-Century Europe*. New York, 2010.
Bermejo, Ildefonso Antonio. *La Estafeta de Palacio, historia del último reinado; cartas trascendentales dirigidas al rey Amadeo*. Madrid, 1872.
– *Historia de la interinidad y guerra civil de España desde 1868*. Madrid, 1875.
Bermejo Martín, Francisco. *Espartero. Hacendado riojano*. Logroño, 2000.
Boix, Vicente. *Historia de la ciudad y reino de Valencia*. Valencia, 1845–7.
– *Xátiva: memorias, recuerdos y tradiciones de esta antigua ciudad*. Xativa, 1857.
Bolaños Mejías, Carmen. *El Reinado de Amadeo de Saboya y la Monarquía Constitucional*. Madrid, 1999.
Boletín Extraordinario del Ejército Nacional de Operaciones al Sur de Arequipa. 1823.
Borao, Gerónimo. *Historia del Alzamiento de Zaragoza en 1854*. Zaragoza, 1855.
Borrell Merlín, María Dolores. "Historia y Cultura del Rioja: El Marqués de Murrieta." *Berceo* 150 (2006): 169–88.
Botrel, Jean François. "Les 'Historias de Colportage': Essai de catalogue d'une Bibliotèque Bleue espagnole (1840–1936)." In *Les Productions Populaires en Espagne, 1850–1920: Colloque organisé par Pyrenaïca, Faculté des lettres, Université de Pau et des pays de l'Adour*. Paris, 1986. 25–62.
– "Las historias de cordel y la historia del tiempo presente en la España del siglo XIX." In *Roman populaire et/ou roman historique*. Lleida, 1999.
Boyd, Carolyn. "Un lugar de memoria olvidado." *Historia y Política* 12 (2004): 15–40.
– "The Politics of History and Memory in Democratic Spain." *Annals of the Academy of Political and Social Science* 617 (May 2008).
Breña, Roberto. *El imperio de las circunstancias (Las independencias hispanoamericanas y la revolución liberal española)*. Madrid/Mexico City, 2013.
– *El primer liberalismo español y los procesos de emancipación de América, 1808–1824: Una revisión historiográfica del liberalismo hispánico*. Mexico City, 2006.
Breña, Roberto, ed. *Cádiz a debate: actualidad, contexto, legado*, Mexico City, 2014.

Brett, Edward. *The British Auxiliary Legion in the First Carlist War 1835–1838: A Forgotten Army*. Dublin, 2005.
Bullen, Roger. "France and the Problem of Intervention in Spain, 1834–1836." *Historical Journal* (June 1977): 363–93.
Bullen, Roger, and Felicity Strong, eds. *Palmerston*. London, 1985.
Bullón de Mendoza, Alfonso. *La Expedición de Gómez*. Madrid, 1984.
– *La Expedición Real: auge y ocaso de don Carlos*. Madrid, 1986.
– *La primera guerra carlista*. Madrid, 1992.
Burdiel, Isabel. *Isabel II. No se puede reinar inocentemente*. Madrid, 2004.
– *Isabel II. Una biografía*. Madrid, 2011.
– "Historia política y biografía: más allá de las fronteras." *Ayer* 93 (2014): 47–83.
– "Monarquía y nación en la cultura política progresista. La encrucijada de 1854." In *Culturas políticas monárquicas en la España liberal. Discursos, representaciones y prácticas (1808–1902)*. Valencia, 2013. 213–32.
– *La Política de los Notables. Moderados y Avanzados durante el Régimen de la Estátua Real*. Valencia, 1987.
Burdiel, Isabel, and Roy Foster, eds. *La Historia Biográfica en Europa*. Zaragoza, 2015.
Burguera, Mónica. *Las Damas del Liberalismo Respetable*. Valencia, 2012.
– "Mujeres y revolución liberal en perspectiva. Esfera pública y ciudadanía feminina en la primera mitad del siglo XIX en Espana." In Encarnación García Monerris, Ivana Frasquet, and Carmen García Monerris, eds., *Cuando todo era posible: liberalismo y antiliberalismo en España e Hispanoamérica (1740–1842)*. Madid, 2016. 257–96.
Buxeres, Antonio. *Barcelona en julio de 1840: sucesos de este periodo*. Barcelona, 1844.
Caballé, Anna. "La biografía en España: primera propuesta para la contrucción de un cánon." In I. Burdiel and R. Foster, eds., *La Historia Biográfica en Europa*. Zaragoza, 2015. 89–118.
Caillet-Bois, Ricardo. *La mission Pereyra-La Robla al Rio de la Plata y la convención preliminar de paz del 4 de Julio de 1823*. Buenos Aires, 1940.
Calderón de la Barca, Fanny. *The Attaché in Madrid*. New York, 1856.
Callahan, William J. *Church, Politics and Society in Spain, 1750–1874*. Cambridge, 2014)
Canal, Jordi. *El Carlismo*. Madrid, 2000.
– *El Carlismo. Dos siglos de contrarrevolución en España*. Madrid, 2004.
– "La primera guerra carlista." In Aróstegui, Canal, and González Calleja, *El Carlismo y las guerras carlistas*. Madrid, 2003.
Cañas de Pablo, Alberto. "Espartero y Prim, o cómo España buscó su 'Capitán del Siglo.'" *Revista Historia Autónoma* 7 (2015): 67–82.
– "Personificando la Revolución de 1840 y su llegada a la Regencia." *Vínculos de Historia* 5 (2016): 270–89.

Carballés, Jesús Alonso. "La evolución de la memoria de la Guerra Civil en el espacio urbano de Bilbao: una mirada comparativa." *Cahiers de civilisation espagnole contemporaine. De 1808 au temps present* (Autumn 2009). http://ccec.revues.org/3000.

Cardeñosa y Mir, Alejandro. *Vida militar y política de Espartero*. Barcelona, 1846.

Carrillo, Victor. "Marketing et edition au XIXe siècle." In *L'Infra-Litterature en Espagne aux XIXe et XXe siècles*. Grenoble, 1977.

Castelar, Emilio. *Discursos parlamentarios de Don Emilio Castelar en la Asamblea Constiuytente*. Madrid, 1877.

Castells, Luis. "Celebremos lo local, celebremos lo nacional. Política estatuaria en el País Vasco, 1860–1923)." In *Procesos de nacionalización en la España contemporánea*. Salamanca, 2010. 355–78.

Castro, Demetrio. *Los males de la imprenta*. Madrid, 1998.

Cazorla-Sánchez, Antonio. *Franco. La biografía del mito*. Madrid, 2016.

– *Las Políticas de la Victoria: la consolidación del Nuevo Estado franquista, 1938–1953*. Madrid, 2000.

Censo de Floridablanca. Madrid, 1986.

Cepeda Gómez, José. "Don Manuel de Mazarredo y Mazzaredo: la sombra de Narváez," *Revista de la Universidad Complutense* (1979): 77–104.

– "El general Espartero durante la 'década ominosa' y su colaboración con la política represiva de Fernando VII." *Cuadernos de historia moderna y contemporánea* (1981): 147–64.

– *Los pronunciamientos en la España del siglo xix*. Madrid, 1999.

Chambers, Sarah C. *From Subjects to Citizens: Honor, Gender and Politics in Arequipa, Peru, 1780–1854*. University Park, 1999.

Chao, Eduardo. *Espartero. Páginas contemporáneas escritas por él mismo*. Madrid, 1846.

Chasteen, John C. *Americanos: Latin America's Struggle for Independence*. New York, 2008.

Christiansen, Eric. *The Origins of Military Power in Spain, 1800–1854*. Oxford, 1967.

Chust, Manuel. "Héroes para la nación." In Victor Mínguez and Manuel Chust, eds., *La construcción del héroe en España y Mexico (1789–1847)*. Valencia, 2003.

Clonard, Conde de. *Memoria histórica de las academias militares de España*. Madrid, 1847.

Condori, José Victor. "Guerra y economía en Arequipa: las actividades del español Lucas de la Cotera en una coyuntura de crisis, 1821–1824." *Revista de Indias* 71, no. 253 (2011): 827–58.

– "Lucas de Cotera: Financista del Gobierno Virreinal 1821–1824," *Revista de Indias* 71 (2011): 109–23.

Contestación a un papel que circula impreso bajo el titulo de Dictamen que dió el Excmo Sr. D. Baldomero Espartero, comandante general de las provincias

Vascongadas al Excmo. Sr. general en gefe de los ejército de operaciones y de reserva. Madrid, 1836.
Convenio de Vergara y confirmación y modificación de los fueros de Navarra decretadas por las Cortes. Madrid, 1841.
Coroleu, José. *Memorias de un menestral de Barcelona, 1792–1854*. Barcelona, 1916.
Corrales, Laura. "L'estampa i la primera guerra carlina a Catalunya (1833–1840)." PhD thesis, Universitat Autònoma de Barcelona, 2014.
Cortés, Alonso. *Juan Martínez Villergas bosquejo biográfico-crítico*. Valladolid, 1910.
Costello, Edward. *Memoirs of a Soldier*. London, 1841.
Coverdale, John. *The Basque Phase of Spain's First Carlist War*. Princeton, 1984.
Dardé, Carlos. "Los partidos y la vida política, 1836–1868." In Dardé, ed., *Liberalismo y romanticismo en tiempos de Isabel II*. Madrid, 2004.
de Felipe, Jesús. *Trabajadores, lenguaje y experiencia en la formación del movimiento obrero español*. Ciudad Real, 2012.
de la Fuente Monge, Gregorio. "La figura del general Espartero en el teatro decimonónico." *Historia y Política* 29 (2013): 103–38.
– *Los revolucionarios de 1868*. Madrid, 2000.
de la Pezuela, Joaquín. *Memoria de gobierno*. Seville, 1947.
de Torija y Carresse, Antonio. *El guirigay, los ministros y Espartero*. Madrid, 1839.
Delgado, José. *Relato official de la meritísima expedición carlista dirigida por el general andaluz, don Miguel Gómez*. San Sebastián, 1943.
Dérozier, Claucette. "La caricatura en la prensa satírica ilustrada de la regencia de Espartero: *El cangrejo* (1841), *La posdata* (1842–43), *Guindilla* (1842–43)." In Jean-René Aymes, Albert Dérozier, et al., eds., *Revisión de Larra: ¿protesta o revolución?* Paris, 1983. 117–32.
Díaz Marín, Pedro. "La construcción política de Espartero antes de su Regencia, 1837–1840." *Cuadernos de Ilustración y Romanticismo*, no. 14 (2006): 301–27.
– "Espartero: el regente plebeyo." In Emilio la Parra López, ed., *La imagen del poder*. Madrid, 2011. 177–209.
– "Espartero en entredicho. La ruina de su imagen en las elecciones de 1843." *Ayer*, no. 72 (2008): 185–214.
– *La Monarquía tutelada. El progresismo durante la Regencia de Espartero (1840–1843)*. Alicante, 2015.
Dichos y opiniones de Espartero en conversación con sus amigos. Madrid, 1868.
D.M.H. y D.J.L. *Espartero, su vida militar, política, descriptiva y anecdótica*. Madrid, 1863.
Doña Jacinta y Sinforosa. *La Mujer en el S. XIX*. Logroño, 2015.
Donoso García, Santiago. *Baldomero Espartero*. Granátula, 2009.

- *Iglesia Parroquial de Santa Ana*. Granátula, 2004. http://oretum.es/iglesia/iglesia.pdf.
Duncan, Francis. *The English in Spain, or, the Story of the War of Succession between 1834 and 1840*. London, 1877.
Durston, Alan. "Quechua Political Literature in Early Republican Peru (1810–1876)." In Paul Heggarty and Adrian J. Pearce, eds., *History and Language in the Andes*. New York, 2011. 165–86.
Echaide, Martín. *Reseña histórica sobre los preliminaries del Convenio de Vergara*. Madrid, 1846.
Elogio fúnebre que en las solemnes exeqias [sic.] celebradas por la M.H. villa de Madrid en la Iglesia de San Isidro el día 5 de Febrero de 1837, a la digna memoria de las esclarecidas víctimas sacrificadas por la patria en la inmortal Bilbao en los tres memorables sitios. Madrid, 1837.
Elogio fúnebre que … en sufragio de los valientes del ejército, guarnición de Bilbao y milicia nacional que han perecido en su último y glorioso sitio … el dia 5 de Febrero de 1837. Zaragoza, 1837.
Epistolario militar de la primera guerra civil carlista. Madrid, 1950–2.
Esdaile, Charles. *Outpost of Empire: The Napoleonic Occupation of Andalucia, 1810–1812*. Norman, 2012.
– *The Peninsular War: A New History*. London, 2003.
Espartero, Baldomero. *Exposición del General D. Baldomero Espartero, Conde de Luchana a S.M. la reina, respecto de los sucesos producidos en Sevilla, con presencia del teniente general D. Luis Fernández de Córdova*. Madrid, 1838.
– *El Regente del Reino a las Españoles*. Madrid, 1843.
– *Representación elevada a S.M. por el Escmo. Señor Conde de Luchana … a consecuencia de la Real Orden de 23 de octubre, por la que se determina la organización de un egército de reserva de cuarenta mil hombres*. Madrid, 1838.
Espartero. Études biographiques nécessaires à l'intelligence des faits qui ont préparé et déterminé la dernière révolution d'Espagne. Paris, 1841.
Espartero. Su pasado, su presente, su porvenir. Madrid, 1848.
Espina, Antonio. *Espartero, o ¡Cúmplase la voluntad nacional!* Madrid, 1949.
Estado Mayor General del Ejército Español: historia del ilustre Cuerpo de Oficiales Generales, hechas con las biografías de los que más se han distinguido e ilustrada con sus retratos de cuerpo entero. Madrid, 1851–4.
Estevánez, Nicolás. *Fragmentos de mis memorias*. Madrid, 1903.
Evans, Luis de. *Memorias sobre la Guerra de Navarra*. Barcelona, 1837.
Ezquerra del Bayo, Joaquín. *Retratos de Mujeres Españolas del Siglo XIX*. Madrid, 1924.
Fernández Cuenca, Carlos. *Espartero*. Madrid, 1932.
Fernández de Córdova, Fernando. *Memoria justificativa que dirige a sus conciudadanos el general Córdova en vindicación de los cargos que por la prensa*

nacional y extrangera se han hecho a su conducta militar ó política en el mando de los ejércitos de operaciones y de reserva. Paris, 1837.
— Mis memorias íntimas. Madrid, 1889.
Fernández de los Ríos, Angel. *1808–1863. Olózaga.* Madrid, 1863.
— *Estudio histórico de las luchas políticas en la España del Siglo XIX.* Madrid, 1864.
Fernández García, María de la Soledad. "Universidad de Almagro: enfrentamiento por la forma de proveer las cátedras." *Cuadernos de estudios manchegos* (1989): 213–26.
Fernández Mirez, Rafael. "La forja del rey conciliador: Alfonso XII bajo el prisma de *La Época* y *La Ilustración Española y Hispanoamericana.*" In José Antonio Caballero López et al., eds., *Entre Olózaga y Sagasta.* Logroño, 2011. 355–70.
Ferrer, Melchor. *Historia del tradicionalismo español.* Seville, 1943.
Fisher, John R. "The Royalist Regime in the Viceroyalty of Peru, 1820–1824." *Journal of Latin American Studies* 32, no. 1 (2000): 55–84.
Florez, José Segundo. *Espartero: historia de su vida militar y política y de los grandes sucesos contemporaneous.* Madrid, 1844.
Ford, Richard. *Letters to Gayangos.* Exeter, 1974.
Fradera, Josep María. *Cultura nacional en una sociedad dividida.* Madrid, 2003.
Fraser, Ronald. *Napoleon's Cursed War: Spanish Popular Resistance in the Peninsular War, 1808–1814.* London, 2008.
Fuentes Aragonés, Juan Francisco. "Afrancesados y liberales." In Jordi Canal, ed., *Exilios: los éxodos políticos en la historia de España: siglos XV–XX.* Madrid, 2007. 137–66.
Galería Militar Contemporánea. Madrid, 1846.
Gallego Franco, Henar, and Mónica Bolufer Peruga, eds. *¿Y ahora qué? nuevos usos del género biográfico.* Barcelona, 2016.
Gárate Ojanguren, Montserrat. "Financial Circuits in Spain: Merchants and Bankers, 1700–1914." In Alice Teichova, Ginette Kurgan-van Hentenryk, and Dieter Ziegler, eds., *Banking, Trade and Industry: Europe, America and Asia from the Thirteenth to the Twentieth Century.* Cambridge, 1997. 69–88.
García Balañà, Albert. "À la recherche du *Sexenio Democrático* (1868–1874) dans l'Espagne contemporaine. Chrononymies, politiques de l'histoire et historiographies." *Revue d'histoire du XIXe siècle* 52 (2016): 81–101.
— *La Fabricació de la fàbrica.* Igualada, 2004.
— "Patria, plebe y política en la España isabelina: la Guerra de África en Cataluña, (1859–1860)." In E. Martín Corrales, ed., *Marruecos y el Colonialismo Español 1859–1912.* Barcelona, 2002. 13–77.
— "El primer Balaguer o la temptativa populista a la Catalunya liberal (1859–1869)." *L'Avenç* 262 (2001): 36–41.
García Camba, Andrés. *Memorias para la historia de las armas españolas en el Perú.* Madrid, 1846.

García de Paso García, Ignacio. "El 1848 español. Una excepción europea?" *Ayer* 106 (2017): 185–206.
García Gutiérrez, Antonio. *El Sitio de Bilbao. drama de circunstancias en dos actos, en prosa y verso*. Madrid, 1837.
García Rovira, Anna Maria. "Eugenio de Aviraneta e Ibargoyen (1792–1872). El paroxismo de la conspiración." In Isabel Burdiel and Manuel Pérez Ledesma, eds., *Liberales, agitadores y conspiradores. Biografías heterodoxas del siglo XIX*. Madrid, 2000.
– *La revolucio liberal a Espanya i les classes populars (1832–1835)*. Barcelona, 1989.
García Ruiz, Eugenio. *Historias*. Madrid, 1878.
Garrido, Fernando. *Espartero y la revolución*. Madrid, 1854.
– *Historia del reinado del último Borbón de España*. Barcelona, 1869.
– *El Pueblo y el trono*. Madrid, 1854.
Garrido Muro, Luis. *Guerra y paz. Espartero durante la regencia de María Cristina de Borbón*. Madrid, 2016.
– "El Nuevo Cid. Espartero, María Cristina y el primer liberalismo español (1834–1840)." PhD thesis, University of Cantabria, 2016.
Gil Novales, Alberto. *El trieno liberal*. Madrid, 1980.
Glorias de Azara en el Siglo XIX. Madrid, 1854.
Great Britain, *Foreign and State Papers*. London, various years.
Gracia Albacar, Mariano. *Memorias de un zaragozano*. Zaragoza, 2013.
Gueniffey, Patrice. *Bonaparte*. Cambridge, 2015.
Haigh, Samuel. *Sketches of Buenos Ayres, Chile, and Peru*. London, 1831.
Haverty, Martin. *Wanderings in Spain*. London, 1847.
Higueras Castañeda, Eduardo. *Con los Borbones, jamás. Biografía de Manuel Ruiz Zorrilla (1833–1895)*. Madrid, 2016.
Historia del General Baldomero Espartero, Duque de la Victoria y de Morella. Madrid, 1851.
Hoja de Servicios del Duque de la Victoria y Morella. Madrid, 1852.
Hoja de servicios del Excmo. Sr. Capitán General D. Baldomero Espartero, Duque de la Victoria y de Morella. Madrid, 1861.
Hortelano, Benito. *Memorias*. Madrid, 1936.
Ibo Alfaro, Manuel. *Historia de la interinidad española*. Madrid, 1872.
The Illustrated Letters of Richard Doyle to His Father, 1842–1843. Columbus, 2016.
Inarejos Muñóz, Juan Antonio. "El aura del general Espartero. Construcción, deconstrucción y apropiación de los perfiles carismáticos de un prohombre." *Historia y Política* 30 (2013): 205–23.
– *La revolución de 1854 en la España rural*. Ciudad Real, 2010.
Irving, Washington. *Letters*. Boston, 1982.
Izquierdo Navarrete, José, et al. *La Academia General Militar*. Zaragoza, 2002.
Kiernan, Victor. *La revolución de 1854 en España*. Madrid, 1970.

- *The Revolution of 1854*. Oxford, 1966.
Koontz, Stephanie. *Marriage: A History*. New York, 2006.
Lafuente, Modesto. *Historia general desde los tiempos primitivos hasta la muerte de Fernando VII por Modesto Lafuente, continuada desde dicha epoca hasta nuestros dias por Juan Valera*. Madrid, 1869.
Lanza Ruedas, Jesús, ed. *Baldomero Espartero. Granátula de Calatrava, el pueblo que le vió nacer*. Ciudad Real, 2005.
La Parra, Emilio. *Los Cien Mil Hijos de San Luis. el ocaso del primer impulso liberal en España*. Madrid, 2007.
- *Fernando VII: Un rey deseado y detestado*. Barcelona, 2018.
- *Manuel Godoy. la aventura del poder*. Barcelona, 2002.
- "La restauración de Fernando VII en 1814." *Historia Constitucional*, no. 15 (2014): 205–22. http://www.historiaconstitucional.com.
Lario, Ángeles. "La monarquía de Isabel II y el liberalismo post-revolucionario. Una necesaria renovación historiográfica," *Ayer* 56 (2004): 271–82.
Lawrence, Mark. *Spain's First Carlist War*. London, 2014.
- *The Spanish Civil Wars*. London, 2017.
Lázaro Torres, Rosa María. "La fortuna de Espartero." *Aportes* 30, no. 1 (1996): 62–77.
Leerson, Joep. "When Was Romantic Nationalism? The Onset, the Long Tail, the Banal." *NISE Essays* 2 (2014). http://nise.eu/news/new-publication-on-romantic-nationalism/.
Lilti, Antoine. *Figures publiques. L'invention de la célébrité (1750–1850)*. Paris, 2014.
López, Joaquín Maria. *Exposicion razonada de los principales sucesos políticos que tuvieron lugar*. Madrid, 1845.
López, María Isabel. *El General Infante: un Liberal Español en Bolivia*. Cáceres, 2010.
López Alós, Javier. "Ensayo sobre los afranceados." In Antonio Rivera García and José Luis Villacañas Berlanga, eds., *Gonzalo Díaz y el archivo de la filosofía Española*. Murcia, 2013. 123–210.
Luengo, Jorge. "Las élites liberales en la España del siglo XIX: entre biografía, prosografía y redes." In Burdiel and Foster, eds., *La Historia Biográfica en Europa*, 219–40.
- *Una sociedad conyugal. Las élites de Valladolid en el espejo de Madeburgo en el siglo XIX*. Valencia, 2014.
Lynch, John. *San Martín: Argentine Soldier, American Hero*. New Haven, 2009.
- *Simon Bolivar: A Life*. London, 2006.
- *The Spanish American Revolutions, 1808–1826*. New York, 1986.
Lyttleton, Adrian. "The Hero and the People." In Silvana Patriarca and Lucy Riall, eds., *The Risorgimento Revisited* (London, 2012).
Marcuello Benedicto, Juan Ignacio. *La Práctica Parlamentaria en el reinado de Isabel II*. Madrid, 1986.

Marks, Patricia. *Deconstructing Legitimacy: Viceroys, Merchants and the Military in Late Colonial Peru*. University Park, 2007.
Marliani, Manuel. *La Regencia de Espartero, conde Luchana, duque de la Victoria y de Morella, y sucesos que la prepararon*. Madrid, 1870.
Martín Arranz, Raul. "Espartero: Figuras de legitimidad." In José Álvarez Junco, ed., *Populismo, caudillaje y discurso demagógico*. Madrid, 1988. 101–28.
– *Galdós y Espartero. La huella en los Episodios Nacionales*. Madrid, 2014.
Martínez Baeza, Sergio. *Vida del General Juan Gregorio de las Heras*. Buenos Aires, 2009.
Martínez Gallego, Francesc A. "Democracia y república en la España isabelina: el caso de Ayguals de Izco." In Manuel Chust, ed., *Federalismo y Cuestión Federal en España*. Castellón, 2004. 45–90.
Martínez Moreno, Silvia. "El Espolón de Logroño: pasado y presente." In Blanca Fernández and Jesús-Pedro Lorente, eds., *Arte en el espacio público*. Zaragoza, 2009.
Martínez Riaza, Ascensión. "'Para Reintegrar la Nación': el Perú en la política negociadora del Trienio Liberal con los disidentes Americanos, 1820–1824." *Revista de Indias* (2011): 647–91.
– "El peso de la ley. la política hacia los españoles en la independencia del Perú (1820–1826)." *Procesos: revista ecuatoriana de historia* 42 (2015): 65–97.
Mendiburu, Manuel de. *Diccionario historico-biografico del Peru*. Lima, 1887.
Michonneau, Stéphane. *Barcelone: Mémoire et identité 1830–1930*. Rennes, 2007.
Millán, Jesús. "Els militants carlins del País Valencià central. Una aproximació a la sociologia del carlisme durant la revolució burgesa." *Recerques* 21 (1988): 101–23.
Millán, Jesús, and María Cruz Romeo. "Iglesia y religión en el liberalismo anterior a la sociedad de masaas." In S. Calatayud, J. Millán, and M.C. Romeo, eds., *El Estado desde la Sociedad*. Alicante, 2016. 149–83.
– "La Nación Católica en el Liberalismo. Las Perspectivas sobre la Unidad Religiosa en la España Liberal, 1808–1868." *Historia y Política* 34 (July–December 2015): 183–209.
Millán García, J.R. *Sagasta, o el arte de hacer la polítca*. Madrid, 2001.
Mina, Juana Vega de. *Apuntes para la historia del tiempo en que se ocupó los destinos de Aya de S. M. y A. y camarera mayor de palacio*. Madrid, 1910.
Mínguez, Raúl. *Evas, Marías y Magdalenas. Género y modernidad católica en la España liberal (1833–1874)*. Madrid, 2016.
Miraflores, Marquis of. *Memorias para escribir la historia contemporánea de los siete primeros años del reinado de Isabel II*. Madrid, 1843–4.
Miranda Calvo, José. "La Universidad de Toledo en 1808: el Batallón de Voluntarios Universitarios y la preimera Academia Militar." *Militaria. Revista de Cultura Militar* (1989): 39–56.

Molina, Fernando, and Miguel Cabo Villaverde. "An Inconvenient Nation: Nation Building and National Identity in Modern Spain: The Historiographical Debate." In Marten Van Ginderachter and Marnic Beyen, eds., *Nationhood from Below: Europe in the Long Nineteenth Century*. London, 2012. 47–72.
Moliner Prada, Antonio. "Anticlericalismo y revolución liberal." In Emilio La Parra and Manuel Suárez Cortina, eds., *El anticlericalismo español contemporáneo*. Madrid, 1998.
Monerri Molina Beatriz. "Las Cortes del Estatuto Real (1834–1836)." PhD thesis, Universidad Complutense de Madrid, 2017.
Morayta, Miguel. *Historia general de España, desde los tiempos antehistóricos hasta nuestros días*. Madrid, 1886–96.
Moreno Luzón, Javier. *Romanones, caciquismo y política liberal*. Madrid, 1988.
Moreno Luzón, Javier, and Xosé M. Núñez Seixas. *Los colores de la patria*. Madrid, 2017.
Muñoz López, Pilar. *Sangre, amor e interés*. Madrid, 2001.
Napier, William. *History of the War in the Peninsula*. New York, 1882.
Nido y Segalerva, Juan de. *Historia política y parlamentaria de S.A. D. Baldomero Fernández Espartero*. Madrid, 1916.
Nombela, Julio. *Impresiones y recuerdos*. Madrid, 1909.
Núñez Muñoz, María F. *El Bienio progresista y la ruptura de relaciones de Roma con España*. Madrid, 1993.
Núñez Seixas, Xosé Manoel. *Fuera el invasor: nacionalismos y movilización bélica durante la Guerra civil Española*. Madrid, 2006.
Ollero Vallés, José Luis. *Sagasta, de conspirador a gobernante*. Madrid, 2006.
Oman, Charles. *A History of the Peninsular War*. London, 1908.
Oración fúnebre . . que dijo el Dr. D. Miguel Moragues. Palma, 1837.
Palomas i Moncholí, J. *Victor Balaguer. Renaixença, Revolució y Progrès*. Vilanova i la Geltrú, 2004.
Papers Relating to Lord Eliot's Mission to Spain in the Spring of 1835. London, 1871.
Paredes Alonso, Francisco Javier. *Pascual Madoz, 1805–1870*. Pamplona, 1982.
Pareja de Alarcón, Francisco. *El abrazo de Vergara: reflexiones sobre la pasada revolución y la paz que se nos acerca*. Madrid, 1839.
Parry, E. Jones. *The Spanish Marriages, 1841–1846: A Study of the Influence of Dynastic Ambition upon Foreign Policy*. London, 1936.
Pastor Díaz, Nicomedes. *Galería de Españoles Célebres*. Madrid, 1844.
Patriarca, Silvana, and Lucy Riall, eds. *The Risorgimento Revisited*. London, 2012.
Peiró Martín, Ignacio. *En los altares de la patria*. Madrid, 2017.
Pérez Galdós, Benito. *Cádiz*. Madrid, 2010.
Pérez Garzón, Juan Sisinio. *Las Cortes de Cádiz*. Madrid, 2007.
– *Milicia Nacional y Revolución Burguesa*. Madrid, 1978.

Pérez Núñez, Javier. "Los amigos de Espartero: La construcción de la red de los Ayacuchos." *Ayer* 105 (2017): 77–102.
– "1839: Madrid ante los Fueros Vascos." In *El Poder de la Historia: Huella y legado de Javier Ma Donézar de Ulzurrun*. Madrid, 2014.
– "La revolución de 1840: la culminación de la Madrid Progresista." *Cuadernos de Historia Contemporánea* 36 (November 2014): 141–64.
Peyrou, Florencia. "Familia y Política. Masculinidad y Feminidad en el Discurso Democrático Isabelino," *Historia y Política* 25 (January–June 2011): 149–74.
– "A Great Family of Sovereign Men: Democratic Discourse in Nineteenth-Century Spain." *European History Quarterly* 43 (2013): 235–56.
– *Tribunos del pueblo. Demócratas y republicanos en el period isabelino*. Madrid, 2008.
Peyrou, Florencia, and María Cruz Romeo. "Mitos, símbolos y monumentos de la memoria de la españa liberal en el Siglo XX." In Ismael Saz and Ferrán Archilés, eds., *La Nación de los españoles*. Valencia, 2012.
Piñeiro, A.A. *Las Heras, Espartero y la paz con España*. Buenos Aires, 1957.
Pirala, Antonio. *Historia contemporánea: Anales desde 1843*. Madrid, 1875–9.
– *Historia de la Guerra Civil y de los partidos Liberal y Carlista, aumentada con la Regencia de Espartero*. Madrid, 1891.
– *Historia del Convenio de Vergara: artículo publicado en la Enciclopedia Moderna del señor Mellado*. Madrid, 1852.
– *El Rey en Madrid y en provincias*. Madrid, 1872.
Poco Mas. *Scenes and Adventures in Spain*. London, 1845.
Pro Ruiz, Juan. *Bravo Murillo: política de orden en la España liberal*. Madrid, 2006.
– *El Estatuto Real y la Constitución de 1837*. Madrid, 2010.
Puell de la Villa, Fernando. *Historia del ejército en España*. Madrid, 2000.
Puigdollers, Bernat. "Pau Gibert i Roig, un escultor oblidat." *Butlletí de la Reial Acadèmia Catalana de Belles Arts de Sant Jordi* 26 (2012): 97–116.
Rebelión de Aznapuquio por varios jefes del ejército español. Rio de Janeiro, 1821.
Reclus, Elie. *Impresiones, de un viaje por España en tiempos de Revolución: Del 26 de octubre de 1868 al 10 de marzo de 1869, en el advenimiento e la República*. Logroño, 2007.
Remesar Betlloch, Antoni, and Núria Ricart Ulldemolins. "Estrategias de la Memoria. Barcelona, 1977–2013." *Scripta Nova* (November 2014). http://www.ub.edu/geocrit/sn/sn-495.htm#_edn1.
Reseña historica del último sitio y defensa de Bilbao, con pormenores muy interesantes: sobre los memorables acontecimientos ocurridos en los dos meses que ha durado. Madrid, nd.
Reyero, Carlos. "El reconocimiento de la nación en la historia. El uso espacio-temporal de pinturas y monumentos en España." *Arbor* 135, no. 740 (2009).
– "Sevilla y las políticas de propaganda visual durante la regencia de Espartero." *Laboratorio del Arte* 25 (2013): 701–14.
Riall, Lucy. *Garibaldi: Invention of a Hero*. New Haven, 2005.

- "Travel, Migration, Exile: Garibaldi's Global Fame." *Modern Italy* (February 2014): 41–52.
Richardson, John. *Journal of the Movements of the British Legion*. London, 1837.
Río Aldaz, Ramón del. "Peseteros y radicales, el asesinato de Sarsfield en agosto de 1837 en Pamplona." *Hispania* 57, no. 195 (1997): 183–211.
Riquer i Permanyer, Borja de. "La débil nacionalización española del siglo XIX." *Historia Social* 20 (1994): 97–114.
Risques, Manuel J. "La insurrecció de Barcelona pel novembre de 1842." *Recerques* 10 (1982).
Rivas, Natalio. "Un asistente de Espartero." *ABC*, 30 June 1944.
Roca, José Luis. *Ni con Lima, ni con Buenos Aires: la formación de un estado nacional en Charcas*. La Paz, 2007.
Roca Vernet, Jordi. "Fiestas cívicas en la Revolución Liberal: entusiasmo y popularidad del régimen." *Historia Social* 86 (2016): 71–90.
Rodriguez, Moises. *Under the Flags of Freedom: British Mercenaries in the War of the Two Brothers, the First Carlist War and the Greek War of Independence (1821–1840)*. Lanham, 2009.
Rodríguez Marcos, Javier. "La hora de la biografía." *El País*, 4 April 2012.
Rodríguez O, Jaime, ed. *Las Nuevas Naciones: España y México, 1800–1850*. Madrid, 2008.
Romanones, Conde de. *Espartero. El General del Pueblo*. Vitoria, 2007.
Romea Castro, Celia. *Barcelona romántica y revolucionaria. Una imagen literaria de la ciudad (1833-1843)*. Barcelona, 1994.
Romeo Mateo, María Cruz. "De patricios y nación. Los valores de la política liberal en la España de mediados del siglo XIX." *Mélanges de la Casa de Velasquez* 35, no. 1 (2005): 119–41.
- "Domesticidad y Política. Las Relaciones de Género en la Sociedad Posrevolucionaria." In María Cruz Romeo and María Sierra, eds., *La España Liberal* Madrid, 2014. 89–127.
- "Joaquín María López. un tribuno republicano en el liberalismo." In Javier Moreno Luzon, ed., *Progresistas: biografías de reformistas españoles: (1808–1939)*. Madrid 2006. 59–98.
- "Juana de la Vega, Condesa de Espoz y Mina." In Adrian Shubert and José Álvarez Junco, eds., *The History of Modern Spain*. London, 2018.
- "Juana María de la Vega, Condesa de Espoz y Mina (1805–1872): por amor al esposo, o por amor a la patria." In Isabel Burdiel and Manuel Pérez Ledesma, eds., *Liberales, agitadores y conspiradores*. Madrid, 2000. 209–38.
- "Memoria y política en el liberalismo progresista." *Historia y política: Ideas, procesos y movimientos sociales* 17 (2007): 69–88.
- "La tradición progresista: historia revolucionaria, historia nacional," in Suárez Cortina, ed., *La redención del pueblo: la cultura progresista en la España liberal*. Santander, 2006. 81–113.

- "¿Y éstos en medio de la nación soberana son por ventura esclavos? Liberalismo, nación y pueblo." *Alcores: revista de historia contemporánea* 7 (2009): 13–37.
Rubio, Carlos. *Historia filosófica filosófica de la revolución española de 1868*. Madrid, 1869.
Rubio Jiménez, Jesús. "José María Gutiérrez de Alba y los inicios de la revista política en el teatro." *Crítica hispánica* 16 (1994): 119–40.
Ruiz de Morales, Joaquín. *Historia de la Milicia Nacional*. Madrid, 1856.
Ruiz Torres, Pedro. "Political Uses of History in Spain." In J. Revel and G. Levi, eds., *Political Uses of the Past: The Recent Mediterranean Experience*. Portland, 2002. 95–116.
Salcedo Olid, Manuel de. *Ramón María Narváez (1799–1868)*. Madrid, 2012.
San Miguel, Evaristo. *Sobre las ocurrencias de Madrid desde principios hasta el 23 de julio del presente año*. Madrid, 1843.
Sánchez de la Nieta Santos, Dámaso. *La Universidad de Almagro: tres siglos de actividad, 1574–1821*. Ciudad Real, 1982.
Sánchez García, Raquel. "Héroe y Martir. La Construcción del Mito de Diego de Leon." *Revista de Historia Militar* 112 (2012): 45–66.
Sánchez Mantero, Rafael. *Fernando VII: su reinado y su imagen*. Madrid, 2001.
Santirso Rodríguez, Manuel. "Barcelona. Rueda del progreso (1840–1843)." In Juan Sisino Pérez Garzón, ed., *Los Bombardeos de Barcelona*. Madrid, 2014.
- "El Convenio de Vergara y otras paces descartadas." *Hispania* 55, no. 191 (1995): 1063–92.
- *España en la Europa liberal (1830–1870)*. Barcelona, 2008.
- "Revolución liberal y guerra civil en Cataluña (1833–1840)." PhD thesis, Universitat Autònoma de Barcelona, 1994.
Selections from the Correspondence of the Earl of Aberdeen. London, 1858.
Semprún, José, and Alfonso Bullón de Mendoza. *El ejército realista en la independencia americana*. Madrid, 1992.
Serrano, Carlos. *El Nacimiento de Carmen*. Madrid, 1999.
Sevilla, Rafael. *Memorias de un oficial del Ejército*. Madrid, 1916.
Shubert, Adrian. "Baldomero and Jacinta: Scenes from a Nineteenth-Century Spanish Marriage, 1827–1878," *Journal of Modern History* 89 (December 2017): 749–71.
- "Being – and Staying – Famous in 19th-century Spain: Baldomero Espartero and the Birth of Political Celebrity." *Historia y Política* (July–December 2015): 211–37.
Sicilia de Arenzana, Francisco. *Un Monarca … y la República, o Espartero Rey*. Logroño, 1868
Sobrevilla Perea, Natalia. *The Caudillo of the Andes: Andrés de Santa Cruz*. Cambridge, 2011.
- "From Europe to the Americas and Back: Becoming Los Ayacuchos " *European History Quarterly* 41 (2011): 472–88.

- "Loyalism and Liberalism in Peru 1810–1824." In Scott Eastman and Natalia Sobrevilla Perea, eds., *The Rise of Constitutional Government in the Iberian Atlantic*. Atlantic Crossings. Tuscaloosa, 2015. 111–32.
Solís, Ramón. *El Cádiz de las Cortes*. Madrid, 1969.
Somerville, Alexander. *History of the British Legion, and War in Spain*. London, 1839.
Spiers, Edward. *Radical General: Sir George de Lacy Evans, 1787–1870*. Manchester, 1983.
Stoat, Stephen K. *Pablo Morillo and Venezuela, 1815–1820*. Columbus, 1974.
Suárez, Federico. *Donoso Cortés y la fundación de El Heraldo y El Sol: (con una correspondencia inédita entre Donoso Cortés, Ríos Rosas y Sartorius)*. Pamplona, 1985.
Subirachs i Burgaya, Judit. *L'escultura del segle XIX a Catalunya: del romanticisme al realisme*. Montserrat, 1994.
Sucinta relación de las honras fúnebres que conforme al Real Decreto de cinco de enero de 1837 tributó la fidelísima ciudad de Cervera en los días 11 y 12 de febrero del mismo año a los héroes defensores y libertadores de la invicta Bilbao. Cervera, 1837.
Thompson, Guy. *The Birth of Modern Politics in Spain: Democracy, Association and Revolution, 1854–75*. London, 2009.
Tomás Villaroyo, Joaquín. "La Ley de Ayuntamientos y la Renuncia de María Cristina de Borbón a la Regencia." In *Estudios de historia moderna y contemporánea: homenaje a Federico Suárez*. Madrid, 1991.
Tone, John L. *The Fatal Knot: The Guerrilla War in Navarre and the Defeat of Napoleon in Spain*. Chapel Hill, 1994.
Torata, Conde de. *Documentos para la historia de la guerra separatista del Perú*. Madrid, 1894.
Toreno, Conde de. *Historia del levantamiento, guerra y revolución de España*. Madrid, 2008.
Torras Elías, Jaime. *La Guerra de los Agraviados*. Barcelona, 1967.
Urbiztondo y Eguía, Antonio. *Apuntes sobre la guerra de Navarra en su última época, y especialmente sobre el Convenio de Vergara*. Madrid, 1841.
Urquijo y Goitia, J.R. *La Revolución de 1854 en Madrid*. Madrid, 1984.
Valdés, Gerónimo. *Exposición que dirige al Rey D. Fernando VII el General Gerónimo Valdés*. Madrid, 1894.
Van Halen, Antonio. *Diario razonado de los acontecimientos que tuvieron lugar en Barcelona desde el 13 de noviembre 1842, con reflexiones que sirven para dilucidar su naturaleza*. Perpiñán, 1843.
Varela Ortega, José. "Políticas de la Memoria: Desde la Transición y con la República." Fundación José Ortega y Gasset, Documento de Trabajo 2011/17.
Varela Suanzes-Carpegna, Joaquín. "La Constitución española de 1837: una Constitución transaccional." *Revista de Derecho Político* 20 (1983–4): 95–106.
Vida de Joaquín María López. Madrid, 1857.

Vida militar y política de Espartero: obra dedicada a la ex Milicia Nacional del Reino. Madrid, 1844.

Vida y hechos de don Tomás Zumalacárregi. Madrid, 1845.

Vidal Delgado, Rafael. *Entre Logroño y Luchana. campañas del General Espartero.* Logroño, 2004.

– "Espartero. Una figura de leyenda." *Revista de historia militar* (2001).

Viejo-Rose, Dacia. *Reconstructing Spain: Cultural Heritage and Memory after Civil War.* Brighton, 2014.

von Rahden, Wilhelm. *Andanzas de un veterano de la guerra de España (1833–1840).* Pamplona, 1965.

Zurita Aldeguer, Rafael. "El Progresismo. Héroes e Historia de la Nación Liberal." In M. Cruz Romeo and M. Sierra, eds., *La España Liberal, 1833–1874.* Madrid, 2014.

Index

Page numbers in *italic* refer to figures.

Aberdeen, Earl of, 175, 198, 199, 392n26
Abrantes Manifesto, 68
African War, 258, 279, 282
Agreement of Vergara, 125–6, *127*, 128, 131; commemoration of, 142, 249, 320, 332, 336, 337–8, 339; and Espartero, 100, 145, 146–7, 216, 317–18; in 1930s, 344, 345–7, 348, 349, 421n79
Aguirre, Joaquín, 270, 284, 286
Agulhon, Maurice, on "statuemania," 337
Ajuriaguerra, Juan, 350
Alaix, Isidro: in government, 112, 114–15, 119, 131, 374n137; military roles, 92, 113; and peace talks, 122, 123, 124
Albacar, Mariano Gracia, 225
Albacete, 191, 194, 205, 209, 272, 307
Albornoz, Álvaro de, 344
Alcalá Galiano, Antonio, 25, 30
Alegría, Ciro, 56
Alfonso XII (king of Spain): death of, 339; and Espartero, 319, 322, 323, 325–30, 336, 418n79; and Isabel II, 288, 311; and monarchy competition, 293, 298, 301, 309, 310, 314; as "Peacemaker," 329–30, 334. *See also* Restoration
Alicante, 299, 308–9, 335, 336
Allende Salazar, José, 226, 227, 228, 233, 236, 326
alliances. *See* treaties
Almodóvar, Count of, 85, 161
Alvarado, Rudecindo, 43, 44
Álvarez de Toro y Molina, Josefa (mother), 16, 17, 18
Álvarez Junco, José, 20
Álvarez Robles, Mariano, 260
Amadeo I, Duke of Aosta (king of Spain), 313–14, 315–20 *passim*, 343, 416n7
Amarillas, Marquis of las, 79
American colonies: and the Cortes, 29, 39, 45–6; coup in, 41–2, 44; expeditionary force, 33–4, 35; peace talks, 46–50; uprisings in, 32–3, 35–9, 40–1, 43–5, 50–1. *See also names of countries*
amnesty, 67, 186, 187, 188, 205, 271, 282, 284
Andreu, Jaime de, 311
Anguera, Pere, 303

anniversaries. *See* commemoration
Aosta, Duke of. *See* Amadeo I, Duke of Aosta
Aragón, 101, 115, 130, 133, 271. *See also* Zaragoza
Arequipa, Peru, 42–3, 56, 65
Argentina, 36, 33, 45
Argüelles, Agustín, 161, 163, 164, 167, 174, 185
Arístegui y Vélez, Rafael, Count of Mirasol, 103
Arlabán, battles of, 84, 85, 86
Army of the North: in Bilbao, 4, 94, 96, 97; conditions, 81, 90–1, 101, 105, 108, 112, 116, 117; Espartero commands, 9, 85, 86, 92–3; finances improved, 115, 119; in Third Carlist War, 319, 320, 321, 324. *See also* First Carlist War
Army of the Reserve, 79–80, 113, 115
Arrache, Juan de, 54, 58
art and artists, 20, 194, 201, 250, 287, 418n79. *See also* monuments; portraits
artisans, 17, 18, 211, 213, 214, 241
Asensio, Calvo, 251, 252, 266
Askwith, Lieut. William H., 176
assassinations, 173, 315, 352; attempted, 73, 277
Aston, Arthur Ingram: and Espartero, 148, 150, 191, 201, 390n144; and Jacinta, 183; and María Cristina, 144; and regency issue, 158, 160, 161; and regency of Espartero, 14, 164, 166–7, 169, 171, 172, 175, 179, 187–8; on revolution of 1843, 192, 193
atrocities. *See* executions; war crimes
autographs, 243, 264, 275
Aviraneta, Eugenio, 122, 205
Ayacucho, battle of, 52, 56, 57
ayacuchos, 59, 76, 164, 189, 204

Ayguals de Izco, Wenceslao, 178, 214–15, 230
Aymar, Agustín, 269, 279
Aznar, José María, 352
Azpiroz, Francisco Javier, 144, 191–2

Bacon, John Francis, 73
Balaguer, Victor: in elections, 266; and Espartero, 255, 257, 264–5, 269, 277–9, 282, 305; and Vigues, 260
Baldomero, Saint, 154. *See also* birthday celebrations
Balmaseda, 76, 119
Bañeras, 60, 61, 63, 364n6
Barcelona: debates of 1840, 136–8, 140, 141; labour unrest, 240–1; memorial, 336–7; reception in, 139–42, 147, 242, 246, 290, 330; street names, 348, 350, 351; uprisings and, 172, 177, 179–82, 190, 253
Bardaji, Eusebio, 102, 103, 105
Barrio Ayuso, Manuel, 108
Basque Country: and Carlist Wars, 9, 74, 77, 79, 89, 319, 329, 345; and Carlos, 67; and Espartero, 129; *fueros*, 72, 123, 131, 139, 176, 177, 338; peace campaign, 99–100, 121–6, 129. *See also* Bilbao
Bautista Topete, Juan, 288
Belgium, 77, 207, 301
Bellsolá y Gurrea, Teresa, 332
Bermejo, Ildefonso Antonio, 213–14, 274, 316
Bernardin, Benito, 224, 225
Bienio Progresista. *See* revolution(s): of 1854
Bilbao: in Carlist Wars, 3–4, 68, 69, 70, 71, 72–3, 75–6, 80, 94–7, 320, 324 (*see also* Luchana, battle of); monument proposal, 342–3; rebellion of 1841, 173; shopping in,

155; street names, 348, 350, 422n105
biographies, 10; early, 17, 28, 30, 31, 33, 53–4, 71, 212–17, 380n88, 395n128; of 1868, 22, 23; of 1879, 336; of 1930s and 1940s, 56, 344–5, 348–9, 352
birthday celebrations, 242–3, 246–7, 259, 261, 279–81, 305, 328, 330, 331, 409n174
black people, 35, 155. *See also* slaves
Bolívar, Simón, 35, 52, 55, 56, 57
Bonaparte, Joseph (king of Spain), 20, 21, 25
Bonaparte, Napoleon. *See* Napoleon I
Borrega, Andrés, 140
Borso di Carminati, Cayetano, 173
Bourbons. *See* Restoration; *specific royals*
Boves, Tomás, 35
Bravo Murillo, Juan, 219–20
British ambassadors, 196, 206, 211, 264. *See also* Aston, Arthur Ingram; Caradoc, John Hobart; Villiers, George
British press, 99, 197–8, 201, 220, 221, 236, 258, 286, 321–3, 329
Bruil, Juan, 224, 244, 260
Bulwer, Henry, 206, 211
Burdiel, Isabel: on Carlist War, 86; on Espartero, 248; on history, 11; on liberalism, 183; on politics, 202, 235–6, 237; on royals, 137, 140, 223, 262
Burgos, 92, 108, 219, 249, 274, 305
Burguera, Mónica, 12
Burrell, Julio, 342

Caballé, Anna, 348
Caballero, Fermín, 188
Caballero, Francisco Largo, 346

Cabrera, Ramón, 103, 129, 131, 134–5, 203, 204, 330
Cádiz: economy, 24; and Espartero, 231, 236, 269, 277; publishing in, 25–6; and revolution, 288; siege of, 24–5, 28–9. *See also* Constitution of Cádiz
Calatrava, José María, 88, 93, 97, 102
Calatrava, Ramón, 179
Calderón de la Barca, Fanny, 222, 227, 229, 238
Canning, Charles, Earl (Viscount), 199, 201
Cánovas del Castillo, Antonio, 221, 301, 326, 332, 343, 352
Canterac, José de, 41, 44, 52
Cantero, Manuel, 310
Caradoc, John Hobart, Baron Howden, 220, 233, 234, 235, 236, 237–8, 242, 244, 246–7
Carlist Wars. *See* First Carlist War *et al.*
Carlos IV (king of Spain), 19, 20, 21, 416n18, 428n18
Carlos VII, Duke of Madrid, 322, 329
Carlos de Areizaga, Juan, 22–3
Carlos María Isidro Benito de Borbon (Carlos V, Infante): and Carlist War, 3, 9, 67–8, 77, 78; Durango Decree, 74; and Isabel's marriage, 171; and peace talks, 122, 125; pursuit of, 129; and Royal Expedition, 100–1, 103, 116
Carlos Sebastián. *See* Charles III (king of Spain)
Carratalá, José Manuel de, 106, 108
Carsi, Juan Manuel, 180, 181
Casa-Palacio, 210, 256, 334
Castaños, Francisco Javier, 175
Castelar, Emilio: and African War, 258; and Espartero, 146, 313, 335, 336; vs. monarchy, 301, 302; as president, 296, 321, 323

Castro, Alejandro, 109, 111, 112
casualties, 22–3; in Carlist War, 70, 75, 78–9, 91, 99, 135, 365n38; in uprisings, 180, 253, 285
Catalan language, 259, 277, 278, 292, 335, 342
Catalonia: in Carlist War, 31–2, 89, 100, 113, 133; and Carlos, 67; and Espartero, 194, 262, 265, 269, 277–83, 292, 305; literature of, 216–17; María Cristina and, 136; and monarchy campaign, 305–6; politics in, 250, 271, 281–3; trade in, 172, 183–4. *See also* Barcelona
Catholic Church: and Carlist War, 7, 81–3, 87; and constitutions, 242, 359–60n52; and ecclesiastical policies, 123, 241–2, 243, 262, 282; Espartero on, 51, 72, 248, 256, 273; and Isabel II, 171, 233, 311; and politics, 12, 26, 67, 116
Catholic press, 170, 318, 341, 346, 419n23
Cea Bermúdez, Francisco, 67, 87
Ceballos Escalera, Rafael de, 103, 104
censorship. *See* freedom of the press
Centro Progresista, 248
Chao, Eduardo, 215
charity, 249, 260–1, 280, 281, 282, 409n174. *See also* philanthropy
Charles III (king of Spain), 18, 36, 265
Charles IV. *See* Carlos IV (king of Spain)
Chasteen, John, 32
Chile, 33, 36, 39, 41, 44, 46, 48, 49
"chorus of voices" (Burdiel), 11, 298
Cincinnatus: compared to, 231, 295, 296, 298, 308, 309; image as, 15, 152, 202, 210; and retirement, 273, 277

civil wars, 99, 258, 344. *See also* First Carlist War *et al.*; revolutions(s); Spanish Civil War
Clamor Público, El, 201, 204–5, 208, 261–2, 264, 265, 406n82
Clarendon, Earl of. *See* Villiers, George
Cochrane, Thomas, 39, 41
Colombia, 33, 44, 46, 48
colonies. *See* American colonies
commemoration: of Carlist War, 6–9, 97, 152–3, 314, 325, 342; of Constitution of Cádiz, 157; of liberalism, 352–3; of Vergara, 142, 145–6, 249, 336, 345–6. *See also* monuments; public memory
commemoration of Espartero: in Francoist Spain, 345–50; monuments, 337–9, *340*, 341–3; plays, 8–9, 144, 145–6, 292–3, 312–13, 343; poems, 135, 145, 146, 259–60, 278; post-Franco, 350–3; in the press, 294–5, 325; in songs, 139, 144, 147, 320; street names, 144, 290, 348, 350–1, 422n105. *See also* biographies; cult of Espartero
Conservative Party, 198, 221, 341, 342
conservative press, 170, 208, 236, 332, 335
constitutional monarchy, 200, 269, 272, 338; return to, 301; and revolution of 1868, 288; royals and, 315, 327; support for, 298
Constitution of Bayonne, 20
Constitution of Cádiz (1812), 29–30, 359–60n52; commemoration of, 157, 353; and Espartero, 87, 92; nullified, 32, 39–40, 50; restoration of, 88

Constitution of 1837: and Agreement of Vergara, 125; approval of, 100; and Espartero, 8, 120, 152, 139, 163, 166, 191, 282; and Isabel's accession, 202; and municipal government, 135; uprising to restore, 203
Constitution of 1845, 202, 217; revision of, 262
Constitution of 1854, 241–2
Constitution of 1856, 284
Constitution of 1869, 291, 301
Córdova. *See* Fernández de Córdova, Luis
Corona de Aragón, La, 277–8, 290
Coronado, Carolina, 146
Corradi, Fernando, 261–2, 264. See also *Clamor Público, El*
Cortes Generales. *See* government
Cortina, Manuel, 144, 149–50, 158, 177, 178, 183, 186, 208
Cotera, Lucas de la, 53, 54, 60, 65
Crespi, Manuel, 182
Cross of San Fernando, 44, 55, 327–8, 329, 366n78
Cruz Romeo, María, 156, 350
Cuba, 188, 212, 222, 342
cult of Espartero, 11, 145–8, 353; in Catalonia, 277–83; in families, 213, 225, 264, 269; in literature, 146–8, 216–17, 240–1, 388n90; and politics after 1854, 265; and retirement, 273–7, 313; and virtues, 277–9. *See also* plays; poems; songs
culture. *See* art and artists; popular culture
Cutchet, Lluís, 255, 257, 258, 277

Delgado, Justo Tomás, 286, 302–3
Delgado, Vidal, 71
democracy, 301, 350, 353

Democratic Conservative Party, 317
Democrats: in government, 252–3, 289, 291, 292, 298; and María Cristina, 234; and monarchy competition, 301; and Pact of Ostend, 285; vs. Progressives, 217; press, 257, 263, 265; and revolution of 1854, 223
demographics, 16–17, 24. *See also* population
de Walden, Baron Howard, 196
diaries, 13, 140–1, 182, 207–8
dictators, 88, 288, 293, 323, 351. *See also* Franco, Francisco; Primo de Rivera, Miguel
Diego de León, Don, 118, 119, 141, 174, 175–6
disentailment, 123, 241–2, 243, 262, 282
Domingo de Santa Cruz, Juan, 24, 61–2, 64, 323
Donoso Cortés, Juan, 167–8, 172
Donoso García, Santiago, 55
Doyle, Richard, 199
Dulce, Domingo, 174, 175, 221, 298
Durango, 69, 70, 73, 98, 121
Durango Decree, 74

ecclesiastical policies, 170. *See also* disentailment
Eco del Comercio, El, 76, 108; manifesto, 131, 132; and regency, 158, 161, 177, 178, 179, 183, 185, 186; on return from exile, 208; on retirement, 210
Eco del Progreso, El, 295, 318
Eco Nacional, El, 286
economics of marriage, 18, 54–5, 61–2, 63–4
economy, 16, 43, 110, 248, 250, 256. *See also* trade
education, 12, 18–19, 62, 184, 217; military training, 23–4, 26–9. 30–1

elections: of 1834 and 1836, 87, 100; of 1839 and 1840, 119, 131; of 1841, 157; of 1843, 183, 185, 186; of 1854, 235–6; of 1857, 262–3; of 1863, 266; of 1864, 271; of 1867, 285; of 1869, 291, 298; of 1871, 315–16; of 1872, 318

Elío, Joaquín, 32, 123

Eliot, Edward, Earl of St. Germans, 74

Eliot Convention, 74–5

Embrace of Vergara. *See* Agreement of Vergara

Enrique of Borbón (prince), 302

Época, La, 262, 313, 322–3, 326, 329, 332, 335, 339, 342

Escosura, Patricio de la, 211, 246, 250, 252, 261

Espartero, Francisco (brother), 18, 332

Espartero, Joaquín Baldomero: appearance of, 55, 155, 238, 251; author and, 10–14; bio in brief, 9–10; birth of and background, 16–18; character of, 13–15, 33, 53, 74, 99, 110, 164, 221; comparable figures, 14–15, 145, 273–4, 278 (*see also* Cincinnatus; Garibaldi, Giuseppe; Napoleon I; Washington, George); death of and funeral, 332, 334–7, 339, *340*; deference to authority, 60–1, 72, 126, 241; dynastic loyalty of, 55, 59, 60–1, 67, 137, 235, 245, 254, 286, 316; early education of, 18–19; ease with children, 58, 197–8; finances of, 33, 64, 65, 72, 81, 178, 220, 334, 364n18; and gambling, 53–4, 110; and gardening, 169, 193, 257 (*see also* viticulture); image of (*see* portraits; public image); informality of, 169, 326; lack of offspring, 154, 293,

294; letters to Jacinta, 13, 70–1, 75–128 *passim*, 133, 134, 138, 142, 152, 153–5, 156–7, 183–4; manly voice of, 5, 104, 128, 163, 181, 226; marriage of, 61, 63–5, 153–7, 364n17; model of masculinity, 155–6; motives of, 14, 22, 33, 51, 76; namesakes of, 146; nicknames of, 70, 73, 179, 192, 335 (*see also* "Patriarch of Freedom"; "Peacemaker of Spain"; "sword of Luchana"); philanthropy, 211, 256–7, 336–7; popularity of, 10, 97, 206, 220, 221, 247, 302, 316, 317, 341 (*see also* cult of Espartero); as "public man," 102, 262, 271, 278; sense of self, 9, 14, 106, 107, 152, 202, 210, 244

—military career in America, 32–58; action(s), 36–9, 40–1, 42–3, 44–5; diplomacy, 46–50; on experiences, 57, 258; finances after, 53–5; health, 44, 53, 56, 58, 60, 364n6; honours and promotions, 42, 44, 45, 53, 55; joins expeditionary force, 32, 33–4; and Olañeta's revolt, 50–1; pastimes, 40, 43, 53–4; return to Peru, 55–7; return to Spain, 57–61; support network, 59 (see also *ayacuchos*)

—military career in Spain: academy training, 23–4, 26–9, 30–1; action(s) in Carlist War, 3–4, 76, 68–73, 76, 79–86, 94–7 (*see also* First Carlist War); and the British, 77–8, 172; *chapelgorri* controversy, 81–3, 87; commands northern army, 9, 85, 92–3; concern for recognition, 69, 80, 110, 131; concern for soldiers, 37, 75, 81, 96, 98, 142; decision to enlist, 22; defeat at Monte Descarga, 75; on discipline,

82–3, 89–90, 94, 104–5; dislike of paperwork, 85, 101, 110, 115; dislike of politics, 88, 114, 119, 120–1, 123; first action(s), 22–3, 28–9, 31–2, 36; first command, 66–7; and government, 105–6, 108, 111–15, 131–2; health, 4, 70, 79–80, 81, 92, 93, 99; honours, 7, 80, 97, 110, 118, 134, 366n78; Logroño posting, 61, 65–6; popularity among troops, 97–8, 105; proclamations, 74, 99–100, 110, 135, 371n41; promotions, 61, 69, 73, 86, 93, 109, 368n141; and queen regent, 72, 79, 86, 101, 108, 109, 113–14; and Royal Expedition, 100–1, 103; and royal gratitude, 55, 69; strategy of, 71, 98–100, 106, 115, 116–17, 131; threats to resign, 79, 84, 105, 108

—political career: and Constitution of Cádiz, 30, 92; early interest, 87; elections in Logroño, 100, 157, 263, 298, 315–16, 318; exile and intrigue, 196–207; first independent action, 51; first term as leader (1837), 101, 102–3; as governor, 142; health, 201, 206, 207, 238, 249; honours, 182, 219, 227, 242; and marriage, 61; Mas de las Matas Manifesto, 132–3, 378n25; meets with US emissary, 222; negotiations of 1840, 136–8, 140, 141, 145, 148–50; on own record, 202–3, 254; political views, 40, 105–7, 116–17, 152, 321–2; press opposition, 236, 247, 257–8; and Progressives, 131–2, 143, 217–21, 247–8, 262; railroad tour, 248–50; resignation in 1856, 241, 252; return from exile, 208–10; and revolution of 1840, 143–5; and revolution of 1854, 217, 224–31, 261–2, 273, 278, 290; second term as leader (1840–1), 150–2; showdowns with Isabel II, 242, 243–4; third term as leader (1854–6), 10, 223, 233–48; threats to resign, 140, 149–50, 237–8, 245

—as Regent of the Realm (1840–3), 163–95; debate over regency, 158–62; domestic and foreign issues, 167–71; election and first days, 161, 163–4, 385n4; elections of 1843, 185; government debates, 166–7; health, 183, 311–12; and Linaje, 187–8; overview of term, 164–5; political views, 185; post-election Cortes, 185–9; press opposition, 178–9, 182–3, 189, 190–1; and princesses, 152, 168–9; rebellion of 1841, 172–6; resignation contemplated, 188; and revolutions of 1842–4, 180–2, 189–93, 194–5; trade issue, 171–2, 178–9, 181, 184

—retirement (1843–8 and 1856–76): and cult, 273–83; health, 257, 325; honours, 256, 261, 281, 282; Isabel II appeals to, 320; last years, 331; letters from admirers, 209, 218, 219, 229–30, 231, 258–60, 264, 268–9, 272–3, 275, 276, 394–5n104; life in Logroño, 10, 209–12, 216, 217, 256–8; manifesto of 1857, 263–4; monarchy campaign, 294–6, 297, 298–300, 302–9, 313–14, 414n114; named Prince of Vergara, 317–18, 416n18; party crisis of 1864, 266–73, 407n138; politics of 1857–63, 261–6; proposed as head of state, 293–4; refuses crown, 310, 313; refuses political roles, 272, 317; return to politics,

Espartero (cont'd)
233; and revolution of 1868, 283–7, 289, 290, 291; royal visits, 283, 316, 326–9, 330, 332; on second retirement, 255–6; sought after by Bourbons, 319–20; support for Alfonso XII, 319, 322, 323
Espartero, Manuel José (brother), 17, 22
Espina, Antonio 348–9
Espoz y Mina, Francisco, 60, 62, 66, 73, 93
Esquivel, Antonio María, 165, 194, 274
Estevánez, Nicolás, 289, 395–6n129
Europe, 24, 51, 75–7, 337
Evans, George de Lacy, 77–8, 93, 95, 98, 99, 199
Evans, Luis de, 90
executions: in America, 42; in Carlist War, 66, 69, 70, 103–4, 111, 115–16; military, 173, 176; uprisings and, 182, 250, 274, 393n47. *See also* war crimes
Ezpeleta, Joaquín, 79–80

families, 146, 182, 213, 253, 277
fashions, 74, 110, 148, 155, 169, 225, 326, 334
Federal Republicans, 292, 298, 301
Felix Domenech, Jacinto, 160
femininity, 12, 184. *See also* women
Ferdinand VII. *See* Fernando VII (king of Spain)
Fernández Álvarez, Vicente (brother), 17, 19
Fernández Cuenca, Carlos, 345
Fernández de Córdova, Luis: in Carlist War, 74, 78–9, 82; end of command, 85–6, 87–8, 92, 370n178; and Espartero, 84, 92–3, 111, 113, 114, 119–20; in government, 107–8; and revolution, 190

Fernández de Gamboa, Agustín, 122, 152
Fernández de los Ríos, Ángel, 14, 222, 239–40, 251, 252. *See also* *Novedades, Las*
Fernández de Luco, Vicenta, 332, 334
Fernández Espartero, Antonio (father), 16, 17–18
Fernández Espartero y Blanco, Eladia (niece), 154, 184, 198, 199, 201; inheritance, 332, 334
Fernando VII (king of Spain): arrest of, 19; and Constitution of Cádiz, 30, 32, 39–40, 50; death of, 68; and Espartero, 55, 59, 137; and expeditionary force, 33; marriage of, 66; and Narváez, 113; plot vs., 60–1; policies, 67; restorations of, 31, 52, 58, 59; and War of Independence, 20, 21, 25, 26
Fernando de Abascal, José, 36
Fernando of Saxe-Coburg and Gotha, 301, 302, 309
Ferraz, Valentín, 137, 141
Ferrer, Joaquín María, 65, 82–3, 143, 150
First Carlist War: battles of, 4–9, 75, 78–9, 80, 84–5, 86, 96–7, 117–18, 355n5; beginning of, 68; Bilbao siege, 3–4, 75–6, 94–7, 342; brutality of, 3, 73, 105; capture of Morella, 134, 145; capture of Peñacerrada, 109–10; Carlists and, 88–9, 115–16; casualties of, 70, 75, 78–9, 91, 99, 135, 365n38; *chapelgorri* controversy, 81–3, 87; commemoration of, 6–9, 97, 152–3, 314, 325, 342; compared, 68, 76, 346; and Eliot Convention, 74–5; end of, 135; "English plan," 98–100; foreign involvement in,

76–8, 116; Jacinta's role in, 83, 84, 87, 120, 122, 325; Maestrazgo campaign, 133–5; mutinies in, 102, 103–4; peace talks, 121–8; political questions of, 86–7; pursuit of Carlists, 88–92, 108–9, 113, 117–19, 121, 129, 134–5; Royal Expedition, 100–3, 116
First Spanish Republic, 14, 146, 215, 319–20, 325
Flores, Antonio, 274
Florez, José Segundo, 28, 30, 53–4, 66, 214, 215
Ford, Richard, 201
foreign legions, 77–82 *passim*, 89, 98, 99
foreign relations, 169–71.
  See also British ambassadors; French ambassadors; Spanish ambassadors
Foxà, Count, 323
France: in Carlist War, 77, 132, 137; invasion of 1823, 46, 47, 51–2, 65; Isabel II and, 171, 227, 243, 264, 289, 310; Jacinta and, 204; press in, 221, 286, 305. *See also* French ambassadors; War of Independence
Francisco de Asís, Duke of Cádiz, 171, 203
Francisco de Eguía, General, 32
Francisco de Paula, Infante, 151, 171
Franco, Francisco, 57, 347
Francoist Spain, 13, 345–50, 352, 420n72
freedom of the press, 26, 29, 120, 185, 187, 191, 212, 220–1, 247, 292
French ambassadors, 172, 180, 227, 235, 238, 243, 255, 264, 285, 288, 310
French Revolution, 9, 19–20, 24, 159, 337
Frías, Duke of, 112–13, 114

Fuentes y Altafago, Pascuala, 260
fueros, 72, 123, 131, 139, 176, 177, 338
funerals, 7, 209, 263, 334–7

García Camba, Andrés, 37, 41
García Goyena, Florencio, 205, 206
García Santa Olalla, Santiago, 259, 330
Garibaldi, Giuseppe, 11, 258, 273–4, 301, 353, 395n126, 395–6n129
Garrido, Fernando, 231, 235, 295
Garrido Muro, Luis, 103, 108. 115
Gay, Vicente, 345
gender, 11–12, 138, 153, 155–6, 352.
  See also women
George IV (king of England), 74
Gibert i Roig, Pau, 338, 419n41
Gil Blas, 286, 317, 319
Gil de Bernabé, Mariano, 26–7
Glorious Revolution. *See* revolution(s): of 1868
Godoy, Manuel, 19, 416n18
Goicoechea, Baldomero, 256, 257, 278
Gómez, Sgt. Alejandro, 88–92, 113
Gómez, Manuel, 267
Gómez Becerra, Alvaro, 188, 189
González, Antonio, 56, 141, 145, 166–7, 171, 173, 177, 183
González Bravo, Luis, 160, 175, 285, 288
government: of 1808, 21–2, 23, 24, 26 (*see also* Constitution of Cádiz [1812]); of 1811, provisional junta, 36; of 1820–3, constitutional, 40; of 1830s, and instability, 111–15; of 1839, and *fueros*, 131; of 1840, debates, 136–8, 140, 141, 145, 148–50, 158–62; of 1840–1, regency and revolution, 166–7, 177–9, 180, 183; of 1843, 185–9, 244; after 1843 revolution, 193, 197, 202, 205–6, 392n13; of 1852–4, and instability, 219–21; after 1854,

government (cont'd)
  222–3, 226, 227, 228, 233, 234, 235;
  of 1855–6, constitutional, 235–42,
  244–6, 252–3; of 1857–63, 264,
  265; of 1868, provisional, 290–2;
  of 1869, 300–2, 307, 309–10, 313–14,
  414n114; of 1871–2, and Republic,
  315–17; of 1874, and coup,
  323–4; of 1937, and Vergara, 346–7.
  See also elections; legislation;
  municipal governments
Goya, Francisco, 20, 250
Graham, Sir Thomas, 28, 29
Gran Cruz de Isabel la Católica, 80
Gran Cruz de San Fernando, 44, 55,
  327–8, 329, 366n78
Granés, Salvador María, 293
Granátula de Calatrava, 9, 16–17, 55
Grant, Ulysses S., 14–15
Great Britain: and Carlist War, 3,
  74, 77–8, 92, 93, 123–4, 172; and
  ecclesiastical policies, 170; exile in,
  9–10, 71, 197, 198–203, 206–8,
  215, 251; and French Revolution,
  19, 24; and Isabel's marriage,
  171; and rebellion of 1841, 173,
  175–6; and War of Independence,
  21, 25, 28–9, 32. See also British
  ambassadors; British press
Greece, 159, 295, 301
Guergué, Juan Antonio, 109, 115, 116
Guernica, 69, 71, 75
Guerra dels Matiners, 204, 351
Gurrea, Ignacio: and Espartero, 210,
  236, 240, 253, 255; in London, 201;
  and O'Donnell, 246, 248, 249; titles
  stripped, 392n13; uprising and,
  224, 225
Gurrea Arrieta, Jacinta, 256, 332
Gurrea de Bellsolá, Jacinta, 332
Gurwood, Col. John, 74
Gutiérrez de Alba, José María, 293

Gutiérrez de la Concha, José, 288,
  289, 331–2
Gutiérrez de la Concha, Manuel,
  173–4, 190, 194–5, 220, 289, 339;
  commemoration of, 342, 351

Hamilton-Gordon, George. See
  Aberdeen, Earl of
Hardman, Frederick, 221, 236,
  397n170
Haro, 79, 108, 249, 290
Hay, Lord John, 95, 111, 123, 124
Hera, José Santos de la, 51, 76, 78
Heraldo, El, 188, 205, 420n72
Heras, Juan Gregorio de las, 46–51
Heredia y Begines de los Ríos, Narciso,
  Count of Ofalia, 103, 105, 122
Heros, Martín de los, 159
Hezeta, Colonel, 123
historical memory, 12–13, 311, 334,
  337, 347–8, 351. See also public
  memory
Holland, 25, 171
Hortelano, Benito, 208–9, 212–14, 215
Howden, Lord. See Caradoc, John
  Hobart
Huelva, 242–3, 290

Ibarreche, José María, 72
Iberia, La, 183, 235, 272, 325, 330, 335,
  339. See also Sagasta, Práxedes
  Mateo
identity, 10–11, 202, 210, 275
Iglesias, Pablo, 348
Imparcial, El, 204, 335, 339
Indigenous people, 29, 33, 36, 38
Infante, Facundo, 56, 392n13
Irving, Washington, 180–1, 184, 193
Isabel II (queen of Spain):
  abdication of, 310; accession of,
  202; birth of, 67; and Carlist
  War, 3, 7, 9; commemoration of,

353; and Espartero, 10, 14, 223, 233, 246, 310–11, 320, 323; and Espartero's regency, 152, 168–9; and Espartero's return, 205, 207, 209, 210; guardianship and tutorship, 151, 167–9; marriage of, 170–1, 180, 203–4; and political power, 357n36; and politics of 1854, 236, 237, 241–2, 243–4; reputation of, 204, 220, 285, 290, 316; uprisings and, 173, 174–5, 191, 192, 226–8, 262, 264, 265, 288, 289
Istúriz, Francisco Javier de, 88, 112, 137, 138, 205, 206, 207, 392n27
Italy, 154, 258, 284, 302, 313, 395n126
Izquierda Republicana, 347, 348

Jacinta (wife). *See* Martínez de Sicilia y Santa Cruz, María Jacinta Guadalupe
Jones, John Edward, 201
journalists, 220–1. *See also* Moore, John; press
Jovellar, Joaquín, 289
Juliá, Santos, 166
Junta Central of 1808, 21, 23, 24, 26
Junta de Salvación, 227, 228, 233, 234, 235
Junta Provisional Revolucionaria, 290–1

Kiernan, Victor, 248
Koontz, Stephanie, 64

labour unrest, 240–1
Lacunza, Román de, 279
La Granja revolt, 88, 100, 105, 141, 370n178
La Peña, Manuel, 28–9
Latre y Huarte, Manuel de, 73, 76, 107, 108, 111
leadership, 278, 407n115. *See also* morality

Leerssen, Joep, 337
legislation: conscription, 238–9; of first Cortes, 29–30; and *fueros*, 131, 176, 177; gutted by Narváez, 262; on historical memory, 351; for monuments, 338, 339, 341–2; municipal government, 135–6, 137, 140, 143, 149; for workers, unrealized, 241. *See also* ecclesiastical policies; Pragmatic Sanction
Leon, Ramón, 398n12
Leopold of Hohenzollern Sigmaringen, 309, 310, 313
Lesseps, Ferdinand de, 180
"liberal," applied to politics, 29
liberalism: of Espartero, 33, 60; and Franco, 347, 350, 352; and politics of Carlist War, 87; and women's place, 12; and the year 1843, 183. *See also* Moderates; Progressives
Liberal Party, 335
Liberal Union: and *Bienio* politics, 235, 236, 239; Corradi's support for, 264; and Espartero, 248, 282, 285; in government, 289, 291, 319; and monarchy competition, 295, 301
Linaje, Francisco: death of, 209; and Espartero, 92, 141, 158, 160, 203; government program of, 138; manifesto, 132–3; and peace talks, 125; proposed dismissal, 187, 188; titles stripped, 392n13
literature, 8, 12, 56, 146–8, 216–17, 277–8. *See also* biographies; novels; plays
Logroño: celebrations, 130, 205, 249, 319; funeral, 336; military and, 91, 101, 103; monuments, 337–8, 339, 340, 341–2, 420n54; petitions, 307–8; politicians, 202; population, 256; posting in, 61, 65–6; retirement in,

Logroño (cont'd)
10, 152, 210–12, 216, 217, 256–8, 316; and revolution of 1868, 289–90
London, 60–1, 211
Londonderry, Marquis of, 198
López, Joaquín María, 6–7, 156, 159, 160, 177, 183, 186–7, 193, 202, 390n142
Loriga, Sabine, 10
Louis XIII (king of France), 47, 87
Louis Philippe I (king of France), 155, 171, 203, 301
Lowe, Lieut. Frederick, 197, 198
luchana (facial hairstyle), 148
Luchana, battle of, 4–9, 96–7, 145, 314, 342, 355n5
Luisa Carlotta of Naples and Sicily, 151
Luisa Fernanda, Infanta, 67, 152, 167, 168–9, 173, 174–5, 191, 301; marriage of, 205
Lynn, Lieut. J., 109–10, 134, 176

Madoz, Pascual: in elections, 263; and Espartero, 270–1, 286; in government, 243, 244, 253, 266, 269, 289; and monarchy competition, 302, 305–6, 314; and Progressives, 218, 272, 282, 284; repentance of, 230, 241; and workers, 240
Madrid: and Carlist War, 7, 75, 98, 99; memorial, 336; monuments, 338–9, 348, 419n41, 419n43; public memory, 343; reception in, 101–2, 144–5, 164, 182, 229, 230, 246–7, 255; siege of 1843, 191–2, 194; street names, 350, 421n102; uprisings, 20, 142–3, 173–5, 177, 181, 188, 221–3, 226–9, 252–3, 285
Magraner, Mariano, 68–9

"magic prestige," 98, 106, 107, 109, 111, 112, 160, 234, 284, 309
Marés, José María, 215, 216
María Cristina of Borbon–Two Sicilies (queen regent): assumes regency, 68; vs. the Carlists, 100–3; commemoration of, 332, 334; defamed by the press, 120; departure of, 234–5; and Espartero, 69, 111, 112, 118, 143, 223, 283, 368n141; Espartero's appeals to, 79, 86, 108, 109, 113–14; and government, 87, 88, 92, 136–8, 140, 141, 145, 148–9; and Isabel II, 151, 167–9, 202; and Jacinta, 140, 150, 378n24, 382–3n135; marriage of, 66, 67; and Miraflores' peace plan, 123; municipal government law, 136–40; and political power, 357n36; regency debate, 158–62; resignation of, 149–50, 382–3n135; uprisings and, 143–5, 172–6, 190
María Luisa (queen of Spain), 19, 85
Marliani, Manuel, 150, 162, 183, 187
Maroto, Rafael, 109, 115, 116, 117–19, 121; and peace talks, 122, 123–8
marriage, economics of, 18, 54–5, 61–2, 63–4
Martín Arranz, Raúl, 344
Martín de Olías, Joaquín, 336
Martínez Campos, Arsenio, 325
Martínez de Irujo, Carlos. *See* Sotomayor, Duke of
Martínez de la Rosa, Francisco, 87, 112
Martínez de Sicilia y Santa Cruz, María Jacinta Guadalupe: appearance of, 62, 154–5, 184, 207; background, 61–2; Baldomero's letters to (*see under* Espartero); bio in brief, 12; death of, 331–2,

339, *340*; in exile, 196, 197, 198–9, 100, 201; honours, 85, 130, 184; as intermediary, 83, 84, 87, 120, 122, 138, 140, 156–7, 183–4; on Isabel II, 311–12; letters of, 260–1, 267–8; life in Logroño, 210, 211, 256–8, 320, 325; marriage of, 61, 63–5, 153–7; philanthropy, 184, 211, 239, 256–7, 260; political role, 143, 152, 157, 175, 206, 352; on politics, 88, 263, 270, 272, 407n115; portraits of, *62*, *63*, 155, *333*; and queen regent, 150, 283, 378n24, 382–3n135; reception of, 130, 136, 139, 141, 260; regency and revolution, 152, 163, 168–9, 183, 184, 193–4; return to Madrid, 239

Martínez de Tejada, Diego, 268
Martínez Villergas, Juan, 208, 215, 396n147
Martín-González, Xabier, 350
Marx, Karl, 229
Masadas, Ponciano, 269
masculinity, 155–6
Mas de la Mata Manifesto, 131, 132–3, 378n25
Massa y Sanguinitti, Carlos, 212
Mazarredo y Mazzaredo, Manuel de, 102
medicine, 56, 92, 312, 317
Mendizábal, Juan Álvarez: in government, 85, 88, 98, 171, 188, 241; monuments, 260, 348; and public memory, 343; on regency issue, 159
merchants, 16, 17, 50, 53, 60, 73, 97, 201, 203. *See also* trade
Mexico, 33, 212, 348
Michonneau, Stéphane, 337
middle class, 54, 180, 184, 332
Milans del Bosch, Lorenzo, 190

military: of Alto Perú, 41–2; and conscription, 233–9; expeditionary force, 33–4, 35; modernization of, 59; mutinies, 37, 44, 100, 102, 103–4; officer training, 26–8; and revolution of 1843, 189–93; royal concerns about, 87; shipboard conditions, 57–8; statistics, 23, 133, 135, 142, 143, 182; Tiradores de la Patria, 180, 182; vs. Vergara in 1930s, 347. *See also* Army of the North; National Militia

Miller, William, 44
Mina, Countess of, 62, 169, 174–5, 184, 192, 352, 388n101
Miraflores, Marquis of, 122–3, 266
Mirasol, Count of, 103
Mitchell, Col. Edward, 134
Moderates: about, 12; and de León martyr cult, 176; in elections, 157, 183; and Espartero, 103, 119; manifesto, 219–20; and municipal government law, 135–6; vs. Narváez, 262; and regency issue, 162; and revolution of 1854, 223; and royals, 172–3, 202, 204; on trade treaty, 179
Mojón, Camilo, 305
Mola, Emilio, 345, 347, 348, 420n72
Molins, Marquis of, 326–8
Mon, Alejandro Pidal y, 109, 111
monarchy: and colonies, 32–3, 42; and Constitution of Cádiz, 29–30; crisis of 1868, 285, 286 (*see also* constitutional monarchy); and Espartero, 236, 245, 254, 261; and government, 21, 237, 291–2; and the Pragmatic Sanction, 67. *See also specific royals*
monarchy competition: candidates, 301–2, 309–10; press and, 294–6; pro-Espartero campaign, 297,

monarchy competition (cont'd) 298–300, 302–9, 313–14, 414n114; results, 314
Monet, Juan Antonio, 67
Montemolín, Count of, 171, 203, 204
Montesino, Cipriano (nephew-in-law), 160, 184, 257, 262, 267, 271, 303, 310, 318
Montesino, Pablo, 184
Montpensier, Duchess of, 314
Montpensier, Duke of, 203, 294; comparison, 295; and monarchy competition, 301–2, 309–10, 313, 314, 414n114, 415n142; and Prim's death, 315
monuments, 324, 332, 334, 337–9, *340*, 341–3, 419n41, 419n43, 420n54; destroyed, 32, 320, 348
Moore, John, 101, 117, 121, 126–8, 135
Morales del Progreso, 290, 299
morality: and Espartero, 11, 206, 230, 277–9, 294, 323, 336; and government, 120, 132; of Isabel II, 204, 220; and theatre, 292. *See also* virtues
Morella, 110, 111, 112, 134, 145, 147, 336
Morillo y Morillo, Pablo, 34, 35, 36
Moriones, Domingo, 319–20
Morón, Fermin Gonzalo, 236
Muñagorri, Juan Antonio, 110, 121–2, 123
municipal governments: in colonies, 20, 41; and Constitution of 1837, 100; and independence, 12, 321; law, 135–9, 140, 143, 149; petitions, 307–9, 414n114; monument proposals, 337–8, 342–3
Muñoz López, Pilar, 64
Muñoz Torrero, Diego, 266–7
Muro, Salvador José de, Marquis of Someruelos, 105, 108

Murrieta, Francisco, 43, 53, 54, 60
Murrieta, Luciano, 210, 211–12, 256, 257, 261, 332
mutinies, 37, 44, 100, 102, 103–4

Napier, William, 22
Napoleon I: compared to, 14, 191, 215, 274, 342, 345, 349; cult of, 11, 353; in War of Independence, 19–20, 23, 25, 31; speech plagiarized, 385n4
Napoleon III (king of France), 258, 289, 310, 320
Napoleonic Wars, 36, 159, 190
Narváez, Joaquín, 274
Narváez, Ramón María: books about, 215, 343, 344, 396n147; in Carlist War, 113–14, 115, 374n137; death of, 285; and Espartero, 133, 209, 211, 266; in government, 105, 202, 203, 206, 262, 264, 265, 271, 284, 285; Jacinta on, 193; and revolution of 1843, 190, 192, 194
National Guards, 176, 181, 182, 192, 229
national identity, 10–11
nationalism, 11, 20, 29, 142, 334, 348
Nationalist Spain, 13, 345–50, 352, 420n72
National Militia: and Carlist War, 3; celebration, 419n43; disarmed, 182; Espartero and, 226, 230–1, 243, 330, 337; and manifesto, 221; O'Donnell vs., 245–6; and Progressives, 12, 187; uprisings and, 142, 173, 180, 181, 191, 192, 221, 235, 254
national symbols, 10–11, 13
national unity, 14, 131, 152, 308, 310
"national will" slogan, 60, 226, *232*, 233, 236, 293, 295, 305, 319; used against Espartero, 308, 318

Navarra: and Carlist Wars, 9, 68, 71, 74, 103, 320, 329; and Carlos, 116; and Espartero, 73, 88, 93, 176, 307; *fueros*, 123, 131; peace campaign, 100, 129. *See also* Pamplona

Navarro, Francisca, 145–6

Negri, Count Ignacio de, 108–9

Negrín, Juan, 346–7

Nelson, Horatio, 24, 25

newspapers. *See* press

nobility, 21, 27, 29, 173

Nocedal, Cándido, 236, 247

Nogués y Milagro, Romualdo, 146

Nombela, Julio, 227

Nordenflich, Capt. Pedro, 42

Novaliches, Marquis of, 289, 319, 320, 323–4

Novedades, Las, 221, 251. *See also* Fernández de los Ríos, Ángel

novels, 15, 25–6, 213–14, 215, 274, 343–4

Ocaña, battle of, 22–3

O'Donnell, Leopoldo, 403n166; and African War, 279; in Carlist War, 111, 133; death of, 285; and Espartero, 111, 148, 248, 249; in government, 234, 235, 244, 245–6, 250, 252–3, 264, 265, 284, 285; in hiding, 220–1; Jacinta and, 193, 263; and public memory, 343; uprisings and, 144, 173, 190, 222, 223, 228–9, 233, 254, 261, 262

Ofalia, Count of, 103, 105, 122

Olañeta, Pedro, 50–1, 52–3, 362n48

O'Leary, Daniel, 45

Olloqui, Damiana, 331, 334

Olózaga, Salustiano de: banquet controversy, 266–73, 407n115, 407n138; on Bilbao, 7; biography, 352; in elections, 183, 263, 298, 318; and Espartero, 156, 201, 218, 220, 244, 284; in government, 131, 177, 178, 186, 188–9, 301, 309–10, 390n150; Jacinta on, 263; in London, 203, 211; and Progressives, 248, 282, 407n115; and regency, 159, 160, 165, 166; and revolution of 1843, 193; scandal and exile, 202

Oman, Charles, 23, 31–2

Oráa, Marcelino, 5, 110, 111, 112

oral tradition, 146, 179, 216, 259

Orense, José María, 296

Otway, Loftus Charles, 245

Pact of Ostend, 285

Palacio, Manuel del, 265

Palmerston, Lady, 199, 207

Palmerston, Lord, 12, 93, 119, 206, 207, 210–11; in London, 199, 201, 203

Pamplona, 60, 63, 65, 104, 173, 228, 249, 314

Pando, Manuel de, Marquis of Miraflores, 122–3, 266

Pareja de Alarcón, Francisco, 135

Paris, 64–5, 155, 172–3, 190, 221, 286, 289

Partido Liberal Esparterista, 306

Partido Socialista de Catalunya, 353–2

"Patriarch of Freedom," 308, 309, 324, 329

patriotic hymns, 110, 139, 144, 205, 243, 279–81, 290, 293, 312, 313, 320. *See also* songs

Pavía y Lacy, Manuel, 289, 319, 320, 323–4

"Peacemaker of Spain," 143, 147, 208, 230, 246, 249, 260, 268, 281, 287; and cult, 275, 277; in monarchy campaign, 295, 299, 302, 305, 308, 313; taken by Alfonso XII, 329–30, 334

Peel, Robert, 198, 199
Peiró Martín, Ignacio, 337
Peninsular War. *See* War of Independence
Pérez, José Antonio, 268
Pérez Alonso, Francisco, 59–60, 61, 66, 364n6, 364n18
Pérez de Castro, Evaristo, 115, 148
Pérez Galdós, Benito, 25–6, 314, 343–4
Peru, 36–9, 40–1, 43–5, 46, 48, 50–1, 52–3, 56, 65
Peyrou, Florencia, 350, 408n168, 410n22
Pezuela, Joaquín de la, 39, 40, 41–2, 44
philanthropy, 12, 184, 211, 239, 256–7, 279, 336–7. *See also* charity
Philip V (king of Spain), 16, 177
photography, 274–5, *276*, 316
Pi i Margall, Francisco, 298
Pirala, Antonio, 302, 314, 316, 337
Pita Pizarro, Pío, 120
plays, 8–9, 144, 145–6, 292–3, 312–13, 343
poems: by admirers, 135, 145, 146, 208, 259–60, 261, 281, 299; by Espartero, 40, 43, 63, 65; vs. Espartero, 179, 265, 388n92; to Jacinta, 136, 260; on Luchana, 8; in the press, 278, 346; by Quintana, 263
political culture, 10–11, 281–3
political theatre, 293. *See also* plays
popular culture, 146–8, 179
population, 16, 24, 256, 365n38
portraits, *165*, *276*; admirers and, 146, 148, 217, *219*, 227, 260, 269, 274–5, 304, 343, 395–6n129; destruction of, 194, 254; discussed in letters, 155; displayed, 142, 145, 240, 243, 274, 281, 290, 305, 325; of Jacinta, *62*, *63*, 155, *333*; in the press, 335;
publishers and, 213, 396n145; and self-identity, 275
Portugal, 19, 30, 67, 77, 196–7, 286, 301–2
Portugalete, 70, 95, 96
Pragmatic Sanction, 67
press: author and, 13; and Carlist Wars, 74, 76, 83, 84, 92, 99, 105, 119–20, 321, 325; in Catalonia, 277–8; on Espartero's birthdays, 278, 286; on Espartero's death and after, 335–6, 339, 341; vs. Espartero, 178–9, 182–3, 189, 190–1, 236, 247, 257–8, 261–2, 265; on exile and return, 201, 204–5, 208, 209, 221, 394–5n104; foreign, 47, 197, 221, 229, 305 (*see also* British press); on Jacinta, 136, 201, 332; and manifestos, 132–3, 263–4; on meeting with Alfonso XII, 326–9; and monarchy competition, 294–6; on political death, 261–2; pro-Espartero, 398n12; on reception in Madrid, 102, 229; and regency issue, 158, 160, 161; on Vergara in 1930s, 345–6. *See also* Catholic press; freedom of the press; Republican press
"Pretender, the." *See* Carlos María Isidro Benito of Borbon; Carlos VII
Primo de Rivera, Miguel, 337, 344, 345, 348
Prim y Prats, Juan: commemoration of, 258, 282, 290, 343, 352–3; death of, 315; and Espartero, 267, 271, 286; Jacinta on, 268; and monarchy competition, 301, 302–3, 304, 306, 309, 313; in politics, 263, 266; uprisings and, 190, 283, 284–5, 288, 390n152
private lives. *See* public vs. private spheres

Progressives: about, 12; in Catalonia, 250, 280–3; in elections of 1843, 183; and Espartero, 131–2, 133, 143, 209, 215, 217–21, 247–8, 262, 269, 272–3, 279; in government, 144, 145, 289, 291; internal conflicts, 266–73, 315, 317; vs. Isabel II, 202; in London, 211; manifestos of, 218, 219, 248, 272, 406n82; and monarchy competition, 301, 302, 306; and municipal government law, 135–6, 139; and O'Donnell, 264, 265–6; and Pact of Ostend, 285; and regency, 162, 164, 165, 166; and revolution of 1854, 223; on trade treaty, 179; and virtues, 408n165
propaganda, 7, 179, 305, 329, 345, 348
public art. *See* monuments
public image: embodying liberty, 219, 229–31, 272, 273, 324, 335; embodying morality, 11, 206, 277–9, 294, 323, 336 (*see also* virtues); as a father figure, 75, 82, 259, 314, 339; as a peacemaker, 230, 308, 353; revived in 1930s, 344–5; as a veteran, 293, 328. *See also* cult of Espartero
"public man," 102, 262, 271, 278
public memory, 231, 300, 343–5. *See also* historical memory
public reception: after battle of Luchana, 6–9; after Carlist War, 139–42, 144–5; as commander in chief, 101–2; in exile, 198–200; after peace of Vergara, 129–30; on railroad tour, 248–50; as regent, 163–4, 182–3; on retirement, 255; on return from exile, 205, 229–31; on royal tour, 316. *See also* birthday celebrations

public vs. private spheres, 156, 157, 167, 209; as permeable, 352, 356–7n35; politicians and, 279, 408n168; for women, 11–12, 184
publishing, 26, 212–17, 395n126. *See also* literature; press
Puig y Salazar, José María, 231, 268–9

Quadruple Alliance, 76–7
Queipo de Llano, José María, Count of Toreno, 25, 28
Quintana, Manuel José, 263, 395–6n129

Radical Progressive Democratic Party, 317, 318, 319
railways, 248–50, 256, 334, 404n9
Rando de Boussignault, Catalina, 259
rebellion of 1841, 172–6, 187
Reclus, Elie, 293
Republican press, 179, 180, 189, 201, 296, 316, 319, 335–6, 341
Republicans: in elections, 157; and Espartero, 172, 204, 320, 336; in monarchy campaign, 295–6, 299, 305; and Pact of Ostend, 285; and Prim's death, 315; in regency, 177, 214, 388n92; and revolution of 1854, 223; and Vergara, 346. *See also* Federal Republicans
Restoration, 64, 325–6, 332, 334, 337, 352. *See also under* Fernando VII
revolution(s): of 1808, 20; of 1840, 142–5, 159, 170, 191, 216, 231; of 1841 (*see* rebellion of 1841); of 1842, 172, 179–82, 187; of 1843, 189–91, 194–5, 231; of 1854, 217, 221–3, 224–6, 248, 252–3, 261–2, 273, 278, 290, 337–8; of 1868, 283–93, 298

Reyero, Carlos, 337
Riall, Lucy, 395
Ribot y Fontseré, Antonio, 179, 215, 388n90
Ricafort, Mariano, 38, 42
Richardson, John, 80, 81, 82
Rico y Amat, Juan, 235
Rico y Amat, Pedro, 7
Riego, Antonio de, 221, 222
Riego, Rafael de, 40
Río de la Plata, 35, 36, 46–50
Rioja, La, 24, 116, 296. See also Logroño
Riva Agüero, José de la, 44, 45
Rivadavia, Bernardino, 46
Rivas, Duke of, 248
Rivera, Antonio, 352
Rivero, Captain General, 224, 225
Roca de Togores, Mariano, Marquis of Molins, 326–8
Roche, Col. Phillip K., 22
Rodil, José Ramón, 55, 92–3, 94, 178, 182
Rodríguez, Antonio, 269–70
Rodríguez, Gregorio, 299
Rogers, Nicholas, 363n80
romances, 146–8, 240–1, 388n90
Romanones, Count of, 56, 344–5, 352
"Romantic Nationalism" (Leerssen), 337
Roncali, Federico, 102, 156, 175
Rossell, José, 318
Rubio, Carlos, 267
Ruiz, Casimiro Rufino, 233–4
Ruiz Zorrilla, Manuel, 270, 284, 315–19 passim, 416n7

Saavedra, Ángel de, Duke of Rivas, 248
Sagasta, Práxedes Mateo: in elections, 298; in government, 246, 266, 284, 286, 315, 316, 318; press opposition, 341; statue of, 338; visits Espartero, 267, 270. See also *Iberia, La*
saints, 155, 213, 274, 343. See also Baldomero, Saint
Salamanca, 243, 295, 296; petitions, 307, 308
Salamanca, José de, 211
Salic Law of Succession, 67
Salmerón, Francisco, 295, 301, 303, 396n147
Salmerón, Nicolás, 321
Salvador, Amos, 341
Salvador, Miguel, 331
Sánchez García, Raquel, 212
Sancho, Vicente, 144, 166, 198, 199
San Martín, José Francisco de, 39, 40–1, 42, 43, 46
San Miguel, Evaristo, 3, 103, 145, 191, 209, 226–7, 237
Santa Cruz, Andrés de, 44–5
Santa Cruz, Francisco Javier de, 87, 91
Santa Cruz, José, 224
Santa Cruz, Marquise of, 168–9, 382–3n135
Santirso Rodríguez, Manuel, 66
Sarabia, Colonel (aide-de-camp), 241
Saravia, Rafael, 271
Sarsfield, Pedro, 92, 93, 98, 99, 103–4
Sartorius, Capt. George, 196
Sartorius y Tapia, Luis José, 220
satire(s), 247, 265, 285, 312–13, 347. See also Ribot y Fontseré, Antonio; *Gil Blas*; *Tío Camorra, El*
Second Carlist War, 204, 351
Second Italian War of Independence, 258
Second Republic. See Spanish Republic
Segundo Ruiz, José, 202
Seoane, Antonio, 42, 45, 56, 83, 88, 101, 192, 194

Serna e Hinojosa, José de la, 41–2, 43, 44, 46–50, 51–3
Serrano, Francisco: in government, 187, 188, 190, 192–3, 290–1, 300, 319, 323, 324; Isabel II and, 204; and Prim's death, 315; as regent, 301, 302; in Third Carlist War, 324–5; uprisings and, 221, 253, 289
Seville, 23–4, 236; greetings from, 259, 330, 394–5n104; uprisings and, 114, 190, 194
slavery or slaves, 33, 35, 112, 209, 214, 277
slogans, 240, 285, 296, 318, 321. *See also* "national will" slogan
Smith, John Abel, 201
social classes, 16–17, 21; Espartero and, 106, 177, 208, 210, 221, 225, 241, 259, 280, 395–6n129; Jacinta and, 239; politics and, 265. *See also* middle class; nobility; working class
Solano, Col. Ramón, 75
Soler, Juan Pablo, 296
Someruelos, Marquis of, 105, 108
songs, 8, 10, 147, 179, 200, 204, 225, 226, 240, 250. *See also* patriotic hymns
Sotomayor, Duke of, 201, 204
Soulé, Pierre, 222
Soult, Jean-de-Dieu, 22, 28, 31
South America. *See* American colonies
souvenirs, 8, 100, 213. *See also* portraits
sovereignty: and constitutions, 29, 241, 300, 301; and the Cortes, 25; national, 308, 317, 319, 338; of the people, 20, 293
Spanish ambassadors, 122–3, 178, 201, 204, 205–6. *See also* Istúriz, Francisco Javier de; Olózaga, Salustiano de; Sancho, Vicente

Spanish Civil War, 13, 68, 76, 345–7, 349–50, 365n38
Spanish Republic, 166, 344–5
State Society for Cultural Commemoration, 353
statistics: on celebrations, 280, 409n174; on conscription, 229; on letters, 153, 209, 259, 394–5n104; on wine, 199, 267. *See also* elections; military: statistics; population
statues. *See* monuments
street names, 144, 290, 348, 350–1, 421n102, 422n105
Suárez Ponte, Wenceslao, 243
Sucre, Antonio José de, 45, 52, 56, 57
"sword of Luchana," 226, 253, 286, 335

Téllez-Giron, Joaquina. *See* Santa Cruz, Marquise of
Temple, Henry John. *See* Palmerston, Lord
Third Carlist War, 319, 320–5, 329–30, 334
Tío Camorra, El, 205, 208, 215
Tiradores de la Patria, 180, 182
Topete, Juan Bautista, 288
Torata, battle of, 44
Toreno, Count of, 25, 28
Torre, Simón de la, 124, 125
Torrejón de Ardóz, battle of, 192, 194
Tortosa, 32, 242
trade: American, 24, 41, 43, 48; Espartero and, 200, 212, 247, 258, 282, 299; treaty issue, 171–2, 178–9, 181, 184. *See also* merchants
Trafalgar, battle of, 24
treaties: colonial, 45–6; commercial, 171–2, 178–9, 181, 184; Eliot Convention, 74–5; of Fontainebleau, 19; Quadruple Alliance, 76–7; of San Idefonso,

treaties (cont'd)
19; of Valencay, 31; of Villafranca, 258. *See also* Agreement of Vergara
Turner, Lieut. George, 103, 123

unions, 182, 235, 240–1, 346, 347
United States, 33, 222, 229; Civil War, 258
universal suffrage, 12, 227, 247, 285, 291
University of Almagro, 17, 18–19
University of Toledo, battalion, 23–4, 26
Urbiztondo, Juan Antonio de, 125, 126, 128

Valdés, Gerónimo: in America, 42, 45, 51, 59, 362n58; career of, 43–4, 115; in Carlist War, 69, 74, 75, 93; in government, 138, 140, 188
Váldez, Manuel, 58
Valencia: in Carlist War, 100, 130, 133; and Carlos, 67; and Espartero, 145, 157, 205, 336; and Fernando VII, 32; politics and, 145, 148–50, 151, 236, 296; street names, 248; uprisings in, 190, 194, 222, 283
Valladolid, 248, 250
Vallejo, José Mariano, 312
Valle-Umbroso, Marqués of, 45
Van Halen, Antonio, 115; in London, 201; and political unrest, 141, 177, 180, 182; postings of, 109, 132, 189; on strategy, 194–5
Varela Ortega, José, 350
Vega, Juana de la, 62, 169, 174–5, 184, 192, 352
Vera y Ramos, Manuel 324
Vergara, 71, 176. *See also* Agreement of Vergara
Vergara, Prince of, 317–18, 416n18
Vicars, Lieut. Edward, 5, 6

Victoria (queen of England), 199, 207–8
Vidart, José, 57
Vigues, Domingo, 260–1
Vila, Antonio, 7
Vilardell, Juan, 269
Villacampa, Pedro, 32
Villalonga, General, 187, 390n144
Villiers, George: on Alaix, 114; on Carlist War, 73, 94, 111; and Córdova, 92; on Espartero, 93, 95, 97, 98, 109, 115, 371n41; in London, 199; on treaty, 171
virtues, 47, 219, 260, 277–9, 304, 305, 307, 309, 335, 408n165. *See also* morality
viticulture, 212, 216. *See also* wine
Vitoria, 103, 110, 155, 173, 176, 208
Vizcaya, 71–2, 75

war crimes, 35, 37, 38, 73–4. *See also* executions
"War of Bread and Cheese," 274
War of Independence: battles of, 22–3; Cádiz siege, 24–5, 28–9; causes and context, 19–21; commemoration of, 353; compared, 36; and the Cortes, 21–2; last days of, 31–2. *See also* Junta Central of 1808
"War of the Aggrieved," 67
War of the Matiners, 204, 351
Washington, George: aspirations, 227, 231; compared to, 15, 143, 152, 200, 215, 269, 296, 282, 300, 335, 349; and retirement, 273–4, 277
Wellington, Duke of, 14, 22, 28, 74, 77, 199
William II (king of Holland), 171
Wills, Garry, 15
wine, 199, 239, 256, 267. *See also* viticulture

women: as admirers, 259–60; and philanthropy, 184; politics and, 209, 240, 250, 352, 357n36; and the Pragmatic Sanction, 67; and public respectability, 11–12, 184. *See also* gender
working class, 16–17, 179, 213, 217, 265, 281, 335. *See also* artisans; unions
Wylde, William: and Bilbao siege, 4, 95, 96, 97; on Carlist War, 89, 111, 119, 121, 130–1; and Espartero, 93, 98, 104–5, 171–2, 199, 207; and peace talks, 123, 124, 125; replaced, 134

Yglesias Veguer, José, 293

Zambrano, Marquis of 59
Zapatero, Juan, 240, 250
Zaragoza: and Castelar, 296; elections, 236, 262, 298; and Espartero, 7, 204, 249–50, 299, 300, 316; and Jacinta, 136, 257; memorial, 336; and Olózaga, 218; proclamation of, 230; uprisings and, 143, 145, 173, 176–7, 190, 221, 222, 224–6, 228, 245–6, 253, 324
Zavala, Pedro José de, 124–5
Zavala y de la Puente, Juan de, 228, 324
Zumalacárregi, Tomás, 68–78 *passim*, 88, 343
Zurbano, Martín, 173, 188, 190, 192, 203

Toronto Iberic

CO-EDITORS: Robert Davidson (Toronto) and Frederick A. de Armas (Chicago)

EDITORIAL BOARD: Josiah Blackmore (Harvard); Marina Brownlee (Princeton); Anthony J. Cascardi (Berkeley); Justin Crumbaugh (Mt Holyoke); Emily Francomano (Georgetown); Jordana Mendelson (NYU); Joan Ramon Resina (Stanford); Enrique García Santo-Tomás (U Michigan); H. Rosi Song (Durham); Kathleen Vernon (SUNY Stony Brook)

1 Anthony J. Cascardi, *Cervantes, Literature, and the Discourse of Politics*
2 Jessica A. Boon, *The Mystical Science of the Soul: Medieval Cognition in Bernardino de Laredo's Recollection Method*
3 Susan Byrne, *Law and History in Cervantes'* Don Quixote
4 Mary E. Barnard and Frederick A. de Armas (eds), *Objects of Culture in the Literature of Imperial Spain*
5 Nil Santiáñez, *Topographies of Fascism: Habitus, Space, and Writing in Twentieth-Century Spain*
6 Nelson Orringer, *Lorca in Tune with Falla: Literary and Musical Interludes*
7 Ana M. Gómez-Bravo, *Textual Agency: Writing Culture and Social Networks in Fifteenth-Century Spain*
8 Javier Irigoyen-García, *The Spanish Arcadia: Sheep Herding, Pastoral Discourse, and Ethnicity in Early Modern Spain*
9 Stephanie Sieburth, *Survival Songs: Conchita Piquer's* Coplas *and Franco's Regime of Terror*
10 Christine Arkinstall, *Spanish Female Writers and the Freethinking Press, 1879–1926*
11 Margaret Boyle, *Unruly Women: Performance, Penitence, and Punishment in Early Modern Spain*

12 Evelina Gužauskytė, *Christopher Columbus's Naming in the* diarios *of the Four Voyages (1492–1504): A Discourse of Negotiation*
13 Mary E. Barnard, *Garcilaso de la Vega and the Material Culture of Renaissance Europe*
14 William Viestenz, *By the Grace of God: Francoist Spain and the Sacred Roots of Political Imagination*
15 Michael Scham, Lector Ludens: *The Representation of Games and Play in Cervantes*
16 Stephen Rupp, *Heroic Forms: Cervantes and the Literature of War*
17 Enrique Fernandez, *Anxieties of Interiority and Dissection in Early Modern Spain*
18 Susan Byrne, *Ficino in Spain*
19 Patricia M. Keller, *Ghostly Landscapes: Film, Photography, and the Aesthetics of Haunting in Contemporary Spanish Culture*
20 Carolyn A. Nadeau, *Food Matters: Alonso Quijano's Diet and the Discourse of Food in Early Modern Spain*
21 Cristian Berco, *From Body to Community: Venereal Disease and Society in Baroque Spain*
22 Elizabeth R. Wright, *The Epic of Juan Latino: Dilemmas of Race and Religion in Renaissance Spain*
23 Ryan D. Giles, *Inscribed Power: Amulets and Magic in Early Spanish Literature*
24 Jorge Pérez, *Confessional Cinema: Religion, Film, and Modernity in Spain's Development Years, 1960–1975*
25 Joan Ramon Resina, *Josep Pla: Seeing the World in the Form of Articles*
26 Javier Irigoyen-García, *"Moors Dressed as Moors": Clothing, Social Distinction, and Ethnicity in Early Modern Iberia*
27 Jean Dangler, *Edging toward Iberia*
28 Ryan D. Giles and Steven Wagschal (eds), *Beyond Sight: Engaging the Senses in Iberian Literatures and Cultures, 1200–1750*
29 Silvia Bermúdez, *Rocking the Boat: Migration and Race in Contemporary Spanish Music*
30 Hilaire Kallendorf, *Ambiguous Antidotes: Virtue as Vaccine for Vice in Early Modern Spain*
31 Leslie Harkema, *Spanish Modernism and the Poetics of Youth: From Miguel de Unamuno to* La Joven Literatura
32 Benjamin Fraser, *Cognitive Disability Aesthetics: Visual Culture, Disability Representations, and the (In)Visibility of Cognitive Difference*
33 Robert Patrick Newcomb, *Iberianism and Crisis: Spain and Portugal at the Turn of the Twentieth Century*

34 Sara J. Brenneis, *Spaniards in Mauthausen: Representations of a Nazi Concentration Camp, 1940–2015*
35 Silvia Bermúdez and Roberta Johnson (eds), *A New History of Iberian Feminisms*
36 Steven Wagschal, *Minding Animals in the Old and New Worlds: A Cognitive Historical Analysis*
37 Heather Bamford, *Cultures of the Fragment: Uses of the Iberian Manuscript, 1100–1600*
38 Enrique García Santo-Tomás (ed), *Science on Stage in Early Modern Spain*
39 Marina Brownlee (ed), *Cervantes'* Persiles *and the Travails of Romance*
40 Sarah Thomas, *Inhabiting the In-Between: Childhood and Cinema in Spain's Long Transition*
41 David A. Wacks, *Medieval Iberian Crusade Fiction and the Mediterranean World*
42 Rosilie Hernández, *Immaculate Conceptions: The Power of the Religious Imagination in Early Modern Spain*
43 Mary Coffey and Margot Versteeg (eds), *Imagined Truths: Realism in Modern Spanish Literature and Culture*
44 Diana Aramburu, *Resisting Invisibility: Detecting the Female Body in Spanish Crime Fiction*
45 Samuel Amago and Matthew J. Marr (eds), *Consequential Art: Comics Culture in Contemporary Spain*
46 Richard P. Kinkade, *Dawn of a Dynasty: The Life and Times of Infante Manuel of Castile*
47 Jill Robbins, *Poetry and Crisis: Cultural Politics and Citizenship in the Wake of the Madrid Bombings*
48 Ana María Laguna and John Beusterien (eds), *Goodbye Eros: Recasting Forms and Norms of Love in the Age of Cervantes*
49 Sara J. Brenneis and Gina Herrmann (eds), *Spain, World War II, and the Holocaust: History and Representation*
50 Francisco Fernández de Alba, *Sex, Drugs, and Fashion in 1970s Madrid*
51 Daniel Aguirre-Oteiza, *This Ghostly Poetry: Reading Spanish Republican Exiles between Literary History and Poetic Memory*
52 Lara Anderson, *Control and Resistance: Food Discourse in Franco Spain*
53 Faith Harden, *Arms and Letters: Military Life Writing in Early Modern Spain*
54 Erin Alice Cowling, Tania de Miguel Magro, Mina García Jordán, and Glenda Y. Nieto-Cuebas (eds), *Social Justice in Spanish Golden Age Theatre*

55 Paul Michael Johnson, *Affective Geographies: Cervantes, Emotion, and the Literary Mediterranean*
56 Justin Crumbaugh and Nil Santiáñez (eds), *Spanish Fascist Writing: An Anthology*
57 Margaret E. Boyle and Sarah E. Owens (eds), *Health and Healing in the Early Modern Iberian World: A Gendered Perspective*
58 Leticia Álvarez-Recio (ed), *Iberian Chivalric Romance: Translations and Cultural Transmission in Early Modern England*
59 Henry Berlin, *Alone Together: Poetics of the Passions in Late Medieval Iberia*
60 Adrian Shubert, *The Sword of Luchana: Baldomero Espartero and the Making of Modern Spain, 1793–1879*